THE AMERICAN ECONOMY:

AN INTRODUCTORY ANALYSIS

BY George W. Zinke

PROFESSOR OF ECONOMICS
UNIVERSITY OF COLORADO

330
Z 66a

THE RONALD PRESS COMPANY · NEW YORK

2

1109056

To my granddaughter

SUZANNE ELLEN UHLMANN

Preface

Why is economics studied and taught? Because it is concerned with the operational truths about man's efforts to overcome want and to preserve abundance. It is a truism by now that, unlike the physical sciences, economics cannot discover its truths by sifting the facts of external nature alone; on the contrary, its truths emerge primarily by reference to the ever-changing arrangements of human affairs. In consequence, there can never be one set of economic principles that will be valid for all time. Economics must be taught and studied as a continuing search for principles that will aid us to come to grips with the current economic problems of our society.

As an introduction for the newcomer to the discipline of economics, this book seeks to present those principles that will be operationally useful in the next few decades. In this endeavor its aim is twofold: to familiarize the student with the principles and institutions that are vital to the American economy today, and to provide a solid basis for more refined speculation in advanced courses.

Although this study of the American economy contains much detailed information and analysis, it is a purposeful departure from the encyclopedia-type text. The basic course in principles, it is widely felt, has tended to become overloaded with facts which cannot be properly assimilated in the time that is available. Therefore some of the traditional materials have been purposely omitted. On the other hand, material on natural resources has been included, in summary form, to meet a long-standing need. Thus, by concentrating on the fundamental features of our economy, time is left to stimulate group discussion and investigation of prime issues and ideas and to encourage the much-neglected superior student to independent study.

To equip the student with the tools of thought for coping with economic problems, abstractions must necessarily be made from the staggering complex of relevant and irrelevant factors of daily experience. As a foundation for making abstractions, Parts I and II present a simplified accounting view (both national and private) of our economy, and an inventory of the base of natural, human, and man-made recources that the economy manages. After the student has acquired an ability to take a comprehensive look at our institutions and real resources, he is introduced to employment theory in Part III, followed by price theory in Part IV and income theory in Part V. For those instructors who prefer a different sequence of topics, this order can easily be altered by the omission of a few pages of transitional material.

The theoretical presentation, it will be readily noted, is built on the foundations of established economic thought in its present-day forms. The view of the microeconomic and the macroeconomic process of production unfolds from the concept of the marginal transformability of real resources and relates this to the money-cost criteria of resources allocation. The aim is to foster an appreciation of input-output analysis, although this "Ricardianism in modern form" is not developed to the extent practiced by econometricians.

In the explanation of consumer choice, the cardinal view of marginal utility is employed in preference to the ordinal utility-isotopes approach. This calls for an open admission that utility is neither measurable nor interpersonally comparable. This candid confession is not required of indifference-curve analysis, which subtly circumvents the problem of the measurement of utility. Is this a problem, however, when understanding, not measurement, is at stake?

A fundamentally Keynesian approach is made to the analysis of economic instability, chronic unemployment, and distress in certain "pockets of poverty" in the national economy. However individual economists may regard Keynes' practical conclusions, his extension of the method of marginalism to analyzing the relations of economic aggregates is generally accepted.

The plan of the book, as well as its contents, has been tested in classes over a substantial period of years. Among other things, experience gained with the use of graphs has led me to use them in strict conformance with the admonition of Alfred Marshall, the innovator in the popular use of graphs, namely: "It is to be remembered that graphical illustrations are not proof." May my sins on this score be few and "minor." Some of the testing of the book involved experimentation under a recent grant of the Ford Foundation's Fund for the Advancement of Education.

Full acknowledgment of my intellectual indebtedness over a period of 25 years is impossible, but a few names must be mentioned. I owe gratitude to Professor Ira B. Cross of the University of California at Berkeley for an inspiring example of the effective teaching of eco-

nomic principles; to Professors M. M. Knight and Frank H. Knight; to
the United Nations economists Michael Kalecki and Sidney Dell; and
to the late Professor Leo Rogin. In England, Piero Sraffa and Maurice
Dobb of Cambridge University, where I studied, and Ed Nevin of the
University of South Wales are gratefully acknowledged.

Needless to say, there have been classmates, colleagues, and precious crops of patient, trusting students. Foremost among them is my
daughter Martha who aided me, often unknowingly, in the way only
a daughter can. My thanks go to my mother for consistently encouraging me in the career of teacher, and finally, all the gratitude of
a husband to my wife Barbara for tedious hours spent in helping with
the preparation of the book and for her general moral support of the
venture.

G.W.Z.

Boulder, Colorado
September, 1958

Contents

List of Illustrative Material   xi

Part I. INTRODUCTION
The Nation's Economy

1   The Structure of the System   3
2   National Income and National Prosperity   22
3   National Prosperity and Private Capital Accumulation   47
     Appendix: Elements of Business Accounting, 65
4   National Income and Private Accounting   77
     Appendix: Major Sources of Economic Information, 95

Recommended Further Reading   100

Part II. THE STRUCTURE OF RESOURCES

5   Natural Resources: Land and Water   105
6   Natural Resources: Minerals and Energy   125
7   Human Resources   155
     Appendix: Construction of a Total Factor Productivity Index, 174

8   Man-Made Resources   179
Recommended Further Reading   197

Part III. THE ABUNDANT USE OF RESOURCES
Employment and the Principle of Effective Demand

9   Supply and Demand as Employment Determinants   203
10   Employment Problems in Theory   227

11   The Role of Government in Stabilizing Employment   248
12   Government Debt and Tax Management   265
13   Monetary Policy for Economic Stabilization   289
     Recommended Further Reading   329

Part IV. THE EFFICIENT USE OF RESOURCES
Price and the Principle of Diminishing Yields

14   A Summary Explanation of Price Analysis   333
15   Individual Choice as a Basis of Commodity Demand   343
16   Individual Costs of Production and Industry
       Supply Schedules   362
17   Elementary Theorems of Price Determination   387
18   Monopoly   427
19   Limited Competition   463
20   Product Competition   484
     Recommended Further Reading   515

Part V. DISTRIBUTION OF THE NATIONAL INCOME

21   Income and Wealth Distribution   521
22   General Theory of Distribution   546
23   Property Incomes   583
24   Labor Incomes   624
25   Modern Methods of Wage Determination   638
       Appendix: Structure of the AFL-CIO, 657
26   Public Policy and Collective Bargaining   661
27   The United States Labor Code Revised   678
     Recommended Further Reading   692

     General Index   695

Illustrative Material

GRAPHS AND CHARTS   Page

Chapter 2
Consumer prices, 1952–57 28
Gross national product in constant and current dollars, 1929–57 31
Relation of gross national product and national income, 1957 33
Disposable personal income and consumption 44

Chapter 3
Calculation of gross profit—Form 1040 52
Calculation of net profit or loss—Form 1040 54
Calculation of capital—Schedule M, Form 1065 56

Chapter 4
Capital accumulation of a large corporation, 1929–56 81
Capital accumulation of a large corporation compared with turnover of
  production and inventories, 1929–56 82
Capital accumulation of all American private corporations compared with
  aggregate turnover of production and inventories, 1929–55 86

Chapter 8
Business expenditure on new plant and equipment, 1929–57 194

Chapter 9
Employment determined by supply and demand equilibrium 206
Derivation of economy-wide supply function under linear output ex-
  pansion 209
Aggregate supply curve on linear expansion assumptions 209
Two hypothetical consumption functions 212
The American consumption function, 1929–57 212
Investment function of American corporations, 1946–57 218
Government spending related to national income 220
Aggregate real costs, total real consumption, and employment 222

Chapter 10
Major components of the national income flow 231
Schedule of marginal efficiency of capital in general 242
Marginal efficiency of capital and the interest rate 243
Increasing aggregate investment exactly compensating for tapering aggre-
  gate consumption 244

GRAPHS AND CHARTS

Chapter 13

Federal Reserve System—Districts and their branch territories 304
Federal Reserve System—Organization chart 305
Changes in Federal Reserve holdings of government securities and other
  market factors affecting level of reserves 316
Graph of a typical schedule of liquidity preference 323
Keynesian interest rate determination 324
Increase of Keynesian interest rate caused by stronger economy-wide
  liquidity preference 325
Purely formal model of interest rate determination 326

Chapter 15

Hypothetical demand schedule 348
Illustration of an increase of demand 354
Elasticities of demand for butter of three types of family 357
Total demand for a commodity 358

Chapter 16

Total cost for an individual firm 374
Aggregate sales income for an individual firm 375
Profit maximization for a competitive single firm 377
Average total unit cost of production for the individual firm 379

Chapter 17

Supply curve for a commodity drawn from its industry supply schedule.... 389
Demand curve for a commodity drawn from its market demand schedule   389
Supply and demand determining price 390
Prices equating supply and demand 391
Computing marginal cost 396
Average revenue curve equals marginal revenue curve 397
Price and cost relationship of individual firm under pure competition 398
Effect of increased demand on price and sales income 400
Increased demand, price, and cost 402
Short-run production increase of the firm 403
Long-run price and output under conditions of tight resources 407
Emergence of rent from ownership of absolutely fixed factor 409
Price determination for representative firm and industry, pure competi-
  tion under conditions of flexible resources 419
"Envelope" or "planning" curve of feasible plant sizes 422

Chapter 18

Monopoly average revenue and marginal revenue 438
Monopoly output and price equilibrium 443
Monopoly price maximization, total cost and income analysis, and unit
  cost and income 444

Chapter 19

Price determination and resource utilization under crowded service competition 467
Profit impact of price rivalry, first move 472

GRAPHS AND CHARTS   Page

Chapter 20
Total output for steel fabrication industry and trend lines for three component parts, 1876–1956 486
Price movement and output increase in first and second phase of a product life cycle 494
Product decline under competition 498
Profit cycle of one selected chemical venture 503
Growth in terms of physical output 505
Rate of growth of physical output, du Pont, 1927–57 506

Chapter 21
Distribution of the consumer dollar, 1957 compared with 1857 525

Chapter 22
Service-supply schedule of resource z 551
Service-demand schedule of resource z 566
Equilibrium price of resource z 569
How factor price rations 573
Equalization of rewards to units of resources 576
Commodity price equilibrium 579
Factor price equilibrium 579
General equilibrium 580

Chapter 23
Present values of $200 to be received a number of years in the future.... 591
Capital demand determining interest 593
Capital demand still determining interest 594
Technology and national income really determine interest 595
Productivity and the Federal Reserve rediscount rate 597
Productivity and the long-term rate of interest 598
Land values before and after urbanization 599

Chapter 25
Structural organization of the AFL–CIO 658

TABLES

Chapter 1
Volume of business by and among transactor groups, 1939, 1953, 1956   8
Income-generating expenditures by each U.S. transactor group for labor, property owners, and other groups, 1953 9
Borrowing and lending activities in the U.S., 1953 12
Balance of all transactional flows in the U.S., 1953 13

Chapter 2
Implicit price deflator for selected years............ 30
Real and nominal gross national product for selected years............ 30
Gross national product and national income, 1957............ 32
Final product, intermediate product, and value added in production........ 36
National income by industrial origins............ 40
National income by type of economic organization............ 41

TABLES

Page

Chapter 3

Company X: Simplified statement of consolidated income for 1958........... 66
Company X: Consolidated balance sheet, December 31, 1958................... 69

Chapter 4

The nation's income, expenditure, and savings, 1955–57......................... 98

Chapter 5

Land surface of the continental U.S... 108
Private land by capability class, continental U.S., 1950............................. 114

Chapter 6

Readily accessible minerals originating in North and Central America...... 127
South American minerals with secure access... 130
Minerals imported from overseas... 131
North and Central American mineral supplies expansible by subsidized
high-cost production 132
Index of electricity bill for residential user compared with index of con-
sumer retail prices, 1935–57... 143
Primary energy sources for electricity, U.S., 1925, 1950, 1975................. 144

Chapter 7

U.S. labor force of gainfully occupied and experienced persons 14 years
of age and over, March, 1958.. 157
Total of gainfully employed or experienced workers, and those in farm
occupations, 1820–1957 159
Productivity index for a steel mill, 1951–58.. 170
Indexes of output per man-hour in a single industry, in all nonagricultural
industries, and in agriculture, 1948–57... 171

Chapter 8

Estimated national wealth, by type of asset, 1955..................................... 180
Man-energy compared with equipment-energy, 1850, 1900, 1950........... 183
Relation of business investment and business savings, 1929–57............... 193

Chapter 9

Average outlays of American families for current consumption, 1935–36 214
American spending units owning liquid assets and paying on life insurance
policies, 1957 215

Chapter 10

Net savings and investment, U.S., 1929–33.. 232
Computation of marginal propensity to consume....................................... 235

Chapter 11

Budget expenditures of federal government, by major functions, 1958...... 250

Chapter 12

Ratio of federal debt to GNP, 1947–57... 270
Percentages of income paid as tax by families and individuals, 1957......... 279
Impact of federal income tax on income groups, 1947............................... 280
Relation of highest U.S. income group to lower groups, before and after
taxes, 1947 280

TABLES   Page

Role of the federal government viewed budgetwise, 1958........................... 284
Percentage distribution of budget receipts of federal government............... 285

Chapter 13
Simplified illustration of bank clearing... 296
Bank X's balance sheet at outset.. 298
Bank X's position after increase of deposits.. 299
Bank X's position after expanding its business... 299
Credit expansion in the economy (hypothetical illustration)....................... 301

Chapter 15
Individual demand schedule for meat at different prices, U.S., 1950's........ 343
Demand for butter by three income groups and in total............................. 353

Chapter 16
Average diminishing yields to inputs of direct labor................................... 369
Average returns with reference to fixed plant and equipment.................... 371
Average diminishing returns with reference to both fixed and variable
    inputs of factors of production.. 372
Total cost of production of a firm (at $1.00 per man-hr.)......................... 373
Aggregate sales income of a firm at two prices of its product.................... 375
Derivation of average total unit cost of production..................................... 378
Types of average cost... 381
Hypothetical schedule of marginal costs at different levels of output of a
    firm 382

Chapter 17
Emergence of rent from ownership of absolutely fixed resource................. 408
Change in demand schedule with given industry supply schedule.............. 413
Short-run excess profit of the representative firm....................................... 414
Long-run equilibrium price, 122 firms in the industry, each producing
    nine units of product.. 416

Chapter 18
Typical percentage distribution of nonfarm and nonprofessional business
    firms of different sizes... 428
Percentage of total volume of business done by 20 largest firms in selected
    industries, 1954 429
Elasticity of demand and monopoly power to raise prices.......................... 435
Income from sales... 436
Cost of production 439
Equality of marginal cost and marginal revenue.. 440
Total monopoly profit... 441
Monopoly equilibrium 442

Chapter 19
Demand for the product, and costs and profits for its two producers........ 471
Total cost for each producer.. 472
Demand, marginal revenue, and marginal cost schedules for the single-
    firm monopoly 474
Competitive price and output.. 477

TABLES

Page

Chapter 20

Rate of return on investment during growth phases of a product............... 495
Cost reduction for the firm.. 496
Change of price and output because of cost reduction, under monopolistic profit maximization 497
Operating profit history of eight products... 507

Chapter 21

Some components of the current American standard of living, in the perspective of world conditions... 524
Average distribution of personal consumption expenditure, U.S., late 1950's 526
Food, clothing, and shelter as shares of family expenditure in three representative American cities.. 527
Size of income and proportionate consumer expenditures......................... 528
Level of aggregate disposable income and proportionate consumer expenditures, on the average... 529
Distribution of American households by total money income, 1929, 1935/36, 1944, 1957.. 530
Absolute and percentage change of income distribution, 1935/36 to 1947, 1947 to 1957.. 532
Definitions of need for different spending units, 1956............................... 533
Mid-twentieth century poverty.. 534
Rural farm families and their total money incomes, 1954.......................... 535
Growth of consumers' assets, U.S., 1957.. 537
Housing status of nonfarm families, 1958.. 538
Automobile ownership within income groups, 1958.................................. 539
Liquid asset holdings and their composition, by income groups, 1958........ 541
Life insurance provisions of families surveyed in 1954............................. 542
Life insurance premiums within income groups, 1956............................... 544

Chapter 22

The American distribution ledger, Aug. 1957 and Aug. 1958.................... 547
Service-supply schedule of resource z.. 551
Total marginal revenue products of three factors...................................... 562
Entrepreneurial resources demand at given factor prices........................... 562
Entrepreneurial demand for factor z at three different prices..................... 565
Hypothetical demand schedule for units of resource z............................... 566
Factor-price determination for units of resource z.................................... 569

Chapter 23

Progress of rent and profit.. 604
Percentages of commercial farms in different size categories, 1950.......... 610
Rural farm families by source of money income, 1955............................. 610

Chapter 24

Static analysis of specific wage rate determination................................... 635

I
INTRODUCTION
The Nation's Economy

1　The Structure
of the System

Seventy million gainfully occupied persons staff the
economy of the United States. It is expected that this
number of jobholders will rise to ninety million in less
than twenty years. These gainfully occupied individuals do not work
merely to ward off hunger; they are not faced with sheer scarcity.
Quite the contrary, they are abundance-minded, and they will continue
to be abundance-minded. If abundance is, can be, and ought to be the
rule, is there a need for economizing?

THE CONCEPT OF ECONOMY

To economize means to minimize waste in using human and material resources so as to maximize the contributions these resources can
make to abundant living. Why is it necessary to economize?

The usual explanation is that we must be provident because human
wants are insatiable; hence, never enough resources can be mustered
to satisfy all wants. It follows logically that we must make resources
go as far toward want-satisfaction as possible. Given America's
capacity to produce, *absolute* scarcity has been overcome. But individuals and families must still make choices to forego an enlarged
consumption of some things in order to possess an ample supply of all
things. *Relative* scarcity persists.

Though logically not wrong, this explanation is so abstract as to be
easily misleading. In reality, individual wants are not insatiable. Our

3

cultural environment and our desire for social approval within it set limits of acceptability on what an unrestrained, egocentric imagination might cause us to want.

On the other hand, resources are not forbiddingly limited *provided that* they are used freely and efficiently. Surely one cannot complain of a lack of resources during recessions or depressions, when the available ones are not being fully utilized. And at times of full employment who will deny that the existing practices of resource utilization can in many instances be improved? With this proviso understood, the concept of relative scarcity is useful in that it emphasizes the wisdom of choosing carefully among alternative means to anticipated want-satisfaction so that human opportunities to enjoy abundant living may ceaselessly be broadened for the people.

Economics accepts the concept of relative scarcity as one of its fundamental points of departure. The term "relative abundance" could equally well be used, because the reference in the case of any particular good or service is not to the physical limitation of its supply. Instead, *relative scarcity* (alternatively, *relative abundance*) is defined as *a condition in which the purchase and further production of units of particular goods and services retard the expenditure of income and the use of labor and materials in other ways, although everything may be plentiful.*

ECONOMICS, A SOCIAL SCIENCE

Economizing is recommended personal behavior. However, much of one's success in this matter depends upon one's economic environment. By this term we designate the rules and customs of technical and human relations which society develops as guideposts for individual and cooperative economic efforts. Great personal frugality will not accomplish much for an individual in any society which places no incentive on improving methods of production, which sanctions the wasteful use of valuable resources by a favored few to the detriment of the unfavored many and at the expense of future generations. By contrast, there is no visible limit to the economic progress which can be made when the members of a society impartially have access to knowledge and to opportunities to earn, and have the right to participate in shaping the economic environment through free voting.

For the average citizen to participate responsibly in the conduct of the economic life of a nation, it is necessary that he understand the working rules of the economic organization. Only then can he conform or intelligently propose reform.

Economics is the specialized intellectual discipline which strives to serve individuals in their efforts to participate intelligently in general (rather than purely personal) economic affairs. Specifically, economics teaches an individual to think about the daily business affairs of his life in the broad perspective of the technical and social working rules for getting at and using resources efficiently and abundantly. Because of this orientation, *economics* may be defined as *the practical and theoretical study of individual and group behavior related to full and efficient resource utilization insofar as social organization and democratic control are involved.*[1]

Economics, then, is distinctively a social science. Some authorities prefer to label it an art rather than a science, but this raises no vital issue. It is the social nature of economics which provides the distinguishing characteristic, not whether it is an art or a science.

THE SCOPE OF ECONOMICS

As a specialized field of study within the domain of the social sciences, economics typically deals with the following five problems:

1. What kinds of goods and services are to be produced?
2. In producing a selected list of goods and services, how may human, natural, and man-made resources be utilized fully and effectively?
3. Who shall obtain the goods and services produced? in what amounts? on what terms?
4. How shall the basic production facilities—factories, farms, power dams, etc.—be kept from running down?
5. How might the living standards of all citizens improve, through investment in human beings and material equipment, so that better-educated persons will be able to work with improved means of production?

Most of these problems would confront an isolated individual in a lost wilderness; yet it is easy to understand that their solution must be of a highly complex nature in modern economies. Here men organize by the tens of millions in order to broaden their individual opportunities through associated action in producing, exchanging, and distributing goods and services.

[1] A study of economics includes learning a set of general principles of resource-allocation, employment, and income distribution. These principles—e.g., the law of diminishing returns—have been formulated in increasingly refined form by many generations of economists. Those which will serve the beginning student have been selected and will be presented in an accessible form according to the best economic tradition. Principles of economics are aids to thought about real-life economic problems and policies and issues. That is, economic principles do not furnish answers although they are useful in arriving at answers. And that is why the above definition does not single out the principles of economics but broadly identifies economics as the study of the working rules of the American economy as viewed practically and with the aid of theoretical principles.

ECONOMIC INTERDEPENDENCE

If an economic system were just being organized, the five main economic problems might be approached one after the other. But in our long-established economy some businessmen are deciding to manufacture a new product; some who are satisfied that they are producing wanted goods consult efficiency engineers to learn how to produce more economically; accountants are deciding how to make proper depreciation allowances so that industrial plants do not run down; while somewhere else in the economy certain entrepreneurs may be conferring with investment bankers about launching certain major economic development projects. At the same time organized labor and management groups are conducting collective bargaining negotiations. And government officials are studying current economic trends in contemplation of taking, or not taking, such action as may be required if economic growth is to be sustained.

This is only a bare indication of the fact that the five typical economic problems are approached simultaneously. Not only that, but the decisions which must be made in coping with these problems are all interrelated. The kinds of goods that are to be produced depend upon who shall obtain the goods and services, upon the methods of production used, upon how much of the annual national income will be used for investment rather than immediate consumption, and so forth. This necessarily calls for extensive economic information and networks of economic communication. If, then, all the main lines of economic question-raising and decision-making are (1) acted on at the same time, (2) interrelated, and (3) served by networks of economic communication, it should be possible to observe the *whole* economy operating at any moment as a total "going concern."

A Sketch of the American Economy

PRELIMINARY REMARKS

In preparation for taking a total view of the economy, we must remember that most individuals or economic groups specialize in furnishing one or a limited number of goods or services. This is a fact of modern economic history, commonly referred to as *the division of labor*. Of this more will be said later; at present only the fact of specialization is to be noted.

All the products of specialized labor are coordinated in a total stream of goods and services, which is called the *national output*. This is a physical aggregate of real things and personal services—tons of coal and hours worked, for example.

The many goods and services which make up the nation's physical output enter into an elaborate process of exchange as goods are sold and services performed for hire. In this exchange process each person, typically specializing in the production of one or a limited number of goods or services, acquires during a year literally thousands of other goods and services which he needs in order to enjoy his standard of living.

Goods and services are characteristically exchanged for money; they are not directly exchanged for each other. Thus the national physical output becomes a financial magnitude in the total process of monetary exchanges of goods for money and money for goods.

If one were to add the financial value of all cash and credit transactions in the United States for a year, the sum total would be a staggering figure of thousands of billions of dollars. But this would be like examining what occurs in every house, street, and alley of a city in order to obtain an impression of that city. We need to observe only the main features of a city's life to receive an impression. Likewise, in economic analysis we need not witness every detailed transaction but can "break down" the economy into the chief sectors of transaction.

STREAMS OF ECONOMIC TRANSACTIONS

The main flows of exchanging goods and services for money, and vice versa, are conducted among the following principal sectors of the economy: consumers, corporations, unincorporated business firms, farmers, the federal, state, and local governments, banking and insurance firms as well as nonprofit organizations such as hospitals or labor unions, and persons and firms outside of the United States who are doing business here.

Each of the named economic sectors is understood to do business with all the other sectors. Thus the corporate sector sells to consumers, to unincorporated business firms, to farmers, to government agencies, and so forth. Again, governments—federal, state, or local—collect taxes from consumers and businesses and render government services in return. Farmers buy from corporations, from unincorporated firms, from the rest of the world, and so on through and among the various sectors.

The sum totals of these transaction flows were $1.3 trillion in 1953 and $1.6 trillion in 1956, in rounded figures. However, the sum totals are not significant figures for the present purpose. Here we are not concerned with measuring (at market prices) the total of all the values created by current productive activity. For ascertaining this there exists a superior survey method, to be explained in Chapter 2.

At present the reader is asked to concentrate on the composition of economic activity, not its gross volume or even the specific absolute magnitudes of the various streams of transactions. It is the *relationship* between the ingredient magnitudes which is of significance in appraising the composition of economic activity.

The illustrative data which follow are representative of the composition of total economic activity during the 1950's. This composition is not expected to change radically in the calculable future. In the ensuing discussion, 1953 data are used extensively because the authoritative publication on, and the "dictionary" of, money-flows national accounting is the Federal Reserve Board study cited in Table 1–1, covering the period 1939–53.

Table 1–1. Volume of Business Done By and Among Major Transactor Groups, United States, 1939, 1953, and 1956

Transactor Group	Revenue Received ($ billions)		
	1939	1953	1956
Corporations	130.0	550	652
Nonincorporated business firms	57.0	216	249
Farmers	9.0	32	34
Federal government	7.5	78	85
State and local governments	14.0	40	53
Banking, insurance, and nonprofit organizations	13.5	52	77
Rest of the world	3.5	18	26
Consumers, considered as selling productive services	72.5	303	376

SOURCES: Board of Governors of the Federal Reserve System, *Flow of Funds in the United States, 1939–1953* (Washington, D.C.: Government Printing Office, 1955), p. 38; *Statistical Abstract of the United States, 1958,* p. 310.

It will be observed that except for the farming and small business sectors of the economy, which have fallen behind percentagewise, and the financial and government sectors, which have gained relative to the other sectors, there is a substantial similarity in the composition of the total flow of transactions in 1939 and 1953 and 1956.

These flows in transactions are expressed in terms of current market prices—which raises the interesting question: How are current market prices established? Before we enter into this crucial question, even in a most general fashion, the nation's total economic activity should be observed in terms of another vital aspect of social organization.

NATIONAL OUTPUT AS NATIONAL INCOME

In the process of exchange every specialized seller of a good or service acquires a claim to a fraction of the total output of all goods and services—that is, insofar as he is able to obtain a price for his specialty at all. These claims on the national output are the sellers' incomes. Thus the national output, being delivered by all who come to market, can also be conceived as the mass of commodities and services available to all who manage to establish income claims in the market.

The price-exchange process now appears as one in which incomes are generated to the total of the available national output. We see that the other facet of the national output is its appearance as the national income. It is in terms of output that income claims are generated, and it is in terms of income claims that the national output is divided. To illustrate this insight with economic data, we next view the flows of economic transactions in terms of income generation rather than, as before, in terms of output-selling activities.

Table 1–2 shows how each main transactions group in the economy creates income for labor and property owners and for sellers of goods

Table 1–2. Income-Generating Expenditures by Each Major Economic Transactor Group for Labor, Property Owners, and Other Groups, United States, 1953

($ billions)

Transactor Group	Paid to Labor for Direct Employee Services	Paid to Owners for Use of Property	Paid to Other Groups for Goods and Outside Services	Total Spending
(a)	(b)	(c)	(d)	(e)
Consumers	3	16	283	303
Corporations	119	20	417	556
Nonincorporated business firms	30	40	146	216
Farmers	3	13	17	33
Federal government	19	6	60	85
State and local governments	13	1	26	40
Banking, insurance, and nonprofit organizations	9	4	29	42
Rest of the world	....	2	14	16

SOURCE: Board of Governors of the Federal Reserve System, *Flow of Funds in the United States, 1939–1953* (Washington, D.C.: Government Printing Office, 1953). The above data have been assembled from various chapters.

and services in the other sectors. For example, column (d) of Table 1–2 shows corporations buying $417 billion of goods and outside services—freight insurance, consultants' services, and so on. Column (b) shows that at the same time corporations directly hired $119 billion worth of labor services, which were used under the direct supervision of the corporate managers in their respective plants and offices. In addition, the corporations paid $20 billion to owners of property in the form of rent for land, interest, and dividends.

Simple addition of all the figures in Table 1–2 yields roughly $1.3 trillion, the amount of total income that was generated, which equals the $1.3 trillion of the volume of business done by all transactor groups, as shown in Table 1–1.

Attention is called to the fact that this figure of $1.3 trillion is useful only as a tally mark for reconciling the output-selling and income-earning aspects of the economic process. The meaningful information contained in Table 1–2 concerns the structure of income flows originating in each particular sector, not the total of these income flows. Again, as in the case of volume of business done, there is a superior method of recording the total national income measured at current rates of wages, rent, interest, and profits.

FINANCIAL TRANSACTIONS

Thus far the economy has been viewed primarily as a goods-producing and goods-purchasing system. No attention has been paid to purely financial transactions in which not goods, but money and credit transfers are involved.

Such transfers take place when consumers, businessmen, and government agencies wish to purchase more goods and services than the income at their disposal permits. Borrowing is therefore necessary if purchasing is to be carried out as planned.

The would-be borrowers now approach either (1) persons or groups commanding more disposable money income or wealth than they wish to spend, or (2) banking institutions which have the right to create money. (Trade credit—for example, charge accounts—may also be given by sellers to buyers.)

Upon transferring money or credit to borrowers, the lenders, in return, acquire financial claims on the incomes or wealth of the borrowers. These claims take the form of *promissory notes* when short-period loans are involved. *Bonds* are issued by industrialists, merchants, and governments when they borrow money for long periods. *Mortgages* are assumed by consumers, businessmen, farmers, and other borrowers when they pledge real estate or other forms of property as security for their loans. In all cases the borrower undertakes to pay interest at specified rates and at stated periods and to repay (amortize) the loan under stipulated conditions. *Stocks* are securities which corporations issue with the promise to pay dividends (shares of profits) to persons or groups subscribing money. Stock purchasers become co-owners of the issuing corporation. These, in brief, are the legal forms for transfers of money and credit between borrowers and lenders.

The economic significance of transfers of money and credit rests in their stimulating effect on expenditure for goods and services. For example, when an individual consumer borrows money to buy a house or incurs instalment debt, his expenditure obviously increases. However, the stimulating effect of total consumer borrowing in any given year cannot be measured simply by adding all new consumer borrowing during that year. While some consumers are newly borrowing, others are making repayments on debts incurred in the past. This reduces the purchasing power available for purchasing new goods. Therefore it is necessary to deduct repayments on the existing debt from new consumer borrowing in order to ascertain the *net* stimulating effect of borrowing on consumer spending. When this is done for the year 1953, the *net* amount of consumer borrowing is seen to be $11 billion. This might not appear to be an appreciable amount of added consumer expenditure compared with the total outlay of the consumer sector from its own financial resources, $303 billion in 1953. However, one need only imagine a deduction of $11 billion of purchasing power to realize that this would have had a severely depressing economic effect. The net borrowing of all the listed economic transactions groups amounted to $42.5 billion in 1953.

Mindful of the definite impact which purely financial transactions of net borrowing have on the flows of goods and services in the economy, we must take these financial transactions into account in this preliminary sketch of the total economy. They are recorded in the left-hand column in Table 1–3.

To record borrowing only would not afford a full view of the flows of financial transactions. The other side of borrowing is lending. As in the case of borrowing, money-flows accounting records only the *net* amount of new lending during any given year. This is ascertained by deducting repayments of loans received by creditors from the amount of new total lending. When this is done for the year 1953, the net amount of lending is seen to be $42.5 billion, after a technical allowance is made for a decline of cash balances held at banks by the government.

Intersector borrowing. In the aggregate, net borrowing must of course equal net lending. Yet there may be more persons or groups in one economic transactions sector who are lending than there are persons in that sector who are borrowing, or vice versa. Having more people lending than borrowing in a sector means that one or more other economic sectors are indebted to the sector with an excess of lenders. On the other hand, when the number of borrowers in any given sector of the economy, say the farm sector, exceeds the number of lenders therein, it will be in debt to one or more of the other sectors.

Information about debtor-creditor relationships between major transactions groups provides vital insights into the structure and problems of an economy. To illustrate: for many years the farm problem in the United States was closely definable in terms of the chronic indebtedness of farmers as a whole to other transactions groups. In recent times the chronic indebtedness of the federal government has posed problems of inflation, of distribution of the tax burden, and many more. Being illustrative, these remarks are not meant to generate controversial discussion at the moment. At present the aim is only to outline the economic system. Table 1–3 furnishes a complete view of the nation's purely financial transactions.

Table 1–3. Borrowing and Lending Activities in the United States, 1953

Net Borrowing Resorted to for Supplementing the Sector's Disposable Income ($ billions)	Sector	Net Loans Made by Persons or Groups in the Sector ($ billions)
11.0	Consumer	13.0
8.0	Corporate	2.0
3.5	Nonincorporated business firms	3.5
1.0	Farmers	......
5.5	Federal government	−1.5
3.0	State and local governments	3.0
10.0	Banking, insurance, and nonprofit organizations	20.0
.5	Rest of the world	2.5

SOURCE: Board of Governors of the Federal Reserve System, *Flow of Funds in the United States, 1939–1953* (Washington, D.C.: Government Printing Office, 1955), p. 38.

THE COMPOSITE VIEW OF THE AMERICAN ECONOMY

Having viewed the flows of goods and services as well as financial flows (both types being measured at market prices), the reader now can grasp the overview of all the transactions combined. In Table 1–4 note how each transactions sector is brought into balance and how all the sectors balance when (1) borrowing as a source of funds is added to revenue received from the volume of business done; and (2) lending is added to spending, as an additional use of funds. The table also shows which sectors are in debt to the others and which are the characteristic creditor sectors.

Table 1–4. Balance of All Transactional Flows in the United States, 1953
($ billions)

Source of Funds to the Sector		Transactor Sector	Use of Funds by the Sector		Debt (—) or Credit (+)
Revenue (Table 1–1)	Borrowing (Table 1–3)		Spending (Table 1–2)	Lending (Table 1–3)	
550	+ 8	Corporate	556	+ 2	—6
216	+ 3.5	Nonincorporated business firms	216	+ 3.5	......
32	+ 1	Farmers	33	......	—1
78	+ 5.5	Federal government	85	— 1.5*	—7
40	+ 3	State and local governments	40	+ 3	......
7	+ 5 of "created" checkbook money†	Banking	6	+ 6	+1
33	+	Insurance	24	+ 9	+9
12	+ 5	Nonprofit organizations	12	+ 5	......
303	+ 11	Consumers	303	+ 13	+2
18	+ 0.5	Rest of the world	16	+ 2.5	+2

SOURCE: Board of Governors of the Federal Reserve System, *Flow of Funds in the United States, 1939–1953* (Washington, D.C.: Government Printing Office, 1955).
* This is explained by a reduction of federal government cash balances.
† The credit which banks give their customers, allowing them to draw checks against the bank, is not revenue, but neither is it borrowed money. It constitutes, however, funds which banks use to advance to their customers and which are there-upon spent by the customers. Bank credit will be explained in some detail in Chapter 13.

Let it be also noted that the composition of the exhibited flows of goods, services, and finance is determined by habits, customs, technology, and other elements of human behavior which remain quite stable over long periods. Consequently the picture presented in Table 1–4 should be descriptive of the economy for years to come; that is, it should not be too narrowly interpreted as being true only of 1953. Of course, the particular magnitudes change from year to year, but the relations of flows are not easily upset, except when war or depression intervenes.

THE MATTER OF PRICE

In Table 1–1 the main lines of output-selling activities were portrayed in terms of current market prices. Again, in Table 1–2, the incomes generated in the exchange process were shown in terms of current levels of wages, rents, interest, and dividends. The financial transactions pictured in Table 1–3 are conducted by people mindful of prices; for example, the value of a home loan mortgage depends on the price of residential housing. Table 1–4, being merely a composite table, alters nothing in this respect. Thus, the national flow of transactions is commensurable only in terms of prices, whether we view the matter in terms of output prices, input prices, financial prices, or all of them together.

Again the crucial question arises: How are prices established? At this stage a broad general view of the process of price determination is called for. Of course, the reader is asked to bear in mind that the following general remarks about price determination are made only to aid in the present task of sketching the economic system so as to set the stage for detailed descriptions and explanations.

The Pricing Process: a Fundamental Rationing System

Prices are items of economic intelligence—messages to inform producers, consumers, and people who wish to borrow or lend money where they stand in the economic order of things. Prices are ratios of money to specified units of goods or services. By observing prices, one can readily imagine which of the many possible patterns of expenditure to adopt for the purpose of attempting to maximize satisfaction or profit from expenditure.[2]

Thus for a household consumer the information about actual prices of different kinds of goods and services is all that is required for him to select one of a number of alternative patterns of spending an actual or anticipated income (perhaps supplemented by borrowing). This will be the pattern which, under the circumstances, promises the most of good living. On the other hand, production planning for the kinds of goods to turn out, and in what quantities, is conducted in terms of a number of alternatives seen in the light of information on expected sales prices per unit of varying quantities of different goods.

Now, it is evident that different potential production and expenditure plans made by millions of individuals and groups imply differing

[2] *Attempting* to maximize satisfactions or profits is the best that can be done, for we live in a world of uncertainty and formidable complexity. Substantial advances in economic analysis have been made since this fact of modern life was first acknowledged.

uses of national resources. Of course, consumer expenditure plans and business development plans depend not only on what output prices are but also on anticipated income and on the changes that are expected in that income. In this sense there are millions of generals on the economic field only waiting to see what the economic price intelligence reports convey in order to determine which particular expenditure or production plan to put into action. It follows that the adaptive behavior of millions of persons to current and prospective price trends signifies the specification, in the aggregate, of one over-all pattern of resource utilization for the nation, that is, one particular way of allocating social resources.

This, then, is the function of prices, both commodity output and service income prices. Considered in the abstract, the phenomenon of price is a method of allocating social resources in an exchange process of people selling goods for money and purchasing goods with money in the market places of the nation.

But a mechanism for allocating resources must have human purpose and be expressive of constructive human values lest there be "a price on everything"—a man's life, virtue, his self-respect, and so forth. Our general purpose in the American democracy is that resources shall be allocated for the "greatest good for the greatest number." By "good" we do not mean frivolous pleasure, and the term "greatest number" need not invite huckstering to a mass of marching morons. The end sought is creative unfolding or development for as many people as possible so that they are able to face life's joys and tribulations as mature individuals.

Neither our price mechanism nor any other mechanism can create human values of dignified individual living in the midst of society. A price mechanism can but give expression to such better or worse human values as do exist. We must rely on our homes, our schools, our churches, and all other centers of ethical culture to imbue individuals and families with worthy desires and to equip them with socially useful productive abilities. To the extent that this is accomplished, resource-allocation as monitored by the purchase and sale of goods at market prices is a method whereby men organize in order to make mutually efficient use of the resources.

DEFINITION OF MARKETS

Economic markets should not be conceived primarily as physical locations. They are better defined as patterns of regularly recurring trade relations between consumers, producers, and investors—whether conducted by mail or teletype, in buildings or outdoors. There are commodity markets (retail and wholesale), labor markets, real estate markets, capital markets, and so forth.

Ways and means of administering resource-allocation vary in different parts of the world. In order to highlight the special nature of resource-allocation through a market pricing process it is useful first to glance at another method of performing this vital economic function.

DIRECT RATIONING BY PLANNED DECISIONS

During wartime there exists a very directly shared common purpose of maximizing the armed forces' striking power, thereby minimizing the war's duration. This requires converting into military hardware all possible resources that can be cut from civilian consumption. Claimant agencies representing the military and civilians therefore get together to allocate known resources and to plan for developing new ones. What remains for civilian use is thereafter rationed (1) by a system of ration coupons which entitle everyone who has purchasing power to a share of necessary food, clothing, shelter, and transportation, and (2) by a method of officially controlling prices in such a manner as to assure people that they can buy at reasonable prices the things to which their ration coupons entitle them. This amounts to guiding the fundamental pricing system in harmony with the ration coupon system.

Rationing is superimposed on the price system because long experience has shown that the uncontrolled impact of artificial wartime scarcities on economies organized on peacetime patterns of consumption and production disrupts economic life. It lowers the morale of civilians and soldiers alike, and even deteriorates the health and productivity of the labor force and the business population, thus diminishing the war effort. To the extent that wartime rationing and price controls are administered in a generally fair and equitable manner (that is, in conformance with what responsible citizens understand wartime necessities to be), these controls (1) prevent black market prices from being established, because they act to pull back into civilian consumption basic resources needed for war production; and (2) permit the absorption of the shocks of wartime restrictions instead of letting them convulse the normal economic system. This is a lesson that was bitterly learned during the Civil War and not fully acted on until World War II.

Direct rationing under normal peacetime conditions can be found in modern socialistic societies where the basic means of production, such as steel mills, are publicly owned and operated. The rationing, however, is most likely to apply only to these basic means of production, not to ordinary consumers' goods. Some cooperative settlements (for example, the *kibbutzim* in Israel) also practice a degree of direct rationing. In these modern instances (for example, the socialist economy of Yugoslavia) techniques of government consultation with factory managers and worker representatives are adopted both as a means of realistic planning and to furnish incentives for the managers and workers to reach the targets of economic planning. This being a controversial statement, a simpler form of direct rationing will be described for the purpose of illustrating the meaning of direct peace-time rationing. It is the case of a primitive tribal community or of an isolated frontier family.

In the primitive community a council meets to decide what shall be produced and how it shall be parceled out. In a frontier household in which "usufacture" (home production for home consumption) is the rule, the family head makes these decisions. Under the circumstances an independent price system would exist only in an incidental form. Some ardent hunters in a tribe might exchange fishing tackle for arrows with fervid fishermen; in a frontier family the members might swap particular possessions. It must be evident that such prices as may be established in side exchanges do not determine the community's or family's production. Incidental exchanges under direct rationing may slightly modify the personal distribution of planned production; they cannot alter its fundamental pattern.

INDIRECT RATIONING THROUGH PRICES

In a peacetime economy people do not for the most part get together to decide who is to do what and who is to get what and how much. To be sure, now that the United States is a worldwide political and military power, there is always the shadow of production planning for national security. It takes the form of directly allocating certain rare strategic raw materials, of stockpiling, and of letting out defense production contracts to those concerns that fit best into the industrial aspects of the national security program. These matters entail personal economic relations between government authorities and private producers.

As concerns the bulk of ordinary, peacetime production, *goods and services,* rather than the *persons* who own or command them, have direct economic relations, that is, market-price exchange relations. Of course people *do* control these price relations among goods—there is no known record of goods having desires for each other. But the control is a remote one which operates through millions of separate bargaining transactions all over the nation. In other words, except for purposes of national security production, Americans do not act centrally through representatives to form a national economy, conceived as an ongoing productive and cooperative whole. Coordination is expected to result from the operation of markets in which goods, services, and loan funds are exchanged *at a price*.

This imposes on price a vital function which has no equivalent in systems of direct rationing. Mark well that in a market-price economy, production still has to be guided so that the economy may be maintained and expanded. But in a price system the processes of consumption, production, and investment planning are quite decentralized, being done by many consumers, businessmen, and investors throughout the land. Some form of communication must unite them lest they work at cross-purposes.

OUTPUT PRICES

So far as commodity production is concerned, prices ideally establish the needed communication between productive entrepreneurs, permitting them to compete with each other without wastefully duplicating productive efforts. The entrepreneurs rarely meet, but their wares do. Meeting in the market places, the wares put each other to competitive tests of strength of consumer appeal. This means, ideally, that no commodity or brand of commodity can qualify as a staple article of consumption simply because it is better than nothing or only because time and energy were consumed in fabricating it. The commodity has to be better than something else that might have been made, using the same amounts of basic manpower and natural resources, and ideally the commodity must be made as inexpensively as possible.

On the other hand, people must not be allowed to acquire goods too cheaply if as a consequence valuable social resources are depleted merely to gratify their momentary whims or if wants are satisfied for which consumers are not really willing to pay. As an example, consider the fishing and canning trade of prewar imperial Japan. Workers contracted out for long periods to labor on incredibly insanitary cannery boats, some of which hovered off the coast of California. Canned seafoods were shipped into Los Angeles at half the prices of domestically prepared seafoods. It meant that Japan was sapping some of its vital manpower resources for the benefit of some American consumers and a handful of Japanese profiteers.

INCOME (OR "INPUT") PRICES

Regarding the prices which are paid for the services of labor or to property owners, it is self-evident that they must be at least high enough to make it possible for income-earners to afford a minimum level of decent living—otherwise, social deterioration will set in. Actually, the idea of a static minimum level of social existence is a strange and unacceptable one to Americans, for Americans are typically abundance-minded and have gone a long way in providing abundance for themselves. Though pockets of poverty remain, production as *mass* production is sensitively geared to needed mass consumption.

From this it follows that the labor and property services which people render and from which they derive incomes must be rewarded liberally. Prosperity can be sustained only if purchasing power is widely distributed and freely exercised. Today we know that poverty is not only unnecessary but positively dangerous. Therefore we have elevated the concept of spending to the status of a leading principle of economics. And statisticians everywhere, whether employed by the government or private industry, are always watching the trends of personal-consumption expenditure as a prime indicator of the direction in which economic activity is moving, up or down.

This newer economics, however, does not make any inference that income (or "input") prices should be high merely for the sake of being high. The reason we can afford a high-income philosophy is the great degree of technological efficiency which has been achieved by labor, management, and scientists, as well as sympathetic government officials, all working together effectively, imbued with a progressive tradition of mass democracy, and well educated by our extensive system of free public education.

To maintain and improve incomes and production, labor and management, in particular, must very consciously regard themselves as mutual trustees of the nation's technological heritage. This means that income prices for particular kinds of goods or services rendered must be relatively high in industries or occupations where solid improvements in methods of production are being made, but relatively low in declining industries or in occupations which essentially sanction a squandering of human effort and material resources. It is needless to repeat that income differentials based on productivity differences should exist at high levels of income (because in our economy of abundance this is not only desirable but necessary).

In brief, a price system in its role of generating income must guide the deployment of the labor force and productive property in such a way that people will use their labor, or let their property be used, not only in any manner they prefer but along lines which are socially useful and necessary.

IN CONCLUSION

The foregoing remarks have brought forth basic qualitative considerations pertinent to any appraisal of resource-allocation by a method of selling and buying goods, services, and finance at market prices. Previously the quantitative aspects of American economic activity, as mediated by market prices, were comprehensively examined.

The particularities of theoretical and actual output-price determination will be explained in Part IV of this book, and the theory and reality of our income distribution in Part V. The generalizations projected in this introductory chapter are meant to acquaint the reader with the quantitative dimensions of the American price system and with the qualitative standards by which it must be judged.

For Discussion

1. The Reverend Thomas Robert Malthus, in his *Essay on Population,* first published in 1798, advanced a theory that population increases in a geometrical progression (1, 2, 4, 8, 16, etc.), whereas the means of subsistence increases in an arithmetical progression (1, 2, 3, 4, 5, etc.). At present, with the great technological progress since Malthus' time in producing means of subsistence, it would appear that his theory might well be stated the other way around. Why, then, is there any need for economizing in the use of resources?

2. One authority has said that "economic science investigates what the individual is confronted with and what he does in getting a living and getting rich by transfers of property ownership." How, if at all, does this differ from the definition of economics in this book?

3. The following figures are presented for your use in thinking about the statement made on page 8: "This composition [of total economic activity during the 1950's] is not expected to change radically in the calculable future."

Volume of Business Done By and Among Major Transactor Groups, United States, 1940 and 1955

Transactor Group	Revenue Received ($ billions)	
	1940	1955
Corporations	145	603
Nonincorporated business firms	62	240
Farmers	9	32
Federal government	9	81
State and local governments	14	49
Banking, insurance, and nonprofit organizations	14	72
Consumers, considered as selling productive services	79	354
Rest of the world	4	22

a. Translate the table into percentage terms by obtaining the total for each year and expressing the revenue received by each transactions sector during the respective year as a percentage of the total for that year.

b. What is your over-all impression as the result of making a comparison of the two years in percentage terms?

c. What are some of the significant differences in the detailed aspects of the composition of total economic activity during these two years?

d. What accounts for the large differences in absolute dollar magnitudes of money flows as between the two years?

4. The total flow of goods and services and financial transactions amounted to precisely $1.333 trillion in 1953. Of this amount only $42.5 billion, that is, $0.0425 trillion, was in the form of purely financial transactions. Why elaborate on this apparently trivial item in the description of total economic activity, as is done in the body of this chapter for several pages?

5. To define a price system as a rationing system seems to invite at least verbal confusion, since we habitually *contrast* pricing and rationing. What is the way out of this apparent verbal difficulty?

6. Of the five main functions of an economic system, listed on page 5, which do you believe a price system can perform adequately and exhaustively? Which, if any, do you think it cannot?

7. Accepting the definition of "market" which is given in this chapter, try to envision what different types of markets exist in your home town. Envisage not only trade relations of a purely local character but also the relations of your community with other American centers of economic activity and with the rest of the world. To what extent, if any, does this analysis alter your perception of the economic life of your home town?

8. In the section on output and income (input) prices it is said in several places that these prices "ought to be" this or that. This implies that there is a relation between ethics and economics. Do you think there ought to be such a relation? Why not accept the "facts of the market place" as they are revealed to us by statistical analysis?

2 National Income and National Prosperity

In Chapter 1 the economic system was described in terms of the major flows of economic transactions at current market prices. The function of market price in allocating resources and distributing income was *institutionally* sketched, that is, as a customary way in which exchanges are made in the American economy. (The theoretical analysis of the pricing process will be presented in Part IV.)

Can a market-price system of economic organization serve all the major economic functions, not only those of resource-allocation and income-distribution, but especially the functions of maintaining full employment and stimulating economic growth? One may wonder why the question is even posed, as our economic market system is something most people simply take for granted, or so it seems.

As a matter of fact, a significant change in attitudes toward the capability of a price system in the matters of employment and economic growth has taken place since the 1930's. New ways of economic thinking emerged when persistent unemployment, lasting over a decade, cast strong doubt on the belief that when the economy has fallen into depression it will soon generate its own automatic forces of revival. There was a widespread feeling that, if left alone, the economic system might leave us in the doldrums forever.

Many persons experienced this feeling as a matter of grave practical concern. To others (that is, younger persons) the American economy's predicament during the 1930's is only a historical fact. Years of lively economic activity since 1941 directed attention to problems that are characteristic of times when full employment or nearly full employment is the rule. Following World War II, businessmen were largely preoccupied with supplying markets, not with finding them. The prime concern of wage-earners was not finding jobs, but improving conditions on and off the job. On the negative side, postwar conditions caused anxiety about high levels of prices, not about low prices and wages, as was the case during the Great Depression.

The problem of full employment nevertheless remains basic. For example, the concern people feel about constantly rising prices is based on the awareness that boom and bust are causally related. In the decade following World War II there were two recessions, those of 1948–49 and 1953–54. They proved to be neither deep nor prolonged, but this was not known at their outset. A third recession began in October, 1957, when in six months industrial production dropped almost as much as during the year-long 1948–49 recession and approximately twice as much as during the 1953–54 recession. During these six months, October, 1957, to April, 1958, the value of all goods and services produced in the nation declined by 5 per cent—nearly as much as it had fallen, percentagewise, in the prewar recession of 1937–38 (when the drop was 6.5 per cent). Industrial operations were reduced to two-thirds of capacity, or less, in many key industries, for example, in basic metals production, in machinery building, and in the manufacture of major consumers' durables.

Late in 1958 it was seen that business investment in new plant and equipment would most likely be one-sixth below 1957, at best, assuming an immediate upturn. This hope was based on surveys of businessmens' investment plans for the near future. But businessmen had, since recession set in, twice promised about 10 per cent more new investment than they later actually undertook. Government expenditure increased in 1958 and further increases were planned for 1959. Was the recession over at the end of 1958?

In these circumstances there is a continued interest in the practical and theoretical knowledge which has been gathered about possible ways and means of maintaining full employment. A prerequisite for accomplishing anything in this regard is, of course, the collection and classification of statistical data which have a direct bearing on the problem of sustaining employment and national output and income at high levels. The need is being met by a progressive refinement of national income and output accounting for the special purpose of recording the aggregate effects of economic decision-making by consumers, businessmen, and government officials on the national level of employment and output activity.

Types of National Economic Accounting

Prior to 1936, national accounting had not extended much beyond the problems of the individual firm, with careful calculations being made to disclose the impact of business decisions on the firm's private profit or loss position. Public enterprises, such as municipally owned and operated water and power districts, accounted for their income from operations also; and federal, state, and local governments gave some accounting of their use of appropriations—accounts which, when assembled, showed whether there was a balance or imbalance of government finances.

Since 1936, national accounting is being done for the economic system as a whole. We have already observed the money-flow system of national economic accounting, which furnishes a comprehensive view of the characteristic methods of conducting our economic affairs, that is, of how we "sector" our economy according to legal and functional types of organization and how we borrow and lend.

Money-flow national accounting could serve as an aid in coming to grips with the problem of economic instability. However, a less-detailed form of national income and output accounting is customarily employed. In this less-detailed system, which is simply known as *national income accounting,* purely financial transactions are ignored and the goods-purchasing, goods-selling sectors are more broadly defined; that is, some data are combined which are separately accounted for under the method of money-flow accounting. These simplifications are made because national income accounting primarily serves a special purpose, that of highlighting the direct effect on national income of all the separate economic decisions made by consumers, businessmen, and government officials. If the effect is to raise the national income, there will be lively economic activity leading to a state of full employment; if the effect of economic decisions is to lower national income because the decisions are made in a pessimistic mood, unemployment is most likely to ensue. The emphasis in national income accounting lies on the economic activity generated under our institutions, not on the structure of these institutions.

In this chapter the concept, as well as the general method, of national income accounting is explained. Different ways of measuring national income for different purposes will be elucidated. And the social significance of national income accounting will be pointed out. Its significance resides in the fact that slowly but surely decision-makers, in studying accounting which is done on an economy-wide basis, are forming their decisions in terms of the effect they might have on the size of the national income and the level of employment, as well as estimating the effect of these decisions on their private profit or loss position. When this is done, many knotty problems of the economic environment (specifically, employment and unemployment) can be much more easily tackled by mutual agreement of business, government, and labor leaders than was possible when people only dimly sensed the general economic forces operating in the environment and had no quantitative conception of them. This chapter will also explain how economic leaders use national income data individually and in conference with one another.

The aim of national income accounting is to observe the *end results* of how the economy operates as a goods-producing and goods-purchasing system. That is to say: Is current productive activity at a sufficiently high level to provide employment for every person able and willing to work or to put his property to productive use? What is the aggregate final output of goods and services? How are the fruits of production allocated? These are the questions national income accounting asks with the practical aim of furnishing the decision-makers in the economy with the kind of information they need in order to determine whether by their choices of action (or inaction) they are contributing to the maintenance of full employment.

To summarize, there are two closely related types of social income accounting. One is the system of money-flow accounting. It facilitates our understanding of our institutional arrangements for goods-purchasing, goods-selling, and borrowing and lending. Money-flow accounting was discussed in Chapter 1 for the purpose of indicating the institutional characteristics of the American economic process. The other system of social accounting is called national income accounting. It focuses attention on the problems of economic stability. It is of simplified design and directly aids private and public economic decision-makers in arriving at policies favoring sustained full employment. The remainder of this chapter is devoted to a particularized explanation of this widely used system of national income accounting.

The Concept of National Income

Economic production lies at the heart of a nation's general welfare and common defense. It is the *final*, usable output realized by current productive activity and constitutes the real income of the nation.

The total output of goods and services may be measured from two points of view: as the sum total of final products created by the economy, and as the sum total of costs incurred in turning out the goods and services. The distinction is pointed up by observing the operations of a typical business firm. On the one hand, the firm produces and sells a flow of product values. On the other hand, it pays out, or retains, incomes that accrue to the firm in the course of its operations. This double aspect of the activities of the single business firm suggests that the measurement of national output, largely produced by business firms, can be approached in a twofold manner—either by summing product values at current market prices or by summing income flows.

GROSS NATIONAL PRODUCT (GNP)

When national output is measured in terms of the aggregate market value of all flows of goods and services to their final users, a figure is obtained which is called the *gross national product* (GNP). Expressed in current prices, the GNP reflects the total dollar value of production—$440 billion in 1957, $234 billion in 1947, $91 billion in 1937, for example.

So stated, the figures for GNP in different years cannot be directly compared. The amount of goods and services flowing to final users in 1957 was not nearly twice as large as it was in 1947, nor was it almost five times as large as in 1937. This appears to be the case only because a different yardstick of prices was used to measure the value of the nation's gross output in different years. Different aggregate amounts of goods and services are produced in different years, to be sure. If a dollar always purchased the same amount of the same or similar types of goods and services, the fluctuations of GNP would indicate fluctuations of the national gross product correctly.

The purchasing power of the dollar is notorious for its instability. As a result, raw data showing the value of goods and services at current market prices register the influence not only of changing quantities produced but also of fluctuations in the purchasing power of the dollar. For instance, it was possible in 1937 to buy for a dollar almost twice as much of the same or similar kinds of goods as could be commanded with a dollar in 1957.

Measuring the purchasing power of the dollar. Statisticians have developed methods for determining the purchasing power of the dollar in different years. It is done by selecting a representative large number of different types of goods commonly bought by consumers at retail. Another measurement of the value of the dollar is made in terms of goods which producers typically buy at wholesale prices. The selected goods are considered to fill a typical market basket. These market baskets, one for consumers and one for producers, are constituted so as to be reasonably comparable between different years. Then the consumers' and producers' market baskets are priced; that is, it is determined how much they would have cost at different times.

When pricing a market basket of consumers' or producers' goods, the prices of the component items cannot be simply averaged. Supposing, for simplicity's sake, that the consumers' market basket were comprised only of bread and neckties, the bread costing 20 cents a loaf and the neckties $2.00 apiece. Clearly, the price of this market basket cannot be $2.20, the simple sum of 20 cents per loaf of bread and $2.00 per necktie. This amount would not express the relative importance of either article of consumption in a typical consumer's budget. Let us say that consumers normally buy 175 loaves of bread annually per person, and three neckties. The average price of this simplified market basket during a year would be only 23 cents. This is the magnitude of a *weighted* average of the price of bread and neckties during a year, that is, an average weighted in proportion to the importance which each article assumes in a representative consumer's budget.[1]

If the price of bread rises to 25 cents a loaf in a subsequent year and neckties to $3.50 per unit, the same market basket will cost 30 cents. The same quantities of goods being involved in either year, a change in the purchasing power of the dollar stands revealed. To determine by how much the value of the dollar changes, one may use a cost of living "index number" or an index number of wholesale prices. These index numbers are prepared by government and private statisticians. They are constructed by the use of weighted averages of the prices of numerous articles.

The construction of index numbers requires the selection of any one year, or average of years, as the *base period* in some reasonably close succession of years. (It would be absurd to use the year 1817 as a base period, for example, since consumer wants and methods of production have drastically changed since that early time.) The weighted average of the prices of representative and comparable articles in the base period is stated as being 100 per cent. The price of the same or a

[1] To arrive at a weighted average one multiplies the number of units consumed of each of different articles by their respective per unit prices. The total amount of expenditure, thus ascertained, is next divided by the total number of articles purchased. In the above example 175 loaves of bread are assumed to be the typical amount purchased annually per person. At 20 cents per unit, 175 loaves of bread yields $35. Three neckties per year are also assumed to be in the typical annual consumer's budget. At $2 per unit this (or perhaps some closely equivalent article) adds $6 to the budget. The simplified market basket costs $41 for the year. Divided by 178, the number of articles bought, this yields 23 cents as the *weighted average* price of the market basket. For realism one need only expand this illustration to include a large number of items which characteristically enter into the American consumer's budget—not only basic staples, but TV sets, etc.

similar budget in subsequent and earlier years is then expressed by percentages in relation to the base period. To illustrate, the officially recorded consumers' price index for 1957 is 122 per cent of the 1947–49 base period; in relation to this period, the consumers' price index for the single year 1947 is 95.5 per cent; and 61.4 per cent in 1937, a year of abnormally low prices. Figure 2–1 illustrates changes in the cost of living during five successive years as regards the total consumers' budget and its chief components.

Figure 2–1. Consumer Prices, 1952–57

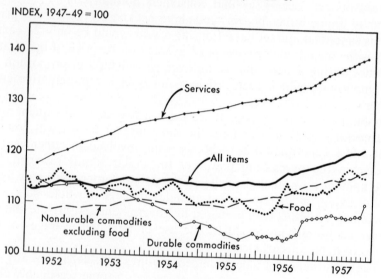

Cost of living indexes, or wholesale price indexes, can be used to ascertain the purchasing power of the dollar. To do this one must visualize how many representative articles a dollar will buy, rather than think of how many dollars are required to buy a given amount of goods. Thus, if in 1957 the cost of living has risen to 122 per cent of the 1947–49 base period, it is evident that any one dollar will buy only as much as 82 cents did in the base period. (The simple arithmetical procedure is to take the reciprocal of the cost of living, that is, to divide 100 by 122 in order to ascertain the 1957 purchasing power of the dollar in terms of the 1947–49 base period.) The index of wholesale prices, which is the businessman's general cost of living, is prepared in a similar manner. The purchasing power of the dollar is reported from both the consumers' and the producers' point of view by government statisticians.

Real GNP contrasted with nominal GNP. The index of consumer prices explains the pressure we experience as individuals when the cost of living is rising. The index furnishes a measure of the real value of a person's income, as compared to the nominal amount which is measured by the number of dollars gained. However, neither the cost of living index nor the index of wholesale prices should be applied in correcting the gross national product for price changes. Both indexes apply only to a part of the total flow of goods and services; but the GNP measures this flow in its entirety. Hence an index is required which is based on price trends in all the sectors of the economy.

Statisticians have developed such an over-all index. Goods and services transactions are first classified in four broad categories: (1) personal consumption expenditures, (2) expenditures for private domestic investment inclusive of home-buying, (3) foreign investment expenditures, and (4) government expenditures. Each of these broad categories of goods and services expenditures are subdivided. Thus, in reference to people's personal consumption expenditures, price indexes are separately constructed for changes in the prices of durable goods, nondurables, and services. Price indexes for new residential construction and for producers' durable equipment are ascertained. Changes in prices of goods typically bought by government—for example, military hardware—are observed. Each broad category, such as new residential housing, is analyzed for price movements with respect to particular types of housing. The index for this and the other categories is arrived at by combining these separate observations. Finally, an over-all index is constructed by combining the broad categories mentioned.

The refined index is used, instead of the index of consumer or wholesale prices, to adjust the value of the gross national product to changes in prices, so that a direct comparison can be made, year by year, to reveal actual changes in the quantity of goods and services. The procedure, once this refined index is available, is simply to divide any given annual magnitude of GNP by the index. The procedure is known as "deflating" the GNP, and the refined index is known as the *implicit price deflator.* (It is implicit in all the separate indexes of which it is comprised.) The most readily accessible implicit price deflator to translate nominal GNP into real GNP is that prepared by the Department of Commerce. Here the single year of 1954 is used as the base period. The instability of the purchasing power of the dollar, *with respect to total GNP,* is disclosed in Table 2–1.

With this information it is easy to correct the GNP for changing dollar values so as to make a comparison of different years possible.

Table 2–1. Implicit Price Deflator for Selected Years
(1954 = 100)

Year	1937	1942	1947	1954	1957
Price Deflator	49.5	59.6	83.0	100	108.2

SOURCE: U.S. Department of Commerce, *Survey of Current Business*, July, 1958, Table 8, pp. 10–11.

It is only necessary to divide the nominal GNP, the brute total money value of all goods and services in any year, by the implicit price deflator for that year. When this is done in the case of the years cited in Table 2–1, the result is striking. It is emphasized in Table 2–2 by showing the nominal GNP in comparison with the real GNP as computed by the use of the appropriate price deflators.

Table 2–2. Real and Nominal Gross National Product
for Selected Years
($ billions)

Year	Nominal GNP (current dollars)	Real GNP (Dollars of constant 1954 value)
1937	90.8	183.5
1942	159.1	266.9
1947	234.3	282.3
1954	363.1	363.1
1957	440.3	407.0

SOURCE: *Survey of Current Business*, July, 1958, Table 7, pp. 10–11.

Figure 2–2 pictorializes the differences between the nominal and real GNP for the period 1929–57.

By comparing GNP values in constant dollars for different years, one is in effect observing the over-all output performance of an economy at these different times. This is one of the principal uses of GNP data, and such comparisons are made currently, even in periodicals for popular reading, so that the concept and also the label "GNP" have become established in the ordinary vocabulary of most Americans.

In many circles the historical record of the expansion of the *real* GNP, as shown in Figure 2–2, is called a record of economic growth. This is inaccurate, because growth is a matter of quality as well as quantity. By no means all the goods and services which are produced improve the quality of our American culture. In particular instances

Figure 2-2. Gross National Product in Constant and
Current Dollars, 1929-57

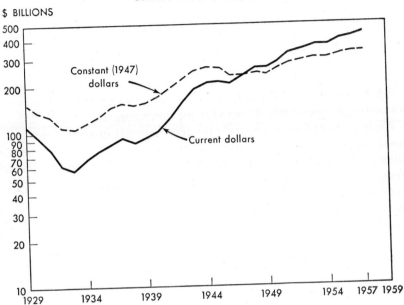

SOURCE: *Survey of Current Business,* July, 1958, Table 7, pp. 10-11.

we may differ in our judgments of whether a commodity, or service, really furnishes genuine want-satisfaction. One should refer to historical increases of GNP simply as physical output expansion, allowing individuals to make up their own minds whether or not the economy is really growing in its ability to serve the needs of the American culture for survival and enrichment. Other uses of the concept of gross national product will be explained later.

NATIONAL INCOME

The total output may also be measured in terms of the cost factor of producing it: labor costs, land costs, and capital costs, to mention only the principal factor categories. Measuring the total output in terms of the factor costs of producing it yields the *national income,* that is, the aggregate earnings of labor and property as paid to job-holders and property owners for participating in current production. This measure of national welfare differs from the gross national product in disregarding two types of cost charges against the total value of production. These cost burdens are: (1) depreciation charges and other allowances for wear and tear of durable capital goods (factories, machinery, farm buildings, and so on); (2) excise taxes, customs, luxury taxes, and some other types of taxes which consumers pay as part of the price of articles they purchase. These are the so-called "non-income" charges against value received from production. They are charges which businessmen must make to consumers, but which they cannot treat as income freely spendable at their discretion. For if capital consumption allowances were spent on anything other than the replacement of capital goods, the plant would run down. And taxes which businessmen collect on behalf of the government obviously do not constitute spendable income for the entrepreneur.

An important fact to remember is that national income is not computed simply by deducting the nonincome charges from the market value of the total output of consumable goods and services. National income is computed by ascertaining the sum total of labor and property incomes paid—the aggregate of wages, salaries, rents, royalties, and the like. Table 2–3 shows GNP and national income separately ascertained.

Table 2–3. Gross National Product and National Income in 1957
(billions of current dollars)

OUTPUT		INCOME	
Gross National Product in Terms of Major Components		National Income in Terms of Major Components	
Personal Consumption Expenditures:		Compensation of employees	254.6
On durable goods	40.0		
On nondurables	138.0	Noncorporate business and professional persons' incomes	31.7
On services	106.5		
Consumer and Business Investment:		Farmers' incomes	11.6
Residential housing	17.0	Rental incomes	11.8
Other new construction	19.0		
Producers' new investment in durable equipment	27.8	Interest incomes	12.9
Change in business inventories	1.0	Corporate profits before taxes	43.4
Government Purchases of Goods and Services:		Inventory re-evaluations	—2.0
Federal government, national security expenditures	46.5	Total National Income	$364.0
Other federal expenditures	4.8	Add: Nonincome charges to the value of production:	
Outlays of state and local governments	36.3	Capital consumption	37.8
Net Foreign Investment by Americans:	3.5	Indirect business taxes	37.7
Total (rounded):	$440	Total (rounded):	$440

SOURCE: *Survey of Current Business*, July, 1958, Tables 1, 2, 4, pp. 4–7.

THE RELATIONSHIP OF GNP AND NATIONAL INCOME

When the final output and income values generated in the course of current production are separately surveyed and calculated, it is evident that national output and income values must balance after suitable allowances for nonincome charges against production have been made. In other words, although independently determined, national income will equal gross national product *minus* nonincome charges for capital consumption and indirect business taxes. Alternatively, gross national product will equal national income *plus* the nonincome charges. This is a formidable way of saying, merely, that no more can be distributed in the aggregate than is produced in the aggregate for current consumer, business, and government consumption. The relationship is graphically illustrated in Figure 2–3.

Actually, for a short time more can be consumed than is produced for current consumption by failing to replace worn-out plant and equipment or by using productive equipment for immediate consumption purposes. But this is the road to ruin and is resorted to only by warring nations already well on the road to ruin. For example, in

Figure 2–3. Relation of Gross National Product and National Income in 1957

(In $ billions, at current prices)

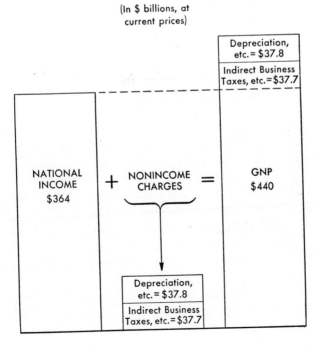

Germany in 1917, anything containing copper was commandeered, and the copper was extracted and used in weapons production.

The matter of final output values balancing with aggregate national income values may also be put in another way. We desire to have a measure or index of national economic activity to inform us as to whether or not current production is at a rate that provides jobs for all willing and able persons. Let us take, as a simplified example, the case of a farmer selling wheat to a miller, who grinds it into flour and then sells flour to a baker. The baker finally sells bread to housewives. What is the value of the employment-determining economic production involved in this example? Is it the value of the wheat *plus* the value of the flour *plus* the value of the bread made from the flour?

Value added. Offhand this might seem to be true, but brief reflection will show it to be erroneous. For a moment let us pause to consider what is involved in this illustration. Between the farm gate and the consumer's table, a number of handling and processing steps take place, each of which must be paid for. A bushel of wheat moves from the farm into a country elevator, and from there to a flour mill as much as 1,600 miles distant. On the way the wheat may temporarily come to rest at a terminal elevator; this entails storage charges. Carriage charges have already been incurred for moving the wheat on rails; these transportation charges will continue until the wheat reaches the flour mill.

First, processing of the wheat is done at the flour mill, where the wheat is ground and emerges as flour of different types. Grain mill production workers must be paid at the mill, and other production costs must be covered. From the flour mill a 100-pound sack of flour moves by rail or truck to a bakery. There the number of services performed multiplies rapidly. Before the finished loaf of bread is placed in a supermarket, its ingredients have been stored, processed for baking, and baked; the bread itself has been sliced, wrapped, and delivered by a driver-salesman. At the supermarket the bread must be displayed, inventoried, and sold. The process of bread production has not ceased until the bread is on the consumer's table.

Now let us determine how much value was added at every step of the process. The farmer receives sales revenue in commercially disposing of his wheat. From this he must deduct certain costs directly associated with the production of the wheat: the cost of seed, the cost of gas and oil used in operating farm machinery, a repair bill for farm buildings, and others of a similar direct nature. We shall assume the farmer gathers his own seed instead of buying it and has money on hand with which to meet the other out-of-pocket costs. Hence we may

1109056

ignore these running costs which must be met immediately, long before the wheat is sold. Consequently, when the wheat is sold, we can consider the entire revenue received by the farmer at that time as "value added" by the farmer to production. Out of this value added by his productive efforts the farmer pays wages to his farmhands and to himself, interest on borrowed money, and rent on leased acres of land.

What is the value added to production by the miller when he sells flour made of the farmer's wheat? Of course, the price which the flour-miller charges his customer, the baker, includes the cost of the wheat used in producing the flour. But that part of the miller's sales revenue —the cost of the wheat—is not a measure of value added to production by the miller. Only if the flour-miller owned and operated a wheat farm and grew his own supplies would this be true. In that case he would have paid, or would be obligated to pay, wages, interest, and rent to cooperating owners of productive services who help him grow the wheat. But we have supposed that he lets a farmer do this and simply buys the wheat from him. Therefore, if we counted the cost compensation which the miller received from the baker for the wheat bought, as though it were value added to production by the miller, we would be counting the value of wheat production twice over: once for the farmer, once for the miller when only the farmer had carried on this production. It goes without saying that this would seriously mislead us in estimating how much employment was furnished by the activity of wheat production.

To prevent double counting at any stage of production it is necessary to distinguish between *final product* and *intermediate product* at every stage of production. Thus the wheat in our example is the final product of the farmer. To the miller, the wheat, which he grinds into flour, is an intermediate product. The flour is the miller's final product, but to the baker it is the intermediate product; the bread is the baker's final product. This, in turn, becomes an intermediate product to the supermarket operator, whose final product is his retailing service.

The price of an intermediate product is classified as "cost of material" by its user. To obtain the unduplicated value which is added, for example, in bread production, simply deduct from the sales value of the final product at each stage of production the price of the intermediate product, that is, the cost of material. Table 2–4 demonstrates the procedure.

Column (*b*) in Table 2–4 shows the price of the intermediate product at each successive stage of production. This price equals the sales value *at the previous stage,* at which it was a final product. By observ-

Table 2–4. Final Product, Intermediate Product, and Value Added
in the Production of a 1-Pound Loaf of Bread*

Type of Producer	Sales Value of His Final Product (a)	Cost of Material (b)	Value Added (c)	
			In Cents	As a Percentage
Farmer	+ 3¢	......†=	3	17
Grain elevator, transport agency, and flour miller	+ 5	— 3¢=	2	11
Bakery, wholesale	+15	— 5 =	10	55
Supermarket	+18	—15 =	3	17
Total	+41	—23 =	18, the unduplicated value added by bread production	100

SOURCE: U.S. Department of Agriculture, Agricultural Marketing Service, *Marketing Margins for White Bread,* Misc. Pub. No. 172 (Washington, D.C.: Government Printing Office, March, 1956), pp. 5–6.

*A bushel of wheat yields enough flour to make about sixty-six 1-pound loaves of white bread.

†Negligible for the small amount of wheat required for making a 1-pound loaf of bread. Cost of seed, fuel for tractors, etc. are incurred but are figured for the wheat crop as a whole.

ing the diagonal lines it will be noticed that intermediate products cancel out, being marked with a (+) sign in column (*a*) and a (—) sign in column (*b*). In column (*c*) the desired information is furnished, namely, the unduplicated value added at every stage of production. When summed, column (*c*) reveals the total unduplicated value added by the entire process of bread production. This equals the price of the end product delivered to the housewife.

Generalized view of value added. When the value added by each of many thousands of specific production processes is correctly ascertained, then summed for the entire economy, the nature of national income is clearly revealed and its relation to GNP unmistakably seen: (1) The value of the final product of the economy as a whole evidently equals the sum of the total product of each producing entity in the economy *less* its purchases of materials; and (2) for each producing entity, the sales value of the product less the cost of materials purchased equals income earned by labor, land, capital, and management, *plus* whatever nonincome charges of depreciation and indirect business taxation were incurred and will be passed on to the consumers. Hence it follows that (3) for the economy as a whole the total value of final product equals the sum of incomes accruing in production *plus* nonincome charges against the value of production; that is, gross national product equals national income *plus* nonincome charges.

NATIONAL INCOME CONCEPTS IN COMPARISON WITH MONEY-FLOW ECONOMIC ACCOUNTING

Being oriented toward the end results of economic operations rather than their institutional nature, national income accounting does not report transactions in such refined detail as does money-flow accounting. For example, gross national product accounts contain only one consolidated business sector, comprised of all the varieties of business organization. In other words, GNP does not distinguish in terms of sales and costs between corporate, noncorporate, farm, and financial sectors in the economy as does the money-flow accounting system. Also, national income accounting procedure is to include in the business sector all commercial government transactions, such as those of municipal water and power districts or of the federal post office system. The reason is that a main purpose of national income accounting is to shed light on how commercial transactions contribute, or fail to contribute, to full employment and economic expansion, regardless of whether these transactions originate in the private business community, in government, or even in private households. Transactions are also consolidated in the government and consumer sectors of the economy.

When the different types of business transactor groups are consolidated (for example, life insurance companies, farmers, the post office), flows of money between them naturally fall into the category of "intermediate product values" and are consequently eliminated from national income accounting. Offhand, the startling result is a great reduction of the magnitude of recorded economic transactions. For example, in the more detailed money-flow accounting system, the recorded business transactions total $890 billion for 1953. For the same year, national income accounting records less than a third of that amount. Even when all commercial transactions of federal, state, and local governments are added into the business sector, the final product values generated by the business sector of national income accounting total only $321 billion for that same year of 1953. Product values generated by government through noncommercial activities total $31.7 billion in the national income accounts of 1953, as against a total of $116.4 billion recorded under the procedure of money-flow accounting. The upshot of these consolidations (made to center attention on the values of products for end consumption by consumers, businessmen, and federal, state, and local governments) is a gross national product magnitude of $365.5 billion, as compared to a total of $1.3 trillion ($1,300 thousand billion) in transactions recorded under the method of national money-flow accounting.

It is precisely this smaller figure of $365.5 billion of final output values which gives us the information we require in order to compare GNP's from year to year and, above all, to help us determine whether the national economy is heading toward or away from full employment.

How can a simple gross national product datum or a national income total inform us of this vital matter? Readily enough. Knowing what the prevailing rates of wages, interest, and rent are, as well as understanding current methods of production, one can estimate quite closely how much it would cost to produce national output at a rate at which our human, natural, and man-made resources can be utilized to the full extent that employees, self-employed persons, and property owners freely wish to have their personal or material resources used. Thereupon it is a matter of comparing the actual national gross product, or national income *trends*, to determine whether or not a full-employment national income is likely to be established or maintained. By the same token, it is possible to estimate whether or not national income trends are in the direction of inflation; that is, whether the private and public decision-makers in economic matters are planning for more production than there are resources available for realizing expanded production.[2]

[2] The reader should beware of concluding that it is a simple matter to appraise the feasibility of planned production in the aggregate against the available resources base. It can only be accomplished by using national income accounting in conjunction with a third type of social accounting, that known as "input-output analysis." This system takes into account the technological relations between physical inputs and physical outputs at every stage of the productive process. That is to say, it focuses on inter-industry relations at the production level. For each industry the important factor is the amount purchased from other industries in relation to its own production, and the allocation of its output to other industries and sectors of the economy. If certain bills of goods are planned for production, the analysis reveals the existence of bottle-necks of labor, raw materials, and component parts. And the analysis permits viewing a planned production program not only in the light of individual limiting factors but also with an eye toward the interdependence of these factors and the prospects for breaking some of the bottlenecks. Progress along these lines was made by the War Production Board in 1942, when an originally overambitious military program was

PRIMARY USES OF GNP AND NATIONAL INCOME MEASURES

Numerous aids to economic decision-makers are furnished by national income accounting in addition to its pre-eminent utility in facilitating informed discussions about the problems and policies of maintaining full employment.

GNP. As a measure which focuses on the over-all performance of an economy, GNP can be used in wartime to estimate the outside limits of feasible war production, given certain irreducible basic civilian requirements. Also, in reflecting depreciation allowances, GNP allows us to judge whether we are conserving our material resources by setting aside enough productive effort to replace them as they wear out, or whether we are living in a fool's paradise, "eating up our capital."

The item of indirect business taxation is an interesting inclusion in GNP. Actually, it records the value of most government services which we pay for, not at the time of using them (if ever), but when purchasing certain goods (for example, gasoline or cigarettes) from private businessmen or when paying property taxes. (Home-ownership is considered to be the business of furnishing oneself with housing services.) The fact is that whether or not one uses public libraries or sends children to public schools, whether or not one drives on a road through a national park, and so on, these are things one pays for when paying federal excise taxes, state sales taxes, and local property taxes. Conversely, when actually using parks, public schools, state or national highways, one does not pay at the time for this specific instance of use as one would when crossing a private toll bridge, sending one's youngsters to private schools, and so on. In recording indirect business taxes (including property taxes), GNP gives some indication of the proportion of our over-all current productive effort which is being devoted to establishing and maintaining generally available public services—the misleadingly called "free public services."

National income. The national income measures what we can consume without using up our capital or reducing the public services that are generally available. At the same time, national income informs us directly about the earnings of individuals and groups in the aggregate. By relating the two, it may be seen that the national income shows how many goods and services individuals and groups can

---

reduced to feasible dimensions. A satisfactory explanation of input-output analysis can be made only with the use of mathematics; hence this material is only for advanced study.

have in return for individual or group productive efforts without undermining the bases of future wealth and public welfare.

Because national income is the measure of the value of national production at the factor costs of production, national income fluctuations disclose variations in people's willingness (or ability) to work or to have their property used productively. Since this variability in people's willingness to engage in productive activity is far more of a causal factor in producing business cycles than are variations in capital consumption allowances or in the provision of general public services, economists habitually think in terms of national income rather than GNP when concerned with employment and economic growth problems.

Another highly significant aspect is that national income is shown not only in terms of the factor costs of current production but also in terms of its origins in the various industries of the national economy and by different legal types of economic organization as well. As to the first—national income by industrial origins—Table 2–5 shows the breakdown in 1954.

Table 2–5. National Income by Industrial Origins

Industry	Per Cent of National Income Generated (Approx.)
Agriculture, forestry, and fishing	5
Mining	2
Construction	5
Manufacturing	32
Wholesale and retail trade	17
Finance, insurance, real estate	9
Transportation	5
Communications, public utilities	4
Private services	10
Government services	11
Rest of the world	Less than 1
	100

SOURCE: U.S. Department of Commerce, Office of Business Economics, *National Income, 1954 Edition—A Supplement to the Survey of Current Business* (Washington, D.C.: Government Printing Office, 1955), Table 13, pp. 176–77.

This type of information is extremely useful in spotting economic troubles that encompass a whole industry, from where they could sweep on to affect the total economy. Thus, in recent years farming has suffered an income setback which could easily spread to manufacturing through a drop in orders to farm machinery manufacturers, who in turn could reduce their orders of steel, and so on. Of course, other influences in the economy could offset troubles in any one industry, but to spot difficulties and set in motion recovery policies is surely preferable to hoping that economic trouble spots will somehow be offset by unexpectedly bright spots elsewhere in the national economy.

Table 2–6 shows national income as it originated in the different *legal* forms of economic organization in the mid-1950's.

Table 2–6. National Income by Type of Economic Organization

Type of Economic Unit	Per Cent of National Income Generated
Corporations	55
Sole proprietorships and partnerships	25
Mutual insurance companies, mutual savings and loan associations, cooperatives, etc.	5
Commercial-type government enterprises	1
Total, private business	86
Income generated by general government operations	10
Income originating in households and nonprofit institutions	4
	100

SOURCE: U.S. Department of Commerce, Office of Business Economics, *National Income, 1954 Edition—A Supplement to the Survey of Current Business* (Washington, D.C.: Government Printing Office, 1955), pp. 174–75.

Changes in types of economic organization by legal form (for instance, the growing predominance of corporations) are of considerable importance in explaining the impact of, say, sales fluctuations on the level of national employment. This will be discussed at length later, but to illustrate it briefly we may consider the fact that before the rise of corporations, falling sales typically stimulated entrepreneurs to lower prices in order to revive sales. Today's trend of corporations is, however, to maintain prices at or near their current level.

OTHER MEASURES OF INCOME

While the national income measure of the final value of aggregate production is the general "work-horse" concept of economic analysis, it is occasionally desirable to break down this measure further. This is done when one wishes to know how much money individual families and unrelated individuals have for spending and for paying taxes. One might think that this is measured by the national income, but the fact is that not all the earnings to which individuals have a claim are distributed to them in any given accounting period. On the other hand, some individuals receive income payments without having participated in current production. Thus, the *personal income* of Americans, in the aggregate, differs from their rewards for participating in current production.

Personal income illustrated. In the latter part of the 1950's national income was in the neighborhood of $350 to $400 billion. However, not all of this was distributed to the people who had gained it. Thus the tax on corporate profits absorbed $5 out of every $10 of profit gained by corporations; the managers of the corporations typically retained another $2 out of every $10 of corporate profits and plowed it back into the business. The remaining $3 out of every $10 of corporate profit was received by the stockholders as personal income. Owners of unincorporated enterprises are not required to pay a tax on their business profits but are allowed to treat these as personal income. However, the owners and/or managers of noncorporate firms do not withdraw all their business profits; they characteristically leave from one-fourth to one-third of them in the business. As a result of taxes on corporate profit and plowbacks of earnings in 'corporate and noncorporate enterprises, the amount of national income actually received by persons was reduced from $364 billion to $326 billion in 1957.

This diminished amount does not constitute the nation's aggregate personal income. Just as there are many persons who do not receive as income all that is gained by their investment of time and/or money, so are there people who receive income without having rendered services during the current accounting period. These are retired persons drawing social security benefits, their survivors, temporarily unemployed persons, war veterans in receipt of military pensions or military disability and educational allowances, and civil service pensioners. These kinds of payment as well as similar ones by state and local governments and, to a far lesser extent, by business firms are called *transfer payments.* They are so named because they literally transfer money claims on available goods and services from persons currently active in production to persons not currently engaged in production. (This statement carries no moral connotation of people necessarily "getting something for nothing," for could this be said to be true of a disabled veteran, or a person drawing unemployment compensation because he cannot find suitable employment which he is perfectly able and willing to perform?)

Transfer payments rose to nearly $20 billion in the mid-1950's and continued to rise thereafter, standing at $22 billion in December, 1957. Most transfer payments are made by the federal, state, and local governments. Retirement benefits and other payments made under private business pension, health, and welfare plans are also considered to be transfer payments, although classified as wages and salaries earned in the past.

Having observed how the national income is reduced by corporate taxation and earnings retained by business before becoming available to persons, we now add to the reduced amount the total of transfer payments. To illustrate, transfer payments totaled $22 billion in 1957. This is added to the $326 billion of earnings which were actually distributed to persons during that year. The resulting rounded total of $348 billion is, finally, the nation's aggregate *personal income*. It is defined as the total sum which people had available for spending, and for paying taxes.

The concept of personal income has significant practical application. For instance, the measure of personal income reveals what the tax-bearing ability of the people is, given reasonable basic living standards on which encroachment by taxes would be strongly opposed, politically, by the citizens of the nation. To illustrate, let us suppose that the United States wished to finance through taxes a large foreign aid program. Our Congressmen would have to determine what might be the average minimum living standard with which the voters would be content. Deducting this minimum per capita figure, multiplied by the number of individuals in the nation, from the aggregate personal income would indicate the feasible size of the foreign aid fund. Needless to say, the personal income measure becomes vital in case of war, when taxation has to be carried to the ultimate.

Disposable personal income. This is the income remaining to persons after the deduction of personal tax (largely federal income tax) and nontax payments (fines, penalties, donations) to government. As such, personal disposable income indicates most directly the people's standards of living, for it is the amount of money which they freely spend at their individual discretion, and of which they save a part. In 1957, personal tax payments amounted to $43 billion, which, when deducted from the cited figure of $348 billion personal income, leaves $305 billion as the nation's disposable personal income. Figure 2–4 shows disposable personal income in relation to people's aggregate personal consumption expenditures.

We have come a long way from the amount of $440 billion gross national product, the over-all value of the final output of goods and services at current market prices, to $305 billion, the aggregate amount of money which people can freely dispose of as they individually see fit. Disposable personal income is 70 per cent of GNP.

This is not a finding of sinister import. It is simply what is, and nothing more. Out of every dollar of gross national product we first

Figure 2–4. Disposable Personal Income and Consumption

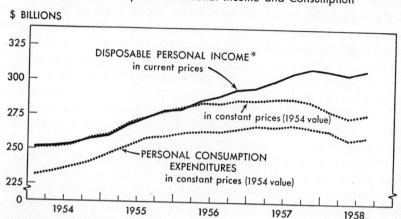

NOTE: Disposable income rose during 1956 and most of 1957, but its buying power increased little because of price advances.

SOURCE: *Survey of Current Business,* July, 1958, Table 3, pp. 6–7.

set aside 8 cents to keep our productive plant and equipment in good condition. Then we spend one-fourth of the remaining 92 cents for government services and government transfer payments. We finance this expenditure by paying business and personal taxes. That is why we usually have 70 cents left per GNP dollar for individual and/or group spending and saving.

Out of this freely disposable 70 cents per GNP dollar, 65 cents was actually spent on personal consumption in 1957. Accordingly it was possible for "the average American" to save 5 cents out of every GNP dollar. In addition, our corporation managers *and other businessmen* did some "automatic saving" for the owners of our business concerns. This was done by management's retaining billions of dollars' worth of earned profits to be plowed back into the businesses, instead of paying out to the owners every dollar of profit gained.[3] Averaged over the whole gross national product, this automatic saving for stockholders and other owners of firms amounted to roughly 4 cents out of every GNP dollar value added by production in 1957.

[3] This amounted to $17 billion in 1957: $9.5 billion retained by corporations for the needs of business and an estimated $8 billion plowback by owner–managers of unincorporated enterprises. Undistributed profits markedly decline in less-prosperous years, since corporations, attempting to maintain dividend payments undiminished, are likely to pay out a reduced profit income in its entirety. At such times small business owners and/or managers may also be forced to withdraw all profits gained, in order to maintain their living standards.

Adding all the separate savings totals—8 cents for capital consumption, 4 cents for business plowback, 5 cents for individual financial saving—we arrive at a total of 17 cents which Americans were able to realize as savings out of every dollar's worth of the over-all market value of their productive activities.

The Theme of the Next Chapter

Mark well the wording in the above sentence, where it is said that ". . . Americans were able to realize as savings . . ." Old-school economists would have given the act of business and individual saving an altogether more active and causal emphasis. Our usage allows one to infer that saving is in the nature of a residual outcome of national prosperity and national income. But the old-school economists would have stoutly maintained that it was these 17 cents savings per GNP dollar which, when added to savings made in previous years, were the most important single cause of setting industry in motion to the extent of producing a $440 billion GNP, a $364 billion national income, a personal income of $348 billion, and a disposable income of $305 billion.

This writer "sees it the other way around," expressing thereby the consensus of modern economists. We have come to learn this: Suppose that at the beginning of 1957 Americans had definitely planned to save, on the average, 17 cents out of every GNP dollar. Their savings plans would not have materialized had not a high level of economic activity first been achieved, measured by a GNP of $440 billion or, more directly, by a national income of $364 billion.

This shift in the interpretation of business and individual saving as being the effect rather than the cause of prosperity and national income is a major conceptual development of our time. It is laden with the most profound changes in attitudes toward private decision-making and government policy-making. How this came about and what it means for the future are the subject matter of the next chapter.

For Discussion

1. When we are concerned with aggregate effects of economic decision-making by consumers, businessmen, and government, we are studying "macroeconomics." What would be the subject-matter of "microeconomics"?

2. In national income accounting we do not record the values of transactions in which the purchase price of a product paid by a buyer is treated by him as a current cost of operations to be repaid by subsequent customers of the firm during the current accounting period. What is the technical term for goods which are thus bought to be resold after having been processed during the year?

Why are not the values of these goods recorded for the purpose of national income accounting? What is the name applied to goods whose values are recorded? How does this distinction aid us in thinking about the determination of the level of employment?

3. Distinguish between the two ways of viewing national income, verifying that they are merely two ways of looking at the same thing.

4. The nominal value of GNP is widely publicized in periodicals, newspapers, and business letters. The cost of living index also receives wide publicity. To ascertain the real value of GNP, why not use the cost of living index to adjust the nominal GNP in any year by the cost of living index for that year?

5. Jones correctly deflates the nominal values of GNP over a period of years and finds that the real GNP has been increasing over these years. He offers this as evidence that there has been economic growth. Hearing this, Smith objects, saying that Jones is begging numerous questions. What might prompt Smith in raising the objection? Examine your personal environment and determine whether you would go along with Jones or with Smith, and to what extent in either case.

6. Suppose that Congress wished to support a huge program of technical aid to underdeveloped countries, the cost to run into tens of billions of dollars. You are an economist on the staff of a joint Congressional committee for investigating the feasibility limits of such a proposed program. Which one, or several, national income measures would you consult? If more than one, what would be their order of importance in your thinking?

7. On several occasions Congress has passed a law permitting businessmen to accelerate their depreciation and amortization of capital equipment over artificially shortened periods of time. This means that a businessman, for tax purposes, can write off a machine which will last for ten years as if it will be useless in five years. By doubling the capital consumption allowance cost, less profit is recorded and less business income tax need be paid. The result is that investment in new equipment becomes more profitable. The aim of Congress in passing such laws has been to stimulate increased investment. What effect, if any, would a sudden rise in capital consumption allowances have on (a) the national income at factor prices, and (b) on GNP?

8. Discuss the following statement: "Slowly we seem to be entering an era in which the scope of conscious calculation extends beyond the individual firm to the economic system as a whole. . . . [This] means that economic decisions are made in terms of their effect on the size of the national income rather than upon the profits and losses of private business. When accounting is made in terms of national income, many of the most difficult economic problems are automatically solved." Why should this be the case? Do not attempt to come to a definitive conclusion at this moment. See how many interesting questions are suggested by the statement. List the kinds of further information and explanation you feel are required for discussing this statement adequately.

3 National Prosperity and Private Capital Accumulation

The Role of Private Capital Accumulation

Before national income accounting was perfected, the chief measure of prosperity was private capital accumulation. Boom or bust were predicated on business confidence, a subjective entrepreneurial response. The prime determinant of this response was considered to be the firm's capital account. If high profits were earned for a few years and public policies were deemed favorable to private money capital accumulation, a "new era of prosperity" was heralded.

As each of the "new eras" successively drew to a close, the general cause was sought in the encroachments of rising costs on business profits. Rising money costs of production were held to blame in the final analysis, especially the money wages of labor. In effect, this placed the responsibility for full employment squarely on labor, for the logical inference was that there would always be jobs if the working-man would occasionally offer to work for less, thereby encouraging capital accumulation. The nub of the argument assumed that reduced money costs, especially the prime variable of wages, would augment business savings and personal savings—naturally not the savings of working people, but the personal savings of property owners who might thereby be paid higher dividends, more rent, or more interest income. These supposedly augmented money savings of businessmen, and of owners of stocks, bonds, and other forms of property, were conceived as automatically constituting prosperity-nourishing private capital accumulation.

That this is no longer the prevailing economic point of view has already been stated. It has ceased to dominate public and business opinion regarding government welfare activities, labor unions, and other social-economic developments formerly considered incompatible with private capital accumulation.

Still, the only fundamental notion which has been rejected in modern times is that private money-making solves all economic problems, that it is an end in itself. Today's prevailing interpretation of the causes of national prosperity favors private and public policies which stimulate high-level consumption and a broad, equitable distribution of purchasing power, as well as policies which encourage private capital accumulation.

The modern idea is to maintain a careful balance between stimulating consumption, ensuring a fair division or sharing of the fruits of production, and activating business investment. It should be noted that the present-day emphasis on consumption and fair sharing is not new, although it is contemporary and therefore modern. Actually this attitude came to the fore politically in 1893, when the "captain of industry" Andrew Carnegie earned a profit of $23 million and was not required to pay a cent of income tax on it. Others, too, earned fortunes in 1893 and in the preceding years; yet there was a major depression then.

From that time on, the thesis that private capital accumulation is an unmixed social blessing has never again enjoyed the status of an unchallenged truth. In 1894 the United States Congress passed a law with a rider to tax the incomes of individuals and corporations. The intent of this law was not primarily to give the federal government added tax revenue. Rather, the fundamental intention of Congress was to redistribute income when it becomes heavily concentrated in the hands of the few. This was to be accomplished by taxing incomes on a graduated scale, the rate of taxation rising with the size of income. The Supreme Court nullified the 1894 income tax a year later, but agitation for it found sufficient response to legitimize the tax by means of the Sixteenth Amendment. As of 1913, a graduated income tax has been collected by the federal government, and later on by states and by a few cities as well.

The desirability of widespread, high-level consumption as a means of furnishing a broad home market for American producers was a part of the argument in these earlier demands for progressive income taxation, but the consideration of distributive justice was uppermost in the minds of its advocates. It was in the depressed 1930's that consumption was widely recognized as a prime determinant of the volume of aggregate employment, that is, as an autonomous means to prosperity rather than a process functionally dependent on private money-making. This newer insight furnishes the topic of the next chapter, wherein it will be explained as a characteristic of the modern economic system. The insight is analyzed at length in Chapter 10, which explains the theory of employment determination.

Although private capital accumulation is no longer considered an *end* in itself, much of modern economic analysis is aimed at furnishing an understanding of the *role* which it does play in contributing to national income and prosperity—the ways in which, the extent to which, and the conditions under which such a contribution can be made. To understand the *role* of private capital accumulation in our economic system it is necessary first to have a good understanding of the *nature* of private capital and its accumulation.

Capital Accumulation Defined

THE PRIVATE PROPRIETORSHIP POINT OF VIEW

In the broadest sense *capital accumulation* refers to any process of increasing a stock or fund of possessions beyond that which exists at a particular moment of time. *Stock* or *fund* refers to the assets of a business, which are held with the object of earning an income by their use and not for the purpose of sale in the ordinary course of business. Thus goods on the shelves of a store are not part of a stock, or capital, but the shelves are.

To a private individual, *capital* means proprietary interest or, alternatively stated, a proprietary equity, in personal belongings of a durable nature. Thus a man's house is part of his capital, as is his deepfreeze, cash that he has in the bank, and so forth. Of course, he may not fully own his house or his car. In this case what he does own is a residual *equity*, corresponding nominally to what he has paid off but really depending upon the secondhand value of the property he uses but does not fully own. For if he should fall behind in his payments and the bank should seize his home or car, the sale of the asset may yield only just enough to cover the unpaid balance. Thus the individual's residual equity turns out to be zero.

To a businessman capital is measured in a broad sense by all the financial resources available for carrying on operations, regardless of source. Business capital thus comprehensively defined includes all money invested by the owners of the firm as well as money which has been borrowed from creditors of the business. Excluding the liabilities to creditors, business capital consists of money invested originally and subsequently by the owner or owners and augmented by earned business revenue reserved for the internal needs of the business by managerial decision with majority consent of the owners. The sum total of money originally invested by the owners *plus* subsequent investment and/or *minus* withdrawals constitutes a value of ownership which is known as proprietary equity. It is a residual equity, that is, an amount of money which is left after allowance has been made for outstanding claims against the business.

PROPRIETARY CAPITAL AND INCOME

The concept of "business capital" is distinguished from the idea of "business income" on the basis of an essential accounting principle. The principle is the fundamental requirement that the money capital contributed by the proprietors of the business should be preserved. In a *real* sense this would require managers of enterprises (if they are not the owners) to conduct the affairs of the business so that satisfactory profits are earned on the investment as appraised in terms of the current level of prices, not in terms of an amount of money contributed by the owners at the time they made the investment.

For example, say that in a given year $1,000,000 is contributed by the owners of a firm, and the managers immediately spend it for an amount of plant and equipment. Some years later the general level of prices has risen by 50 per cent. The plant and equipment are still in operation. Momentarily ignoring depreciation, the investment in these properties can now in a real sense be said to be worth $1,500,000. The owners' capital will then be preserved in terms of its general purchasing power at the current level of prices.

The practical effect of accounting for the value of capital in this manner would be to reduce the percentage of profit which is earned on investment. Thus if $50,000 is earned in the year in which capital is reappraised as being worth $1,500,000, the rate of profit is 3⅓ per cent. If the profit is figured in terms of the original amount of capital contributed by the owners of the firm ($1,000,000), the rate of profit will appear as 5 per cent. This might make a difference to the entrepeneur in deciding what products to make and how many units of these products. Suppose that the average rate of profit earned in the economy is 5 per cent. If the entrepreneur figures his profit in terms of the original money amount of investment, he may rest content with his present lines of activity. If he uses the purchasing-power approach and values the investment in operating properties at $1,500,000, the 3⅓ per cent rate of return may cause him to search for new and more profitable ways of using the plant and equipment.

The purchasing-power approach to appraising the value of capital is called "stabilized accounting." However, it is not the usual form of accounting. For one thing, the government does not permit it to be followed in accounting for profits and capital gains for the purpose of taxation. Nor is it a simple procedure, for it requires deflating *all* types of assets by suitable index numbers, e.g., the value of buildings by an index of construction costs.[1]

From this it does not follow that businessmen, as a group, fail to take account of the impact of changing price levels on the value of capital invested in their enterprises. However, they respond to this not by reappraising the value of the capital but by searching for unusually profitable means of utilizing their plant and equipment. This has been shown, in the preceding paragraph, to be the practical outcome of reappraising the real value of capital in terms of the current level of prices. In other words, many entrepreneurs behave *as if* they actually engaged in "stabilized," real-capital accounting, although they record the value of plant and equipment at its original money value at the time it was purchased with money contributed by the owners of the business. A formalized system of real-capital accounting would undoubtedly be helpful to entrepreneurs as a supplement to their accounting records wherein capital value is recorded at the original dollar-cost value of plant and equipment, as is required by the government for taxation purposes. Supplementary real-capital accounting would provide a more precise approach to production decision-making than that which is likely to be followed when an entrepreneur takes account of price-level changes apart from his formal accounting records.

In this chapter we are concerned, however, with the manner in which entrepreneurs actually operate, not with what might be the best recommended procedure. Hence the discussion now proceeds in terms of the usual practice of money-capital accounting rather than real-capital accounting.

To understand what is meant by preserving proprietary money capital, one should picture a concern when it is just starting in business. At that moment nothing exists other than capital. As soon as the concern begins operations, the money capital contributed by the owners is virtually "transformed" into goods. Henceforth, in the go-

[1] See, for example, *The Accountancy of Changing Price Levels* (London: Institute of Cost and Works Accountants, Ltd., 1952).

Figure 3–1. Calculation of Gross Profit—Form 1040

Line

1. Total receipts $.............., less allowances, rebates, and returns $..............

2. Inventory at beginning of year $..............

3. Merchandise purchased $.............., less any items withdrawn from business for personal use $..............

4. Cost of labor (do not include salary paid to yourself) ....

5. Material and supplies ....

6. Other costs (explain separately) ....

7. Total of lines 2 through 6 ....

8. Inventory at end of year ....

9. Cost of goods sold (line 7 less line 8) ....

10. Gross profit (line 1 less line 9) ....

ing concern, the great stream of revenue takes over, as production is followed by the exchange of the goods in the market at current prices. The goods being sold, streams of revenue fow into the business. Economists and accountants alike understand that these streams consist not merely of cash payments but primarily of *accounts receivable.* On the security of accounts receivable the businessman can borrow money.

As rivulets of revenue flow in, to swell into aggregate revenue, the capital originally contributed by the proprietors is returning—augmented if a profit has been earned, diminished if a loss has been experienced.

For a moment the proprietors are in the same position as they originally were. At that time, when they entrusted the managers with their money capital, a sequence of commercial events was set into motion which has now been completed. The regained capital, plus or minus profit or loss, can be used to "recycle" another sequence of physical production and subsequent money exchange. The owners of the business have the legal option as to whether they wish to "recycle" the commercial operations of the firm. In any short historical period this may not be feasible. But in principle. and over a long enough period, it is possible for the owners to withdraw their entire capital (or whatever fraction of it they can rescue when the firm is operating at a loss). In other words, the owners of the business could conceivably exercise their option to withdraw not only the profit earned, if any, but every cent of revenue which belongs to them, that is, which is not owed either to other persons who have made advances to the business or to the government for taxes.

If the owners decide to withdraw revenue from the firm or if the managers declare some of it to be free for withdrawal, business is thereby converted into proprietary income.

At this point it is important to be consciously aware that what is under discussion is the business income of proprietors, not the so-called "gross income" of a business. Gross income, or gross profit, is what is left of inflowing aggregate revenue after the direct cost of the goods sold is deducted. Of course, this leaves the accounts far short of revealing the proprietary interest of the owners in the business. Figure 3–1, part of a United States government tax form (Form 1040), clarifies this point for the individual proprietorship business.

Notice that what is calculated as "cost of goods sold," on line 9, includes only direct outlays of cash or accounts payable. The only exception is the so-called "inventory adjustment," carried out by first adding the estimated value of the inventory at the outset of the accounting period (in this case a calendar year), then subtracting the value of the inventory held at year-end. If there has been a decrease

Figure 3–2. Calculation of Net Profit or Loss—Form 1040

OTHER BUSINESS DEDUCTIONS

11. Salaries and wages not included on line 4 (do not include any paid to yourself) .... $ ......

12. Rent on business property ......

13. Interest on business indebtedness ......

14. Taxes on business and business property ......

15. Losses of business property (attach statement) ......

16. Bad debts arising from sales or services ......

17. Depreciation and obsolescence (explain separately) ......

18. Repairs (explain separately) ......

19. Depletion of mines, oil and gas wells, timber, etc. (attach schedule) ......

20. Amortization (attach statement) ......

21. Other business expenses (explain separately) ......

22.   Total of lines 11 through 21 ......

23. Net profit (or loss) (line 10 less line 22) ...... $

in the value of inventory, actually more will have been paid for the goods sold than is indicated by the costs recorded on lines 3 through 7. The reason is that the originally warehoused goods also involved costs of production. By contrast, if the value of the inventory held at the close of the accounting period is higher than the beginning inventory value (assuming no appreciable change in prices), then the cost of producing all the goods, those sold and those held in warehouse, must be reduced by the increase in inventory to arrive at the actual cost of the goods which were sold. If the prices of the firm's goods change appreciably upward, an "inventory profit" is realized, which is treated by accountants the same as any other profit. Estimating the pecuniary value of goods as yet unsold, however, raises knotty problems of accounting and taxation. The estimate would be reflected in the value of year-end inventory entered on line 8 of the partial federal tax schedule in Figure 3–1. The interesting fact is that this appraisal is a key factor in determining the amount shown as gross profit on line 10 of the schedule.

The Internal Revenue Service's Form 1040 for individual proprietors reveals further, in lines 11 through 22, how raw a datum the gross profit shown on line 10 really is because it fails to show what the proprietor's interest in his business is. Recorded in Figure 3–2 are various business deductions which must be made from gross profit before there can be any discussion of the value of the proprietary interest. (Monetary entries opposite the listed accounting categories have been purposely omitted, because the aim at this moment is to illustrate the *nature* of these categories.)

The final line, numbered 23, reveals whether the sole proprietor realized a net profit or suffered a net loss. Does this figure of net profit (or loss) disclose the owner's proprietary interest in his business? It does *not*. The owner has yet to pay his federal revenue tax. Line 23 has been computed for the very purpose of enabling him to determine what it will be. By adding the net profit shown there to other income (if any) that he may have derived from sources outside the business, his total obligation to the federal government in taxes can then be ascertained.

Federal taxes do not exhaust the proprietor's obligation in this regard, however. State and local taxes must be paid. Only after deducting all taxes from the net profit does one reach a figure which defines the proprietor's unencumbered monetary interest in his business, that is, the residual revenue which he can freely dispose of.

The process of arriving at the residual proprietary interest in a business, that is, the residual equity of one or more owners, is illustrated in a summary fashion in an explanatory schedule which the

Figure 3—3. Calculation of Capital—Schedule M, Form 1065

Schedule M—RECONCILIATION OF PARTNERS' CAPITAL ACCOUNTS

	1. Capital account at beginning of year	2. Capital contributed during year	3. Separate income	4. Ordinary business profit	5. Losses	6. Withdrawals and distributions	7. Capital account at end of year
Partner (a)...............							
" (b)...............							
" (c)...............							
" (d)...............							

Internal Revenue Service asks partners in a business to fill out. This is Schedule M of the Partnership Tax Return (Form 1065). Here capital is explicitly defined (see Figure 3–3, columns 1 and 7).

In column 1 the partners (that is, the joint proprietors) are regarded *as if* they had actually contributed certain amounts of money at the beginning of the year which would be recorded under (*a*), (*b*), (*c*), and (*d*) if there were four partners. This is an arbitrary assumption, because the productive and marketing processes are continuous for a going concern. In other words, some capital is always going into these ongoing processes while other capital is returning in the form of revenue. Consequently, any cut-off period chosen for accounting would be as arbitrary as the customary period of a year.

To the capital attributed to the proprietors at the beginning of the year may be added new capital coming from the outside—for instance, when another partner is taken into the firm. If additional capital has been contributed during the year, it will be shown in column 2; if not, the column remains blank.

In column 3 the government requires the partnership to report gains or losses which are not experienced in the ordinary course of business. For example, a piece of used property might be sold above or below what it has been estimated to be worth on the firm's books, that is, above or below *book value*. (How book value is determined is a technicality which may be taken for granted at this moment.) To illustrate further, one or all of the partners may have invested some of the firm's money in the stocks of a corporation that failed; consequently the stocks have become worthless. Quite evidently, this would diminish the value of the partners' proprietorship, individually and as a whole. However, "separate income" factors are not likely to be large by comparison with revenue gained in the ordinary course of business.

Ordinary business profit, entered in column 4, is the partnership equivalent of the net profit (or loss) which an individual proprietor must report on his Form 1040 personal tax return. The detailed differences need not be elaborated here, since they are primarily technical.[2] The figures entered are derived essentially along the same lines as in the case of a sole proprietorship, that is, principally by (1) ascertaining gross profit by deducting the cost of goods sold from sales

---

[2] The main difference is this. The partners may own some securities in common or some real property which is rented to outsiders, although rental is not the business of the partnership. Incoming revenue from such "separate" sources must be added to the partnership's sales revenue received for its primary goods or services before the firm's net profit is calculated. A sole proprietor of a business would compute his net business profit without including income from separate sources. In either case, however, the tax liability to the government is increased.

proceeds and making an inventory adjustment, if required; and (2) thereafter subtracting the usual business deductions.

Column 5, the loss-record column, is self-explanatory. Real difficulties of appraising loss of business property may arise under practical circumstances.

Now appears the interesting disclosure of withdrawals made by the partners during the year. Mark well that the amount is withdrawn, or withdrawable, by the partners as *proprietors*. The withdrawals are therefore in addition to the salaries which the partners have agreed to pay themselves.

By comparing the withdrawals made by the proprietors with the net profit which would be shown in column 4, minus losses, the firm's capital at the *end* of the year is precisely measured. If withdrawals exactly equaled the net profit earned, the firm would have no internal sources for an enlarged scale of commercial operations. If less was withdrawn than the amount indicated in column 4 (again, minus the loss amount of column 5, if any), the capital of the firm has increased. This information is conveyed in column 7, which shows the partners' respective capital accounts at year's end. When combined, they reveal the firm's aggregate year-end capital.

SOME REASONS WHY BUSINESS CAPITAL AND BUSINESS INCOME ARE DISTINCTIVELY DEFINED

When the whole sequence of commercial production and marketing events is considered in the case of a going concern, the central fact which stands out is the stream of aggregate revenue from sales and financial investment. Money capital is this continuous business process seen from an ownership point of view; that is, invested money originally started the sequence as capital and returns as revenue. The money which remains after debts and taxes have been paid is once again considered capital. It continues to be capital *until a decision is taken.* That decision occurs when the proprietors resolve to withdraw some of the unencumbered, therefore freely disposable, revenue. If they do not deem this to be a wise course of action, the disposable revenue remains as capital in the business. Everything depends, however, upon the incoming stream of revenue. If this is not available, there is nothing to decide about what is capital and what is income.

Why, then, in this broad view of continuous commercial operations, is it necessary to distinguish proprietary capital and income? There are three technical reasons from the broad viewpoint of economics.

The first technical reason is that the government attaches a part of incoming business revenue in order to finance many of its protective and welfare functions. But in doing so, the government is not permitted to diminish the proprietary interests of the owners of private businesses; to do so would be to undertake a capital levy. Hence the government must be informed about the state of capital accounts of businesses at the beginning of each year.

The second technical reason for ascertaining business capital is that there are usually creditors who advance money or real goods to a firm and who expect in return to be paid interest or rents, besides receiving back in due course the principal of their loans or the property they made available for use by the firm. Such creditors desire to know the extent of the proprietary interest of the owners of the firm, should the firm fail in repaying its debts. In that event the creditors would be entitled to seize the capital of the owners. Naturally, therefore, the creditors want to know what that capital is.

A third technical reason is that the owners themselves have contributed money capital to the firm in the expectation that this capital will be preserved, that is, that their proprietary equity will not be diminished below the amount of money which was originally contributed. Of course, this is not done by hoarding the contributed money capital. The original capital will be spent in an effort to create an aggregate stream of incoming sales and investment revenue. Thereupon careful decisions must be made to allow enough of that stream of aggregate revenue to remain within the business to equal at least the amount of the capital originally contributed.

This third reason points directly to the basic reason why capital, as an aspect of incoming business revenue (that is, as a decision concerning it), must be defined distinctively in separation from proprietary income. Let us suppose, for example, that a railroad company regards its permanent trackage as something always to be maintained and replaced out of the general revenue which comes in during the year as repair and replacement needs occur with respect to particular sections of the permanent trackage. In other words, the railroad company makes no provision for depreciation or obsolescence of the permanent trackage.

To provide for depreciation and obsolescence means setting aside a certain amount of incoming business revenue and treating it as capital to be accumulated, so that when sections of the permanent trackage wear out or need to be modernized, funds will be available for the purpose. The original cost will not be recoverable when the trackage is worn out or obsolete, of course. Consequently, this cost must be recovered either while the trackage is wearing out or in anticipation of its becoming outmoded.

That is accomplished by reserving a portion of incoming passenger and freight revenue year by year, starting with the year when the present trackage was installed. The revenue earmarked for depreciation and obsolescence is not hoarded, not kept idle. Instead it is placed in use, that is, invested—usually in the business itself.

Reserving as capital and investing the annual earmarked sums of incoming passenger and freight revenue normally results in the creation of extra business revenue. This extra revenue grows to the extent that it will suffice to meet the necessary replacement and/or modernization cost when that falls due.

Suppose, however, that the described provision for depreciation and obsolescence had not been made. In that case more of the annual incoming freight and passenger revenue could have been declared free for withdrawal by the proprietors of the railroad during all the years while the trackage was wearing out. Later, the railroad company's service would have deteriorated, because in previous years too much of the then-current business revenue had been freed for withdrawal, too little reckoned as capital. With the deterioration of the company's service, the worth of the business to the proprietors would also have declined.

Modern methods of production require the use of much plant and equipment which, however durable, wear out sometime. Long-lasting facilities for production are often labeled *fixed assets*. Yet, all assets are "wasting assets" if we consider a long enough span of time. Incoming revenue must be reserved, even now, to replace so apparently permanent a productive facility as the Hoover Dam, for one day it will be completely silted and unusable.

The management of depreciation and obsolescence shows that capital is not a natural fact but something which has to be accumulated originally, and then again and again. That which is true of capital with regard to a firm's plant and equipment is true of capital in every respect.

Fixed capital implies the corresponding existence of durable things —durable, however, only in relation to an accounting period of the customary one-year length. For any given firm, fixed assets may include long-term securities of other corporations, that is, fixed financial assets rather than fixed physical assets. Fixed financial assets held by a concern, however, imply the existence of durable physical plant and equipment somewhere else in the economy. Of course, if the security concerned is a bond, its cost is fully recoverable when the bond matures, the principal normally being repaid at that time.

Next there is *working capital*. This is the excess of money, and of things that could be readily converted into money, over and above obligations to pay which the firm must meet in the current accounting period. Working capital therefore represents the firm's net current resources that are available to continue operations. That part of the working capital which exists in the form of cash is usually referred to as *liquid capital*.

In addition to fixed and working capital, there are *capital reserves*. These are the funds which are earmarked for replacing, modernizing, and expanding the firm's stock of plant and equipment, such as the permanent railway trackage in the foregoing illustration.

In all these business matters action must be taken to preserve capital by placing incoming business revenue back into the business. In this perspective capital is seen as comprised of monetary funds which were originally contributed by the owners of a firm, then augmented as time goes on, perhaps by added capital contributions of newly added owners but chiefly by earned business revenue which the managers of the firm earmark and invest, rather than disburse to the owners. This is done by the managers to prevent the originally and perhaps subsequently contributed funds from draining away. In this respect the managers act as trustees for the owners.

If, then, the proprietary interest lies in the preservation of capital (the owners expecting to be paid a return on investment, but not at the expense of the investment), the following definition clearly emerges. *Private capital accumulation* is the augmentation of an owner's proprietary interest, or equity, by reason of conservative management of the firm.

THE ECONOMIST'S INTERPRETATION OF CAPITAL AND CAPITAL ACCUMULATION

In approaching economic affairs from the viewpoint of the general welfare and common defense, proprietary interest in an enterprise is not of prime concern to the economist. The economist regards *capital* in the sense of the nation's productive power, independent of any financial claims which individuals or groups may have to the things (the machines, power plants, and the like) which help to generate this productive power.

Economists regard the whole community as beginning an accounting period with a store of "real" assets which are the source of production during the period; at the end of the period the store is normally increased or reduced by the difference between production and consumption. The store at the beginning is not regarded as a money value or as a proprietorship interest, but as a "real" item consisting of physical goods, the legacy of past production carried on to serve as a source of productive power for the current year. Similarly, the net increase or reduction during the year is regarded in "real" terms.[3]

Specifically, capital accumulation connotes to the economist the augmentation of the community's store of assets during the year, regardless of who owns them.

This whole matter of capital accumulation in social-economic welfare terms will be fully explored in Chapters 11, 12, and 13. Here it is mentioned because of its rather obvious relation to national income and national prosperity. Businessmen measure their success by realized results in accumulating capital, and they shape their job offers to wage-earners according to the prospects for further accumulation.[4] The United States government takes steps to create conditions favorable to private and/or community capital accumulation in several ways. At the behest of businessmen, for instance, it improves roads, grants "protective" tariffs, and the like. Also, when business confidence is low, it can issue money and credit on easy terms and undertake public works on its own initiative. Nothing is plainer than the fact that full employment requires sustained capital accumulation, and vice versa.

Private Accounting for Capital Accumulation

By habit and association, most persons have come to look upon capital accumulation as something measured in the private accounting records of business concerns. But these records mention real, *economic* capital formation (that is, productive equipment added to the community's store of real assets) only tangentially.

For one thing, private accounting systems document many financial transactions which have little to do with physical production and/or construction activities, the real bases of national income. That is to say, besides recording *operating income* from the sale of goods and *operating costs* incurred in the purchase of goods and services, the books of corporations, partnerships, and sole proprietorships also convey information about *nonoperating incomes* and *nonoperating outlays* as shown in the following list.

---

[3] Quoted from: "Some Accounting Terms and Concepts," a report of a joint exploratory committee appointed by the Institute of Chartered Accountants in England and Wales and by the National Institute of Economic and Social Research (London, England: Cambridge University Press, 1951), p. 26.

[4] Much has been written recently with the avowed intention of showing that considerations of power, status, technological interest, and social responsibility influence business decision-making. This is perfectly true. But in no way is it at odds with the fact that businessmen are still in business to make money

Nonoperating Income Sources	*Nonoperating Outlays*
Dividends received from subsidiaries and miscellaneous trade investments	Any exceptional loss or expense, such as an uninsured loss of inventory by fire, or money having to be paid as damages awarded to some other person who has won a legal suit
Interest or dividends received from investment in securities of other corporations or government securities	
Interest on money lent, including interest on deposits left with bankers	Interest on money borrowed
Capital gains on plant or equipment sold at more than book value or original cost, whichever is lower	Capital losses, such as a loss on the sale of plant or equipment at less than its book value

Because these nonoperating incomes and outlays influence business decision-making, some persons regard them as part of economic capital accumulation. However, this is a misconception. For what is added to the economy's store of productive equipment when, for instance, one person pays interest and another person receives it? The creditor's ownership of money is increased, whereas the debtor's financial ownership is decreased. The transaction represents a reshuffling of income yielded by already existing productive equipment. This may significantly affect the structure and amount of production in the future. The recipient of interest income may spend it to buy consumption goods, whereas this amount of money might have been applied to the purchase of additional machinery had the entrepreneur been able to retain the money instead of being obliged to disburse it as interest on borrowed money. However, the redistribution of purchasing power, from the entrepreneurs to their creditors, does not in itself alter the community's store of productive goods during the current accounting period. There is a transfer of value, but no value added in the economist's sense of increased current production. Observe that in either event there will be private capital accumulation, either by the machine manufacturers or the makers of consumption goods. However, there is not *economic* capital accumulation, because a financial transaction does not directly change the source of the community's productive power.

Inventory gains realized in times of rapidly rising prices also illustrate the difference between the accountant's and the economist's conceptions of capital accumulation.

A businessman might have the same quantity of stock at the end of the year as he had at the beginning, as well as the same amount of cash, credits, and debts. Yet, if there has been a considerable rise in prices, the identically sized inventory of goods he holds could be valued at a higher amount because of the rise of prices. The markup would in no way reflect any change in the firm's productive activity and therefore would not register an increase in the community's stock of goods.

On the other hand, suppose that the cost of replacing worn-out equipment is higher than the original cost of the equipment; this is generally the case in periods of rising prices. Even if the scrapped equipment is replaced by identical equipment, the replacement cost must exceed the amount of income nominally earmarked for the purpose of covering depreciation expense. This would not create an operating loss, but it would require the firm to retain more of its profits rather than pay so much out to stockholders. Otherwise the firm would be forced to borrow money to cover the difference between the original cost and the actual replacement cost of plant or equipment. Here we have another financial datum, namely, the depreciation deficiency, which has nothing to do with current productive activity.

Private accounting statements sometimes show "too little" from the standpoint of the economist's concept of social capital accumulation. Here one touches the subject of the planned results of business investment as compared to the actually realized results in accounting terms. Let us say that a firm ordered a given quantity of productive equipment, several batteries of machines, early in 1929. Before the machinery was delivered and installed in good operating condition, October had come, and with it the onset of depression. Considering the expected low depression prices at which the output of the new equipment would have had to be sold, the ownership of the equipment would not have been worth as much as had been anticipated when it was ordered. Expressing this disappointing reality, the books of the firm would have shown a degree of capital decumulation. Yet, from the community's viewpoint, its store of productive equipment would have been increased.

A CLOSER SCRUTINY OF PRIVATE ACCOUNTING CONVENTIONS

What does private accounting for capital accumulation reveal which is of general economic significance and not merely of particular interest to the owners of a given concern? This is a vital topic. As already mentioned, the motivation of the owners and managers of American enterprises, large or small, is to increase monetary proprietorship, that is, to accumulate capital in the private accounting sense. This urge remains the single most important driving force of the goods-producing and goods-purchasing transactions which both money-flows national accounting and national income accounting reveal—the latter, uniquely.

In the past, this was interpreted to mean that prosperity was assured so long as the records of business enterprises showed increases in ownership values. That would permit savings to be made which could be plowed back, thus promoting not only private proprietorship augmentation but, at the same time, social capital accumulation. From this belief stems the old-school slogan: "Work hard, be thrifty—prosperity will come."

This view (namely, the mere accumulation of ownership value) now having come under constructive criticism—not for its moral content, but for its usefulness—is no longer considered a safe economic weather vane by itself. If it were, the evolution of national income accounting and the use made of it not only by government, by academicians, and by labor unions, but most of all by the business community itself would be inexplicable.

What is the relation of private enterprise accounting, for proprietary capital accumulation, and national income accounting which records the aggregate effect of private and public economic decision-making on the national level of employment? This is the subject matter of Chapter 4. An elementary knowledge of the general nature of private enterprise accounting is required for understanding its relationship to national income accounting. The following Appendix acquaints the reader who has no knowledge of business accounting and its basic conventions and may serve to refresh the memory of others who have a basic knowledge but have not recently applied it.

Appendix

Elements of Business Accounting

To show the nature and elements of private enterprise accounting, Tables 3–1 and 3–2 present basic accounting data for a hypothetical Company X. It is a company of considerable financial and productive stature, as is indicated by the size of the money transactions recorded in the two accounting statements. In the interest of simplicity, the figures are rounded off to the nearest millions.

Table 3–1. Company X: Simplified Statement of Consolidated Income for the Year 1958

Operating Income		$2,100,000,000
Other Income		
Dividends from subsidiaries	$ 50,000,000	
Miscellaneous trade investments	15,000,000	
Interest on government bonds	10,000,000	
Other dividends	25,000,000	
	$100,000,000	
		100,000,000
Total gross income		$2,200,000,000
All Expenses		
Materials and supplies	$ 600,000,000	
Wages and salaries	450,000,000	
Depreciation	150,000,000	
Selling costs and administration	100,000,000	
Bonuses to employees	50,000,000	
Interest and amortization on bonds outstanding	100,000,000	
Taxes		
State and local	75,000,000	
Federal corporation income tax	275,000,000	
Total, all expenses	$1,800,000,000	
		1,800,000,000
Net Income (or Profit)		$ 400,000,000
Allocation of Net Income		
Dividends to stockholders	$250,000,000	
Retained for needs of business	150,000,000	
	$400,000,000	
Earnings on Total Investment		
Plant and equipment (operating assets)		$2,500,000,000
Financial assets		1,000,000,000
Total investment		$3,500,000,000

Net income of $400,000,000 on an investment of $3,500,000,000 yields the company's rate of return: 11.4%.

THE INCOME STATEMENT

A firm's income statement (often called profit and loss statement) shows how the managers have fared in anticipating sales, investment, and cost conditions as they are related to one another. In other words, an income statement shows how, by adroit anticipations, the managers have tried to realize increased holdings of assets for the owners of the business. In short, they have tried to earn a net profit.

The following paragraphs explain the various items and amounts summarized in Table 3–1, the 1958 income statement for Company X.

Operating income of $2.1 billion is the value of the goods the company sold during 1958. It is the net sales figure after all discounts and rebates have been deducted.

But Company X had other sources of income, apart from its own operations in manufacturing and selling. From its investment in subsidiary companies over whose operations it has a considerable measure of control, Company X received $50 million in dividends. It received $15 million income from miscellaneous trade investments and $10 million interest on the U.S. government bonds it holds. Company X also holds securities of other corporations in the management of which, however, it has no direct control; these other dividends amounted to $25 million. Thus, the nonoperating income amounted to $100 million in all and, added to operating income, yields a total gross income for Company X of $2.2 billion.

Out of this gross income the company had to meet its expenses, charges, and taxes. For each of the 100,000 employees, the company bought, on the average, $6,000 worth of raw materials, semimanufactured goods, tools, office supplies, and the like. It paid, therefore, $600 million for materials and supplies. Wages and salaries averaged $4,500 per employee, making a total annual payroll of $450 million. The company set aside $150 million to replace worn-out and obsolete property, such as plant and equipment. There were selling and advertising costs, as well as necessary administration and "housekeeping" expenses, which include hundreds of items, such as maintenance of a sales force, telephone bills, price catalogs, fees for legal and engineering consultants, provision for employee pensions; all these came to $100 million. Under a Treasury-approved incentive plan, bonus payments were awarded to employees in the amount of $50 million. Fixed interest on the company's own bonded debt had to be paid—a sum of $100 million. Finally, $350 million in taxes had to be paid: $275 million to the federal government under the corporation income tax; $75 million for applicable state and local taxes. The grand total of all these expenses was $1.8 billion.

After paying all the foregoing bills, charges, and taxes and after providing depreciation and pension reserves, the company's net income (or profit) from all sources in 1958 was $400 million ($2.2 billion *minus* $1.8 billion). Although revealing the conditions under which capital accumulation becomes possible (that is, by making a profit during the year), the income statement shows only what money or money equivalents, if any, are *available* for capital accumulation. Thus, at the end of the year 1958, Company X had $400 million more than was available in 1957 for capital accumulation. (For simplicity's sake we assume that it is in money form.) However, $250 million was paid out in dividends to stockholders, so that really only $150 million was used for capital accumulation—or so it would appear.

Actually, more of the firm's gross income could have been used for capital accumulation than the apparent $150 million which was "plowed back" by the management instead of being paid out to the stockholders. To understand how this could have been the case we must examine the same firm's balance sheet of assets and liabilities.

THE BALANCE SHEET

The statement of assets (Table 3–2) is divided into three categories: current, durable, and financial. Among its current assets the company possessed $185 million in cash; and it held readily marketable securities of other corporations and of the United States government in the amount of $250 million. Accounts receivable—that is, money owed the firm by some of its customers—totaled $285 million. The company's inventories of goods as yet unsold—valued at cost or at market price, whichever is lower—were deemed to be worth $250 million. Finally, deferred charges for services rendered but not yet billed would amount to $30 million. All together, the current assets add up to $1 billion.

Durable assets are the company's plants and equipment. They are reckoned at approximately their original cost, this being presumably the least for which the present repaired and modernized, or replaced, properties could be sold. Plant and equipment thus carried a "book value" of $1.5 billion.

Together, the current and durable assets constitute the company's operating assets. Their combined book value was $2.5 billion.

Among the financial assets the company owns are securities of various subsidiaries over which the company exercises control. These securities had a cost (not a market value) of $600 million. The company holds some of its own stock in its treasury for the purpose of paying bonus awards to its employees in the future at the management's discretion, and the value of this stock was $50 million. The company's "good will," with its customers, its trademarks, and its patents, was judged to be worth $50 million. Company X also owns securities in other corporations in the management of which, unlike its own subsidiaries, it has no direct control. These other securities cost $300 million. Financial assets, then, add up to $1 billion. All the assets of Company X—current, durable, and financial—total $3.5 billion.

The asset side of the consolidated balance sheet more or less speaks for itself concerning the private wealth of Company X. What it does

Table 3–2. Company X: Consolidated Balance Sheet, December 31, 1958

ASSETS

Current Assets

Cash	$ 185,000,000	
Marketable securities	250,000,000	
Accounts receivable	285,000,000	
Inventories	250,000,000	
Deferred charges	30,000,000	
Total	$1,000,000,000	
		$1,000,000,000

Durable Assets

Plant and equipment		1,500,000,000
Total operating assets		$2,500,000,000

Financial Assets

Securities of subsidiaries	$ 600,000,000	
Own stock for paying bonus awards to employees	50,000,000	
Good will, patents, and trademarks	50,000,000	
Securities of other companies	300,000,000	
Total	$1,000,000,000	
		$1,000,000,000
Total, all assets		$3,500.000,000

LIABILITIES

Current Liabilities

Accounts payable		$ 200,000,000	
Estimated taxes	$350,000,000		
Less: U.S. government securities and other cashable securities	$350,000,000		
Other accrued debt		50,000,000	
Total current liabilities		$ 250,000,000	
			$ 250,000,000

Fixed Debt

Bonds outstanding		500,000,000

Provisions

Bonus funds	$ 35,000,000	
Pension trust funds	25,000,000	
Total	$ 60,000,000	
		60,000,000
Total current and fixed liabilities		$ 810,000,000

Reserves

Depreciation	$ 875,000,000	
Obsolescence	50,000,000	
Insurance and contingencies	15,000,000	
Total	$ 940,000,000	
		940,000,000
Total liabilities		$1,750,000,000

NET WORTH

Capital stock	$ 750,000,000	
Surplus	1,000,000,000	
Total net worth	$1,750,000,000	
		$1,750,000,000
Sum Total: Liabilities and Net Worth		$3,500,000,000

not divulge, however, is the ownership condition of the firm. If a concern has debts to outsiders, these must be deducted before the pure ownership of the people who have invested their money in the firm can be ascertained. The claims against an enterprise are known in business terminology as *liabilities*. From what has been said, it is plain that: Ownership equals assets *minus* liabilities.

At this point, the main categories of business liability are discussed in connection with the balance sheet for Company X. The most obvious types of liability are money claims which outsiders have against a firm. This refers, first of all, to other merchants and manufacturers who have delivered goods to the firm but have not as yet received payment for them. Company X's accounts payable (that is, money owed for goods and services purchased but not yet paid for) totaled $200 million. Should a firm, however, fall behind in paying wages to its employees, under our "mechanics' lien" laws (enacted under the pressure of early trade unions more than a hundred years ago), their claims to compensation would take priority over even the accounts payable to other businessmen.

Next come the claims of federal, state, and local governments for applicable taxes. In many instances these are contingent on the volume of business done and on whether a profit is earned. Most firms earmark certain sources of cash that could be quickly realized to pay taxes if need be (for instance, United States government bonds). Since estimated tax payments are secured, at least under good business practice, this particular liability is not necessarily shown on the balance sheet. It is, however, shown as a "cleared entry" in Table 3–2.

The most intimate creditors of a concern are its bondholders—persons who have invested money in the firm with a guarantee that they will receive a stipulated rate of interest on their investment and will be repaid the amount of their investment as well at a certain date in the future. Should the management of the concern be unable to fulfill this guarantee, the bondholders could insist that the business be sold so that they might recoup their investment—that is, if enough value is left in the concern to make this possible *after* the prior claims of accounts payable, taxes, and, perhaps, the claims of workmen have been satisfied. The face value of the bonds that Company X has outstanding is $500 million; this is the amount the bondholders could demand if interest were not paid regularly on it.

A third direct type of liability arises when a firm commits itself to its employees to operate a pension plan, an incentive bonus plan, and perhaps a straight-out profit-sharing plan. A concern having such arrangements, and most modern firms do, need not set aside funds for paying pensions, bonus awards, and so on. But when these payments fall due, the firm will be liable for them. As a matter of fact, if these plans were instituted under the pressure of trade unions in collective bargaining, they become a part of the "contractual" relations between management and the work force covered by the labor agreement. In that case, the agreed-on welfare payments are almost bound to be considered as a part of wages and thus could establish a top priority claim under the mechanics' lien laws. The situation is not so clear where the plans are instituted and operated at the sole discretion of the management, but if the plans be long continued in operation, the tendency of the courts would undoubtedly be to consider payments under unilateral employer welfare plans as a part of wages also.

Company X has set aside $35 million in bonus funds to be awarded at management's discretion to employees, and it has paid $25 million into a separate trust for employee pensions. The bonus and pension provisions amount to $60 million. Added together, current liabilities, bonded debt, and bonus and pension provisions total $810 million (Table 3–2). From these current and fixed commitments the managers and owners of Company X cannot be extricated, legally or morally.

Today, in every going concern, the managers see to it that not everything is considered as profit which is earned above the costs of wages, salaries, materials, daily running expenses, and other forms of immediate, direct costs of operation. Instead, the managers assiduously set aside certain *reserves,* to provide for repairing plant and equipment and replacing them when worn out, and for insurance and unforeseen contingencies.

These reserves are classified as liabilities, too. In a peculiar sense one might say that they are the liabilities of the owners of the firm to the concern itself—so that it remains a going concern, rather than running down. Naturally, a factory is only a congeries of plants, tools, machinery, and so on, with no ability, will, or voice of its own to insist it be kept intact. The human beings who have this responsibility are the managers, who are protecting their positions when they prevent the owners (in case the two are not the same persons) from "eating up capital." Conceivably, the owners of a concern could demand that they be paid everything that is earned above daily "out-of-pocket" operating expenses—and sometimes they do when dividends have not been paid for some time.

Apropos of this consideration, it is interesting to note that in the early nineteenth century economists could not quite make up their minds whether depreciation reserves should or should not be considered as part of profit or as necessary operating expense. By contrast, many modern economists not only consider depreciation reserves as absolutely necessary expenses to keep a business going, but even insist that the amount of such reserves should be based upon not the original cost of installing and maintaining present plant and equipment but rather upon the replacement value at current prices. Businessmen and accountants, however, rate the depreciation burden at the original, historical cost of plant and equipment for a very practical reason. Much replacement cost will be incurred only in the future, and so one would have to speculate on what future prices of replacement parts and equipment might be. On that basis, some firms might never pay dividends while general prices are rising; this would be an undue burden on the present stockholders. The best business practice is to mark depreciation at the original cost of the plant and equipment as they wear out, but to retain some of the earned gross income to meet increasing replacement costs as they occur.

However reckoned, depreciation and obsolescence reserves are to be considered *valuation* reserves, not liabilities in the sense of accounts payable and the other fixed commitments already described. There is a direct relation between depreciation and obsolescence in that obsolescence is a factor which limits the service life of plant and equipment just as is wear and tear from age and use—that is, depreciation. Obsolescence therefore can logically be taken into account in estimating the service life of plant and property and in establishing a schedule of retirement charges. Many business concerns report depreciation and obsolescence reserves in a single account, a practice which is justified by Paton in the following words:

> Generally in scheduling depreciation no effort is made to trace separately the effect of each factor influencing service life; if a reasonable estimate is assumed there is no occasion for such tracing. If expected life in a particular case is five years, for example, the depreciation program should call for systematic absorption of cost during the anticipated period of service, without regard to the possibility that under other circumstances the effective life might be ten years.[5]

Obsolescence estimates can easily be exaggerated; for that reason the government carefully specifies the nature of tax-allowable obsolescence. In Table 3–2 depreciation and obsolescence reserves are separately reported in order to emphasize that wear and tear from age and use normally is a factor in limiting the service life of plant and equipment which far outweighs the factor of obsolescence.

Since purchasing its present plants and equipment, Company X has been setting aside portions of its annual gross incomes in the reserves accounts for meeting tax-allowable obsolescence charges and the costs

[5] W. A. Paton (ed.), *Accountants' Handbook* (3d ed.; New York: The Ronald Press Co., 1953), pp. 731–32.

of replacing worn-out facilities. At year's end these reserves, represented by the improved value of plants and equipment, total $875 million for depreciation and $50 million for obsolescence. In addition, funds of some $15 million have been set aside for insurance and unforeseen contingencies.

Now we arrive at what may be called the *pure ownership value* of the going concern, or its *net worth*. This is represented first of all by the company's *preferred stock*—a number of ownership certificates which entitle the holders to a regular rate of return on the par value of these certificates. *Par value* is a financial worth the company set on these certificates when it issued them. By no means is it necessarily what they are bought and sold for in the market. If the par value of a preferred stock is $100 (regardless of whatever its actual demand and supply market value might be) and if the agreed rate of return is 7 per cent, then a holder of one share of preferred stock is entitled to $7 per year. If that is not forthcoming, preferred stockholders have the right to participate in the management of the firm—perhaps to demand that it be sold even though the hired managers strongly disagree. The sum total of the par values of preferred stock issued by the firm is considered a liability, though it is not such in the direct sense of the outside claims of tradesmen wishing to be paid and of bondholders. Company X has 20,000 holders of preferred stock, and the total par value of their subscription is $750 million.

The final category of liability to specific persons is the liability of the managers of the firm to the holders of the common stock. Common stock is "pure ownership" in the purest sense of the word. Whoever owns common stock is entitled only to whatever earnings the management may decide it is wise to distribute *after all* the outside, committed, and internal liabilities have been satisfied. For that reason, most common stock has no par value at all, since this would commit the management to pay the stockholders some return on the par value, in contradiction to the general idea that common stock earnings are never promised. Of course, what is left after all other claims are satisfied may be a very ample sum, much of which management may feel it proper to distribute. Thus we find that common stock is often highly desired and bid for, and therefore acquires a high market value even though it has no formal par value. In a broad sense, common stock issued is also a liability of a going concern. If no dividends were ever paid on it, it would obviously be difficult to attract capital.

There are 100,000 shares of common stock in Company X. But because this stock creates no specific income claim (as do bonds and preferred stock), the value of the common stock is recorded only at the legal minimum of $1 a share. Thus the $100,000 of common stock is ignored as a negligible sum in financial statements (Table 3–2) where amounts are expressed in even millions of dollars.

If, now, the total assets and the total liabilities of a firm are compared after the preferred stockholders have been paid their stipulated dividend and the common stockholders have received a dividend as well, it is often found that there is still a significant difference. It could not for any prolonged period be a negative difference, showing an excess of liabilities over assets. But for all going concerns which are not operating at a loss, there remains what is characteristically called a *surplus*. The use of the term "surplus" in this connection is unfortunate because it suggests such synonyms as "superfluous," "extra," and "spare cash." Nothing could be more misleading.

In the first place, the residual-value equivalent of assets shown as "surplus" is rarely, if ever, an amount of cash. This might be true of a part of a year's net income which the managers of a business decide not to pay out to the owners of the business but to retain for the needs of the business.

Such a judgment could be challenged by the owners or, in given instances, by a labor union. Apropos of the latter, the Steelworkers' Union in 1956 claimed that the steel companies had "ability to pay" higher wage increases than contemplated because of certain amounts of retained corporation incomes. The companies, however, took the position that this amount of retained earnings constituted funds transferred to special reserves for meeting the increasing costs of replacing worn-out and obsolete equipment. What the steelworkers considered surplus the companies considered necessary cost, even though in that particular period of rising prices the companies were prepared to meet the increased replacement cost out of profits. Thus the argument between the steelworkers and the steel companies turned out to be one over profit-sharing. The same would have been true had some stockholders challenged the management's judgment in retaining a part of the annual net income to meet increasing replacement costs of plant and equipment, rather than paying these funds out in the form of dividends.

Actually, there may be some room for debating the specific disposition of annual net income over and above that part of it which is reserved by management as an annual contribution to so-called "surplus." But the same could not possibly be true of the total "surplus" account which is shown in the liabilities statement. This is really a historical record of the portions of net income retained for the needs of business over past years and *spent,* presumably in ways which helped bring the firm's grand total of assets up to the current level.

Thus, glancing at the entry for surplus in Table 3–2, it is seen that Company X has reserved $1 billion worth of net income over the years, including the year 1958. Yet, on glancing at the current asset entry of the balance sheet, it is seen that only $185 million of cash is immediately on hand. The surplus could not possibly be paid out without forcing the company (1) to cash in some other assets which it may have planned to hold, (2) to borrow money from banks, (3) to issue new capital stock, or (4) to perform any combination of these three alternatives.

To summarize, then, the surplus account of Company X: In addition to capital which was subscribed by preferred and common stockholders, the company has plowed back earnings over the years. The latest addition to surplus was $150 million, in the form of income "retained for needs of business," as shown at the end of the income statement (Table 3–1). Recorded in balance sheet form:

Surplus at the beginning of 1958	$ 850,000,000
Net income for 1958	400,000,000
Available for surplus	$1,250,000,000
Less dividends paid for 1958	250,000,000
Surplus at 12/31/58	$1,000,000,000

The total net worth or pure ownership of Company X—capital stock and surplus—is $1.75 billion. Total liabilities are another $1.75 billion. Their sum, the combined amount of liabilities and net worth, is $3.5 billion, which equals the amount of all the firm's assets. Thus, the balance sheet, by definition, balances.

For Discussion

1. What is the residual equity which you, a friend, or your family has in a car? What is your, or your family's, residual equity in the home? Calculate proprietary equity for other items to which the concept applies under your circumstances.

2. When a businessman is asked what happened when he sold goods, he will typically reply: "I have added to my capital." Is this a correct manner of speaking, a loose manner of speaking, a misleading statement, a totally incorrect one? Explain the reasons for your answer.

3. What is "stabilized accounting," and why will not the government permit its practice for the purpose of business income-tax reporting? If you, or your family, sold your residence, realizing a gain above what it cost you when acquired, what amount of gain would be taxable?

4. You would be justified in investing money in Company X, whose income statement and balance sheet are shown in Tables 3–1 and 3–2. How would the income statement and balance sheet of a company in unsound financial condition appear? What specific entries might reveal the unsound condition?

5. What is the relation of depreciation and obsolescence (a) qualitatively? (b) quantitatively?

6. Why is an inventory profit not of *economic* significance?

7. If a company sells a number of punch presses from its equipment, should the proceeds from this sale be considered as income and entered (a) in the income statement as part of operating income, and (b) on the balance sheet under Accounts Receivable? If so, why? If not, how and where should the transaction be entered? What does this example illustrate about the concept of "capital" as compared to the concept of "income"?

8. Identify those assets in Company X's balance sheet which not only constitute capital in the private accounting sense of the word but can be reckoned as parts of the community's store of "real" assets.

9. The following information about economic conditions in the prosperous 1920's was prepared retrospectively and published in 1941. Which of these four types of economic information do you believe was most readily available at the time? Which type was most likely to be used as a basis for interpreting the then-current situation and for forecasting? What kind of predictions would you expect to have been made (a) by a leading statesman, say, the nation's President? (b) by a business leader? (c) by a labor leader?

You may check your answers by referring to the files of the U.S. *Congressional Record*, e.g., the issue of December 4, 1928, page 20; to *The New York Times*; and to the *American Federationist*, official organ of the American Federation of Labor (AFL), for that period.

Here are the data:

Percentage Increases of Four Key Factors in the Equation of the 1920's Prosperity

		Economic Categories		
Year	Dividends	Other Property Income	Wages	Aggregate Consumer Spending

(The figure for each year marks the *relative** percentage increase (+) or decrease (—) in that year over the immediately preceding year.)

Year	Dividends	Other Property Income	Wages	Aggregate Consumer Spending
1923	+ 12.0	+ 2.0	+ 11.0	+ 6.0
1924	— 2.0	+ 4.0	(no incr.)	+ 4.0
1925	+ 9.0	+ 3.0	+ 2.0	— 1.0
1926	+ 5.0	(no incr.)	+ 5.0	+ 7.0
1927	+ 6.0	+ 4.0	+ 3.0	(no incr.)
1928	+ 7.0	+ 9.0	+ 2.0	+ 4.0
1929	+ 13.0	+ 7.0	+ 5.0	+ 4.0

Source: This table is based on data given in Simon Kuznets, *The National Income and Its Composition* (New York: National Bureau of Economic Research, 1941).

*In each case, 1929 is taken as 100 per cent, and 1922 at whatever percentage of 1929 it happened to be. By reading each column from the bottom to the top, one observes that dividends in 1922 were one-half their 1929 value—actually $3 billion in 1922 and $6 billion in 1929. The actual magnitudes do not matter for the thinking which should go into answering this question.

4 National Income

and Private Accounting

Any meaningful relationships which may exist between national income accounting and private accounting can be detected through abstract thinking.

In speaking of private accounting as a general proposition and of
national income accounting as a method of generalization, we have
already abstracted from the bewildering details of more than four million sets of books kept by businessmen and from hundreds of millions
of spending decisions made by the nation's consumers. Now we must
move to a higher level of abstraction to determine the *relation* which
exists between the two general propositions, national income and private accounting.

Abstract Thought and Economic Understanding

Because of man's gift for abstract thinking we are not forced to
take things as they come. Instead, we can operate with general propositions that can be discerned as underlying the distracting camouflage
of particular economic events. An abstract term names a selected
quality, attribute, or condition of a thing, which allows us to view the
thing in relation to other things. An abstract term stands in contrast
to a concrete term, which names the thing itself. If we were able only
to name things, instead of relating them to each other by the process

of abstract thinking, our existence would be like that of the amoeba. Our days would be spent in withdrawing from things found to be harmful and absorbing or resting on things which favor our survival. We might survive, but not on the basis of understanding ourselves in relation to the world around us.

Abstract thinking means penetrating the mass of undifferentiated facts. The aim is to discern the significant facts which shape our destiny. We think abstractly not with the aim of ignoring facts but in order to think about them more efficiently. We sift facts, selecting those which have quality—that is, which have an influential and not merely incidental relation to the scheme of economic life by which, to a significant extent, we are governed.

In trying to reach economic understanding we start with a hunch, a hypothesis, then test it in the strong, clear light of up-to-date economic information. This test permits us to select the significant facts of economic life and at the same time to reformulate our original hypothesis in the light of observed evidence, which in many instances will be contrary to some of our original assumptions about the scheme of economic life, whose nature and purpose or drift we are trying to grasp. Thus we approximate ever more closely an appreciation of reality, casting out irrelevant considerations and concentrating on the relations of things which really matter. We are now prepared to cope more efficiently with particular daily problems as they arise. In this real sense the selective abstraction from facts, properly safeguarded, brings us close to the facts of life by first removing us from the undifferentiated mass of sense impressions.

Logical Thinking in Economic Matters

Mankind's gift for abstract thinking not only furnishes the opportunity for advancement but creates a danger as well. This is the danger of straying from matter-of-fact reality in the process of selective abstraction. It happens whenever men permit their prejudices or preconceptions to guide their investigation of matter-of-fact human relations. When this happens, the investigation bypasses objective evidence. It ceases to be a scientific investigation and produces nothing more than propaganda for doing things in a way in which the person, or group, felt they ought to be done in the first place.

There is a safeguard against this danger. It is the use of logic in a scientific manner. The objectivity of scientific thought is well known. Hence the use of logic in a scientific manner means that all arguments should be judged by their relevance in the context of what is actually and significantly happening.

There is a safeguard from this danger in economics, as there is in all lines of scientific endeavor. The British logician P. H. Nowell-Smith instructs us how to minimize the danger of being swayed by our personal or group preconceptions. He does this by stating three rules of logical discourse, namely:

1. When a statement is made, the speaker must believe it to be true; that is, he must believe that the statement has some constructive relation to reality.
2. A speaker contextually implies to his listeners that he has good reasons for making the statement, unless he uses guarding phrases such as: "I'm inclined to believe . . ."; or "I read somewhere that . . ."; or "So-or-so says that . . ."—in which case one can check the source of the statement.
3. What a speaker says may be assumed to be relevant to the interests of his audience. To this rule Nowell-Smith adds: "This is the most important of the three rules; unfortunately it is also the most frequently broken. Bores are more common than liars or careless talkers."[1]

How these rules apply may be illustrated by appraising the following conversation, which actually occurred in 1957 after the onset of a recession:

Jones: Why are you worried?
Smith: Because I am a trained machinist but must sell magazines from door to door because of the industrial unemployment.
Jones: Why worry? The factories are still making money, and statistics show that GNP is still increasing.

In applying the modern rules of logical discourse to this conversation, several observations need to be made. First, Jones passed full muster under rule 1: he believed that capital accumulation has a constructive relation to prosperity. He should, however, have qualified his statement under rule 2 by saying that "there is reason to believe that you won't have to sell magazines for long." On the grounds of relevance in the context of the actual economic situation (rule 3), Jones was for all practical purposes illogical. Perhaps he felt that Smith lost his job because he did not work hard enough as a machinist, or that Smith could have retained his job by offering to work for less, or that by saving more, Smith could at least have gone into business for himself when he lost his job. However, a bit of careful thought should have convinced Jones that any or all of these defaults could not possibly hold true for the massive number of five million unemployed persons.

[1] P. H. Nowell-Smith, *Ethics* (London: Penguin Books, Ltd., 1954), pp. 81–83.

ECONOMIC CHANGE AND LOGICAL THINKING

The example shows that logical discourse in economics involves not only the display of mental agility but a willingness as well to expose one's accustomed views to the test of up-to-date economic information. That is not an easy assignment. "Times change"; that is, society never stands still. Specifically, there are continuous changes in our economic institutions, our organized ways of conducting economic affairs. These social changes are *facts*.

Now, facing facts requires strong self-discipline. True as this is of personal matters, it is even more true in matters of social change. Actually, that which in the circumstances of the recent past warranted certain statements, not only as suitable abstractions but as concrete propositions, may have given way to a new order of things, in whole or in part. Yet, what is more comfortable than trying to persist in accustomed attitudes based on past conditions?

Still, this type of argumentation signifies the making of improper abstractions, however refined or emotionally appealing the line of talk may be. For to ignore or to try to evade the facts of modern social-economic development is to abstract incorrectly from vital aspects of reality. The more usual manner of refusing to face facts is to assert carelessly that times have not really changed. Many are the sinners against sound contextual logic who tediously dwell on "the good old days." These are all overt or clandestine ways not only of renouncing logical economic reasoning but also of shirking one's moral and intellectual responsibility to change with the time.

In summary, the prerequisite of sound logical thinking is to test, and recheck, one's own economic abstractions for their veracity, probability, and applicability.

ECONOMIC INFORMATION AND STRAIGHT THINKING

Can one honestly say, at any given time, that a cherished view, traditionally held, is still true? What reasons exist to support a certain view of some economic process, either in its original form or in a modified form? Is a given interpretation of economic events supported by unrealistic special assumptions?

The approach to answering such conscientious questions, either for oneself or for others, lies in consulting available economic information —and demanding more of it if not enough is available. In the following pages an application of the foregoing criteria for logical economic thinking is made; later in this chapter it will be shown how the majority of Americans practice sound logic when confronted by the changing facts of modern economic life and organization.

What Do Private Accounting Records Show?

THE CASE OF A SINGLE CORPORATION

Figure 4–1 exhibits the facts of capital accumulation for one of America's 200 largest corporations.

Figure 4–1. Capital Accumulation of a Large Corporation, 1929–56

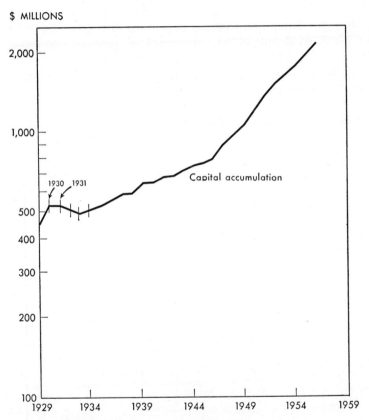

SOURCE: Actual company data on capital stock and surplus.

This record of capital accumulation is not totally misleading. It does show that there was a leveling off between 1930 and 1931, then an absolute decline until 1933—the year which also marked the depth of the depression for the whole national economy. Thereafter the company's record is one of sustained capital accumulation.

Actually, all the data are deceptive. In the first place they do not register the full impact of the deep depression of 1929–33, even in the case of this firm. In the second place, they entirely fail to register several sharp recessions which occurred after 1933. Now, in the real terms of fluctuating output and employment, even the particular company here used for purposes of illustration was not exempted from the vicissitudes of the general economy.

This can be shown, graphically, by superimposing on the chart of capital accumulation a curve tracing the physical (not financial) record of the company's real turnover of goods produced and stored during the same period, 1929 to 1956. The broken line in Figure 4–2 furnishes this latter information, permitting the desired comparison. (The technical details of how the physical turnover curve was constructed need not be explained at the moment.)

This chart has been drawn on specially prepared graph paper, so designed that equal percentage changes in the magnitudes of the two

Figure 4–2. Capital Accumulation of a Large Corporation Compared with Turnover of Production and Inventories, 1929–56

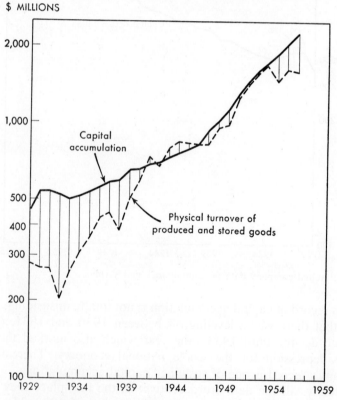

SOURCE: Actual company data.

factors involved are revealed by identical slopes of the respective curves. The reader should not be distracted by the coincidence of the two curves overlapping between 1951 through 1953. This is the sort of fact from which one can properly abstract in the present context. The significant fact is that capital accumulation for the firm and its real physical activity *moved* in an identical fashion in only four out of thirty years.

Now, it would not be necessary to show an identity of movement in every single year in order to justify the traditional view that capital accumulation is the prime cause of national prosperity. But surely there should be a closer conformance than that which appears in Figure 4–2. Even when physical economic activity and capital accumulation are seen to move together in an upward direction, they frequently do so at strikingly different rates (specifically, during almost the entire period from 1929 to World War II). And in numerous instances they can be observed moving in *different* directions. A diminution of output and employment in the face of increasing capital accumulation is an unnatural event, a sheer irregularity, along traditional lines of economic thinking. That is why traditionalists typically interpret the causes of actual discrepancies as emanating from outside the business system; that is to say, they place blame on allegedly external factors such as government intervention in private economic affairs.

Business programing for capital accumulation. Arguments which attribute the nature of things to unnatural causes are not impressive. More to the point would be challenging the procedure of simply comparing the two curves in Figure 4–2. It can be reasonably asserted that the capital accumulation curve should be viewed abstractly, not as a mere concrete record of certain quantities of private capital that are amassed. That is to say, the accumulation curve should be seen as reflecting dynamic human decision-making which influenced the movements of the other curve—the physical activities curve. This might be done by considering every successive pair of points on the accumulation curve in relation to each other and to a logically corresponding pair of points on the physical goods-turnover curve. To illustrate, the 1930 point on the accumulation curve seen in relation to the next, the 1931 point, would indicate that the managers of the firm expected capital accumulation to level off during 1930. As a consequence, they might order a leveling of output between 1930 and 1931, that is, during the year 1930. Close inspection of the chart will show that this actually happened.

Mark well that it would be absurd to pretend that the business decision-makers actually forecast the exact *amounts* of capital accumulation which were later realized. But there is no reason to suppose that businessmen do not try to estimate the likely trend of capital accumulation *primarily on the basis of past performance.* Nothing more than that is implied; each year the decision-maker departs from the results of recently accomplished capital accumulation in making an estimate of what the future might hold in relation to the recent past.

In that sense the actual amounts of capital accumulation shown on the chart have meaning—but only as trend bases, not as evidence to suggest that the managers of this firm always correctly anticipated future capital accumulation. This confusion is easily avoided by bearing in mind that the center of attention is whether the broken-line physical activity curve for the firm can be explained by the capital accumulation curve, as an abstract proposition rather than as a mere statistical record of past events.

It has been seen that in the case of 1930 there was a remarkable correspondence. Between 1931 and 1932 the same is also true: the estimated trend of capital accumulation is downward, and so is the level of production and sales out of inventories. The picture then changes. Forecasting the future in 1933 from the vantage point of 1932, the managers apparently took a pessimistic view. Yet the physical activity of the firm shows a striking upturn. This can only mean that a factor, or factors, other than the original capital accumulation, intervened to influence the firm's actually realized economic activity in 1933. That external factor is known; it was the advent of the National Recovery Administration (NRA)—a politically sponsored business arrangement. (The NRA will be described in a later chapter.) To this recovery effort the firm at first gave hearty support.

From 1933 to 1937 the accumulation and activity curves move together in an upward direction, but at strikingly different rates. Again other factors intervened to give the firm's recovery, in physical terms, an altogether more pronounced impetus than the accumulation curve, conceived as a planning curve, would have predicted. For 1938 the firm, in this interpretation, "foresaw" the general recession of that year, but not its severity. On the other hand, between 1939 and 1940, the accumulation-estimate curve shows a leveling off, but physical activity increased at a high rate. After the war years (which we pass over because of the abnormal conditions) a lag of activity behind the hypothetical accumulation-estimate curve is to be observed. Thereafter the correspondence of the two curves is at first close; then, during the Korean war, it is perfect. In the years 1954 and 1956, immediately following the Korean war, there is no correspondence at all.

The sum and substance of this thumbnail analysis is that data on private capital accumulation exclude a vital economic factor which strongly influences the output which the firm produces or sells out of inventory and therefore also affects the employment which a firm can offer to wage-earners. What, then, is left out of the accounting?

THE ACCUMULATION PICTURE ON A NATIONAL SCALE

The economic factor of which private records do not take explicit cognizance is national purchasing power. The economist's technical term for this is *aggregate effective demand.*

A definition. Effective demand is *the level of total monetary demand of all the people for all goods and services at which it proves to be just profitable for a majority of business enterprises to supply their customers.* At other levels of aggregate monetary demand the entrepreneurs either (1) do not feel that the net worth of the business will increase sufficiently to warrant filling all the orders they might accept; or (2) are prevented by tight supply conditions from filling all orders, so that a backlog is created. Obviously, in situation 1 the total demand is not effective because customers are not offering adequate price inducements to producers. In situation 2 the aggregate demand is not effective because there are not enough basic resources to go around.

What determines aggregate effective demand? The volume and flow of aggregate effective demand are determined by the interaction of many social-economic processes, but above all by the spending attitudes of consumers, businessmen, and the government. This interplay of spending decisions by consumers, business, and the government generates the primary economic force causing the economic environment of a firm, or of business as a whole, to be healthy or stagnating.

No individual firm, however large, can manipulate the general effective demand for goods and services so as to build it to the right strength and consistency for national full employment. Total national purchasing power is an environmental, external factor for the entrepreneur in the daily management of his affairs. The fact that businessmen, *in the aggregate,* are instrumental in generating much of the national income is not a consideration for the individual businessman in taking his actions. He is under the necessity of making practical policy decisions aimed at maintaining and augmenting the proprietary interest of the owners of the particular business. As an intelligent layman-economist, he will appreciate the fact that the whole business community powerfully influences the economic environment; but as a practical individual decision-maker, he can ill afford to act on this general proposition. There is no place on a company's books for recording external factors beyond the firm's direct control, nor is there any known way of doing so. The books are kept to record the management's aptitude in handling the economic variables under its immediate control, that is, costs of production, the firm's specific marketing problems, its personnel relations—certainly not the broad variable factor of national purchasing power.

It follows, both theoretically and in fact, that all the accounting records of individual firms, when combined, cannot furnish an adequate measure of national income movements nor furnish a full explanation, such as Figure 4–3 will show.

Figure 4–3. Capital Accumulation of All American Private Corporations Compared with Their Aggregate Turnover of Production and Inventories, 1929–55

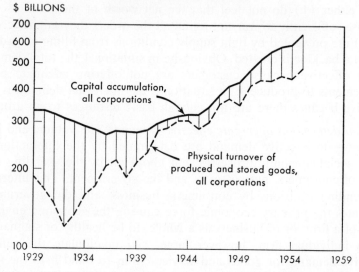

SOURCES: On capital accumulation of corporations, see United States Treasury Department, *Statistics of Income,* Part 2, published annually. Physical turnover of corporations is computed from data on corporate sales in United States Department of Commerce, *National Income,* Table 29.

The findings. In this graph capital accumulation not only includes capital stock and surplus (as was exclusively the case in Figure 4–2), but considers as capital invested in the totality of the nation's corporate enterprises the following items as well: (1) increased indebtedness to outsiders, and (2) increased provision for depreciation and depletion. The reason is that when these items increase for any single firm, they may simultaneously decrease for some other firm. This would make it impossible to say that there was any increase of money capital for the national economy as a whole. But here the perspective is that of the total economy. Obviously, then, when all the enterprises go more heavily into debt, there is no place where business indebtedness could decrease, so that more money capital will actually have been invested. The same is true of depreciation. When one firm increases its provision for that purpose, another firm might be doing the opposite; but this cannot be true for the economy as a whole. The accumulation curve in Figure 4–3, then, is more comprehensive than the one in Figure 4–2.

Nevertheless, the accumulation curve in Figure 4–3 follows essentially the same path as the one in Figure 4–2 and exhibits the same lack of theoretical correspondence with the other curve in Figure 4–3 —that which shows the physical turnover of goods produced by all the nation's corporations. The lack of correspondence is especially pronounced for the period of 1933 to 1941. Still, if one glanced at only the capital accumulation curve, it would be easy to gather the false impression that the period 1933–41 was one of gentle fluctuations. Then, in the post-World War II period there is a signal rise of the capital accumulation curve that is not associated with any parallel acceleration of the physical turnover of goods.

Interpretation of the findings. The relative flatness of the curve of aggregate business accumulation prior to World War II does not, in the light of national income data, divulge economic stagnation. It simply means that capital accumulation was not the prime factor in the increase of economic activity. We know that it was by the government's stimulating aggregate effective demand that recovery was started from the 1933 depression low, by means later to be explained. The accumulation data confirm this, for they could not have accounted for the pace of the actual recovery.

In the postwar period, the rapid rise of the money capital curve is explained by (1) corporation managers' retaining a great deal more of earned profits than they had done in the past, that is, treating more incoming business revenue as capital rather than as withdrawable income; (2) a rise in business indebtedness compared to former times; and (3) more ample depreciation allowances, especially under the incentive given by the 1950 and 1954 federal revenue acts.[2] Whether the sharply increasing capital accumulation, largely self-financed by

2 Under these acts, qualifying entrepreneurs working along defense production lines may write off, over a five-year period, roughly three-fifths of new plant and equipment certified as eligible, even though the things involved may last many more years. From an accounting point of view this is the equivalent of adding to money capital for the business community as a whole.

the corporations, was warranted in the post-World War II period is controversial. It would be less debatable if the preponderance of private capital accumulation had been oriented to improving national welfare standards in terms of slum clearance, eliminating the over-crowding of schools, and other necessary projects.

Traditional Reasoning on Full Employment

When one is confronted by the discrepant facts of physical output performance and private capital accumulation, a question naturally arises. How could people ever have relied on private accounting records, or even general reports about capital accumulation, to guide all policies, both private and public, toward the end of increased private money capital accumulation? How could they have considered it the exclusive means of solving all economic problems? Yet this was the prevailing approach from the time of Alexander Hamilton's *Report on Manufactures,* submitted to Congress in 1791, until the early 1930's.

The answer is surprisingly simple. The traditional view rests on an assumption that in the structure of the economy there is a built-in mechanism which automatically connects the accumulation of money capital to the aggregate national demand for goods and services, and it does this with the effect of creating full employment throughout the nation.

One can readily infer that this factor linking the two concepts would have to be a part of the general price mechanism, that is, a specialized type of market price arising out of economic transactions between private individuals. The price would have to originate in private transactions unaffected by government. Along older lines of economic thinking, private economic transactions, conducted at market prices, will not only suffice to select goods, allocate resources, and distribute incomes, but will assure full employment and economic growth as well. As is well known, in the traditional manner of thinking of past times there was no place for government transfer payments or public works as a means of stimulating aggregate effective demand. In fact the slogan was: "Hands off, government!"

THE CLASSICAL RATE OF INTEREST

The specialized type of price which the classical economists thought of as an automatic means to full employment and economic growth is the market rate of interest. In the classical analysis this is the price paid by entrepreneurs for using other people's saved money. Or, if entrepreneurs use their own funds for financing the expansion of their business, they are expected to credit themselves with an amount of money equivalent to what they would pay if they borrowed the money capital at the going rate of market interest.

In this theoretical perspective capital accumulation is plainly a direct function of personal and business savings. It is a basic premise of earlier economic thinking. A second fundamental premise follows, namely, that a "sound" kind of prosperity depends upon the balance, *on a nation-wide scale,* between the savings which people plan to make and the investment plans of productive entrepreneurs. And it is averred that this balance can be struck only when the national output at current market prices (or alternatively stated, the gross national product) is at a full-employment level—when current productive activity engages every person willing and able to work.

From this proposition it follows that planned savings and planned investments, in the aggregate, will be *out of balance* at any level of national income which is less than full employment, that is, when current productive activity does not provide jobs for all. But an imbalance between aggregate planned savings and aggregate investment decisions cannot last—and that is the nuclear concept of the old school.

What will remedy the situation to bring aggregate saving and investment into balance and therefore restore full employment? The traditional answer is the price mechanism operating through the rate of interest, which is the income price paid for the use of money capital.

The argument proceeds as follows. Should planned savings in the aggregate exceed, for any reason whatsoever, the total investment planned by producers, the owners of unused savings would feel a mounting pressure to have their savings borrowed by producers. The reason is that interest accumulates over time, and money not invested means time lost from accumulating interest. Rather than lose interest-bearing time while holding out for high rates of interest, the savers would offer to lend their money at lower rates, and would do so competitively. With asked-for interest rates declining, businessmen would eventually find it profitable to invest in ventures which they had been unwilling to undertake at the previously higher rates of interest.

The classical balance of savings and investment. Along this line of reasoning the problem of full employment resolves into a matter of leveling planned investments up to planned savings. By definition this provides full employment. Leveling investment up to planned saving also assures economic growth. For investment is not to be conceived as merely using saved money to buy stocks, bonds, or other types of securities. In the classical conception investment inevitably means that borrowed money will be used for new factory construction, for manufacturing new equipment, and in many other ways by which production and consumption facilities are improved.

Note well that problems of full employment and economic growth are held to generate their own solutions primarily by the action of the specialized type of privately arranged *price* known as the market rate of interest. This does not imply that other parts of the price mechanism would be inoperative in an economic readjustment. The price mechanism is indivisible, and so in traditional theory it is expected that wages and prices will also be falling as market rates of interest decline. One might suspect that the falling prices would discourage businessmen from undertaking new investments.

However, prices will not fall in proportion to wages, according to the traditional view as rather recently expressed by A. C. Pigou.[3] He points out that the general price level in any one nation is determined not only in the home markets but to some degree also in the markets of the world. On the other hand, wage levels are purely determined within the nation. Hence prices will hold up better than wages unless there is a worldwide depression. Older economists added to this the consideration that as prices fall, persons living on fixed incomes will be able to purchase more goods. Doing so, they will help to maintain prices at a relatively high level compared to falling wages. In effect, there is a redistribution of income, from wage-earners to fixed-income recipients.

With prices falling less than wages, employers of labor have an inducement to hire more hands, at the same time taking advantage of the declining market rate of interest in order to finance expansion. Employers may hold off from offering increased employment so long as they expect wages to keep declining. However, this will not last. In Pigou's words: ". . . when the impulse driving real wage-rates down comes from the pressure of unemployment, everybody will know that, once a *sufficient* cut is made, the pressure will cease and, therefore, the downward tendency will stop."[4] At this point all employers will actively compete in the labor market.

Thus in the classical conception every part of the price mechanism functions so as to aid the market rate of interest in leveling investment up to planned savings. In this equation of adjustment the category of aggregate planned saving is the independent variable. To this variable the investment plans of producers must adjust, and will adjust, by the mediation of changes in the market rate of interest.

[3] A. C. Pigou, *Employment and Equilibrium* (London: Macmillan & Co., Ltd., 1941), pp. 85–87.
[4] *Ibid.*, p. 87.

Fluctuations in the interest rate cause investment plans to be revised. They will be revised upward when planned savings exceed planned investments and the interest rate declines; they will be revised downward when the opposite is the case, for then the interest rate will rise to bring about a constriction of investment.

A PROBLEM OF THEORY

The lingering depression of the 1930's was a patent indication that something was wrong with accepted theory. Money rates of interest declined to unprecedented lows; prices and wages were reduced by fully one-third, on the average, and in some instances much more drastically.

In the depression of the 1930's it seemed that about everything happened the wrong way. The aggregate amount of predepression personal savings did not remain constant, to be offered for loan at a lower market rate of interest. Instead, personal savings declined until, in 1932, the aggregate amount was actually negative. Business savings increased, which was tragically ironic. It meant that unused savings, instead of exerting a pressure to stimulate investment, were being held by businessmen for the purpose of *avoiding* investment.

When, in 1929, businessmen slackened in their willingness or ability to invest, there was a loss of jobs. The impact of this on total national spending was at first dampened as people drew upon their savings. Sooner or later, though, the unemployed reduced their buying at the neighborhood stores. This had repercussions all along the line of economic activity. Retailers failed to order as much as the wholesalers had expected; the wholesalers cut down on their orders from the manufacturer; and so on in a widening circle of distress. Unemployment, having been precipitated by a loss of willingness to invest, later diminished the ability of businessmen to invest as losses began to mount.

This is what the American populace discovered in the Great Depression. Some relatively isolated economists had pointed it out much earlier, but their views had not found wide acceptance. Still, if the depression of the 1930's taught one lesson more thoroughly than any other, it is that a functional relationship exists between consumer, business, and government spending on the one hand and actually realized business capital accumulation on the other—not, as had previously been thought, between saving and accumulation.

THE LOGIC OF OLD-SCHOOL REASONING

Saving represents a laudable abstention from consumption, in the traditional conception of saving. It is laudable because in effect it informs the owners of scarce human and natural resources: "You are released from using your labor or property services in the production of currently consumable output. You may instead apply your labor or property to the production of technological means such as new steel mills, or to the discovery of new ore deposits for increasing future outputs of consumption goods."

In the economically backward, underdeveloped areas of the world this may be a very helpful conception of saving. In those areas almost all production is for immediate consumption; most production, as a matter of fact, is simple agricultural production.

Under such economically primitive conditions it would measurably aid the advancement of living standards if upon any manifestation of increasing economic activity—say by reason of oil exports from Arabia to Europe—people would abstain from increasing their consumption for the time being and use their oil revenues for buying machinery and so forth from Europe. With this they could then produce their household wares, textiles, and the like more efficiently and thus raise their standards of living in the long run. The point is that even now in some countries of the world up to 95 per cent of the output of goods and services is on an immediate consumption basis; yet the resources are fully, if inefficiently, utilized. Thus, resources for industrial development must be taken from the area of personal consumption—by buying industrial equipment in Europe rather than French perfumes or British pajamas.

By marked contrast, the productive capacity of highly industrialized nations is never so fully occupied simply with the production of goods for immediate consumption. A great deal of factory construction, new machinery manufacturing, and so forth can be undertaken without any encroachment on the output of consumption goods. On the contrary, we experience sales and marketing problems. These resolve into a matter of persuading consumers to use an enlarging flow of household products, the augmented production having been made possible by investment which improves the facilities for mass production. What a far cry this is from the necessity of requiring people to abstain from consumption on the grounds that otherwise real investments in new, improved plants and equipment could not be undertaken.

As a matter of fact, modern technology—science applied to the solution of industrial problems—seems to produce progress which is self-accelerating. Technology might almost be said to live its own life in research laboratories and experiment stations. And modern technology cries for customers to take its increasing flow of products off the market; this is the major problem, not that of having to beg for real and financial resources to keep industrial investment going. The traditional conception of savings was valid at past stages of our economic development. It appears illogical when applied in the context of present American economic circumstances.

A CONSTRUCTIVE, NEW WAY OF UNDERSTANDING SAVING

Real difficulties arise under modern economic circumstances when saving is conceived simply as nonspending—as a postponement of consumption *now* to afford the means for enjoying certain things later. Parsimony is more likely to damage business investment than to level it up to savings. So keenly are Americans aware of this fact that an adaptive change has been made in our conception and our practice of saving.

The change consists in this: funds which are budgeted for making payments on mortgages, goods bought on the instalment plan, premiums paid on life insurance policies, and so on are all considered as money saved. These are earmarked funds which cannot be spent to acquire additional current output of industry. To earmark funds is to set money aside as surely as one does when saving it. Only in this case one does not postpone consumption. One actually enjoys it from the moment one begins to save in this modern sense.

The new conception of saving meets the needs of an economy of abundance. For it allows us continuously to "upgrade" our wants *in proportion to the technological availability of increasing streams of goods and services.*

It is not to be inferred from this statement that some saving in the old sense of postponing personal consumption is not advisable. It is always well to have on hand certain amounts of liquid money funds: for a rainy day; for taking advantage of a good cash bargain; for meeting unanticipated emergencies, for example. This is wise household economics.

But is it a truth of universal application that economic progress causally depends upon saving in the strict sense of first downgrading one's wants in order to be able to upgrade them later on? Yes, say the economists of the old school; otherwise we shall have inflation. No, say the newer economists, goods must be bought as they become available; they cannot with profit be warehoused until the consumers can "afford" them. For want of a nail a kingdom was lost, and for want of a hoarded penny prosperity might be lost.

However this controversy may be settled in theory, there remains little question of how it has been concluded in fact. The emphasis of business and government decision-makers is on spending. The latter is the more surprising because "government economy" has long been a watchword in the American tradition. To be sure, numerous Americans continue to cherish a traditional preference for a government which holds its spending to the minimum. Many Americans also prize the traditional conception of savings considered as thrift and the laudable abstention from consumption.

Whatever their sentiments, however, few Americans have proved themselves prepared to return to a strict discipline of saving in the old-fashioned sense of postponing consumption, downgrading current wants in order to upgrade living standards later. The same lack of correspondence in thought and action may be observed in the matter of government spending. It has wisely behooved many politicians to promise government economy if elected, only to be confronted with a possibly disastrous loss of votes if vigorously attempting to fulfill their campaign promises after being elected. It was symbolic of modern times when America's most ardent advocate of curtailed government spending early in 1958 asked that the federal debt ceiling, imposed by law, be raised only $3 billion instead of $5 billion. In general it appears that Americans react to the logic of events in the way they act and vote, if not in their manner of thinking and speaking.

America's practical emphasis on spending to preserve prosperity has resulted in, among other things, a new habit for economic decision-makers. An emphasis on spending focuses attention on the need for maintaining full employment as the source of high-level national purchasing power. Unemployed workers contribute nothing to the national income and are severely limited in their spending. With this in mind, businessmen and government and labor officials are concerned with obtaining economic information which reflects the trends of employment and spending.

GROWING USE OF NATIONAL INCOME ACCOUNTING DATA IN ECONOMIC DECISION-MAKING

General information about trends of aggregate spending by consumers, businessmen, and government is gaining more and more the attention of alert businessmen. To be sure, broad general economic information will never be absorbed by a businessman with the same intense interest with which he scrutinizes the particular bookkeeping information in the private ledger of his own firm. For upon this specific knowledge an entrepreneur must fundamentally base his production and marketing decisions. But a farsighted businessman knows well that only in the rarest instances can an individual concern move counter to firmly established national income trends. One such exceptional case is the shoe repair industry. In depression times an abnormally high proportion of consumers have their shoes mended rather than buying new ones, for an obvious reason. But how many industries are there of this kind?

What is the significance of this slowly developing habit of economic decision-makers of conducting their affairs with an eye to national income accounting as well as private enterprise accounting? It is a new *fact* of American economic organization, as much a characteristic as older institutions in our economic system. Indeed, the development of future ways of conducting economic affairs seems destined to follow the path of an increasing reconciliation of national income and private accounting.

Appendix

Major Sources of Economic Information

DATA ON CONSUMER SPENDING

To assist private and public decision-makers in their planning, the Federal Reserve Banking System periodically conducts studies of consumer expenditures and the future plans of the nation's *spending units*. These are the nation's households—families or pools of unrelated individuals, or just single individuals keeping house for themselves. A representative sample of United States households is personally and systematically interviewed and asked such questions as: (1) whether prices are about right for buying at the present or whether it would be better to wait; (2) whether the head of the household thinks he or she will be financially better off next year than now; (3) whether there are some deep-felt needs the consumer has which he considers still unsatisfied.

When thousands of answers to such questions are assembled and their statistically significant similarities and differences are analyzed, a sort of "spending barometer" can be constructed in the form of an index of "Consumer Attitudes and Buying Intentions." The analysis is done at the University of Michigan's Survey Research Center, through which the Federal Reserve System conducts its surveys of consumer finances; the results are usually published in the June issue of the *Federal Reserve Bulletin*.

The published results of consumer spending plans do not relieve a businessman of the responsibility for making decisions on whether to expand or contract his operations. For one thing, consumer spending is only one variable factor in the business-judgment equation. True, it is ultimately the most significant variable factor, but at any one time supply conditions enter in, such as the availability of certain types of machinery, labor rates, transportation costs, and so on. And in many industries the final consumer demand for end products of manufacture or agriculture is a rather remote consideration. An instance would be the metal-mining industry—it is a long way from a pound of extracted iron ore to an iron frying pan. But although general data on aggregate consumer spending plans do not supplant independent business judgment, the data, if carefully used, are certainly of great value not only to businessmen but also to financial agencies, labor union leaders, farmers, and government officials. For these data reveal the high or low "ceilings" of consumer confidence. In the new school of economics this is an even more sensitive gauge for estimating future short-run economic conditions than is the element of business confidence—the only behavioral datum past generations of economists and businessmen really wanted to know.

The Federal Reserve Board's studies constitute only one among many sources of information on consumers' behavior, on their actual and desired planes of living. Research findings in this matter are made by the United States Department of Labor and published in the *Monthly Labor Review*, a periodical, as well as in special pamphlets. Other federal, state, and local government agencies collect and publish information which has a bearing on consumer spending. Private foundations subsidize research of the same general nature—for example, the Heller Committee of the University of California at Berkeley. Significant findings about consumer budgets have been made by persons working under the auspices of this organization. Not to be ignored is the vast amount of marketing research done by private corporations. Much of all this research work on consumer behavior is publicized in the nation's newspapers and leading periodicals.

BUSINESS SPENDING

The United States Department of Commerce, through its Office of Business Economics, not only supplies records of past business spending for investment purposes but also publishes elaborate studies on business *plans* for future investment in new plant and equipment. Often these studies attempt to determine the relation between business investment plans made in the past and the amounts that were actually invested thereafter—whether according to plan or in deviation therefrom. Here the government is observed in an effort to arrive at an actual capital accumulation planning schedule of the type illustrated earlier.

In studies of business spending plans and their later realization or modification, many valuable insights will be suggested to businessmen in the future. The studies, published monthly by the United States Commerce Department in the *Survey of Current Business,* feature a nicety of procedure and detailed analysis.

As in the case of data on consumer spending, the Department of Commerce is only one of many sources of information on business spending. There is a veritable host of trade associations, industrial institutes, and economic consultants' organizations which publish general and particularized studies of trends of business investment. In addition, numerous books and articles are published on the subject by economists. A number of leading periodicals, such as the *United States News and World Report,* are dedicated primarily to business reporting, as are such specialized newspapers as the *Wall Street Journal, Commercial and Financial Chronicle,* and others printed in leading cities for local circulation.

The President's *Economic Report*

Most persons are familiar with the fact that corporations issue annual financial statements to their stockholders. Not nearly as generally known is the annual economic report made by the President of the United States. This is directly transmitted to Congress and thereafter made available to the citizens at large. Far from being a dull, forbidding government document, it is a lively account—a bit colored, perhaps, by the ruling Administration's economic philosophy, but no more so than is true of any report submitted by any administrative group, public *or* private.[5]

One of the chief attractions of the *Economic Report of the President* is its annual recapitulation and reconciliation of the nation's income, saving, and expenditure. The data are classified by major transactor groups—namely, consumers, business, government, and the rest of the world.

The President's *Economic Report* abounds in detailed references to aggregate spending. Careful notice is taken of increases (or decreases) in instalment plan buying and changes in mortgage debt. Population projections are presented which have a direct bearing on probable levels of spending in years to come. Then too, spendable

[5] The *Economic Report of the President* (the official title) is submitted to Congress in January of every year. It can be obtained from the Superintendent of Documents, Washington, D.C., for a modest price.

Table 4–1. The Nation's Income, Expenditure, and Savings, 1955–57 ($ billions)

Economic group	1955 Receipts	1955 Expenditures	1955 Excess of receipts or expenditures (−)	1956 Receipts	1956 Expenditures	1956 Excess of receipts or expenditures (−)	1957* Receipts	1957* Expenditures	1957* Excess of receipts or expenditures (−)
Consumers									
Disposable personal income	270.2			287.2			300.0		
Personal consumption expenditures		254.4			267.2			280.4	
Personal net savings			15.8			20.0			19.6
Business									
Gross retained earnings	39.8			40.9			44.0		
Gross private domestic investment		60.6			65.9			63.6	
Excess of investment (−)			−20.8			−25.0			−19.6
International									
Net foreign investment		−.4			1.4			3.3	
Excess of receipts or investment (−)			.4			−1.4			−3.3
Government (federal, state, and local)									
Tax and nontax receipts or accruals	101.1			109.0			115.7		
Less: Transfers, interest, and subsidies (net)	21.5			24.0			27.5		
Net receipts	79.6			85.0			88.2		
Total government expenditures		98.6			104.2			114.1	
Less: Transfers, interest, and subsidies (net)		21.5			24.0			27.5	
Purchase of goods and services		77.1			80.2			86.6	
Surplus or deficit (−) on income and product account			2.6			4.8			1.7
Statistical discrepancy	2.1		2.1	1.6		1.6	1.7		1.7
Gross National Product	391.7	391.7		414.7	414.7		433.9	433.9	

SOURCE: Based on the national income and product statistics of the Department of Commerce (except as noted). *Preliminary; fourth quarter by Council of Economic Advisers.
NOTE: Detail will not necessarily add to totals because of rounding.

earnings of workers in industrial production are recorded, as well as a balance sheet for agriculture to indicate the status of the farmers' purchasing power. Among other highlights, private business debt and the public debt are described—information which has a direct bearing on private enterprise spending for investment purposes and on government spending. Business expenditures on new plant and equipment are documented in specific detail.

Only a generation ago most of these data were not available; they simply were not collected. The *Economic Report* is the capstone of an abundant and refined flow of national economic information. Table 4–1 exhibits a synopsis of the *Report*, the nation's economic budget.

For Discussion

1. Would you call the American economic system a "mixed system"? Why or why not?

2. Since there is no room for national income accounting data on the books of private firms, by what means can a businessman establish his own regularized procedures for taking advantage of national income information? Should he hire an economist, use the services of specialized economic consultants, or turn to some other means? In general, what outside sources exist to which he can have recourse in attempting to appraise the bearing of the economic environment on his individual affairs? What are some of the practices of business concerns in your vicinity in this regard?

3. Why are the old-school, traditional views of such things as the cause of prosperity, the relation of government and business, etc., worth considering if these views have been superseded in the popular mind?

4. If an economic factor of the magnitude of aggregate effective demand could have eluded even the best of economic experts until the 1930's, what are the odds that another great depression might not simply reveal another huge gap in our current flow of economic information?

5. In the seventeenth century a book was written which bore the title *Money Solveth All Things*. Eighteenth-century writers were somewhat more sophisticated and argued that restraining the interference of *monarchical* forms of government with the business community would solve all things. Many nineteenth-century writers had a tendency to argue that the price mechanism solves all economic problems. But it has been argued that this view of those nineteenth-century writers was not logically sound, in terms of actual circumstances, after the onset of the mass-production phase of the Industrial Revolution. When did this phase begin? Do you agree with the critics of those nineteenth-century economists who argued that the economic system is self-regulating? Do you disagree? Is there some intermediate position? Check your answer to this question with the one which you have given for the first question in this set.

6. A leading twentieth-century economist had this to say: "If our poverty were due to famine or earthquake or war—if we lacked material things and the resources to produce them, we could not expect the Means to Prosperity except in hard work, abstinence, and invention. In fact, our predicament is notoriously of another kind." Of what kind? This statement was made during the Great

Depression. Has post-World War II expansive economic activity furnished the grounds for an opposite opinion?

7. Is an increasing reconciliation of national income and private accounting the road to socialism? Do not attempt to answer this question once and for all, but concentrate on the questions it raises in your mind.

8. Ascertain whether your local library has a copy of the *Economic Report of the President*. Check to see how many of your friends and acquaintances have heard of it, or read it. Determine how many economic decision-makers in your acquaintance consult a publication known as *Economic Indicators*, which is published monthly by the Council of Economic Advisers and contains the latest information on national income trends. So far as you can determine, what kind of economic information, and how much, do people actively engaged in economic life actually use? What kind of a problem does the state of affairs in this regard reveal? What will you do about it?

Recommended Further Reading for Part I

On the Economic System

AYRES, C. E. *The Theory of Economic Progress.* Chapel Hill: University of North Carolina Press, 1944.

BOARD OF GOVERNORS OF THE FEDERAL RESERVE SYSTEM. *Flow of Funds in the United States, 1939–1953.* Washington, D.C.: Government Printing Office, 1955.

CLARK, COLIN. *Conditions of Economic Progress.* London: Macmillan & Co., Ltd., 1940.

CLARK, JOHN MAURICE. *Economic Institutions and Human Welfare.* New York: Alfred A. Knopf, Inc., 1957.

DOANE, ROBERT R. *The Anatomy of American Wealth, The Story of Our Physical Assets (Sometimes Called Wealth) and Their Allocation as to Form and Use Among the People.* New York: Harper & Bros., 1940.

GOLDSMITH, R. W. *Measuring National Wealth in a System of Social Accounting.* Vol. XII in a series sponsored by the Conference on Research in National Income and Wealth. New York: National Bureau of Economic Research, Inc., 1938, Part I, pp. 23–101. See also second entry under Kuznets, Simon Smith, below.

KATONA, GEORGE. "Effects of Income Changes on the Rate of Savings," *Review of Economic Statistics,* May, 1949.

KING, WILLFORD ISBELL. *Wealth and Income of the People of the United States.* New York: The Macmillan Co., 1915.

KUZNETS, SIMON SMITH. *Income and Wealth of the United States—Trends and Structure.* Papers by Simon Kuznets and R. W. Goldsmith. London: Bowes & Bowes, Publishers, Ltd., 1952.

———. *On the Measurement of National Wealth.* With discussion by R. T. Bye, Gerhard Colm, M. A. Copeland, and E. E. Martin. Vol. II in a series sponsored by the Conference on Research in National Income and Wealth. New York:

National Bureau of Economic Research, Inc., 1938. See also Goldsmith, R. W., above.
————. *National Product Since 1869*. New York: National Bureau of Economic Research, Inc., 1946.
LERNER, ABBA P. *The Economics of Control*. New York: The Macmillan Co., 1944.
SCHELLING, THOMAS C. *National Income Behavior*. New York: McGraw-Hill Book Co., Inc., 1951.
WRIGHT, DAVID MCCORD. *A Key to Modern Economics*. New York: The Macmillan Co., 1954, chs. IV, V.

Private and Social Accounting

POWELSON, JOHN P. *Economic Accounting—a Textbook in Accounting Principles for Students of Economics and the Liberal Arts*. New York: McGraw-Hill Book Co., Inc., 1955.
PYLE, WILLIAM W. *Fundamental Accounting Principles*. Homewood, Ill.: Richard D. Irwin, Inc., 1955.
U.S. BUREAU OF THE BUDGET. *The United States at War—Development and Administration of the War Program by the Federal Government*. Washington, D.C.: Government Printing Office, 1946.
U.S. DEPARTMENT OF COMMERCE, BUREAU OF THE CENSUS. *Historical Statistics of the United States, 1789–1945*. Washington, D.C.: Government Printing Office, 1946. See also successive issues of the *Statistical Abstract of the United States*.
————. *Census of Manufactures*. Washington, D.C.: Government Printing Office. See latest edition.
U.S. DEPARTMENT OF COMMERCE, OFFICE OF BUSINESS ECONOMICS. *National Income—a Supplement to the Survey of Current Business*. Washington, D.C.: Government Printing Office. See latest edition.
————. *Business Statistics*, Washington, D.C.: Government Printing Office, 1957.
U.S. DEPARTMENT OF HEALTH, EDUCATION, AND WELFARE. *Statistics of Higher Education: Faculty, Students and Degrees, 1951–52*. Washington, D.C.: Government Printing Office, 1955.
U.S. DEPARTMENT OF LABOR. *Military Manpower Requirements and Supply, 1954–60*, Bulletin No. 1161. Washington, D.C.: Government Printing Office, February, 1954.
U.S. FEDERAL TRADE COMMISSION. *National Wealth and Income* (published pursuant to Senate Resoluton No. 451, 67th Congress). Washington, D.C.: Government Printing Office, 1926.
WIXON, RUFUS, and KELL, WALTER G. (eds.). *Accountants' Handbook*. 4th ed.; New York: The Ronald Press Co., 1956.

II

THE STRUCTURE
OF RESOURCES

5 Natural Resources:

Land and Water

Definition and Description of Resources

Resources are material objects of nature which we have learned to use in gaining a livelihood, as well as the human skills which permit us to use these materials. This definition has two main implications.

First, the physical properties of materials accessible to man are not resources unless he has a working knowledge of them. For example, in an article on radioactivity in the 1910–11 edition of the *Encyclopaedia Britannica* it is stated that "the atoms of matter must . . . be regarded as containing enormous stores of energy which are only released by the disintegration of the atom." Einstein had discovered the relativism of mass and energy in 1905. Others had long since discovered special properties of uranium with respect to radioactivity. But in 1911 the atom was not as yet a power resource, because man did not know how to split the atom.

Second, it follows that man's primary resource is his own developing insight and his appreciation of what use can be made of the materials of nature. In other words, at the center of economic development is the unfolding of human knowledge in its practical applications.

Resources may be classified as follows:

1. *Natural resources* are land, forests, water, minerals, and so forth, in the production of which man has largely had no part. In economics, these are frequently grouped under the term *land*.

2. *Human resources* consist of human energy, skills, abilities, and intelligence. In economics, these resources are called *labor*.
3. *Man-made resources* are natural resources after they have been reorganized, treated, modified, fabricated, processed, or changed in some respect by man so that they are usable for the satisfaction of wants. Man-made resources range from simple items of household equipment such as can openers, through consumers' durables such as electric dishwashers, to heavy industrial equipment such as blast furnaces in steel mills. Resources of the last-named type are called *intermediate goods*—because they serve consumers indirectly—or *capital goods*—because they are bought with invested money; they are also frequently called "tools," "plant and equipment," and "producers' goods."

The problem of efficiently using and developing resources, whether given ones or man-made ones, is basically a global problem. The earth is a single great complex of elements and forces that exist in an untold number of combinations, known and yet to be discovered. Some of these combinations and forces are directly useful to mankind: water, wind power, and so forth. Other combinations and forces can be contrived (for instance, synthetic rubber and nuclear fission), or we may ingeniously harness potentially destructive natural forces. When falling water is used to generate electrical energy or natural elements are combined in new ways to help raise living standards by such inventions as nylon, we speak of technological progress.

Since man is by nature a researcher and a developer, the products of his scientific imagination are perhaps as natural as anything can be. Hence, in talking about natural resources one must always do so with reference to the technological efforts and achievements in extending the limits of available resources. For example, present industrial practices in steel-making generally specify a high chromium content in the basic iron ore. For purposes of assessing potential steel production, this means ignoring vast resources of "low-grade" iron formations such as taconite. Yet taconite may be one of the commercial ores of the future.

As a matter of fact, mankind does not ever take its natural environment simply as given. The physical environment is something which man is continuously shaping into configurations that spell different levels of civilization by virtue of the social organization (or institutions) and the technology applied to them.

The American Resources Base

Going concerns not only keep book-records of their affairs but also take inventory of their resources. The knowledge having been acquired of how accounting is performed for the American economy conceived as a going concern, the next logical step is to make a physical inventory of our national resources—the land, the labor force, and our technical equipment.

It is important to take stock, not so much because of the numerical description of national resources at the moment but because of the questions that description raises. How well are we conserving the rich heritage of the past so that it can be passed on to future generations, enriched by our passing contribution? On the other hand, to what extent and in what ways are we squandering our patrimony? What is the structure of wants which has evolved in the march of progress mixed with spoliation? What is considered a culturally approved standard of comfort and decency in our time? And do we share the fruits of production, through various processes of income distribution, in such a way as to bring culturally desirable living standards within the reach of the broad masses of the population? If so, to what extent? If not, how far are we falling short? These are the questions posed. Official data are supplied as material for reflection, and specific directions are given on where, and how, to supplement the facts presented.

Natural Resources: The Surface of the Earth

Werner Sombart, in his monumental book *Der Moderne Kapitalismus,* explained the eighteenth-century Industrial Revolution as the transition in economic activity from dependence on vegetable power to dependence on mineral power. This brilliant insight is a valuable aid to thinking about the development of the Western economic complex. The technology of the past two hundred years has shifted the emphasis of economic activity from agriculture (or the exploitation of surface soils) to industry. It should be remembered, nevertheless, that primary agricultural exploitation remains the predominant form of economic activity throughout most of the world. Even in the United States the growth of industry has rested firmly on the ability to exploit the soil in such a way as to support the growing industrial population with the food it needs.

What kind of use has been made of the arable land that has been carved out of the forest, prairie, and the shrub and desert country which America once was? (See Table 5-1.) The fact which must be appreciated in this connection is that the continental United States has a great deal more sloping land than Europe. This is particularly true of the prairie land which gently but persistently slopes downward from the eastern edge of the Rocky Mountains to the Great Lakes.

Table 5–1. Land Surface of the Continental United States
(millions of acres)

Type of Utilization Before Settlement, 1400 A.D. (a)		Type of Utilization in 1954 (b)	
Forest vegetation	900	Forest and woodland	550
		Suitable for timber	355	
		Used for pasture	120	
		In farms, not pastured	75	
Grass vegetation	750	Pasture and grazing land	700
		Not plowable	460	
Shrub vegetation	155	Not in farms	240	
		Cities, towns, farmsteads, parks, roads, military land, and	
Desert, rock, and other barren lands	95	desert or barren land	190
		Cropland	460
		Cultivated	335	
		Fallow	60	
		Plowable pasture	65	
Total	1,900	Total	1,900

SOURCES: Column (a), see: J. Frederic Dewhurst and Associates, *America's Needs and Resources* (New York: Twentieth Century Fund, 1955), p. 514; column (b), see: U.S. Department of Commerce, Bureau of the Census, *Statistical Abstract of the United States, 1957* (Washington, D.C.: Government Printing Office, 1958), p. 616.

Without in any sense meaning to discredit the great efforts of hard-working American farmers, past and present, the words of the United States Soil Conservation Service may be quoted in this respect.

Land capability has to do with the suitability of land for specified uses.... Probably most farmers have made at one time or another in their own minds some kind of classification of the capability of their land. They know that some fields can be used for cultivated crops and that others are too steep, too stony, too thin, or too wet, for cropping....

Many farmers, however, have failed to realize that steeply sloping land cannot be farmed safely with level-land methods. They have plowed straight furrows and planted straight rows rather than change their farming to fit the land. This makes some of the rows run uphill and downhill, and every rain falling on an unprotected slope removes part of the soil. A few farmers, watching muddy water flow from their fields, have appreciated how valuable and how irreplaceable their thin layer of topsoil really is and have taken steps to check this kind of waste. But losses of soil for the most part come about so gradually that they are not fully realized. Farming habits, like any others, are difficult to change; moreover, precise recommendations for soil-saving measures have not been generally available to farmers. Therefore, it is not surprising that in the past farmers in classifying their land for use more often than not have neglected to consider the full significance of soil erosion.[1]

It may be added that the problem of managing *gently* sloping land was even less foreseen or understood than that of steeply sloping land; hence our "dust bowls."

EXTENSIVE AND INTENSIVE CULTIVATION

Europeans husband their land resources very carefully. Why then, as their descendants basically, have we not done so too? To answer this question we must appreciate the difference between *extensive* and *intensive* agriculture. The latter is prevalent where there is a high ratio of labor to land. German and French vineyardists, Northern Italian general produce farmers, and other Europeans terrace their land almost by hand. In the United States it is not safe *anywhere* to cultivate land beyond a ten-, twelve-, or at most a fifteen-degree gradient except with highly unusual conservation treatment. But in the American economy the land-to-manpower ratio has been exactly the reverse of what was true of Europe. Labor has been the scarce factor of production, whereas for many decades it seemed that land could be had almost for the asking. Hence, whereas much labor was used in Europe for conserving land, it was used in the new country for breaking open more land. That happened not merely in colonial and post-revolutionary days but with especial momentum between 1850 and 1920. During those seven decades the land acreage used for growing crops approximately quadrupled, from 113 million acres to 375 million acres. During that same period the population of the United States increased from 23 million to 106 million persons.

Since 1920 American agriculture has become oriented to intensive cultivation so far as obtaining additional output is concerned. (We continue to operate extensively as compared to Europe, but modern cultivation in America is intensive when compared to our past practices.) Marked increases in yield per acre, that is, in agricultural productivity, have taken place in the recent past. It has been possible to feed and clothe a population which grew from 106 million in 1920 to 170 million in 1957 with no increase at all in the amount of land used for crops and land used to sustain cattle. (There was a shift from open-range grazing land to cultivated grassland and pasture land.) This progress continues. It is estimated by the U.S. Department of Agriculture that by 1975 harvested cropland will increase to 400 million acres, a very considerable increase over the approximate 350

[1] U.S. Department of Agriculture, Soil Conservation Service, *A Manual on Conservation of Soil and Water*, Agriculture Handbook No. 61 (Washington, D.C.: Government Printing Office, June, 1954), p. 23.

million acre cultivation of the mid-1950's. In 1975 the population is expected to be 207 million (the lowest official estimate), an increase of over 20 per cent.

In terms of increased yield per cropland acre, agriculture has staged a "productivity breakthrough," along with industry, during the last decade. If we take the average crop production from 1947 to 1949 as 100 per cent, it is seen that the per acre yield (of 28 leading crops) was: 102 per cent in 1951; 108 per cent in 1953; and 123 per cent in 1956.[2]

The farmers' remarkable capacity to increase yields per acre is attributable to:

1. Personal capacity to get work done
2. Improvements in crop varieties
3. Increased use of fertilizers
4. Expansion of irrigated and well-drained areas
5. Advances in control of plant insects and diseases
6. The use of modern power equipment

To appreciate the last-named point note that the number of tractors on farms was 246,000 in 1920, as compared to 4.5 million in 1956; yet the acreage of land used for producing crops was a little less in 1956 than it had been in 1920.

A NECESSARY CAUTION

The real achievements of present-day farmers must not blind us to the fact that in some instances we are only recouping by productivity gains what was previously lost by careless land utilization. Thus, corn yields were greatly increased in the 1930's when hybrid corn was introduced. But early-day farmers could tell of yields of ordinary corn on virgin soil fully equal to modern hybrid yields.

Speaking generally, some changes in American land utilization will have to be made if further *net* productivity gains are to be made. As a matter of fact, merely getting better crop yields by using improved varieties and applying chemical stimulants to the soil does not tell a full story. It is also important to know whether or not yield-per-acre gains are being made at the expense of the soil itself. Crop yields depend not only on what is done *on* the land but also on what is done *to* the land. Damage to the land may proceed very gradually; yet it must sooner or later reduce yields.

A process of soil depletion is taking place in the United States. It is caused by overworking, or failure to safeguard, the soil in order to

[2] U.S. Department of Agriculture, Agricultural Marketing Service, Crop Reporting Board, *Crop Production, 1956,* Annual Summary (Washington, D.C.: Government Printing Office, December 17, 1956), p. 41.

achieve high per-acre yields. For example, the prices of farm products rose by 152 per cent between 1940 and 1950, whereas the wholesale prices of *all* commodities rose only 105 per cent. Did this comparative rise of farm prices mean that the farmers were enriched? No, because a substantial part of the rise in farm prices was brought about by increased costs of achieving high yields.

SOIL EROSION AND THE FERTILITY SITUATION

The early economists used to talk about the "original and indestructible fertility of the soil." But now we know that this can be true only with regard to nature's over-all favorable soil balance. Soil destruction in particular spots was no greater than soil creation by solar radiation elsewhere—*before man came on the scene.* Soil erosion, whether by wind or water or both, means rainfall, running water, or airborne particles scouring and cutting at the earth's surface, dislodging and scattering soil particles. Under natural conditions, but at a very slow rate, this has happened throughout the ages. At first the Grand Canyon of the Colorado probably was little different from hundreds of other small valleys in the same region. Erosion has carved this tremendous gorge by abrading each day through many ages a little more rock and soil from the area—and the Grand Canyon is still growing. But this kind of erosion is not a human problem.

Soil erosion, with which we must be very seriously concerned, is an abnormal and undesirable process started by man's activities, yet subject to his control. It manifests itself most strikingly in gullies that may develop from rills in cultivated fields, ruts in roadways, cattle trails, ditches, or other depressions along which running water is concentrated, eventually becoming a cutting force and a carry-off vehicle. Starting as a small channel across which a man can step, a gully may rapidly increase in size until it is large enough to hide a cow or even a house. But gullies which are even a few feet in depth interfere with cultivation; the land becomes so gullied that one cannot get equipment across it. Recovery from erosion is extremely slow.

What is called *sheet erosion* is even more vicious than the kind just described. It is less obvious and attacks the rich topsoil first, perhaps removing only a cubic yard each week from an acre. This would scarcely be noticed, but if it continued for only thirty years, it would cause a loss of about eleven inches from the entire surface. It is caused by thin sheets of water flowing across unprotected, clean-cultivated fields or across bare spots in hillside pastures during heavy showers or during man-caused flooding of a stream's channels, and so forth.

Wind erosion occurs in areas where there is not enough vegetation to cover and protect the soil, a natural condition in arid lands and along the sand shores of lakes, oceans, and rivers. Sand dunes are great hazards, since they are free to move with shifting winds to invade valuable croplands and forests. The dry-farming plains regions in the United States have suffered heavily in severe drought, when unprotected fine-grained topsoil, blowing easily because loose and dry, was carried great distances. It filled the air, clouding the sun for days and giving a weird characteristic to the light. In heavy blows or "dusters" the fine soil gets into everything; tightly closed houses or cars offer no adequate protection, and the blowing sand is choking and blinding to animals and humans alike. In the plowed land from which the loose material is blown away there may be nothing left but hard subsoil, with dunelike drifts several feet high piled up elsewhere.

Certain types of crop are harder on the land than others. Thus, expanded production of grain and forage at the middle of the twentieth century increased the drain on our land. From 1942 to 1949, expanded acreages of wheat and intertilled crops speeded up soil depletion, even though more attention was paid to conservation practices. It was a race between conservation and depletion, with the latter forging ahead. The Department of Agriculture has prescribed the following measures for maintaining the nation's soil fertility:

... essential protective measures for cropland are as follows: (1) Cover crops are needed annually on more than 30 million acres; (2) green-manure crops on 55 million acres; and (3) crop rotations on more than 200 million acres.

If these measures are to be carried out, a reduction in grain and other soil-depleting crops will be necessary to permit planting cover and green-manure crops and to install rotations containing hay and pasture crops.

If the requirements for protection and maintenance of the land are to be met, it will mean slowing down production of grain crops and of many other cultivated crops. An equivalent of 20 million acres or more of cropland is estimated to be necessary to permit working space for proper rotation with year-long cover and soil-improvement crops to maintain and increase production. *Otherwise, present production rates cannot be maintained nor can needed increases in productivity be achieved.* [Italics supplied.]

Cover and soil-improvement crops would make suitable for occasional cropping much eroded and depleted, moderately sloping land. In the long run, this treatment would be less expensive than developing new land by clearing, drainage, or irrigation. But shifts of many steep slopes and rough or rocky areas permanently to grass and trees would be necessary.[3]

The prescription is not stronger than the need of the agricultural situation. Since the beginning of cultivation in this country, about 20

[3] U.S. Department of Agriculture, *Land,* Information Bulletin No. 140 (Washington, D.C.: Government Printing Office, June, 1955), p. 83.

per cent of our original tillable area (approximately 120 million acres out of an original 600 million acres) has been ruined for further cultivation purposes. With approximately 460 million acres of really good, high-grade cropland left in the United States and approximately 400 million wanted for direct tillage as early as 1975, it is plainly in the public interest to use wisely what we now hold abundantly.

Potential Agricultural Production

In measuring potential agricultural production the useful concept of *land capability* is employed. This refers to the systematic arrangement of different kinds of land according to specific properties which determine the ability of the land to produce on a virtually permanent basis.

Soil conservation experts have developed eight main categories of land. After they have been defined, we shall see how much of our land falls into the respective classifications.

LAND CAPABILITY CLASSES

Most of our *tillable* cropland falls into Classes I, II, and III of land capability. Class I land is very good, nearly level land with deep, easily worked soils that can be cultivated safely in using ordinary good farming methods. Class II land is good but has some limitations. It needs moderately intensive treatment if it is to be cultivated safely; for example, contouring, cover-cropping to control erosion, or simple water-management operations to conserve rainfall. Class III is moderately good and can be regularly used for cultivated crops in a good rotation if plowed on the contour of sloping fields. It requires intensive treatment such as terracing or strip-cropping to control erosion, or intensive water management on flat, wet areas.

Class IV is fairly good land, but its safe cropping use is very limited by natural features such as slope, erosion, adverse soil characteristics, or adverse climate. As a rule its best use is for pasture or hay, but some of it may be cultivated with proper safeguards.

Class V, VI, and VII lands are not suited for cultivation at all but may be used for grazing or forestry, according to their adaptability. Class V land has few natural limitations for such uses and needs only good management. Class VI needs protective measures, usually because of slope or shallow soil. Class VII needs extreme care to overcome or cope with its major limitations, which are usually steep slopes, very shallow soil, or other very unfavorable features.

Class VIII land is suited for wildlife, recreation, or watershed protection. It is usually characterized by such features as extreme steepness, roughness, stoniness, wetness, sandiness, or erosibility. These characteristics make it unfit for any safe or economical cultivation, grazing, or forestry.

With this explanation of land capability classifications, and bearing in mind that these characteristics are not concentrated as between different large regions but may appear within given regions, the following breakdown of land acreage can now be readily understood. Table 5–2 certainly furnishes food for thought about the conditions under which our farmers furnish food for our tables. Only about a tenth of our cropland is such as may be cultivated with ease and abandon. Fully 80 per cent has to be cultivated with some degree of intensity,

Table 5–2. Private Land by Capability Class, the Continental United States, 1950

Class	Cropland (471 million acres)	Grassland and Pasture (461 million acres)	Woodland (338 million acres)
	(as percentages of these respective totals)		
I	11%	2%	2%
II	36	8	10
III	34	13	18
IV	10	9	10
V	1	4	10
VI	5	31	19
VII	3	31	31
VIII	negligible	2	negligible

Source: Adapted from *Land Facts—a Compilation of Facts and Estimates on the Extent, Nature, and Use of Land Resources in the Continental U.S.;* for use of Soil Conservation Service workers (Washington, D.C.: processed, November, 1953).

ranging from moderate to high—in other words, with educated forethought, good equipment, and careful labor. A bottom tenth of our cropland should not be in cultivation at all. About two-thirds of our grassland also has to be wisely managed, one-third of it with the adoption of protective measures and the other one-third with extreme care. Half of our woodland requires the same kind of attention.

In view of this evident requirement to husband wisely and not merely extensively (though that is our tradition), what is the actual state of our land? Here we shall refer only to the 471 million acres of privately owned arable land (including rotational pasture).

Roughly, one-half of our arable land is in good shape, there being only a slight danger, or none at all, of its dropping into a lower capability classification because of erosion or other kind of soil damage. A quarter of our land is in serious danger of dropping into a lower capability classification unless some real conservation efforts are made within fifteen to thirty years. Another, the final quarter of United States land, is in a critical condition. It will have deteriorated years before 1975 unless steps are promptly taken to save it.

CAN MORE LAND BE PROVIDED?

Official estimates are that 17 million acres of land might be added for crop cultivation by irrigation in the West. In the East, particularly the Southeast, 20 million new acres could be developed as farm land by draining wet lands not presently available to agriculture. Uncleared Class I and II lands suitable for cultivation and now in farm woodland and woodland closely adjoining farm areas (exclusive of the wet-lands potential already mentioned) amount to another 25 million acres. Thus 60 million acres of new land are available, to which may be added 65 million acres of plowable pasture not presently cultivated.

However, this abstract potentiality raises a truly economic question. Is valuable labor and capital to be used to obtain more production by adding more land, or shall at least some of that labor and capital be used to improve the use of established land?

Several observations in this connection can be made. (1) Extra acres newly brought into cultivation will be a *net* addition only if we keep our presently cultivated acres intact; otherwise we shall be developing land with one hand and destroying or impairing land with the other. (2) The feasibility of bringing substantial areas of new cropland into production by *clearing* is severely limited, except in the case of some very high-priced specialty crops. (3) Bringing in new land by the medium of *irrigation*, particularly in the western states, is by no means universally feasible compared with the practicability of giving supplementary irrigation to established farm land in other parts of the nation. (4) Obtaining new land by *drainage* of some 20 million acres (mostly in the lower Mississippi Valley) seems to be an expensive procedure in view of the fact that in that same area another 30 million acres *already in farms* could be improved by drainage.

What is being done? The state of affairs regarding 1.4 billion acres of privately owned farm land in the United States was reported definitively in the mid-1950's. At that time—and there is no conclusive evidence that the situation has been greatly ameliorated—the facts were: (1) 300 million acres of farm land of all types received adequate conservation treatment; (2) 900 million acres were still in need of conservation treatment—more than three times as much as the land receiving attention; (3) 200 million acres of privately owned farm land needed no conservation practices at all and thus presented no problem. In other words, 10 per cent of our agricultural land was not in need of attention. Another 20 per cent needed treatment and was receiving it. Seventy per cent of the land needed some or a great deal of conservation care but was not getting it.

It is encouraging to note that as of July 1, 1953, 87 per cent of our farmers belonged to cooperative and democratic land planning associations. These associations—that is, the individuals belonging to them—are assisted by state and federal agricultural experts, research stations, and educational associations. However, the above data reveal that much work remains to be done. The estimated *annual* soil loss during the mid-1950's was still 400,000 acres by soil erosion and blowing, and another 100,000 acres lost because of other preventable causes of soil deterioration. The fact that this constitutes a marked improvement over the situation twenty years earlier, when land was being wasted at an annual rate of a million acres, offers only cold comfort.

Water as a Resource

Water management is a *must* for the American economy. Westerners know this as they more or less grumblingly abide by sprinkling regulations even on the privacy of their own lawn; and people in the industrialized East have every reason to be just as seriously concerned. For in the East the user of water for industrial purposes is steadily encountering higher real costs because the supply is increasingly inadequate to meet the rising demand.

The withdrawal of water for all uses in 1955 was 262 billion gallons per day; by 1975 this is expected to increase by 75 per cent—up to 453 billion gallons per day.[4] At present the nation's annual water bill totals $3 billion, approximately 1 per cent of the national income. The total investment in reservoirs, aqueducts, and other works for using or controlling water was $50 billion in 1956 (this figure may be appreciated by comparing it with a total outlay of $32 billion for building the nation's railroads). The Department of Agriculture has estimated that we can expect further investments of from $50 to $75 billion over the next fifty years.[5] This large addition to our present $50 billion plant will be made by private, state, and federal interests.

WHO USES THE WATER?

Farmers are the biggest users of water; normally they make one-half the total of water withdrawals in a year. Approximately two-fifths

[4] This figure is based on the lowest official estimate of the 1975 population (207 million) and assumes that there will be 50 per cent more industrial production.
[5] U.S. Department of Agriculture, *Water, the Yearbook of Agriculture* (Washington, D.C.: Government Printing Office, 1955), p. 7.

of all the water withdrawn is used for irrigating arid and semiarid farm lands in the seventeen western states alone. With a population of 40 million, these states use as much water daily as 31 eastern states with more than three times that much population. On the other hand, whereas the western states use only 3 billion gallons daily for industrial purposes, the eastern states use 65 billion gallons per day.

INDUSTRIAL WATER

Industry uses water primarily for cooling which is required as a consequence of intensely high and often prolonged heating processes in manufacturing. Statistics for several industries demonstrate the use of water as a coolant. The steel industry alone consumed about 16 per cent of the industrial water used in 1950, or about 8 per cent of all the water used that year for all purposes. The chemical industry is a heavy user. That is why it is visionary to think of great chemical installations in the vicinity of Denver, say. Instead, Philadelphia and its surrounding region seem destined to remain centers of chemical enterprise. The reason is that the Delaware River is one of the world's finest industrial cooling systems; the same is true of the Monongahela, Ohio, and Allegheny rivers for steelmaking centers in and around Pittsburgh. Petroleum refining, a big user, absorbed 9 per cent of all industrial water in 1950. Water use here, as well as in the chemical industry, may be expected to increase rapidly. Steam-electric generating plants used 44 per cent of industrial water in 1950, most of it for condenser cooling. In general, three-fourths of industrial water is used for cooling —that is, somewhat more than a fifth of *all* of our water. After cooling, washing, grading, and waste disposal account for the largest volume of water used by industry.

To illuminate the concept of "industrial water" it may be mentioned that 18.33 barrels of water are required to make one barrel of oil, no less than 65,000 gallons of water to make one ton of steel, and 300 gallons of water to roll out a barrel of beer. Much of this water is returned to streams or the ground. If not too polluted or overheated, the water can be re-used.

IRRIGATION WATER

One out of every eight acres of harvested cropland depends completely upon being irrigated. However, this does not tell a full story. When the *sales value* of harvested crops, rather than the amount of acreage, is noted, irrigated crops account for one-third of the total income from annual crop sales. The reason is that crops which are grown on irrigated land are typically high-priced agricultural commodities. As was already mentioned, most of the land which depends totally upon irrigation is in the 17 western states.

Irrigation of a supplementary kind is practiced in 31 states of the Midwest and East—in Louisiana, Arkansas, Florida, Georgia, and to some extent even in Wisconsin, Michigan, and Minnesota. As a matter of fact, irrigating to supplement regular water flows is a rapidly spreading practice in the humid areas of the nation.

Irrigation in the West varies with the amount of rainfall and the type of farming. In the three Pacific Coast states, 70 per cent of the crops, measured by value, are grown under irrigation. In the eight Mountain states as a whole the figure is 60 per cent; in Utah and Wyoming, specifically, between 75 and 85 per cent; in Arizona and Nevada nearly all crops are irrigated. The percentages are much lower in Nebraska and the North Dakota-Texas tier of states. One of the chief reasons is that dry-farming of wheat has proved commercially successful, reducing the reliance on irrigation.

As for the types of crops grown by irrigation, in nearly all the western states rice, sugar beets, and citrus fruits depend on irrigation. Two-thirds of the cotton grown in the chief western cotton states of Oklahoma, Texas, New Mexico, Arizona, and California comes from irrigated land—a percentage double that of 1939, only a generation before. About one-half of western feed crops and four-fifths of western fruits and vegetables depend upon irrigation.

Further expansion of irrigated land surface is to be expected, though at a much slower rate than in the recent past. Such lands as are likely to be brought under irrigation will be more expensive, because competition for unutilized water supplies is keen and is growing keener.

The United States Bureau of Reclamation has done much to aid irrigation in the West. Between 1950 and 1954 the Bureau's projects added 282,000 acres of new-land irrigation and provided supplemental water to an additional million acres.

Projects under construction and authorized by Congress as of January 1, 1955, included about 6.5 million acres of *new* irrigation in the West and provided for *supplemental* water for nearly 4 million acres. It has been estimated that 15 million acres remain available for irrigation development in the West, potentially bringing the West's ultimate total to better than 40 million acres of irrigated land as against 26 million acres or thereabouts at present. About 5.6 million newly irrigated acres can be developed in the Columbia River Basin, and 3.4 million acres in California's Central Valley and 6 million in the Missouri Basin are irrigable.

One might wonder why all this emphasis is laid on irrigation in the West when so little acreage is involved. But it must be remembered that man "liveth not by bread alone"; many of the western crops are specialty crops, good things of life that we treasure. Nor is the West so far removed in this respect from the more populous centers as one might think; for example, New Yorkers get the most and best of California orchard and strawberry crops.

WATER PROBLEMS

Americans are never more voracious than they are in their consumption of water. The total daily requirement of persons living in ancient European villages was perhaps 3 to 5 gallons a day. The modern American uses 60 gallons a day directly for household and lawn-watering purposes in the average electrified farm or urban home. This is not counting the industrial water needed to furnish finished products of industry or the irrigation and other water used to furnish agricultural products to consumers.

Difficulties were bound to develop with the high rates of water utilization. The problems are, naturally, localized ones that differ case by case, according to the type of water use. Thus, in Arizona, an extreme case, 60 per cent of the water supply comes from over-pumped wells. Southwest of Los Angeles there is a depletion of ground-water. This has invited a contaminating intrusion of salt water, which recently was moving inland at rates up to 300 feet per year, spoiling fresh water supplies.

In a six-county area of the High Plains of Texas the water table is dropping so much that it is now considered possible that the economically recoverable water in that area will be totally exhausted. The ground-water supply in the Antelope Valley in California appeared to be inexhaustible in 1910, owing to the presence of high-pressure artesian wells. Many of these ceased flowing by 1920; in 1950 the annual pumping rate was 110,000 acre-feet, but the estimated replenishment rate was only 65,000 acre-feet. The water level in the wells had been declining at the rate of three feet a year.

On the other hand, a problem also appears when the water table rises, as is usual when irrigation is brought in from canals rather than being pumped from artesian wells. When a water table rises too near the surface, it can produce problems of drainage, salinity, and alkali which will cut down the size of the crop.

Soil erosion is a great menace to irrigated land in arid regions, since the soils there are shallow, light in texture, and low in organic matter, making them highly vulnerable to wind and water erosion. Erosion is threatening the continued productivity of more than half of all our irrigated land. Some 250,000 irrigated acres are losing topsoil at the rate of an inch every three years; another 500,000 acres at the rate of an inch every five years. As topsoil is lost, the total soil structure is broken down, making the remaining soil less able to take water after row crops have been grown for some time.

Much damage to irrigated land can be done by building irrigation runs which are too long. Delivery of irrigation water in open ditches adds heavily to water loss. The loss may be as high as 70 per cent. Some of it is due to seepage or to heavy weed growth in canals. Such growths slow down the flow velocity of the water, increasing the loss due to seepage and evaporation. Actually, the efficiency with which farmers apply their irrigation water to the land ranges from 15 to 90 per cent of the water they turn onto a field; the remainder (from 85 to 10 per cent) is lost as runoff, deep percolation, and evaporation. Improper methods of logging and heavy animal grazing on the watersheds which produce the irrigation water have created other problems. Enough has been said to indicate that irrigation agriculture must be a scientific undertaking: Topsy "just growed"—not so our irrigated crops.

Drainage. This is perhaps not a water scarcity problem, but it is certainly a problem of avoidable scarcity due to water. Agricultural drainage may be defined as the removal of excess water from the soil profile by artificial means in order to enhance agricultural production. On many farms the bottom lands have the most fertile soil. But because they are wet during some of the year, they produce only part of the yield which they could produce. A wet soil is a cold soil, one that is likely to be compact and dense. Plant roots cannot spread easily through such soil. Sweet clover and other soil-building crops will not grow; thus a balanced crop rotation cannot be followed. Liming, also, is often useless in soggy soils.

When soil is drained, air replaces the water that is removed; it takes relatively little heat to warm this air; and so the soil loosens up. Seeds germinate faster and a better stand is obtained. The plants do not drown out after a rain. Moreover, the roots go down deeper. Thus the plants can draw on deeper moisture and are therefore better able to withstand summer drought.

Excess water can be drained from land either by open surface drains or by subsoil drains. The latter (usually of tile) are relatively expensive but truly economical. Some kind of drainage is now practiced on about 2 million farms, covering 103 million acres in forty states. Much of it is under public auspices. Thus, more than 155,000 miles of outlet ditches, 56,000 miles of outlet tile drains, 7,800 miles of levees, and pumping plants of 110,000 horsepower have been constructed under public drainage improvement projects. In addition to a total of 103 million acres of publicly served lands, 50 million acres of wet farming have been drained by individual private projects.

Every state has some land that can be improved through drainage, but the largest areas of wet land are in the eastern half of the country. An estimated 20 million acres of fertile undeveloped land needs to be drained if new farm land is to be developed from it. A large total acreage that could be drained lies in the creek and river bottoms of the Southeast and along the Atlantic Coast. The Mississippi Valley has additional thousands of alluvial acres which can be improved for farming as needed. In the Lake states and the Corn Belt there is still much potentially good land which could be put in better shape for the plow by drainage. Once again we see that agriculture is a truly scientific undertaking.

There are many other farm water problems. A recent one has been brought about by the rapid strides of rural electrification. This has caused so heavy an increase in the use of water for household and production purposes that the limited well-water supplies of many farms have been severely strained.

Some industrial water problems. In this respect trouble stems from the unsound practice of building factories without prior studies to determine whether water would be available to operate them and to provide for the communities around them as well. Then, too, there is a persistent lowering of water tables in nearly all populous industrialized areas, not only in arid regions where irrigation is practiced in agriculture. Even where water is plentiful, some serious shortages have developed because the water supply is not fit to use. In part this is due to gross uncleanliness—using streams and rivers as open sewers. Industrial water problems are due to natural pollution,[6] and also to refuse disposal of concentrations of acids or alkalies from mines or industrial plants.

Now as never before, industry is requiring more and more pure water—water free of organic matter, minerals, acids, or gases. The trend toward synthetic materials and the rapid growth of chemical industries accentuate this demand for pure water, because these industries cannot operate with anything else. Cases are already known in which industries requiring relatively clean water have been discouraged from locating along heavily polluted rivers even though good plant sites, a labor supply, and other attractions existed. Some plants whose water supplies have deteriorated have even moved to other localities rather than incur high costs of purification. Industries today

[6] One-fifth of industry's intake of water is brackish water.

are spending millions of dollars (where once they spent little or nothing) treating intake water to bring it to adequate quality standards, and treating outgoing wastes so as not to destroy the water's usefulness for the next downstream consumer.

Perhaps the problem of water pollution had best be viewed in a *qualitative* perspective—what pollution does to public health—rather than primarily in terms of dollars and cents. This is especially necessary now, because a new dimension has been added to the problem—that of protecting municipal and rural water supplies from radioactive wastes. The new problem does not refer so much to atomic blast residues as it does to the more subtle and pervasive effect of the increasing use of radioactive materials in manufacturing, for electricity generation, and for experimentation in medicine, agriculture, and industry.

The operation of nuclear power reactors alone will produce a manifold increase in the amount of radiation released into the air. Even more is released by the increasing multitude of small industrial and professional devices involving radiation. Be they ever so humble, they contribute a sizable share of aggregate noxious radiation, and such devices are becoming more and more widely used and scattered throughout the country. Radioactive materials released into the air are deposited sooner or later on the surface of the earth, including streams and lakes. It is said that most of what enters municipal water reservoirs or other surface waters is rendered harmless by the application of modern detection and treatment methods. Even if that is so, not enough is known about the long-time, cumulative effects on human beings of minimal amounts of radiation that still remain in the water we drink *after* it has been treated.

By contrast, much is already known about watershed management aimed at favoring the slow movement of water through the soil into underground storage. In the opinion of one expert it may be from this direction that an offset to contamination of water by airborne materials will come—provided radioactively contaminated solids are not placed underground in misbegotten, separate efforts to get rid of radioactive waste!

Water pollution is a problem of national dimensions and should therefore be coordinated on the level of federal government. The federal Water Pollution Control Act of 1948 does provide for federal cooperation with states and interstate groups such as associations of state governors. Upon examination of the Act, however, its enforcement provisions are found to be weak and time-consuming. Moreover, its positive feature, that of providing federal aid to pollution abatement projects, allows only minimal sums to be spent by the federal government in assisting the states. The United States Public Health Service has estimated that an initial expenditure of from $9 billion to $12 billion will be required to rid our rivers of pollution. Another $12 to $15 billion should be spent to keep them clear of pollution thereafter.

In addition to many new types of water problems, there is still the ancient one of runaway flood waters. People, generally, acknowledge this creates a collective need for protection; hence large public invest-ments have been made for levees, dikes, reservoirs, and other means of curbing floods. Here again, however, a lack of federal coordination must be noted. To be sure, the Army Corps of Engineers fights in this matter as valiantly in peace as it does on other fronts in time of war. Still, there have been deplorable jurisdictional disputes for want of over-all federal flood control planning—crippling disputes between localities, state governments opposing particular federal projects, and contentiousness even between different federal agencies. As a result, flood damage costs the nation $1 billion a year, in addition to which human lives continue to be needlessly lost.

WATER MANAGEMENT

Planning in advance is needed to prevent towns, cities, industries, and farm areas from expanding beyond the safe limits of the water reasonably available to them. Lack of city and countryside planning entails expensive, makeshift, or long-term efforts to cope with emer-gencies that should never have arisen in the first place.

Civic planning must comprehend all aspects of the water utilization problem from a multipurpose point of view—water for industrial use, for navigation, for power generation, for flood control, for land reclamation and irrigation, and not least from the viewpoint of good water, for household consumption. Unless water-use planning is com-prehensive, progressively severe emergencies will have to be met by incurring high real costs in coping on a crash basis with the water needs of our growing population.

For Discussion

1. The terms *factors of production* and *economic resources* are often used interchangeably. List the three main categories of economic resources, define each category in a phrase, and write beside each the name of the factor of production which corresponds to it.

2. "All of our resource problems would be well in hand, and gains already achieved would be well secured, if inanimate objects were no longer falsely worshipped or, alternatively, carelessly abused because they are conceived as 'things'—rather than as resources improved by people, to be conserved for the people." Discuss.

3. "Land is not soil." Explain this statement, placing special emphasis on the factors which can cause erosion.

4. Farm output per head of American population has increased more slowly than total farm output. Which of the following two explanations is true? (a) Population has increased while farm output has decreased; (b) population has increased at a relatively rapid rate, thus offsetting the total increase of farm output.

5. In the past, much land has been wasted; at present, agricultural production is not as mechanized as is industrial production. Yet the rise of agricultural productivity exceeds the growth of productivity for industry as a whole. Is there a simple explanation for this?

6. What is the relation between the concepts of extensive cultivation, intensive cultivation, and land capability classes?

7. Which of the following developments do you favor as means of improving agricultural productivity in future years: increased ability of the farmers to buy more land; the growth of cities, whereby massive market opportunities are furnished to farmers; shifts in types of land use; growing size of individual farms? What other factor or factors should be considered?

8. If water is a resource, why is not air? Can you think of circumstances under which "air management" is necessary and knowledge to that effect has been developed or is being developed? Generally speaking, air is not considered a resource but rather a free good, i.e., something always to be had for the asking. Why?

9. "Few activities have so clearly brought out the interdependence of all individuals, communities, and nations as have our harried concerns with water, this product of the heavens." Illustrate this statement by first envisaging your home community's water situation, then broadening this view.

10. Industrial users of water have typical water problems, and farmers have other specific water problems. Show some interrelationships of these seemingly divergent problems.

6 Natural Resources:

Minerals and Energy

According to the official census of manufactures, the value added by bread manufacturing in 1954 was $1.5 billion, whereas the voraciously steel-consuming automobile industry added four times as much value, $6 billion. This is but one token of the fact that although bread continues as the staff of life, steel gives our civilization its peculiar technological quality. In point of fact, civilizations have long been classified according to the material of their civilian and military hardware. There was a Stone Age, remnants of which remain, for example, in the southwestern part of the United States among Indians occasionally situated adjacent to atomic energy projects. There was a Bronze Age, a Copper Age, an Iron Age; remnants of the last may be found in Africa.

As modern Americans we are living in a "steel age." In many respects this is a late, refined phase of the Iron Age, since steel is iron ore transmuted. More significantly, we are limited, as were our primitive Iron Age ancestors, to exploiting ore deposits which exist in high, rich concentrations near the surface of the earth; that is to say, we do not know how to use the iron which exists limitlessly in the oceans, although in extremely low concentrations, that is, two parts out of 1 billion.

Like anything refined—whether a personality or a product—steel is very demanding. No steel can be made without manganese, or without a hardening alloy, principally tungsten. Fluorspar is required as a flux when steel is produced by the widely used open-hearth method. Cobalt, a prescribed alloy for steel to be used under high-temperature conditions, will be strongly demanded in years ahead. Chromite is an essential alloy in stainless steel production.

International Interdependence

In distributing rich concentrations of metallic ores, nature did not anticipate the existing political subdivisions of the earth. Thus the United States depends upon foreign sources of supply to supplement domestically mined alloys for transmuting iron into steel and to furnish certain alloys entirely. Good basic iron ore exists in abundance, although higher-grade and more cheaply produced ores are increasingly imported from Canada, from Venezuela, and from overseas.

International interdependence characterizes not only steel-making but other main lines of metal production, a prominent example being that of lead. There is an even higher degree of dependence for antimony used as a hardening element of lead to be used in storage batteries, type metal, and bearings.

The following pages analyze the American minerals position in terms of the ease or difficulty which might be experienced politically in getting access to additional or unique sources of certain mineral supplies produced in other countries.

In assessing the minerals position of our economy at mid-twentieth century, two assumptions are made. The first is that no major technological, economic, or political changes are in the offing. Second, not only are home-produced minerals considered, but also those which are nearby and readily available to the United States on commercial terms. In other words, this means counting our domestic mineral resources *plus* what can be imported from Canada and Mexico without, however, cutting back their requirements. In these terms, then, the American economy seems to be assured of ample supplies, either through domestic production or through economic purchase, of the minerals listed in Table 6–1.[1]

In addition to North and Central American minerals to which access is almost completely unimpeded, there are minerals in South America

[1] Much of the following material is based on testimony presented at hearings before the Senate Committee on Interior and Insular Affairs. See the printed transcript bearing the title *Long-Range Minerals Program*, Parts 1 and 2, a record of hearings in June, July, and August, 1957 (Washington, D.C.: Government Printing Office, 1957). See also the documents entitled *Stockpile and Accessibility of Strategic and Critical Materials to the United States in Time of War*, 8 parts (Washington, D.C.: Government Printing Office, 1954); also, Senate Document No. 83 of the 84th Congress, 1st Session, entitled *Critical Materials* (Washington, D.C.: Government Printing Office, 1956).

Mineral	Annual Domestic Production	Annual Home Consumption	Annual Imports	Chief Sources of Imports	Domestic Reserves	Future Developments
Arsenic	12,000 s.t. (+ 2,000 s.t. from stocks)	20,000 s.t.	6,000	Mexico (89%) Canada (9%)	2,500,000 s.t.	New uses in large quantities.
Asbestos	50,000 s.t.	750,000 s.t.	700,000 s.t.	Canada (94%)	1 million s.t.	Synthesis of asbestos.
Barite	1.2 million s.t.	1.6 million s.t.	400,000 s.t.	Canada (52%) Mexico (30%)	40 million s.t.	Steady growth.
Boron (borax)	1.1 million s.t.	900,000 s.t.	None. U.S. exports boron	....	Very large	Many new uses.
Cadmium	10 million lb.	11.5 million lb.	1.5 million lb.	Mexico (66%) Canada (20%)	42.5 million lb.	Improved methods of recovery.
Fluorspar	300,000 s.t.	600,000 s.t.	300,000 s.t.	Mexico (57%)	22.5 million s.t.	Recovery of waste fluorine from phosphate rock.
Gold	2 million oz. t.	1.5 million oz. t.	Varies widely	North America (74%)	50 million oz. t.	Continually rising production costs.
Iodine	Negligible	1.4 million lb.	1.4 million lb.	Chile (65%)	....	....
Lead	750,000 s.t. of primary and recovered lead	1.2 million s.t. cont.	450,000 s.t. cont.	Mexico (20%) Canada (15%) Other Latin America (25%)	3 million s.t. cont.	Declining industry? Improved recovery needed, as richer ore bodies are depleted and costs of production are rising. Plastic substitutes for lead sheathing are developing.

(Continued)

Table 6–1. Readily Accessible Minerals . . . (Continued)

Mineral	Annual Domestic Production	Annual Home Consumption	Imports	Chief Sources of Imports	Domestic Reserves	Future Developments
Magnesium	68,000 s.t. from sea water	61,000 s.t.	200 s.t. U.S. exports magnesium	Canada (52%)	Annual production capacity is 130,000 tons	Evolution of low-cost continuous thermic process of producing the metal.
Molybdenum	60,000 lb. cont.	40,000 lb. cont.	None. U.S. is the world's largest exporter of molybdenum	....	Over 2 billion lb.	New process of producing massive ductile molybdenum, by electrodeposition.
Nickel	5,000 s.t.	125,000 s.t.	130,000 s.t. (net imports)	Canada (81%) Cuba (11%)	550,000 s.t.	Continuing world shortage?
Phosphate rock	13.5 million l.t.	11.3 million l.t. (+ 2.2 l.t. to stock)	Negligible (100,000 l.t.)	Netherlands Antilles	13.5 million l.t.	Utilization of low-grade materials presently wasted in manufacturing phosphatic fertilizers.
Silver	40 million oz.	110 million oz.	70 million oz.	North America (57%) South America (18%)	600 million oz.	Greater use of silver in chemical and metallurgical industries.
Sulfur	7 million l.t.	5.5 million l.t.	United States normally exports sulfur.	....	50–70 million l.t.	Obtaining supplies from off-shore deposits, from salt dome deposits free

Titanium	14,500 s.t.	11,000 s.t. (+5,000 to private stocks and government stockpile)	1,500 s.t.	Japan	500 million tons of ilmenite = 5-year supply; 1.9 million tons of rutile = 40-year supply	Improved quality and uniformity of the metal; new applications; better fabricating techniques.
Uranium (U_3O_8)	7,500 s.t.	Security classified information		Canada Union of South Africa Belgian Congo	60 million s.t.	Improved recovery methods; government health and safety regulation for uranium mines.
Vanadium (an alloy)	7,000 lb.	4,000 lb.	U.S. exports vanadium	··············	By-product of uranium ores	Discovery of physical properties of pure vanadium.
Zinc	550,000 s.t.	1 million s.t. (+250,000 s.t. to stocks of producers and consumers)	700,000 s.t.	Canada (40%) Mexico (30%) Peru (15%)	13 million s.t.	Declining industry? Faces increasing competition of aluminum and magnesium. Relatively high costs of production have not heretofore been reduced.

SOURCE: U.S. Department of Interior, Bureau of Mines, data submitted at the Hearing of the Senate Committee on Interior and Insular Affairs, 85th Congress, 1st Session; see: *Long-Range Minerals Program, June 4, 1957* (Washington, D.C.: Government Printing Office, 1957), Appendix 1, pp. 4a–153a.

Table 6-2. South American Minerals with Secure Access

Mineral	Annual Domestic Production	Annual Home Consumption	Annual Imports	Chief Sources of Imports	Domestic Reserves	Future Developments
Aluminum Ores (Dried-bauxite equivalent)	1.8 million l.t.	7.8 million l.t.	6 million l.t.	Jamaica (48%) Dutch Guiana (47%) British Guiana (5%)	70 million l.t.	Treatment of low-grade ores, increasing reliance on imports.
Copper	1 million s.t.	1.5 million s.t.	500,000 s.t.	Chile (40%) Mexico, Peru (15%) Canada (20%)	25 million s.t.	Treatment of low-grade and complex ores.
Iron ore	95 million l.t.	125 million l.t.	30 million l.t.	Canada (45%) Venezuela (30%)	2.5 billion l.t.	Blast furnace operation techniques to justify use of low-grade domestic iron ores.
Platinum metals	25,000 oz. t.	725,000 oz. t.	700,000 oz. t.	Canada (35%) Union of South Africa (35%)	....	....
Rare earth metals	Security classified information			Belgian Congo	U.S. has ample supplies and can be self-sustaining	New large-scale uses and cheaper production methods.

SOURCE: U.S. Department of Interior, Bureau of Mines, data submitted at the Hearing of the Senate Committee on Interior and Insular Affairs, 85th Congress, 1st Session; see: *Long-Range Minerals Program, June 4, 1957* (Washington, D.C.: Government Printing Office, 1957), Appendix 1, pp. 4a–153a.

which are readily accessible because the transport routes are militarily secure. Table 6–2 lists the principal minerals in this category.

Another category of supply includes minerals whose commercial production in the Western Hemisphere does not suffice to meet the domestic demands of the United States and the other countries in our economic orbit. Table 6–3 lists the most important minerals whose supply is supplemented by importation from overseas.

Table 6–3. Minerals Imported from Overseas, Late 1950's

Mineral	Percentage of Total Supply Imported	Chief Overseas Sources, with Percentages of Total U.S. Supply
Antimony	80	Union of South Africa and China (50)
Cobalt	85	India and Africa (60)
Chromium	93	Philippines (32) Africa (40) Turkey (21)
Columbium-tantalum (used as high-temperature alloy)	99	Africa (75) Other (24)
Graphite (for military use)	100	Madagascar (45) Ceylon (30) Other (25)
Industrial diamonds	100	Africa
Jewel bearings	100	Switzerland
Manganese	70	Africa (33) India (25) Other (11)
Mercury	50–75	Italy and Spain
Mica (for military use)	98	India (80) Other (18)
Tin (primary)	75	Malaya (55) Indonesia (10) Other (10)
Tungsten	35	Korea and China (30) Portugal (5)

SOURCE: U.S. Department of Interior, Bureau of Mines, data submitted at the Hearing of the Senate Committee on Interior and Insular Affairs, 85th Congress, 1st Session; see: *Long-Range Minerals Program, June 4, 1957* (Washington, D.C.: Government Printing Office, 1957), Appendix 1, pp. 4a–153a.

The Potential Minerals Position

Now let us suppose that technological and economic changes of a basic nature permit us to use known submarginal resources such as the so-called "low-grade" (taconite) iron formations or shale oil. In these *potential* terms our minerals position would change considerably.

Taking into consideration what may reasonably be expected to be available for our consumption from Canadian and Mexican sources, the minerals shown in Table 6–4 would be added to the list of ample resources that are already easily at hand (as shown in Table 6–1).

Table 6–4. North and Central American Mineral Supplies
Expansible by Subsidized High-Cost Production

Aluminum ore	Fluorspar
Bismuth	Graphite
Antimony	Iodine
Copper	Jewel bearings
Iron ore	Quartz crystal (radio grade)
Manganese	Rare earth metals*
Mercury	

SOURCE: U.S. Department of Interior, Bureau of Mines, data submitted at the Hearing of the Senate Committee on Interior and Insular Affairs, 85th Congress, 1st Session; see: *Long-Range Minerals Program, June 4, 1957* (Washington, D.C.: Government Printing Office, 1957), Appendix 1, pp. 4a–153a.

*The specific nature of these metals is classified information, but some rare earth metals are presently used for high-luminosity carbon electrodes, principally in the motion picture industry as a light source in film projectors and in the glass industry as glass decolorizers (glass additive to cut out ultraviolet light) and as a glass polisher. They are also used in the production of various chemical and medical supplies and in the electric industry in the manufacture of lamp filaments and vacuum tubes for special purposes.

To supplement our resources we would continue to import from overseas chromite, cobalt, platinum metals, tungsten, asbestos, and high-grade mica. Our complete supply of tin and industrial diamonds would still have to be imported. With technological developments to permit the use of known submarginal resources in South America, however, we would be completely dependent on overseas imports only for industrial diamonds. Chromite, cobalt, tin, tungsten, and asbestos would move into the category of resources for which only *additional* quantities are brought in from overseas if the Western Hemisphere supply were to take care of part of the need.

It must be emphasized, however, that the potentiality of using known submarginal resources easily leads one into the temptation of spelling out a possible self-sufficiency for the Americas, regardless of what it might cost. To the economist that would mean staging *Hamlet* without the Danish prince. In other words, that would be forgetting about *real* costs, the expenditure of extra manpower and capital equipment needed to be "self-sufficient."

REAL COSTS TO THE ECONOMY

Any expansion of output entails an additional, *incremental cost* of obtaining the extra units of a product. There are two main versions of this incremental cost. One is the *real cost* version. The other is *money cost*. The chairman of ex-President Truman's Materials Policy Commission illustrates the difference in these words:

> The individual businessman or consumer thinks of costs in terms of the dollars he must pay, under existing levels of prices and wages, to secure a given amount of labor, materials, energy, and so on. In inflation, such costs rise; in depression, they fall. These costs are vital economic factors, but they differ sharply from what we term real costs. Real costs are measured in the amount of labor, the amount of capital investment it takes to produce a pound of material or a unit of energy. For instance, if the quality of ore declines, it will take more man-hours of work, or more capital investment in machinery or new processes or both, to produce a pound of finished metal.[2]

Tangible real cost. Extra real cost is the added cost of extra output viewed in terms of the additional quantities of land, labor, and capital required to achieve enlarged output. This version of cost is *real* because it narrates the physical circumstances of expanded production—how many extra man-hours of labor were employed, what quantities of materials were consumed, the types and amounts of additional equipment needed, and so forth.

In the case of minerals extraction a true report of real cost must also include any amount of the mineral resource itself which was sacrificed in the effort to get some amount of the resource out of the ground. An illustration of this is the waste of natural gas in early days of oil-well drilling, when the gas was allowed to blow off, with the result that large portions of underground pools of oil could not be recovered for lack of pressure. This was a costly way of extracting crude oil, skimming the top of the underground deposits only. The natural gas which merely escaped and the residual oil which can never be recovered must be considered as having been consumed in producing the oil which was actually extracted.

A quantitative definition of real cost. From the viewpoint of immediate problems of resources utilization, *real cost* is defined as *the physical quantitative measurement of amounts of certain resources used in the production of units of another resource or of goods for final*

[2] Testimony of William S. Paley before the Senate Subcommittee on Minerals, Materials, and Fuels Economics, 83d Congress, 2d Session, April 9, 1954, in *Stockpile and Accessibility of Strategic and Critical Materials to the United States in Time of War*, Part 8 (Washington, D.C.: Government Printing Office, 1954), section on "Real Cost Principle," pp. 31–33.

consumption. This measurement must include units of the resource to be produced which are used as intermediate products not available for final consumption. Such use of a resource for the further production of units of its type may be necessary, as when steel is consumed in constructing furnaces used for further steel production. By contrast, units of a resource may be wastefully consumed in production, as when good pine timber is destroyed by lumbermen in a haste to get at stands of harder woods.

When quantitatively defined, real cost is readily measured by comparing the increase in money costs of minerals with the rise of money costs of all the commodities produced in the American economy. Then we find that whereas wholesale prices of commodities in general advanced an average of 105 per cent from 1940 to 1950, in that same decade:

> Zinc rose 119 per cent.
> Petroleum rose 149 per cent.
> Lead rose 157 per cent.
> Lumber rose 218 per cent.

Other materials, such as aluminum, iron ore, nickel, sulfur, and even copper, moved up less than the general wholesale price level, indicating that real costs *were* being lowered by technological advance. This should be the prescription for *all* our minerals (and other commodities): Overcome rising real costs, do not burden the consumers with them. It might be necessary to produce at excessively high real costs in time of war when we are cut off from access, but even then it is a good idea to count costs just to know what we are up against. This is even more urgently required in regard to peacetime defense production. The proper economic attitude is that of the Secretary of Interior in 1957, when he said:

For ... beryl, columbium-tantalum, and chromite, domestic production is now almost entirely related to defense programs. It is believed, however, that competitive domestic industries may eventually be developed in these commodities. Known reserves of these minerals are substantial, but the grade of ore is so low that production at this time is not profitable at world prices.[3]

Mindful of the high real costs of producing under the current conditions, the Secretary of Interior proposed "that a continuing program be established to pay bonuses for a limited production of these commodities *as research continues to seek ways of making these industries competitive* [italics supplied].

[3] *Long-Range Minerals Program,* June 4, 1957, p. 8.

Other aspects of real cost. When the mineral resources situation is being appraised, the statistics of physical inputs of land, labor, and capital to achieve output furnish important criteria for judging the situation. However, we must also inquire along other lines to obtain a rounded view of the situation. It is important to know about the men who manage the mines and the operatives and laborers who work in them. Are their rewards adequate? What are their working conditions? Also, we must take note of the impact of the process of mineral extraction on the life of the community. For example, early British coal mining combined bad features in all these respects. Narrow shafts and narrow and crooked tunnels were constructed to follow only the very richest seams, perfectly good seams being ignored or cut through in order to get at the richest seams. Workers eked out a miserable existence crawling through these honeycombs of carelessly constructed tunnels, sifting coal by hand, plagued by dripping water and endangered by explosions. British coal towns are to this day notorious for their uniformly uninspiring appearance.

It appears, then, that real cost actually has at least four aspects, two of them quantitative, the other two qualitative. The first and most generally understood aspect is the quantitative dimension of real cost: How much of a resource is being used? The other quantitative dimension is that of reward: Are wages sufficient for the wage-earner's needs of maintaining a standard of living? The first qualitative aspect of real cost involves the question of the working conditions under which resources are used: Are these conditions conducive to the maintenance and/or improvement of the resource? The second qualitative aspect of real cost is that of social welfare: How is the community affected by the characteristic use of natural and human resources? The last-named aspect of real cost is frequently referred to as the "social cost consideration."

MONEY COSTS

Another view of cost is to consider how much money must be paid in order to secure the services of the owners of productive resources which are to be used in production. Here the emphasis lies on wage rates, rates of rents and royalties, and interest rates. The real quantities of needed productive services are ascertained or estimated and multiplied by the remuneration which must be paid to the owners of the productive services. This gives us the money value of the real quantitative costs of production, as defined. Incremental money cost is the extra money outlay required to expand production.

Money cost differs from real cost in that money cost reflects contracts which are made between people to pay specified amounts of money for the use of resources, or amounts of money which they charge when personally using their own resources. Money cost does not directly or necessarily express the physical or human facts of production as real cost does. As a consequence the state of a nation's resources may not be accurately reflected in terms of money costs. Thus in the case of early British coal mining, money costs were inaccurately low, since the use of good coal as an intermediate product (for example, as a pillar support instead of timber) simply was not accounted for. Money costs of coal to its consumers were also out of line with real costs to the extent that miners were badly underpaid and mining towns were ill-designed to contribute toward the growth of a healthy and educated population.

Money cost is defined as *a pecuniary measurement of amounts of money paid, or contracted to be paid, by users of productive services to the owners of these services.*

A detailed explanation of the behavior of real and money costs of production is reserved for Part IV, where the influence of costs in the determination of prices is analyzed. For the moment the purpose of drawing the distinction between real and money costs is to aid in the description of the state of our national resources.

COST IMPACTS OF EXPANDED MINERAL PRODUCTION

The concept of real cost is implicit in the foregoing discussion of land resources, where the question was raised as to the extent to which new land should be brought into cultivation, by clearing, irrigation, or new drainage when existing land is being impaired by lack of conservation practices. To the extent that production on newly opened land merely offsets preventable soil deterioration, the amounts of land, labor, and capital involved are diverted from better uses.

This aspect of the resources situation confronts us even more strikingly in the case of mineral resources. Mineral deposits are unlike acres of soil. Soil exhaustion is an abnormal phenomenon which can be prevented by conservation practices. By contrast, the depletion of mineral deposits (that is, their utilization to the point of exhaustion) is the normal order of affairs in mining. Wasteful farming practices result in depletion, but wasteful mining practices consist mainly in unnecessarily accelerating depletion. Once the damage is done, there is no remedy other than to move on to the exploitation of new deposits.

The question is: How long can this continue? The answer is: So long as real costs are not counted. There is no real check on wasteful exploitation of mineral resources when prices received cover money costs of production which are abnormally low because real costs of wasted resources are ignored. Then it remains for future generations to discover the real costs at which their ancestors supported the living standards of their time—a sad heritage.

Another form of waste which complicates a nation's mineral resources position is expanding minerals extraction when this is not really commercially feasible. This is apt to happen when domestic producers are pressed by the demands of an increasing population—demands fortified by the voracious appetites of American consumers for the products of mineral resources. The question now arises of how to supplement the flow of the supply of minerals. Where shall new deposits be opened, and what kinds of deposits?

The customary solution has been to import supplementary supplies of minerals from foreign countries where rich deposits can be tapped. However, this arouses political opposition. Usually, there are domestic producers whose financial resources will not permit them to participate in resources development abroad—development which they may consider as threatening, if not to their continued existence, at least to their chances for expanding their domestic production. Major producers are usually liberal in their attitude toward foreign resources development; they participate in it and see in importation a means of conserving some of their productive underground resources for future use. Other producers, generally those who feel they must turn every resource to immediate account, argue in a different vein. Since they are neither in the circumstances to participate in foreign trade and investment nor in the habit of doing so, they contend that expanded production to accommodate increasing domestic demand should be undertaken at home even though this incurs high incremental money costs.

The argument converges on real cost considerations in several of its aspects. In terms of the quantitative definition of real cost as given on page 133, the expansion of domestic minerals output at high incremental money cost appears wasteful. This view is aptly expressed in these words:

I said some time ago that we probably could produce almost every material that we need in this country at a cost. But that cost could easily be prohibitive. ... If we can get material abroad at a lower cost than we produce it here this would allow our industrial machinery to produce finished goods at lower cost and increase our consumption of those goods. We should have a stronger economy than if we use our own labor to produce those same materials at a higher cost and, in so doing, take that labor and capital away from other material or other products that could be produced with higher product value.... If we insist on being self-sufficient instead of importing when it is more economical to do so, it will cost us heavily in man-hours of work, or in investment or both. ... If we do this on a very extensive scale, we will weaken our economy, and reduce our potential for war or peace.[4]

4 William S. Paley, *op. cit.*

The particular Senator who conducted the hearing during which this statement was made objected to this point of view. He maintained that money costs of foreign sellers of minerals are abnormally low because wages in countries from which we import mineral resources are too meager to permit foreign workers to enjoy anything approaching an American standard of living. This too is a real-cost consideration. Are different aspects of real costs irreconcilable? Actually this is not the case.

In the given instance the fact is that the highest-grade American copper mines put out an ore that is about 1 per cent copper, whereas 5 per cent copper is being mined in Africa today. Hence labor alone or the difference in living standards is not enough to make up for the differences in the money costs of production in America as compared with Africa. And, therefore, it would be wasteful to expand American production to the extent that imports would not be required.

Another example was furnished when, in a study of the General Services Administration, it was found that even if the current price of antimony were doubled (presumably by steeply raising the tariff on imports), the domestic producers would receive little benefit and the national economy would soon suffer. With an American price double the world market price, the production of primary requirements supplied from domestic mines was estimated to rise from 5 per cent to 25 or 30 per cent. At the increased rate of production it was believed that our known resource base in antimony would probably be exhausted in a few years.[5]

What Can Be Concluded
About the American Minerals Situation?

The American economy has developed historically in the context of a startling abundance of virgin mineral deposits. For a long time abundance minimized our dependence upon international trade and investment to supplement economically exploitable domestic sources of supply. It also permitted wasteful practices, the effects of which are beginning to be felt. This complicates a minerals situation already affected by the impact in the past of a rapidly increasing population, which placed strong pressure on mineral resources even when they were efficiently developed, as the Secretary of the Interior pointed out in 1957:

The greatest problems faced by the domestic mining industry today are the depletion of its easily accessible high-grade reserves, the substantially increased costs that go with the mining of low-grade ores, and the difficulties encountered

[5] *Long-Range Minerals Program,* June 4, 1957, p. 9.

in the search for and mining of more deeply buried ore deposits. It is generally conceded that the obvious large and easily worked mineral deposits in the United States have been found.[6]

Material Energy Resources

In *The Education of Henry Adams* (written in 1906), the auto-biographer writes:

At the rate of progress since 1800, every American who lived into the year 2000 would know how to control unlimited power. He would think in complexities unimaginable to an earlier mind. He would deal with problems altogether beyond the range of an earlier society.... The historian could see the new American—the child of incalculable coal-power, chemical power, electric power, and radiating energy, as well as of new forces yet undetermined.... The new forces would educate ... and the style of education promised to be violently coercive ... it would require a new social mind. Thus far, since five or ten thousand years, the mind had successfully reacted, and nothing yet proved that it would fail to react—but it would need to jump.

Since Henry Adams wrote these words, the population has doubled; nevertheless there is two and a half times as much power, from all sources, for every American man, woman, and child.

Sources and Uses of Power

We remain closely bound to the hard crust of the earth for most of our sources of energy, as we do for food, fiber, and metallic ores. Crude petroleum, exploited from concentrated subsoil land and offshore deposits, accounts for 40 per cent of the total energy; natural gas, found in close conjunction with petroleum, accounts for another 25 per cent. Coal, the foundation on which earlier industrial empires were built, still furnishes 30 per cent of total energy annually supplied in the United States. The rest (5 per cent) is water power, used to generate electricity.

This is the total overview of American material energy. It includes power used to operate factories and their machines, and power to transport goods to market—about ten times as much power as is required to produce the goods. Expressed in terms of the horsepower equivalent of our total energy, it is found that industry and agriculture together use better than 1.5 billion horsepower annually. And the households of the nation use three times that much, more than 4.5 billion horsepower, which includes all domestic uses of power, from the car to the electric shaver.

[6] *Ibid.*, p. 7.

The internal combustion engine which propels trucks, tractors, and planes, as well as many stationary devices, accounts for much of the command which the average American has over physical power. Still, electricity is the true symbol of the age of potential plenty. It not only constitutes brute force but can be used to produce incredible high-voltage-induced manifestations whose implications are only beginning to be apprehended, much less comprehended. At the same time, electrical energy can be used at very low levels to refine our communications systems and our complicated control instrumentations—that is, automation. And of all forms of energy, electricity generates most prolifically from relatively modest inputs of raw materials, thus providing the most genuine phenomenon of abundance economics which mankind has so far discovered. It is through the medium of electricity that nuclear fission will most comprehensively serve a peaceful world for many years to come—to power ships and planes without the need for refueling, to bring prime energy to remote locations uneconomically distant from coal, oil, or natural gas fields and feasible means of transportation. For this reason, the following discussion of power centers on electricity, with special reference to the development of nuclear fission in its principal role of electricity generation.

THE ADVENT OF ELECTRICAL ENERGY

Since the time of Henry Adams, the production of electricity, measured in billions of kilowatt-hours, has progressed as follows:

Year	Kwh (billions)
1900	6
1925	85
1945	270
1955	625
1956	685

This includes, in addition to electricity produced by utility concerns for public use, a much smaller amount produced by some industrial plants for their own use. The Federal Power Commission has estimated future requirements, up to 1980, and the probable production of electric energy to be supplied by utilities for public use only.[7] To make these estimates commensurable with the data already given requires an assessment of future amounts of electricity to be produced by industrial plants and railways having their own generating facilities. When this is done, and based on past trends in the relationship of

[7] U.S. Federal Power Commission, *Statistical Abstract, 1958* (Washington, D.C.: Government Printing Office). Estimates are based on Table 670, p. 528, therein.

electricity produced for sale and for direct use, these future supply situations can be reasonably anticipated:

Year	Kwh (billions)
1960	880
1965	1,100
1970	1,400
1975	1,700
1980	2,000

Prosperous, peacetime conditions are assumed throughout.

By contrast with the consumption of power in all forms, most of which takes place in American households, the bulk of electricity consumption occurs in industry. Thus, in 1956 approximately 450 billion kilowatt-hours were used for industrial purposes, as against 165 billion kilowatt-hours for residential, domestic, farm, and other household purposes. (Additional electrical energy is used by the utilities.) There has been a striking rise of household consumption, although this appears modest when compared with the industrial use of electricity. In 1925 only 6 billion kilowatt-hours were sold to residential consumers. Nearly six times that much was sold in 1945, namely, 34 billion kilowatt-hours. Then, after World War II and through 1956 another fourfold increase took place; in 1956 residential consumers bought 133 billion kilowatt-hours of electrical energy.

Farm electrification is another example of the modern "electricity breakthrough." Only yesterday, in 1940, a mere one-third of the farms in the United States were served with electricity. At present, practically every American farm is electrically equipped. One third of the farms are served by private profit enterprises, another third by public authorities, and the final third by rural electrification cooperative associations. In 1955 the federal government owned and operated 15 per cent of the nation's total installed generating capacity; this included well-known federal projects such as the Bonneville Power Administration in the Pacific Northwest, the Hoover Dam project, the Tennessee Valley Authority, and others.

PROSPECTIVE NEEDS FOR ELECTRICITY

The need for electricity in 1980 is estimated as three times the amount produced in 1956. One of the chief reasons for this is the advent of the age of light metals. Aluminum is already copiously used, magnesium is coming into use, and an increasing consumption will be found for titanium, to say nothing of the other light metals yet to be developed.

Production of these so-called "light" metals (they are actually strong structural materials) involves heavy consumption of electricity. When metals must be assembled from low concentrations (for example, as with magnesium which is obtained from sea water), a low cost of energy used in processing must "compensate" for the disadvantage of using ores found in low natural concentration. Titanium, for example, is a voracious consumer of electricity: 40,000 kilowatt-hours are required per ton of titanium product, as compared with less than one-tenth of this (that is, 3,400 kilowatt-hours) per ton of electrolytically produced zinc. In the 1950's titanium, a low-density, high-strength silver-white metal noted for resistance to corrosion, was used mainly for military purposes. But it can well be used for peacetime production in the manufacture of machine tools, textile machinery, food handling and processing equipment, and even sports equipment.

The available quantities of titaniferous ore are remarkably large as compared to ore supplies of older metals—copper, lead, zinc, and even the more abundant iron ore. Vast bauxite deposits, the raw material of aluminum, exist in the neighboring territories of Cuba, Jamaica, and Haiti; and aluminum ore is abundantly found in the United States and Canada. It, too, requires much electricity. The great need for electricity in the future to process the new light metals poses no special or critical problem. For the fact is that the real costs of producing electric power generation have consistently declined in the past. There is no reason why this trend should be reversed.

THE EXCEPTIONAL ECONOMICS OF ELECTRICITY

Considered as a natural resource, electricity is unique. In a sense it is not a natural resource, but rather one which we have created from natural phenomena—from lightning, for example, which our ancestors experienced in terror. Electricity is a natural resource only in the sense that, starting as a man-made resource, it is so integral a factor in our daily lives and is so abundantly supplied that it falls into the category of something "natural." For all this we have many people to thank, not the least being Benjamin Franklin with his kite and his colossal luck in not getting killed while experimenting with it.

The economics of electricity is singular in that it is a problem not of preventing real costs from rising, but of keeping them going down. Other products at some late stage of mature development not only pose the usual problems of efficient production but present the producer with a serious predicament of steeply rising real costs. The rule has been to extricate oneself from the maturity predicament of a product by developing new products for which labor and capital can be more efficiently combined with natural resources.

Electricity has never created a real cost predicament. The broader its use, the less are the proportional amounts of land, labor, and capital which are required on the average to produce a kilowatt-hour of electrical energy. This is proved by the data shown in Table 6–5; though they are money-price data, they clearly reflect a unique real cost situation.

Table 6–5. An Index of the Electricity Bill for a Residential User of 250 Kilowatt-Hours a Month, Compared with an Index of General Consumer Retail Prices, 1935-57
(1935 = 100 per cent)

Year	Consumers' Price Index	Electricity Index
1935	100	100.0
1945	131	77.4
1955	195	79.0
19ʾ7	ʹ0ʷ	79.9

SOURCE: U.S. Department of Commerce, Bureau of the Census, *Statistical Abstract of the United States, 1957* (Washington, D.C.: Government Printing Office, 1958), Table 429, p. 339.

Perhaps this singular performance is due to the fact that electricity may not be a product at all, but rather something bigger, a natural force or a physical law. This suggests an examination of the primary sources of electricity to determine whether the real costs of producing electricity are likely to continue to decline, and if so, for what reasons. At this point, the new process of nuclear fission enters the discussion.

Table 6–6 presents a record of the relative importance of the main sources of electrical energy in the recent past and for the calculable future.

FUELS FOR ELECTRICAL ENERGY

The costs of generating electricity are, of course, as vitally influenced by the technology of handling the basic fuels as by the costs of the fuels themselves. Assuming for a moment that these processing costs, as well as labor costs, are given, the crucial factor in the movement of real and money costs of power generation will be the future prices and real expense of the raw materials. Here is how the cost outlook for the fuels shapes up.

Coal. Commercially feasible, known reserves of coal are good for 2,000 years in terms of the present rates either of consumption or of production. There are tremendous possibilities for improving tech-

Table 6–6. Primary Energy Sources Used for Electricity Production
in the American Economy, 1925, 1950, and 1975

Energy Source	1925 (a)	1950 (b)	1975 (projected with nuclear fission)* (c)	1975 (without nuclear fission) (d)
	(Billions of kwh Produced)			
Coal	52	191	800	800
Hydroelectric (waterpower)	26	101	250	300
Oil and gas	7	97	195	300
Nuclear fission	......	......	155	......
Total	85	389	1,400	1,400

SOURCE: "The Outlook for Energy Sources," *Resources for Freedom, Report of the President's Materials Commission, June, 1952.* Vol. II (Washington, D.C.: Government Printing Office).

*Figures in column (c) are based on an estimate of B. R. Prentice of the General Electric Company when seen in the light of the Paley Committee's estimate of electrical energy production, independent of nuclear fission in 1975; this latter estimate is shown in column (d). Prentice estimated that 11 per cent of total installed electricity-generating capacity would be in the form of atomic reactors privately owned and operated. Atomic reactor plants would be most appropriate in serving where the cost of transporting or otherwise dispatching fuel to generating plants is relatively high, so far as we can now see. Therefore it would appear (again so far as we can now see) that this source of fuel for electricity would crowd oil, gas, and hydroelectric power more than it would coal, in the case of which the "cost of distance factor" is not so controlling. Consequently, the encroachment of nuclear fission on oil and gas, and hydroelectric power, is rated by the present writer higher than it would be on coal. The 1975 total projected power requirement of 1,400 billion kwh is not, of course, affected by these considerations, since it is a demand projection, not a supply projection. The Prentice estimate was made in a report entitled "A Forecast of the Growth of Nuclear Fueled Electric Generating Capacity," submitted to the Panel on the Impact of the Peaceful Uses of Atomic Energy, an advisory body to the Congressional Joint Committee on Atomic Energy; 84th Congress, 2d Session; the Panel's report was printed as a government document, January, 1956. The Prentice estimate, unlike that made in this table, does not include electricity generated for private use rather than sale.

niques of coal production, preparation, transportation, and utilization. For instance, new industries using electroprocess materials which require many kilowatt-hours per pound or ton might locate generating equipment near mineheads and transmit the power instead of shipping the coal. Significantly, productivity (that is, output per man-hour) in the predominating bituminous (soft) coal mining doubled between the end of World War I and the beginning of World War II, then doubled again in the ten-year post-World War II period. Notice that the earlier doubling of output per man-hour required twenty years, whereas the most recent doubling occurred in ten years.

Other sources of raw materials for power generation do not appear to have the same high expansion potential as coal. The most economical sites for generating hydroelectric power have already been developed. Natural gas and oil are frequently cheaper than coal in the vicinity of oil fields and refineries, but coal quickly regains the price advantage when distance is involved. There are more coal sites than oil and refinery sites. These are some of the reasons why coal is expected to keep carrying the heaviest part of the burden of generating energy.

Oil. Unlike coal, oil fuels are quite vulnerable to real cost increases for special reasons. In addition, these fuels are prone to increases in money cost so far as their specific use for electrical generation is concerned.

In the case of oil, the tendency of real costs to rise is revealed by the fact that the number of years of "working inventories" we carry in the form of proved reserves has been declining. This can reasonably be argued to reflect rising costs of discovery. In the decade 1900–1910 the working inventory of proved reserves was twenty-seven times the volume of annual production; in 1957 it was a twelve-year equivalent. This does not mean that the American economy will be out of oil in twelve years. Proved reserves are like reservoirs; there is not only outflow but also inflow. The inflow is *discovery*. What a twelve-year reserve means is that it is not economically or commercially warranted to push discovery further than is required to assure a twelve-year supply. In other words, that much lies ahead, year after year.

But what the decline in the oil reserve ratio to annual production may very well imply is an increasing cost of discovery which operates to limit the number of years of proved reserves considered to be worth establishing. There are other indications that discovery costs and also development costs are rising. Together the two account for 80 per cent of the total cost of crude oil. The other 20 per cent is the cost of lifting the oil; this has been steadily declining because of improved recovery methods, even though it has been necessary to drill deeper. This factor may retard the rise of the total real cost of obtaining crude oil but is unlikely to prevent a rise altogether.

Experts consulted by the federal government have agreed that the real costs of recovering oil can be expected to rise in the future, but there was considerable difference of opinion as to the probable magnitude of the cost increase. Importation may ease the rising real cost burden directly, as when we obtain oil from Venezuela (where most of our imported oil comes from). Or it may happen indirectly when some of our companies having overseas properties supply Europe with relatively inexpensive oil from rich Middle Eastern fields, thereby relieving the United States from having to export oil to Europe. Direct *net* imports of oil into the United States constituted one-eighth of the volume of domestic production in 1956. (We export oil but import more than is exported.)

Any pressure of rising real costs in the oil industry as a whole will be felt with multiplied force by the electricity-generation industry. Only 3 per cent of total oil consumption is for generating electricity, whereas no less than 48 per cent is consumed in transportation uses. Liquid fuel is a basic necessity for transportation, so that any burden of increasing real cost would readily be assumed there. That is not the case with electricity generation, where switching to solid fuels is technologically feasible for many installations. This will happen if and when the transport industries start "raiding" oil supplies by stiff price-bidding.

Natural gas. The competitively cost-raising factor of alternative use bears with special force on the price of natural gas when it is used as a fuel for generating electricity. Actually, this is considered an inferior use for natural gas, as compared to its use for heating homes, for cooking, and other general utility purposes.

The reason gas has been used as a fuel to generate electricity is that electrical generating plants have been able to buy gas at bargain rates during off-peak nonheating seasons. Some gas producers in the West have been willing to make "dump sales" to large nearby industrial consumers during summertime. When pipelines were still being rapidly expanded and markets for high-grade uses of gas were just being promoted, it paid gas producers to attract the trade of local low-grade users to aid in carrying development costs. These opportunities for low-grade users to obtain gas more cheaply than other technically competitive fuels are bound to be curtailed. Underground storage facilities for gas are rapidly being expanded in the East; pipeline and market development costs are not so high as they were, since markets for high-grade uses such as house-heating have now been firmly established; and the demand of general utility users of gas (as compared to industrial users) is increasing substantially. In many cases of household and commercial use, or in industries in which natural gas has a pronounced advantage (for instance, where delicate automatic temperature control is of the essence), consumers were apt to choose gas over technically competitive fuels, even when the price of gas was comparatively higher. (For example, heating the home with gas made "life with father" easier than even the best automatic coal stoker.)

The production of natural gas is naturally joined with oil production, so that the same uncertainties that cloud the long-run prospects of future real cost in the case of domestically produced supplies of oil also affect the developing gas prices. It has been estimated that by 1975 natural gas may be in short supply *relative to the increased demand*—note well the italics. That is to say, no *absolute* shortage of natural gas is in the offing, any more than in the case of oil. But here we are interested in the question of real costs to the economy as a whole and money costs to the electricity industry in particular. The market forces of our demand and supply price system seem destined to guide natural gas into high-grade uses to an increasing extent. Hence it would appear that natural gas could not be relied on to help keep real and especially money costs of electricity production declining, any more so than oil.

Hydroelectricity. Technically speaking, falling water as a source of energy is an inexhaustible resource, because it is constantly replenished by the flow of water in rivers and streams. Spectacular advances had been made in developing hydroelectricity by mid-twentieth century, so that all the great river drainage basins had been equipped with facilities to generate electricity or were in the process of being harnessed. Thus, in 1956 the St. Lawrence Seaway and Power project was undertaken.

This is not to say that huge *potential* amounts of electricity could not be generated, after 1956, at sites already established or in the process of being established. But to the economist the problem is that of getting *low-cost* hydroelectricity, not just getting it. In that respect the important fact is that a definite limit exists to the number of sites at which low-cost hydroelectricity can be developed. Most of the best sites have already been developed. Though these sites could, and most certainly would, in the future be *more fully* utilized, it would appear that the American economy has already seen the rock-bottom in real costs of hydroelectricity production. We ought not to count on hydroelectricity for further aid in keeping real costs of electricity declining.

Nuclear Fission as a Source of Electricity

In the 1950's the use of the atom as an ally in the struggle to keep electricity costs declining was as yet a topic for discussion, not an immediate problem, let alone a scarcity predicament. As the figures given in Table 6–6 on energy sources show, the American economy can serve its estimated 1975 electricity needs without the use of any nuclear fission whatsoever.

What is the economic feasibility of using atomic energy as a source of electricity generation? An informed judgment was expressed by the McKinney Panel, a body of experts which until 1955 assisted the Joint Atomic Energy Commission of Congress in an appraisal of the peacetime uses of nuclear fission. Commenting on an Atomic Energy Act which was passed in 1954 to implement President Eisenhower's "Atoms for Peace Program," the Panel said:

Drafted under pressure so as to open rapidly the peaceful uses of atomic energy to private enterprise, the language of the 1954 act sometimes seems to confuse hope for eventual development of a flourishing private industry with the misconception that such an industry is already in being.[8]

The Panel's judgment was confirmed by an action of the United States Department of Justice in 1956. Late in that year the Anti-Trust Division exempted private firms which cooperate for the purpose of developing nuclear fission for peacetime uses from any liability under the antimonopoly laws of the nation. This gave certain testimony, if implicitly, to a belief that it will be a long time before nuclear fission processes can be sufficiently competitive with the conventional fuels to permit the developers of atomic energy to interfere with competition!

SOME PROBLEMS

There is no need for haste in developing nuclear fission as a means of generating energy for peacetime uses. The American economy faces no predicament of power scarcity, and even if it did, caution must be the order of the day. For a long time to come there will be many serious public health problems pertaining to the use of radioactive materials and processes. Among these the major ones are the following:

1. The disposal of radioactive wastes.

2. The reprocessing of partially spent fuels. This is a highly specialized process in which it is necessary to guard against a spread of radiation. Not every industrial plant using nuclear fuels can afford to or will know how to reprocess properly its partially spent fuels.

3. Atomic accidents in nuclear energy industrial installations. Although the risk is remote, a serious calamity in one community might conceivably destroy lives and property beyond the community. This raises a monetary insurance problem, besides the problem of real social cost. Claims arising out of a catastrophe could easily exceed the

---

[8] Robert McKinney, *et al., Report of the Panel on the Peaceful Uses of Atomic Energy* (Washington, D.C.: Government Printing Office, 1956), p. 102.

resources of any private insurance underwriter, or even a group of underwriters.

4. Training problems. These are being met in large atomic installations but can easily be neglected in small plants because of the personnel management costs involved. This would especially be true when the use of radioactive materials and processes was peripheral and not at the core of the industrial operation. The dangers already experienced with the incidental use of X-ray machines (for example, for metal inspection) emphasize the need not only for safety inspection of plants and equipment in the future but above all for education to prevent leukemia and other diseases from affecting workers. This is not merely a matter of pointing out dangers; the human instinct for self-preservation unfortunately does not extend far enough to prevent workers from "taking short-cuts" when unobserved—removing protective eyeglasses, for example.

5. Problems of transporting radioactive materials.

6. Problems of plant location. Considerable agitation has been created when nuclear installations of an industrial nature were located in close proximity to densely settled urban centers. Yet, if atomic energy plants are to be serviceable in generating electrical energy, they must be located in reasonable proximity to their energy outlets.

THE ORGANIZATION OF AN ATOMIC ENERGY GENERATING INDUSTRY

Nuclear materials are owned by the federal government, whether they exist in a natural state or are processed. Indeed atomic resources are a part of the public domain and are so described even in the Atomic Energy Act of 1954, which favored private enterprise development of atomic energy. Because of this, it would not be unconstitutional for the government to own and operate atomic energy plants for peacetime as well as for military purposes. The constitutionality of the government's developing, transporting, and marketing resources of the public domain was established by the Supreme Court in the *Ashwander* case in 1936.[9]

A publicly owned and operated atomic energy industry such as that of England is not the most likely prospect for the United States. However, the generation of electricity by the use of atomic fuel must necessarily fall into the category of "public utility"; that is to say, it will be considered public business even though conducted by private corporations. For it is a long-established principle in American law that in the fields of transportation, communication, light, heat, power,

[9] 297 *U.S.* 288.

or water, a private company "is the substitute for the state in performance of a public service, thus becoming a public servant."[10] A peace-time public utility industry furnishing atomic energy therefore takes its place with all other public businesses in the normal course of events.

The health and safety problems unique to nuclear energy installations lend special emphasis to the need for close government regulation. Thus, in the matter of insurance one industrialist expresses the belief that the risk is so large that no agency except the government is capable of assuming it. That is to say, the people of the United States as a whole must do so in the case of every installation. If this is the case, it is to be expected that the government will exercise close control in order to minimize the risk the people must carry.

In the same vein, the reprocessing of partially spent fuels is most economically and safely performed at large-capacity reprocessing plants conveniently located to handle the fuels from several power plants. This requires huge capital investment to build centrally located reprocessing plants; the minimum outlay for a reprocessing plant is high and does not vary appreciably with the site of the plant that is actually built. It is doubtful whether particular private enterprises generating electricity by the use of atomic energy could afford to build reprocessing plants except on a cooperative basis. More likely, such plants will be publicly owned and operated, as is now the rule in supplying cities with water, bridges, harbors, and similar central public services. This leaves the industrial users free to avail themselves of the central services for their own purposes as they see fit, but under uniform conditions prescribed by law. In the case of atomic energy the control would be somewhat more intimate; for example, regulations for transporting partially spent radioactive fuels to reprocessing plants can influence the design of privately owned and operated nuclear reactors in a more direct manner than is the case when ships must be designed to conform to certain clearance and loading specifications or vehicles to conform with given conditions imposed on users of public highways.

ATOMIC ENERGY AS ECONOMIC RESOURCE

The great economic advantage conferred by atomic energy is power made accessible to the most remote regions, in mobile form, and for limited durations. Atomic energy is capable of decentralization to an extent unparalleled by energy generated from other and more conventional sources. An early example is the Army's "package power reactor." This hot package has an extraordinarily long fuel-life charge; it is designed to be transported; and it can be operated by General Issue

[10] *Southwestern Bell Telephone* case (262 *U.S.* 276, 291); also *Olcott v. Supervisors* (16 *Wall.* 695).

mortals, not necessarily experienced power plant operators (though safety training is of the essence). The readily conceivable peacetime uses of the "package" include its functioning as a pinch-hit power supplier in local emergencies or in connection with temporary development projects, especially in remote regions. It is this type of invention and innovation which gives the modern conception of power a new dimension of free mobility.

Atomic energy is fast becoming a resource, soon to be joined by solar radiation as a source of energy. At this stage, when we are exploring the new dimensions of power with mature caution, the best which this author can state is what the economics historian Werner Sombart said with reference to electricity in 1905 when the industrial implications of that force were just being glimpsed:

I do not wish to attempt to anticipate my successor, the man or woman who in the years to come will put together the most important events in his account of the evolution of the economy. My task is, rather, to facilitate his work, by handing him an end of thread, to which he can then attach the overview of the resources developments which have occurred by his time.[11]

The General Summary on Natural Resources

Resources are material objects and human skills we have learned to use in gaining a livelihood. They may be classified as: (1) natural resources, to include land in its broadest sense of earth surface, minerals, water, and power; (2) human resources; and (3) man-made resources, which are usually referred to as capital goods.

With regard to land, it is important to understand that it can be destroyed by improper utilization. Ruinous processes of man-induced erosion continue to present critical problems for human welfare. Thus, the resources base is as much a matter of social organization as of natural endowment. In the American economy, a publicly and privately organized conservation movement has made progress in the past fifty years. With 70 per cent of our privately owned farm land still needing conservation attention but not as yet getting it, much remains to be done.

In the matter of minerals, the American economy has developed historically in the context of startling abundance. For a long time this minimized our dependence upon international trade and investment to supplement economically exploitable domestic sources of supplies. At present consumption rates and in the present state of the industrial

[11] *Die Deutsche Volkswirtschaft im Neunzehnten Jahrhundert*, 6th ed. (Berlin: Georg Bondi, 1923), p. 167.

arts, two alternatives exist for meeting current and reasonably projected demands. One is to supplement the supplies of certain strategic raw materials with imports; the other is to exploit known submarginal reserves. Each of the alternatives poses the question of appropriate social organization and public policies to establish the conditions of the most efficient exploitation of mineral resources, both nationally and internationally.

Industrialization, commercial agriculture, urbanization, and rural electrification in the United States have placed water in the category of a costly economic good whose supply has to be managed. The problem is not one of an absolute shortage but one of management to prevent rising real costs due to such factors as local shortages, floods, seepage and silting, and pollution. Perhaps more than any other resource, water illustrates the need for a coordinated, multipurpose program of conservation.

Energy resources are not in a strict sense natural, but our whole scheme of want-satisfaction has become so crucially dependent upon vast energy supplies which derive from natural resources that we may treat energy as a natural resource itself. Electricity has come to be our major form of energy and presents the unique problem of maintaining constantly *declining* real costs. This is a far different problem compared with preventing *rising* real costs as in the case of minerals, or resource destruction as in the case of soil. Not only is our mode of power generation primarily electrical, but new materials of production are absorbing more and more electricity in their transformation; for instance, the strong, light-weight metals of the future: titanium, aluminum, and magnesium. The welcome addition of these and other products of exploration and research poses no problem, *provided only* that we can keep on getting electricity more cheaply.

Coal will doubtlessly continue to be the major source of raw materials for the production of electricity. Past technological and organizational improvements in coal mining, processing, and handling are expected to continue to help bring electricity costs down. Natural gas and fuel oil are likely to continue in heavy use for generating power, especially in the vicinity of fields and refineries; however, it is probable that they will furnish a somewhat decreasing proportion of all the fuel needed for electrical generation. The rapid depletion of domestic pools at current and prospective rates of consumption, having made our economy a net importer of oil even now, raises again the question of rising real costs. Great potential shale oil reserves brighten the prospects for the future, but they are still only technologically possible, not economically feasible. Now that the best sites for hydroelectric power generation have been developed, this resource, like gas and oil, will probably furnish a somewhat smaller proportion of our expanding requirements for the raw materials of generating electricity.

Nuclear fission as a source of electrical energy is at present in a very early pioneer stage. According to the Paley Committee, it will not make a substantial contribution to electrical generation in the immediate future. Although there may be bright prospects for the long pull, the safest statement to make is that the atomic program, whether for peace or war, will for a long time continue to consume more electrical energy than it will generate.

For Discussion

1. How many of the minerals listed in Table 6–1 (p. 127) do you recognize? How well? Check *Webster's New International Dictionary* and/or any standard encyclopedia.

2. In real costs we are talking about and measuring the production potential of the country. Explain.

3. Let us assume that an expansion of crude petroleum and natural gas extraction involves hiring 5,000 workers in addition to 100,000 already employed. The average straight-time hourly wage rate in the industry is $2.50. We shall assume that no overtime will be worked; also we take it for simplicity's sake that no incremental cost is involved other than that of hiring the extra workers. What is the incremental real cost per 8-hour day? What is the incremental money cost? Suppose that because so many new workers have to be attracted to the industry, the wage rate is raised to $2.60 an hour. What is now the incremental real cost? Is it different from before? What is now the incremental money cost? It is different from before, but by how much?

4. Jones is a tungsten mine operator who is experiencing difficulty in making a profit selling tungsten at the price established in the world market, plus the existing American import tariff. ($40.00 per short ton unit plus 36 per cent *ad valorem* [i.e., by value] import duty = $54.40.) He argues that either the government should buy tungsten from domestic miners at a higher price or the import duty should be increased. The higher home price as compared to the world market price should be set so as to make up the difference between the cost of mining tungsten at home and the presumably lower costs in competing foreign nations. He says that it will cost the nation very little because only a small amount of tungsten is used per ton of steel which is improved by the use of tungsten as an alloy. "In other words, it is like the soda and the biscuit. Whether you pay 10 cents a package or 50 cents a package, it does not make much difference. There is only a pinch of it in there anyway." Jones claims that there is more tungsten in the United States than could be used in a hundred years and that it could be produced if only it were profitable to do so.

The estimate of reserves is true only if we assume that annual consumption will never exceed the rates of the late 1950's. Let us accept it for the sake of argument. What can be said in refutation of Jones' line of reasoning, if anything?

5. Suppose that Congress were to pass a bill authorizing the Department of the Interior to construct and operate demonstration plants to determine how eco-

nomically, how competitively, liquid fuel could be made from coal and oil shale. Do you believe that such a step would be desirable? Necessary? Constitutional? Argue *pro* and *con,* having in mind the actual resource situation and how it came about and is being handled. Keep your notes and reserve final judgment until you have finished your course of study.

6. Why need we feel concerned about the fact that the richest and most easily worked ore deposits have been found when electricity generation is progressing at a rate to sustain almost any conceivable production of the new metals such as magnesium?

7. Resources do not just exist; they *become* resources. Is solar radiation an energy resource?

8. In December, 1957, there were 70 nuclear reactors in the United States, as compared with 20 in December, 1952. Of the nuclear reactors in 1957, 53 were federally owned and 17 were privately owned, whereas in 1952 all reactors were federally owned. The first peacetime atomic energy plant for the generation by private industry of electricity for peacetime uses was placed in operation in 1957; it was one of 17 privately owned reactors. Half of the government reactors and 16 of the privately owned reactors were research reactors. Was the nation at the beginning of 1958 behind in its atomic energy development?

9. List some of the unique problems of atomic energy development and add considerations not mentioned in this chapter. In doing so, apply the concept of real cost in all of its dimensions.

7 Human Resources

Economic Value and Human Effort

It is only by virtue of human activities as directed by human wants and aspirations that the bulk of our natural resources acquire *value*. The things of nature have no intrinsic worth unless they are shaped, or at least gathered, by the hand of man. Of course, this refers only to economic value, not aesthetic or religious value.

Let us illustrate the character of economic value. In Los Angeles there is a park featuring a natural exhibit known as the LaBrea Pits. These are asphalt pits which contain fossil remains of many extinct animals. Many primitive men must have passed these pits by, for to them asphalt was worthless. They did not know what to do with it. Today the fast-moving Wilshire Boulevard traffic which speeds past the Pits is powered by a petroleum technology. Had primitive man possessed this technology, he would have known that native asphalt is evaporated petroleum residue, the presence of which indicates oil deposits exist somewhere nearby. The point is not that there would have been an early oil boom, but that most natural resources might as well not exist, so far as mankind is concerned, if there is no known use for them.

At present there are some effects caused by ultra-high velocities and solar radiation phenomena inside and outside the earth's atmosphere which we are only beginning to understand. They will be of *value* to future generations. Why? Because future men will know how to apply human effort to the development of what we now only glimpse.

In this light we can understand what the pre-eminent modern economist, the late John Maynard Keynes, meant when he said: "It is
preferable to regard labour, including, of course, the personal services
of the entrepreneur and his assistants, as the sole factor of production,
operating in a given environment of technique, natural resources,
capital equipment and effective demand." In this chapter we place the
primary economic emphasis where it belongs—on persons, their numbers, and the quality of their productive efforts.

Population as a Resource

Actually, the founder of modern economics put "the car of economics" on the right track two hundred years ago. The very title of
his book, *Inquiry into the Nature and CAUSES of the Wealth of Nations* (emphasis supplied), reveals an intention to discuss the essence
rather than the symbols of wealth. Consequently, we find him arguing
that the wealth of a nation is its labor force, the value of educated,
healthy, human efforts, and not its hoard of precious metals, nor the
extent of its arable land.

Adam Smith's broad conception of the basic value of human effort
brought to the fore the first statement in modern history of a higher-
wage doctrine. That is to say, speaking in the historical context of his
time, Adam Smith advocated a policy of increasing the production
of the articles of staple consumption, specifically foodstuffs, which
were then the principal items in the budgets of workers. In the terms
of his times, this corresponded with the modern abundance theory of
mass consumption and mass production. We call it "consumers'
capitalism" because into the category of "articles of staple consumption" now fall such durable equipment items as cars, refrigerators,
radios, and other products of the manufacturing technology. Adam
Smith talked in terms of "the wages-fund" which, when increasing
from progressively ample bases, would have the following desirable
consequences:

A plentiful subsistence increases the bodily strength of the labourer, and the
comfortable hope of bettering his condition ... it animates him to exert that
strength to the utmost. Where wages are high, accordingly, we shall find the
workmen more active, diligent, and expeditious than where they are low—in
England, for example, than in Scotland; in the neighbourhood of great towns
rather than in remote places. ... The same cause which raises the wages of
labour, the increase of stock, tends to increase its productive power, and
though, in consequence of the flourishing circumstances of the society, the real
price of labour should rise very considerably, the great diminution of the quan-

tity of labour needed to produce [a given amount of output], will generally much more than compensate the greatest rise which can happen in the price of labour.[1]

Seen in the Smithian view of labor as the ultimate source of human welfare, Table 7–1 gives the official estimates of the wealth of the United States in March, 1958:

Table 7–1. The Total United States Labor Force of Gainfully Occupied and Experienced Persons of 14 Years of Age and Over, March, 1958

Classification by Occupation	Number (millions)	Percentage of Total
Farm	5.0	7.0
Nonfarm	57.2	82.0
Armed Forces	2.6	3.5
Unemployed	5.2	7.5
Total	70.0	100.0

Classification by Sex	Number (millions)	Percentage of Total
Male	48	68.5
Female	22	31.5
Total	70	100.0

SOURCE: *Statistical Abstract of the United States, 1958,* Table 254, p. 203.

The government apparently appreciates Adam Smith's profound insight: labor force data are the *only* census data kept strictly up to date on a monthly reporting basis. In addition, the size of the labor force at various future dates is officially estimated to be, at the minimum:

Expected Total Labor Force

Year	Millions of Persons (male and female)
1960	73
1965	78
1970	84
1975	91

This forecast is based on a total population increase up to a minimum of 207 million souls by 1975 and on an assumption that Amer-

[1] In *The Wealth of Nations* (New York: Modern Library, Inc., 1937), pp. 81, 86, 243.

icans will continue to be as actively interested in working as they were from 1920 to 1958.

A HISTORICAL SIDELIGHT

Two characteristics of the American labor force stand out: (1) the fact of "womanpower"—one out of every three workers is a woman; and (2) the relatively small number of persons working in agriculture.

The present extent of women in industry may be fully appreciated by consulting official historical data. They show that in 1920 only one out of *five* workers was female; in 1890, only one out of every *six*. The forecasts in this report are that the present ratio of men to women in industry is expected to prevail in the future.

As for the relatively small number of persons gainfully occupied in agriculture, this represents liberation from mankind's early bondage to the soil and the whims of weather.

More people are free to contribute to the production of industrial goods by being released from the struggle for their daily bread. It might be added that the farmer himself is no longer a bondsman to harsh nature, but often an agricultural technologist operating with a sizable investment in productive equipment. As for yesteryear's hordes of permanent farmhands and casual farm laborers, their modern equivalent is working to produce tractors and combines in the factories of Detroit, Racine, Moline, and other centers manufacturing agricultural implements. Even in gathering field crops, "stoop labor" is being replaced by mechanical devices—for example, in harvesting the sugar beet.

Column (e) of Table 7–2 traces the progressive liberation of men and women from hard labor on the land and from backbreaking home production of clothes, bedding, candles, and the like.

Here are a few special characteristics of the gainfully employed labor force of experienced persons—meaning managers, farmers, professionals, as well as laborers in the narrow sense of the word. In 1957, only 40 per cent of persons 14 to 20 years of age were working. Standing in marked contrast to earlier years of American history, this relatively low percentage of adolescent labor means that the nation is making a real effort to educate its people highly before they enter the labor force.

As to the other end of the age scale, it may be noted that a full *third* of *all* gainfully occupied persons are forty-five years of age or over. In earlier years, with their sixty-hour weeks instead of the current forty-hour week, most workers were old by the time they reached the age of forty-five—if indeed they reached it. In 1880 the average life expectancy at the age of five was only 41.3 years. In 1920 life ex-

Table 7–2. Civilian Labor Force: Total of Gainfully Employed or Experienced Workers and Number and Percentage in Farm Occupations, 1820–1957

Year (a)	Population (b)	Total (c)	Farm Occupations Number (d)	Farm Occupations Percentage (e)
		Persons 10 Years Old and Over		
1820	6,487,815	2,881,000	2,068,958	71.8
1830	8,639,412	3,931,537	2,772,453	70.5
1840	11,629,006	5,420,000	3,719,951	68.6
1850	16,452,835	7,697,196	4,901,882	63.7
1860	22,429,625	10,532,750	6,207,634	58.9
1870	29,123,683	12,924,951	6,849,772	53.0
1880	36,761,607	17,392,099	8,584,810	49.4
1890	47,413,559	23,318,183	9,938,373	42.6
1900	57,949,824	29,073,233	10,911,998	37.5
1910	71,580,270	37,370,794	11,591,767	31.0
1920	82,739,315	42,433,535	11,448,770	27.0
1930	98,723,047	48,829,920	10,471,998	21.4
		Persons 14 Years Old and Over		
1930	89,100,555	48,594,592	10,161,212	20.9
1940	101,102,924	51,742,023	8,833,324	17.1
1950	112,354,034	59,015,464	6,837,652	11.6
1957	120,445,000	65,011,000	6,222,000	9.6

The header row for the "Gainfully Employed or Experienced Civilian Workers" spans the Total, Number, and Percentage columns.

SOURCE: *Statistical Abstract of the United States, 1958*, Tables 252 and 254, pp. 202–203.

NOTE: Table 7–2 differs from Table 7–1 in two respects: (1) it is on an annual basis; (2) it excludes the unemployed and members of the Armed Forces.

pectancy at birth was 52 years for males and 55 years for females; in 1954 it was 67.5 years for males, 73.5 for women. The average life span of Americans was exceeded at mid-twentieth century only in Norway and Sweden, and there only for men—an oddity that warrants further investigation. In underdeveloped regions average life expectancy at birth stood at tragic lows of 36 years in Guatemala and 32 years in India. A most interesting aspect of the American labor force is that four out of every ten males at 65 years of age continue to work.

Lost Wealth: the Extent of Unemployment

If human effort is really a most basic aspect of the nation's wealth, then people who are willing and able to work should have the opportunity to find employment. What are the facts in this respect? First of all, it may be noted that since the end of World War II an appreciable number of persons have been involuntarily and totally unemployed during every year, for periods of from ten to fifty-two weeks in any one year. The mildest involuntary unemployment was reached in 1953, when 1.6 million were unemployed, most of them for less than ten weeks. The high year of post-World War II unemployment was 1949, closely rivaled by 1954, and exceeded after 1957. Postwar unemployment does not compare with the duress which many Americans experienced in the 1930's. However, unemployment is galling and personally impoverishing, and it signifies a loss of social wealth.

The total story of unemployment is not told by government estimates based on the number of people claiming unemployment compensation due them by law. As a matter of fact, only 55 out of every 100 persons in the labor force worked from fifty to fifty-two weeks at full-time jobs even during the prosperous year of 1956. Another 25 out of every 100 gainfully occupied persons worked at jobs for which they were hired on a full-time basis but in which they were active only from fourteen to forty-nine weeks because of slack periods.

The government manages to count with a fair degree of accuracy the persons who become totally unemployed against their will. But a difficulty arises in counting the time lost when people have to work part time when they are prepared to work full time. For example, there were 13.5 million part-time workers in 1956. Some of these persons chose to work part time only, others were forced to do so because they could not find a full-time job. If we assume that only 1 million out of the 13.5 million part-time workers were unable to find work for more than four hours per day during the entire year, this would be equivalent to 500,000 persons being totally unemployed for the year. This amount should be added to the official count of 2.5 million persons who were totally unemployed sometime during 1956. They were unemployed for eleven weeks on the average. With 2.5 million having been unemployed for eleven weeks on the average, and an equivalent of 500,000 persons for fifty-two weeks, the weighted average duration of unemployment for an equivalent of 3 million persons becomes eighteen weeks. (This may be verified by multiplying 2.5 million by eleven weeks, 500,000 by fifty-two, adding the results, and dividing this total by 3 million.)

Our widely publicized official data on unemployment unfortunately are not computed in this manner. This is a grave shortcoming in times of recession, when part-time work is imposed on many workers by cutting the work week back to thirty-two hours or less. The loss of wealth by reason of unemployment is usually understated.

Loss of Wealth: the Problem of Population

On July 1, 1947, the United States population numbered 145 million; only ten years later, July 1, 1957, it stood at 170 million persons. This 17 per cent population increase during a single decade would have been welcomed by Adam Smith. To him an increasing population portended an enlarged labor force, which, by producing more wealth, automatically laid the foundation of a further increase of the population, and so on, in ever widening circles of human prosperity.

By marked contrast, many students of society refuse to view the rise of population as an unmixed blessing. For example, in 1953 the eminent philosopher Bertrand Russell anxiously asked, "What is the inevitable result if the increase in population is not checked?"[2] "The Malthusian law will reign," said this philosopher.

A CLASSICAL PRINCIPLE OF POPULATION

The law to which Russell referred was projected in 1790 by the Reverend Thomas Robert Malthus, a fellow of Cambridge University's Jesus College. Malthus was struck by what, in his view, appeared to be a fallacy in Adam Smith's optimism on the subject of population. To Malthus it appeared that Smith had completely overlooked the possibility of a growing population outpacing the increase in a nation's food supply. What if there be, in the nature of things, a limiting factor which applies to the increase of food production and no corresponding limiting factor to operate on increases of population?

Malthus asserted this to be the case. He was, of course, aware of the fact that new croplands might be opened, but he referred pessimistically to "the barren quality of land as yet uncultivated," "our limited knowledge of the quality of land," and so forth, in his *Essay on Population,* first published anonymously in 1798.[3] By contrast, Malthus could see nothing to restrain parents from bringing children into the world without first having the means to support them; this behavior Malthus had observed as a parish parson in his work with the poor.

Reflecting on his experience and on the poverty problem of his time, Malthus emerged with this philosophical conviction: Such is the ease of multiplying the human species, in comparison with the difficulty of increasing output from cropland, that one might well speak of population increasing in a *geometric* ratio, while land (considered as food-producing capacity) can increase only in an *arithmetic* ratio.

[2] *Impact of Science on Society* (New York: Simon & Schuster, Inc., 1953).
[3] An excellent modern edition is in the Everyman's Library series, published by E. P. Dutton & Co., Inc., New York, 3rd ed., 1933.

At some time or other in the history of a nation, population would press against food supply. There would be overpopulation. No measure of social relief could alleviate that situation. Redistribution of wealth would only impoverish the well-to-do while bringing more paupers into existence. Sooner or later everybody would be living on the margin of starvation. Thereupon any fluctuation would cause starvation; vice would flourish, as would wars between have-nots and haves.

On the other hand, it might be possible rather accurately to plan one's family decisions, exercising prudential restraint as a preventive check on population to avoid the cruel checks of misery, vice, and war. To substantiate his point logically Malthus posited a model situation in which one starts, for purposes of argument, with a state of full employment and a condition of high wages. Then, under a system of free competition and in the absence of any social security law, a man could very closely estimate his future earning power, Malthus argued. The prospective parent would enjoy considerable, if not perfect, knowledge of the state of the labor market, for wages would be completely determined by the naked forces of demand and supply; there would be no transfer payments—that is, no unemployment compensation, no minimum wage legislation, no aid to dependent children, no old age pension system.

Because nothing of a humanitarian nature can be done about the demand for labor, Malthus' argument continues, it follows that the remedy for poverty must reside in changing the supply of labor. Here again, social action will not do. For example, combinations or unions of laborers who desire to raise their wages would only reduce the profits employers expected to make.

This would diminish the quantity of labor demanded. The sole remedy Malthus had in mind was for the workers to diminish the supply of labor, not by joint action but by reducing the sizes of their families. As Malthus saw it, a man could time the age of his marriage to correspond with the age at which he had established a solid basis for earning an adequate income for supporting a family. In general this would be the age of 26, Malthus thought. With smaller families to support, workers would not be hard pressed to accept work on any terms. Future workers would be in a better individual bargaining position because of the elimination of an oversupply of labor.

A CRITIQUE OF MALTHUSIAN REASONING

There was a large increase of population in Malthus' time. However, the reason for it was not an increased birth rate among poverty-stricken people. Parish statistics available even in Malthus' time prove that birth rates were actually lower in the most pauperized parishes than in rich ones. The reason for the increases was, first and foremost, a declining death rate. This came about because of such factors as improved public health practices, higher living standards, and cultural conditions.

Today it is a widely acknowledged fact that "the enemy of the poor is their poverty." That is, poverty creates a vicious circle of social circumstances which deprive the poor of opportunities and condemn their children to an unpromising start in life. Consequently, democratic governments strive to aid underprivileged citizens in overcoming the despotism of economic exploitation by guaranteeing workers the right of freely forming and joining unions of their own choosing, by enacting minimum wage legislation, and by putting an end to economically deleterious racial discrimination, which is bound to perpetuate poverty among minority groups. And free public education bears prime witness to the government's desire to combat ignorance so that children in low-income families might know their civil and political liberties and enjoy them not merely in the abstract but concretely.

NEO-MALTHUSIANISM

The idea that population may press against food supply and thereby diminish wealth has not been abandoned. However, modern expressions of this pessimism are distinctly subtle. They may take the form of studied estimates of what might be the optimum size of a given national population under existing trends of that nation's technology. In this instance it is not the food supply which is considered as a limiting factor but the entire standard of living, comprised of all the articles of "necessity and luxury" for which men strive. In another version of Neo-Malthusianism, in which the human propensity to multiply and to be fruitful is pessimistically viewed, the problem is not related to the number of people but to their cultural standards, which are said to be declining. Thus Henrik DeMan writes: "Our culture is like a healthy brute of a man, but there is a lack of individual differentiation, initiative, originality . . . modern mass-man has quantity without quality."[4]

Other versions of Neo-Malthusianism are confined to regional population problems; specific historical situations are examined rather than general propositions being projected. In this more limited type of inquiry, particular attention is called to the agricultural and industrial production problems of underdeveloped areas of the world. Rapid

[4] *Vermassung und Kulturverfall* (Berne, Switzerland: A. Francke A.-G. Ltd., Co., 1951), p. 46.

growth of population may complicate the problem of the economic and social development of underdeveloped areas in several ways:[5]

1. There is increasing pressure of population on land which is already densely settled. As farms and villages become overcrowded, agricultural productivity has been seen to decrease because of accelerated soil depletion, waste of labor, and inability to use farm machinery on small tracts.

2. Accelerating population growth aggravates the existing capital shortages which are typical in underdeveloped countries. If population grows rapidly in these areas, a greater share of the national income must be used for increasing productive equipment of the type already in use so that the enlarged labor force will have tools with which to work. This means that less national income is left for current consumption and that income which might be invested in improving farm and industrial equipment must be used for merely producing more rakes and hoes and shovels.

3. Disposable personal income diminishes per head of population when agricultural productivity decreases and when a smaller share of national income can be used for current consumption. This encourages family heads to put young children to work in order to increase the family's income; at the same time people continue to work beyond the age at which retirement is customary in highly developed countries. Thus in underdeveloped areas one out of every three male children ten to fourteen years old is working, as compared to only one out of every twenty-five in industrialized countries. Child labor lowers the national level of education and may stunt the physical growth of the young workers.

4. A rapidly growing population requires that employment opportunities must be continuously expanded in order to avoid mounting total unemployment or enforced part-time work. This calls for programing not only agricultural expansion but industrial expansion as well. Yet underdeveloped areas are frequently not at all well organized for initiating national development programs or to execute them. For example, population pressure on settled land frequently occurs in backward areas at the same time that potentially productive land lies idle. This is due to landholding systems which concentrate land ownership in a few hands while impoverished persons have not the means to buy land or would not be permitted to do so under native customs. Lack

[5] See *Report on the World Social Situation,* prepared by the Bureau of Social Affairs, United Nations Secretariat, in cooperation with the International Labour Office, the Food and Agriculture Organization, UNESCO, and the World Health Organization (New York), United Nations Publication, Sales No.: IV-3 (1957), pp. 21–27.

of equipment for opening and cultivating new rich land, or lack of knowledge, may also retard development.

5. Housing, medical and health facilities, and other social services and amenities must be provided at a quickened rate if crime and plagues and deterioration of morale are to be prevented in areas under population pressure.

6. Increasing population signifies an enlarged number of children to be schooled. This necessitates designating an enlarged share of national income to building schools, buying equipment, and training teachers.

The discerning reader will have noted that these problems, which are characteristically emphasized in a Neo-Malthusian view of population increase, do not only arise in underdeveloped countries. They are encountered in the United States as a consequence of the postwar population explosion. They appear in an accentuated form in certain depressed urbanized and rural areas—for instance, in the cut-over timberland area of northern Wisconsin and Michigan.

The lasting influence of Malthus. Neo-Malthusianism shades imperceptibly into general resources analysis when it finds expression in studies oriented toward understanding the total of human and natural resources in given areas and under specific institutionalized social practices. Such research has in the past yielded major contributions, exposing waste in using resources or in failing to develop them. When aimed at removing individually caused and institutionally wrought barriers to economic progress, Neo-Malthusianism does not invite the bitter criticism once voiced by a leading Indian economist who remonstrated that "the time spent in lamenting the inordinate increase in the population of the poor would be far better spent in arranging effective measures for the removal of their destitution."[6]

The lasting influence of Malthus is not his emphasis on regulating the size of a population. That recommendation was derived from a prior consideration of the social circumstances some 200 years ago— circumstances viewed by Malthus in terms of his particular social preferences. Those times have passed, as has Malthus. But are there not parts of the world which are now in a stage of development similar to that of Malthus' England? To assert this would be to fall into one of the gravest errors of historical interpretation—the pre-Darwinian fallacy that evolution proceeds by classifiable stages.

Malthus' scientific and, therefore, lasting insight is the idea of the man-resources ratio, which must be kept track of so as to prevent any

[6] Pramathanath Banerjea, *Study of Indian Economics,* 5th ed. (London: Macmillan & Co., Ltd., 1940), p. 112.

waste of resources which are needed to feed the population. That is to say, the emphasis in Malthus has at present been transferred from a concern with population to such proper matters for action as soil conservation, resources development, and fundamental research to aid in preserving and expanding America's natural wealth. Above all, it has been recognized that the only sensible way to worry about population is to think about it in *qualitative* terms. Are sufficient educational facilities available to help people improve their skills and knowledge? Only when so equipped can people participate creatively in improving technology—which remains as the only *immediately* manageable cause of economic growth. Then population will not threaten society with a loss of wealth.

Gain of Wealth: Productivity

There are two ways of thinking about population, one in terms of its numbers, the other in terms of a community's technology. A mere increase in the number of people may cause a gain of wealth, but it may also lead to a loss of wealth, as has been seen. Many people believe that the actual outcome is determined by things—by natural resources and capital goods, depending upon their availability. However, the decisive factor is a *process*, not a stock of things. It is technology. *Modern technology is the process of applying abstract scientific principles to the solutions of practical day-to-day problems of maintaining and improving the living standards of the people.*

Scientific thought is a product of creative human imagination. As such it has its origin in the remote past of mankind, though the strict objective discipline of observation, classification, generalization, and verification is of relatively recent inception. Technology, a way of turning general ideas to practical account, is also an ancient human attribute. It manifests itself in the use by primitive communities of artifacts in production, which, however simple, reflect insight into general principles such as thrust, friction, and leverage.

Technology is a cultural, cooperative phenomenon, not the product of individuals working in isolation. It begins in the schoolroom, where individuals pick up the strands of scientific thought which has come to us from the past; it flourishes by cross-fertilization of ideas; and it passes in an advanced form to future generations. The pattern of technological insight and efficiency current in any given culture is its chief economic asset and is held in common trust even though the community's economic capital, the store of productive goods, is privately owned and operated. Actually, productive goods, machinery, transportation and communication systems, and so forth, are the material results of applied human knowledge and skill, as is demonstrated by the fact that when better ideas of machine construction and other means of production are developed, the existing equipment becomes obsolescent.

Because technology is a social fact, an individual would be helpless without access to it. This was emphasized by the American economist Thorstein Veblen (1857–1929) when he wrote:

It is none too broad to say that [an individual] is a workman only because and so far as he effectually shares in this common stock of technological equipment. He may be gifted in a special degree with workmanlike aptitudes, may by nature be stout or dextrous or keen-sighted or quick-witted or sagacious or industrious beyond his fellows; but with all these gifts, so long as he has assimilated none of this common stock of workmanlike knowledge he remains simply an admirable parcel of human raw material; he is of no effect in industry.[7]

When people are freely trained to understand their community's technology and have the opportunity to use and to help improve it, the result is *productivity*. Productivity is an action word denoting mankind's increasing control of the forces of nature in making them serve industrial development. It follows that productivity can be measured by the physical returns to human efforts applied in production, and in terms of material objects used in production.

The term "productivity" is used in the language of economics, not in the sense of explaining technological progress but of measuring it. Accordingly, *productivity denotes the ratio of the output of physical goods to a corresponding amount of input of one or several factors of production*—land, labor, and capital, of different types and in certain combinations. For example, one may speak of wheat output per acre of wheat land placed into production, output per machine-hour (per hour of a machine's operation), thrust per unit of rocket fuel, and so forth.

Most commonly, however, the term "productivity" is used to designate measures of output per unit of labor input. Productivity records showing changes in output per employee or per man-hour are widely used in the discussion and study of various economic topics—for example, wage-cost-price relationships, the rise of living standards, technological progress, and the outlook for production and employment.

It is important to note that this technique of appraising productivity as measured in output per man-hour is not meant to convey the false impression that the particular employees at work at any given moment are causally responsible for the ratio which their inputs of labor bear

[7] *The Instinct of Workmanship* (New York: B. W. Huebsch, 1918), p. 138.

168THE STRUCTURE OF RESOURCES

to the output of the product. It is the *organization* of the employees in
their use of natural resources and man-made equipment and of their
personal efforts which causes the output. This can be illustrated by the
words of a record-breaking test pilot who, in a network TV interview,
kept using the pronoun "we" in reference to his accomplishment.
Asked why, he simply pointed to the designers, the technicians, and
his chase pilot, who were gathered around him.

CHANGES IN PRODUCTIVITY

In a dynamic economy of potential abundance the *growth* of productivity, rather than current productive efficiency, is the interesting
consideration. This results from several main causes. An obvious cause
is scientific *invention*. However, this is only a necessary cause of technological progress, not a sufficient cause. The necessary *and* sufficient
cause is *innovation*. This means that greater knowledge gained by
invention is brought to bear on production problems by the managers
of firms either on their own initiative or by adopting advanced practices as applied in other areas of the economy.

A second principal cause of productivity growth is the enlargement
of the share of the market which a producer can serve, and/or the
extension of the size of the market for all the producers in an industry
or in the nation as a whole. Larger-scale operations often permit
savings to be made in both the private and social sense. An individual
firm may be able to organize its work flow more effectively by specializing certain functions which formerly had to be done by one person
or department handling all of them. The larger firm may be able to
take advantage of certain freight services available to bulk shippers,
or it may be able to locate at a more convenient site. For the economy
as a whole, a scale increase of production may justify building improved highways, harbors, and other communication facilities that
would not be feasible under backward economic conditions.

For the individual firm, scale increase may have either an active
or a passive origin. Scale increase has an active origin when a firm
adopts improved production methods, lowers the price of its output,
and thus, by extending its share of the market, also expands the scale
of its operations. Scale increase has a passive origin as, for example,
when the firm simply benefits from the over-all growth of the economy,
manifested by increased aggregate effective demand which, among
other effects, also strengthens the demand for the product of the particular firm. Or the firm may benefit and expand its scale of operations
simply because better public transportation, light, power, and other
facilities such as harbor facilities have become available in its area.

Third, growth in productivity may be due to substituting one productive factor for another. Improved working combinations of human and natural resources are thereby achieved, with correspondingly increased yields of output throughout the nation.

MEASURING PRODUCTIVITY

For the individual firm. Numerous entrepreneurs compute index numbers which reveal the rate of productivity increase in their operations. This is usually done in terms of output per man-hour, or man-shift, for the plant as a whole. Since output per man-hour is a ratio, a production numerator and a labor denominator must be calculated. The production numerator is computed by taking a weighted average of the output of the different varieties of a basic product. For instance in the case of steel, different types are averaged—ordinary steel for use in construction, high-temperature alloy steel, steel for rails, and so forth. That is to say, each type of output is assigned the importance which it has in the firm's pattern of production. If, for instance, high-temperature alloy steel production is only a minor part of the firm's total output, it receives a low weight as compared with construction steel, should that be the firm's major type of output.

In constructing the labor denominator to be used in arriving at the productivity ratio (that is, in estimating the total input of labor hours), it is a typical procedure to take a simple average of all man-hours applied in production regardless of the difference in skill or reward of different kinds of employees. (Needless to say, this is not the most precise manner of treating labor inputs to production, but the benefits of following a more refined procedure are generally not considered sufficient to warrant its adoption.)

The production numerator and the labor denominator of the productivity ratio are, of course, computed for an identical period of time. A period of time which is reasonably close to the year of current production is chosen as the base period and designated as 100 per cent of productivity performance. (If a remote date were chosen, there would be too many changes in production methods and types of output to make year-to-year comparisons feasible.)

Given the base period, rated as 100 per cent, productivity measurements are made in succeeding years (or for shorter intervals) and compared with the productivity measure of the base period. Table 7–3 illustrates an index number series for an individual firm.

A table such as this yields valuable information in many respects. It permits the entrepreneur to distinguish at a glance between productivity changes caused by factors operating in the outside environment and changes due to factors under his direct or at least partial control.

Table 7–3. Productivity Index for a Steel Mill, 1951–58

(1951 = 100)

Year	Labor Productivity (accumulated tons per man-shift)
1951	100
1952	95
1953	105
1954	101
1955	109
1956	105
1957	105
1958	97

SOURCE: Based on actual company data.

Thus the setback to labor productivity in 1952 and 1956 was due to nationwide steel disputes eventuating in work stoppages during those two years. This factor of labor relations is under the partial control of any one entrepreneur in the steel industry. The lowered productivity rates for 1954 and 1958 were due to recession, a factor not under an individual entrepreneur's direct control. The consistent tendency toward an upsurge of productivity, which is evident in Table 7–3, reflects to a significant extent a successful manipulation of factors directly under the individual entrepreneur's control. To some extent, however, the tendential rise of productivity is also due to general developments which benefit the whole industry—for example, advances in steel technology, improved power facilities, or improvements in the mining and shipping of iron ore. Depending on how many of these productivity variables are actually under his control, the entrepreneur can seek ways and means of bettering his plant's situation.

Productivity indexes for an industry. The construction of productivity indexes for an entire industry involves the described basic procedure, but in a more complicated form. Although producing the same kind of product or products, different firms use different specifications of size or weight. This renders the construction of a homogeneous product numerator difficult; that is, products may have to be assigned to classifications which are too broad to take account of significant differences in the quality of the products of different firms. Again, different entrepreneurs combine land, labor, and capital in dissimilar proportions. And again, this makes it difficult to obtain an approximately accurate labor-input denominator for the industry's productivity ratio; it is like comparing the style of two baseball pitchers in terms of the length of their arms. However, these and similar difficulties can be and are overcome. The U.S. Bureau of Labor Statistics as well as private industry associations prepare productivity indexes; these are found particularly useful by entrepreneurs in an industry, allowing them to compare changes in their productivity with those typical of the entire industry. The indexes are also used by economists to make interindustry comparisons of productivity changes and for other purposes. Table 7–4 presents a typical productivity index for an industry.

Table 7–4. Indexes of Output per Man-Hour in a Single Industry, in All Nonagricultural Industries, and in Agriculture, 1948–57

(1947 = 100)

Year	Rayon and Other Synthetic Fibers Industry	All Nonagricultural Industries	Agriculture
1947	100.0	100.0	100.0
1948	112.1	101.7	123.7
1949	114.4	104.2	113.8
1950	151.6	111.5	131.4
1951	162.3	115.7	129.0
1952	166.6	119.2	138.0
1953	171.7	122.2	152.7
1954	185.9	125.1	166.3
1955	....	129.8	168.9
1956	....	130.6	175.0
1957	....	132.6	183.4

SOURCE: *Statistical Abstract of the United States, 1958,* Table 280, p. 226.

Productivity measurement for the national economy. What does productivity growth mean when seen from the vantage point of the American economy conceived as a totality of productive operations? In that perspective productivity growth signifies *real* savings made in the use of our abundant human and natural resources. The savings must be *net* savings. That is to say, nothing is accomplished from the viewpoint of economic welfare if the various kinds of natural and human factors of production are simply reshuffled.

To clarify, let us suppose that a producer, or group of producers, substitutes machinery for labor because a given output can be produced more cheaply in that manner. For the sake of argument, let us say that the released labor is hired elsewhere, but for less productive uses—waiting on tables rather than making tables, for example. In the meantime the firm, or group of firms, adopting machinery in the place of labor continues to produce a given output, sells it at the same prices, and nets a profit by being able to produce the given output less expensively.

This example shows why simply defining productivity as "output per man-hour" is an inferior measure of total national productivity. In the manufacturing firms involved, there will be a definite increase of output per man-hour, but this will be due to the measure used, and not to increased output from the social point of view. The released labor, now employed in secondary or tertiary uses, actually works with lower productivity. It is a well-known fact that productivity in the service trades is necessarily lower than productivity in the manufacturing trades. To be sure, when working as dishwashers, waiters, chauffeurs, etc., these people would not diminish the productivity in that sector of the economy; they would, however, add to the number of persons working under conditions of low productivity.

By contrast, let us suppose that the firm, or group of firms, enlarges its volume of business by lowering prices on the basis of the cost-reduction achieved by using the new machinery. Or let us suppose that entrepreneurs, aggressively using improved equipment, raise wages all over the nation, perhaps conjointly with reducing prices. In that case labor may not be released from manufacturing at all; it would be needed to help furnish the enlarged output made feasible by increased aggregate effective demand and broadened markets for specific goods. Perhaps a few concerns start this, and the rest follow their example.

A productivity index which relates the whole national output to the aggregate of production factors used (human and natural resources) would differentiate between the first and second cases here supposed. For in the first case, that of a transfer of labor out of manufacturing, no net savings would be made in the use of national resources. Hence nothing would be registered on an index which relates *all* output to *all* resources. (Such an index of productivity differs considerably from one based on observing output per man-hour ratios in particular firms and then adding the results.) But in the second hypothetical case there would actually be more national output from the aggregate of resources, and it would therefore be registered on what economists call a "total factor productivity index."

How can an over-all, national-scale productivity index be constructed? The general principle may be apprehended in this manner. Let us say that in a given year, say 1960, a certain amount of national output is produced. Now what if this output were produced with no more efficiency, on the national average, than it could have been produced in an earlier year, say 1955? Then the aggregate output in 1960 would, on the assumption of a dollar of stable value, cost the entrepreneurs no more than it would have cost had it been produced in the earlier year, 1955. For entrepreneurs pay for the services of resources needed to make goods, in accordance with what it is worth to the entrepreneurs to use resources to one extent or another. In the entrepreneurs' determinations of the worth of units of resources to them, productivity is the uppermost consideration; so, if productivity of resources does not change, on the national average, a given amount of national output would cost the entrepreneurs the same regardless of when that output is produced, earlier or later, give or take a little.

But what if productivity increased throughout the nation on the average—not in every shop, but by and large, between, say, 1955 and 1960? Resources would then be worth more to the entrepreneurs and so the national output, in the aggregate, would cost more than if it had been produced at 1955 rates of reward to the factors of production.

Of course when productivity increased, between 1955 and 1960, it became quite impossible to produce the 1960 national output at 1955 rates of rewards to owners of land and labor and capital resources, precisely because resources are rewarded in line with their productivity. The only point in mentioning 1955 rates of reward at all is to emphasize this very fact—from which we can then deduce the following. If in any given year a national output costs the entrepreneurs more than the same output would have cost in the past, then, on the assumption that the purchasing power of the dollar has not changed, productivity must have increased—not in every shop, but on the average throughout the nation. Bear in mind that we are dealing with money costs, not real costs, and with total money cost of the entire national output, not with the per unit cost of goods or services. Actually, when productivity increases, real costs decline as well as per unit money costs of products; that is why the entrepreneurs can afford to reward the owners of productive resources more liberally.

Evidently, then, to determine whether or not productivity has increased on a national scale, it is only necessary to determine whether or not, *in fact,* the national output in any given year costs more than if it had been produced at the rates of remuneration paid to the factors of production—land, labor, capital, and all varieties thereof—in some previous year. The steps which must be taken to make such a determination are fairly involved; because of this they are described in the *Appendix* to the present Chapter (pp. 174–77). For the generally well informed person it suffices to know that productivity *can be* measured, and compared year by year, not only for the individual firm or industry but for the entire nation.

Appendix

Construction of a Total Factor Productivity Index

This type of index[8] has been developed by the National Bureau of Economic Research, a privately endowed research organization. For this purpose the Bureau establishes two broad factor classes to include all materials and skills which enter into production. These are labor (including management and proprietors active in production) and capital (which, in the Bureau's approach, includes natural resources).

The Bureau's total factor productivity index is constructed by taking these steps:

1. For any given year ascertain the number of persons in each of the number of job classifications customarily designated in practice—toolmakers, assembly line workers, unskilled workers, white collar workers, and the many other classifications.

2. In each case multiply the number of persons in the job classification by the earnings paid for that type of work *in some chosen base period* other than the year for which the number of workers is ascertained.

3. Apply the procedure of steps (1) and (2) to proprietors according to leading types—farm proprietors, owners of businesses, independent professional persons. (This will include only proprietors actually engaged in production, not stockholders of corporations, or landlords, or lenders of capital.)

Multiplying the number of persons in each job and proprietorship category during a given year, say 1959, by their earnings in a chosen base period, say 1947, yields a *weighted* total amount of income. This is the aggregate amount which wage-earners and working proprietors would have earned in the chosen base period if production had been arranged in the same way during the base period, say 1947, as it actually was arranged in 1959.

---

[8] See John W. Kendrick, "Productivity Trends: Capital and Labor," *The Review of Economic Statistics* (August, 1956), pp. 248–57.

4. The next step is to ascertain what would have been the total money value *during the chosen base period* of all the real inputs of capital goods which were actually applied in production during a subsequent year. This is accomplished by first removing the influence of changes since the base period, in the prices of land, plant, equipment, and business inventories. To eliminate the factor of price changes in capital goods, their prices in the year to be compared with the base period are translated into the prices charged for these or similar goods during the base period. This is done by reducing (or increasing) the current prices of capital goods by the percentage of price change since the base period, using "implicit price deflators" available for the purpose. (See Chapter 2, pages 29–30, where the concept and use of implicit price deflators are explained.)

When the current prices of capital goods have been expressed in dollars of constant purchasing power, the *real* value of capital goods in any given year is observed. It is what it would have cost to produce the stock of capital goods actually used in, say, 1959 at prices in the chosen period, say 1947. Now we have a measure of the *weighted* total income which would have accrued to suppliers of capital goods if production had been arranged in the chosen base period as it actually was during the other years, say 1959, to be compared, productivity-wise, with the base period.

5. The aggregate income gained by persons furnishing labor and capital inputs to industry, respectively, has now been measured *at base period prices*. Adding these subtotals, what is the meaning of the grand total? The answer to this question is to be found by inquiring into what would happen if, for example, the productive efficiency of an economy were to decline between some chosen base period and the next year. Necessarily, less output would be produced during that next year by labor and capital used in the same amount and in identical proportions. By the same token, an increase of national productive efficiency would cause a larger output to be produced by an identical amount and composition of labor and capital inputs. (The identity has been construed in the preceding four steps of this explanation.)

6. It follows that to ascertain productivity growth we must express, in dollars of constant purchasing power, (a) the computed aggregate cost value (not sales value) of the output of an identical aggregate labor-capital input in a chosen base year and (b) the actual cost value of the realized output in another year; then compare these two figures. If the figure in the later year is larger than that of the base year, there will have been productivity growth. Alternatively, if there has been no productivity growth as between a base year and a subsequent year, the stable-dollar cost value of the outputs of an identical amount and

composition of labor and capital inputs will be in one-to-one correspondence. In that case the productivity index number will be 100
for both the base year and the year which is compared with it. Productivity growth will be indexed for years after the base year by
figures larger than 100.

FINDINGS ON NATIONAL PRODUCTIVITY

The analysis of productivity growth, using a total factor productivity index, yields significant insight into the nature and amount of
American productivity growth over long periods of years. The chief
finding is that the *net* productive efficiency of the American economy
increased at an annual rate of 1.75 per cent during the period from
1899 to 1953. Throughout that same period the gross national product
(GNP) increased at a rate of 3.3 per cent annually. Thus, net increases
in efficiency accounted for about one-half of the nation's growth in the
annual current output of goods and services. The rest of the increase
of GNP happened simply because the United States grew. As a matter
of fact, a part of the growth not accounted for by increasing efficiency
was undoubtedly bought at the cost of wasted resources.

The National Bureau's total factor productivity index is approximately 15 per cent more conservative than conventional estimates of
the output per man-hour ratio. Since the subject matter is one involving
billion dollar equivalents of waste or savings, this difference is truly
significant, especially in regard to the resources and know-how heritage we are likely to leave to future generations of Americans. The
population increased by 20 per cent from 1946 to 1957; it is expected
to increase by another 20 per cent by 1975; and after 1975 another
large spurt is expected to take place. By estimating the outputs of
goods and services which will be wanted, it is possible to project the
probable production factor inputs which will be needed in terms both
of the changes in advanced knowledge applied to production and of
progressive factor substitutions which increase output. The Bureau's
total factor productivity index, however, does not serve only to project
resources requirements on the basis of given estimates of future output.
It also improves the quality of the estimates of future output. Projections of output are necessarily based on historical trends. Now, changes
in total factor productivity have been observed to be less variable over
time than output per man-hour in individual plants or in whole industries. As a consequence, a projection of future output, when based on
the less fluctuating total factor productivity, is subject to smaller error
than the conventional projections based on man-hours.

What practical idea emerges from this discussion of productivity,
its growth, and its measurement? Simply this: As Americans who are

living in a consciousness not of scarcity but of abundance, we have become prone to exaggerate our productive achievements. Nothing is easier than to confuse increased production with productivity; nothing is more gratifying—and nothing is more dangerous to the future course of a civilization.

For Discussion

1. The labor force does not always increase in proportion to the number of young persons who have reached working age during any given year and are willing, able, and eligible to accept jobs. Was Adam Smith wrong in supposing that increased population signifies increased social wealth created by an increasing labor force?

2. In numerous states of the Union more persons are gainfully employed in agriculture than in manufacturing, or at least as many. Per capita personal incomes in most of these states (not all) are below those of the industrial states. Which of the following generalizations is the most nearly true, if at all warranted? (a) The agricultural states are backward areas. (b) The agricultural states are deprived of benefits of industrialization because these benefits are monopolized in the centers of industry. (c) Although the agricultural states cannot become centers of industry, they could be aided by forms of industrialization adapted to primarily agricultural situations.

3. What, presumably, would Malthus have had to say about automation?

4. Our high living standards and our preference for democracy with its emphasis on the dignity of the individual tend to blind us to the fact that death and misery are still powerful regulators of the population in most of the world. How does a Neo-Malthusian approach this problem?

5. When productivity increases in an individual firm, the management does not always take full credit but may acknowledge the contribution of the employees, and of the stockholders for allowing management to plow earnings back and for investing additional money in the firm. What other factors may be involved when the productivity of a firm increases?

6. The Warren Timber and Pulp and Paper Company, a Pacific Northwest corporation, finds that its productivity index stands higher than the average for its industry. Does this prove that the officers and the company's employees work more efficiently than people in that industry elsewhere in the nation?

7. When productivity increases in industry as a whole, or in agriculture, where shall the credit go? To the abundance of natural resources? To the improved technical education of the labor force? To the persons and groups who have saved and invested? Which is most nearly true?

8. Under which of these circumstances will an increase of productivity in industry as well as agriculture result in more leisure time for the population: (a) if the population declines; (b) if gross national product remains constant (being measured in dollars of constant purchasing power); (c) if total production increases throughout the nation with a constant amount of man-hours of labor input; (d) if total production increases with a constant amount of labor and capital input?

9. Suppose that instead of measuring *national* productivity growth by the total factor input method, we simply take a weighted average of the separate output per man-hour productivity indexes of our various industries. That is to

say, we would weight each separate productivity index by the contribution each separate industry makes to GNP, then combine the results and divide by the number of industries. What would be the difference in the ascertained national productivity rate, if any?

10. What is wrong with using output per man-hour as a measure of national productivity, inasmuch as human effort is the ultimate basis of value? Does a total factor productivity measure overlook this basic fact?

8

Man-Made

Resources

The American economy certainly appears as a busy one, with most people either working, getting ready to do so, or enjoying an Indian summer of life after having made a contribution to production. The United States therefore is a wealthy nation. But in the legal sense of the word "wealth," *things* rather than persons are considered national wealth, and only *tangible* things at that. The reason is that people's abilities, their health and intelligence, are properties so personal that they could not possibly be transferred by sale or purchase without the person's being transferred too. This would of course strike at the very heart of our traditional abhorrence and prohibition of involuntary servitude.

Alienations or acquisitions of title to things are confined to the transfer of goods. Titles, such as stocks, bonds, and mortgages, are *records* of wealth; they are not wealth in themselves. What is customarily considered national wealth is illustrated in Table 8–1.

The total of $1.3 trillion in Table 8–1 is the community's store of real assets, the legacy of past and present production. It is a rough measure of the economist's welfare definition of capital, as given in Chapter 3, page 61. The present chapter is written entirely in terms of capital considered as one of the bases of the community's productive power and independent of the financial ownership claims to that same store of assets which constitute capital in the private accounting sense. To avoid confusion in the matter of the growth of capital, reference

Table 8–1. Estimated National Wealth, by Type of Asset, 1955
(at 1947–49 prices)

Asset	Value ($ billions)
Class I: Reproducible Tangible Assets	
a. Structures:	
Nonfarm residences	321
Nonfarm nonresidential buildings	140
Underground mining	24
Farm structures	33
Institutions	20
Government structures (including nongovernment operated projects)	131
b. Equipment:	
Producers' durables (including government owned nonmilitary)	160
Consumers' durables:	
Automobiles and other (including TV, air-conditioning)	144
c. Inventories:	
Livestock	11
Crops	7
Nonfarm, private	87
Public (including government stockpile)	7
d. Monetary gold and silver	26
Class II: Nonreproducible Tangible Assets	
Farm land	69
Forests	10
Urban and mineral land	98
Public land (including land for defense purposes)	37
Class III: Net Tangible Assets Held in Foreign Countries	15
Grand Total	$1,340,000,000,000 (or approx. $1.3 trillion)

SOURCE: This table is based on official estimates of the component parts of 1955 United States wealth as given in: U.S. Department of Commerce, Bureau of the Census, *Statistical Abstract of the United States, 1958* (Washington, D.C.: Government Printing Office, 1958), Table 412. p. 323.

will be made here to "capital formation" rather than to "capital accumulation."

Wealth as Service Value

Wealth, viewed as a whole, is never consumed in the American economy. Quite to the contrary, it generally keeps growing. Naturally, particular items of wealth are consumed; yet the *whole* national wealth is not being consumed so long as our *total* equipment of man-made resources, or capital goods, is not diminishing. In our economy this is generally prevented by employing a sufficient amount of labor and materials in maintaining and expanding the nation's basic productive equipment. Thus, although particular items of wealth are always wearing out or becoming obsolete, the general wealth remains permanently established. Or we might better say that each article of wealth has its own specific life cycle, but the nation's aggregate wealth is as permanent, continuous, and growing as the American economy itself.

This is one of the least consciously known or understood facts of our economic life. Fortunately, though, we *act* as if we grasped it. That is to say, people in the aggregate do not at any moment contemplate using, for immediate consumption, all the income of money and services they might have. Thus, a home-owner could let his house run down and stand unprotected; instead he most generally invests some money in buying fire and theft insurance or in having repairs and improvements made or in making them himself. A factory manager does not draw as profits all that part of his sales revenues which he does not need for paying wages or for buying raw materials and current supplies. The factory's executive committee does not tell the production managers to keep producing to the same specifications but invests money in research and development. Even the majority of investors save not only to be able to *spend* more later but also to be able to *save* more later. Otherwise, instead of buying stocks and bonds, they would all buy annuities. That is to say, with a bond one ultimately is repaid the full value of one's original investment. This means that one has gone without spending the principal sum, which might have been spent during the period while the security was held. By comparison, with an annuity the periodic payments one receives are so arranged that one uses up the capital as one goes along, so that at the end of a stipulated number of years nothing at all is left. Although with an annuity one does not spend everything at once, one keeps on disinvesting. Even this, however, means that one is not using all one might spend at any moment.

THE REASON FOR SAVING

Why do not people consume all they might at any moment but, in the aggregate, set some funds aside, thus allowing our national wealth to be continuously and permanently maintained and expanded?

The most general answer is that people are as much interested in getting ahead as they are in having "all the fun in the world" at any given time. The home-owner wants to retain his status in the neighborhood and give objective evidence of making progress through improving his grounds. The factory works manager knows that he is going to be rated by the appearance of his shop and equipment—even by the men who work under him. And the executive committee seeks prestige as well as profit in "making better things for better living."

That is the general answer. The specific reason is something about the equipment itself. The fact is that productive equipment is nothing other than man's power extended far beyond his individual capacities. As a physical force man is certainly limited, but for brain power he will do. In fact, man is unexcelled as a dreamer and schemer of mechanical things. The things thus wrought are not objects in an ordinary sense. Man-made resources are products of the imagination—man's embodied labor, in the highest sense of the word.

Sometimes we become confused and act as if man-made resources somehow had their own, totally independent, existence. Perhaps it is because of the huge amount of wealth which comes to us from the past that we fall into the error of assuming that capital goods are things in themselves. Many items of capital equipment which we enjoy were virtually given to us by our forefathers, with nothing more required, for instance, than that we keep the Flatiron Building clean and in repair. By this token our successors will be using the facilities of Hoover Dam, say, having only to add their own efforts to keep it from silting. But even this minor effort will be a link in the chain of ideas which prompted our generation to devote a massive amount of manpower and materials to the construction of the project.

Thus wealth flows on perpetually, for it is nothing other than a product of man's continuous activity in thinking—looking ahead for himself and his children—while working with his fellows. This understood, we may proceed to examine what at mid-twentieth century the American economy holds in man-made resources, fully appreciating this inventory's deeper meaning.

Society's Capital Possession

A crude but effective way of showing how man has greatly increased his productive power is to ascertain the mechanical work-energy he employs in production. Table 8–2 presents a historical view of the matter.

Table 8–2 should be appreciated in the light of the tremendous increases in total power utilization between 1850 and 1950. In 1850 there were 10 billion horsepower-hours used; in 1900 the amount was 75 billion; in 1950, no less than 675 billion. Of course, the population also increased, from 23 million in 1850 to 63 million in 1900, up to 151 million by 1950. Hence the *per capita* increase of power use

Table 8–2. Man-Energy Compared with Equipment-Energy,
1850, 1900, and 1950

(as percentages of all power used in production)

Source of Energy	1950	1900	1850
Human	1.0	5.5	12.5
Hydroelectric	7.5	1.5	......
Coal	33.0	68.0	7.0
Petroleum	37.0	1.0	......
Natural gas	20.0	......	......
Other mechanical sources (direct-drive water wheels)	1.0	3.0	9.0
Animal and wind power	0.5	21.0	71.5

SOURCE: Computed from Table L, Appendix 25–3, in J. Frederic Dewhurst and Associates, *America's Needs and Resources* (New York: Twentieth Century Fund, 1955), p. 1116. (Totals are purposely omitted.)

was not so large as power totals as the respective dates might seem to indicate.

The telling figures, however, are those which show the small proportionate use which is being made of human energy at mid-twentieth century. Then, too, animal and wind power constitute an insignificant proportion of total use of power in 1950. Yet animal and wind power combined accounted for 71 per cent of all power in 1850, and 21 per cent as late as 1900.

Another frequently used measure of the amount of productive equipment used in industrial production is the dollar sum of investment which stands behind each person employed in an enterprise. Thus one large chemical corporation had in 1956 an average investment of $25,200 per employee; a large steelmaking concern had $15,000 invested per employee; and a leading automobile manufacturer had increased his investment from $3,700 per employee in 1940 to $13,200 in 1957.

Increasing investment per employee has been the rule of modern industry since Adam Smith's day. He was the first to articulate, in writing, the important discovery made about 300 years ago that the contents of jobs performed by craftsmen could be separated into component routines of a simple nature, the elementary subroutines then being repetitively performed by specialists needing no particular skill or training. When this insight was widely understood and applied, it was only a short step to the recognition that detailed specialized job operations were of so simple and repetitive a nature that they could be performed by a mechanical contrivance. Hence, directly after Adam

Smith, we entered the age of *machinofacturing*. Machine manufacturing, however, requires substantial investment. At the same time, many practical ways and means of utilizing physical forces and controlled chemical reactions are special to specific tasks of delivering work-energy in concentrated form and of tremendous magnitudes. For this reason, too, heavy investment in expensive plant and equipment is required.

Geometrical Increase of Man-Made Resources

Investments made in technological facilities during the past two centuries—always replaced when obsolescent—have brought us to a point where the supply of goods and services tends to increase in a geometric progression along with the population. Some people believe that technological progress is actually self-accelerating. However, this is an exaggeration. The most intricate apparatus wrought by modern automation is still in essence a result of human specialization. The human factor accounts for the design of the electronic computer, that extremist specialist which solves a thousand mathematical problems in millionths of a second. Yet the task performed is simple enough, one of saying yes or no in selecting from a high-speed flow of specialized information fed to the machine. If anything other than a simple task were to be performed, we would hardly entrust it to a mindless creation. The thrust which sends a rocket to outer space is also the ultimate effect of the work of the human hand at the drawing board and in the laboratory.

The evolution of modern machine and power specialization, dating back to the eighteenth century, must be understood in order to appreciate our current man-made resources situation, its promises, and the problems which it presents to us.

LABOR SPECIALIZATION BY TASK AND TOOL

The first major forward step in the modern division of labor is what may be called Adam Smith's manufacturing division of labor. With the thought in mind that "manufacture" literally means "doing by hand," what was found in the eighteenth century was an increasing tendency to shape tools to perform routine hand and arm motions. The great era of labor-saving devices was ushered in as the *economic* expression of the great eighteenth-century spirit of rationalism.

This new look in the division of labor was dramatically brought to public notice by Adam Smith, the father of modern economics, in his *Inquiry into the Nature and Causes of the Wealth of Nations,* first published in 1776. The following excerpt is from chapter I, Book I. The text may appear trivial to the younger reader who has been brought up in a space suit. But in 1776 this description was as exciting as the announcement of a new principle to control an earth satellite is now.

... The greatest improvement in the productive powers of labour, and the greater part of the skill, dexterity, and judgment, with which it is anywhere directed and applied, seem to have been the effects of the division of labour.

. . . .

To take an example, therefore, from a very trifling manufacture, but one in which the division of labour has been very often taken notice of, the trade of pin-maker, a workman not educated to this business, (which the division of labour has rendered a distinct trade), nor acquainted with the use of the machinery employed in it, (to the invention of which the same division of labour has probably given occasion), could scarce, perhaps, with his utmost industry, make one pin in a day, and certainly could not make twenty. But, in the way in which this business is now carried on, not only the whole work is a peculiar trade, but it is divided into a number of branches, of which the greater part are likewise peculiar trades. One man draws out the wire, another straights it, a third cuts it, a fourth points it, a fifth grinds it at the top for receiving the head: to make the head requires two or three distinct operations: to put it on is a peculiar business, to whiten the pins is another; it is even a trade by itself to put them into the paper; and the important business of making a pin is, in this manner, divided into about eighteen different operations, which, in some manufactories, are all performed by distinct hands, though in others the same man will sometimes perform two or three of them. I have seen a small manufactory of this kind where ten men only were employed, and where some of them, consequently, performed two or three distinct operations. But though they were very poor, and, therefore, but indifferently accommodated with the necessary machinery, they could, when they exerted themselves, make among them about twelve pounds of pins in a day. Each person, therefore, could be considered as making about 4,800 pins per day, as against perhaps only one, and certainly not 20, had he wrought separately and independently.

The three chief factors in Adam Smith's division of labor were, as he listed them: (1) the improvement of the dexterity of the workman as he reduces his business to a simple operation; (2) the saving of time commonly lost in passing from one sort of work to another; and (3) the stimulus given to inventing labor-saving machinery by observing routine human motions performed after a division of labor.

MASS PRODUCTION

Production by the use of standardized and interchangeable parts came into vogue in the 1840's, not long after the division of labor as publicized by Adam Smith had won widespread acceptance. Rifles and sewing machines inaugurated this new order of production. But it required the development of electricity, as a decentralized power source to permit plugging ordinary machinery on or off, to get modern mass production really under way. This development took place toward the end of the nineteenth century. Electricity also made it possible to achieve highly sensitized machine control on a precision-measurement basis not to be achieved by human operators. This was accomplished by low-energy conversions for the purpose of relaying control information *through* mechanical *control* apparatus *to* mechanical *operation* apparatus and to human operators.

The name of Henry Ford is associated with this new development of combining high-energy power with low-energy control to obtain suprahuman results. "In the Ford organization," a competent observer wrote, "human beings are expected to do the things that human beings normally do. For example, the function of checking thousandths of an inch in tolerance on large-scale production is not a normal thing for workmen to do. Consequently, machines are developed to check these tolerances automatically. By following this system, a minimum of effort is left to human abilities. Workmen start, stop, and check operations, but no workman performs an operation which can be better performed by a machine."[1]

Mass production is mechanized simplicity. It has three main aspects:

1. The planned, forward, process-to-process movement of the item being fabricated.
2. Mechanical delivery of his work to the human operator, who, therefore, does not have to look for it.
3. A never-ending analysis of work-flow into increasingly refined constituent elements that can be mechanically performed and then mechanically laced into a totally coordinated over-all work-flow.

The high degree of refinement in production, as compared even to Adam Smith's ingenious pin factory, may be appreciated by observing just one minor process contributing to a finished automobile as long ago as 1928. This is the story of a spring leaf.

1. Beginning as a strip of steel prepared by the steel mill, it is placed in a punch press until it hits a stop, then trips the press. The cut-off and pierced piece falls on a belt conveyor which runs along the loading end of a series of heat-treating ovens.
2. A second workman takes the pieces from the belt conveyor and places them on a conveyor which passes through the furnace (in which the temperature is automatically controlled); thence they are deposited at a certain temperature by this conveyor at the unloading end of the furnace.

[1] Hartley W. Barclay, *Ford Production Methods* (New York: Harper & Bros., 1936), p. 219.

3. The heated piece is lifted with tongs by a third operator and placed in a bending machine which gives the leaf its proper curve and plunges it in oil, the temperature of which is maintained at a definite degree by apparatus beyond the operator's control.
4. As the bending machine emerges from the oil bath, the same operator takes out the leaf and sets it aside to air-cool.
5. The leaf is then drawn by a fourth operator through molten nitrate kept at a regulated temperature.
6. A sixth workman removes the leaf from the conveyor which carries the molten nitrate and inserts a bolt through this and the other leaves required in the spring.
7. A seventh workman puts the nut on the bolt and tightens it.
8. An eighth workman puts on the right- and left-hand clips and grinds off the burrs.
9. A ninth workman inspects it.
10. He hangs the spring on a conveyor.
11. The spring passes the tenth workman, who sprays it with paint; the conveyor carries the spring above the ovens where it was originally heated, and the radiated heat "force dries" the paint. (Note the economy of heat involved.)
12. The conveyor continues to the loading dock, where the eleventh workman removes it.

Under older systems of production one workman would have attended the leaf through all these phases, or would even have made a complete spring. Naturally his production would have been severely limited.

Mass production is the clever organization of human efforts in effective relation to natural resources. But Henry Ford did not stop there. He was keenly aware that the human effort itself would have to be improved as a part of the over-all process of increasing wealth by these means. Indeed, he personally believed that mass production would not prove to be feasible unless it operated as an educational system to enable men to improve their insights into the industrial process, and in so doing, to get new ideas and win social approval as well as material reward. Machine operators, foremen, and supervisors were encouraged to study their work instead of just doing it, to report their findings, and to feel that their constructive ideas would be as readily received and rewarded as would the recommendations of trained mechanical experts. The latter were to be considered as advisors, not forbidding superiors. Henry Ford personally was distinguished by an amazing ability to walk through the works, and upon noticing an operator who had applied an idea, jot down his name in a notebook, never to forget the man thereafter. Ford measured efficiency in machine-hours—not in terms of a low price of man-hours that, being cheap, might be used wastefully. Moreover, he stated specifically that mass production justifies itself only in an economy whose benefits may be passed on to the worker through high wages and to the consumer through low prices of quality products.

AUTOMATION

This is a term which means many things to many men. To the electronics engineer automation means a closed system of process control as compared with an open system. The difference is illustrated by comparing a thermostat, which feeds back its own observations of temperature automatically to control the furnace, with a thermometer, which by registering temperature informs a human operator to do something about the heat in the house. To another person automation may mean a set of instrument boards and panels. To yet another it may mean computing machines which someday could set production schedules and activate other controls to run a continuous production process, not without a human supervisor or a human maintenance man, but without a human operator. To the ordinary mortal, however, automation probably means only the difference between doing things by machine and doing these same things *automatically* by machine—that is to say, without human work-handling between successive production processes.

The canning industry has long featured the continuous-flow production in which human beings do things to products as they come by in increasingly finished form, rather than different crews of operators handling the product completely for certain processes and then passing it on to the next crew. The latter is the case in house-building, where the plumbers take over after the carpenters are finished, and so on. A modern continuous steel mill furnishes marked contrast to an old-fashioned iron works, as do oil refineries to yesterday's chemical works. Many other examples readily come to mind to illustrate the difference between doing things by machine and doing them more or less *automatically* by machine.

Is automation a new industrial revolution? If so, the examples given, and many others, reveal that this so-called second industrial revolution has been in the making ever since the coming of the tin container—either as a container for food or, in the form of the "Tin Lizzie," as a vehicle for human beings intent on running down chickens and then, with increasing speeds, each other. But even before mass production there were stirrings of automation.

The Reverend Edmund Cartwright, who lived in the eighteenth century, invented a mechanical weaving loom that had built into it three standard moves of hand-loom weavers. (But the power loom was only a copied combination of human movements and embodied no self-regulation at all; feed, speed, and tie-in with succeeding operations, as well as color printing, were all regulated from the outside by a human operator.) Cartwright, incidentally, made his discovery after he had seen a chess-playing automaton in London performing twelve moves. He felt that he could certainly build just three observed standard movements of handloom weavers into a machine, which also might be hooked up to a good deal more power—steam power—than the muscle power of the handloom weaver. At about the same time James Watt was progressing toward automation by inventing the mechanical governor. Upon any variation of the speed of a shaft from a standard constant speed, the governor controlled a throttle which, by regulating steam pressure, brought the shaft speed back to normal. Later, the rudders of steamships were equipped with connections to a steering engine. When a ship went off course, the rudders were motivated in such a manner that the deviation itself instructed the steering engine, through valve control, to bring the ship back to course. But, of course, it remained for the "Tin Lizzie," and its assembly line, to bring automation to the masses.

It is difficult to make one single definition of automation, because it overlaps all previous technological achievements and adds new ones. Automation performs all the old tasks of job-shop production as well as of mass production, but does so with a simpler and yet more comprehensive approach which reaches out to include many new functions. There are three major types of automation; they may be labeled "Detroit," "feedback," and "electrothink" automation.

"Detroit automation." This refers to a continuous-process operation involving the use of stationary multiple tools on workpieces that are automatically transferred from one to the next in a sequence of stations that are stretched out in a straight line. An illustration is the Cross Company's Transfer-matic, a device for machining V-8 cylinder blocks. This multiple-station machine is 346 feet long and performs 539 operations on 104 workpieces in process at one time; each workpiece is automatically handled in seven different positions, with a capacity of 100 pieces at 100 per cent efficiency.

This sort of automation was invented by an unknown person who first thought of placing two tools on a lathe carriage to cut two diameters at one time. Being simultaneously performed on a single workpiece, these cutting operations so speeded up production that hand loading and unloading could not keep pace. Hence expensive machinery had perforce to stand idle while waiting on the human operators. Load-transfer machines were next developed. In the case of the Transfer-matic, the entire 346-foot line is under the control of one operator. But plans are under way to perfect an automatic work-banking unit between each two sections of the line to eliminate manual handling of workpieces while tools are being changed; and an installation is being considered for the beginning of the line to displace the sole operator.

"Feedback automation." This involves control of a machine on the basis of its actual performance rather than its expected performance, as, for instance, when an automatic elevator allows its doors to be opened only after having received information *from itself* that it has reached a floor-level. How far this technology has advanced beyond Adam Smith's pin factory may be observed by watching a modern automatic pin-making machine. It regulates its own cutting and its jet-streams of oil, and it literally tumbles the pins out. The human operator strolls among his battery of machines and in a manner of speaking "produces" so many pins that modesty forbids making a numerical comparison with the great Scotsman's eighteenth-century pin-makers.

Feedback has now progressed from mechanical to electrical forms. Vacuum tubes are used, for example, to carry back to a generating station reports of actual performance miles away, and then, by suitable amplifying devices, to step up the low energy of the conveyed message into power to motivate a suitable response of the distant generating equipment.

"Electrothink automation." In its most primitive forms this is the simple tape-feeding of instructions into a machine which carries out the orders, mindless of the results of behaving as it was instructed to do. In a more complicated design the machine scans the results of its own behavior and becomes a logic machine in drawing consequences, so that it will automatically stop itself or give a red alert to a human operator when self-destruction or spoilage threatens. In a yet more complicated arrangement the machine changes its own behavior as a result of having come to a logical conclusion that the ordered behavior is wrong.

However impossible it may seem for machines to "learn by doing," this is what happens every time a naval gun is fired. The gun compensates with an extra push for any lag between the order its pointer gives it and the carrying out of that order because of the presence of an obstruction like frozen grease. Prudently, a feedback control is built in to ensure that the gun will not lag behind orders for even a split second—long enough to let the target get by.

For another fresh example of electrothink automation one may take the case of camera-rockets that zoom up to a height of many miles in order to photograph sun phenomena that cannot be observed at ordinary atmospheric levels. The rocket not only keeps its camera arm pointed to the sun but shifts its position, acting on some 160 reports which it receives every thirty seconds through its electronic eyes, both as to purely external conditions and as to the results of its own behavior in responding to external stimuli. The rocket not only draws logical conclusions and goes by them but courteously radios them to a mechanical ground-recording station for future reference. The human element enters only into the design, fabrication, transportation, and firing of the rocket.

Automation goes further than solving complex operational and abstract problems. Computers can be used for data-processing in ordinary commercial operations. There they have the great advantage of working *directly* in terms of raw data when analyzing the results of business operations, whereas the feeble mind (which, however, invented these machines) has to work with averages and estimates in order to handle any flood of information. One trade union has such machines to inform its officials about dues collections and other union business matters, so that the officials have more time and energy to spend in organizing workers and concentrating on essential aspects of economic information on which they base their demands on employers.

Benefits of automation. In the long run, automation seems destined to contribute to the enrichment of human personality. For by its very nature, automated equipment is nonfunctioning without the effort of *educated* persons. The equipment is expensive, so it will always pay an employer to hire only the most qualified labor, exactly as was foreseen by Alfred Marshall. That eminent British economist pointed out in 1890 that "when expensive machinery is used which has to be proportioned to the number of workers, the employer would often find the total cost of his goods lowered if he could get twenty men to turn out for a wages bill of £50 as much work as he had previously got done by thirty men for a wages bill of £40."[2]

Specifically, the work of human machine-surveillance that will remain, once automation is in full sway, will be characterized by constantly changing job contents. These changes will affect jobs from the bottom to the top level of work performance. Consequently, only flexible and adaptable individuals can man the jobs. Flexible and adaptable individuals are educated individuals. Trade unions recog-

[2] *Principles of Economics* (8th ed.; London: Macmillan and Co., Ltd., 1930), Bk. VI, ch. iii, p. 550.

nize this and are offering their members retraining courses of a broad general nature to fit them for working in the new context of automation. American management is alert to the broad general educational implications of automation. Mark the words of a prominent business leader who says: "Technology actually begins and derives its greatest strength in the universities, for its most dynamic fuel is the flow of human initiative and human imagination shaped and developed in the careful training of human minds."

Capital Formation

The community's technology finds concrete expression at any one time in capital goods of particular specifications. As time passes specific capital goods wax and then wane, but the flow of a community's technology is essentially continuous though it is sometimes interrupted. At any one time the production of specific capital goods requires: (1) a willingness to invest in capital goods and their construction; (2) available savings which can be transformed into investment.

The second condition is relatively easy to fulfill. In times of recession there are at the outset hoards of savings. Credit to supplement savings can be extended by the banks and by the government. In good times savings are facilitated by the rise of national income and personal disposable income.

As for the first consideration, the transformation of savings into investment is contingent upon the expectation that capital formation will not work at cross-purposes with capital accumulation. That is to say, new plant and equipment is installed on a broad scale only when capital formation promises to preserve or enhance the financial value of a firm's proprietorship.

Table 8–3 shows that at repeated intervals the transformation of savings into investment has been retarded. Even the savings made by businessmen out of their firm's financial resources (liquid capital and retained profits) have not been freely used for acquiring new capital goods at such times. Some amount of acquisition of new capital goods of course takes place continuously. Most businessmen replace worn-out equipment unless they are on the verge of bankruptcy. However, severe constrictions on the aggregate flow of business savings into investment recur. A part of aggregate business savings then comes to rest in idle hoards, a phenomenon evidenced by an excess of total business savings over aggregate business investment. Needless to say, outside funds are not borrowed then by the business community as a whole. In Table 8–3 the years of excessive business savings are marked

Table 8–3. Relation of Business Investment and Business Savings, 1929–57
(deflated series, 1947 = 100)

Year	Aggregate Gross Business Investment as Percentage of the Value of Total Business Product	Aggregate Business Savings as Percentage of the Value of Total Business Product	Excess or Deficit of Business Investment Compared with Business Savings
1929	14.7	12.2	+2.5
1930	10.7	11.0	—0.3
1931	7.6	7.7	—0.1
1932	1.7	5.3	—3.6
1933	1.0	5.3	—4.3
1934	2.8	8.6	—5.8
1935	10.0	10.0	=
1936	9.3	9.0	+0.3
1937	13.7	9.7	+4.0
1938	6.4	10.4	—4.0
1939	8.2	10.4	—2.2
1940	11.2	11.7	—0.5
1941	12.8	10.5	+2.3
1942	6.4	10.4	—4.0 ⎫
1943	2.8	10.3	—7.5 ⎬ War
1944	3.6	5.3	—1.7 ⎪
1945	5.4	9.4	—4.0 ⎭
1946	13.5	8.3	+5.2
1947	11.2	9.8	+1.4
1948	14.1	11.8	+2.3
1949	9.5	12.5	—3.0
1950	14.5	9.0	+5.5
1951	14.5	10.0	+4.5
1952	11.8	10.0	+1.8
1953	10.9	9.4	+1.5
1954	10.3	10.3	=
1955	11.8	10.5	+1.3
1956	12.4	10.1	+2.3
1957	11.0	10.2	+0.8

SOURCE: U.S. Department of Commerce, *Survey of Current Business,* National Income issue, February, 1958.

with a minus sign; those with a plus sign denote periods of lively investment activity when business savings were completely transformed and outside sources of funds were tapped. The table is constructed by the simple device of expressing both the aggregate of internal business savings and aggregate business investment as percentages of the national volume of business sales, then comparing the two percentages.

The data in Table 8–3 do not measure capital formation directly. But successful transformation of savings into investment lies at the basis of the creation and installation of new plant and equipment. This is verified by Figure 8–1, in which the dips of business expenditure on new plant and equipment closely match the minus signs of Table 8–3, which designate excess saving.[3]

Figure 8–1. Business Expenditure on New Plant and Equipment, 1929–57

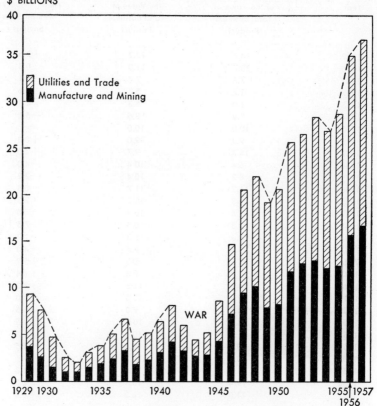

SOURCE: *Economic Report of the President,* January, 1958, p. 150.

The trouble with this chart is that, although it records dollar amounts, it overlooks changes in the "purchasing power of the dollar," which has notoriously decreased since World War II. As a consequence, the amount of investment, stated in "wooden nickels," appears greatly exaggerated as compared with prewar days.

[3] The outstanding exceptions occur in the years 1934 and 1944–45. In the year 1934 the rise of business expenditure on new plant and equipment was minimal and was therefore quite consistent with business hoarding in the aggregate: only the most progressive companies expanded. In the years of 1944–45 there were shortages of construction facilities, so that savings could not be freely spent for expanding the stock of capital goods.

The most informative data regarding capital formation, according to an economist's definition, is to be found in individual trade journals. Take, for instance, figures or comments on *new* orders for machine tools, such as can occasionally be gleaned by reading such periodicals as *Machine Design* or *Tool Engineer*. Machine tools are generally ordered in conjunction with factory expansion; hence *new* orders tend to reflect the presence or absence of business confidence. An example of the absence of business confidence is that of new orders for machine tools being halved between July, 1937, and July, 1938.

Figure 8–1 indicates reduced activity for 1938 but does not reveal as sensitively the sharp impact of the 1937–38 recession. However, the distress of that short, but sharp, depression stands out clearly in Table 8–3. Specific data on machine tool orders for transportation equipment and some other sensitive "barometers" serve to show in precise detail what happens to the production of capital equipment during years when businessmen do not fully use their own investment funds.

AN ECONOMIC PARADOX

A meaningful generalization emerges when data on segmental or total business fluctuations are viewed in the light of the relations between aggregate business savings and investment, as shown in Table 8–3. We observe that lapses in United States capital formation are explained by the lack of investment *opportunities,* not by the lack of investment *funds.*

With the preceding generalization this discussion of national resources has come full circle. Again we face the problem of the relation of savings and investment, which was raised in Chapter 4. However, the state of our national resources has now been depicted. The savings and investment problem in this nonfinancial, real perspective appears paradoxical. We possess a wealth of natural and human resources; that is, real sources of productive power abound. Yet at repeated intervals economic activity is throttled for fear that investment opportunities are lacking.

The paradox is as much man-made as are our capital resources. It exists primarily in terms of "induced investment." Here lies the clue to the amelioration of the repeated interruption of the economy's technological progress for periods of more or less prolonged duration.

Induced investment is a phrase which specifically refers to new capital formation caused by an increased rate of aggregate consumer spending. When new capital formation is retarded by lack of business confidence, why cannot extra investment be induced by government policies of encouraging consumer spending?

There can be "autonomous investment" as well as induced investment. *Autonomous investment refers to new capital formation which is activated independently of businesslike profit and loss considerations.* For the most part autonomous investment is undertaken by the government. Military spending is the outstanding example. Few persons would wish the government to expand the construction of military plant and equipment as the means of shoring up new capital formation. However, autonomous investment is also made for many peacetime purposes. When private capital formation is lagging, cannot slum clearance, the building of new schools, highway construction, and so forth, be accelerated? Is it possible to sustain the community's technology undiminished by government's autonomous investment as a supplement to private investment?

The overwhelming majority of economists answer "yes" to these important questions. They support this affirmative response with careful theoretical reasoning.

For Discussion

1. All but one of the following items are included in national wealth: structures, equipment, monetary silver and gold, government property, stocks and bonds, inventories. Find the category under which each item is included. Which is excluded, and why?

2. Which sta'ement is true and why? (*a*) Conserving and developing our resource base is a matter of individual decision. (*b*) Conserving and developing our resource base is an obligation because we have received this resource base from previous generations and "owe it" to future generations. (*c*) There is an obligation, but because of technological progress it is not so pressing as it used to be.

3. When seen from a resources point of view, savings and investment are two facets of one continuous social process of people, in the aggregate, sustaining the nation's technology. Yet, from a financial point of view, savings and investment may be quite sporadic and are prompted by purely personal reasons. Discuss.

4. Which of these attitudes toward machinery is most compatible with the author's position and why? (*a*) Machines should be viewed as the accumulated product of men throughout the ages seeking to improve their environment by technology. (*b*) Machines are the particular contributions to society of owners of capital funds who by their savings and investments cause machines to be invented. (*c*) Machines determine human values and institutions; therefore they should be studied in order to understand society. (*d*) Men are human, machines are not; hence machines should be used to improve the conditions of the human beings who projected them in the first instance.

5. "Automation is a robot pushing a worker from the assembly line into the breadline." Discuss this statement of a British worker.

6. "Automation raises no problems not already created by the eighteenth-century Industrial Revolution, and solved thereafter." In what respects is this statement inadequate?

7. "Automation is the control of machines on the basis of their own perform-ance, either by human control or by the machine's correcting itself upon its discovery of its prime error." Reformulate this definition until you arrive at one which you find satisfactory.

8. What is the relation as well as the lack of relation between the concepts of "capital accumulation" and "capital formation"?

9. What, in the final analysis, constitutes progress? (*a*) A rising GNP? (*b*) Developing natural resources? (*c*) Increasing the standard of living? (*d*) Im-proving ourselves as human beings? (*e*) Adding to the stock of capital goods as the means of an improved use of natural and human resources? Select what you consider to be the prime criterion.

10. With all the resources problems that confront us now and will confront us in the future, how can there ever be any lapses from full employment for want of investment opportunities? Do not attempt to answer this question definitively; instead, list the specific kinds of explanation you feel that you will require in order to answer the question.

Recommended Further Reading for Part II

On Natural Resources

BROWN, HARRISON S. *The Challenge of Man's Future.* New York: Viking Press, Inc., 1954.

CHASE, STUART. *Rich Land, Poor Land—A Study of Waste in the Natural Resources of America.* New York: McGraw-Hill Book Co., Inc., 1936.

DEWHURST, J. FREDERIC, and ASSOCIATES. *America's Needs and Resources—A New Survey.* New York: Twentieth Century Fund, 1955.

Full Prosperity for Agriculture. Washington, D.C.: Conference on Economic Prog-ress, 1955.

GARNSEY, MORRIS E. *America's New Frontier: The Mountain West.* New York: Alfred A. Knopf, Inc., 1950.

GOODALL, MERRILL R. *Administration and Planning for Economic Development—Three Lectures.* Occasional Papers No. 5 of the Delhi School of Economics. Delhi, 1952.

GUSTAVSON, REUBEN G. "Resource Problems and Research Possibilities," *Annual Report, Nineteen Fifty-five.* Washington, D.C.: Resources for the Future, Inc., 1955.

ISARD, WALTER, and WHITNEY, VINCENT. *Atomic Power—An Economic and Social Analysis.* New York: McGraw-Hill Book Co., Inc., 1952.

LILIENTHAL, DAVID. *TVA: Democracy on the March.* New York: Pocket Books, Inc., 1945.

MCKINNEY, ROBERT, *et al. Report of the Panel on the Peaceful Uses of Atomic Energy.* Washington, D.C.: Government Printing Office, 1956.

The Nation Looks at Its Resources. Report of the Mid-Century Conference on Re-sources for the Future. Washington, D.C.: Resources for the Future, Inc., 1954.

NATIONAL RESOURCES COMMITTEE. *The Structure of the American Economy.* Washington, D.C.: Government Printing Office, 1939.
OSBORN, FAIRFIELD. *The Limits of the Earth.* Boston: Little, Brown & Co., 1953.
———. *Our Plundered Planet.* Boston: Little, Brown & Co., 1948.
PALEY, WILLIAM S., et al. *Resources for Freedom.* A Report to the President by the President's Materials Policy Commission. 5 vols. Washington, D.C.: Government Printing Office, June, 1952.
RAUSCHENBUSH, STEPHEN. *Our Conservation Job.* Public Affairs Institute, Report No. 4. Washington, D.C.: 1949.
RUSSELL, SIR E. JOHN. *World Population and World Food Supplies.* London: George Allen & Unwin, 1954.
SHAPLEY, HARLOW (ed.). *A Treasury of Science.* New York: Harper & Bros., 1946.
TAYLOR, HENRY C. *World Trade in Agricultural Products.* New York: The Macmillan Co., 1953.
TENNESSEE VALLEY AUTHORITY. *Annual Report, 1955.* Washington, D.C.: Government Printing Office, 1956.
U.S. DEPARTMENT OF AGRICULTURE. *Farmers in a Changing World.* The Yearbook of Agriculture. Washington, D.C.: Government Printing Office, 1940.
———. *Water.* The Yearbook of Agriculture. Washington, D.C.: Government Printing Office, 1955.
———. *A Manual on Conservation of Soil and Water.* Soil Conservation Service, Agriculture Handbook No. 61. Washington, D.C.: Government Printing Office, 1954.
———. *Agricultural Land Resources.* Agricultural Information Bulletin No. 140. Washington, D.C.: Government Printing Office, 1954.
U.S. DEPARTMENT OF INTERIOR. *1954 Annual Report—Resources for Tomorrow.* Washington, D.C.: Government Printing Office, 1955.
World Economic Survey, 1957. New York: United Nations, 1958.
WOYTINSKY, W. S., and WOYTINSKY, E. S. *World Population and Production.* New York: Twentieth Century Fund, 1953.
ZIMMERMAN, ERICH W. *World Resources and Industries.* New York: Harper & Bros., 1933, and later editions. This is the classical work in this field.

On Population

CARR-SAUNDERS, A. M. *World Population: Past Growth and Present Trends.* London: Oxford University Press, 1936.
GRIFFITH, G. TALBOT. *Population Problems of the Age of Malthus.* London: Cambridge University Press, 1926.
MALTHUS, THOMAS ROBERT. *An Essay on Population.* New York: E. P. Dutton & Co., Inc., no date. Everyman's Library edition by Ernest Rhys. First published in 1798.
———. *Principles of Political Economy Considered with a view to their Practical Application.* Oxford: Basil Blackwell & Mott, Ltd.; New York: Augustus M. Kelley, Inc., 1951. First published in 1820.
OSBORN, FAIRFIELD. *Our Plundered Planet.* Boston: Little, Brown & Co., 1948.
ZIMMERMAN, ERICH W. *World Resources and Industries.* New York: Harper & Bros., 1933, and later editions.

On Productivity

ABRUZZI, ADAM. *Work Measurement.* New York: Columbia University Press, 1952.
CORDINER, RALPH J. Testimony on Automation. Given before the Subcommittee on Economic Stabilization, Joint Congressional Committee on the Economic Report, Washington, D.C., October 26, 1955. Copies obtainable from the General Electric Company, Department 2-119, Schenectady 5, New York.

DAVIS, HIRAM S. *Productivity Accounting*. Philadelphia: University of Pennsylvania Press, 1955.

DIEBOLD, JOHN. *Automation*. Princeton, N.J.: D. Van Nostrand Co., Inc., 1952.

DRUCKER, PETER F. "America's Next Twenty Years" (article on automation), *Harper's*, April, 1955, pp. 41–47.

Economic Growth in the United States—Its Past and Future. New York: Committee for Economic Development, February, 1958.

FRIEDMANN, GEORGES. *Industrial Society: The Emergence of the Human Problems of Automation*. With an introduction by Harold L. Sheppard. Glencoe, Illinois: The Free Press, 1955.

HAGEDORN, GEORGE F. *Productivity, Gauge of Economic Performance*. New York: National Association of Manufacturers, 1952.

HUTTON, GRAHAM. *We Too Can Prosper: The Promotion of Productivity*. London: George Allen & Unwin, 1953.

Industrial Productivity. Publication No. 7, Industrial Relations Research Association. Champaign, Ill.: 1951.

KENDRICK, JOHN W. *National Productivity and Its Long-Term Projection*. Washington, D.C.: U.S. Department of Commerce, Office of Business Economics, 1951. Mimeographed.

MAVERICK, LEWIS A. *Productivity—A Critique of Current Usage*. Carbondale, Ill.: published by the author, 1955.

The Measurement of Productivity. Bulletin No. 14, Machinery and Allied Products Institute, Council for Technological Advancement. Chicago, 1953.

MILLS, FREDERICK C. *Productivity and Economic Progress*. New York: National Bureau of Economic Research, 1952.

Production and Progress. Prepared for the 13th Annual Meeting of the Conference Board. New York: National Industrial Conference Board, 1946.

ROSEN, S. MCKEE, and ROSEN, LAURA. *Technology and Society; the Influence of Machines in the United States*. New York: The Macmillan Co., 1941.

ROSTAS, LASZLO. *Comparative Productivity in British and American Industry*. London: Cambridge University Press, 1948.

STEINER, PETER O., and GOLDNER, WILLIAM. *Productivity*. Berkeley: University of California Institute of Industrial Relations, 1952.

U.S. GOVERNMENT, INTERAGENCY COMMITTEE ON PRODUCTIVITY ESTIMATES. Established January, 1957 under the auspices of the Bureau of the Budget. Publications will be forthcoming.

U.S. GOVERNMENT, NATIONAL RESOURCES COMMITTEE. *Technological Trends and National Policy*. Washington, D.C.: Government Printing Office, 1937.

III

THE ABUNDANT USE
OF RESOURCES

Employment and the Principle
of Effective Demand

9 Supply and Demand

as Employment Determinants

Depending on the structural detail to be emphasized, many different models of an economic system can be conceived. Nevertheless, every model must convey the general idea of how the economic system is organized. In America the forces of supply and demand give fundamental direction to the national output of goods and services, and, consequently, to the employment of the labor force.

There are different possible levels of employment, some stable and others unstable. At some levels of total output, for instance, production becomes unprofitable because the proceeds realized by the business community from sales are less than the aggregate of costs which businessmen must cover at the very minimum. Consequently, employers will not hire the relatively large amounts of labor required to produce the unprofitable amounts of aggregate output. At certain other levels of employment, excess profits can be realized. Individual firms are then tempted to enlarge their sales turnover by raising trade-in allowances and by other means of cutting prices, even though the *rate* of excess profit is thereby diminished. Enlarged sales-turnover results in more employment.

UNEMPLOYMENT AND FULL EMPLOYMENT DEFINED

Production requires the use of natural and man-made resources as well as the employment of a labor force. But natural resources and capital goods are the passive agents of production; man is the active agent. The relation of man to material resources is expressed by technology. Obviously an individual must have access to the nation's technology in order to contribute his share of production, and men are deprived of access to the community's technology when a measure of general unemployment exists or when local or seasonal job scarcity occurs. *Unemployment is a social condition in which people are unable to participate in socially necessary production although able and willing to do so, even at reduced wages.* (When a person is unwilling to work at the going rate of wages, he is not unemployed. He may prefer not to work or he may be on strike; characteristically, striking workers, in most states, are not officially classified as unemployed and are therefore not eligible to receive unemployment compensation benefits.)

Full employment is a social condition of free access to jobs. Sometimes under this condition the economy strains to use resources to an extent which is not currently feasible. This results in inflation, as more money than goods is being added to the economic circulation.

ASSUMPTIONS

Our analysis of unemployment and full employment will be confined to what can happen at any time and for periods of limited duration.[1] This is of primary concern, for the long sweep of history depends on how we face our immediate problems.

To construct a model analysis of the American employment process we must temporarily leave aside all considerations other than what determines the *amount* of national employment. In other words, problems of work efficiency, safe and healthy working conditions, and so forth, must be disregarded for the time being. We must also hold in abeyance all problems connected with the use of natural and man-made resources. Thus we shall take as *given*:

1. The existing skill and quantity of the currently available labor force.
2. The existing quality and quantity of available capital goods and raw materials.
3. The desires and habits of consumers.
4. The work-preferences of the labor force (including management personnel and self-employed proprietors).
5. The organization of American management and labor.
6. Our general economic institutions.
7. The fundamental characteristics of aggregate supply and aggregate demand (to be explained).

---

[1] Time is the great healer, but this is cold comfort in economic matters. It is no more reassuring than the knowledge that nature in the long run remedies the damage wrought by man-caused soil erosion.

All these factors influence the size of the national output and, therefore, the national income and its distribution. Taking them as given does not mean that we are assuming them to be unchanging even for periods of limited duration. For example, the labor force may change from year to year as young people reach the age when they are ready and eligible for work. New and improved capital goods may be installed to increase the nation's productive capacity. All we are assuming is that at any time these changes are not of an overwhelming magnitude. Consequently, we can leave the actual and relatively minor changes out of account when studying the employment process during any period of limited duration. By so doing we bring to the forefront factors already observed as directly shaping employment situations, namely, consumption, saving and investment, government spending, and costs of production.

Having isolated these "strategic factors," each will be considered in terms of a theory to explain their observed variations. It is then possible to speculate on the possibilities of influencing or offsetting these variations when their undisturbed impact would produce unemployment or inflation.

THUMBNAIL SKETCH OF CHAPTER 9

This chapter on the determinants of employment brings to the forefront a special conception of supply and demand. Although the terms "supply" and "demand" usually refer to one commodity, in employment theory the terms denote biddings for and offerings of the entire amounts of goods and services which could be produced currently.

Aggregate supply. Total money costs of producing national outputs of different amounts are treated in a simplified fashion in this chapter. Entrepreneurial money costs of production, when aggregated for the entire economy, are the basic determinants of the varying national supplies of goods and services which might be produced currently if market conditions warranted doing so. A schedule can be made of different aggregates of money costs of production for variously sized national outputs. Such a schedule is called, simply, an *aggregate supply schedule.*

Aggregate demand. That component of national income labeled "personal consumption expenditure" is analyzed in this chapter. A theory is advanced to show that there is a characteristic relationship between people's incomes and their spending and saving. This relationship which exists for all families and individuals is seen as reflected in a typical relationship between national income and aggregated personal consumption expenditure.

Another typical and general relationship exists between national income and gross private domestic investment. In the present chapter this relation will be presented as an empirical generalization from observed data; a theoretical explanation is reserved for Chapter 10. Government spending as an element of aggregate demand will merely be mentioned as a supplement to private consumer and business spending. The reason is that 80 per cent of the national income is generated by the private economy, so it is there we must seek the causes of employment fluctuations. (Government may of course attempt to play a role in employment stabilization.)

Equilibrium of aggregate supply and demand. As has been said, there can be various levels of employment, many of them unstable. But there is also a tendency for the economy to approximate one stable level of employment. This is the point at which the totality of consumer, business, and government spending provides that amount of aggregate income which the businessmen feel they must be paid, at the minimum, for supplying the customers. Figure 9–1 clarifies this by showing that at most levels of output and employment there is either an excess of aggregate demand or the business community is offering to supply more than is wanted.

Figure 9–1. Employment Determined by Supply and Demand Equilibrium

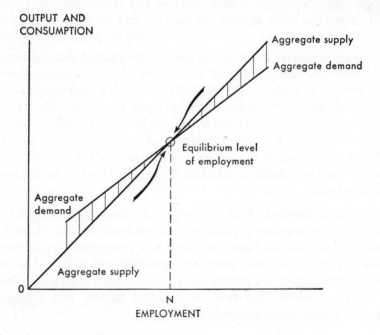

The unique level of output and employment toward which an economy tends is referred to as the *equilibrium level* of output and employment. However, since output is intimately related to employment, reference will henceforth be made simply to the *equilibrium employment level*. The question which employment theory has to answer is whether the equilibrium level must necessarily also be at any time the full employment level. The arguments developed in the rest of the present chapter lead to a negative conclusion.

The Foundations of Aggregate Supply

ENTREPRENEURIAL MONEY COSTS

The most general requirement which consumers must meet in order to have their wants supplied is that entrepreneurs be able to meet their own costs of production. This means that at the very minimum, prices and sales volume must suffice to cover "out-of-pocket" costs for current wages and materials of the individual firms. However, most firms would balk at supplying output on such low terms; instead, they would attempt to maintain prices by cutting back output and employment.

By observation of businessmen's reactions to the different prices which might be offered for specific products at different levels of output, supply schedules can be constructed, industry by industry. But the products of different industries differ in quality; tons of steel are not commensurable with ounces of fine gold. For that reason product supply schedules cannot be aggregated to yield a total supply curve for the economy.

There is one element, however, which all products have in common. They all require human labor to be applied to their production, directly and/or indirectly. Thus we derive an aggregate cost-based supply schedule, not in terms of commodity output, but in terms of the total employment needed to produce that output. A utilization schedule for labor exists for every individual firm. For theoretical purposes we need not know the actual details of all the individual labor-utilization schedules. Knowing that they exist makes it easy to conceive all of them being added, not only for industries but for the economy as a whole. The aggregation is possible because all these schedules are cast in the same terms, namely, in terms of the employment of standard work services. For example, whether employed in making refrigerator parts or parts for rocket engines, a machinist is a machinist. Thus, when an aggregate supply schedule for the nation's output of goods and services is being conceived, employment can be made an *indicator* of national output. By making some simplifying assumptions we can logically derive from the nation's total wages bill the aggregate money costs to the economy of variously sized national outputs of goods and services. Of course, these imagined data are useful only for purposes of illustrating the theory of employment.

Aggregating entrepreneurial money costs. These are the simplifying assumptions:

1. We take the annual wage bill per employee as given and constant; for the United States economy of 1975 let us suppose the average annual wage or salary to be $6,666.

2. We assume that labor and other factors of production are combined in fixed proportions, which will not alter during any period to which this type of analysis applies.

3. We assume that of the total cost of production of the nation's output of goods and services 66⅔ per cent is labor cost, while 33⅓ per cent covers other costs, including normal profit. (National income has been divided in this proportion between labor and property incomes for many years.) This means that for every $6,666 of average wage or salary received by the nation's employees (and attributed to self-employed persons), the total amount of value added by production is $10,000.

On these assumptions we obtain a *linear increase* of the total cost of producing the nation's output as it increases. In other words, the aggregate costs at which larger and larger outputs of goods and services will be supplied increase in direct proportion to the increases of output. To express increasing total supply costs in employment terms on the above assumptions, we find that when 10 million persons are employed, the resulting output will be supplied at an aggregate price of $100 billion. When 20 million are employed, the total supply price of output will be $200 billion; and so forth, up to 80 million employed, with the national output price at $800 billion. Plotting these data on a graph shows a series of enlarging squares (Figure 9–2).

Figure 9–3 shows the result of connecting the top right-hand corner of each square in Figure 9–2 with that of the succeeding square. A straight line emerges, every point of which is equidistant from both axes of the graph. *This is the economy's supply function under the foregoing linear expansion assumptions.* The aggregate supply function is labeled Z. Henceforth it will be referred to as a curve, in the mathematical sense of a line which can be described by an equation.

Another way of thinking about this straight-line version of an aggregate supply curve is that it would reflect national production conditions which, on net balance, are characterized neither by rising real costs nor by declining real costs. This is a simplifying, not a falsifying, assumption; it is, incidentally, not inappropriate to an economy of abundance.

Figure 9–2. Derivation of an Economy-wide Supply Function
Under Linear Output Expansion

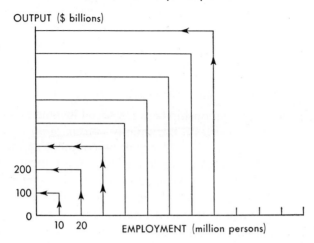

Figure 9–3. An Aggregate Supply Curve on Linear Expansion Assumptions

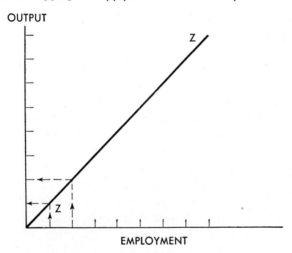

The Foundations of Aggregate Demand

THE CONSUMPTION FUNCTION

The British phrase *propensity to consume* is customarily applied to the inclination which consumers display collectively toward spending their money incomes. The propensity to consume is measured by comparing total consumer expenditure with gross national product (GNP), national income, or disposable personal income. When comparisons are made over a period of years, it is immediately seen that aggregate consumer spending has a definite character; it varies from year to year, but not at random. There is, instead, a distinctive relationship between social income and personal consumption expenditure. *Aggregate demand for consumption goods and services always increases as an absolute amount when social income rises, but the growth of total consumption does not keep pace with the rise in social income.*

An assertion. Any relationship between social income and total consumer spending is known as a community *consumption function.* (A function connotes the interdependence of two or more variable magnitudes.) To state that a characteristic attribute of a typical community consumption function in the American economy is a lagging of consumer spending behind increasing social income is to assert a significant proposition. It means that as the national income rises, the rate of private and/or public investment must rise in order to compensate for a *relative* lag of consumer spending. A further implication is that investment must increase in the face of *retarded* consumer spending. This may be profitable under given circumstances, but not so under other circumstances. If increased private investment is not profitable and is not undertaken, the rise of national income will be arrested unless public investment is immediately accelerated to compensate for retarded consumer spending and the failure of private investment.

The American economy is typically geared to expansion by virtue of numerous firms and millions of wage- and salary-earners being employed in producing capital goods which add to the nation's productive capacity. It follows that the economy cannot level off on a static plateau of economic activity. When levelling off of national income makes further economic expansion unprofitable, a decline of economic activity must occur and with it unemployment.

The proposition that personal consumption expenditure typically lags in an era of economic expansion quite evidently has profound social implications. However, before elaborating them let us see whether the proposition, as stated, is factually true.

Graphic proof. The proposition that aggregate consumption lags behind increasing social income can be visually demonstrated. The first step in the proof is to see what would happen if consumers always increased their spending in direct proportion to increases of their disposable incomes. If this were the case, then starting with no consumption whatsoever, $10 billion of disposable income would entail

$10 billion of aggregate consumption; $20 billion of disposable income would result in $20 billion of total consumption; and so on. Expressing this relationship in a schedule, it would appear as follows:

Disposable Income	Personal Consumption Expenditure
($ billions)	
10	10
20	20
30	30
..	..
..	..
..	..
100	100

Each pair of corresponding values can be considered as locating a point on a graph. Each point would obviously be equidistant from the vertical and horizontal axes of the graph. We know that when equidistant points on a graph are connected by a line, it must be a straight line rising at a 45-degree angle. The line pictures the consumption function on the assumption that aggregate demand never lags behind increasing social income.

Now let us suppose that, although increasing, personal consumption expenditure does so at a slower rate than disposable income. In that event the lag-relationship would be expressed in the following type of schedule.

Disposable Income	Personal Consumption Expenditure
($ billions)	
10	10
20	19
30	27
..	..
..	..
..	..
100	80

Each point located on a graph in terms of the above pairs of corresponding values would not now be equidistant from the axes of the graph. Instead, the resultant line would slope upward and to the right at less than a 45-degree angle.

It follows that if both the line portraying full consumption of disposable income and the line picturing a partial consumption are

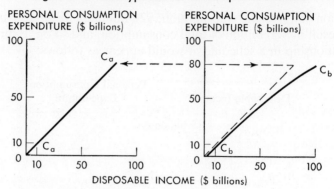

Figure 9–4. Two Hypothetical Consumption Functions

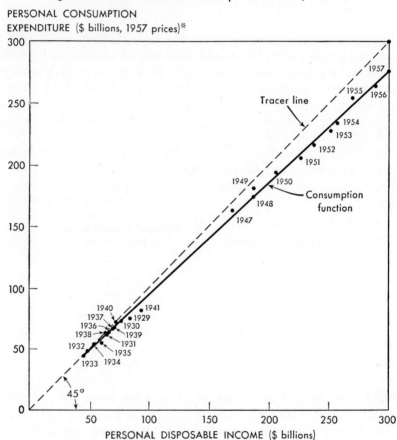

Figure 9–5. The American Consumption Function, 1929–57

SOURCE: *Economic Report of the President,* January, 1958, p. 131.
NOTE: World War II years omitted as abnormal.

212

plotted on the same graph, a gap will be seen to develop between the 45-degree line and the one which rises at a lesser angle. Figure 9–4 illustrates this, using the hypothetical magnitudes in the schedule on page 211.

So much for hypothesis. What are the facts of the matter? In Figure 9–5 an actual consumption function of the American economy is shown for the years 1929 to 1957. Each dot on the graph is a point which has been located by observing the amount of disposable income in each separate year, as well as the aggregate value of personal consumption. Thus, in 1929 disposable income was $83 billion and personal consumption expenditure $79 billion; in 1930 disposable income was $74.4 billion and total consumption outlay $71 billion; finally, in 1957 disposable income was $305 billion and personal consumption expenditure $284.5 billion. Plotting all these points yields what is known as a "scatter diagram," a dispersion of separate points. The points are connected by a line (either a computed one, or one drawn on the basis of visual inspection).

Next a tracer line with a 45-degree angle is inserted on the graph, not because such a line exists or could exist, but to enable us to visualize the increasing gap which must be filled by private and/or public investment if the economy is to remain in forward motion. Figure 9–5 proves that the American consumption function typically produces such a gap. It does *not* prove that the gap is fatal to prosperity. However, the question is raised whether the economy has a built-in mechanism for filling the consumer spending gap with an adequate amount of private and/or public investment.

INDIVIDUAL CONSUMPTION FUNCTIONS

A community consumption function reflects the expenditure patterns of the spending units in a region or in the nation. The characteristic lag of aggregate demand shown in Figure 9–5 must therefore find explanation in terms of individual and family consumption expenditures. Obviously, the particular ways in which different spending units dispose of their incomes vary considerably. There is, however, a uniformity of spending behavior in regard to the question which here concerns us. The fact is that when a spending unit's income increases, a diminishing proportion of it is spent for current consumption. Table 9–1 illustrates this fact.

The relationship between income and expenditure illustrated in Table 9–1 for families also holds true of unrelated individuals who pool their funds to meet expenses or who live alone. In the latter case one

Table 9–1. Average Outlays of American Families for Current
Consumption, 1935–36, by Family Income Levels

Income Level	Percentage of Family Income Spent for Current Consumption
Less than $1,000	More than current income
$ 1,000 – 1,250	100
1,250 – 1,500	97
1,500 – 1,750	94
1,750 – 2,000	92
2,000 – 2,500	89
2,500 – 3,000	85
3,000 – 4,000	80
4,000 – 5,000	75
5,000 – 10,000	65
10,000 – 15,000	54
15,000 – 20,000	53
20,000 and over	35

SOURCE: U.S. Department of Commerce, *Consumer Expenditures in the United States, Estimates for 1935–36* (Washington, D.C.: Government Printing Office, 1939), p. 20.

speaks of spending units of several persons or single-person spending units. Families are of course spending units of related persons. The Federal Reserve Board summarizes a survey of consumer finances made in 1957 by pointing out that "while spending units in the lower income brackets tend to spend most or all of their incomes, those in the upper brackets are able on balance to save a larger amount."[2] Actually this typical relationship between size of spending unit income and expenditure was reported scientifically by the Saxon statistician Ernst Engel a hundred years ago, in 1857.

When cash spending is retarded as the income of a spending unit rises, savings increase, whether in the older form of holding cash in reserve or in the newer form of making contractual repayments on instalment purchases or paying insurance premiums. Cash funds or bank and savings deposits, or readily marketable securities and mortgages, are called *liquid assets*. Table 9–2 reveals that consumers' liquid assets, as well as life insurance owned and being paid for, are more prevalent among higher-income spending units than among those with low incomes.

The sizable percentage of spending units of small income who have savings is attributable to retired persons who accumulated savings when their incomes were higher. Many of the younger spending units

[2] *Federal Reserve Bulletin*, August, 1957, p. 881.

Table 9–2. American Spending Units Owning Some Liquid Assets and Paying Premiums on Life Insurance Policies, by Income Groups, 1957

Money Income Before Taxes	Percentage of Spending Units Owning	
	Some Amount of Liquid Assets	A Life Insurance Policy on Which They Are Paying Premiums
$ 1,000 or less	45	43
1,000 – 1,999	54	53
2,000 – 2,999	66	67
3,000 – 3,999	68	81
4,000 – 4,999	80	91
5,000 – 7,499	90	93
7,500 – 9,999	97	97
10,000 and above	100	96

Source: *Federal Reserve Bulletin,* August, 1957, supplementary Tables 6 and 12, pp. 894 and 898.

in the lower income groups hold no liquid assets at all, and an appreciable number of them have no life insurance policy.

Aggregating spending units. Because high-income families and individuals spend a smaller proportion of their incomes than low-income units, it is reasonable to suppose that people will *relatively* decrease their spending when they move from a lower to a higher income bracket. If this is the case, consumer spending must necessarily become retarded, relatively speaking, when the entire national income rises. For this means that most people are moving up on the income ladder and, in the aggregate, will therefore save more and spend less.

There are, of course, some difficulties with this simple explanation. A rising social income may be due to the fact that the population has increased, so that there is more output without any person receiving a larger share of national output. In that event, aggregate consumer spending keeps pace with increasing social income (unless productivity increases faster than the population).

Another reason for consumer spending possibly keeping pace with rising incomes is the desire for emulation. When people move up on the income ladder they may find that they must indulge more expensive wants to keep up appearances. It could happen that the larger income now serves them less well than did a previously lower one, for now they must keep two cars and enlarge the garage or buy a new and costly home. However, a rise of income may also have the reverse implications. A person or family who never saved before may find that an increased income permits doing so, especially in the form of buying things on credit now that a credit standing has been established. Being able to buy on credit also permits people to preserve liquid assets which they would have to expend if they had to pay cash for every purchase.

With this dynamic possibility of easing dollars to support credit, the aggregate of savings in the old-fashioned sense of *not-spending* has naturally diminished. When, in 1950, average outlays of city worker families *having the same real income* were studied and the findings compared with a similar analysis of 1934–36, it was seen that the 1934–36 survey group had a small surplus of $9, on the average, whereas the families in the 1950 survey drew on past savings and bought on the instalment plan to the extent that they had a cash deficit of $200 on the average. But note these words of the analyst:

> If ... it had been possible to calculate the extent to which their purchases of durable consumer goods (in addition to dwellings) exceeded current depreciation on their stocks of such goods, and to include the resulting difference in savings, it would have been found that ... the 1950 group made, on the average, much the larger savings. Their expenditures on new automobiles and on house-furnishings and equipment were very much larger than those made by the employed wage clerical workers surveyed in the mid-1930's.[3]

Liquid assets which can be cashed to boost current-income spending must, of course, either be accumulated out of income already earned or be in the form of bank loans made in the light of a person's expected future income. The same is true of instalment buying. To obtain a credit standing one must have the demonstrated ability to earn and to continue to earn. Thus all spending is ultimately based on income.

In 1936 John Maynard Keynes expressed the savings condition of a rich society as a "fundamental psychological law, upon which we are entitled to depend with great confidence both a priori from our knowledge of human nature and from the detailed facts of experience, namely: that men are disposed, as a rule and on the average, to increase their consumption as their income increases, but not by as much as the increase in their income."[4]

On this principle Keynes based much of the modern theory of employment. In this respect the newer forms of saving do not alter the fundamental proposition; they only accelerate the economic process. That is to say, there is more spending by consumers, but it absorbs

[3] Faith M. Williams, "Standards and Levels of Living of City-Worker Families," *Monthly Labor Review,* Sept., 1956, p. 1020.

[4] *General Theory of Employment, Interest, and Money* (New York: Harcourt, Brace & Co., Inc., 1935), p. 96.

additional production which would not be feasible without credit buying. Spending increases and so does saving, even in the older form of laying away money. The gap of aggregate consumption, exhibited in Figure 9–5, remains a problem.

BUSINESS INVESTMENT

Consumer spending generates by far the largest part of aggregate demand, approximately 65 per cent. By comparison, about 10 per cent of total spending is business spending for investment purposes. (The other 25 per cent is accounted for mostly by government spending.) The business sector's total money flow of transactions is of course several times that of the consumer sector, but most of these are derived, rather than autonomous, transactions. That is to say, businessmen spend the greatest part of the money which they receive from consumers in meeting payrolls and incurring other costs of current production. Over and above this there is an autonomous business demand which does not depend upon immediate consumer spending. This is the demand for new plant and equipment, whether for replacement purposes or for increasing current productive capacity. It is only this autonomous *investment demand* which at any time constitutes an addition to the aggregate demand generated by consumer spending.

THE INVESTMENT FUNCTION

Business investment fluctuates more widely, from year to year, than does aggregate consumption. Nevertheless, a characteristic relationship exists between national income and gross investment. The typical experience is that there will be more aggregate investment at progressively higher national income levels.

Figure 9–6 exhibits the investment function from 1946 to 1957 of American private corporations engaged in manufacturing, transportation, and furnishing public utility services. These production corporations undertake over 70 per cent of total business investment in new plant and equipment. If corporations always plowed back every cent of profit gained, the investment function would be the dotted straight line which in Figure 9–6 rises at a 45-degree angle. However, in years other than those of recession, corporations pay out dividends and thus do not use the firm's entire income for the needs of business.

There are four principal reasons why business investment, in the aggregate, rises along with increasing national income:

1. The simplest reason is that managing an enlarged volume of business requires, among other things, operating more equipment or operating the given equipment at hand more intensively by employing double shifts, speeding up machine performance, etc. This alone

Figure 9–6. Investment Function of American Corporations, 1946–57

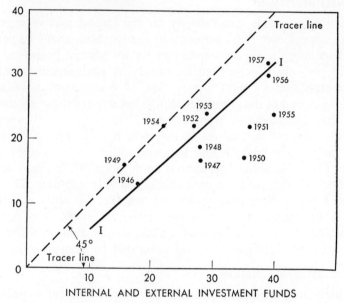

OUTLAYS OF CORPORATIONS
FOR NEW PLANT AND EQUIPMENT
($ billions, 1957 prices)

INTERNAL AND EXTERNAL INVESTMENT FUNDS

SOURCE: *Economic Report of the President,* January, 1958, p. 183.

increases aggregate investment because of a more rapid depreciation of the intensively used production facilities. By the same token there is less need for replacement during a depression; less equipment will be installed, and the given equipment will not be worn out so quickly.

2. Another factor which operates to increase investment as national income rises is business confidence. During periods of rising national income, businessmen place more orders for new equipment. To illustrate, the GNP rose from $397 billion in 1955 to $419 billion in 1956. Managers of business firms had anticipated this and consequently ordered 22 per cent more plant and equipment in 1956 than they did in 1955. The 1956 amount of gross investment was accentuated because in 1955 businessmen were still somewhat hesitant because of the 1954 recession; that is, to some extent there was a "catching up" of investment in 1956. Sometimes this catching-up factor produces a hectic situation. In Great Britain recent years of rising national income caused business confidence to rise so high that orders for new plant and equipment soared beyond the capacity of the

manufacturers of the new plant and equipment to meet the demand. As a result some firms ordering new facilities could not be assured of receiving delivery until eight years later.

3. A very modern reason for investment rising when national income does is the American government's policy of allowing facilities devoted to, or used in relation to, defense production to be amortized at an accelerated rate. Thus, a businessman whose facilities are certified for defense production purposes may charge for depreciation on the assumption that the certified equipment will be worn out or obsolete in five years, although the equipment will probably last longer than that. This permissible surcharge for depreciation cost reduces the amount of computed profit on which a tax must be paid. It is expected that the tax savings will be invested in buying additional equipment, and this is frequently done.

4. An important reason for investment to rise with national income is the capital-output ratio for the economy. If $100 billion of plant and equipment is required to produce $300 billion of consumer goods and services, the capital-output ratio is 1:3. Suppose that personal consumption expenditure is 90 per cent of disposable income. This means that when personal consumption expenditure amounted to $300 billion, disposable income was $333 billion. If disposable income rose to $355 billion, personal consumption expenditure would rise to $320 billion were people to continue spending 90 per cent of disposable income. However, people save more and spend less with rising incomes. Let us assume that with the $355 billion of disposable income they spend only 85 per cent of it. This leaves a personal consumption expenditure of $312 billion. With a 1:3 ratio of capital to output, this would mean that if the same methods of production are to be used, investment in capital goods must rise to $104 billion in order for entrepreneurs to accommodate the extra demand for goods and services.

GOVERNMENT PURCHASES OF GOODS AND SERVICES

The substantial demand added by government (federal, state, and local)—some $85 billion's worth—is *politically* related to rising national income. Figure 9–7 shows that when a certain major political party is in office, government spending invariably rises. When the opposition party assumes control of the Congressional committees and the White House, it accepts the heightened level of spending but tries to confine government expenditure to that level. The rising curves and the horizontal lines in Figure 9–7 are marked with year identifications of the points relating to government spending and national income, to permit confirmation of what has been said about the rule of the respec-

Figure 9–7. Government Spending Related to National Income

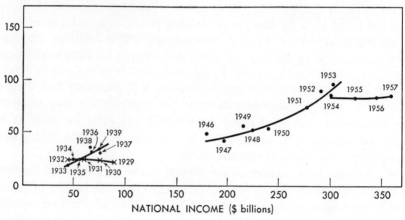

AMOUNT OF GOVERNMENT
SPENDING ($ billions, 1957 prices)

SOURCE: *Economic Report of the President,* January, 1958, p. 119.

tive political parties; it will be found true regardless of whether the
bulk of government spending is for peacetime or military purposes.

SYMBOLS

Aggregate supply is referred to with the symbol Z both in forthcoming graphs and in the text of the discussion. Aggregate demand is symbolized with the letter D. Since it is comprised of consumer and
business and government spending, the symbols D_1, D_2, and D_3 may
be assigned to these components in the order mentioned. Thus aggregate demand:

$$D = D_1 + D_2 + D_3$$

Alternatively, one may use the symbols C and I and G for consumer
and business and government spending. Then:

$$D = C + I + G$$

The only difficulty with this usage is that it makes aggregate demand
appear to determine the gross national product, for, as explained in
Chapter 2:

$$GNP = C + I + G$$

and so it is reported in official statistics (including the additional element of foreign investment). There is no danger in using either set of

symbols to denote aggregate demand *D*, provided one bears in mind that although aggregate demand plays an important role in employment determination, it does so along with aggregate supply.

Aggregate Supply and Demand Seen in Conjunction

PROPOSITION 1

There would always be full employment under the following conditions:

a. If consumers were to spend their disposable incomes in entirety, saving only in the sense of buying on credit but making no savings in the form of laying away money.
b. If businessmen plowed back every cent of profit gained.
c. If government were to spend exactly the amount received in taxes, no more nor less.
d. If output increases in a linear fashion as previously explained.

Under these conditions, aggregate supply and aggregate demand would be equal at every level of output, consumption, and employment. Every dollar gained by persons or government in connection with the production of national output would be spent in buying the entire output. That is to say, the consumption function would be 100 cents spent out of each consumer income dollar; the investment function would be 100 cents invested out of each net business revenue dollar, and 100 cents spent by government out of each tax dollar. Graphically, each function would be represented by a straight line rising at a 45-degree angle. Thus all spending, when added, would be represented by a line at a 45-degree angle. The aggregate supply curve under our linear increase assumption is also rising at a 45-degree angle and from the same zero point of origin. The two lines overlap, simply informing us that under the above assumptions everything gained in production is spent on the fruits of this production. (It is suggested that the reader draw a graph to fit the above assumptions and to illustrate this abstract proposition.)

The condition (d) that output increases in direct and fixed proportion to the number of persons employed in industry is not unrealistic for periods of limited duration. Obviously abstract, however, are the conditions (a), (b), and (c) of individuals, business, and government spending and investing 100 per cent of disposable income. However, the actual circumstances can be more clearly understood when compared with this abstract 100 per cent spending and investment model.

PROPOSITION 2

The actual community consumption function lags progressively behind national income. Figure 9–8 shows that as a result, aggregate supply and demand are equal at only one point rather than at all levels. Is this unique equilibrium level of aggregate supply and demand indicative of sufficient economic activity to furnish opportunities for full employment? In Figure 9–8 observe that if there were only consumption demand, D_1, then $Z = D_1$ at very low amounts of output, consumption, and employment. If we add investment demand, D_2, the intersection point of $Z = D_1 + D_2$ lies at higher levels. An even higher level of output, consumption, and employment is achieved with the addition of D_3, government spending. This still does not inform us whether $Z = D_1 + D_2 + D_3$ signifies full employment. In Figure 9–8, a hypothetical $240 billion represents the money value of the employment resulting from the $Z = D$ equilibrium. In the late 1950's at least another $60 billion would have been required to finance full employment for hired as well as self-employed persons.

Figure 9–8. Aggregate Real Costs, Total Real Consumption, and Employment (Based on assumed data)

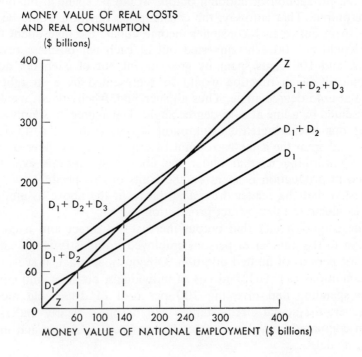

PROPOSITION 3

Aggregate supply and demand come into balance by economic processes which have little if anything to do with the national employment situation. This is proved by examining some main attributes of the balance of Z and D.

a. The prime characteristic of $Z = D$ is that a position of profit maximization has been achieved by the entrepreneurs. This has been stated and illustrated (see page 203, and Figure 9–1). Profit maximization is by no means inconsistent with maximum employment levels, but neither is there a necessary relation between the two. In Chapter 4 it was learned that when accounting for its capital accumulation, the individual firm must be preoccupied with factors that lie within the firm's direct control. Accounting describes the firm's specific supply problems and the expectations of the managers concerning the specific demand for the firm's specific products. Accounting does not record the opinions of the managers about the economy's aggregate demand for the entire national product.

Businessmen are, of course, aware that full employment is good for the nation and the nation's business. If upon the onset of every recession businessmen ignored their accounting records and hired back the unemployed, they would *in the aggregate* find it profitable. Each businessman would have to feel certain that all others would follow suit; no businessman could be presumed to have special problems which prevented him from doing so. On several occasions in the past the highest political authority in our land has appealed to businessmen to act as one in stemming the tide of unemployment, so far without success. Until such a time as the appeal for confidence beyond accounting data finds a response, profit maximization realized through the balance of aggregate supply and demand need have no relation to employment maximization.

b. Another characteristic of $Z = D$ is that it designates that the aggregate of personal savings *plus* business savings equals aggregate business investment. In other words, when aggregate supply and aggregate demand are equal, so are aggregate national savings and investment. This may appear mysterious. However, one need only bear in mind that money which people plan to save is received by them as part of their incomes. To the entrepreneurs who paid out these incomes, they appeared as money costs of production. Evidently the entrepreneurs cannot recover their full money costs of production unless all the money paid out is spent by consumers or turned over to the entrepreneurs for investment. If consumers planned to save more

than entrepreneurs wish to invest, some of the money which entrepreneurs must recapture to cover their costs will not reach them. They
do not receive for their output as much as they spent to produce it.
In effect the entrepreneurs have produced more output than the consumers are willing to use; the consumers planned extra savings. Next
the entrepreneurs cut back the unprofitable amount of output. This
involves for some persons a loss of their jobs and brings about a
diminution of aggregate savings. In the end, savings are reduced to
a level which is even lower than the amount the entrepreneurs originally
wished to invest. Since this happens in the process of aggregate supply
coming into profit-equilibrium with aggregate demand, it is natural
that when $Z = D$, so also must $S = I$.

Mark well that in this entire process there is no direct consideration
of the level of employment. It changes in the process of equilibration
but only as an incidental result of adjustments of profit, savings, and
investment.

c. An often overlooked attribute of the balance of supply and demand is technological. Where $Z = D$, the total amount of spending
for new capital goods is sufficient to maintain the output capacity of
plant and equipment or to alter it only slightly. If at any time plant
and equipment were modernized so as to expand greatly the productivity of capital, the new and more productive equipment would make the
older equipment which remains in use appear unprofitable in competition with the new equipment of higher output capacity. That is to say,
proportionately more output could be realized from new equipment
per dollar invested in it, and the additional output therefore could be
sold at lower prices. But this could not be done with the output of the
older equipment; yet all output must be sold at the same prices. Once
a level has been reached at which new equipment not only replaces
worn-out capacity but adds net productivity, the competition of the
new equipment with the remaining old equipment will lead entrepreneurs to consider that they are producing an unprofitably high
level of output. Orders for new equipment may then be cut back, to
the point where in the future new equipment just suffices to maintain
over-all capital productivity, or only slightly to alter it. Since this happens in the process of Z and D coming into balance, elimination of the
competition of new against remaining old equipment is an attribute
of the aggregate supply and demand balance.

We notice that this adjustment is made in consideration of capital
productivity, not in any direct consideration of labor force employment. As a matter of fact, this sequence describes the process of technological unemployment. The new equipment replaces manpower,
which *at the time* cannot be used to produce further equipment (be-

cause the augmentation of the stock of capital goods is retarded to moderate the competition of new and old equipment). Here is an aspect of $Z = D$ which shows better than the others that a balance can be reached which not only has no regard for the state of employment but which is actually adverse to it.

FINAL PROPOSITION

In America the forces of supply and demand which give fundamental direction to the economic process do not operate automatically to assure the labor force of full employment. There is a built-in mechanism for balancing aggregate supply and demand by the medium of profit maximization. This self-balance of supply and demand forces can occur at different levels of employment. In other words, the determinants of employment—consumption, savings and investment, costs of production—are part of an apparatus of supply and demand which is not purposefully geared to the achievement of full employment. Employment stabilization, at the high level on which there is a job for every able and willing person, is a problem, not something which at any time can be taken for granted.

For Discussion

1. What effect, if any, do you suppose a relative income redistribution which took place in the United States after 1933 has on the economy's consumption function?

2. What considerations justify the omission of government spending from the listing of the active factors causing fluctuations of aggregate demand? Does not this falsify the whole approach in view of the fact that government spending is a large part of total spending?

3. In John Maynard Keynes' *General Theory* (on page 30) there is reference to "the special assumption of the classical theory according to which there is some force in operation which, when employment increases, always causes investment demand to increase sufficiently to fill the widening gap between aggregate supply and aggregate consumer spending." What would you think was the nature of these assumptions? (Start by asking yourself whether assumptions made by classical economists a century ago were likely to be far-fetched or whether they were reacting to different times and different cultural values.)

4. If the Great Depression showed large gaps not only between aggregate demand and supply but also in economic theory, what assurance do we have that a possible future depression will not reveal shortcomings of the employment theory originally projected by Keynes? In what respects do you think these gaps might be revealed?

5. In terms of the concepts presented in this chapter, would you agree that the American economy has experienced inflation after World War II with the cost of living rising from 123 per cent of the 1936–39 average of consumer prices to approximately 200 per cent of that average? Would you compromise by calling this "creeping inflation"? If so, exactly what do you mean by this? Can you invent a better term to describe the postwar situation?

6. "The fear of under-employment equilibrium has been rendered obsolete by automation." Discuss.

7. "Creative salesmanship and rapid obsolescence are the answers to the relatively lagging consumption function." Discuss.

8. On the basis of the type of analysis presented in this chapter some people feared that directly after World War II there would be unemployment. Why did they fear this? For what reasons were they wrong?

10 Employment Problems in Theory

Theory, like a map, is useful for finding one's way. But a map is never confused with the territory to be traversed. Similarly, theory cannot be expected to extricate an economy from actual unemployment predicaments. To accomplish this, practical judgments and decisions must be made in consideration of the particular circumstances. These judgments will be based on observation, experience, intuition, and experimentation. Theory improves the quality of practical judgment by allowing economic decision-makers to think more efficiently about their observations, their experience, and experimentation. A theoretical approach spares enormous amounts of time and energy which would otherwise be spent in groping toward the central cause-and-effect relationships that tend to produce and perpetuate unemployment in our system of economic organization.

Properly understood, then, what is the significance of a model of aggregate demand and aggregate supply coming into balance at a point short of the level of full employment? It does not mean that such a situation must occur. Still, if it does occur, the theory indicates that we must direct our thinking to the various factors which determine aggregate demand and supply in order to arrive at the cause of the trouble. Of course, the decision-makers of a nation need not await an employment predicament; theory can be applied in efforts aimed at preventing unemployment.

PLAN OF CHAPTER 10

In this chapter the reader is introduced to problem areas of employment stabilization seen in a theoretical setting. In Chapter 9 we traced shortcomings of aggregate demand to their root causes. In Chapter 10 the aim is to show in a general manner how specific shortcomings, or overages, of aggregate demand can be located. The first step in this approach is to view the total stream of economic transactions with the aim of spotting points at which the economy may be diverted not only into temporary distress or inflation but possibly also into permanent stagnation or continuous inflation.

Having acquired a general understanding of where the origins of unhealthy economic diversions lie, the next step is to scrutinize in close detail what happens at such points of diversion. What small changes in consumption at any given level of national income may set in motion a chain of events which cumulatively diminish employment? Major problems of national employment do not usually stem from large changes in consumption, such as are involved, for example, when people change their consumption habits—as they did in the second decade of the twentieth century to become automobile buyers. Sectional and regional strains are involved in large shifts of consumption or investment patterns, but most of these economic strains are eliminated by a reallocation of resources. In other words, there is a change in the composition of specific sectional or regional outputs, but not necessarily in the volume of output and employment for the nation.

The employment problems which plague us are those which originate with small quantitative changes of the *rate* of consumption or investment. Small changes at the margins of given levels of consumption and/or investment are absorbed by corresponding changes in the total amount of employment. This effect, however, may serve as a further cause for making other economic adjustments. Massive unemployment or inflation may result from an accumulation of minor causes. The importance of scrutinizing employment problems in the precision focus of *marginal* analysis is indicated. The greater part of this chapter is devoted to the explanation of the marginal analysis of employment problems.

GENERAL LOCATION OF TROUBLE SPOTS

The first point of departure into problem areas of employment is an elementary insight, namely: The total flow of money incomes earned by spending units should return to the business world in the form of consumer outlays, business investment, and government expenditures.

For when this does not happen, money must be flowing out of economic circulation. The result is a widening gap between aggregate demand and supply which, if nothing purposeful is done, will be closed at some level of *un*employment equilibrium.

Employment theory is primarily concerned with gaps which might develop in the economic circulation of money—gaps that are indicative of the fact that money is leaking out of circulation. When gaps develop, the leakage of money causes a fall of prices which can easily lead to unemployment. Merchants and manufacturers find themselves "overstocked" or "overproduced." They may offer to sell their wares at reduced prices, or they may attempt to maintain prices by cutting back production and employment. In either case the aggregate money-flow volume of transactions is reduced. When money is leaking out of circulation, we speak of the situation as being *deflationary*.

Gaps in the economic circulation of money from consumers to the business world and back to the consumers. There are many causes for gaps in the flow of money from the business community to consumers through wages and back again to business through the medium of spending. One type of gap is caused when families and individuals substantially curtail their consumption expenditures in order to increase their liquid holdings. Another type of gap exists when government collects more in taxes than it spends for purchases of goods and services. A third type of gap may occur if the citizens of a country persistently import more goods from abroad than they export. The difference will have to be paid to foreign businessmen in money; under certain conditions this could be a one-way outflow of money. Yet another type of gap can be created by business savings exceeding investment.

In the ensuing analysis of the flow of national income, the international account will be ignored, not because the United States balance is minimal,[1] but for the sake of simplifying the exposition. The assumption will also be made that the government balances its budget; that is, it spends no more or less than it collects in taxes. Finally, it is assumed that all internal business savings in the form of depreciation reserves and retained profits are immediately reinvested in the business.

Overages in the economic circulation. Overages or surpluses can occur along the same lines as gaps, indicating that too much money is flowing into circulation. Then we speak of *inflation*.

A spectacular example of overage was furnished by the German economy immediately following World War I. German businessmen were anxious to reconstruct war-depleted production facilities and to

---

[1] The annual average was $2 billion, plus or minus, between 1948 and 1957.

get back into world competition. However, consumer incomes were at so low an ebb that people generally were neither willing nor able to make appreciable savings. Consequently there was a great excess of planned investment over planned savings. Factories, warehouses, office buildings, shops, etc., sprang up; but while being erected, they necessarily could not contribute to the flow of consumption goods to the market. However, labor and property incomes were being earned by persons engaged in designing and constructing the new production facilities and getting them ready for use. This extra money-income went into strong competition for consumers' goods in the markets. The supply of consumers' goods being limited (as compared with the money demand for them), prices soared. Millions of persons were rationed with increasing severity by skyrocketing prices, especially those whom the war had rendered poverty-stricken.

Inflation always threatens when there is war. For then there is an overage of investment demand for the construction of war production facilities. In addition, the output of war plants is in the form of rifles, tanks, planes, and all sorts of military equipment, which, obviously, are not brought to market. Yet the producers earn incomes which *are* spent in the markets of the nation. If controls on prices and wages and profits were not imposed by the government, inflation would be inevitable.

THE FLOW OF NATIONAL INCOME

When there are gaps or overages in the economic circulation, the system of money-flow accounting explained in Chapter 1 would reveal the institutional nature of the leakage or overage. That is to say, money-flow accounting would indicate in what sector or sectors of the economy the difficulty has arisen.

For employment theory, however, the more general concept of national income accounting explained in Chapter 2 is preferred. The reason is that it highlights the possibility of discrepancies between aggregate planned savings and total planned investment. Figure 10–1 clarifies this advantage.

The two halves of the circular flow in Figure 10–1 are different aspects of the national income. It is easy to see that for the bottom half and the top half of the circle to be equal, savings must equal investment. And it is a simple inference that the two halves must always become equal. For what would be the consequence if savings were to leave the income stream without reappearing as investment?[2]

---

[2] The assumption, it will be recalled, is that savings made by businessmen in the form of retained profits and depreciation funds are sure to be invested in the business. That is, the business sector has a balanced budget as well as the government. This assumption does not affect the quality of the argument but renders it less complicated.

Figure 10–1. Major Components of the National Income Flow

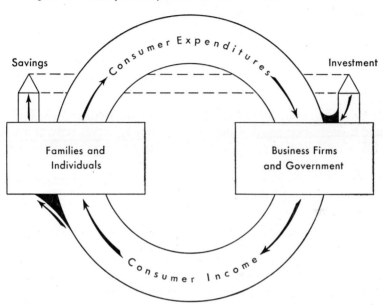

Consumer incomes would shrink and, therefore, also the aggregate amount of consumer expenditures. Contracting effective demand would depress business confidence so that extra investment would not be made to utilize the increased amount of savings which are presumably newly available for investment (all other things being equal).

To illustrate, let national income be designated as Y, aggregate domestic consumption expenditures as C, savings as S, and total domestic investment expenditures as I. Then $Y = C + S$, and $Y = C + I$. Therefore, $S = I$.

Supposing now that for some reason or other an amount of personal savings wanders out of the stream of circulation altogether, whereupon businessmen become so discouraged that they stop ordering new productive equipment and do not even replace that part of their equipment which wears out during the year. The outcome would be that the economy would produce only consumption goods. Yet millions of Americans depend directly or indirectly for their jobs on active capital formation. There would be widespread unemployment, forcing people to use up their savings. With the economy producing only consumption goods, and in the absence of investment and savings, the above equations would now read: $Y = C + (S = 0)$, and $Y = C + (I = 0)$. Therefore, $S = I$, as before, but this equation is equal to zero!

232

(It must be because, both S and I being equal to zero, $(S = I) = 0$, by the elementary principle of algebra.)

In practical language this means that the economy has adjusted itself to the low level of national income which corresponds to the production of consumption goods and services but without new capital formation. There the economy might remain indefinitely since it is in balance; this is the practical meaning of $Y = C$, when $S = I$ at the level of zero.

Is such a state of affairs possible? In the theoretical form just presented a stagnation equilibrium of the economy serves only as a warning of what might happen, in the extreme situation, if nothing were done to halt the downdrift of investment during a depression. After two years of depression during the early 1930's, this was, in fact, the actual situation (see Table 10–1).

Table 10–1. Net Savings and Investment, United States, 1929–33

Year	Personal Saving		Business Investment	
	$ Billions	Percentage of Disposable Income	$ Billions	Percentage of GNP
1929	4.2	5.0	12.6	12.0
1930	3.4	4.6	8.2	9.0
1931	2.5	3.9	3.0	4.0
1932	minus 0.6	minus 1.3	0.3	0.5
1933	minus 0.6	minus 1.4	0.9	1.7

SOURCE: *Economic Report of the President,* January, 1958, pp. 118, 130. Residential housing construction is deducted from the total of gross private domestic investment given in this source on p. 118.

Table 10–1 ends with the year 1933 because recovery action undertaken with government participation was well under way by the beginning of 1934. The facts disclose, however, that at no time during the 1930's did investment rise to its customary predepression level of approximately 12 per cent of GNP. Millions of Americans therefore felt a personal impact closely resembling that which the theoretical possibility of a balanced $Y = C$ low-income economy gives warning of. Real GNP declined one-third from $149.3 billion in 1929, to the low level of $103.7 billion in 1933 (both amounts expressed in dollars of 1947 value).

Questions naturally arise: Why would businessmen rest content with low levels of economic activity corresponding to low-level GNP's? The millions of unemployed do not have effective demand and therefore would not be heard in the market places of the nation. But what about the manufacturers, merchants, and bankers? They do not all go into bankruptcy during a depression. Many have funds for investment even during depressions; why would not at least these funds actually be invested?

To take these questions in order: Investment for the purpose of creating additional income need not necessarily take the form of producing capital goods for industry or houses or other consumers' durable assets. But investment must be made, if only because the unemployed and the distressed businessman will bring political pressure to bear toward this end, even though their economic power is at a minimum. And this investment might take the form of "leaf raking, building battleships, fighting wars, or . . . refunding income taxes paid in previous years" (in the hope that the refunded money will be spent to stimulate business), as Professor Dudley Dillard points out.[3] There is also the possibility that the jobless workers and their wives would accept positions as domestic servants of more fortunate persons. Payments made for domestic services are considered consumption expenditures, so that it is conceivable that national income would stem entirely from consumption ($Y = C$) at a point where there was no unemployment, but no capital formation either. The millions who formerly made capital goods would be occupied in menial capacities.

Such a situation would be most unprofitable for the business community. Still, under the circumstances, abstention from new investment could be the means of minimizing losses in proprietary capital.

A TENTATIVE CONCLUSION AND A PLAN FOR FURTHER DISCUSSION

When national purchasing power is at low ebb, protracted curtailments in the output and employment of individual firms are the means of minimizing operating losses. This completes a *general version* of why it is possible for the economy to find balance at a level of economic activity at which there is no capital formation, that is, where Y (the national income at some low level) equals C (aggregate consumption expenditure). The result would be one of the three following conditions or a combination thereof: (1) a hard core of persistent unemployment; or (2) unproductive use of labor formerly occupied in capital formation; or (3) employment of that same labor in menial capacities.

This general idea, however, offers no possibility of thinking one's way out of a depressed situation; obviously it indicates a need for a more particularized approach. To return to the fundamental employ-

---

[3] "Keynesian Economics after Twenty Years," Papers and Proceedings of the American Economic Association, 69th Annual Meeting, *American Economic Review*, XLVII, No. 2 (May, 1957), p. 82.

ment-determining equation, $Y = C + I$, the procedure which recommends itself is to cease viewing consumption and investment as aggregative billion-dollar amounts which register the end results of economic behavior. Instead they are to be understood in terms of the motives which caused the human behavior that finally resulted in certain aggregate amounts of income, consumption, and investment. For that reason the symbol C will be used[4] when the emphasis is on the psychological aspect of the consumption *function*. This is a relationship of mutual dependence between private incomes as well as national income on the one hand and aggregate consumer expenditures and the savings which people plan to make on the other.

By the same token, I is now to be understood as emphasizing psychological aspects of the investment *function*. The interdependence in the case of investment is between business decision-makers and their specific economic environments, as well as between them and the economic environment in general. The environment has an impact on businessmen as individuals, and their aggregate responses to these impacts have a reciprocal effect on the national economy.

Thus, by considering C and I as behavioral categories, the national income, Y, becomes a living record of economic events. Moreover, a basis is established for requiring and/or inducing changes of behavior in case chronic unemployment should occur again.

THE CONCEPT OF "MARGINAL PROPENSITY TO CONSUME"

In a lively, going economy one simply takes for granted that there will be a huge total amount of consumption, even during a depression. The interesting fact to observe is what occurs when the economy's income increases. How much is spent and how much is saved at that point (that is, "at the margin") where an enlarged income exceeds a previously more limited one? To ascertain this, one need only divide the extra consumption by the corresponding extra amount of income to find the "marginal propensity (or tendency) to consume." Alternatively, one can divide the additional amount of saving in the community by the additional national income to emerge with a measure of the "marginal propensity to save."

Increases in national income are characteristically associated with increases in the number of people employed. In Table 10–2 a hypothetical series of employment figures is shown and, corresponding to these, increasing levels of national income. Next are shown rising amounts of aggregate personal consumption. First, we take the difference between each successive pair of these consumption expenditure

[4] The symbols D_1 and D_2 have been used to denote the *quantitative* aspects of the consumption and investment functions; they will be further so used.

levels; then we ascertain the difference between successive national income levels. Dividing the expenditure differences by the national income differences yields the schedule of the marginal propensity to *consume,* shown in column (d) of Table 10–2. Mark well that the marginal propensity to *consume* declines as national income increases. This experience is logically implicit in Keynes' psychological principle of consumption.

Table 10–2. Computation of Marginal Propensity to Consume

N—Employment (millions of persons)	Y—National Income	C—Aggregate Personal Consumption Expenditure	$\frac{\Delta C}{\Delta Y}$ = Marginal Propensity To Consume
		($ billions)	
(a)	(b)	(c)	(d)
30	100	100.0	
			.90
33	110	109.0	
			.80
36	120	118.0	
			.75
39	130	125.5	
			.70
42	140	132.5	
			.65
45	150	139.0	
			.60
48	160	145.0	
			.55
51	170	150.5	
			.50
54	180	155.5	
			.45
57	190	160.0	
			.40
60	200	164.0	

THE IMPLICATIONS OF DECLINING MARGINAL PROPENSITY TO CONSUME

Inspection of column (d) in Table 10–2 brings the realization that as the national income increases, more and more people will have to be employed in making productive equipment or go without jobs. For obviously not all are wanted for producing consumers' goods.

It is not valid simply to assume that businessmen will automatically order an increasing amount of productive equipment because national income is increasing. To be sure, an augmented volume of money savings is momentarily in existence, money which businessmen might wish to borrow and invest in new equipment. However, this raises two questions: Is there an inducement for the businessmen to borrow the money? And are they willing to borrow it on the terms on which the potential lenders of the money are willing to make it available for investment?

The mere existence of savings funds does not indicate whether they are to be invested. As a matter of fact, the first impact of increased saving is a relative (not absolute) diminution of consumption. Under certain circumstances this might be considered discouraging by businessmen, leading them to slow down on further investment. At this point it is necessary to examine what considerations induce businessmen to invest, or to abstain from investment.

Investment as a Source of Employment Problems

HOW AN INDIVIDUAL FIRM DECIDES TO INVEST AND TO WHAT EXTENT, IF ANY

No business investment is ever undertaken unless it promises to be profitable, because individual firms are in business to make profits for the owners. Realizing a profit depends fundamentally on the relation between (1) costs incurred in producing output and (2) sales income derived from the sale of that output at current market prices. That is to say, no firm will buy new productive equipment or even replace worn-out equipment simply because it can be bought cheaply or because labor can be hired cheaply to operate it. The businessman must also be confident that he can sell the extra output from the new equipment and do so at a remunerative price.

A number of factors should be noted. The businessman cannot expect to be certain of making a profit; he can only estimate this. But he must have confidence in his ability to evaluate his prospects for making a profit. This implies two criteria of investment decision-making, one objective and the other subjective. The objective step is taken by ascertaining the supply price of the equipment whose purchase is contemplated. The subjective estimate is complex. It involves the businessman's appraisal of his skill in managing the equipment in the future; whether he thinks better equipment will be produced less expensively in the future and used by his competitors; what he thinks the political and economic climate will be; and so forth.

Given the current supply price of new equipment and the businessman's expectations as to the future, there emerges an evaluation of the probable net profit which the contemplated investment might yield. This estimated net yield is next compared with the going rate of interest to determine whether the contemplated investment should be undertaken. The reason for making this comparison is simply this: It certainly would not pay to use one's own money capital for financing enlarged production if as much return, or more, could be earned by lending the money at interest. And it would be even more ill-advised to borrow money for expanding production, paying the current rate of interest, if the use of this money were to yield less than it costs to borrow the money.

THE CONCEPT OF THE "MARGINAL EFFICIENCY OF CAPITAL"

To estimate the probable net future yield of current investment is to determine the *"marginal* efficiency of capital." That is to say, in any going concern a good deal of equipment is already installed and being operated; hence, the decision to be made is only whether one should go beyond the present limit (margin) of productive capacity.

Then, too, in ascertaining the supply price of the additional unit (or units) of equipment which might be purchased, the prospective buyer must estimate the price required to be paid to the manufacturer of the equipment in order to induce him to produce the extra (marginal) equipment. For only thus can one be sure of being supplied, even though it may occasionally be possible to acquire equipment at abnormally low prices.

Given the normal supply price of the equipment, a further consideration arises. When buying the equipment, the businessman will in reality be purchasing the right to a series of future net returns to be obtained by selling the output from the equipment, over and above the costs of operating the equipment. Let us say that the equipment is expected to last two years. The businessman then estimates what he thinks the net return of using the equipment will be for each of the two years.

Here is where the subjective element enters. The businessman cannot simply regard his current yield from the use of similar equipment as a measure of what he is likely to earn by the use of additional equipment. He must diminish this current yield in his appraisal for the future if he thinks there is a likelihood of such events as increases in real costs of materials or labor which might reduce profit; lower prices per unit of output in some future year of recession; new inventions or better methods of production which might render his equipment prematurely obsolete; increases in business taxes which might diminish the margin of profit; possible new foreign competition; a good customer ceasing business or an apparently good one defaulting on his obligations; and so forth.

The businessman makes these considerations, and others, year by year for every future year. His view will naturally have less definition the farther away lies the prospective income year; obviously, it becomes increasingly difficult to estimate the increasingly distant future. Let the evaluation of a probable net return for a year's use of the equipment be labeled Q. Then, for equipment expected to last two years a series of different Q's is obtained, namely, Q_1, Q_2. If this series, when added, gives a sum total which is higher than the supply price of the equipment, the businessman will actively consider buying the equipment. If not, he will dismiss the matter from his mind. Thus, the relation between the current supply price of the equipment and the sum total of the expected yields from future sales of the output of the equipment is the marginal efficiency of the capital to be invested in the equipment.

A numerical illustration of marginal efficiency of capital. Let us suppose that a businessman is contemplating the purchase of an additional small punch press which will cost him $750 and is expected to last two years. The entrepreneur estimates the chances of the punch press paying for itself by establishing first of all a mental rating scale. If, for instance, there is only a very remote danger of losing on an investment rather than making any gain at all, this chance will be rated, say, at 5 per cent. The particular bench marks chosen depend upon the individual; in and of themselves they do not matter, although their relationship does. In this example a remote chance is rated as a 5 per cent probability; a fairly remote chance as a 10 per cent probability; a good chance is rated at 20 per cent and a strong chance at 30 per cent.

With this mental rating scale the businessman now proceeds to evaluate the prospective profit yield from a punch press with a supply price of $750 and built to last two years. He rates the chances of the punch press paying for itself in the manner outlined in the following paragraphs.

1. During the first year there is a fairly remote chance that the net return *above cost* will amount to $1,000. There is another fairly distant chance that the sale of the output of the press will yield a net return of $800. Both opportunities are rated at the 10 per cent level of probability. The chance of reaping a net yield of $600 from the machine during its first year are fairly good, so it is rated as a 20 per cent probability. Most likely, though, the machine will net $400; hence this chance is rated as a 30 per cent probability. Now, there is a real possibility that business might not expand as much in the next year as it has been expanding in the past. Hence the probability of a net yield of only $200 must be rated at 20 per cent to indicate that the businessman is not disposed to delude himself in a mood of unreasoning optimism. Finally, there is an off-chance that times will really be depressed,

so that no profit at all will be earned above the cost of operating the punch press. This remote chance is rated with only a 5 per cent probability.

The businessman now has the following table in mind:

(Row 1)				Alternative possibilities:		
Expected net earnings from the punch press during the first year: $1,000	$800	$600	$400	$200	$0

(Row 2)						
Estimated Probability %: 10%	10%	20%	30%	20%	5%

How much is the punch press expected to yield during the first year? The businessman must come to some decision. This he does by multiplying each of the above dollar amounts by the percentage probability corresponding to it. Thus another row of figures is obtained:

(Row 3)			Alternative possibilities:		
Weighted expectation of earning power for the first year:.... $100	$80	$120	$120	$40	$0

The rest is easy. The businessman simply adds these various amounts to arrive at what is known as a "weighted average estimate of earning power." In this case the estimate amounts to $460, the most probable yield of the punch press during its first year.

2. For the second year the businessman's hopes are not so strong as for the first, so let us say that he weighs his chances at 5%–10%–15%–20%–30%–20%, instead of at the higher values shown in *Row 2* above. Accordingly, the punch press is expected to yield only $360 in the second year.

The total estimated yield over the machine's two-year life is $820, the sum of $460 for the first year and $360 for the second year. The purchase price is $750. Offhand it would seem that the businessman will buy the punch press without further question. But the comparison is not quite that simple.

At the moment of the investment decision the businessman commands $750 cash as the equivalent of the purchase price of the equipment. This hard cash he could spend in a variety of ways. Therefore he must estimate not only the prospective yield of the punch press but also the probable yields of alternative ways of using the $750. Let us suppose that he has done so and has found the punch press expenditure to be the preferred alternative.

There is also the consideration that the $750 of money capital could be lent at interest rather than being used in the business. Buying equipment means tying up money capital for the life of the equipment—in this case for two years. How much could be earned by lending $750 at compound interest? That is to say, what would be the interest-income for lending $750 for one year and then lending this sum *plus* the accrued interest for another year?

We shall suppose the going rate of interest to be 5 per cent. At 5 per cent compounded annually over a two-year period, $750 grows to $827; this is the amount of money capital which would be returned to the businessman after two years. The sum of $827 may be considered to be the *opportunity cost* of the punch press. The designation is appropriate because the businessman foregoes the opportunity of realizing $827 when he spends $750 for buying the punch press instead of lending out that amount of money.

Quite obviously the prospective yield of equipment must at least equal its opportunity cost if the equipment is to be purchased. In the instant case the estimated yield is $820 and the opportunity cost is $827. It would seem that the punch press will not be bought.

So far, only the businessman's estimated yield has been calculated. Practical entrepreneurs, however, give expression to their *confidence in estimates*. In the present case the prospective yield may have been underestimated; it might be $840. Or the future yield may have been overestimated; it might be only $800. Assume that our hypothetical businessman allows himself a margin of error of $20, give or take. This means that he stands prepared to buy the punch press if its opportunity cost (supply price plus imputed interest) lies within a range of $800 to $840. In the present example the opportunity cost is $827, well within the purchasing range. The punch press is bought.

To recapitulate:

  Cost of the machine.....................................$750
plus Interest that might be earned by using
  the money elsewhere.................................. 77
    equals ....$827 (the opportunity cost).
  Expected income from the use of the
  machine
    1st year $460
plus 2nd year ....$360 (total prospective yield).
    equals $820
  Margin of estimate-error: *Plus* or *minus* $20.
  Consequent purchasing range: $800–$840.
  Investment decision: *Affirmative.*

It may appear incredible that a business executive performs such detailed operations; but in a manner of speaking this is "all he has to do," and it is what he had best do as a matter of "first things first." Of course, in real life, businessmen "spice" their calculations (for the most part made subconsciously) with impulsive speculative reactions to the current scene. Thus when talk is rife about a "new era" having arrived, caution is apt to be cast to the winds—even by the conservative businessman who may personally harbor misgivings. As Keynes trenchantly remarked: "Worldly wisdom teaches that it is better for reputation to fail conventionally than to succeed unconventionally."[5]

THE AGGREGATE SCHEDULE OF MARGINAL EFFICIENCY OF CAPITAL

What would be the result of asking many potential users of a given type of productive equipment this question: "What would be the marginal efficiencies, to you, of successively adding one, two, three, or more units of this equipment to your present stock of equipment?" A broad range of different responses would be encountered because businessmen, as individuals, differ according to circumstances, outlook, and temperament.

Upon assembling and classifying the answers, a whole schedule of marginal efficiencies would emerge for each of a series of additional amounts of investment in the particular type of equipment. This schedule would exhibit a characteristic pattern; it would not merely register a random scattering of replies.

The pattern would reveal from the outset a continual decline of the marginal efficiency of successive amounts of capital invested in the equipment. There are two reasons for this.

1. The more equipment of a particular type that a firm installs or expects to install, the less each additional unit increases the firm's prospective profit yield *in comparison with* what could be accomplished by applying other types of equipment or spending the money capital in alternative ways.

2. A businessman ordering a large number of additional units of the equipment, or contemplating doing so, would expect his competitors to be doing the same. Therefore he would anticipate being required to pay a higher supply price. This, of course, diminishes the prospective profit yield.

The pattern of declining marginal efficiency applies to all types of productive equipment collectively. It is therefore possible to combine the schedules of marginal efficiencies of particular kinds of equipment. Then one emerges with an aggregate schedule of the marginal efficiency of money capital invested in equipment in general. Just as

---

[5] *General Theory of Employment, Interest, and Money* (New York: Harcourt, Brace & Co., Inc., 1935), p. 96.

in the case of its constituent parts, this general schedule will be a declining function of increasing investment, as Figure 10–2 shows.

The pattern of declining marginal efficiency holds true for an individual firm as well as for the business community as a whole. Figure 10–3 clarifies this. First observe the aggregate marginal efficiency schedule for capital in general, that is, the economy's business-investment demand schedule; this is the same as in Figure 10–2. The

Figure 10–2. Schedule of the Marginal Efficiency of Capital in General, for Any Given Period of Time

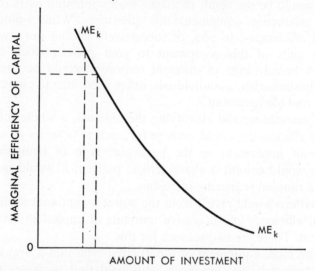

EXPLANATORY NOTE: The curve ME_k shows the relationship of the volume of business investment and the marginal efficiency of capital in the aggregate, for the economy. It does not portray the total amount of investment but discloses only the changing attitudes toward additional investment as more and more is undertaken. Because the demand for investment is based on these attitudes, the curve ME_k is often referred to as the community's schedule of investment demand.

new feature is the solid horizontal line intersecting the business-investment demand schedule. This is merely a "tracer line" drawn horizontally to an arbitrary level of the rate of interest, marked on the vertical axis of the graph along with the different rates of marginal efficiency. The rate of interest chosen in this illustration is 6 per cent, but this has no special meaning. The significant point is where the horizontal tracer line intersects the marginal efficiency schedule. From this point a vertical broken tracer line leads to the horizontal axis of the graph, where it is seen that the volume of investment is OM. With the given marginal efficiency of capital as portrayed by the curve ME_k, more investment would have been undertaken had the rate of interest been lower, say 4 per cent; less if the rate of interest had been higher.

It must be clearly understood that neither the rate of interest nor the marginal efficiency of capital solely determines the volume of investment. They *codetermine* it. In other words, aggregate investment demand is shaped on the basis of considerations proper to each businessman—criteria which have no direct connection with the fact that

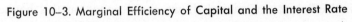

Figure 10–3. Marginal Efficiency of Capital and the Interest Rate

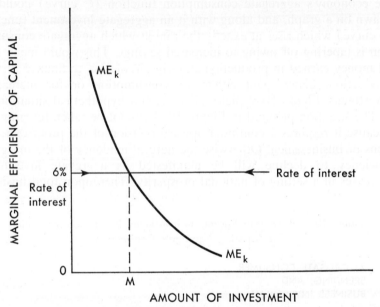

AMOUNT OF INVESTMENT

as the nation's consumers enjoy rising incomes they tend to save a greater proportion of these incomes. To be sure, this might prompt the savers to offer to lend their augmented savings at a lowered rate of interest. However, the businessmen would still have to reassure themselves that the future demand for their products might warrant expanding output through investment; this they would seek to estimate regardless of how cheaply money capital could be obtained at the moment. In other words, *savings do not automatically create investment.*

IMPLICATIONS OF TYPICALLY DECLINING MARGINAL EFFICIENCY OF CAPITAL

When the economy is operating at full employment, the problem of maintaining employment is to keep consumption and investment in such a relation that all money earned by businessmen and collected by government, then paid to consumers, stays in circulation. This was illustrated in Figure 10–1, which, for the moment, may be regarded as a total monetary circulation corresponding to a state of full employment.

Full-employment monetary circulation does not allow one to infer that savings are automatically creating investment to the entire extent of the money savings. But a full circulation does show that savings are not detracting from consumption to the extent of discouraging businessmen, that is, to the extent of causing them to revise downward the marginal efficiency of capital. If we could count on this happening, the economy's aggregate consumption function (*C* curve) could be drawn on a graph, and along with it an aggregate investment function (*I* curve) which rises at exactly the rate at which aggregate consumption is tapering off owing to increased savings. This would mean that all money earned in production stays in circulation to finance further production, being spent either for consumption or for increasing investment. Figure 10–4 pictorializes such a hypothetical situation.

The situation pictured in Figure 10–4 cannot be taken for granted, because it requires a continual upward revision of the profit expectations of businessmen. Otherwise the natural tendency of the marginal efficiency to decline will be manifested as aggregate investment increases in a setting of national prosperity. Thereupon total business

Figure 10–4. Increasing Aggregate Investment Exactly Compensating for Tapering Aggregate Consumption

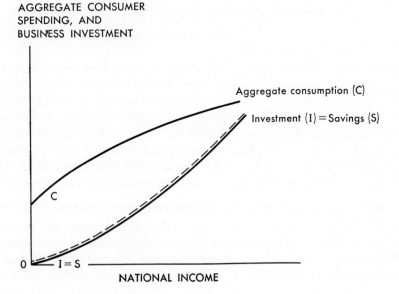

AGGREGATE CONSUMER SPENDING, AND BUSINESS INVESTMENT

Aggregate consumption (C)

Investment (I) = Savings (S)

C

0   I = S

NATIONAL INCOME

investment could still increase but only at a decreasing rate. Thus the business community's investment function would behave in a manner similar to the economy's aggregate consumption function. Obviously it could not then compensate for the tapering off of the consumption function in a national prosperity setting. As a result, increased savings would exert a depressing influence on business confidence—a slackening of investment demand. In an economy in which millions of jobs depend upon investment, the end result would be deleterious.

Circumstances under which businessmen continually revise *upward* their profit expectations can be generated by a great variety of fortuitous and/or planned economic and political developments. Leading among these are economic factors such as a wave of inventions that reduce real costs; a broadened dispersion of national purchasing power; or, from the political side, heavy military spending, and so on.

By the same token there are many circumstances under which businessmen find their confidence in future earning prospects diminished. These are caused by economic factors such as rising real costs of production (owing to the wasteful utilization of resources); increasing wealth and income concentration; or, from the political side, loss of foreign markets owing to social upheavals abroad.

Should depressing circumstances predominate, any appreciable increases in the rate of consumer savings would be felt by businessmen as constituting deductions from anticipated levels of market demand. For there would be no compensations to the tapering of the consumption function. Consequently, businessmen would be discouraged from expanding their operations; this might be the final straw in a sequence of events characterized by a relative inadequacy of spending.

As a matter of fact, a conservative approach to the employment problem is to recognize that savings are always *in the first instance* deductions from consumption. When this is understood, it is not necessary to trust to luck to provide required offsets. Instead, private and public investments can be planned ahead to assure a sufficient volume of aggregate investment. In that way, savings would furnish opportunities to undertake, among other things, such long-neglected social investments as slum eradication and the elimination of congestion in schools.

If savings can be subordinated to the role of a negative influence on consumption, we can drop the equation $Y = C + S$, and concentrate on the other equation, $Y = C + I$. In this equation the consumption function and the investment function stand forth as the prime codeterminants of national income and therefore also of the volume of employment.

In Conclusion

The prime determinants of the volume of employment have been analytically derived and may be summarized in the following manner.

$$Y \text{ depends on} \begin{cases} C \text{ depends on} \begin{cases} \text{personal incomes} \\ \text{and} \\ \text{marginal propensity} \\ \text{to consume} \end{cases} \\ + \\ I \text{ depends on} \begin{cases} \text{marginal efficiency} \\ \text{of capital compared with} \\ \text{rate of interest} \end{cases} \end{cases}$$

If action to prevent or remedy unemployment is to be taken by the government and/or voluntary associations, these prime determinants of employment must be influenced, directly and/or indirectly.

For Discussion

1. What is meant by saying that "the national income is the active factor in bringing savings and investment into balance"? Does this have favorable, unfavorable, or neutral implications?

2. In which way, if any, is employment theory related to business cycle theory—the theory that the economic process undergoes periodic fluctuations, with the "turning points" of boom and bust being discernible?

3. Is it not contradictory to assert that full employment is the normal state of an economy operated on the basis of private capital accumulation through profit realization? Why would businessmen persist in employing all the available labor if this should not happen to be the most favorable situation in which to make money or to avoid losses?

4. Discuss: "Consumers who make money-savings and businessmen who invest money in plant and equipment are doing so for entirely different reasons. The consumer who saves does so to achieve income security, whereas the businessman is interested in accumulating capital. Hence it is not surprising that there is no automatic correspondence between saving and investment."

5. Complete the flow-chart diagram below to show the flow of money, goods, and services in the economy.

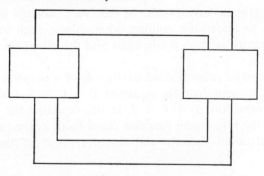

6. "Two pyramids, two masses for the dead are twice as good as one; but not so two railways from London to York." How did J. M. Keynes, in this telling sentence, mean to explain the occasional breakdown of the marginal efficiency of capital?

7. After World War II there was a backlog of capital goods, originally stemming from the 1929 depression. Under those circumstances would not savings automatically create investment, since businessmen wish to overcome the shortage of capital goods? Is this what happened between 1946 and 1959?

11

The Role
of Government in
Stabilizing Employment

What is remarkable about current attitudes and theories concerned with employment problems is the task of guidance assigned to democratic government. Keynes, for example, stated as a dictum that there is a "necessity of central controls" for "the task of adjusting *to one another* the propensity to consume and the inducement to invest"; and he reached the conclusion that both "the propensity to consume and the rate of investment" need to be "deliberately controlled in the social interest." He envisaged "a system where we can act as an organized community for economic purpose and to promote social and economic justice, while respecting and protecting the individual—his freedom of choice, his faith, his mind and its expression, his enterprise and his property."[1]

In America the responsibility of government for promoting high-level business activity and maximum employment opportunities is expressed in the declaration of policy of the *Employment Act of 1946*; there it is stated:

The Congress hereby declares that it is the continuing policy and responsibility of the Federal Government to use all practicable means consistent with

[1] The first two quotations are from *General Theory of Employment, Interest, and Money* (New York: Harcourt, Brace & Co., Inc., 1935), pp. 380 and 219; italics supplied. The last quotation is from "Democracy and Efficiency," *New Statesman and Nation*, January 28, 1939, p. 121.

its needs and obligations and other essential considerations of national policy, with the assistance and co-operation of industry, agriculture, labor, and State and local governments, to co-ordinate and utilize all its plans, functions, and resources for the purpose of creating and maintaining, in a manner calculated to foster and promote free competitive enterprise and the general welfare, conditions under which there will be afforded useful employment opportunities, including self-employment, for those able, willing, and seeking to work, and to promote maximum employment, production, and purchasing power.[2]

One is well advised to heed the warning that "it would be a mistake to read too much into the declaration of policy as marking a change of economic philosophy."[3] On the other hand: "The Act is more than an essay in wishful thinking." It "constitutes an attempt to bring the tools of economic science . . . to bear more effectively in the formulation of practically successful policies for the conduct of the nation's business."[4]

The Employment Act of 1946 should also be understood in the light of the fact that the various agencies of American government already participate in the nation's economic life. As a result the mandate of Congress can in part be met simply by varying government expenditures as might be necessary to strengthen the employment situation. This requires careful timing but reduces the need for creating many new government functions. For example, the federal government is currently influencing consumption patterns for welfare purposes by such means as old-age assistance, aid to dependent children, unemployment compensation, farm relief, home-owners' and veterans' loans, and so on, or for stabilization purposes by imposing or changing minimum down payments on automobiles and homes or by changing tax rates or tax exemptions. Modern governments also own and operate productive assets for the purpose of providing collective want-satisfaction. On the federal level such assets are the facilities for national security and multipurpose federal development projects such as the Tennessee Valley Authority (TVA); on the state and municipal levels they include schools, harbors, water and power districts, hospitals, sometimes municipal transport systems, and so forth.

The broad scope of government operations in the United States at mid-twentieth century is shown by the fact that in 1957, federal, state, and local governments in combination spent $114 billion, the equivalent of one-fourth the gross national product for that year. Purchases

---

[2] *United States Statutes at Large,* 79th Congress, 2d Session, 1946 (Washington, D.C.: Government Printing Office, 1947), Vol. 60, Part I, p. 23.

[3] Jacob Viner, "The Employment Act in Operation," *The Review of Economic Statistics,* May, 1947, p. 76.

[4] Edwin G. Nourse, *Economics in the Public Service* (New York: Harcourt, Brace & Co., Inc., 1953), p. 5.

of goods and services at all levels of government for 1957 amounted to $87 billion; about 60 per cent of these purchases were made by the federal government. The role of government as a big spender is evident, as well as the disastrous effect of any sudden curtailment of government spending—for it is pervasive in its influence on and throughout the national economy. The difference between $114 billion total government expenditure at all levels and $87 billion spent for goods and services is accounted for mainly by interest and transfer payments. The latter take the form of veterans' pensions, social security benefits, federal grants-in-aid to states for old-age pensions, and the like.

Types of federal expenditures. In the case of the federal government, the main item of outlay is for national security. This accounts for 60 per cent since the Korean War—for example, $45 billion out of $73 billion federal expenditure budgeted for 1958. The rest is for welfare, interest, and general government administration purposes. Table 11–1 is a breakdown of budget data for 1958; the figures are not identical with the actual outlay distribution but substantially reflect it.

Table 11–1. Budget Expenditures of the Federal Government—Percentage Distribution, by Major Functions, 1958

Major Function		Per Cent of 1958 Budget
Major national security		62
International affairs and finance		2
Welfare and conservation		23
Veterans' services and benefits	7	
Labor and welfare	4	
Agriculture and agricultural resources	7	
National resources	2	
Commerce and housing	3	
Interest		11
General Government		2
		100

SOURCE: This type of data may always be found in current issues of the *Statistical Abstract of the United States* indexed as Section 14: "Federal Government Finances and Employment."

These are the types of federal government outlays for which checks have been issued—to a total amount of $73 billion in 1958, for instance. But that is not the amount of cash which the government adds to the general monetary circulation. In the first place, a small part of the $73 billion was used to finance intragovernmental expenditures, some $3 billion worth; the checks issued in this connection do not circulate in the ordinary sense of the word. Of much greater importance is the large amount of money which the government handles when acting in its capacity as the trustee of the American social security system, and as the trustee of certain other funds such as those of the Federal Mortgage Association (which assists persons in buying homes), the reserves of the veterans' life insurance program and of the railway retirement and federal employees' retirement system, funds appropriated in advance for the highway program, and a few other minor funds. Acting as the trustee of these funds the federal government handled, in 1958, some $15 billion worth of expenditures pertaining to the listed programs. This $15 billion is in addition to the $73 billion for which the federal government, in 1958, issued checks to sustain its own, specific operations. Thus the 1958 total of federal expenditure was $85 billion which entered the general circulation—$73 billion for budgeted operations *minus* $3 billion of intragovernmental transactions *plus* $15 billion handled on trust account.

This total $85 billion of federal government *payments to the public* is the amount which enters into general economic circulation. To *payments to the public,* there are, of course, corresponding *receipts from the public.* These are principally comprised of tax revenues and, to a lesser extent, contributions to the social security system and so forth.

The impact which the expenditures of federal government make on the economy is measured by the balance (or imbalance) between receipts from the public and payments to the public—not by the balance (or imbalance) of the federal government's budgeted expenditures for its own specific purposes and disregarding the money flows involved in the operation of the social security program and other trust-fund programs. The federal government's budget for its specific, internal operations is often referred to as the *conventional budget.* It is of interest largely because it informs us of the *kinds* of spending activities which the federal government carries on in its own behalf, as shown in Table 11–1. By comparison, the information about the government's receipt of cash from the public and about its cash payments to the public reflects a broader type of budget—the nation's *economic budget* of forwardgoing goods-selling and goods-purchasing activities and of saving and investment. (This total economic budget was illustrated in Table 4–1; a useful reconciliation of the conventional budget and the government's role in the total national economic budget is published every year in the President's *Economic Report.*)

The balance of governmental receipts from, and payments to, the public should really be struck in terms of governmental activity at all levels—federal, state and local. (This is done in the President's *Eco-*

nomic Report, 1958, Table F-52.) To illustrate, in the fiscal year of 1957, federal government receipts from the public overbalanced payments made by federal government to the public by the amount of $2 billion in rounded figures. But the states and localities spent $2 billion (in rounded figures) in excess of what they received from the public. Consequently there was no net effect of government spending on the economy at all. The federal government was draining money from the general circulation—which is what happens with a government cash surplus—and the states and localities were pumping an equal amount of cash into the economy—as is the case when governments run deficits.

State and local expenditures. Whereas the federal government carries the bulk of the cost of developing natural resources, practically the entire cost of veterans' services, and all of the national defense cost, the states support the public institutions of higher learning, the larger part of the highways, public assistance programs of a specialized nature, and about half the nation's public hospitals. Local governments sustain the elementary and secondary schools (though with state assistance); they render general public assistance to the indigent; they carry 80 per cent of housing and community redevelopment programs; they furnish four-fifths of the nation's police protection and, of course, all the local fire protection, sanitation, and local park and recreation facilities.

Stimulating Aggregate Consumption

PUBLIC WELFARE EXPENDITURES

If certain economists who lived and wrote during the early days of the Industrial Revolution could return to earth, they would be surprised (most of them also gratified) to observe a new social attitude toward the problems experienced by families and unrelated individuals in securing their incomes against interruption and loss. In earlier times these problems of diminished or vanished incomes (because of sickness, accident, unemployment, or old age) were faced by the individual person or family unaided by public assistance other than the degrading charity of the poorhouse. Today we still make a person's success in life depend largely on his own effort. But it has been recognized that individual and family economic survival depends not only on nature but even more on the organization of society. And in our democratic society it has become an acknowledged human right to look to government for some measures of income security.

Since 1939 the federal government has become the trustee for social insurance expenditures reaching, by the end of the 1950's, the high level of $12 billion for unemployment compensation, old-age and survivors' and disability insurance, veterans' life insurance, and railway and federal employees' retirement programs. In addition, direct federal farm programs aimed at agricultural income support cost about $1.5 billion, and aids and special services to businesses in connection with direct federal civil (not military) programs cost almost $1 billion. At all levels of government there are outlays for education, veterans' programs, and for public assistance. The President's cabinet includes a full-fledged Department of Health, Education, and Welfare. Federal, state, and local welfare outlays total over $40 billion.

The new attitude of social responsibility also involves the average citizen's feeling that government has some positive contribution to make in maintaining stable economic growth so that a person may enjoy job or profit opportunities. Social welfare expenditures are seen to be directly related to this goal. The relationship was clearly expressed in the January, 1957, *Economic Report of the President,* in which he said:

The maintenance of high levels of employment and income in recent years has been a powerful aid to Americans in making better provision for their own and their families' security. Because good times and a stable dollar are our best formula for accomplishing this result, Government makes its greatest contribution to the strengthening of personal security when it pursues policies that promote stable economic growth and price stability. But Government also contributes to the vigor and stability of the economy by measures designed to assure retirement and survivorship incomes and to alleviate certain severe forms of personal misfortune.[5]

THE SOCIAL SECURITY SYSTEM

Enacted in 1935 and actively organized since 1937, the federal social security system now has three main branches: old-age and survivors' insurance (OASI), unemployment compensation, and public assistance by such means as grants-in-aid to states having old-age pensions, giving aid to dependent children and the blind, and so forth.

OASI. By the end of the 1950's, nine out of every ten members of the labor force were covered or eligible for coverage under the old-age and survivors' insurance, with only some specific professional groups being excluded, by their own wish. Eligibility requires a worker to show that he has worked half the time between January 1951 and his retirement. Thus a worker retiring in January 1955 needed two years of work to be eligible for benefits; by 1971 all workers will need to show ten years of work, which will from that time on be the stand-

[5] *Economic Report of the President,* January, 1957, p. 67.

ard requirement. (Twenty years is considered a minimum normal work-life.)

Benefits under the old-age and survivors' insurance system are wage-related. Under the original act of 1935, as administered beginning in 1937, monthly benefits were based on each individual's cumulative total earnings before reaching the age of sixty-five and equaled half of 1 per cent of the first $3,000 of total earnings. Benefits of only one-twelfth of 1 per cent could be received on the next $45,000 of accumulated earnings, and so on with less and less percentage benefits for increasing totals of prior earnings. This approach was modified in later years. By 1954 changes had been made in the law to permit one's benefit to be equal to 55 per cent of the first $110 of average monthly wages over the recipient's working lifetime and 20 per cent of the next $240. Earnings over $4,200 could not be socially insured. Effective as of 1959, this formula was liberalized when a "Table for Determining Primary Insurance Amount and Maximum Family Benefits" took the place of the formula, which, however, remained as the fundamental principle underlying the computation of the new Table. Earnings could now be socially insured up to $4,800 per year. Thus, a single person starting covered employment in 1959 and earning the limit of an average of $400 a month over his working lifetime, can receive $127 a month in social security benefits. A married couple receives an additional allowance of 50 per cent of the benefit for the wife; thus, the retired couple would enjoy a combined benefit of roughly $190 a month. If the insured person dies before reaching the age of sixty-five, fractional allowances of his benefit are made to his widow and such dependents as he may legally claim, including a dependent parent in addition to children under 18 or of any age if disabled. Women may receive retirement benefits upon reaching the age of sixty-two. Benefits are available to totally disabled workers aged fifty or over.

At the end of the 1950's approximately half the persons aged sixty-five or over were receiving benefits totaling more than $7 billion annually; another $2 billion was paid to 1½ million children and their widowed mothers and $30 million to some 600,000 women who had been declared eligible when retiring at the age of sixty-two rather than sixty-five, or who had lost their husbands at the earlier age of sixty-two.

Intent of OASI. Notice that the social insurance system, by imposing an insurable top limit of $4,800 annual earnings, gives larger *percentage* benefits to low-income recipients than to high-income recipients; for a person with average monthly earnings of $200 the primary benefit is 42 per cent, while for a $500 income it is 25 per cent. This expresses the original intent of the legislation—namely, to aid those persons in the lower-income brackets who are least likely to be able to save and are most stringently afflicted by income losses.

Employers and workers share the immediate expense of the insurance system jointly; a deduction is made by the employer for the worker's share of the joint tax, and the employer pays an equal amount as a payroll tax. It is fairly well agreed among economists, however, that the employer's payroll tax is ultimately shifted either to consumers in the form of higher prices or to the workers by reason of wage increases being withheld. Thus the system is in effect a true insurance system in that the beneficiaries pay for it, but in another sense it is a *social* rather than individual insurance system. The benefits in many individual cases exceed the contributions and will do so for years to come (until 1975). The government does not make up the difference, but consumers make it up paying higher prices, or, in some cases, the employers absorb it.

The reserve fund problem. The government, acting as trustee, receives the taxes paid by the workers and the employers and credits them to a "reserve fund." However, the incoming monies are spent for current purposes, and benefits are paid out of current over-all taxation. This has led some observers to complain that the system is in a sense a deception, since no earmarked reserve funds exist to pay benefits. Yet this objection loses force if we ask what alternatives the government has. For the government to invest the money in private industry is inconceivable. Many billions of dollars are involved—$23 billion by January, 1958. How would this money be distributed among private firms without charges of favoritism being hurled, or charges that the government is becoming too much of a factor in the private capital markets and in the control of private corporations?

Of course, the government could mark incoming social security taxes for direct expenditure on public projects of a productive nature, low-cost housing, multipurpose river basin developments, etc. This type of social security investment is actually required by law in many foreign countries, but so far it has been considered politically unfeasible in the United States.

One thing the government *cannot* do is to hoard the incoming taxes, for that means taking money out of circulation and setting a *deflationary* process into motion. Thus the only place for investing incoming social security taxes is in government bonds.

The important fact in considering the economic impact of old-age and survivors' insurance is that by 1975 more than 30 million persons will be sixty years of age and over. There are already 20 million persons in this age category. If such a large number of persons were not rendered reasonably secure against want and loss of income, any ripple of recession might swell into depression. The United States economy has in its social insurance system not only an equitable institution, but one of several effective shock-absorbers against depression, as well as a powerful agency for promoting social tranquility.

UNEMPLOYMENT INSURANCE

This second phase of the American social security system operates to provide temporary financial protection to those who find themselves out of work through no fault of their own. The program is administered by the individual states within the framework of standards prescribed by the federal government. These standards require the following:

1. A state shall earmark funds for unemployment compensation only. Ninety per cent of the receipts from a federally collected payroll tax to finance unemployment compensation is deposited in a state's account with the United States Treasury; any unused state funds form part of a trust fund.
2. The system, as administered by the states, must not be used to lower labor standards. For instance, a state may not require applicants for unemployment compensation to apply for work at places paying substandard wages, or at places where a legal strike is being conducted, or for work clearly unsuitable to their previous experience and training.
3. Unemployed persons to whom compensation is denied must have the opportunity for a fair hearing, originally and on appeal.
4. Benefit payments must be made promptly.

The system, as said, is financed in the first instance by employers paying a 3 per cent tax on their payrolls. But an employer may reduce his tax to as low a figure as three-tenths of 1 per cent if he does not have a record of labor turnover. This differential system of the rates charged employers according to their employment records is called "experience rating." Presumably it encourages employers to operate in such a manner as to stabilize employment. But to a significant extent it is unfair to employers in seasonal industries and in heavy-goods industries, which have sharper business cycles than light-goods industries, as well as to businessmen in a highly industrialized city (such as Los Angeles) as compared with a highly commercialized city (such as San Francisco)—commercial activity being considerably more stable than manufacturing activity.

Unemployment compensation is not only an economic depression shock-absorber but an automatic stabilizer as well because it works in what economists call a "countercyclical fashion." When employment decreases, unemployment compensation payments increase, to help support the level of popular purchasing power. For example, when between September and December, 1957, wage and salary payments declined by $3 billion (on an annual basis), unemployment benefits led a rise of transfer payments generally, a total rise of $1.5 billion (also on an annual basis). Thus one-half the personal income decline was offset for the time being.

PUBLIC ASSISTANCE

Here we enter the field of public charity in its modern form, which started in England in 1834, when "poor relief" was for the first time categorized according to the type and cause of income loss involved. Thus old-age assistance is an altogether different problem from aid to persons on the other side of the age scale—dependent children in broken homes. Many persons who place a stigma on old-age pensions would not react the same to the plight of youngsters in households suffering from dire need. Another category of public relief is general assistance—aid to indigent or transient persons stranded without means of support.

The significant difference between social insurance and public assistance is that a person is entitled to social insurance payments without question, whereas in order to receive public assistance a person must submit to a "test of means"—that is to say, he must let himself be investigated in order to determine whether any means of support are being hidden or whether relatives exist who could reasonably be expected to support the indigent person.

Public assistance is financed and administered by the states, though the federal government makes substantial grants-in-aid in the matters of old-age pensions and of aid to dependent children and to the blind. In some states specific sources of revenue are earmarked for pension purposes only, a situation effected by the badly neglected old people who, having lost their savings in the 1930's (or never having had any), asserted themselves through political pressure groups such as the Townsend movement (named after the originator, a retired physician of Long Beach, California).

The tendency in the states is to set maximum limits on the amount of monthly pensions which can be received, and then to provide for additional group medical plans which reduce the costs of meeting the special health problems of aged persons.

Economics of public assistance. The economic impact of public assistance is that of a consumers' subsidy. The question is whether its net effect is to increase, to decrease, or merely to transfer purchasing power in a community. A great deal of controversy has also raged about the effect of public assistance on productive efficiency. However, it is safe to say that in regard to efficiency few "pampered paupers" can be found who are subsidized in idleness; investigation of the records of any city welfare department proves this. Then, too, few aged persons would be valuable to society if they were forced to work against their will and ability after superannuation. It is also hard to believe that the nation's productivity would be increased if youngsters who now receive aid as dependent children were taken from their homes and put to work in public workhouses, to say nothing of the callousness of the proposal.

As for the impact of public assistance on national purchasing power, this depends primarily on the nature of the economic situation. In good times, public assistance most probably constitutes a pure transfer of purchasing power, but this matter cannot really be judged by economic criteria. It is a matter of one's moral and religious persuasions. In times of depression public assistance doubtless has an employment effect, principally through the granting of relief doles. However, no individual will acknowledge more readily than the unemployed person who in the 1930's eked out his dole by leaf-raking in public parks that public works of a constructive nature would be preferable as regards both the recipient's morale and the national productivity.

Unfortunately in the past there has been strong political opposition to the extension of constructive public works projects, rather than of make-work projects, even during depressions. If he "had the power today," Keynes asserted in 1933, he would rebuild the cities of England. He pointed out that "with what we have spent on the dole in England since (World War I) we could have made our cities the greatest works of man in the world."[6]

Stimulating Aggregate Investment
PUBLIC WORKS

Many persons have a tendency to associate public works primarily with the Works Progress Administration (WPA) relief projects of the last depression; yet, actually, public works are among the oldest of government functions. In 1776 Adam Smith spoke of public works as the "duty of the sovereign of a commonwealth," defining them as projects "which may be in the highest degree advantageous to a great society [but which] are, however, of such a nature, that the profit could never repay the expence to any individual or small number of

6 "National Self-Sufficiency," *Yale Review,* Summer, 1933, p. 764.

individuals, and which it therefore cannot be expected that any individual or small number of individuals should erect or maintain." And he added: "The performance of this duty requires very different degrees of expence in the different periods of society."[7]

The total of public construction in 1957 was in the neighborhood of $13 billion, 70 per cent of which was undertaken by state and local governments and 30 per cent by the federal government. Most of the state and local building activity was for nonresidential buildings and highways; most of the federal expenditure was for nonresidential buildings also (court houses, post offices, etc.), for conservation and resources development, and for airfields. Some federal funds were also allocated for loans to local low-rent public housing development authorities. But these were only the civilian public works projects. Military public works and atomic energy facilities caused an expenditure somewhat exceeding the civil public works outlay.

These are all prosperity and defense projects, to which emergency public works could be added in case of depression. In saying this the writer does not wish to be understood as sanctioning depression-time boondoggling. "Shelves of public works" should be prepared ahead of time—that is to say, shelves of blueprints and contracts to be used if a depression situation occurs and cannot be otherwise remedied. There is no reason why very productive public projects cannot be managed efficiently. It is only when public works are instituted in an atmosphere of desperation that "make-work" activity is likely to occur. Under such crash conditions the public administrators of relief projects do not wish to give the impression that they are creating government competition with private enterprise, already in the doldrums.

This said, however, it must be pointed out that by no means all the New Deal works projects were mere makeshift. Educational institutions benefited greatly from government-subsidized construction on a local campus or new sites; airfields were built without which the subsequent war effort would have been impeded; Bonneville Dam, the so-called "Roosevelt's Folly," was a strategic factor in the building of the atomic bomb, while TVA contributed to aluminum fabrication among other things, permitting World War II aviators to do combat in the skies with more safety than if their planes had been sheathed more heavily and less securely.

Many nations other than the United States have developed "shelves of public works"; in fact, all nations of modern Western civilization have. Public works are measures *par excellence* not only for providing

---

[7] *Wealth of Nations* (New York: Modern Library, Inc., 1937), Book V, Part iii, chap. 3.

community want-satisfaction in ordinary times but for helping to restore employment and business confidence in bad times. The theory of how public works may trigger recovery will now be presented.

Employment Theory Applied to Public Works Expenditure

The concept of the marginal propensity to consume gives a clue to the stimulation of investment by way of the government's undertaking public works as a supplementary means of preventing or ameliorating mass unemployment. This we may appreciate by viewing the marginal propensity to consume (increased consumption divided by increased income) in the context of the so-called *multiplier principle*.

This principle takes its departure from the common-sense insight that there is a relation between increased investment and increased national income. Suppose now that at a time of unemployment it is decided by government officials in consultation with business, labor, and farm leaders that it would be well advised for the government to increase its public works expenditure in order to encourage business confidence in the light of increased national income being created by public investment. Compared with businessmen, the government is in a favored position to increase its investment in a time of recession or depression. For the individual businessman, even when he is a large one, must treat the nation's aggregate demand for goods and services as a given datum; no amount of additional employment he can give will create enough extra national income to raise the society's purchasing power. Together, of course, all entrepreneurs exercise an influence on social purchasing power, but businessmen are not organized to act jointly in such an endeavor.

The government, however, can act on a scale large enough to create additional social purchasing power. It can do so by the previously described process of public borrowing, which really amounts to putting extra money into circulation without taxing to obtain it, or without absorbing savings that might otherwise be invested in private enterprise. In other words, a business concern cannot assume a burden of debt in the hope that this will generate purchasing power in a general sense. To assume debt a businessman must have a specific type of demand in view, for some particular good, line of goods, or services. But government, operating on a large scale, can plan its debt with reference to its own capacity to create general social purchasing power. In brief, government can operate to speed recovery by basing policy directly on the huge factor of aggregate demand. Here is how.

Basis of the multiplier. Actual observation studies have revealed that the marginal propensity to consume of United States citizens as a whole (not any particular family or individual) is two-thirds; in other words, out of every added dollar of income 66⅔ per cent will be spent, and the rest saved.

Now let us suppose that the government spends $1.5 billion on additional public works to counteract a threatening recession. This is not an unreasonable assumption, for as the Committee for Economic Development (a businessmen's organization) points out:

> The Federal government is now in a much better position than it was in the 'thirties to increase its public works expenditures rapidly. The Federal agencies maintain continuously revised six-year plans, listing projects they would want to construct in the next six years, and indicating their priorities and state of readiness. In an emergency it would be possible to increase construction by accelerating work on the projects that are most urgent and ready from the standpoint of plans, funds, site acquisition and other prerequisites. It has been estimated that these reserves of projects would permit an increase of about $1 billion in the annual rate of non-military public works within one year and about $1.5 billion in total Federal construction (including military construction).[8]

Operation of the multiplier. The $1.5 billion will be paid by the government to construction entrepreneurs who, in turn, will pay this sum to themselves and the cooperating owners of the factors of production. In the interest of simplifying the illustration we shall ignore, throughout, the following facts. (1) The entrepreneur would normally set aside, say, 15 per cent of the $1.5 billion received, for depreciation and obsolescence, as well as for paying indirect business taxes. Therefore they pass on to the factors of production, including themselves, only $1.225 billion. (2) For the purpose of spending, much of this sum would not be received by the persons earning it, since a part will be withheld in the form of income taxes at the source.

Assume, then, that $1.5 billion of public investment becomes available in its entirety to construction entrepreneurs and the cooperating factors of production. The marginal propensity to consume being two-thirds, we know that $1 billion will be spent on consumption by the persons engaged in constructing the public works. In other words, $1 billion comes into the hands of businessmen furnishing consumption goods and services, who treat this amount of money as income.

The consumption goods entrepreneurs in their turn spend two out of every three dollars which they have received, or $667 million. The recipients of this amount of money again spend two-thirds of their income, or $444 million. And so the multiplier process continues until its effect on total spending becomes insignificant, as ultimately it must by the laws of mathematics. For what we are observing is in the

---

[8] *Defense Against Recession: Policy for Greater Economic Stability.* A National Policy Statement of the Committee for Economic Development, March, 1954.

mathematical sense a decreasing infinite number series in which each
successive number is two-thirds of its preceding number, thus:

$1 billion + $667 million + $444 million + $295 million
+ $196 million + $132 million + $88 million . . . = $3 billion

If all the progressively smaller amounts in this public investment
multiplier series were added, it would be seen that they total $3
billion. In brief, with a marginal propensity to consume of two-thirds,
$1 billion worth of public investment theoretically yields $3 billion of
additional aggregate demand. A formula by which to remember the
multiplier principle may be developed as follows:

Let Y stand for the national income, I for investment, and MPC
for marginal propensity to consume. Then (using the sign $\triangle$ to denote
changes in these factors):

$$\triangle Y = \frac{1}{1 - MPC} \triangle I$$

or in our example:

$$\triangle Y = \frac{1}{1 - \frac{2}{3}} \triangle I$$

Simplifying this equation, we arrive at:

$$\triangle Y = \frac{1}{\frac{1}{3}} \triangle I$$

Now, the additional public investment in this example is $1 billion;
symbolically: $\triangle I = \$1$ billion. Substituting this in the equation:

$$\triangle Y = \frac{1}{\frac{1}{3}} \times 1$$

When solved, this equation shows that:

$$\triangle Y = 3$$

Recapitulation. The multiplier really is the relation of increased
investment to national income, operating through aggregate demand
behavior. This is determined, quantitatively, by the marginal propensity to consume. Retrospectively, the multiplier is defined as the ratio
of additional investment to the additional national income created;
symbolically: $\triangle Y / \triangle I$. The influence of the marginal propensity
to consume is seen in that:

$$\frac{\triangle Y}{\triangle I} = \frac{1}{1 - MPC}$$

However, $\triangle Y / \triangle I$ is a clumsy expression; hence it is customary to substitute for it the. letter K. The general multiplier formula then becomes, simply:

$$K = \frac{1}{1 - MPC}$$

In actual life situations "multiplier effects" of public spending can conceivably be dampened if people hoard money earned in connection with public works projects. This would be the case during any one given period, say a year, even though the hoarded money is later spent. In that case the multiplier effect might be reduced to 2 or even 1—but which is still more than if nothing were done.

When money leaks out of circulation despite spending on purposeful public works, we speak of "truncated multipliers." But there can also conceivably be "explosive multipliers." This would happen if badly timed public works spending added to an already existing overage of investment. So far there has been no historical example of this, unless military spending is falsely considered as public works activity designed to stimulate aggregate demand and the volume of employment. There is a relation, but it would be oversimplifying matters to claim that it exists by intention.

In Conclusion

In this chapter the attempt has been made to describe the role of government in its modern dimensions. As a factor in the creation and maintenance of economic prosperity the government, at federal, state, and local levels, is of vital importance. The founders of our Republic probably did not envision big government as we know it, but we cannot view the phenomenon with provincial alarm. We must remind ourselves, as they would have done, that the ability to create new democratic forms of living under changing environmental circumstances did not vanish with the founding fathers after they had strikingly manifested it. Big government will oppress us if we fear it, because it is here to stay; but it will gladly serve us if we take the trouble to understand it!

For Discussion

1. In the 1952 presidential election campaign one of the candidates said:

So I pledge you this. If the finest brains, the finest hearts, that we can mobilize in Washington can foresee the signs of any recession, and depression, that would put honest, hardworking men and women out of work, the full power of private industry, of municipal government, of state government, of the Federal Government will be mobilized to see that that does not happen. I cannot pledge you more than that.

Was it the Democratic, Republican, or Socialist candidate who made this pledge?

2. Assuming that the economy is in an inflationary situation, would a federal budget of balanced receipts and expenditure furnish evidence that the government is not contributing to an overage of investment-spending? Would you advocate that the government confine its spending to the amount received by the medium of taxation during a depression? If so, why? if not, why not?

3. Is there any evidence that public welfare spending is retarding the advance of productivity in the United States because people have social security coverage and are therefore not inclined to exert themselves to the extent previous generations did?

4. What limitations do you discern on public welfare expenditures as a means of recovery from depression? What about public works?

5. In relating to one another the propensity to consume and the inducement to invest, what difficulties might arise for government in its effort to contribute to employment stabilization? For example, what if social security benefits were reduced in times of prosperity to help in fighting "inflation"?

6. Make a list of items to be included in a blueprint of a "shelf of public works" to be held in readiness for the onset of depression. Indicate priorities. Must this shelf be stocked entirely with projects for physical construction of buildings, etc., or is there room for "investment in human beings"? What would this be?

12 Government Debt
and Tax Management

Where is the money coming from? This is the question which readily comes to the American mind in any matter of public spending. Will the national debt be augmented? Will taxation be increased? It would be vain to pursue further the policy aspects of employment stabilization without dealing with this matter.

Where the money for government expenditure is coming *from* when gaps develop between aggregate demand and supply is not the leading question. The matter of prime concern is where the money is going *to*. The situation is this: A great income stream has been generated by the business world, but some of the income is not returning, either in the form of consumer expenditure or via government purchasing. It would be preposterous to expect families and individuals to engage in spending sprees to overcome this difficulty, or to urge businessmen to increase their spending at such a time. But there is nothing absurd about the government's supplementing an inadequate flow of consumer purchasing power to the business community. Bear in mind that public works in the United States are executed by private enterprises whose owners bid for government contracts, then hire the required labor and buy machinery and materials from other private enterprises.

It follows that public works in support of employment are means of keeping money from being lost to the economic circulation, not devices for taking money out of circulation. Observe that supplementary government spending to fill circulation gaps allows consumers to realize their plans for increasing their liquid savings, by preventing a decline of the national income which would force these consumers to use up their savings.

Public spending can impinge on private spending or investment when there are overages of aggregate demand rather than shortfallings. At such times it is by no means always possible or desirable to curtail public works—highway construction, projects to advance resources conservation, slum clearance, or the like. To do so would be to give priority to private consumption on ideological grounds rather than in terms of the basic social needs of the nation. The public works would, however, need to be financed by tax revenues obtained at high rates of taxation, otherwise there could be disastrous inflation. Observe that high taxes, insofar as they prevent inflation, sustain the purchasing power of people's incomes and the value of their savings.

Government policies to take direct action for maintaining the flows of private income, and the value of such incomes, are called *fiscal policies.*[1] The essential advantage of fiscal policies is their directness in influencing the flows of private income in economic circulation, either by supplementing the flows or by absorbing a part of them for purposes of community want-satisfaction.

Fiscal policies of government have two prime facets: national debt management and taxation.

Government Borrowing

Ordinary debt. The national debt results from the government's use of its credit standing to obtain funds from investors which would otherwise have to be secured by taxation. The national debt may be enlarged by the government's creation of money through the Federal Reserve System in order to meet war expenditures or to speed a recovery from depression. In other words, there are really two kinds of public debts. One kind is caused by the government's borrowing of private savings. Another kind of public debt is caused by government creation of money. The last-named variety of public debt is not available to state and local governments, for the Constitution denies them the power to create money. Hence we shall first discuss the borrowing of citizens' savings by the government, whether done on the federal, state, or local level.

---

[1] The term "fiscal" derives from the Latin word *fiscus,* meaning a basket in which money is collected. This in a political context refers to a government treasury. Thus "fiscal" has become a word applying to the management of treasury affairs, most recently treasury management in aid of employment stabilization.

When we consider ordinary government borrowing (in which case money is not created), it is possible to think of the government as a large individual borrower. This is appropriate whether the reference is to city, county, state, or federal government. In the context of ordinary, nonemergency borrowing, the same rules apply to government agencies as to businessmen. For the businessman, going into debt means issuing notes or company bonds. For local government it means issuing debt certificates, notes, state and municipal bonds, and for the federal government, treasury bonds, as well as various types of savings bonds.

A businessman would not contract through the sale of bonds a debt running over a period of years if he thought equipment bought with the proceeds would be worn out before the loan was repaid. He would have to use part of his future income to pay for things he could no longer use. Likewise, an agency of government, at any level, does not consider itself justified in contracting a long-term debt to meet current expenditures. That would require future taxpayers to meet the cost of an expenditure the benefits of which they cannot enjoy.

There must be a sound relationship between the amounts of money which will be required to meet interest cost and repayment of the principal, on the one hand, and the income generated by the government project about to be undertaken, on the other. Only long-term earning assets justify borrowing. Thus if a city floats bonds to finance a new expressway, the tax basis created by reaching out to suburban and exurban locations should suffice to yield taxes to carry the interest and principal payments on the loan. Twenty-year bonds have sometimes been issued to finance expressway construction when it was known that the entire project would have to be renovated in ten years; taxpayers thus paid interest on a highway for ten years after it had been replaced!

Extraordinary debt. Another type of public debt is emergency indebtedness. (It is called this only by courtesy; there is no borrowing in the real sense of the word.) What happens is that the federal government is confronted with a situation in which it wishes to undertake relatively large public expenditures but finds the taxpayers unable or unwilling to pay increased taxes to the required extent. Increased taxes would be a hardship during depressions. In wartime people and politicians behave irrationally in refusing to finance the emergency on a pay-as-you-go taxation basis. Obviously the real economic burden of war must be carried at the time of the fighting; "guns for butter" is a necessity at the moment. But instead of paring their consumer expenditures of their own accord by paying high taxes, consumers prefer to be paid nominally high incomes and then to be rationed partly by a rise of prices and partly with ration coupons issued by a government authority.

WAR FINANCE

The rational manner of financing a war would be to limit personal disposable incomes to an amount sufficient to provide a healthy and decent living standard for the civilian population on a case-by-case basis. This could be done by deferring the *payment* of all income increases for the duration of the war; that is, unions, for example, could still negotiate for wage increases for their members, but the increases would be payable only in the form of credits to the members' savings accounts which could not be drawn out until after the war. (As is proper in a democracy, a provision could be made for some measure of leniency in proven cases of individual hardship.)

The actual procedure which has been followed is to limit people's purchasing power indirectly. In part there is high taxation during war-time, but for the most part the government purchases wartime supplies by issuing bonds. Some of these are acquired by individuals or businesses; some are bought by state, local, and federal government agencies; and approximately 40 per cent of federal government securities are held by banks. The bank-held bonds are "hot." They can be used as a basis for creating bank deposits either for the government directly or for war contractors who furnish supplies to the government. More than that, when an ordinary neighborhood bank holds government bonds it can use these to obtain more money to buy more government bonds. The neighborhood commercial banks can do this by selling currently held bonds to certain large banks which operate only to serve the needs of smaller bankers. After selling some government bonds or borrowing on their collateral value, the neighborhood bankers are credited with deposits on the books of their regional "bankers' bank"—for example, the Kansas City regional bank.

This places the neighborhood banks in a position to extend credit to the government or to war contractors. War production being done through private entrepreneurs in local communities, the neighborhood banks are naturally used by the military agencies of government who arrange loans and pay for local war production services by drawing checks on the local banks which have granted the government credit. The war contractors pay their bills by first depositing the government checks which they receive and then writing checks on these deposits.

Observe that so far as bank-held government bonds are concerned, there is very little saving, in the sense of postponed consumption, if any. In effect, the government is printing money or allowing check circulation to multiply. This would create no difficulty if the situation were that of a gap in the monetary circulation. But in wartime the reverse is true: there is an overage of aggregate demand. The result is that the government must strive to restrain the use of the very purchasing power which it helps to create by paying its own employees with newly created money at a time when extra goods are not available, and by allowing war contractors to pay their help with "hot money." This calls for wartime price controls, soon followed by wage controls and direct rationing. The civilian morale would be badly damaged if these were not instituted, for then prices would soar and long queues of housewives trying to buy scarce goods would form.

If wartime direct rationing to forestall inflation were the only consequence of government borrowing from banks, it would merely be a way of going without certain civilian goods which in wartime necessarily cannot be forthcoming—new cars, stainless steel kitchens, electronics, home appliances, and so forth. But the inflationary fact is that the government's bond issues become cumulatively larger, even though some of them are always being bought back by the government. The point is that the government, acting through the regional and Washington bankers' banks, only buys bonds back in order to be able to issue several times that amount of new government bonds. Thus the federal government's gross debt rose from $43 billion in 1940 to $259 billion in 1945.

While the tanks, planes, and battleships were all paid for at the time by using the nation's real resources which could have been applied to civilian production in peacetime, the necessary investment in military hardware was not *financially* paid. The goods are gone, but a quarter of a trillion dollars' worth of wartime national debt has yet to be repaid, to bank and nonbank investors. This of course violates all known economic principles of debt incurment and debt repayment— but then, war defies all known principles, not only those of economics.

POSTWAR DEBT

Emerging from World War II with a public debt of $259 billion, the American economy was somewhat in the position of a farmer who has used up some tractors, combines, and other productive equipment but must still pay for them. Fortunately, though, the American owes the debt to himself, so that no outsiders can attach our current productive assets. Moreover, the American economy now has more productive equipment than it did before World War II and therefore has the ability to pay at least the interest on the debt. Still, the heritage of wartime debt is not to be dismissed lightly by saying that we owe it to ourselves and can afford to pay the interest.

In the first place, the interest scheduled to be paid on the national debt in 1959 amounted to $8 billion—not an inconsiderable amount of money. More important than this, government securities held by banks and large corporations exist to add fuel to the fires of inflation, should they be fanned to any intensity. A large national debt imposes definite requirements for debt management by fiscal means, that is, by direct intervention in the stream of private incomes in the nation's economic circulation.

First, it must be frankly acknowledged that there is no known way of retiring an amount of debt so large as to equal one year's total consumer spending without throwing the nation into a terrible depression. Hence the debt is "here to stay." The best which can be hoped is that it will become a diminishing percentage of GNP. As Table 12–1 shows, this is happening.

Table 12–1. Ratio of Federal Debt to GNP, 1947–57,
by Three-year Intervals
(including categories not subject to statutory debt limitation)

Year	Debt as Percentage of GNP
1947	112
1950	95
1953	80
1956	75

SOURCE: U.S. Department of Commerce, Bureau of the Census, *Statistical Abstract of the United States, 1957* (Washington, D.C.: Government Printing Office), Tables 361 and 462, pp. 297 and 386.

The *real* burden of the debt is not completely shown in this table, because during the Korean war part of the rise of national income was due to military purchasing which did not detract from, but also did not add to, living standards. Thus the 80 per cent ratio for 1953 (and also for 1952) understates the matter. However, the tendency of GNP to "overcome" the national debt is definitely in existence. What will have been accomplished by 1975 or the year 2000 the writer leaves for more daring "projectionists" to imagine. To the skeptical mind the matter is somehow reminiscent of Alice's experience in Wonderland when she was getting smaller, and smaller, and . . . .

The national debt is not to be viewed as an isolated factor but must always be seen in relation to the national income, output, and employment. This may best be appreciated by considering what would constitute sound debt management in the case of recession or depression.

DEBT MANAGEMENT IN DEPRESSION

Suppose that 17 million persons (or 10 per cent of our population—the actual unemployment percentage in 1933) were involuntarily unemployed and remained unemployed despite the government's efforts to stimulate business revival by such indirect approaches as lowering taxes. Obviously, then, the government could not raise revenue by taxation. Yet, the government could legitimately view the 17 million unemployed not only as citizens in need but also as a valuable labor force which, when engaged in production, would create real and substantial additions to the national income. Having failed to stimulate recovery in any other way, the government might plan to set some public works projects in motion, perhaps using all of the 17 million unemployed in part-time employment (perhaps some part-time and some full-time).

If this were done, the unemployed would pay their own way. In part they would actually create assets such as schools, hospitals, highways, airfields, housing, and so forth. In part the people on work relief would indirectly pay their way by spending their wages, thus helping to restore business confidence. Sooner or later the people working on emergency public works projects could leave their relief jobs and return to their former positions in private industry.

During the Great Depression the Swedish government employed many people on a vast project of electrifying farms, railroads, and other productive facilities. To this day the Swedes claim that their superb electrified railway system did not "cost them a cent." In other words, they are saying that if they had put the same people on the dole, it would have cost much money without anything being added to the community's store of productive assets. In the United States during the depression there was so much political opposition to constructive public works that many projects were undertaken merely to "make work." But important additions were also made to the nation's real wealth, as has already been mentioned.

To return to the hypothetical case of 17 million unemployed: Up to $35 billion annually could be allocated easily for creative public works activity which could be undertaken. At least $3.5 billion could be applied to low-cost public housing, which in the mid-1950's was allotted only one-seventh that much—with continued ugly evidences of neglect in the blighted sections of our major cities. If health centers were constructed for every 50,000 people, equipped with research facilities, and open to all persons carrying low-cost public health insurance, another $3.5 billion could be spent at the minimum. This would improve health services for 10,000 American communities at least, especially for rural farm and nonfarm communities. It would mean some 600,000 or more hospital beds added throughout the nation. And the added service would not eliminate private medicine; it would simply relieve 20 per cent of our people from chronic medical debts, especially younger people.[2] A billion dollars' worth of investment in improved nutrition and child care would not be an exorbitant price to pay in subsidies to schools for hot lunches and for child-care centers in an age when so many parents are at work during the day. For education an additional $7 billion annual budget for buildings and teacher-training would serve to lift education from the category of one of the few "depressed industries" in an age of potential plenty. Highway construction and conservation projects are ready for $10 billion at least to get improvements under way. Another $10 billion worth of projects could be undertaken for: (1) expanding the nation's recreational and cultural facilities—teenage canteens, adult centers, beaches, civic operas, art galleries, and the like; (2) encouraging home improvements by home-owners and landlords; (3) further extending private and social insurance coverage; and (4) numerous other worthy purposes to improve community life and to secure the freedom of the individual from ugly social surroundings.

These suggested data are estimates; and they are conservative. They are mentioned because many Americans wonder what would happen if "peace should break out," thereby greatly diminishing the need for military spending. When it is considered that military spending presently includes extensive educational training for young persons, the problem is reduced in scope, for much of that work would be continued under civilian auspices. The same is true of much valuable research now being done under military auspices. Besides, there is no apparent political possibility in sight for reducing military spending to any low amount such as was *customary* in the United States up to World War II. However, there is reason to hope that the international armaments race will slow down to a more sensible pace, because the risk of atomic obliteration has now become universal and destruction would not be confined to distant battlefields. In short, if peace is in the offing, economists can only say: "So much the better, we can afford it!"

Financing public works in peacetime. When public works are undertaken to shore up aggregate demand in a depression, the financial procedure closely resembles that of war financing. The federal government would, of course, find it impossible to finance works projects

[2] See *Federal Reserve Bulletin,* June, 1955 (Washington, D.C.: Government Printing Office), supplementary Table 16, p. 620.

by increasing taxation. Hence it would borrow money from the banking community. There is, however, a significant difference between war financing and depression financing. In a depression the government would not first have to buy bonds from the banks and then allow the banks to use the proceeds for credit expansion and for buying more government bonds. Business and personal bank loans are curtailed under depression conditions; consequently, the banks would have free reserves with which to buy government bonds.[3] The multiplier principle would go into effect, though not necessarily to the full theoretical extent of a threefold increase in economic activity for every dollar of public investment. Then the newly acquired government securities would permit the neighborhood banks to extend credit freely to local merchants and manufacturers. The abundance of money also would keep interest rates low, so that investment would be encouraged—provided only that the marginal efficiency of capital did not fall at the same time.

Observe that, of necessity, the national debt will increase as the government issues bonds to finance public works. This is called *deficit financing*. There is, however, no comparison between this kind of increase in the national debt and the augmentation of wartime debt, and this is true both quantitatively and qualitatively. We entered the Great Depression with a net federal debt of $16.5 billion and emerged with a net debt (in 1939) of $43 billion. Calculated in dollars of 1929 purchasing power, the 1939 debt actually amounted to $56 billion (because the dollar's purchasing power increased, owing to the low prices of depression). Thus there was an increase of $40 billion in the national debt. But the National Resources Committee estimates that we lost $200 billion of potential national income which might have been realized if there had been full employment. As it was, there was an average annual unemployment of 10 million persons during that period.

This experience has led to virtual agreement among economists, bankers, businessmen, and labor and farm leaders that deficit financing (that is, increasing the national debt) is the lesser evil of depression.[4] As a matter of fact, the modern interpretation of sound debt management considers the *quality* rather than (within reasonable

[3] Commercial bank loans to businessmen, farmers, and consumers declined from $36 billion at the end of June, 1929, to $16 billion at the end of June, 1933.

[4] In this paragraph I quote extensively from *A Compendium of Materials on Monetary, Credit, and Fiscal Policies,* a collection of statements submitted to the subcommittee on monetary, credit, and fiscal policies by government officials, bankers, economists, and others of the Joint Committee on the Economic Report. 81st Congress, 2nd Session, U.S. Senate Document No. 132 (Washington, D.C.: Government Printing Office, 1950).

limits) the quantity of government investment as the prime criterion. If government investment results in additions to the community's store of productive assets, debt is no more to be feared than in the case of private investment. Total private indebtedness nearly matched aggregate public debt (federal, state, and local) from 1947 to 1950 and since then has exceeded it. Unquestionably, Professor Seymour E. Harris spoke for the majority of economists when he said that: "The guiding principle should be to contribute to a healthy economy. An annual balancing of the budget is undesirable. Debt should be accumulated in periods of decline and retired in periods of overexpansion. So long as debt charge remains in a reasonable proportion to national income, there is little danger in a rising debt." To this the words of industrialist Meyer Kestnbaum may be added: "There are no automatic guides to fiscal policy; the Government must take into account changing conditions, new social forces, and conflicting pressures."

Taxation

Taxes are the prices we pay for community want-satisfaction. Not least among our general wants is the desire of Americans, in the aggregate, for full employment. Still, the subject of taxation is so closely interwoven with feelings of social justice, with productivity, and with general cultural evolution that it would be unwise to treat taxation with sole reference to employment stabilization.

In order that the government may carry on its activities it must resort to varied sources of income. The most general rule is to raise regularly recurring expenditures through taxation, but it has been seen that under extraordinary circumstances governments are justified in incurring indebtedness.

BASES OF TAXATION

Americans are traditionally inclined to view taxes with hostility. However, since taxes are the prices paid for publicly performed services, they should be judged by what one receives in return for one's expenditure. In one respect, however, taxes differ from the prices paid for articles of individual want-satisfaction. A tax is an obligatory price paid for the general benefits of organized community life, however little or much any particular public service may be used by the taxpayer. On the other hand, taxes are not imposed arbitrarily under our democratic way of life but are levied by legislatures in the light of manifest community wants as ascertained by the people's political representatives in the legislatures.

The Constitution, in Article I, Section 8, clause 1, bestows upon Congress the power to lay and collect taxes, and states that they shall be uniform throughout the United States. The Sixteenth Amendment, passed in 1913, further permits Congress to lay and collect differential taxes on incomes, from whatever source derived, and without apportionment among the several states.

The writers of the Constitution were familiar with Adam Smith's canons of sound taxation as presented in the *Wealth of Nations* (1776). Stated with masterly simplicity, they still remain applicable today.

1. *Equity*—a self-explanatory criterion.
2. *Certainty*—making it possible for people to plan their budgets in consideration of their tax obligations.
3. *Adequacy*—avoiding the false economy of not raising enough tax revenue and therefore having either to curtail vital public functions or levy special assessments.
4. *Flexibility*—making it possible for government to operate in terms of the needs of the times, instead of being confined by a rigid, ancient tax formula.
5. *Convenience of payment*—freeing citizens from the need of sacrificing living standards or selling property to meet tax payments.
6. *Economy in collection*—a much violated canon!

To the great Scotsman's tax canons we may add several new ones suited to the needs of our time:

7. Taxes should help to make the economy more stable by restraining aggregate demand in times of overage and stimulating demand when recession or depression threatens to occur.
8. Tax collections in good times should be at a high level so that the national debt may be gradually reduced by using tax surpluses *provided that* no socially necessary government functions are left unperformed.
9. Frequent tax changes should be avoided, for they have unsettling effects on business and personal expenditures planning.
10. A tax shall not transfer purchasing power from persons with a high propensity to consume to those with a strong tendency to withhold money from active circulation.

The additional tax criteria take the employment effect of taxation into account, whereas the original and still valid criteria of Adam Smith emphasize the effect which taxation may have on the efficient utilization of national resources.

Types of Taxes

Some general distinctions may be noted between major types of taxation, for example, the difference between direct and indirect taxation. Direct taxation is clearly visible: so many cents or dollars of tax on an article of consumption or a percentage of the price of that article. Sales taxes furnish the outstanding examples of direct commodity taxes. Indirect taxation means that the tax is added at the producer's level and is charged to the consumer in the form of increased prices of articles, the tax not being perceptible in the price. Cigarette and liquor taxes are of this nature. Another difference is that which exists between progressive and regressive taxation, which will be illustrated with regard to specific kinds of taxes.

PERSONAL AND PROPERTY TAXES

One of the earliest types of taxation was the poll tax—a uniform, direct levy on adult individuals. A poll tax illustrates what is meant by a *regressive* tax, for it may impose definite hardship on persons of limited means, who must pay the same amount of tax as do persons of ample financial standing. A rather recent equivalent of the poll tax is the retail sales tax, under which poor and rich alike pay the same tax on articles of ordinary consumption (shoes, drugs, and so forth); to the low-income recipient this obviously constitutes a relatively high tax burden. If a sales tax is levied merely on luxuries, this argument loses force, as low-income recipients are not likely to spend money on purely luxury items of consumption. The tax then becomes a *proportional* one, since the wealthy person will spend more on his want-satisfaction buying luxuries and his tax bill rises in proportion to his extravagance.

In the case of motor oil and gasoline taxes the verdict as to their equity is not easily made. But on balance such taxes are probably regressive, the automobile not being exactly a luxury article.

State taxes. State governments rely very heavily on sales taxes for about two-thirds of their total tax revenue; most of these are general and motor fuels taxes and taxes on alcoholic beverages and tobacco. But states also derive taxes from individual and corporate revenue, about one-fourth as much as from sales taxes.

Another source of state tax income is money to be spent for unemployment compensation which is collected on a federal level but returned to the states almost in its entirety. The federal payroll tax is collected from employers. It is probably shifted to consumers in the form of higher prices of consumption goods; hence the payroll tax is most likely a proportional one, the total amount which an individual pays varying with his consumption expenditure. Finally, states derive an appreciable part of their revenues from selling auto, business, fishing, and hunting licenses and the like—which are also taxes of sorts.

Inasmuch as most state taxes are either regressive or proportional, it may be said that state taxation systems do not rank high according to the criteria of equity and employment stimulation. Taxes which lie heavily on people's ordinary consumption are relatively unjust and discourage spending, which in turn is a handicap in regard to the maintenance of full employment in an economy geared to mass consumption.

Local taxes. For local governments, taxes on property furnish the main sources of revenue. Thus, 481 cities having 25,000 inhabitants or more collected $4.2 billion in taxes in 1957. Three-fourths of this amount was paid in the form of property taxes.

In earlier times, when the nation was largely agricultural, with small towns as trade centers, the amount of land ownership was perhaps a logical and fairly accurate measure both of one's ability to pay taxes and of the benefits received by the government's protection of one's property. Then a general property tax may have been suitable in all respects. In modern times, however, the value of intangible property such as stocks and bonds exceeds the value of real property, so that in the local government's chief reliance on property taxes, the land-owner and home-owner are penalized as compared with persons who derive their incomes from dividends or other intangible property sources.

INCOME TAXES

When toward the end of the last century it became apparent that property taxation would not suffice and was, moreover, unjust as a prime basis of taxation, a new source adapted to the realities of changing times was seen in a federal income tax. One of the chief recommendations for this sort of tax, from any point of view, was that it could not readily be avoided. Being a federal tax imposed on individuals who earn more than a minimum living wage, it would apply to a person's earnings wherever they originate in the nation, whether from landed, industrial, or natural wealth. Thus there would be no source of income which might escape taxation. The income recipient, to avoid being taxed for his share of the cost of government, would have to leave the United States. This is something few persons enjoying prosperity would care to do.

As for corporations, it was thought that the income tax would lie on net profits. Being taxed, these profits would, of course, be diminished. However, any attempt to shift the tax to consumers by raising prices would reduce sales volume and thereby profits, while at the same time inviting customer resentment. This would especially be the case with the excess profits of monopoly; a monopolist could hardly charge more than the traffic will bear—which he was presumed to be already doing.

Income taxation on a national basis has been used to finance *war* expenditures since the beginning of the eighteenth-century industrial revolution. England collected such a tax during the Napoleonic wars, and the United States collected a federal income tax between 1861 and 1871. In 1909 a federal excise tax on corporations was held to be constitutional, and in 1911 the state of Wisconsin passed a comprehensive income tax without losing citizens or business to adjacent states. Then, in 1913, the Sixteenth Amendment was passed, during the administration of Woodrow Wilson, giving constitutional sanction to the practice of income taxation which has persisted since that time.

FEDERAL INCOME TAX ON INDIVIDUALS

The present federal income tax on individual earnings is a graduated levy on incomes above exempted amounts of earnings (depending on the number of the wage-earner's dependents and certain allowable deductions). The tax obligation increases as the amount of taxable income increases. Taxable income is personal income minus allowable deductions. Say that a married couple has two children and that the income of the family head is $4,950. First he is allowed four exemptions of $600, one for each member of the family. Next the taxpayer is allowed to reduce his income by certain contributions to charity, expenditures for interest, taxes, extraordinary medical and dental expenses, child care, certain losses, and miscellaneous items. The taxpayer may list these deductions or he may take advantage of the provision for a "standard deduction." For persons earning less than $5,000 this is automatically allowed in a tax table attached to Form 1040, the regular income tax return which individuals make out every year. For persons earning $5,000 or more, the standard deduction is 10 per cent of gross income (as adjusted to allow for excluding sick pay and/or certain gains or losses from business or farming operations, including room rentals).

In this example the head of the household has a gross income of $4,950 and exemptions and deductions totaling $2,895. This leaves a taxable income of $2,055. Had the family experienced very unusual medical or dental bills, or losses by storm damage to the home, and so forth, the deductions might exceed $495; in this case the taxpayer would itemize his deductions instead of claiming a standard $495 deduction. Checking with the short-form tax table on the individual income tax return, Form 1040, this taxpayer finds that by not itemizing deductions he pays $416 on his gross income. Comparing $416 with $4,950 of gross income the rate of taxation is seen to be 8.4 per cent. It ought to be $411, or 8.3 per cent; why?

Incremental taxation of family and individual incomes. Observe how tax rates rise on *extra* income earned. Say that a family of four has an income of $7,000. On the assumption that the family head chooses to take the standard 10 per cent deduction, this family has a taxable income of $3,900 ($700 + [4 × $600] of individual exemptions). The tax will be $780, that is, 20 per cent of the taxable income at 1957 rates. Now, if the family head earns another $1,000, the rate on the taxable $900 of this additional amount of income is 22 per cent.

A family having a taxable income (after exemptions and deductions) of $28,000 would pay a federal income tax of $8,520 (in 1957). The *incremental* rate on the next $4,000, which brings this family's income from $28,000 to $32,000, is 47 per cent, making the tax on the $32,000 income $10,400. This incremental income tax acceleration is reflected in an increasing *average* rate of taxation. In the example the average tax rate for the $28,000 income is 30 per cent, but it is 32.5 per cent for the same family's increased income of $32,000. (Observe that the 47 per cent tax increment raises the average tax only by 2.5 per cent.)

Aggregate impact of progressive-rate income taxation. Although the increasing percentage of income taxation is spectacular as very high incomes are reached, the fact is that only 1 per cent of American families receive incomes of $25,000 and over, and only two-fifths of 1 per cent of individuals without dependents. Actually, the lowest income within the upper fifth of the 50 million American spending units, in 1956, was $7,000. Referring to Table 12–2, this means that

Table 12–2. Percentage of Gross Income Paid by Families and
Individuals, United States, 1957

Gross Income Received (before exemptions and standard deductions)	Percentage Paid in Federal Income Tax	
	4-Person Family	Individual with No Dependents
$ 5,000	8.5	20.0
7,000	11.0	23.0
15,000	15.0	30.0
25,000	23.5	39.0
50,000	36.5	53.0
100,000	51.0	67.0

four out of every five families were paying less than 11 per cent of their gross incomes for federal income taxes if there were four persons in the family, less than 13 per cent if there were three persons in the family, and less than 15 per cent if there were only the husband and wife. Individuals without dependents and earning $7,000 paid 23 per cent for federal income taxation, but 98 per cent of the taxpayers without dependents earned less than $7,000. These findings conform to earlier ones made in complete detail by Joseph A. Pechman for the year 1947, when income tax rates were at a high level compared with what they are now and are likely to be in the calculable future.

Pechman's studies also shed light on the effect of income taxation at a progressive rate on the equality of national income distribution. The data, which remain applicable, do not support the frequently heard allegation that federal personal income taxes are *drastically* redistributing income. (See Tables 12–3 and 12–4.)

Table 12–3. Impact of Federal Income Taxation by Income Fifths of Recipients, 1947

Category of Income Recipients	Income Before Tax	Income After Tax	Tax Paid Amount	Tax Paid Per Cent
Lowest fifth	$ 746	$ 737	$ 9	1.2
Second fifth	1,808	1,730	78	4.0
Third fifth	2,810	2,624	186	6.6
Fourth fifth	4,051	3,721	330	8.1
Highest fifth	8,975	7,459	1,516	17.0

SOURCE: "Distribution of Income Before and After Federal Income Tax, 1941 and 1947," in *Studies in Income and Wealth* (New York: National Bureau of Economic Research, Inc., 1951), Vol. 13, pp. 194–95.

Table 12–4. Relation of the Highest Fifth of United States Income Recipients to Successively Lower Fifths, Before and After Federal Income Taxes, 1947

Relation	Before Federal Income Tax (ratio)	After Federal Income Tax (ratio)
Highest fifth to lowest fifth	12.0:1	10.1:1
Highest fifth to second lowest fifth	5.0:1	4.3:1
Highest fifth to middle fifth	3.2:1	2.8:1
Highest fifth to fourth highest fifth	2.2:1	2.1:1

SOURCE: "Distribution of Income Before and After Federal Income Tax, 1941 and 1947," in *Studies in Income and Wealth* (New York: National Bureau of Economic Research, Inc., 1951), Vol. 13, pp. 194–95.

Rationale of progressive-rate taxation. Income taxation on a graduated basis has been justified on two grounds. (1) There is the logical argument of the "ability to pay," by which it is claimed that the utility of additional income to a person or family already enjoying high income is less than the utility of money to low-income recipients. By this reasoning, the $15,000 family paying a $2,250 income tax probably makes no greater sacrifice than a $5,000 family paying a $420 tax. Each tax dollar paid by the lower-income family deprives it of more necessary individual want-satisfactions than that which the higher-income family sacrifices. (2) Another argument for income taxation is the observable fact that most Americans seem to consider the "ability principle" fair and equitable, for they exert no strenuous efforts *as a majority* to have the income tax law repealed. (There exists a strenuously arguing minority which advocates repeal or drastic modification by means of a constitutional amendment which would limit the tax rate to 25 per cent.)

The progressive income tax is one of the means by which modern democratic states have counteracted a marked tendency toward extreme concentration of income and wealth. Gross inequality of incomes developed in America after the Civil War and lasted well into the 1920's. Had not the tendency been retarded, the propensity to consume in the American economy might have declined to such an extent that mass production could have faltered because of a lack of sustaining mass consumption. Indeed, there are those who maintain that the Great Depression was caused by maldistribution of income and wealth; this is an oversimplification, but the assertion has a kernel of truth. That is why a present-day movement to limit federal income tax rates to 25 per cent of individual gross income has not been sanctioned by the responsible and conservative Committee for Economic Development.

CORPORATION INCOME TAXES

Before World War II the ordinary tax rate on corporate incomes was below 20 per cent. During World War II the rate was raised to 40 per cent, then cut to 38 per cent following the war, where it remained until after the Korean conflict. Since that time the rate of corporate income taxation increased to 52 per cent, at which level it has remained for the time being. This present rate is comprised of a 30 per cent normal tax applicable to all taxable incomes of all corporations, and a 22 per cent surtax. If a corporation's taxable income does not exceed $25,000, no surtax need be paid; that is, the rate of taxation is 30 per cent. Four out of every five corporations fall into this category of small corporations exempt from the 22 per cent surtax. Nevertheless, the bulk of the economy's output is produced by the lesser percentage of large corporations which pay the normal tax plus the surtax, that is, 52 per cent of their incomes. Because of the great earnings of large corporations, the weighted average of corporation income tax payments is approximately 45 per cent.

Economics of the tax. Much controversy has raged over the merits or demerits of this tax, but so far it has been found politically acceptable. Economists are inclined to agree that the tax cannot be shifted by the corporation to consumers by charging higher prices for goods. The reason is that the tax is levied on net earned income; it is not a cost of production. In other words, the net income above cost on which the tax is paid is earned on the basis of prices realized for goods. These prices the corporation has no power to fix if it is in strong competition. If, on the other hand, the corporation has a monopoly on its goods, it will presumably charge "what the traffic will bear." To attempt to raise prices beyond that point would be self-defeating, as customers would be lost. No monopolist is in a position of absolute control; there are always some potentially competing products, even though normally they would not be considered alternatives by the monopolist's customers. The monopolist has only the choice of paying the tax or losing money by losing customers, and he prefers to pay the corporation income tax.

Of course, this does not dispose of the issues of whether the corporate income tax is equitable and efficient and whether it has a favorable employment effect. Some argue that it is unfair to tax a stockholder via the corporation income tax and also on the dividends which he receives from the corporation. To this the reply is often made that corporations retain earned profits which, were they distributed in dividends, *would* be taxed. It also is argued that well-situated managements are tempted to incur costs of production which they would avoid if they did not feel that increased profits are to be shared with the government. Another way of stating this argument is to say that the corporate income tax raises tax considerations to a dominant place in business decision-making. But is this necessarily an evil? Some who favor the tax argue that entrepreneurs are led to improve the efficiency of their operations because in that way more profit will be earned, and will be available even though the government also receives a greater amount in taxes.

What of the employment effect of the corporation income tax? Here, too, there is controversy. The tax has been defended on the ground that it neither curbs potential investment overages nor intensifies depressions, for when no profits are earned the tax obligation does not exist. On the other hand, it has been argued that the revenue received, and spent, by the government during good times contributes to overages of effective demand.

Enough has been said to show that the corporation income tax is a matter of much controversial uncertainty. One fact is certain, however: that the tax is estimated to yield one-fourth of the total of anticipated federal cash receipts. The *real* uncertainty, therefore, is where this amount of revenue would come from if the tax were abolished or appreciably curtailed. Alternatively, should government functions be curtailed to the measure of a corporate tax reduction? If so, which functions?

As the matter stands, it is generally acknowledged that (1) the large modern corporation is a key institution of the American economy and it is reasonable to ask that it play a major role in the nation's tax system; (2) profits *after* taxes have been adequate, sufficiently so to permit the corporations to undertake huge investments which have made possible "productivity breakthroughs" along many lines. In brief, the technical ingenuity of American management and the satisfactory state of American labor-management relations have made it possible for the corporations not only to produce massive quantities of goods for individual want-satisfaction but also to become outstanding contributors of taxes used in satisfying many collective wants. In effect this constitutes a new structuring of the American economy, one which, on balance, is acceptable to most people throughout the nation. Moderate reductions of the corporation tax are to be anticipated, but the tax, as a matter of practice and principle, is here to stay.

Tax Policy for Economic Stabilization

On the matter of the proper tax policy for economic stabilization there is a conservative and a liberal position. Both depart from a mature recognition of the fact that high taxation is part and parcel of the institutional structure of twentieth-century capitalism. The conservative approach is to be distinguished from views held by a reactionary minority which desires return to regressive taxation and a heavy "axing" of government welfare functions. The liberal view is not to be confused with the revolutionary aim of "soaking the rich." Because the conservative and liberal views envisage a large role for government and necessarily, therefore, high levels of taxation, it is well to proceed with the explanation of these views using Table 12–5, which recapitulates the federal tax situation.

Table 12–5. The Role of the Federal Government Viewed Budgetwise, United States, 1958

Background Data

1958 federal government receipts from the public, fiscal year	$ 81.9 billion
1958 national income, fiscal-year basis	360.0 billion
Ratio of receipts to national income	23%

Federal Government Programs, Fiscal Year 1958

The over-all picture:

Anticipated receipts	$86.0 billion	Actual receipts	$82.0 billion
Planned outlays	83.5 billion	Actual outlays	$83.5 billion
Planned cash surplus	$ 2.5 billion	Realized deficit	—$ 1.5 billion

Specific programs, classified by function (as percentages of $83.5 billion total outlay):

Protection:		
National security	52.0%	
International affairs	3.5	
Total protection		55.5%
Administration:		
General government (including the post office)	4.0%	
Gross interest on debt	6.5	
Payments to social security, to trust funds, and of benefits	13.0	
Total administration		23.5%
Welfare:		
Human resources development:		
Veterans' services and benefits	6.5%	
Public assistance	2.0	
Housing and community development	1.0	
Public health	0.8	
Public education	0.7	
	11.0%	
Development of man-made and natural resources:		
Highways	2.0%	
Agriculture	6.0	
Natural resources	2.0	
	10.0%	
Total welfare		21.0%
Grand Total, 1958 federal government programs		100.0% ($83.5 billion)

SOURCES: *Statistical Abstract of the United States, 1958,* Table 460, pp. 369–70; *Federal Reserve Bulletin,* September 1958, pp. 1094, 1122.

When the federal tax situation is seen in this perspective, it can be truly appreciated. The sources of the tax funds which will be required for the budgeted federal government activities are characteristically in the proportions given in Table 12–6.

Table 12–6. Percentage Distribution of Budget Receipts
of the Federal Government

Type of Tax	Percentage Contribution to Total Tax Receipts
Individual income taxes	50 to 55
Corporation income taxes	30 to 33
Excise taxes	20 to 12
Customs, employment taxes, etc.	18
Deduct: Transfers to social security funds and refunds of receipts (excluding interest)	—18
Total	100

SOURCE: Executive office of the President, Bureau of the Budget, *Budget of the United States Government.*

The conservative position on tax policy. The conservative point of view on taxation has been succinctly stated by the Committee for Economic Development in these words:

Set tax rates to balance the budget and provide a surplus for debt retirement at an agreed high level of employment and national income. Having set these rates, leave them alone unless there is some major change in national policy or conditions of national life.[5]

This is what economists refer to as the "automatic stabilizer" device for using taxation to support employment. As a family's or an individual's income rises, so does his tax and, therefore, the revenue received by the federal government; both tax and revenue rise automatically. The tax *rates* are constant (at different income levels), but the government's income rises when the national income does and falls when the national income declines. "This automatic fluctuation of government's tax revenues is the aim of the stabilizing budget policy," says the Committee. And it is advocated that even though a recession occurs in total economic activity, tax rates should remain unaltered. For if that involves the government in deficit financing, the effect of the government's incurring a deficit will be to inject additional money into the stream of circulation, thus helping to cushion the fall.

Why is this a *conservative* position? The reason is that it binds the government to an automatic formula instead of granting it free discretion to alter tax rates, that is, to use fiscal policy with the deliberate purpose of influencing the propensity to consume and the inducement

[5] Committee for Economic Development (CED), *The Stabilizing Budget Policy— What It Is and How It Works* (New York: July, 1950), p. 8.

to invest in terms of the actual circumstances at a particular time of prosperity or depression. Or better, it places discretion in the hands of Congress to alter tax rates, instead of giving the President the authority to do so within specified limits. The difference is illustrated by the former and the present management of the tariffs on imports from abroad. In the past these rates were determined by Congress, but in recent times authority has been granted to the Executive Department to make trade agreements with foreign countries under which the President is free to lower existing tariffs by as much as 50 per cent. This gives him latitude in negotiating favorable terms of trade. Likewise, in dealing with threatening unemployment or inflation, the Chief Executive would benefit by being able to proceed, within reasonable limits, without perhaps having first to call Congress into special session.

An example may be given. Supposing the Council of Economic Advisors interprets a downturn in business as the start of a major depression, not simply as a minor inventory readjustment of business. Under the automatic stabilizer policy the tendency of Congress would be to postpone or retard large-scale national development projects such as school construction or river basin development. The reason is that even though total tax revenues are now declining, the tax *rates*, being unaltered, painfully "pinch" reduced incomes. This is the type of political climate in which Congress finds it difficult to vote substantially increased appropriations for a vigorous program of public works expansion, even though it is to be supported by deficit financing. That has been observed time and again, but now the existence of a statutory limit on the present amount of the national debt would make it particularly difficult; it would mean that Congress would first have to vote to remove the debt ceiling! If instead the President were authorized to manage a flexible public works budget, at any time and within limits at his discretion, he could have a reserve list of construction contracts and so forth prepared, ready to be let out immediately.

THE LIBERAL POSITION

The liberal point of view focuses more positively than does the conservative position on the amount and quality of aggregate consumption. An example of this viewpoint is the following excerpt from the President's *Economic Report* of January, 1953, submitted to Congress by Harry S. Truman. Observe the pronounced emphasis on a possibly developing long-run problem of aggregate demand shortage. This emphasis was made at a time when in some quarters almost extreme reliance was placed on automatic decreases of tax collections and automatic increases of social security benefits to protect us in the event of a recession. The *Report* states:

... although consumption levels since 1945 have been high, total real per capita consumption has increased very little. In relative terms, as a percentage of disposable income, consumption was not extraordinarily high in the postwar pre-Korean period, despite the fact that it too was subject to the additional stimulus of accumulated shortages. And as a percentage of total production, consumption held fairly steady in the neighborhood of 69 per cent up through 1950, and then, under the joint impact of the security program and a higher savings rate, tumbled to about 63 per cent in 1951 and 1952—the latter at a time when fixed business investment as a per cent of total output remained at or somewhat above its high postwar pre-Korean rates.

It would be dangerous to try to identify any single ratio between private investment and consumption that would be uniquely compatible with a balanced economic growth at some particular annual rate. However, the rough comparisons just indicated seem to justify a presumption that some relative gain in consumption sooner or later will be necessary.

The liberal point of view is not opposed to private investment. Far from opposing private investment, liberals encourage government efforts to create a favorable climate in which private accumulation may flourish. Still, in return they look to the business community for providing a favorable climate for government policies to work effectively toward the end of economic stabilization.

In the end, tax policies are decided by the freely expressed votes of the people. The current drift of public opinion is distinctly in favor of the use of government tax power to assist in economic stabilization, and to do so on an expanding scope of executive discretion. To the ancient article of faith that "the power to tax is the power to destroy" has been added a proviso, namely, that the nonexercise of this power may also be fatal.

For Discussion

1. What should be the guiding principle of the government's spending policies: to achieve an annually balanced budget even though national income and price levels fluctuate? to achieve a deficit at all times? to achieve a surplus at some times and a deficit at other times? (What other times?)

2. If the budget should not be balanced annually so that national debt will not increase, what principles and general considerations should guide the authorities in determining the amounts of deficit or surplus, and under what conditions to incur a deficit or accumulate a surplus? Are there principles which are likely to hold good for all social circumstances, considering that there is always social change?

3. What are the principal limitations on the effectiveness of fiscal policy as an instrument of economic stabilization?

4. What administrative difficulties do you believe exist under the present setup, with Congress making the major decisions on the nation's debt and the

President able only to make recommendations? Would this matter if the Executive belonged to the same party as the Congressional committee leaders?

5. Since the real economic burden of war must fall on the generation fighting the war and cannot be shifted to future generations, why is there any problem of a war debt?

6. Supposing that a nation were to finance war expenditures solely through a progressive income tax. What would be the probable effect on the economy of the nation? Would there be an increase in the amount of aggregate purchasing power in the nation? Would the supply of money increase? Would there be a change in the distribution of income?

7. "Taxes are paid in the sweat of every man who labors," said an eminent American. Does this mean that the best form of taxation is that which imposes the least amount of taxation?

8. "If the corporation tax were repealed, the general level of prices would decline at least 15 per cent." Discuss.

9. When an aged widow with an independent income of $2,200 pays $150 in income taxes even though receiving double exemption for being over 65, can it be said that our income tax is really progressive? Cite other examples, arguing pro and con.

10. Would raising the federal income tax exemption, per individual, from $600 to $1,000 increase consumption and employment after a recession had set in? Would *repeal* of the Sixteenth Amendment serve as a tonic to overcome recession?

13 Monetary Policy
for Economic Stabilization

There will always be enough money to finance high-level economic activity if the business world is willing to undertake it. Bank credit is the artful invention for satisfying the voracious needs of industry and consumers. It helps circulate ever greater masses of goods, as productivity breakthroughs continue to be achieved in the factories and on the farms. Today we are no longer plagued by money supplies which are too rigid, too erratic, and too perverse to suit the needs of business; we have solved the currency shortage question which Disraeli felt made more people mad than love did.

At present the currency question is whether money which can be made abundantly available will be correctly *used*. It is a question of the demand for money, a facet of the general problem of aggregate effective demand. Will people wish to take advantage of our highly flexible money supply when business confidence is low and unemployment is on the increase? Per contra, when aggregate demand is temporarily excessive (that is, when people want more things than there are resources for making them), can a mere restriction of the *supply* of money stop rises in the cost of living? What guidance can democratic government give in these matters?

The purpose of this chapter is to equip the reader with a firm understanding of the problems of money-use or money-demand in an age of potential plenty. This will involve departures from traditional

thinking, but not from the dedication with which the classical economists aimed to explain the money-supply problems in an age of currency scarcity. In this spirit it may be stated, as a motto for the ensuing
discussion, that money can be no sounder than the expectations of
businessmen, and no more effective than their desire to use it.

The Human Nature of Modern Money

The role which democratic government can play in guiding the
economy's use of money can never be one of applying preconceived
controls which are expected to operate mechanically. In dealing with
money one is dealing with people and must therefore be as much a
student of social psychology as of the statistics of money flow. Curtis
and Townshend have emphasized this in well-chosen words:

... the behavior of money ... is the result of the behavior of a very large
number of human units, all of whom use their own or other people's money,
or fail to use it, for buying from one another. In using money they are
influenced by a complex and varying combination of habit, sentiment, and
rational calculation.[1]

After emphasizing that people sometimes "run herd" by indulging
in common moods of overoptimism or excessive pessimism, these experts go on to say that two means of directing the flow of money are
available to monetary authorities, neither of them being strictly reliable. The government can:

... intervene in the markets as one among all the other buyers and sellers—
one operating on a larger scale and with very much larger resources; but even
so its intentions may be nullified by a considerable movement of other buyers
and sellers in the opposite direction. Or it may act by influencing, as it alone
has the means to do, the expectations, and therefore the decisions, of the other
buyers and sellers; but human minds are of intractable material, and the effort
to mold them may be unsuccessful.

A prime example was the plight of American financial and political
authorities when practically every effort they made to stop money
from flowing out of circulation from 1929 to 1933 was either ineffective or was actually reversed by a distressed business community.
This does not mean that dollar bills were locked in vaults, but that
incoming money was used to pay off debts or to acquire financial
ownership of already existing productive facilities, rather than being
spent to increase the community's store of tangible wealth. The

[1] Myra Curtis and Hugh Townshend, *Modern Money* (New York: Harcourt, Brace
& Co., Inc., 1938). This and the following quotation are from pp. 268–69.

country's chief financial authority had therefore to report lamely, in 1933, that:

Although the abundant credit provided [since 1930] was not effectively employed by business, it would appear that the maintenance continuously of a substantial volume of excess reserves through open-market purchases helped to arrest a powerful deflationary movement and created conditions propitious to business recovery.[2]

The snags in money control in the opposite case of inflation may be gleaned from this remark of the Chairman of the Board of Governors of the Federal Reserve System, made in August, 1957:

Unfortunately, during the past year, as price indexes gradually rose, some segments of the community apparently became reconciled to the prospects of a "creeping" if not a "runaway" inflation. If further inflation is expected, the *pattern* of investment and other spending—the decisions on *what kinds* of things to buy—will change in a way that threatens balanced growth.[3]

Two months later this warning was underlined by growing fears of "creeping *de*flation" stemming from previously unbalanced expansion. Truly, the path of monetary control policy is always a narrow one between the high cliffs of inflation and the deep swamps of depression.

Mindful that the essence of money is the use to which it is put, the following equations are useful in outlining the scope of the practices and problems of monetary control.

AN EQUATION OF MONETARY EXCHANGE

Let us view, *from the money side,* the economy's total stream of the purchasing and selling of goods and of financial transactions (as described in Chapter 1). For this purpose a classical symbolism originated by Irving Fisher is frequently utilized.[4] Let M stand for the quantity of currency in circulation—coins and the familiar paper money (mainly Federal Reserve banknotes and a lesser quantity of silver certificates). Let M' stand for the much larger amount of credit in circulation. This exists in the form of checks drawn on banks and also in the form of credit cards and charge accounts of consumers and businessmen who grant "trade credit" to each other. Bank deposits which are not drawn on or unused charge accounts do not constitute credit for the purpose of our analysis; it is important to bear that always in mind.

---

[2] *Annual Report of the Federal Reserve Board,* 1933 (Washington, D.C.: Government Printing Office), p. 21.

[3] William McChesney Martin, "Winning the Battle Against Inflation," statement before the Committee on Finance of the United States Senate, August 13, 1957, *Federal Reserve Bulletin,* August, 1957, pp. 871–72.

[4] *The Purchasing Power of Money* (New York: The Macmillan Co., 1911).

Now, the active *M* plus the active *M'* comprises the supply of money. This money flow represents the aggregate amount of currency and credit which is utilized in effecting the individual exchanges of all the items which comprise a total physical output of goods and services. Let the *number of* goods and services transactions (including financial transactions) be labeled *T*. Evidently, then, if there is a large supply of money, each unit of the total of transactions may absorb more units of money or credit. This would mean that prices would be higher with a large money supply than with a limited one, *all other things being equal.* Mark well the italicized proviso of "all other things being equal." For if people's desires or preferences or incomes were to change, prices might rise or fall while the money supply remained absolutely stable. At the moment we are concerned only with price changes which may arise from the money side of economic circulation, not with fluctuations in consumer habits or business confidence. Of course the reason for focusing on money is to ascertain how such fluctuations in basic spending patterns might be counteracted by monetary manipulations.

Under the given circumstances the general level of prices must vary with the amount of the transactions as related to the supply of money. Following the foregoing reasoning about the work of money, this might be expressed by the simple equation $(M + M') \div T = P$, where *P* stands for the general level of prices. Thus if there were a supply of coins to the value of $1 million and they were used in conducting 10,000 transactions in each of which only one unit of a commodity or service were exchanged, the unit price of the commodity or service would obviously be $100. (When one deals with millions of transactions in various goods and services which are priced differently, a statistical technique of the *index number* is used to express the general price level. This realistic complication can be overlooked for the moment because the relation of transactions to money supply, as expressed through price, is essentially the same as in the above example.)

Now, the simple equation $(M + M') \div T = P$ assumes that people never change the *rate* at which they use money or credit to conduct transactions. This is an untenable assumption. In times of brisk trade, money is turned over time and again; in depressed times a merchant, for example, may wait quite a while before he buys new merchandise. And the *rate* of money and credit utilization varies in good times, sometimes rising to feverish heights, as in the stock market speculation during the early and middle part of 1929. To illustrate, many corporations at that time lent some of their spare cash to stockbrokers for periods of very short duration rather than keep it in the bank even for forty-eight hours. Dollars literally raced in and out of the stock markets of the nation.

The rate of money and credit circulation is known as the *velocity* of money. When velocity is viewed as incomes generated by economic activity, rather than as concluded sales and purchase transactions, we speak of *income velocity*. Income velocity is measured by comparing the supply of money with the net national product, the value of all *final* output—GNP minus (net of) allowances for capital consumption. In 1957, NNP (net national product) was $402.5 billion and the supply of active money of all kinds was $134 billion. The income velocity was, therefore, 3.00 (402.5 billion divided by 134 billion). Another concept of velocity is that of *transactional* velocity. The author appraises this by comparing money supply to the total of money flows explained in Chapter 1. The money supply, in 1957, was $134 billion, and the total of money flows, preliminarily estimated, was $1.660 trillion. Dividing, we find that the transactional velocity was approximately 12; that is, each dollar was used twelve times in the circulation of goods and services among the economy's institutional transactions groups. This compares with an income velocity of 3.00 for the same year, 1957. Observe that the twin concepts of income velocity and transactional velocity simply represent the two aspects of the total economic circulation; that is, business creates incomes which people spend directly, or through government, to buy the products of business.

In the Fisher equation of exchange the income velocity is a factor to be considered. We now include it and label it V for coin and currency. Ignoring credit for the moment, the more complete equation of exchange (for coin and currency) now is $MV \div T = P$. Stated in words, the amount of money *times* its velocity, when compared with the amount of transactions, determines the price level, all other things being equal. To illustrate, let us again say that there are 10,000 transactions, each involving the exchange of only one unit of a commodity. The money supply is $83,333. However, each dollar is used twelve times in the course of 10,000 transactions. Substituting these amounts in the exchange equation, $\$(83,333 \times 12) \div 10,000 = \$100$, the per-unit price of the commodity in this illustration.

To complete the equation so as to include credit along with coins and currency, we use the symbol V' to stand for the velocity of the use of credit (how readily checks and charge accounts are used). The completed equation is $(MV + M'V') \div T = P$.

Implications of the Fisher exchange equation. The quantitative relationship of the Fisher equation highlights the role of government in supplying cash and currency and the role of the banking system and other financial institutions (such as life insurance companies) in supplying credit. Given the supply of currency and credit money, the equation also permits one to draw inferences as to the flow of trans-actions. Thus, if prices are falling while the supply of money is con-stant, it is obvious that transactions and/or velocity are diminishing. If employment declines, we must trace the cause of this diminution to enable us to take remedial action. On the other hand, if the price level is rising while the index of physical production is constant, there may be an inflationary situation. This may lead the government to attempt to induce the banking system to contract credit or to take direct action aimed at limiting the banking system's ability to expand credit.

Decisions to stimulate or discourage the expansion of the money supply, based on the general level of prices, are what is meant by *monetary policies*. These policies are oriented primarily to controlling credit, because most transactions in the United States are conducted with the use of credit, that is, "checkbook money." Of a money supply of $134 billion, in the second quarter of 1957, $106 billion was in the form of demand deposits which people held at the banks, and $28 billion existed in the form of currency in circulation.

The active bank deposits, which comprise most of our circulating money, do not simply consist of currency which people bring to the bank after having earned it, and which they subsequently make use of by writing checks to pay their bills. By far the greatest part of bank deposits is based on credit extended to a customer of the bank. *Credit* is a difficult word to define. Essentially it means pledging anticipated income to the banker as security for the right to draw checks on the bank immediately.

In that way a businessman can undertake further economic activity at once without waiting until he has actually received money by selling goods previously produced. Thus a farmer who has a sound expecta-tion of selling his crop may get a seed loan on this expectation and proceed to plant another crop. Or it may be that the farmer has sold the previous crop but must wait, say sixty days, before being paid. By receiving a bank loan he can proceed to plant the crop sixty days earlier than he otherwise would be able to do. This may make the difference between planting and not planting the new crop.

Credit, then, is a mobilization or undertaking of economic activity based on people's anticipated earnings. Thus credit provides a means of fitting the supply of money to the needs of business. Suppose instead that the supply of money were based on the amount of gold possessed by a country. The amount of gold in the whole world is quite limited, and the increment that can annually be added by the production of gold is greatly limited. Both the amount of gold produced in the past and the amount which could currently be produced have only a remote connection with the current needs of business. Thus there could be a fall of prices simply because M in the equation of exchange lagged far behind T, the transactional factor. Falling prices tend to discourage output and employment. Obviously it is advantageous to relate the supply of money directly to the needs of business. The following section explains how this is done.

Altering the Supply of Money

CREDIT EXPANSION

Commercial banks are the many local banks of the nation which are, literally, in the business of making money by creating money. Of approximately 14,000 local banks, 95 per cent are in a position to expand or contract credit money. This is done principally by extending short-term loans to customers—loans which take the form of creating a *demand deposit*. Against these deposits the customers draw checks (which are payable by the bank "on demand").

One of the big customers of banks since the Great Depression has been the government. Before that time, most of the credit creation by commercial banks was in response to the needs of private business. The credit granted was mostly short-term, lasting up to six months. Merchants and manufacturers who had sold goods, or had sound prospects of doing so, brought in *commercial paper*—promissory notes obtained from customers or warehouse certificates showing that the businessman has valuable goods on hand. The bank then gave him the right to draw checks against a specially created demand deposit. Observe that this is not a deposit in the ordinary sense of the word. However, receiving people's deposits of currency or checks is also a principal function of a commercial bank. In fact, creating deposits and receiving deposits go hand in hand, as will be seen shortly. In recent times, deposits have also been created for the government; the banks buy government bonds, or treasury notes, and pay for these purchases by creating deposits for government agencies to draw upon.

Creating checkbook money by establishing loan deposits does not mean that economic value is conjured out of the thin air. The new money actually represents "value added," or being added, by (1) private production for individual want-satisfaction, and (2) government service in furnishing community want-satisfaction. The best way to understand this is to eliminate government from the picture for a moment and to view only the process of supplying money for the needs of business.

Commercial credit creation. Business could conceivably be conducted on the basis of merchants' and manufacturers' receiving money for the sale of goods and services and depositing this money with bankers for safekeeping. Then, when bills came due, a businessman could go to the bank, ask for his money, and convey it personally to his creditors. However, this would be cumbersome. A long time ago businessmen discovered it to be more convenient to deposit their incoming revenues at banks and then, when bills came due, to draw checks against their accounts.

When all businessmen follow this practice, the interesting result is that actual money does not have to be conveyed at all to settle obligations. This is illustrated in Table 13–1, in which it is assumed that there is a community of only three merchants, each doing business with the other. It is also assumed that there is only one bank. Of course, there are millions of businessmen conducting transactions in the American economy, and thousands of banks. But this does not alter the fundamental principles of credit utilization.

Table 13–1. Simplified Illustration of Bank Clearing

1. Original Deposits with the Banker

    By businessman A $100
    By businessman B   90
    By businessman C   110

    Total $300

2. Subsequent Flow of Transactions

    A buys $50 worth of goods from B and $40 worth from C.
    B buys $45 of goods from A and $30 of goods from C.
    C buys $40 of goods from B and $50 of goods from A.

3. Orders to the Banker by Writing Checks

    A orders the banker to pay $50 to B and $40 to C.
    B orders the banker to pay $45 to A and $30 to C.
    C orders the banker to pay $40 to B and $50 to A.

    Total payments $255

4. Actions of the Banker

    A's account is credited with: $45 + $50 = $95
    His account is charged with: —($50 + $40)= — 90

    Which leaves a positive balance of: $ 5

    B's account is credited with: $50 + $40 = $90
    His account is charged with: —($45 + $30)= — 75

    Which leaves a positive balance of: $15

    C's account is credited with: $40 + $30 = $70
    His account is charged with: —($40 + $50)= — 90

    Which leaves a negative balance of: $20

5. Implication

    The $300 of deposits simply lies idle as payments are effected by the banker making notations on his books to indicate transfers of ownership title; i.e., A's ownership of money capital is increased by $5 and B's by $15; C's ownership is diminished by $20.

Table 13–1 shows economy being practiced in the use of money. Transactions worth $255 are conducted, but only $40 in money—$A$'s $5 balance plus B's $15 balance plus C's $20 balance—is needed to finance them. Even this $40 is not physically handled. The banker "cleared the balances" of the depositors by simply making entries on their accounts in his bookkeeping ledger. The original aggregate deposit of $300 is left undisturbed, only it is now differently distributed.

To make the illustration more realistic, let us drop the assumption that the original three businessmen, in the aggregate, maintain the deposit of $300. They too appreciate that money is always coming in to them while at the same time they are paying out money. But each, in turn, might find himself in the position of having to pay out more than he is receiving in sales revenue at the moment. To provide for this eventuality, let us say that each places $20 with the bank to cover a possible debit balance to his account. The rest of the money he can invest in plant and equipment or in any way he sees fit to expand.

Each of the three original businessmen consequently reduces his deposit to $20, for a total of $60 instead of the original $300 total deposit. Now we may presume that the three businessmen will continue to do $255 worth of business with each other. How do these depositors make these payments now that there is a total of only $60 on deposit? They do so by paying each other with *bills of exchange* instead of drafts on the banker. A bill of exchange is a promissory note, say of ninety days' duration. At the end of that period each businessman who issues a bill of exchange is obligated to pay the cash amount stated on the face of the bill. The recipient of the bill, however, does not desire to wait ninety days to collect his money. He therefore takes it to the bank as security for a ninety-day loan. The bank accepts his security and instructs him to write checks for the amount of the loan, charging a "discount" for the service of later collecting the money from the businessman's creditor.

The bank and each of the three borrowing businessmen have now become mutually indebted. The bank owes each borrower an immediate amount of money to the extent of his loan-created deposit. Each borrowing customer of the bank owes it a debt to be repaid ninety days later. By the time each businessman has reduced to zero the deposit which he borrowed from the banker, the banker will also have collected the money which was owed to him by these same businessmen.

The important observation is that by this credit arrangement the business community is able to purchase goods and hire services to an extent otherwise impossible. In our example, three businessmen now

transact with only $60 of combined deposits $255 worth of business which formerly was sustained by $300 of deposits. The money which is spared from deposits by the businessmen enters the circulation at once to quicken the wheels of profitable trade and production. But this is only the beginning of the story of credit.

Bank reserves. Throughout the economic system as a whole the withdrawals by checks and the deposits of checks must be in balance (including checks in transit). They are only different ownership aspects of the same total amount of money flows in the economy. That is to say, the money supply is geared to the transactional flows of which debit and credit are records of the mutual financial obligations of people.

However, for *any one individual bank* which does business along with many others, the amount of money flowing out only *approximates* the money flowing in. There may be a gap on some business days; hence it is wise to keep a reserve. A simple balance sheet, ignoring administrative details, may be drawn to illustrate the bank's operations as they are limited by the necessity of keeping, say, a 20 per cent reserve. (This is actually required only of large banks in certain central cities; most "country banks" are required to hold a 12 per cent reserve.) It will be assumed that $100,000 was originally deposited by the founders of a bank—whether in gold, paper money, and/or checks drawn on other banks, it matters not. From the date of the bank's foundation until the time of the beginning of our illustration, a business of $500,000 has been developed in loans and deposits. We take this background business (see Table 13–2) for granted and concentrate henceforth on what happens as the bank expands its volume of business.

Table 13–2. Bank X's Balance Sheet at Outset of Illustration

Assets		Liabilities	
Loans and Investments	$500,000	Capital	$100,000
Reserve (in cash or equivalent)	100,000	Demand deposits	500,000
	$600,000		$600,000

Since Bank X normally maintains a reserve-deposits ratio of 20 per cent, it, clearly, has neither an excess of reserve nor a reserve deficiency. It is loaned just up to its limit.

We now suppose that the bank acquires, through its new business efforts, another $100,000 in cash. The balance sheet will appear as shown in Table 13–3.

Table 13–3. Bank X's Position after Increase of Deposits

Assets		Liabilities	
Loans	$500,000	Capital	$100,000
Reserve	200,000	Deposits	600,000
	$700,000		$700,000

Of the new reserve just received, $20,000 will be required to support the new deposit liabilities of $100,000 that came into being as a consequence of the bank's acquiring new cash or its equivalent. Therefore, the bank at present has an excess or surplus reserve of $80,000. Under these circumstances the bank management will be prompted to increase its loans (and investments). If the borrowing customers of Bank X typically leave on deposit an average of 25 per cent of what they borrow and the bank makes new loans of $100,000, the balance sheet will then appear as in Table 13–4.

Table 13–4. Bank X's Position after Expanding Its Business

Assets		Liabilities	
Loans	$600,000	Capital	$100,000
Reserve	125,000	Deposits	625,000
	$725,000		$725,000

The balance sheet shows that Bank X has exactly $1 in reserve for $5 in deposit; it is again loaned up to the limit. The acquisition of the $100,000 of new reserve coming through deposit channels, when operated upon, finds reflection in increased loans of $100,000 and increased deposits of $125,000. Mark well that $75,000 of reserves was withdrawn by check or in cash after the additional $100,000 deposit (in Table 13–3) permitted the bank to expand its loans and investments.

Table 13–4 shows that an individual bank which operates in competition with many others cannot lend or create more purchasing power than it receives in the form of primary deposits from customers old or new. *Primary deposits* are those which arise from the acquisition by the bank of cash or checks or other cash equivalents brought by customers and deposited without any relationship to loans which these depositing customers might later make from the bank. By contrast, *derivative* deposits are those which would not be made by a customer had the bank not made him a loan. Thus, in computing Table 13–4, we assumed that the new borrowers of $100,000 left $25,000 at the bank on the average. The $25,000 is a derivative deposit; it arose only in connection with Bank X's increasing its loans, not because funds were newly brought to it. The derivative deposits, however, simply shore up the reserve position. Actually, Bank X received $100,000 in primary deposits and lent that amount in its turn.

What happens to the $75,000 which was checked away or carried away after the bank expanded its business?

MULTIPLE BANK CREDIT EXPANSION

By contrast to the above example, observe what happens *in the banking system as a whole* when there is an atmosphere of blatant business confidence. In that instance each of many banks receives checks drawn not only on itself but on other banks as well. The checks drawn on the other banks will be treated by each bank as *new* deposits and used as bases for extending credit. Of course these checks which are drawn against all the banks, and deposited in all the banks, will be sent in for collection. But they are not sent by each bank to the other banks. Instead, they are sent to a central clearing house, which exists, as a cooperative institution, in every large city. Each bank has an account at the clearing house, and on this account the checks drawn on the bank are debited, while money owing to the bank is credited to its account. Therefore the individual bank has only to settle the balance, sending cash or a check to the clearing house if it has a negative balance. The clearing house uses the money thus received to pay the banks which have positive balances. Great economy in the use of money is thereby effected, for the clearing system reduces the use of cash to an absolute minimum. Instead, entries on the books of banks that alter or create or extinguish *demand deposits* are the principal media of making payments and receiving incomes. In America we settle 90 per cent of our transactions not by actually using money but through the banks *in terms of* money.

To understand why bank credit is so pervasive, let us examine what happens to the *net* amount of deposits received by the banks in the form of cash paid by the clearing house to those banks which have positive balances at the end of the business day. Each bank which receives *net* deposits now lends 80 per cent of that amount, keeping 20 per cent in reserve.

The result is truly dynamic. To illustrate, let us say that a large bank, Bank Y, located in a major city, receives a check from the clearing house for a $10 million net deposit. For simplicity's sake it may be assumed that when Bank Y next lends $8 million of this, that entire sum is deposited in another bank, Bank B. Assuming that nothing happens in the banking system other than this particular transaction, Bank B will receive a clearing house check for $8 million. Of this it will lend $6.4 million, keeping $1.6 million (20 per cent) in reserve. To continue with these simplifying assumptions, the $6.4 million is deposited in its entirety in Bank C, which then receives a clearing house check in that amount.

The process continues until all the banks have become involved in it. Quite evidently, as this happens, the original $10 million deposit of Bank Y *virtually* keeps reappearing. That is to say, $8 million of the original $10 million deposited in Bank Y now leaves this bank rather than being merely transferred from account to account on the bank's ledger. Bank B, after receiving the $8 million, releases $6.4 million of this; and so the process continues until all the banks have had a part in it. The cumulative result is that the original $10 million deposit in Bank Y grows to $50 million of money in circulation, as Table 13–5 demonstrates. Observe that no one bank lends or creates more purchasing power than it receives, but that the banking system as a whole manifolds the $10 million originally deposited in Bank Y.

Table 13–5. Credit Expansion in the Economy, Hypothetical Illustration ($ millions)

Bank (a)	Addition to Deposits (b)	Addition to Loans (c)	Addition to Reserves (d)
Y	10.0	8.0	2.0
B	8.0	6.4	1.6
C	6.4	5.1	1.3
D	5.1	4.1	1.0
E	4.1	3.3	0.8
F	3.3	2.6	0.7
All other banks	13.1	10.5	2.6
Total	50.0	40.0	10.0

Column (*b*) of Table 13–5 indicates the scope of credit expansion when all the banks are in a buoyant mood regarding business profit expectations. It is seen that a $10 million deposit in Bank Y generated a total circulation of five times that much. Perhaps Bank Y was founded by a group of local businessmen who felt that the already established banks were overlooking opportunities. With Bank Y exploiting these opportunities as well as calling attention to other neglected earning opportunities for banks and their customers, the other banks were stimulated to produce an effect similar to that shown above. Whatever the circumstances, the above illustrates the nature of bank credit expansion. It can be reconstructed by bearing in mind these simple propositions:

1. A single commercial bank, *among many,* cannot effectively add to the community's supply of money when it attempts to move against the prevailing tide of banking and business sentiment.
2. All banks together can expand the money supply if they are so minded.
3. The theoretical outside limit of credit expansion by commercial banks is indicated by the reserve percentage. Given any particular percentage of reserve required to be kept or customarily kept, the theoretical total increment to the money supply from any given amount of original deposit (made in any form whatsoever) is ascertained by the formula $\triangle M' = 1 \div (1 - lf)$, wherein lf stands for the loanable funds after the reserve has been deducted from the deposit. Thus if the reserve percentage is 20, the formula reads: $\triangle M' = 1 \div (1 - \frac{4}{5})$, the $\frac{4}{5}$ being the part of the original deposit which is loanable. Now $1 \div (1 - \frac{4}{5}) = 1 \div \frac{1}{5}$, which, when solved, yields 5 as the value of what may be called the *credit multiplier.* In actual circumstances, however, there are leakages in this process of credit creation, so that 20 per cent reserves rarely create more than a threefold credit expansion.

Further possibilities for bank credit expansion. The reserves of the leading commercial banks are not kept in their vaults, nor do they necessarily constitute currency or checks. Some reserves can actually be in the form of deposits created by Federal Reserve banks, located in twelve major cities. These are "bankers' banks"; they do not deal directly with the public but only with member banks of the Federal Reserve System. Some 6,700 banks out of a total of 14,000 belong to the System. The member banks make over 90 per cent of all loans and investments because they are the largest banks in the nation.

PURPOSE OF THE FEDERAL RESERVE SYSTEM

The Federal Reserve System was founded as a national agency for providing the economy with a flexible supply of money. There has always been some confusion about what this means. Is the System to serve primarily to accommodate the needs of business or government or any other group with easily and cheaply available money? Or is the System intended to control the American economy broadly so as to prevent inflation or depression? By a "flexible money supply" do we mean one to be controlled at every moment so as to keep M (coin and currency) in the equation of exchange and, particularly, M'

(credit) in a stable relation with T (transactions) so as to preserve a stable level of prices? Or shall the System largely confine itself to the task of always supplying enough money to prevent business or government from suffering for the lack of it, even though prices generally may be rising?

In the early days of its operations (before World War I), the Federal Reserve System interpreted its mandate as requiring it to be cautiously but certainly generous in increasing for the nation's business and farmers the accessibility of credit. The general idea seems to have been that the System would flexibly provide money through loans made by the regional banks to local banks on the security of business or farmers' bills of exchange when the local banks had exhausted their own reserves for making loans and the local need for money was pressing. One region of the country might run low on bank reserves yet need money to move crops or to accommodate other needs of business and agriculture. The System, organized to unite twelve major regions, makes it possible for regions with surplus reserves to come to the aid of those regions which are temporarily short of reserves (for example, New York aiding California during certain western crop-moving seasons).

With war and depression have come demands that the Federal Reserve System also serve the needs of government to finance war or speed recovery from depressions. This has brought to the forefront a concept of "currency management"—the System is seen as an agency of economic control rather than exclusively a bankers' organization.

Structure and background of the Federal Reserve System. The twelve regions into which the country is divided for the purpose of administering the Federal Reserve System are shown in Figure 13–1.

Figure 13–2 presents an organization chart for the entire operation of the Federal Reserve System, including the role which the member banks play in selecting directors for the twelve regional banks and in contributing capital.

Referring to the right-hand side of the organization chart, the nearly 7,000 member banks are most often referred to simply as commercial banks, though sometimes they may be referred to as central city banks or country banks; the present writer occasionally uses the term "local banks" or "neighborhood banks" for member banks. Member banks have their own directors, who are chosen without any governmental requirements, just as are the directors of any private business. The member banks are private enterprises in business to gain profit literally by making money. This distinguishes the member banks from the twelve regional Federal Reserve banks, which are not profit-oriented. Member banks could conceivably terminate their membership in the System if they felt that the Reserve System's policy restricted them unduly in their profit-making. However, the member banks are generally aware that the System's administrators, whom they in part elect, shape their policies only after thorough consideration has been given to the private interests of the member banks, as well as to the public interest. Hence the member banks adopt recommended policies

Figure 13–1. The Federal Reserve System—Boundaries of the Federal Reserve Districts and Their Branch Territories

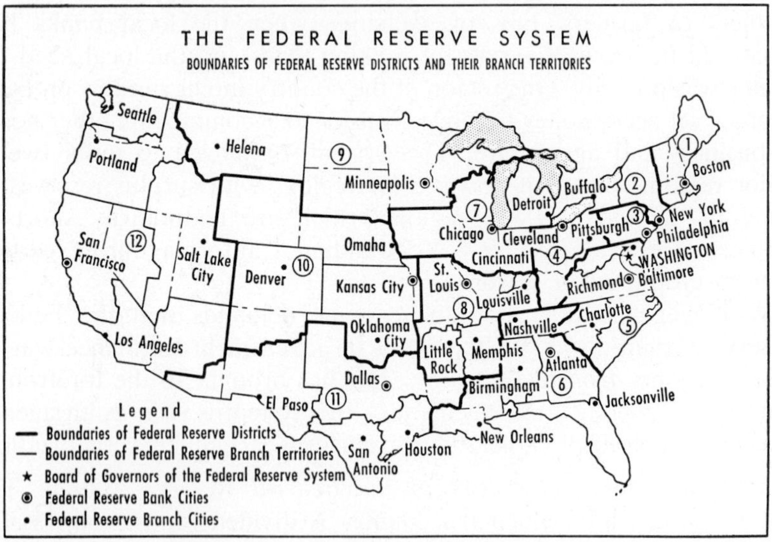

SOURCE: Board of Governors of the Federal Reserve System.

of the central Reserve banks, in the belief that it is a matter of enlightened, long-run self-interest, although it may seem to be costly at the moment.

As for the twelve Federal Reserve banks, each is a corporation organized and operated for public service; however, each bank is privately owned and operated. The stockholders of each bank are the member commercial banks in the region. Since the twelve Federal Reserve banks are organized fundamentally as bankers' cooperatives, they do not seek profit in dealing with their member banks; nor do the member banks receive dividends or enjoy the other powers or privileges of the stockholders of ordinary private corporations.

Of the nine directors of each regional Federal Reserve bank, six are elected by small, medium-sized, and large member banks in that region. The three additional directors, for each region, are designated by the Board of Governors of the whole System.

The Board of Governors of the Federal Reserve System is a *governmental* institution, with offices in Washington, D.C. It has seven members, appointed by the President and confirmed by the Senate. The members of the Board may have a long experience with private banking, which, like any other business, is conducted for profit. But

Figure 13–2. The Federal Reserve System—Organization Chart

ORGANIZATION

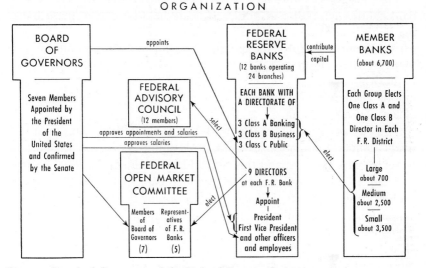

SOURCE: Board of Governors of the Federal Reserve System.

in their capacities as Board members, the seven men are the supreme judges of the nation's *needs* for money to carry on transactions.

PRIMARY FUNCTION OF THE FEDERAL RESERVE SYSTEM

In establishing the System it was thought that there would be times when the ordinary local banks would find their reserves insufficient to support a desired upswing of business activity. In that event it was expected that they would borrow additional reserves from the central bank in their district.

This, of course, requires that the central city Reserve banks have assets which they can use as a basis for extending loans to the member banks of the System. Now, by an ingenious device, these assets turn out to be some of the very reserves which the member banks are trying to supplement. Bear in mind that the member banks are *required* to keep their reserves on deposit at the central city Reserve banks.

Originally, banks held most of their reserves in the form of gold bullion. This gold came—and continues to come—to the banks from the business world, being deposited by miners, foreigners, and Americans engaged in foreign trade. When the Federal Reserve System was organized, all gold reserves of the banks joining the System were deposited in the twelve central banks. Gold is conveyed to the United States Treasury, the owners being paid in promissory notes, the familiar paper money. Since 1934 gold has been withdrawn from ordinary circulation.[5]

The Treasury, however, issues gold certificates to the Reserve banks. For each dollar of gold certificate held by one of these banks, the bank is allowed to issue $3 worth of credit to the member banks. This is "hot money," for the member banks will use the credit afforded them by the central city Reserve bank as additional reserve money. If the whole economy of the region, or of the nation, is in a buoyant mood, each additional dollar of reserve can generate four dollars of circulating medium.

Thus we have an inverted pyramid of bank credit resting on a relatively slender foundation of gold, $21 billion worth of it. Since the Reserve banks can expand this fourfold by lending additional reserves to member banks and since the member banks can together expand each borrowed reserve dollar five times, it may be seen that there is an expansionary potential of twenty times the amount of money originally deposited by businessmen with the member banks of the System. However, as the member banks do not typically expand credit to more than three times their deposits, the outside limit of bank credit expansion is twelve times the amount of the $21 billion worth of gold stock in the Treasury, or $252 billion. This is about double the present supply of money in circulation—$134 billion.

Thus far the discussion has been concerned with only the *amount* of money in circulation. But the *rate of its utilization* can also be significantly increased. Individuals, insurance companies, and other nonbank owners of securities could sell them to commercial banks and use the proceeds for active spending. In addition, if the government

---

[5] In 1933 Congress authorized the President to reduce the gold content of the dollar. This was intended to have the effect of lowering our export prices by making dollars to pay for them more cheaply available. With increased exports, revival of trade was hoped for. The President took action early in 1934. All holders of gold or gold certificates were required to surrender them for paper money. Since each theoretical gold dollar held exclusively by the government thenceforth had less gold content, a surplus of gold was realized. (Gold is usually held in ingot bars by the government, not in the form of coin.) Had not gold been nationalized at the same time that the gold content of the dollar was lowered, the surplus would have been reaped by individual holders of gold.

securities are sold to commercial banks, these banks can in turn sell them to their central bank. The member bank would be given credit by the central bank, thus increasing its reserves.

A TENTATIVE CONCLUSION

By now it must be evident that there will always be enough money to finance high economic activity if the business world is willing to undertake it. Bank credit is the monetary invention which finances productivity breakthroughs in the factories and on the farms. Money itself, however, cannot create economic activity or restrain it; money can only facilitate it. Thus, although the problem of money has been solved on the supply side, the problem of the demand for money is not an easily solvable one. This brings the discussion back to the problem of effective demand. When aggregate effective demand is excessive (that is, when people want more things than there are resources to provide them), the question arises: Can merely restricting the supply of money curb the competitive bidding of people for a relatively limited supply of things whereby prices are driven up, especially the cost of living? Or will they find ways to use money at a high velocity, thus circumventing the reduction of the absolute amount of money? If this were the case—and at present it is—direct fiscal policies of high taxation would be preferable in the fight against inflation, as well as direct measures to halt the diversion of resources to the production of consumption goods and capital goods which have a low priority of social necessity. On the other hand, will people wish to take advantage of our highly flexible money supply when business confidence is low and unemployment is developing? At such times will not public works projects serve to stimulate aggregate demand, while reduced taxation and deficit financing add their impetus to recovery?

These questions define the scope of monetary controls on economic activity. As was said at the outset, money can be no sounder than the expectations of businessmen, and no more effective than the desire of businessmen to use it.

The Controls

In any type of monetary control the aim is to promote the use of money in such a way as to facilitate production and full employment. This involves action by the government through the Treasury, the banking system itself, or both acting together. Say that the Board of Governors is advised by the President's Council of Economic Advisors or its own staff of economists that an unhealthy boom seems in the making. It is almost certain that the member banks will be under pressure from customers for increased loans; the regional Reserve banks will feel the pressure indirectly, and the Board of Governors will experience it either as it filters through the regional banks to Washington, D.C., or as pressure applied directly by Congressmen (who have been besieged by their constituents to bring influence to bear for "easy money").

As said, the Federal Reserve banks and the Board of Governors, especially, are not conducting a banking system for the sole purpose of making profit. Theirs is the public function of guiding the monetary system into support of full employment and away from inflation.

RAISING THE INTEREST RATE

The Board, or any or all Federal Reserve Banks, can send out a primary warning signal when an unhealthy boom threatens. This would take the form of raising the rate of interest at which member banks can borrow additional reserves. Now, as a matter of fact, few of the member banks are in debt to the central city banks; there is a strong tradition that if such debt occurs, it should be speedily liquidated, a tradition to which the member banks adhere. In modern times most banks have excess reserves. The Denver banks, for example, have not been in debt to their Federal Reserve bank in Kansas City since 1929!

However, there is no reason why the commercial banks should not respond to the signal of the Federal Reserve System. The economic storm signal expresses the opinion of the directors of the System that trouble may be ahead if the bank customers in various localities are too easily accommodated with loans. That is, the Federal Reserve banks are saying that our resources are being strained to the point that additional money transactions cannot give rise to additional goods production at a sufficient rate, and, hence, the cost of living must rise.

Increasing the rate of interest at which additional reserves can be borrowed is called *raising the rediscount rate*. The reason for this term is that when the member banks borrow additional reserves, they pledge commercial loan paper and government securities which they have already discounted for their own customers.

If the member banks heed the warnings of the Reserve banks in times of threatening inflation, they may raise their own rates to their customers and bear down on marginal loans (those which have barely been worth making).

When member banks raise their charges to their customers and refuse to make certain marginal loans, they are helping to execute a policy of *tight money*. Theoretically, not many businessmen need to be restricted for some effect to be registered. Perhaps only a fringe of 5 or 10 or 15 per cent of marginal credit spending, when eliminated, may contribute to stabilization. It is the *marginal* influence which the advocates of strong monetary controls rely on, not the total effect. For example, it is argued that tight money policies will cause some businesses to tighten their dividend and profit withdrawal policies, retaining more profit and paying out less in dividends which might be used by the recipients for current spending. A firm which has begun an expansion program may curtail dividends to finance continuation of the program when it becomes costly to go to the banks for additional money under tight credit conditions. Thus credit control, if it is asserted, may increase business savings and indirectly personal savings (by the withholding of dividends for personal spending).

Then again, it is alleged that when money becomes tight, merchants who must carry inventories and borrow money to finance them will cut down their orders for goods so as to reduce the amounts which they must carry at high interest costs on borrowed money. Another effect of tight money is said to be exerted on underwriters who assist businessmen in floating securities. These underwriters are known as "investment bankers." Many business firms who wish to raise money capital by selling securities do not wish to go directly to the general public. Instead, they sell a block of securities to investment bankers who, so to speak, buy the block of securities "at wholesale" and then sell it to the public "at retail" (that is, in small lots). In other words, they act as middlemen between borrowers and lenders.

These middleman investment bankers are loath to undertake new commitments when money becomes tight. They may discourage business concerns from floating new issues and even withdraw pending issues until a more favorable money market situation develops. The reason for this advice is, of course, that at high rates of interest the corporations floating bonds will receive less money from the public than is the case when interest rates are low. If the bond rate of interest is 5 per cent, a bond on which a business firm undertakes to pay $50 a year could be sold for $1,000—the amount on which $50 will be earned (assuming for simplicity's sake that the bond is a perpetual one which will never be retired). If the rate of interest rises to 6 per cent, only $833.33 is required to yield an income of $50 year after year.

Suppose, then, the firm has already announced, through its underwriter, that it will pay $50; that is, the firm has announced a 5 per cent, $1,000 par value issue. It might pay to withhold this issue rather than to receive only $833.33 per bond. The public would not pay more than this, for 6 per cent could be earned by placing one's money in old bonds, rather than risking it in a new business venture. In this way, it is contended, capital expenditures by business and perhaps also by local governments may be postponed owing to the influence of a rise of the Federal Reserve rediscount rate on bond interest rates.

OPEN-MARKET OPERATIONS TO CURB INFLATION

Today it is a rarity for a commercial bank to borrow reserves at its regional Reserve bank by rediscounting promissory notes of businessmen on the security of which a loan was originally made by the bank. But this does not mean that individual banks do not occasionally find themselves short of *primary* reserves on the basis of which to expand credit. The entire national banking picture is one which conforms in principle to the simplified illustration, given in Table 13–1, of three businessmen dealing with each other and the public. But complications do arise when clearings of customer credit balances and interbank balances are made among thousands of banks serving millions of customers. Individual banks occasionally experience large withdrawals of deposits which are not predictable. This may occur when accidents of trade force businessmen to draw down their deposits; or when people draw their money to go on vacation trips over long holidays; or when there are sudden shifts of money to other regions, as when defense production opened in San Diego, drawing people from all over the nation. In these instances, and numerous others, a local bank must be able to obtain supplementary money funds immediately in order to remain in a "liquid position," that is, in order to meet demands for cash, travelers' checks, and so on. Banks prefer to keep some marketable assets which can readily be converted into lendable funds. For ordinary purposes the banks can rely on the usual turnover of maturing loans and investments. But sometimes extra or special customer needs must be met which had not been expected to arise.

The commercial banks rely on the "money market" to enable them to tide over periods of unusually heavy withdrawals and to meet extraordinary customer needs. What is the nature of this financial institution?

The money market. Like all other markets, the money market is not a place but rather a system of contacts through which assets are traded —in this case, lent and borrowed. The stock of "goods" is a complex of credit instruments which the holders believe they can readily liquidate to meet their needs for money. Of course this is only one side of the market. On the other side are persons or groups of persons who are willing to acquire credit instruments as readily marketable investments until such time as they too need "absolute liquidity," that is, money itself. Then they appear on the opposite side of the market. By "credit instruments," in this connection, reference is not made to bank checking accounts of individuals or business firms, nor to savings deposits or savings bonds. The "stock in trade" of the money market's financial transactions is primarily composed of temporary excess reserves (known as "float" and "federal funds") which some banks are willing to lend to others, and of short-term government securities (up to five years' maturity in the largest number of cases).

The trading which is conducted in the money market reflects the economy's basic forces of aggregate supply, demand, and the profit expectations of the business world.

The participants in the money market. The money market is entirely free to access; indeed, it comes closest to what in theory is known as a purely competitive market. The main participants are banks, which number in the thousands, but other financial institutions also enter the money market, such as life insurance companies and sales finance companies.

Then, too, large business corporations issue or buy short-term credit instruments. Periodically they set large amounts of money aside for meeting future tax obligations. Such funds are lent at short term in the money market for the sake of earning interest income. Sometimes when a part of the funds which have been set aside for financing the construction of new plant is not immediately needed, this money can also be lent at short term in the money market. On the borrowing side, a recent example is that of corporations extending more sales finance credit to purchasers of their products through their dealers than the liquid asset position of the firms warrant. This shortage of liquid assets brought corporations into the money market—even some which would ordinarily have no need to obtain outside funds.

In the case of smaller concerns, money market loans are often contracted to finance expansion activities until such time as permanent, long-term financing has been arranged. It has been noted that investment brokers typically enter the money market to supplement their own funds for carrying security issues which they have bought *en bloc* while "retailing" these stocks or bonds to the general public. Individuals or groups administering trust and pension funds sometimes have money to lend for brief periods and at other times are in need of borrowing short-term money. Perhaps the oldest and most constant participants in the money markets are national treasuries, which borrow money in anticipation of tax receipts or lend money at short term when there is no immediate requirement to disburse it. States and municipalities also enter the money market to lend or borrow.

HOW THE FEDERAL RESERVE SYSTEM GETS INTO THE MONEY MARKET

To understand the role of the Federal Reserve System in the money market, it is of utmost importance to realize the difference between the government and the System. The System operates under government supervision and in attempted harmony with government purposes of economic stabilization. But it is, after all, a system of privately owned and operated banks—the member banks as well as the central city Reserve banks which are owned by the member banks. To show how a private banking system may strive to aid in effecting a public purpose, we examine the manner in which the System may handle one of the "goods" traded in the money market, namely, the complex of government securities ranging from three-month treasury bills to bonds of five-year duration. The Federal Reserve System has nothing to do with the issuance of these government securities; that is the business of the United States Treasury. But the System can strive to influence the trading in the money market in an effort to expand or contract the amount of money in circulation. Suppose that the Governors believe that an overage of aggregate effective demand is in the making. Entering the market as a large seller of government securities —the central Reserve banks hold $23 billion of them—the System sets the following financial process in motion:

1. The regional central Reserve banks sell some of their government securities to dealers in securities.

2. In payment, the dealers write checks on commercial banks, making the checks out in favor of the regional central banks.

3. Upon receiving the checks, the Reserve bank in each region deducts the respective amounts from the reserve accounts of the particular neighborhood banks upon which the security dealers drew the checks. This process diminishes the amount of prime reserve which banks are required to hold by law.[6]

4. Because of the reduction of their *legal* reserves held at the central Reserve banks, the member banks must either use their cash and/or secondary reserves or curtail their lending operations. Cash reserves are not usually excessive, so that reducing them is not generally advisable. Secondary reserves (that is, holdings of readily marketable assets) can be converted into cash. But this might not be

[6] At this point it is necessary to interject the explanation that banks carry three types of reserve. One is the usual legally required reserve: 20 per cent for banks in New York and Chicago; 18 per cent for banks in other "reserve cities"; and 12 per cent for the "country banks" in smaller cities and rural areas. The second type of reserve which banks carry is actual cash, as well as deposits made with other banks for various reasons. The third type of reserve exists in the form of readily marketable assets, primarily short-term government securities—the so-called secondary reserves.

possible on a large scale without causing a reduction in the value of these assets. Thus, by converting securities to cash, a capital loss might be incurred, unless a particular bank were to sell some of its securities at a time when most banks were not doing so. Each member bank, however, knows that Federal Reserve operations are conducted on a large scale, so that if in response to Federal Reserve action it sells marketable assets to replenish diminished reserves, other member banks are likely to do so also, whereby capital losses would be invited. Besides, the individual member bankers appreciate that the Reserve will not enter the money market unless it is believed that the action is absolutely necessary in the interest of economic stability. Thus, if the Reserve is selling government securities and diminishing member bank balances, the member banks may very well decide to go along with the policy of credit contraction. This they will do by curtailing loans to marginal customers.

Conversely, when the Reserve is attempting to stimulate credit expansion, the direct approach is for the central Reserve banks to buy government bonds in the money market. Being bought from securities dealers, they are paid for by the Reserve banks with checks to the dealers. The dealers deposit them in their neighborhood banks. These banks forward the checks to their respective Reserve banks. The Reserve banks credit the reserve accounts with the respective amounts of money. Thus, the member banks' legal reserves are increased, and, consequently, their lending power, too. Observe that every dollar of extra reserve thus added to member bank balances can theoretically support $5 of extra monetary circulation by the operation of the "credit multiplier."

Money market operations of the Federal Reserve System are called open-market operations because the money market is indeed open to anyone, so that the Reserve is only one of many buyers or sellers. However, no other sole buyer or seller could possibly operate on so large a scale. Naturally, for open-market operations to be effective it is required that federal securities be possessed in large amounts by banks and nonbank investors throughout the nation.

Prior to the Great Depression government securities played a minor role in the nation's financial structure. Then, in the 1930's, government bonds were freely issued to help finance recovery. Thereafter, in the 1940's, government securities were issued on a massive scale, to help finance World War II. As a result, government securities now play a dominant role in the economy's financial investment structure. The neighborhood banks now have $50 billion of government securities in their portfolios, which can be used as collateral for borrowing from the central Reserve banks or which can be sold in the open market. And the central Reserve banks have $25 billion of them, a large part of which can be used for open-market operations.

OTHER FORMS OF CREDIT CONTROL

In 1935 Congress gave the Board of Governors of the Federal Reserve System the power to double the then-existing percentages in the legal reserve requirements of the member banks. These requirements were 13 per cent for central Reserve city banks (New York and Chicago); 10 per cent for the other ten central banks; and 7 per cent for the ordinary neighborhood banks. This power has been exercised on numerous occasions, and intermediate changes, up or down, have also been made. Such action is taken when the member banks have free excess reserves, which is the case after a depression. Thus, in 1937, the Federal Reserve feared that an inflationary boom was in the making, to be abetted by the commercial banks using their excess reserves. The Reserve therefore decided to absorb these excess reserves and literally doubled the legal reserve requirements. The result was unfortunate; the action of the Reserve contributed to the outbreak of the short-lived, but harsh, 1937–38 recession (though it did not cause it). Since then the Reserve has exercised this authority on several occasions—for example, in 1946, when there was, indeed, a shortage of goods as compared with available popular purchasing power.

The Reserve has also been given the authority to impose direct control of the amount of down payments which stockbrokers must require of their customers. The purpose was to terminate the practice in the 1920's of brokers accepting 10 cents cash for a dollar's worth of stock purchases, using the stock certificate as collateral for a 90-cent broker's call loan. (That is, if the stock went down, the broker would call on the customer to furnish cash to cover the amount of decline.) During the Korean war, the Reserve was given the power to regulate down payments on cars and houses. This particular power has been rescinded, and recent events show the government and the Reserve very loath to use what is called "selective credit controls" of this direct nature.

THE RIDDLE OF OPEN-MARKET OPERATIONS

It is easy to draw the false inference that the essence of open-market operations is simply that the Federal Reserve System buys government securities to make money easy, creating increased central Reserve deposits for the neighborhood banks. Alternatively, it might seem offhand that to make money tight, the Reserve simply sells some of the $25 billion of government bonds in its possession to commercial banks, deducting the proceeds from the commercial banks' reserve accounts at their respective central banks. This is indeed a common impression.

But the matter is not so simple. The central Reserve banks not only absorb or release credit as a matter of planned policy but do so involuntarily merely because they are banks, even though they are "bankers' banks." That is to say, there are natural swings in the amounts of credit instruments held by the central Reserve banks, quite apart from changes in bank reserves wrought by deliberate Federal Reserve System decisions. The natural swings—for example, natural bank reserve reductions—are accounted for by three primary factors:

1. Treasury receipts' falling short of expectations, diminishing the Treasury's balances at Federal Reserve Banks.
2. An excess of payments to be made to the rest of the world. For the time being the money which leaves the country (or is earmarked here for the use of foreigners) diminishes the domestic credit base.
3. Most importantly, an increase of currency in circulation. This means that more money is passing from hand to hand instead of being brought to the banks and deposited so that this money could be used as the basis of credit expansion.

The Board of Governors, especially its Open Market Committee, cannot afford to overlook the operations of these natural credit-tightening factors. Its action may be considered salutary at the time, to be supplemented by deliberate Reserve policy. The supplementary action of the System would, however, appear paradoxical. The System would *buy* bonds, instead of selling them, to help restrict credit. The logic of this is that if the System were to sell bonds at a time when credit is naturally becoming tight, not only might a boom be nipped but a recession might be precipitated. Thus, open-market operations of the System designed to tighten credit will usually take the form not of selling but of buying in the open market—*at a relatively low purchase rate, however, so as not to offset the natural credit constriction.* Figure 13–3 shows that when between July and December, 1955, bank reserves were reduced by increases of domestic currency circulation and for other natural reasons, the Reserve still pursued a tight money policy but did so by buying somewhat fewer securities in the open market than would have been required to offset the natural attrition on free bank reserves during that period.

FEDERAL RESERVE ACTION IN CONTROLLING INFLATION OR DEFLATION

Can Federal Reserve action taken alone be sufficient for counteracting inflation or deflation? Figure 13–3 shows that this could not possibly be the case. Suppose that in 1955 the Reserve had added an extra weight to the already increasing burdens on bank reserves by

Figure 13–3. Changes in Federal Reserve Holdings of Government Securities and Other Market Factors Affecting Level of Reserves (Cumulative changes in daily averages for statement weeks July 6 through December 28, 1955)

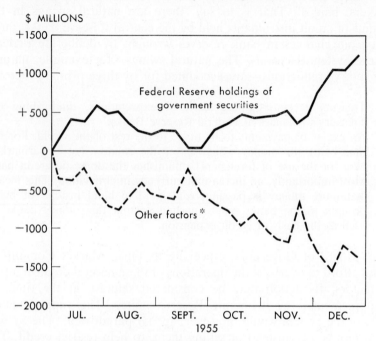

NOTE: (+) or (−) indicates effect on free reserves.

*Excludes member bank borrowing from the Federal Reserve banks.

selling government securities. This would have been to indulge in credit restriction to a punitive degree. The Reserve cannot conduct its affairs on abstract principles of currency and credit. Instead, it must move skillfully in the cross-currents of inflation *and* deflation which exist at any moment of time. Its main function is not simply that of regulation; it is, rather, promotion of the use of bank credit as a propelling force of dynamic economic activity. Its control is *finger-tip control* seeking to balance economic developments in all directions, avoiding any policy which might radically alter business or consumer spending. If more is to be done, it must be accomplished by direct fiscal policies, by debt management, and by altering the rate at which private and public capital construction and development projects are undertaken.

Finger-tip control is exercised on the theory that variations induced by the System in the marginal money supply may go a long way. Thus officials of the System state:

Relatively small reserve banking purchases and sales in the money market will, by adding to or subtracting from bank reserves, affect the capacity of banks to make loans and investments, including investments in government securities. The entire market will feel the effects of this shift in the banking situation and there will be an accompanying change in the market's tone, in the liquidity of all marketable securities, and in the climate of financial and business expectations.[7]

The statement is overly optimistic, although there have been times when it held true. Still, marginal money manipulations by the Reserve affect at the very best only the *supply* of money. The rest (that is, the effect on business expectations and for that matter on consumer expectations) must necessarily be a matter of hope. Marginal restraints on the *supply* of money can be offset by increases in the rate of utilizing a diminished supply of credit. In other words, the *amount* of credit may be reduced by a tight money policy, but the *velocity* of its use may be increased to a degree sufficient to overcome the quantitative restriction, so that the cost of living keeps rising.

This velocity offset to controlling the quantity of money can be accomplished by businessmen and consumers in the normal course of their daily affairs, that is, without any intention of contributing to inflation. Household spending units may cash in savings bonds, using the proceeds to buy goods and services. While they held the securities, the money equivalent thereof was inactive; upon sale, it finances active spending. Thus, velocity of circulation is increased, and if the securities are sold to commercial banks, the money supply is as well, since the commercial banks can add the newly acquired government securities to their reserves. The commercial banks can sell these same bonds and invest the proceeds by buying promissory notes held by sales finance or mortgage companies. These institutions can then make further instalment loans or mortgage loans to new purchasers of consumers' durables or new housing, thus adding to the inflationary spiral.

There are many other possibilities of accelerating the velocities of spending and investment so as to cause pressure on the stock of national resources.[8] One recent development in this respect is the grant-

---

[7] The Board of Governors of the Federal Reserve System, *The Federal Reserve System—Purposes and Functions* (Washington, D.C.: Government Printing Office, 1954), p. 44.

[8] See the article by Warren L. Smith, "On the Effectiveness of Monetary Policy," *American Economic Review,* September, 1956, pp. 588–606.

ing of trade credit by corporations to dealers in their products or to direct purchasers. This is a long-standing commercial practice, but in recent times trade credit has been granted by some large corporations to such an extent as to partially offset the credit stringency desired by the Reserve. As some of the dealers or direct customers of these corporations found access to bank credit restricted, they obtained the desired additional finance in the form of trade credit. The corporations have the means to grant credit because they have possessed large amounts of liquid assets since World War II. These stem from the excess of funds (from operations and temporarily lendable tax accruals) over outlays for fixed and working capital. In 1950 the funds from operations of 198 large manufacturing companies totaled $8 billion, but capital outlays were only $5.3 billion. In 1955 incoming funds of these corporations were $10.5 billion and outlays $9 billion, leaving a surplus of $1.5 billion. In 1950 these corporations made no net bank loans at all; in fact they repaid loans previously made. In 1955, $2 billion was spent on working capital assets (inventory accumulation, and so on), but only $76 million was borrowed at the banks (bank loans are usually contracted for working capital purposes). Thus it is seen that, far from having to use bank credit, corporations are often in a position to extend not bank credit but trade credit. And when, as in 1956, they overextend themselves in this direction, their superior credit lines at banks enable them to make up the difference. All this stimulates investing and spending and thus counteracts the attempts of the Federal Reserve to curb aggregate effective demand through bank credit restriction.

Corporate self-finance can also place investment activity beyond the reach of the Reserve during depressions. During the 1930's, one large American corporation used its liquid assets primarily to purchase properties and other business assets of financially weak concerns in its own and related lines of business. While this contributed to maintaining employment (because the other firms might have ceased operations), it did not constitute the real *new* investment in plant and property which adds to the community's store of wealth and furnishes *additional* employment. New investment is what the Federal Reserve tried to stimulate during the Great Depression by easing credit availability, lowering discount rates, purchasing government securities, and thus augmenting member banks' reserve deposits. However, as was stated at the outset, the mere existence of bank deposits does not constitute money. In order to constitute money, the bank deposits must be used constructively, whether they are customer deposits at the neighborhood bank or commercial bank deposits at the central Reserve banks. In the early 1930's the Federal Reserve made what were, for that time, vigorous open-market purchases. But the banks used them to a large extent merely to pay off their debts to the central Reserve banks and to each other. Therefore the newly created money never really went into active economic circulation. The matter is still controversial; some say that an impact would have been made had open-market purchases been made of several times the actual amount. Somewhere we arrive at the ancient truth that "you can lead a horse to water, but you can't make him drink." What might have happened in the early 1930's, had massive open-market purchases been undertaken, is a moot question; one guess is as good as another. However, it is a known fact that initiating recovery required the undertaking of public works, the adoption of direct fiscal policies for more progressive taxation, institutional changes such as the encouragement of labor-management collective bargaining, social security, and other welfare legislation. And recovery was not complete until the day dawned for that greatest of all public works programs, World War II.

A Theoretical Recapitulation

Consumer spending is the largest quantitative factor in national income, output, and employment. But investment is the cutting edge of economic growth. As seen in Chapter 10, business investment is determined by entrepreneurs by comparing the marginal efficiency of capital with the rate of interest. This is not simply the short-term rate of interest paid on treasury bills or other short-term credit instruments. The rate of interest which determines investment is based on long-run growth expectations.

When Keynes demonstrated that the marginal efficiency of capital and the interest rate are prime determinants of employment, he also contributed a new interpretation of factors which determine the rate of interest. It is in these terms that the subject matter of this chapter can be summarized.

THE CONCEPT OF LIQUIDITY PREFERENCE

Whether times are good or bad, people prefer to hold some of their income and assets in the form of money rather than using it all to buy goods or acquire stocks and bonds and insurance policies and tangible assets. There are three types of motives:

1. The transactions motive. People want to have money on hand to make purchases, perhaps in order to realize an unusually good bargain. Businessmen must have ready cash, or demand deposits, for paying wages and small bills. The amount of cash or demand deposits needed varies with the level of business activity and the customs of a country. (In the United States, wage-earners readily accept checks, but in most parts of the world they still insist at least on banknotes.)

2. The precautionary motive. Consumers prefer to have some liquid assets to guard against a "rainy day" of income lapses.

Businessmen have much the same reasons for keeping some cash in the till. They also prefer to have some readily marketable government and corporate securities which can be readily converted into cash. Should some customer lapse in his payments, for example, the affected businessman would still have to pay his own current bills. Then again, a businessman has to provide against the contingency of his line of credit's being restricted at the bank. Other needs for the precautionary holding of cash, demand deposits, and readily marketable assets will come to mind.

3. The speculative motive for holding money. If the future were certain, nothing would be gained by not spending or investing one's money at practically the same moment as it is earned. For there would be no opportunity of "outguessing" other businessmen or the current purveyors of economic information. But when the future is uncertain, there is always room for a difference of opinion as to whether it is wise to buy now or to buy later.

Now, this observation is most relevant with regard to decisions to buy stocks, bonds, factories, and machinery, and also with reference to consumers' durables. The reader may well have pondered, at one time or another, whether to buy a new car or to wait until prices came down, if he thought that there was a possibility. His behavior, in this possible instance, was one of attempting to outguess the market. The present values of durables reflect the average opinion of future trends of incomes and prices. Reference is made to the example given in Chapter 10, where it was shown how an entrepreneur estimates how much he is willing to pay for a punch press. This was seen to depend on the net income which the machine would yield, which, of course, depends upon the trend of prices, both as regards the future replacement cost of the equipment and the prices expected to be earned when selling the output of the machine. Consumers as well as producers sometimes adopt speculative behavior. When the Korean war began, most people went their accustomed ways, but some could be found who hoarded a number of refrigerators or other durables in their basements, hoping to resell them later at high prices.

The speculative motive may best be observed in the case of purely financial transactions. Say that an investor contemplates buying a bond of $1,000 par value with a stipulated interest rate of 5 per cent, thus yielding $50 per year. This is equivalent to buying an income of $50, year after year, supposing the bond to guarantee a perpetual income like a British consol.[9] There is active trade in these bonds at the $1,000 price; that is, it is the predominating opinion of the market that this $50 income cannot be bought more cheaply in the immediate future. A given investor, however, may differ with the prevailing market opinion, thinking that the rate of interest on this type of security is likely to rise. Suppose he believes that the company will in the future be required to pay 6 per cent in order to attract capital. In that case he would gain by staying out of the market for some limited period of time. For if he should be right, he can later buy the bond for $833.33 and yet earn $50 of annual interest. He will have saved $166.66, and so he might wait until the loss of not earning interest while holding money begins to offset the savings to be made by waiting.

From this simple example emerges a fact which in the 1930's dogged recovery as much as any other factor. Interest rates on long-term bonds were at an all-time low, and many investors held out for a rise, despite the fact that the government announced its intention to continue to keep the rate of interest down. This was expected to make investment in new plant and equipment attractive to entrepreneurs because it meant that loan funds could be cheaply obtained; at the same time a low interest rate was approved as the means to ease the strain of government deficit financing. (If the government could obtain $1,000 by paying only $20 annual interest income, this is obviously preferable to receiving, say, only $500 and yet having to pay $20 of annual interest. In the first case the rate is 2 per cent; in the second, 4 per cent.)

By what means might the Federal Reserve have effectively held down the long-term rate of interest so as to encourage long-term investment in new plant and equipment? The only means would have been for it to sell long-term government bonds every time the general long-term rate of return on private and public investment was expected to rise. The rate of return on investment privately undertaken is related to the rate on long-term government bonds.

But the central Reserve banks have only minimal holdings of long-term government bonds; indeed, very few long-term government securities are issued, in comparison with a large amount of short-term securities having a 5-year or shorter duration. This is due to an ancient

[9] Over a century ago the British Treasury made an issue of consolidated bonds to retire many previously made issues outstanding since the Napoleonic wars. The consols brought all these under one issue with the promise that this issue would never be retired.

custom of national treasuries in all the countries of Western civilization. It is a structural defect of monetary organization. Having no significant stock of long-term bonds with which to operate, the Federal Reserve has no power to enforce long-term low interest rates. People know this and therefore can afford to wait for a rise of the long-term rate of interest, as during a depression. In other words, the speculative motive is strongly supported by the absence of the Reserve's power to influence long-term lending and borrowing decisions.

Combining the transactional, precautionary, and speculative motives for holding income and/or wealth in the form of money, we arrive at the concept of *liquidity preference*. This is the general foundation of the demand for money.

THE MONETARY AUTHORITY AS THE SUPPLIER OF MONEY

Keynes highlighted the important role which central banks play in supplying the economy with money while operating closely under government supervision. This he did by stating that the supply of money at any time is fixed, in an amount given by the monetary authority—in our case by the Federal Reserve System. Although this is an exaggeration, it serves to incorporate into economic analysis the role of monetary policy—its possibilities and limitations. Keynes was emphasizing the policy aspects of money control; action can be taken on this, whereas not much can be done, for example, about the psychological factor of fear which leads people to hoarding. He was, of course, aware of factors which lie beyond the control of monetary policy and which influence the behavior of bank credit. But this awareness only led him to challenge the banking authorities to use what powers they might have to offset adverse effects of "other factors" beyond the control of monetary policy. In formulating the concept of liquidity preference he took full account of the problem of changing velocities of money. The main thought in assuming the supply of money as fixed is that it be fixed at a proper level so as not to interfere with production or employment.

COMBINING LIQUIDITY PREFERENCE AND A FIXED MONEY SUPPLY

Liquidity preference is at the basis of the demand for money. When people wish to hold much money (that is, when they have a strong liquidity preference), entrepreneurs wishing to borrow money will have to overcome the high liquidity preference by offering to pay a high rate of interest. By contrast, if people are anxious to buy things and make investments, enough money is available for borrowing. Hence the rate of interest will be low since entrepreneurs will not have to combat a high liquidity preference. If the rate of interest were high at a time when liquidity preference is low, few entrepreneurs would borrow money. Other people would have cash surpluses which they would be unwilling to hold. Obviously such a situation could not last; the extra money would be lent at lower rates of interest.

The relation between the rate of interest, liquidity preference, and the quantity of money can be portrayed on a curve. Every point on this curve relates a quantity of money to a corresponding rate of interest in terms of an assumed given state of average liquidity preference as is shown in Figure 13–4.

Figure 13–4. Graph of a Typical Schedule of Liquidity Preference

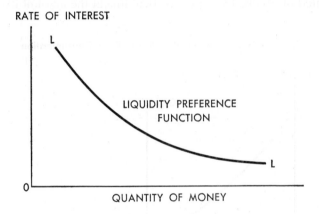

Note that the liquidity-preference curve *L* flattens as it descends. This indicates that a greater total amount of money will be available at lower rates of interest, but only at a diminishing rate. This can be explained in terms of the speculative motive. It has been seen that money might be made by holding out for a rise in the rate of interest. In the case of the bond, this amounted to $166.66, the rate of interest rising from 5 to 6 per cent. However, the person who purchased a claim for a $50 yearly income, paying $1,000, loses only about $17, assuming that the nonpurchaser waits three years for the interest rate to rise. By then the person who proceeded to buy the bond would have earned $150 of interest income, thus receiving only $17 less than the person who waited and reaped $166.66. But if the rate of interest is only 2 per cent, the situation is different. If the rate of interest is 2 per cent, it costs $1,000 to buy a perpetual income of $20. But if the rate of interest should rise to 3 per cent, the same annual income could be bought for only $666.66. In that case the person who waits, say for three years, reaps a gain of $333.33. The person who proceeded to pay $1,000 for the $20 income by that time will have accumulated only $60 in income. Naturally, then, people are much more likely to withhold money at a low rate of interest than at a high rate of interest. This is why the curve shown in Figure 13–4 flattens out. At some very low rate of interest no more loan funds may be forthcoming at all.

The liquidity-preference curve, or money-demand curve, in Figure 13–4 only relates the rate of interest to the quantity of money in a general way. It does not tell what the rate of interest will be at any given time. This will be co-determined by the supply of money which the monetary authority (the Federal Reserve System) makes available at any given time. People cannot create money; they can only use it. The quantity of money made available for use by the monetary authority is represented in Figure 13–5 by a vertical line at the amount fixed by the

Figure 13–5. Keynesian Interest Rate Determination

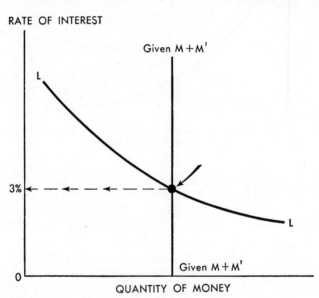

monetary authority. Where this vertical line intersects the schedule of liquidity preference, the rate of interest is determined, as shown in Figure 13–5 by the arrows leading from the intersection point to the vertical axis of the graph.

IMPLICATIONS OF KEYNESIAN INTEREST RATE THEORY FOR MONETARY POLICY

The mere existence of a community liquidity-preference schedule, and of given money supplies, is not informative. Both are normal attributes of modern economic life. But *shifts* of liquidity-preference schedules and of money-supply schedules may tell a story of prosperity or depression. Any one given liquidity-preference schedule describes people's desires in the matter of holding money versus spending and investing it. Suppose, however, that people fear a recession is in the making and therefore determine to hold more money "just in case." The supply of money remaining the same, but the demand for holding money increasing, the rate of interest would increase. Unless at the same time the marginal efficiency of capital were to increase, investment would therefore decline; for investment depends upon comparisons of the marginal efficiency of capital and the rate of interest.

Now, it is unlikely that the marginal efficiency of capital could increase at the same time that people in general are pessimistic about the future. Thus investment would most probably decrease. This sets in motion the entire sequence of declining employment, output, and national income. And this unhappy sequence causes entrepreneurs to revise downward their marginal efficiencies.

But wait a moment! Does not the foregoing formal analysis of how the interest rate is determined imply that the rate of interest could be held stable when liquidity preference increases? Could not this be done by simply increasing the supply of money? In Figure 13–6 an increasing liquidity preference is portrayed by the curve of liquidity preference shifting upward to the right. Hence it intersects the money supply curve at a higher point corresponding to an increased rate of interest.

Figure 13–6. Increase of the Keynesian Interest Rate Caused by Stronger Economy-wide Liquidity Preference

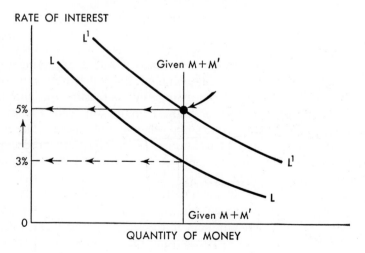

Why not simply shift the money supply to the right, so as to obtain an intersection of the two curves at the previously established lower rate of interest? This is shown in Figure 13–7.

The trouble with this solution is that it is purely formal; it abstracts from real-life circumstances. The increase of the liquidity preference reflects human experiences which have some rational grounds, even though people's fears may be exaggerated. The real reason for economy-wide increases of liquidity preferences is usually that the business

Figure 13–7. A Purely Formal Model of Interest Rate Determination

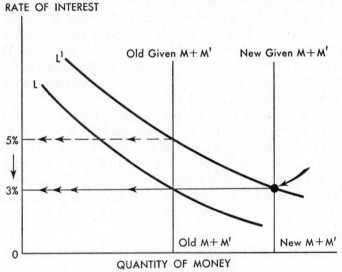

community has already revised downward its marginal efficiency schedule. This could happen for a great variety of reasons, the precise nature of which will vary from case to case. But whatever they might be, they would indicate that the business world is expecting or experiencing a decline of aggregate demand. Even if it were possible to keep the rate of interest from rising, by increasing the supply of money, this established rate of interest might still seem too high in comparison with a reduced marginal efficiency of capital. The monetary authority could attempt to counter by creating yet more lending facilities and ordering the rate of interest charged by the Federal Reserve banks to be lowered. But would the money go into circulation? In some cases, yes. But, in the 1930's a race developed between declining marginal efficiency and a declining rate of interest. The falling marginal efficiency tragically kept in the lead. Interest went down; so did output and employment. The losing race of monetary policy was halted only when direct fiscal and public works measures were taken, beginning in 1933. Even thereafter a monetary policy of cheap credit was relatively impotent, as compared with the effects produced by more direct approaches to economic stabilization.

Per contra, a race can also develop between rising marginal efficiency of capital and rising interest rates. Restrictive "tight-money" policies have at different times been pursued since early 1954, but so far the effect has not been the desired one of restraining the rise of the cost of living.

In this concluding part of the chapter a theoretical foundation has been given to the practical observations made in the opening parts of the chapter. Monetary control was at one time considered the "save-all" formula for economic stabilization. Many people still continue in that view and exert influence to limit government stabilization efforts to "managed currency" policies. Most economists would go farther than this. However, there is practical consensus among economists that skillful money management by the Federal Reserve can prevent monetary factors from worsening matters by avoiding tight money policies when the economy is heading into recession. In the upswing phase of a business cycle it is also hoped that money can be kept from being issued or used so freely as to produce an unhealthy boom.

The question which remains is whether *primary* reliance on policies of tight money to prevent runaway booms spreads evenly the burden of restraint. The period from 1953 to 1958 witnessed the first major attempt to prevent a speculative boom almost exclusively by tight money management. The burden appeared to fall chiefly on persons of small means who are financially "marginal." These people were not necessarily inefficient but had not the financial or credit standing enjoyed by large concerns or wealthy consumers. A list of such persons would include small farmers, temporarily laid-off automobile , and steel workers, permanently separated aircraft workers, men forty years old and over, and persons doing business or performing services in certain distressed areas of the nation, as well as persons trapped in poverty pockets. The burden of tight money also seemed to be falling unevenly on the whole sector of public want-satisfaction. Slum clearance was at a minimum; health facilities were in arrears; and there was no substantial relief in sight for the chronic shortage of classrooms and trained teachers. Public projects to develop river valley basins and other projects to conserve resources were definitely suffering from attrition. All the while there appeared to be no dearth of funds for the financing of articles of individual want-satisfaction, many of a low social priority as compared with the neglected areas of public want-satisfaction.

For Discussion

1. In terms of the monetary equation of exchange, show what is meant by "managed currency."

2. Which of the following is the basic function of the Federal Reserve System: to promote orderly economic expansion? to make money abundantly available to all who seek it for productive use? to support the price of government securities or, in general, the fiscal policies of the Treasury? If none of these categories appears suitable, how would you define the basic function of the Federal Reserve?

3. Member bank reserves are based on the monetary gold stock of the nation, on Federal Reserve credit, and on Treasury currency. Show how member bank reserves would be affected by: (a) an inflow of gold to the United States, decreases in currency in circulation at the same time, and increases in Federal Reserve credit; (b) outflows of gold, increases in currency in circulation, and contractions of Federal Reserve credit; (c) outflows of gold, decreases in circulation, and contractions of Federal Reserve credit; (d) inflows of gold, increases in currency in circulation, and increases in Federal Reserve credit.

4. "The rediscount central bank rate is today an instrument of moral suasion." Do you agree or disagree?

5. How does the Federal Reserve actually engage in open-market operations? Does it simply mop up excess funds by selling securities and insert money into circulation by buying securities? What is the "paradox" of open-market operations? Is it a real paradox?

6. Is liquidity preference a new name for the ancient phenomenon of hoarding? Is it a purely psychological factor, or can it be influenced by a well-executed monetary policy? What is the difference between movement along the curve of liquidity preference and shifts in the curve itself? Give practical illustrations.

7. What if during a decline of business confidence, economic activity, and employment people should stage runs on the banks and demand that their deposits be paid them in cash? Could this demand be accommodated? The answer is yes, in our time, but why?

8. Distinguish between the short-term rate of interest on credit instruments in the money market and the long-term rate of interest which is crucial for economic development. To which of these is the marginal efficiency of capital most intimately related? Which of them does the Federal Reserve System control? Does this indicate an inconsistency in Keynes' reasoning?

9. How is it possible under Federal Reserve System credit control for prices to be rising at the same time that there is unemployment?

10. Articulate in detail how monetary policy can act in support of fiscal policy and how monetary policy can also support long-range community want-satisfaction. How powerful an anti-depression or anti-inflation weapon do you consider the Federal Reserve to be?

Recommended Further Reading for Part III

On Employment Theory

DILLARD, DUDLEY D. *The Economics of John Maynard Keynes.* Englewood Cliffs, N.J.: Prentice-Hall, Inc., 1948.

The Economic Doctrines of John Maynard Keynes. Papers presented at a symposium. New York: National Industrial Conference Board, 1938.

HARRIS, SEYMOUR EDWIN. *John Maynard Keynes, Economist and Policy Maker.* New York: Charles Scribner's Sons, 1955.

KEYNES, JOHN MAYNARD. *The Means to Prosperity.* New York: Harcourt, Brace & Co., Inc., 1933.

MORGAN, THEODORE. *Income and Employment.* Englewood Cliffs, N.J.: Prentice-Hall, Inc., 1947.

OHLIN, BERTIL G. *The Problem of Employment Stabilization.* New York: Columbia University Press, 1949.

PIGOU, ARTHUR CECIL. *Income—An Introduction to Economics.* London: Macmillan & Co., Ltd., 1946.

VEBLEN, THORSTEIN. "The Overproduction Fallacy," *Essays in Our Changing Order.* New York: The Viking Press, Inc., 1945.

WRIGHT, QUINCY (ed.). *Unemployment as a World Problem* (Lectures on the Harris Foundation). Chicago: The University of Chicago Press, 1931.

Public Expenditures and Fiscal Policies

ABBOTT, C. C. *The Federal Debt—Structure and Impact.* New York: Twentieth Century Fund, 1953.

BLUM, WALTER J., and KALVEN, HARRY JR. *The Uneasy Case for Progressive Taxation.* Chicago: University of Chicago Press, 1953.

BOND, FLOYD A., et al. *Our Needy Aged: A California Study of a National Problem.* New York: Henry Holt & Co., Inc., 1954.

BURKHEAD, JESSE. *Government Budgeting.* New York: John Wiley & Sons, Inc., 1956.

BURNS, EVELINE M. *Social Security and Public Policy.* New York: McGraw-Hill Book Co., Inc., 1956.

DOUGLAS, PAUL H. *Economy in the National Government.* Chicago: University of Chicago Press, 1953.

Federal Excise Taxes. New York: Tax Foundation, Inc., 1956.

The Federal Reserve System—Purposes and Functions. Prepared under the supervision of Ralph A. Young. (Washington, D.C.: Board of Governors of the Federal Reserve System, 1954.)

JOINT COMMITTEE ON THE ECONOMIC REPORT, 84TH CONGRESS, 1ST SESSION. *Federal Tax Policy for Economic Growth and Stability.* Washington, D.C.: Government Printing Office, 1955.

NEVIN, EDWARD. *The Problem of the National Debt.* Cardiff: University of Wales Press. Exemplary approach to the problem, although references are largely to British experience.

PAUL, RANDOLPH. *Taxation in the United States.* Boston: Little, Brown & Co., 1954.
SIGAFOOS, ROBERT A. *The Municipal Income Tax.* Chicago: Public Administration Service, 1955.
State Tax Rates and Collections, 1950 and 1955. New York: Tax Foundation, Inc., 1956. See also the previous study *Major State Taxes, 1939 and 1950.*
U.S. BUREAU OF THE BUDGET. "The Federal Budget in Brief." Published every fiscal year and obtainable from the Government Printing Office, Washington, D.C.

Monetary Policy

BROWN, ARTHUR J. *The Great Inflation, 1939–1951.* London: Oxford University Press, 1955. Issued under the auspices of the Royal Institute of International Affairs.
A Compendium of Materials on Monetary, Credit and Fiscal Policies. United States Senate Document No. 132, 81st Congress, 2d Session. Washington, D.C.: Government Printing Office, 1950.
CURTIS, MYRA, and TOWNSHEND, HUGH. *Modern Money.* New York: Harcourt, Brace & Co., Inc., 1938.
FISHER, IRVING. *The Purchasing Power of Money.* New York: The Macmillan Co., 1911. An American classic.
The Gold Standard: An Inquiry into the Function of Gold, and Its Relationship to Money and Credit, with Policy Recommendations. New York: National Association of Manufacturers, 1955. A pamphlet which discusses the feasibility of returning to the gold standard.
GREGORY, THEODORE. *The Present Position of Central Banks.* The Josiah Stamp Memorial Lecture of 1955. London: The Athlone Press, University of London, 1955.
HARROD, ROY F. *The Dollar.* London: Macmillan & Co., Ltd., 1953. Highly recommended.
HART, ALBERT GAILORD. *Money, Debt, and Economic Activity.* Englewood Cliffs, N.J.: Prentice-Hall, Inc., 1947.
HAWTREY, R. G. *Currency and Credit.* New York: Longmans, Green & Co., Inc., 1928.
MISES, LUDWIG VON. *The Theory of Money and Credit.* New ed.; New Haven, Conn.: Yale University Press, 1953. A standard treatise.
NADLER, MARCUS H., et al. *The Money Market and Its Institutions.* New York: The Ronald Press Co., 1955. Introductory description of credit creation with analysis of post-World War II credit and public debt management.
ROBERTSON, DENNIS H. *Money.* New York: Harcourt, Brace & Co., Inc. See latest edition. The English classic.
ROOSA, ROBERT V. *Federal Reserve Operations in the Money and Government Securities Markets.* New York: Federal Reserve Bank of New York, July, 1956.
SPAHR, WALTER E. *The National Association of Manufacturers and Irredeemable Currency.* New York: Economists' National Committee on Monetary Policy, 1955. Criticism of the NAM position stated in the pamphlet *The Gold Standard* (see above).
YOUNG, RALPH A. *Money, Trade, and Economic Growth: Essays in honor of John Henry Williams.* New York: The Macmillan Co., 1951.

IV

THE EFFICIENT USE OF RESOURCES

Price and the Principle of
Diminishing Yields

14

A Summary

Explanation

of Price Analysis

The American economy is characteristically one in which managing and self-employed entrepreneurs hire the personal services of labor of all sorts and the property services of capitalists, large and small. Productive services are engaged by entrepreneurs to assist in making goods and end-consumption services which people then buy with the incomes they receive by hiring out their personal and property services to the entrepreneurs. Entrepreneurs receive incomes in the form of profits, if any, that may be left after costs have been met—direct "out-of-pocket" costs for wages, materials, and so forth, as well as costs of maintaining and expanding plant and equipment over the long pull. The entrepreneurs pay their cooperating factors of production out of the revenues realized in sales and capital transactions. Thus we may observe a whole circular flow system in operation, mediated by the use of money for which goods are bought and sold and with which incomes are paid.

The whole process is really a two-way system of monetary exchanges of goods for money and money for services which are then used to make more goods to be exchanged for money that will be paid to hire productive services; and thus the "wheel of wealth," as Frank H. Knight calls it, spins on and on.

In the normal peacetime economy *prices* impersonally control the orientation of production, the allocation and efficient use of resources, the distribution of the results of production, and the lines of economic development. Prices are ratios of money paid per unit of a good or service. These ratios are established in markets—which are not particular places but spheres of economic influence wherein the price-determining factors of supply and demand operate. The price of a commodity registers its customer appeal. To the greater or lesser extent that goods and end-services possess such appeal, productive power is assigned to creating them—originally in terms of entre-preneur forecasting, and over the long pull under competition. Since this whole system is one which involves two sets of prices—sales and cost prices that are compared—it is known as the *price system*. Its analysis therefore requires first of all the study of the interrelations of these two sets of prices.

Scope and Method of Price Analysis

Anything which happens in nature, society, and history is inextricably bound up with everything else that happens. Hence the brute facts of life and nature do not tell their own stories. They must be arrayed, classified, and used as the bases for generalizations which must then be verified before they can be of use to mankind in its practical efforts to survive on earth and to prosper. Making facts serve human purposes by handling them in this manner is the general method of science. Economics differs not one whit from other sciences in following this fundamental procedure.

Because it deals *directly* with human social relations, economics differs from such disciplines as physics or geology. At most these natural sciences only cope with the relations of man to nature; but economics must also address itself to practical problems raised by man's relation to man. The word "only" in the preceding sentence requires explanation, for it might be interpreted to mean that analyzing man's relation to natural forces is an easy matter. Far from it, as every thinking man well knows. The thought intended to be conveyed has been succinctly expressed by the philosopher Morris R. Cohen, who wrote:

> In passing from scientific method as a whole to scientific method in the social sciences it is well to begin with the general admission that social phenomena are dependent on physical, biologic and psychologic factors. From this it follows that social phenomena are inherently more complex, depending on a larger number of variables. Hence the postulate of determinism, that everything is governed by law, does not assure the discovery in the social field of such relatively simple laws as prevail in physics. For obvious subjective and objective reasons experiments on men and societies cannot so readily be made or repeated

as can experiments on samples of inert carbon or hydrogen. The former cannot be observed with the same degree of freedom, accuracy and detachment as the latter; and in the social field it is impossible to vary one factor at a time and to be sure that the others have remained the same.

In addition to these differences it is important to note that the temporal or historical factors enter into social phenomena to a much larger extent than into purely physical phenomena. Men, communities and customs grow; and the present complexion of such entities is a function of their past history, to an extent which is not true of physical entities. There are, to be sure, certain physical phenomena, such as hysteresis in magnetism, which the past enters. But these are exceptional cases, whose dependence on history is expressible in a relatively simple function. This is certainly not true of religious, moral and political affairs; more history is needed for an understanding of the reaction of a Bulgarian to a Serb than for an understanding of the reaction of water to an electric current.[1]

In view of the apparently forbidding complexity of social events there is a widespread popular belief that a practical man of affairs had best find his way about without relying much on theory. But this is a sheer contradiction in statement; the persons heard professing it will invariably be found to be practicing a theory which they have indeed picked up "by ear" but which does not mean that they are really operating "by ear." Just because everything is related to everything else, in the social as well as in the physical universe, theory is required to enable one to cull out some uniform, constant, and invariable relationships that exist between brute facts, such as, for instance, the law of diminishing yields.

Or take the matter of price. Every price of a particular thing is related in some obscure way to all other prices; for if money were not paid out in one way, it would be expended some other way, changing the whole setup of prices. However, knowing this does not help us in coping with immediate problems in the behavior of the price of bread or meat. To understand the price of meat we have to get at some specific uniform relationship that exists between the supply and demand of meat, between the supply of meat and the methods of its production, between the demand for meat and the desires of consumers and their incomes, and between the demand for meat and the demand for close substitutes in the consumer's budget.

Simplifying Assumptions

To ascertain whether any uniform, invariable relationships exist among closely related facts which influence the price of meat, for example, economists make use of the scientific method of *isolation*.

---

[1] "Method, Scientific," *Encyclopedia of the Social Sciences,* Vol. IX, p. 389.

Thus it is assumed that when people buy a little more meat, this will not cause them to buy less of other things, so that the prices of all other things remain constant. Under these assumptions the only reasons why a little more meat would be bought are (1) a change in people's desire for meat, and (2) an increase in the supply of meat. Assuming there is a given demand for meat (that is, that people have budgeted a meat allowance), the fact that more meat is being bought means that a larger quantity has been brought to market and is being sold at a lower price per pound. With a given allowance for meat assumed, more will be bought when it can be had more cheaply. But if we had not assumed the prices of all other things to remain constant, the extra purchases might be explicable in terms of other things becoming cheaper, leaving more money to be spent for meat. Then we would have had to explore all the factors that led to the decline in the price of the other things, and we could not have established a simple relationship between the quantity of meat brought to market and the demand for it.

Then again, people might buy more meat as a result of an increase in their money incomes. This also would complicate matters, for now we would have to explain all the factors that led to income increases in order to explain the price of meat. Hence economists, interested in the relationship between people's willingness to buy meat and the producers' willingness to supply it, usually take money incomes as given and constant, so that any change in the quantity purchased of a commodity reflects a change either in demand or in supply, and nothing else. Looking at the matter from the viewpoint of supply, however, it could also happen that the price of meat could be lowered and a larger quantity could be supplied at a lower price than had previously been the case—if, say, a flood of immigrants proved themselves willing to work on ranches and in packing houses at low wages. Or methods of production could be improved, permitting the same result. But this means that the price would have to be explained in terms of the events that led to increased immigration or the engineering developments that led to improved methods, and not in terms of the increased quantity of meat alone. To avoid these complications, economists, when explaining the price of a commodity, take the prices of the factors of production as given, and the methods of production as well. Then the only factor which will cause prices to vary as a result of supply changes is the increased or diminished willingness of entrepreneurs to engage in meat production, given people's preferences for meat, their money incomes, and the prices of all other commodities.

Finally, to explain the price of a commodity we must assume full employment of manpower and materials in the total economy. The reason is that there is a law of diminishing returns, that is, of rising real costs. However, this economic law does not come into operation until resources are fully employed. Short of this point, idle resources can simply be put into production and increased supplies can be produced with the same cost. Otherwise stated, a true problem of allocating resources does not exist short of full employment; only then is there a cost-raising tug and pull on resources, with prices serving to ration them in accordance with people's preferred wants and activities.

To recapitulate, the following are the usual *given* (or invariable) factors which economists assume in explaining commodity prices:

1. Rational behavior. This means that consumers try to maximize satisfaction from spending income, entrepreneurs attempt to maximize profits, and wage-earners strive for higher wages and shorter hours; at the same time owners of property seek a maximum return on their investments.
2. Supplies of the factors of production and the prices of these factors, as well as their full employment.
3. Desires and preferences of consumers.
4. Prices of all other commodities than the one being analyzed.
5. People's money incomes.
6. Methods of production (technology).
7. Population.
8. Public laws, tax laws, and so forth.

The Price Which Rations a Commodity

When all these factors are taken as given, one and only one price can be established for a given commodity, regardless of how low a price the consumers might want or how high a price the producers may desire. When the amount of a commodity which consumers are willing to buy at a certain price equals the amount which producers are willing to furnish at that price, the particular price will become established as the prevailing price, the *price current*. At any lower price a greater quantity would be demanded than producers are willing to supply. Thus, it would pay some consumers to outbid some others. At a price higher than the price current—which economists call the *equilibrium* (balance) price—the supply would exceed the demand, so that it would pay producers to reduce their prices in order to sell all their wares. These processes continue until demand and supply are in balance. Still, it is not the balance of the quantities finally bought and sold which accounts for an equilibrium "price current" being established; sales equal purchases whenever a transaction is made at whatever price. That which determines the prevailing price is the fact that at this one price, and no other, is the willingness of consumers to purchase equal to the willingness of producers to supply the market.

What has this balancing of wills to do with rationing? Simply this: Price limits the human activities applied to production at the same time that it limits the people's want-indulgences. There is only one point at which activity intensity and want intensity are equal; the balance price registers this in money terms. At any other point it would pay to produce a little more or to consume a little more; but where wants and activities are being satisfied at equal intensity, an optimum has been reached. The price which expresses this optimum situation in money terms, commodity by commodity, simply informs producers who cannot realize a profit when selling the product at this price to stop wasting their own efforts and society's scarce resources. Consumers who at this price are either unwilling or financially unable to buy the product at all, or as much of it as they might wish, are most obviously rationed in its use (and therefore ultimately in the use of resources to make it). In the latter instance—of persons who are unable to afford certain things, their best efforts notwithstanding—the price system is a hard-hearted phenomenon, with its social welfare significance diminished to the extent that such circumstances exist.

It is in order to highlight the rationing function of price, to let it stand forth clearly, that economists assume the given factors listed above. Otherwise the explanation of any particular commodity would lead us into broad ramifications, entailing the consideration of many remote influences on a price which for theoretical and even for many practical purposes are "matters of a secondary and tertiary order of importance." It should always be borne in mind that when economists speak of price they mean the balancing "price current" which is established under given conditions or under controlled variations of these conditions, not just any price that might accidentally or momentarily be realizable per unit of a product.

Is Price Analysis Realistic?

In the actual everyday world the above-listed *given* factors are usually in a state of change. Moreover, there are private and governmental interferences with the perfectly smooth market bargaining which would bring price to its equilibrium level. Actual conditions of demand and supply are never perfectly known either, and other historical circumstances intervene to prevent a perfect consummation of theory into practice. Is price analysis therefore useless—a mere act of idle intellectual curiosity?

Not at all. Making all the above assumptions does not mean that we ignore the possibility of changes in these given factors. It simply signifies that we intend to discuss the price of the commodity under consideration only in terms of a certain *fixed* relationship with the outside environment, so as to be able to get down to the specific demand and supply factors which most directly shape the price of that particular commodity. It is no more misleading than when a highway engineer making a traffic survey concentrates exclusively on the roads by which a city is linked to the outside. He knows full well that the city is also linked to other places by means of air and rail transport, by telegraph, telephone, and so forth—all of which have some bearing on traffic flows along arterial highways. But for his purpose of understanding the highway problem the engineer can assume that all these other factors are given, to see how the highway system operates *under the given conditions*. Then if any problem arises because of a change in a given condition, say that rail traffic declines and the extra load is shifted to trucks and busses, the highway engineer is in a favored position to trace the impact of the change by having a good understanding of the traffic flow to begin with.

Similarly, if we know what the price of a commodity is likely to be under given demand and supply conditions—not its actual dollar-and-cents amount but its level, high or low—we can estimate in which direction this particular price level is going to change with any change in the given surrounding circumstances. This is important and by no means common-sense knowledge. Let us suppose that people's money incomes increase. Common sense might seem to dictate that those people who have been living on low incomes may now eat more bread. Actually the consumption of bread *per capita* might decline. Low-income recipients may have been eating starchy foods in relatively large quantities because they were unable to afford much, if any, meat. Thus, part of the bread consumption may have been merely in compensation for not having meat and will be abandoned when higher incomes permit the buying of meat.

The need for analytical knowledge of price movements (not just common-sense impressions) may also be appreciated when viewing the matter from the supply side of the price equation. To illustrate: improved methods of production would ordinarily be expected to lower the price of a commodity, but the mass production and consumption which improved technology makes possible may cause problems of costs that will tend to keep the price at a relatively high level. Thus, in the case of meat production in the United States, twice as many people in 1951 consumed the usual annual 140 pounds of meat per capita as did in 1891. In the interim great technical advances were made: control of detrimental weeds on range and pasture lands; coping with animal diseases caused by handling cattle in crowded feed lots; better stockyard and transport conditions; improvements in the equipment of packing plants; more efficiency in the canning of meat products; and so forth.

The price of meat as a percentage of the consumer's budget nevertheless did not decrease. This was not due to an increase in the demand in the sense that people developed stronger desires for meat. In this sense the demand for meat is known to be a very stable one, consumption of meat having been about 140 pounds per capita annually over the sixty-year period 1891–1951. What technological improvements accomplished was to prevent a *rise* of prices. This, however, contradicts the popular belief that improved methods of production must necessarily result in lower prices.

Only by having a precise knowledge of the specific relationships which directly influence the price of a commodity is it possible to understand in what directions the levels of particular prices are likely to move in the course of actual history. The historical changes take the form of changes in the magnitudes of the given factors that have been assumed. Thus when any change occurs in any of the given circumstances, it is possible to trace the impact through and to take informed remedial action should a social problem be created. This is best illustrated by the career of the first precise theoretical economist, David Ricardo, as the following section shows.

Price Analysis and Policy Recommendations

England had regulations on the import and export of small grains (the so-called Corn Laws) which, though originally designed to assure the nation of ample supplies at all times, had the effect of prohibiting the import of grain in the early nineteenth century. Writing at that time, Ricardo contended that this *de facto* policy of excluding grain imports was diminishing the general welfare, and proved it by the means of price analysis. The argument emphasized that because of restricting supplementary grain imports, many English food supplies had to be produced on domestic marginal or submarginal soils, most of them pressed into service during the Napoleonic wars. Crops produced on high-cost soils had to fetch high prices; the high prices of food forced wage- and salary-earners to insist on high money wages; entrepreneurs found that after paying high money wages they had little left as profit. Capital accumulation was thereby retarded and capital export from England encouraged.

Considerable social unrest characterized this period of English history, and through price analysis Ricardo traced some of it to the Corn Laws. The landed gentry (and farmers who had bought land at high prices) argued that the Corn Laws constituted not only a given factor affecting the price of grain but also a constant one; to alter this policy would be to destroy the structure of "merrie olde England." Ricardo acknowledged the Corn Laws as a given factor, but one that could and should be changed. To help bring this change about, Ricardo obtained a seat in Parliament, where he demonstrated that these laws could be repealed without bringing England to ruin, though some particular individuals might suffer a loss of capital.

Thus we see that, from the outset, economists have not been concerned merely with ascertaining in which directions prices will move as the result of certain actions in the business and political communities, given all the factors previously listed. Economists are also concerned with the surrounding circumstances which at first they assume as being given. That is to say, economists try to point out which changes in the *given factors* might benefit the general welfare by increasing abundance.

Price and Welfare

It should be clearly understood that the price analysis in succeeding chapters is but one of several approaches to welfare considerations in the field of economic analysis. Striving to ascertain the causes of economic instability, evaluating types and conditions of income distribution, probing consumer behavior, and other such undertakings rank with price analysis as paramount issues in a full perspective of economic welfare. Indeed, if this book were written to highlight the central economic problems at mid-twentieth century, its major emphasis would be on economic instability in its grave social implications. This book is, however, an introductory one whose aim is to explain the systematic aspects of the American economy rather than to emphasize the problematic aspects. Price analysis explains what system there is in rationing resources by allowing people to freely establish, by bidding and offering in markets, the terms on which they will supply each other with goods and services.

Is the pricing process keeping valuable national resources out of the hands of relatively efficient entrepreneurs? Are consumers required to pay enough for goods and services so that the natural resources used in making the goods can be renewed or replaced, and the human resources kept healthy? These are the kinds of welfare questions which price analysis must answer, let the chips fall where they may.

For Discussion

1. Why trouble to devote three of the forthcoming chapters to abstract price analysis based on the strict assumption in this chapter? Everybody knows that the exceptions to the rules of pure theory are far more numerous than actual instances where the rule of pure demand and supply determination govern.

2. When there is price control and rationing, as during World War II, do you think the price officials of the OPA (Office of Price Administration), all trained in economics or business, paid any attention to theory in formulating regulatory price orders? Discuss this question now and again at the end of this section on price.

3. Is there any bargaining between individuals under a price system? If so, in what manner? Is it perhaps *all* bargaining? Try to defend this latter point of view.

4. When the government makes contracts with entrepreneurs to supply military facilities, what relation is there between prices then established and prices established in the markets of the nation?

5. List the topics which you would like to have explained in more detail after reading this chapter; then, as you proceed to the following chapters, check to see whether they are discussed.

6. After reading the last paragraph of this chapter, Smith exclaims: "Why, here is a contradiction! The author begins the chapter with an explanation of the scientific nature of price analysis, but ends the chapter with imposing on price analysis a general responsibility for contributing toward ethical evaluation of price phenomena." Jones, upon hearing this, asserts that this is no contradiction at all. He points out that ethics is the science of how to make practical judgments—of what ought to be done under given circumstances. Jones maintains that if economists refused to take ethical positions, their findings would be of little if any practical worth. If you were invited to participate in this discussion, how would you proceed?

15 Individual Choice as a Basis of Commodity Demand

If there were such a person as an "average American," Table 15–1 would be his individual preference scale for meat, *given* all those previously listed circumstances which have a bearing on demand—namely, average per capita income, the prices of all other goods, the purchasing power of the dollar, and so forth.

Table 15–1. Individual Demand Schedule for Meat at Six Different Prices, United States, 1950's

Price (a)	Average American's Consumption (b)
41¢	160 lb.
42	150
44	140
46	130
50	120
56	110

SOURCE: Elmer J. Working, *Demand for Meat* (Chicago: The University of Chicago Press, 1954; copyright by the Institute of Meat Packing). This is an actual, not a hypothetical schedule. It is based on observed past behavior, but these observations are applied to the present moment in a scientific statistical procedure. Brought to bear on present circumstances, the findings as shown in this table will of course remain valid only as long as there are no substantial changes in the given factors. A change in the purchasing power of the dollar, of major proportion, would obviously render the price schedule in column (a) obsolete.

What lies behind this individual preference scale—individual choice, free choice, or choice made under the force of circumstances? What are the elements of economic choice?

Utility

Any commodity or service which is not to be had for the asking must be useful in order to bear a price tag. Things which are useful but can be obtained without effort or expense have no economic utility. "Simple utility is not enough," said William Smart. "If useful things are present in superfluity, we think no more of them than we do of the sand on the seashore. It is only when our well-being is not assured that an interest awakens in the things on which it is seen to depend, and that we exert ourselves to acquire these things."

How can a person know that his welfare depends upon possessing one thing rather than another? Strictly speaking, he cannot be sure of this until he uses the preferred item. But he has to choose it before he can use it! Obviously, the best we can do is to *anticipate* want-satisfaction. Thereafter our expectations may be disappointed. Alternatively, one may do something for lack of option, only to experience more satisfaction than one had anticipated. This is a familiar experience of students when rather protestingly they register for a "required course"—to find that it interests them, after all.

Notwithstanding the difficulty of anticipating satisfactions accurately, it is, of course, quite possible to choose rather wisely among goods and services, particularly those which serve the ordinary purposes of life. And, fortunately, we rarely have to make a choice of "all or none"—except, indeed, poverty-stricken persons who must choose, say, between a bit of cultural enjoyment and a meal.

Marginal Utility

Most economic choices are matters of "a little more or less," rather than of "all or nothing." The question ordinarily is: Will another penny spent one way make as much of a contribution to one's well-being as it would if it were spent another way? This is a question of marginal rather than total choice. If marginal choice were not the ordinary experience of life, one would encounter some puzzling paradoxes. For example, if one appraised the value of food by what happens when one eats or goes without eating, then even the plain loaf of bread would possess infinite value—much more than that of a diamond! But if the choice is only between having one loaf of bread more or less, then the final unit of bread will obviously have much less value.

DIMINISHING MARGINAL UTILITY

There is a law of diminishing yields, which applies to consumers as well as to producers of goods and services. Regarding consumers, economists have expressed the law of diminishing yields rather pretentiously—for example, William Smart, when he said: ". . . the first draught of any pleasure is the most grateful, and as the gratification weakens at every repetition, . . . each addition to the stock of a good occupies a lower place."

Theoretically, we carry our consumption of each type of good just so far that, for any good, the marginal utility per unit of expenditure is no higher or lower than the marginal utility of any other good, per unit of expenditure. This implies that we are always measuring the marginal utility of every type of consumption which we propose to undertake.

Now, it is rather difficult to conceive of consumers making careful marginal choices. People simply do not think over their ranges of wants carefully. Also, there is the difficulty of being properly informed. Advertisers of technical products often assert that they are adding some valuable ingredient to the product, yet "selling it at the same price." How is the layman to know whether this is actually so or whether the advertiser is simply mentioning some essential element of his product without which it could not operate or exist at all? On the other hand, consumers not infrequently turn down perfectly well-made products because they are priced low, erroneously believing them to have poor quality. There are many other instances of haphazard or actually "upside down" economic behavior, far removed from a sober weighing of one's expenditures "at the margin."

Still, notwithstanding, the concept of diminishing marginal utility of goods and services is not an empty notion, *provided only* that we apply the concept to the facts of *relative* abundance, i.e. increasing pressure on one's pocketbook, and not directly to consumer psychology.

There is evidence that people *do* make their consumption decisions rationally and consciously *on the whole*. In any given instance they might buy impulsively, imitatively, or imprudently. Rational consumer behavior seems to be a probability rather than a certainty. But it is a strong enough probability to warrant our acceptance of the basic concept of marginal utility if we understand that it is a tool for economic analysis, not a description of actual consumer behavior on any given occasion. As a matter of fact, many of one's doubts about the theoretical rationality of consumer behavior can be dispelled by asking oneself why people trouble to *economize* at all. The obvious reason is that a pinch on the pocketbook is usually felt when one is spending money—money which is felt to be hard-earned and never seems to reach far enough. In other words, people seem to experience not so much a law of *diminishing* psychological satisfactions, but rather a law of *increasing* cost. This is the mounting cost of doing without other things that one also desires on the verge of spending too much on any one thing. In this common-sense view marginal utility is merely the hesitancy one always feels before actually making a purchase.

Individual Demand Schedules

It would be impossible to get a direct numerical measure of any person's utility sensations, but we can observe his consumer behavior in price terms. This we do by simply asking him, or observing, how many units of a product he is prepared to buy at different prices per unit of the product. We assume his income to be given. We observe, for example, how much driving he usually does per week when the price of gasoline is 32¢ a gallon. Then we ask him how much driving he would do should the price go to 50¢, then to 75¢. Lest this sound farfetched, it may be pointed out that Great Britain had this experience during the 1956 Suez Crisis. The price of gasoline rose to 84¢ a gallon, and London traffic dwindled very noticeably. Generally speaking, we expect a diminution in the quantities demanded as price rises and an increase in the quantities demanded as the per-unit price of an article falls.

Putting this in marginal utility terms, we may say (to continue the gasoline illustration) that:

1. A person might be willing to pay 85¢ a gallon rather than not drive at all, but at that price he will not make long trips.
2. Even if gasoline is offered at 20¢ a gallon, say during a "price war," a motorist is unlikely to add much to his customary mileage.
3. When price is at a normal 32¢ a gallon, the enjoyment the motorist receives from making some Sunday outing trips rather than using the car merely for getting around town is just enough to make him willing to pay 32¢ a gallon. If the price he is just willing to pay for any gallon of gasoline may be called a person's *demand price,* then in our illustration the 32¢ a gallon (keeping in mind ordinary and occasional Sunday driving) is the *marginal demand price.*

It follows from what has been said that marginal demand price will be high when a person is just starting on the consumption of an item. In the case of gasoline, for example, when the first need is to use the car for getting to work, a person may be willing to pay a high price. As less important uses are considered, the price one is willing to pay diminishes. In brief: *An increase in the amount of a good or service possessed* (and used) *will diminish the individual's demand price for it*—all other things being equal.

Here we have translated utility into price, for the individual. Price is an objective kind of notation, whereas utility is subjective and cannot be expressed in any sort of unit of measurement which can be verified by outsiders. Having translated utility into price terms, we can draw the individual demand schedules of given persons, schedules which can then be compared with those of other persons. Let the symbol y stand for a list of prices and the symbol x for a corresponding list of quantities of any particular commodity demanded at those prices. Therefore:

y	x
$1.75	10
1.50	12
1.20	16
1.00	18
.75	26
.50	34

This informal manner of notation is, of course, intended only for ready reference. (Figure 15–1, p. 348, pictures the above individual demand schedule.) In presenting the results of any actual statistical survey, one would have to identify the columns fully and reveal exactly how the data were obtained. Bear in mind the assumptions which underlie the drawing up of even the foregoing brief demand schedule. They are part of the general assumptions listed in Chapter 14 (p. 337). For purposes of demand analysis the assumptions specifically involved are Nos. 3, 4, and 5: (3) a given and constant personality structure of the individual, to define his desires and the way he responds to salesmanship and advertising; (4) given prices of all products or services other than those for which demand is being analyzed; and (5) a given income factor which does not vary for the period of the analysis.

With this illustration of how people's preferences are shaped under given conditions, the question arises whether individual demand schedules can be quantitatively aggregated to yield a *composite social* demand schedule (or preference map, so to speak), commodity by commodity.

Summations of individual preference schedules into a composite whole, for each of our hundreds of thousands of commodities, would be of practical value. They could serve as economic "maps" by which entrepreneurs could choose their course of action in coping with marketing problems. But would they be of *social* utility; that is to say,

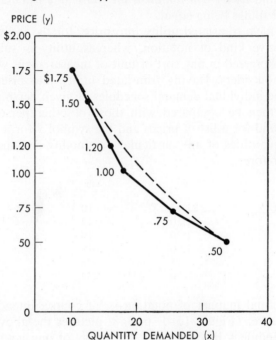

Figure 15–1. Hypothetical Demand Schedule

EXPLANATORY NOTE: Any actual demand schedule would exhibit discontinuity and therefore, when graphed, would have the appearance of the dotted line in the illustration. However, economists usually portray demand as related to price in the form of a continuous function, as shown by the solid curve. This practice will be followed in all subsequent presentations of hypothetical demand curves.

would they reveal the "sum total of happiness" which consumers as a whole expect to derive from consuming different quantities of products at different prices?

Market Schedules of Demand

If the average money income of $4,400 after taxes had been what every spending unit in the United States actually received in 1957, the individual demand schedules of the spending units could easily be aggregated and the sum total could be considered a welfare measurement (to be compared with similar data of past years or in countries abroad). For, with equal incomes, the differences in actual expenditures between spending units would automatically be explained by differences in the personality structures of the individuals in the various spending units. In other words, different spending patterns for families and individuals could be explained by differences in utility, pure and simple. Some spending units would prefer ample housing to possessing two cars; some would prefer two cars; and so forth. It could always be inferred that if one spending unit paid $10,000 for housing and another the same amount for automobiles instead, each would be expecting to derive a commensurable utility, though in a different way.

Now, neither income nor wealth are equally distributed. However, 80 per cent of Americans enjoy a varying plane or standard of living which is modest and adequate or better. Hence there is some sort of functional relation between what they offer to pay for products and the utility they hope to realize by budgeting their expenditures in certain ways. While one must not try to make any exact measurements in this regard, it is safe to say the following: When a consumer who is fairly well off offers to pay only a low price per unit of a product, the probable reason is that he expects a low marginal utility yield per dollar from consumption of a little more of that product. (Alternatively stated, he does not expect to suffer much when foregoing that extra consumption.)

It is otherwise with approximately 9 million low-income families and unattached individuals in the United States—some 24.5 million persons in all. They must spend the little income which they command on more or less fixed quantities of staple articles of consumption which are of the utmost necessity if a bare maintenance plane of living is to be achieved. Hence one cannot infer from the fact that persons so situated may offer a low price for, say, an overcoat that this article is not of great utility to them. It may be, but they have not the means to bid for it in proportion to its expected utility to them.

But why belabor this point? Cannot these low-income recipients bestir themselves or be roused into vigorous action to increase their incomes above the poverty level?

The point is that this is by no means always possible. A mother, as a single head of a household whose father is deceased, may not be able to do more than odd jobs to earn a little extra money without totally neglecting her child-rearing duties. A worthy person living on a minimum social security pension may find it difficult to supplement it appreciably without being penalized for "earning too much"; there are vigorous persons forty-five years of age or thereabouts who find employers unwilling to hire them except on those spotty occasions when a defense boom is under way; and there are people who are trapped in declining industries or regions. These are just some of the minority groups to whom access to more favored earning opportunities is barred.

The existence of persons who are poor for reasons beyond their control forbids making interpersonal comparisons of the marginal utility which people derive from their consumption. For example, older persons will recall how they or their neighbors often walked several miles to work during the Great Depression in order to save a nickel of carfare. At the same time more fortunate people took the streetcar every day. Say that the poverty-stricken person, never sure of his job from day to day, rode on the streetcar six times in two months, whereas a more fortunate person did so eighty-eight times. The marginal utility of streetcar rides to each seems to be equal, being measured by 5 cents. But the poverty-stricken person could spend this nickel only when circumstances demanded (for example, to avoid being drenched with rain), while the more fortunate person paid the nickel merely to avoid the inconvenience of walking.

So aggravated a difference in economic circumstances among persons need not be present in order to make us aware that price cannot serve as a *general* measure of marginal utility. All that is required is for some persons to be rich *relative* to others. Thus when the price of an article declines from $1.00 to 75 cents, one person may extend his purchases from two units to three units but may have no particular feeling about having acquired an extra unit. A relatively poorer person who could not afford the commodity at all so long as it cost more than 75 cents now acquires his first unit of the commodity and is quite delighted that he can now afford it. Undoubtedly 75 cents is the measure of the marginal utility of the commodity to both buyers, but is their combined anticipated yield of satisfaction 300 cents' worth (3 times 75 cents' worth, or $2.25, to the one buyer and 75 cents' worth to the other)? It could be asserted to be, but the figure would have little if any scientific worth or practical meaning. What does follow from our observations is that if there were only the two buyers, we could establish a combined market demand schedule showing the number of units of an article which will be taken from the market at different prices. Thus at $1.00 a unit, two units would be taken; at 75 cents a unit, four units would be taken. This is the general information which can be obtained by adding individual market demand schedules, one to the other, for any number of buyers of a commodity. But we are *not* informed as to how much utility is created throughout this combination of buyers.

Is it useless, then, to draw up market demand schedules in the effort to explain the total demand for particular commodities, or the sum total of commodities, at any time and place? No, if the aim is the modest one of ascertaining the volume of sales that can be made at different list prices—the "activity of demand," as Ricardo called it.

Such schedules are useful in allowing businessmen to judge whether it will pay them to proceed with the production of one or more commodities rather than another or several other commodities—given their costs of production or what they think they can accomplish in efficiently *reducing them* so as to be able to get into markets whose extent and size are revealed by the market demand schedules.

A Milwaukee furnace manufacturer, for example, may have found that average outlays for fuel and heating equipment are as high in Houston, Texas (one of the nation's warmest cities) as they are in Milwaukee (one of the nation's coldest cities). On the other hand, they are lower in New Orleans, which is also a warm city. Looking into the matter, the manufacturer may decide that he was probably wrong in assuming that all warm cities furnish poor markets for heating equipment. He finds that the difference in the demand for heating equipment between Houston, of the New South, and New Orleans, of the Old South, reflects income differentials to a significant extent. In 1958 Houston was a place where weekly incomes earned were almost on a par with those earned in industrial centers (even though hourly rates were somewhat lower). Knowing, however, that the Old South is also industrializing, and that the profitable dairy industry is dethroning King Cotton, the furnace manufacturer may decide that the Old South can also furnish a good market, a better one for expansion purposes than, say, Denver, where his sales are already well established. Scanning his production cost records and potentials, the manufacturer may decide that if he can step up his efficiency to produce a relatively low-cost heating unit, he may very effectively enter the Old South market, where incomes are rising toward industrial levels.

Thus we see that the market demand schedules which the Milwaukee manufacturer had his marketing experts draw up may guide him into profitable but hitherto untapped markets, while at the same time encouraging him to reconsider his cost situation with a view to achieving additional efficiency in production. And in doing well by himself, the businessman will be doing good in the social welfare sense, not only because he contributes more efficient production, but also because he will add to the sum total of satisfaction derived from consumption.

CONSTRUCTING A MARKET DEMAND SCHEDULE

A businessman, a trade association, an economic consulting firm, or a research bureau can ascertain market demand schedules for particular products in several ways. One way would be to send out questionnaires to everybody living in a community, asking them to state how much of the good or goods being surveyed the consumers would buy at different prices. This might be somewhat costly a procedure, and it would probably be an inefficient one, since many people would not bother to answer the questionnaires. A distorted picture would be given if more people from one income group reply than there are such people percentage-wise in the whole community.

A better approach is to make a "stratified sample" based on available United States Census data on the income composition of communities. Instead of sending out 500,000 questionnaires, 10,000 might well suffice. If 92 per cent of the population of a community is above the modest but adequate living level and 8 per cent at that level or below, 92 out of a hundred questionnaires would be sent to people in the upper level, 8 in every hundred to people at the low levels of income. Assuming all of them answered, the sample results would be in the same proportion income-wise as the total population. Or one could study by interview techniques the consumption patterns of the main types of income recipients in the city. Alternatively, one might send out selected questionnaires to some reliable people in each category, asking them to indicate how much of the particular commodity they expect to consume at different prices per unit of that commodity. (If hard-pressed for funds, one can use Bureau of Labor Statistics data that are available on spending patterns by income fifths and tenths; although such data are rarely exactly up to date, they may serve nicely as first approximations, even when an expensive direct survey is to be made.) Given the expenditure patterns for the particular commodity being surveyed in that city, one can ascertain the number of spending units in each income category that has been analyzed and thereupon arrive at some reasonable estimate of the total demand for the commodity *under the given conditions.*

For simplicity's sake, let us assume there are only 1,000 families in a community, with one-third of them at each level—the high-, the middle-, and the low-income level. We jot down for each group their pattern of expenditure for butter in an informal manner (Table 15–2). Assuming the same number of families in each group, namely 333, we add the respective quantities wanted at different list prices and multiply the total by the number of spending units that are actually in the market at different price levels. This provides a reasonable estimate of total demand, as Table 15–2 shows.

From a close reading of Table 15–2 the reader should emerge with a clear and firm understanding of the fact that demand is a *schedule concept.* That is to say, the demand for a product is the whole *list* of price responses shown in column (*c*) of Table 15–2—from the com-

Table 15–2. Demand for Butter in a Community, by Three Income
Categories and in Total

Price per Pound y	By High-Income Families x_1	By Middle-Income Families x_2	By Low-Income Families x_3	Total Demand in Pounds* $x_1 + x_2 + x_3$
	Pounds Taken per Spending Unit			
(a)		(b)		(c)
$1.75	20	0	0	6,660
1.50	25	0	0	8,325
1.25	35	0	0	11,655
1.00	50	10	0	19,980
.75	68	20	10	32,634
.50	120	60	30	69,930
.25	140	120	100	119,880

* These totals are computed by weighing each component group in the market by its purchases per spending unit and multiplying this by the number of spending units, a constant 333 spending units per income group in this example. Thus the total demand at $1.00 is accounted for by 50 lbs. times 333 spending units *plus* 10 lbs. times 333 spending units, or 19,980 lbs., etc.

bined responses to $1.75 a pound for butter to the combined responses at the 25-cent price level.

Demand is never a particular response of buyers at any one particular level of price. People are often confused about this and when the price of a given commodity falls, and the quantity demanded rises, demand is said to have increased. But did the quantity demanded rise to a *greater* or *lesser* degree than was expected in the first place on the basis of the demand *schedule*? If, upon the lowering of a price, more of a commodity can be sold than had been expected, an increase of demand has actually occurred, but it has nothing to do at all with the price decline. Had the price not declined, an increase in sales over what had been expected would have been noticed at the original price level. On the other hand, if upon lowering the price of a commodity, it is found that not as much more can be sold as expected, then a *decrease* of demand will have taken place.

The reader can easily ascertain from the graph, Figure 15–2, that increased demand means more would be bought at an unaltered price. The example can also be read in reverse to show a decrease in demand and its implications. Simply assume D_1-D_1 to be the original level of demand; $D-D$ then becomes the schedule which portrays a diminished demand.

Figure 15–2. Illustration of an Increase of Demand

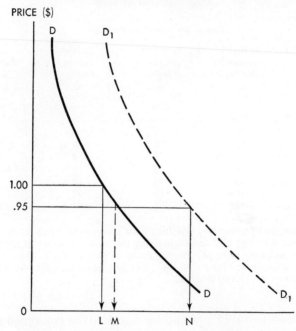

EXPLANATORY NOTE: In this case the price of the commodity is lowered from $1.00 to 95 cents a unit. If the demand had *not* increased, more would have been sold, namely, a quantity *OM* rather than *OL*. But when the demand increased, this was shown by an even larger quantity, *ON*, being sold. Since this represents a new lineup of preferences, the change is reflected in the demand schedule throughout. This is shown on the graph by the whole *D–D* line shifting to the right, where it is labeled D_1–D_1.

The Elasticity of Demand

For many practical and theoretical purposes it is useful to know not only what quantities buyers stand prepared to take off the market at different levels of prices, but also the *sensitivity* of consumer responses to changes in prices. Economists use the phrase *elasticity of demand* to describe price-response behavior. When the reaction to price change is sluggish, we speak of a low degree of elasticity; if the reaction of buyers is intense, we speak of a high degree of elasticity.

ELASTICITY OF DEMAND EXPLAINED AND ILLUSTRATED

In Table 15–2 the demand for butter was shown in schedule form, the total demand as well as the partial demands of three types of families as classified by their incomes. To illustrate the nature of elasticity, attention is directed to the changes in partial and total demand when the price of butter declines from 50 cents to 25 cents a pound (or, alternately, rises from 25 cents to 50 cents). A part of Table 15–2 is reproduced:

Price per Pound y	Pounds Taken per Spending Unit			Total Demand in Pounds $x_1+x_2+x_3$
	By High-Income Families x_1	By Middle-Income Families x_2	By Low-Income Families x_3	
(a)	(b)			(c)
$.50	120	60	30	69,930
.25	140	120	100	119,880

Inelastic demand. Concentrating first on the high-income family expenditure above, note that when the price of butter drops, only 20 pounds more are wanted. This is not surprising, as the high-income family typically uses much butter at relatively high prices. Using more butter is not really important; in fact, some of the extra butter will be put to trivial uses—teaching the youngsters to bake, for example. In other words, under ordinary circumstances the marginal utility of butter is low for the typical high-income family. Therefore the response to a price change is weak. At 25 cents a pound, 140 pounds are bought instead of 120. This can be called either a 16⅔ per cent change or a 14⅔ per cent change, depending on whether one compares the extra 20 pounds purchased with the 120 pounds to which they are added or considers them a part of the new consumption level at 140 pounds. So we simply compromise and call it a 15½ per cent change. Now the price changes from 50 cents a pound to 25 cents. Looking upward from the 25-cent level, this is a decrease of 100 per cent, but, of course, 25 cents is only one-half of 50 cents, so that looking down from the 50-cent price level, there was only a 50 per cent price change. We compromise and call it a 75 per cent change.

To arrive at the coefficient of elasticity, the percentage change in quantity demanded is compared with the percentage change in price. This means dividing the 15½ per cent change of quantity of butter demanded by the 75 per cent price decrease. The quotient, or coefficient of elasticity, is −.2, the minus sign designating that price and quantity change in different directions. This elasticity means that for every 10 per cent change in price there will only be a 2 per cent change in quantity taken. The result in our example of a typical high-income family's demand for butter is rather striking. The price decreases by 75 per cent, but the quantity of butter taken increases by only 15½ per cent—not enough to offset the effect of the fall of price on the butter producers' incomes. When the high-income family bought 120 pounds at 50 cents a pound, the total outlay was $60. Now, at 25 cents a pound, the value of the purchase is only $35 (140 pounds times 25 cents).

This signifies an inelastic demand. It is what the underdeveloped areas of the world encounter when they export agricultural raw materials or ordinary minerals, such as iron ore, to the highly industrialized nations of the world. The demand of these industrialized nations for the raw materials of the backward areas is inelastic. Consequently, whenever producers of raw materials in backward areas have a bumper crop to export, they receive less for it than for the output of a deficient harvest season. But in a deficient harvest season they do not have much to export, so their income is also small. They are caught in the vise of inelastic demand for their export products, and it appears the backward nations can never catch up to the prosperous industrial nations unless they receive technical aid from the more advanced nations. In Figure 15–3, the solid part of curve X_1 illustrates inelastic demand.

Elastic demand. Let us next examine the response of the *low-income* families to a drop in the price of butter from 50 cents a pound to 25 cents. Checking column (*b*) of Table 15–2, it is observed that the quantity demanded by the low-income families (x_3) rises from 30 pounds to 100 pounds. This is not surprising either. When butter is at the low price of 25 cents a pound, the low-income families can afford to use it for cooking, to put it on peanut butter sandwiches, to serve it at every meal—perhaps even to waste some; previously, they would reserve it for Christmas-cookie baking, for father's lunch bucket, and for occasional dinner guests.

The big increase in quantity demanded may either be said to be 233 per cent (70 pounds as a percentage of 30 pounds), or it may be said to be an increase of only 70 per cent (70 pounds as a percentage of 100 pounds). So we compromise and call it an increase of 150 per cent. The price increase we know to be 75 per cent on our compromise basis. Dividing 150 per cent change in quantity demanded by 75 per cent change in price, we arrive at −2.0 as the coefficient of elasticity of butter to low-income families over the price range of 50 cents to 25 cents a pound. This is ten times the elasticity of the high-income families over this range of prices. So lively a response is described by saying that the demand is *elastic* (see the solid part of curve X_3, Figure 15–3).

Figure 15–3. Elasticities of Demand for Butter of Three Types of Family,
Classified by Income

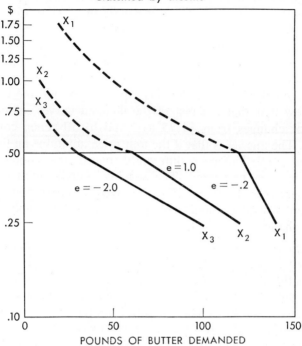

Unitary elasticity. There can also be an elasticity of unitary value. This would mean that for every 1 per cent change in price there would be a 1 per cent change in the quantity demanded. Table 15–2 illustrates this in the case of middle-income families when the price of butter falls from 50 cents to 25 cents a pound. Observe that the quantity demanded rises from 60 to 120 pounds. This is either a 100 per cent increase or one of 50 per cent; we compromise and name it a 75 per cent increase of quantity demanded. The price change is also 75 per cent; hence the elasticity of the middle-income family demand for butter over the given price range is *unity*. This implies that the middle-income family always spends the same amount of money on butter, sacrificing other things when the price of butter rises, buying more of other things or saving money when the price of butter falls. The solid portion of curve X_2, Figure 15–3, illustrates unitary elasticity.

A caution. The general formula for measuring elasticity *between two points* of a market demand schedule is:

$$\text{elasticity} = \frac{\text{percentage change of quantity demanded}}{\text{percentage change of price}}$$

Elasticity of demand should really be measured only over limited price ranges—say over a range of 25 cents in our butter example, which would be the 50- to 25-cent range, the 50- to 75-cent range, and so on. Figure 15–3, a semi-logarithmic chart, centers attention on the elasticities of demand of our three different income-size families. Observe how awkward it would be to fit a smoothed curve to the whole range of price responses of the families, from their responses at $1.75 a pound to their responses at 25 cents a pound. In fact, the reader may wonder how it is that the rest of the demand curves, describing responses for changes from $1.75 a pound to 50 cents, could be so smoothed. The answer is that if the unit price notations on the vertical axis of the graph had been differently spaced, the smoothing effect would have been prevented. The spacing actually used emphasizes what happens over the 50- to 25-cent range of price responses; if more information is wanted about other price ranges, the graph's notations should be changed.

Elasticity and marginal utility. In Figure 15–4 the total demand of column (c) in Table 15–2 is shown. Again the emphasis is on what happens in the 50- to 25-cent price range. The actual elasticity between these two points of price is —.75. The total demand of high-income, middle-income, and low-income families combined is somewhat inelastic. That is to be expected. After all, elasticity of demand gives expression to the rate at which the marginal utility of a product changes. When a product is firmly established in the consumer's budget, the *rate of growth of its marginal utility* is usually at or near maximum;

Figure 15–4. Total Demand for a Commodity (data hypothetical)

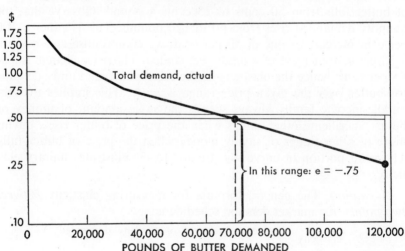

there is no desire to buy much more of it when the price declines, or much less of it when the price rises. This is the position of butter in the high-income family budget in our example. The middle-income family will buy more butter if the price is right, but not at the sacrifice of other goods or services. Only the low-income families are willing to spend money planned for other uses to buy more butter when it becomes sufficiently cheap; that is to say, only among the low-income families is there a rapidly changed rate of growth of marginal utility and, therefore, a high elasticity of demand at low price levels. With two out of every three families in the community the marginal utility of butter is at maximum, or is approaching maximum, so it is not surprising that the demand for butter in the 50- to 25-cent range is somewhat inelastic.

Application of elasticity exemplified. Would the butter producers actually manufacture 119,880 pounds to be sold at 25 cents? If there is competition among them, we cannot tell by merely knowing the demand for the product; we must also know the costs of production. Let us suppose that the aggregate costs of butter production always rise in direct proportion to the increase of production. Thus if producing 70,000 pounds of butter costs the producers $17,500, including 6 per cent of profit (on investment), 119,880 pounds would have cost $30,000 (70,000 : 119,880 = 17,500 : 30,000). Under competition the 119,880 pounds of butter would probably be produced at 25 cents a pound (= $29,970). Competition has the effect of determining prices at the point where they cover costs (including a 6 per cent profit).

If the butter producers are organized in a monopolistic association, they would surely halt the production of butter at the 70,000-pound level, charging 50 cents per pound. For at this point there is the widest spread between total cost, assumed to be growing in a linear fashion, and total income from sales. Cost is $17,500 and sales revenue $35,000. By contrast, at the 119,880-pound production level, cost is $30,000 and so is sales revenue. Could the monopolistic producers cut production back to 32,634 pounds to be sold at 75 cents, as shown in Table 15–2, column (c)? They could, but it would not pay, because the total demand elasticity for butter is −1.5, over the 75- to 50-cent range; that is, the demand is elastic. But monopoly can flourish only in a range of price where the demand is *inelastic*. This reveals one of the most practical uses that can and will be made of the concept of demand elasticity—that of using inelasticity as a measure of the degree of monopoly in any given industrial or commercial situation. The treatment of this is reserved for Chapter 18. Here the concept of elasticity of demand has been introduced with the intention of equipping the reader with a full understanding of demand in all of its aspects of utility, marginal utility, and elasticity.[1]

For Discussion

1. It may be said in general terms that the price of a commodity measures approximately its marginal utility to the purchaser. Is this point of view on the value of an article consistent with the fact that the most useful commodities such as water, iodized salt, and paper towels, are cheap?

2. Explain, in marginal utility terms, that a thing is just worth the price which a rational consumer will pay for it.

3. Most of the prices which we pay are uniform and remain fixed over fairly long periods of time. Moreover, we rarely, as individuals, adjust the amount of a commodity we buy in accordance with its price. How then does the law of demand operate so that prices do vary from time to time?

4. A housewife has arranged her buying schedule rationally, so that the respective marginal utilities which she receives from buying different things are proportionate to their prices. In other words, she pays for each purchase the price it is worth to her considering the alternative purchases she must forego. She now receives an inheritance. We shall assume that she spends this legacy in addition to her previous expenditures solely in buying more of the things she had previously purchased. Is the total utility she now receives smaller or larger than before? Is the marginal utility of each article of her consumption increased or diminished? Since the marginal utilities of the different articles of consumption now change, can all of them once again become proportionate to their prices?

5. In two American cities with approximately the same population, there is this difference of income distribution: in the one city 4 per cent of the population lives at or beneath the poverty level; in the other city, 22 per cent of the population is relatively poor, receiving an income per family of less than $2,500 annually. If, as a children's clothing manufacturer, you avoided doing business in the poorer city, you would have failed to learn the lesson of the principle of marginal utility which underlies market demand, even though market demand is not measurable in a general sense in terms of marginal utility. Explain why you would have failed to learn the lesson.

6. What relation, if any, is there between the concept of demand in this chapter and the concept of aggregate demand as applied in the chapters on employment determination?

---

[1] For advanced study, demand schedules may be conceived as arising in tangencies of iso-outlay, or "budget" lines, with iso-utility contour lines (indifference curves) drawn for various levels of a consumer's indifference to alternative combinations of purchases. As this approach involves only the *ranking* of human preferences, no false inferences about the measurability and interpersonal comparability of utility can be drawn. However, it has not been shown with scientific adequacy just how individual indifference maps can be *non-arbitrarily* aggregated. Thus for the beginning student the simpler marginal utility appears more serviceable. See also Dorfman, Samuelson, and Solow, *Linear Programming and Economic Analysis* (New York: McGraw-Hill Co., Inc., 1958), Appendix A, having reference to possible implications for demand theory of the (also advanced) theory of games.

7. When the elasticities of demand of three types of families, income-wise, were computed from the data in Table 15–2, over the price range of 50 to 25 cents a pound for butter, the elasticities were found to be: .2, 1.0, and 2.0 for the families of high incomes, middle incomes, and low incomes, in this order. But these are only partial elasticities. The elasticity for the combined market demand must be ascertained by consulting column (c) of Table 15–2, that is, by comparing the change in total quantity demanded over the 50- to 25-cent price range to the known price change of 75 per cent for this price range. Ascertain this elasticity. Why is it a different figure than the average of the .2, 1.0, and 2.0 partial elasticities?

16

Individual

Costs of Production and

Industry Supply Schedules

The Basic Meaning of Cost

Production is the processing of resources into useful goods and services. All resources are directly or indirectly transformable into finished goods. Iron ore, for example, is used for making steel; some of the steel is used for building ore-extracting equipment and boats to carry the equipment to the iron ore deposit, bringing more ore to the steel mills in return. Steel is fabricated into household appliances; steel is used in agricultural and transportation equipment; it is used in countless ways to help satisfy human wants directly or indirectly. All economic resources are used together in ever widening circles of productive relationships. To carry on and facilitate aggregate production is the task of labor—the work of those who earn their daily bread, who control automated equipment, who manage, invent, and innovate.

In Chapters 4 through 8 it was seen that the hallmark of the efficient utilization of resources is conservation—using land, labor, and capital sparingly even though we may have them abundantly. *Real cost* was defined as the proportionate amount of valuable resources used to obtain a desired amount of production. Real cost rises when excessive effort is required and declines when natural forces are understood and harnessed for the benefit of mankind. Thus real cost emerges as the fundamental criterion by which to judge performance from the viewpoint of human welfare.

In this chapter the analysis of real cost is carried to the level of the individual firm, where the bulk of decisions about utilizing resources are made. The quantities of wanted goods and services which are brought to market obviously depend in large part on how wisely or unwisely the entrepreneurs can manage to handle resources. Of course, the flow of supplies also depends upon the particular demand for particular commodities and upon the state of aggregate demand for the products of industry. This introduces the criterion of *money cost,* a different consideration than real cost. That is to say, it is not sufficient for an entrepreneur to know that he can manage certain resources efficiently. He must also be assured that he can do so profitably. This is not possible if the resources which the entrepreneur has in mind are urgently wanted for alternative types of production. For then the rate of wages, rent, and interest which the entrepreneur must pay to obtain command over needed units of labor, land, and capital might be unduly high, no matter how efficiently he could manage the resources.

Given data. In the analysis of cost factors which determine the supplies of particular types of goods brought to market, one can safely make the assumption that the main lines of production are well established. The practical problem, therefore, is by how much or how little the flows of supply along these lines are apt to vary (1) in response to consumer demand, and (2) as the result of the producers' learning to use resources more efficiently (or by neglecting to do so). Given the consumer demand for a particular commodity, the problem is reduced to estimating the probable fluctuations of supply due to advancing or regressing entrepreneurial efficiency. For if the consumer demand is adequate, *as given,* the entrepreneur is able to pay the going rate of wages, rent, and interest. The rest depends upon him—that is, whether or not he is able to realize a profit by efficiently managing his production and marketing problems.

Taking the market demand schedule for a product as given, as well as wage rates and rental and interest rates, focuses attention on the cost factors which are directly under an entrepreneur's control. It enables us to observe the entrepreneur who is deciding whether to produce goods of a certain type, how much of them to produce, and in what manner to produce them so that he might realize a maximum of profit.

In the most usual type of business situation the individual firm's problem is not whether to produce goods or not to produce them.

Rather, the problem is whether or not to accept or reject an additional order for a product, *given the current market price for the product.* For the industry as a whole the problem differs. The industry is presumed to be delivering that aggregate supply of the product which it is just profitable to produce at the price current. How much more of an inducement, price-wise, must the industry have to increase its production?

This statement of the problem of the firm and the industry, respectively, reveals that costs of production vary with the rate of operation of one plant and of all the plants in the industry. Let us first consider the case of the individual entrepreneur who is making a supply decision.

Economical Control of Production Costs

How must an entrepreneur proceed in deciding whether to accept or reject an order? He is faced with a subtle problem of "concomitant variation"; that is to say, it may require different proportional amounts of labor, raw materials, and equipment to produce a unit of output when operating at different rates of production. In producing a greater or lesser amount of total output, the entrepreneur's task would be a relatively simple one if all that were needed were the use of certain types of equipment, certain grades of labor, and so on, always combined in the same proportions—only more or less of them. But "baking a large pie" is not necessarily a matter of doing more of the same thing as "baking a small pie."

Usually in business decision-making one or more factors of production are fixed as given; that is to say, in one respect or another, one has to work with what there is. Perhaps the only fixed factor is management ability. But for very many purposes of decision-making the entrepreneur must take his plant and some stock of durable equipment as given to see how well he can manage with it. To this given plant, equipment, and management ability he then adds, figuratively speaking, varying quantities of raw materials, labor, freight services, and the like. The latter resources are referred to as *variable factors of production.* These variable factors he must arrange (1) in adaptation to the fixed equipment and (2) in relation to each other. The aim is to reach the optimal, or best, fixed-plus-variable factor combination. This can be discerned as that unique combination of various possible combinations in which all the fixed and variable production factors are so nicely adjusted that nothing could be gained by rearrangement—by using more of some variable factor and less of another.

How does the entrepreneur arrive at this economical result? It would hardly do for him to grope blindly among various factor combinations, all of which would yield output more or less wastefully, but some of which would push him over the brink of bankruptcy before he had discovered the optimal or even a reasonably economical combination.

THE CONCEPT OF MARGINS

If asked, most practical entrepreneurs would reply that they "play this sort of thing by ear." That may be true, but it should not be inferred that this signifies running industry by chance. What the entrepreneur means is that he learns to recognize the limit to which he should employ each factor of production, which will pay him most in producing units of a particular kind of output. He must, in other words, ascertain that *margin* of utilization for each type of resource which it is economically feasible to use. If he goes beyond this limit, or margin, he will be using that particular resource wastefully, because he could achieve greater output by using less of it. At the same time he will be employing the other resources wastefully, because they could contribute more effectively to production if relatively more of them were used.

But how does one identify the margins of utilization for each economic factor of production, relative to the fixed plant and equipment and relative to all the other variable factors? Again the practical answer would be that one learns about utilization margins by experience. But that is no answer at all. *What kind* of experience?—that is the question. Obviously the only practical answer will refer to some organized pattern of events which may be expected to continue in the future. Practical men of business get to know what constitutes safe operating ratios of tangible assets to the firm's net worth, value of inventory to net working capital, funded debts to net working capital, and so on. The last-named ratio is directly related to the question of how to combine, for profit, indirect and direct man-hours (fixed and variable costs of production). Sometimes these ratios are closely guarded secrets of a successful concern; most often they become known throughout the industry. Thus a person opening a new motel has the benefit of the industry's knowledge about what percentage, roughly speaking, of the investment should be such items as structural parts, electrical installations, appliances and fixtures, and the amount of bedding to be kept in the individual rooms. Every particular motel owner will deviate to some extent. However, the deviations from the industry's representative operating ratios are likely to be relatively small. In the case of a new industry, some original probing must be done to ascertain where the margins lie, that is, the safe operating ratios. Every participant in a new industry may experience difficulty in realizing profit for some time; but when one or a group of entrepreneurs finally discovers safe operating ratios, there is a rapid influx into the industry.

Standard operating ratios (commonly known as industrial efficiency margins) naturally vary from industry to industry. Thus in the men's clothing industry, fixed assets constitute only 16.5 per cent of tangible net worth, showing that much direct labor is used. In the practically automated petroleum industry, by contrast, fixed assets constitute 84.5 per cent of tangible net worth.[1] Sometimes this knowledge is expressed directly in man-hour terms; thus, operating experience shows that for a machine shop which performs expert work, a labor force of 500 production workers is optimal.

Economists have long understood that underlying all the specific operating ratios (that is, resource utilization margins) is a general phenomenon. This is referred to as the *principle* (or law) *of diminishing returns*.

Statement of the Principle of Diminishing Returns

When particular types or grades of resources are combined in certain proportions to produce a certain amount of output, it is not ordinarily possible to increase that amount of output without changing the proportions in which the resources are combined. Let us take as an example an entrepreneur who is operating a factory which has a certain amount of floor space and is equipped with four identical batteries of machines. To obtain an increase of output requires that the entrepreneur hire a number of helpers as well as a few more foremen to aid the operators of the machines. This manifestly changes the proportion in which labor and machinery are combined.

Of course, there are circumstances under which the entrepreneur finds it possible to vary his output without disturbing the ratios of plant space to machinery, labor to machinery, and so on. Let us say that he has been using only two of the four identical batteries of machines. In that case he can double his output simply by using all four batteries and need not alter the proportion of floor space to machine battery, of workers to battery, and so on. Or if the entrepreneur is assured of a permanent increase of the market for his product, he can double his output by building a second plant of exactly the same size and specifications as the original parent plant.

---

[1] See Roy A. Foulke, *Behind the Scenes of Business* (New York: Dun & Bradstreet, Inc., 1952), pp. 159, 165. The appendix discloses median operating ratios for 70 lines of business.

Careful reflection will reveal that all instances when output can be increased without upsetting usual quantitative relations (that is, the proportionalities of different production factors) are cases in which *all* the factors are capable of being varied. But if doubling all the factors is necessary to achieve a doubled production, is it not common sense to realize that production will *not* be doubled if only *some* factors are increased, while one or several others are given and fixed in amount?

Thus the following principle may be stated: *Under a given state of the arts, when equal and homogeneous input units of a variable production factor* (or factor combination) *are successively added to the fixed factor* (or combination of fixed factors), *the result is that total output will grow, but only at a diminishing rate.*

Stated in this generalized fashion (that is, not only with reference to land or other naturally scarce resources), the law of diminishing returns can be applied to any economic situation whatsoever. And what may be considered to be a fixed factor in one given situation may appear as a variable factor in some other situation, or vice versa. Thus an engine lathe may be a fixed factor in a small aircraft-parts plant but may be a variable factor in a large air-frame company which could sell some of its engine lathes if it decided to discontinue producing a certain type of aircraft part and buy this commodity from small machine shops instead.

HOW ENTREPRENEURS ACT ON THE PRINCIPLE OF DIMINISHING RETURNS

Ideally, any entrepreneur who is contemplating a substantial run of production envisions as a first step, or actually experiments with, alternative combinations of productive factors in order to find the one he may expect to operate most efficiently with. Let us say that a foundry operator has a certain amount of factory space, storage capacity, office space, and salaried staff, an electric smelting furnace, a given number of molding benches, sandblasting apparatus, and so on. Given his plant, equipment, and salaried staff, the entrepreneur must now decide how many production workers he will hire. The problem is to determine the optimum-yield combination of the given factors with a variable amount of production workers. By optimum-yield combination is meant the most favorable condition as to output performance of the entire plant.

What will be the results of hiring an increased number of production workers, each to work 8 hours a day? As an example, let us say that the entrepreneur starts with 250 men; less than that would mean that his plant is so seriously understaffed that some equipment would stand idle while the foremen and other supervisors would not have enough to do. Two hundred and fifty production workers employed for 8 hours a day constitutes what economists call a direct "input" of 2,000 man-hours. With this "input of direct labor," 100 units of product are turned out by the end of the 8-hour day. With 2,000 man-hours of work done and a corresponding output of 100 units of product, dividing man-hours into achieved production shows that the average output per man-hour is one-twentieth of one unit of product manufactured during the day.

Is this an optimum yield for the plant as a whole, using all its facilities? The entrepreneur is certain that it is not; in fact, there is much evidence that the plant is understaffed, and seriously so. He hires 188 additional workers, paying them the same rate of wages (because although 188 men is a considerable number for him, it is a small percentage of the normal complement of foundry workers in this labor market area).

The entrepreneur now employs 438 production workers. Working 8 hours, they deliver 3,500 man-hours of work service and show an output of 200 product units. This is double the output of the first 250 workers and an increase from .05 to .057 in the average output per man-hour. The entrepreneur, however, still finds that the plant, as an organization, has not yet reached its full stride, and consequently he hires another 125 men. The total direct labor force now is 563 men, delivering 4,500 man-hours of work services. This process of adding production workers continues until an optimum yield per man-hour is achieved.

Table 16–1 hypothetically illustrates the process of an entrepreneur seeking to determine his optimum yield position, having regard only for the effects of hiring more and more direct production labor. The reader should carefully bear in mind that "all other things" are assumed to remain equal throughout—that is, consumer demand, its size and composition; the price of production equipment; the salaried staff; and the wages to be paid the men who are hired, regardless of how many are hired.

Table 16–1 is constructed by dividing column (b), which shows the output, by column (a), which shows the amount of man-hours directly used to produce that output. This relation is shown for ten different amounts of output in column (c). Thus the first figure in column (c), .05, says that .05 of a unit of output is produced from every man-hour directly used in producing 100 units; but .083 of a unit of product per man-hour is realized when 500 units are produced. Thereafter, the ratio of output falls.

Table 16–1 reveals that the average yield of output per direct labor input in this case reaches a maximum at a 500-unit level of produc-

Table 16–1. Average Diminishing Yields to Inputs of Direct Labor

Man-Hours of Direct-Labor Input (a)	Total Units of Output (b)	Output per Man-Hour of Direct-Labor Input (c)
2,000	100	.05000
3,500	200	.05714
4,500	300	.06666
5,000	400	.08000
6,000	500	.08333
7,500	600	.08000
9,500	700	.07368
12,000	800	.06666
15,000	900	.06000
20,000	1,000	.05000

tion. Does this mean that the entrepreneur should cease operating when he has reached this 500-unit level of output?

The discerning reader will be quick to answer "No" to this question. For to answer "Yes" would be to overlook the fact that the fixed plant and equipment and the salaried staff can also make an additional contribution to the total output if they are more fully used. Of course, the plant and equipment, when used more adequately, do not deliver man-hours of labor in the same direct sense as the hired production workers. However, man-hours of labor were embodied (that is, they were consumed when the plant and equipment were built) in the facilities used for constructing the plant and equipment. At the time the plant and equipment were constructed, the man-hours consumed in doing so could not contribute immediately to any output of finished goods. But now that the plant and equipment are in use, the embodied man-hours are, in a symbolic manner of speaking, released for service in producing the products of the firm. The more effectively the plant and equipment are used, the greater the contribution of the "indirect man-hours"—to use the phrase which is customary in industry.

There is this peculiarity of indirect man-hours: they are available whether the given facilities are used or not. The same is true of the service which the salaried staff can perform. These services have been contracted for in advance for a period of specified duration, say a year; it is up to the entrepreneur to use his staff. He must pay the salaries whether he uses these professional services or not. For simplicity's sake let us say that the entrepreneur has at his command 10,000 man-hours of indirect labor, most of it embodied in the given plant and equipment, some represented by the hours of work for which he has paid the salaried staff in advance. Even if not a single unit of product were to be manufactured, this store of indirect labor would be at the entrepreneur's command. Alternatively stated, it represents a cost of production which he has incurred and which would constitute a total loss if the plant were not placed into operation.

Now, with the hiring of 250 workers the plant starts operations. Naturally, it is not solely the production workers that produce the output. Indeed, without the facilities of the plant and equipment and the salaried staff they could not show an iota of output. Accordingly, the next thing for the entrepreneur to ascertain is the contribution of the given and fixed factors of production at different rates of operation. For this purpose he ignores the fact that production workers are at work and simply concentrates on the increasing yield of his indirect labor represented by the fixed facilities and the salaried staff. As he now operates the plant more and more intensively, he is in effect using an increasing flow of indirect labor hours in combination with the direct man-hours per day delivered by the production workers. When the 10,000 indirect labor hours were not used, they did not contribute any output. When 100 units of the product are produced after 250 production workers have been hired, it is found that each indirect labor hour now contributes one-hundredth of one product unit. (Divide 100 by 10,000.) The contribution of the fixed plant and equipment and salaried staff increases as better, or wider, use is made of these facilities. It continues to increase until a point is reached where these mechanical and human facilities are used to the point of breakdown. (The fixed plant and equipment could not resist this, but the salaried staff certainly would!) In Table 16–2 the results of using given plant and equipment more and more intensively are illustrated hypothetically.

This table is computed in the same manner as Table 16–1, that is, by dividing column (b) by column (a) in order to ascertain the product per indirect man-hour at different volumes of output. Thus .01 in column (c) shows that there is one-hundredth of a product per indirect man-hour when 100 units are produced; but there is one-twentieth (.05) of a product when 500 units are produced.

Actually, there are no diminishing returns in the fixed plant and equipment, but rather increasing returns. When the given factors are used more and more intensively, they naturally contribute more to the total production than if left standing relatively idle. (This holds true until machinery simply breaks down from overuse.)

At this stage of the discussion we might seem to have landed in a quandary. Physical production returns to the average man-hour of *direct* labor applied to the fixed equipment are at a maximum when 500 units of output are produced. To stop there would be to ignore the contribution of the labor indirectly applied by the fixed plant and

Table 16–2. Average Returns as Expressed with Reference to
Fixed Plant and Equipment

Man-Hours of Indirect-Labor Input (a)	Total Units of Output (b)	Output per Man-Hour of Indirect-Labor Input (c)
10,000	0	0
10,000	100	.01
10,000	200	.02
10,000	300	.03
10,000	400	.04
10,000	500	.05
10,000	600	.06
10,000	700	.07
10,000	800	.08
10,000	900	.09
10,000	1,000	.10

equipment. But this contribution keeps increasing. Under these circumstances how can the entrepreneur determine his optimum combination of direct-plus-indirect labor from the viewpoint of physical returns?

The simple answer to this question is that the entrepreneur must reckon returns in terms of the *combined* use of direct and indirect labor. Note well that this cannot be done by adding the figures in columns (c) of Tables 16–1 and 16–2. For these figures reflect two different points of view on the results of increasing production. But now we shall take a third, an over-all, view. In Table 16–3 we consider, as before, the total output of products at different production levels. However, the data are for the *combined* input of direct and indirect labor hours, rather than for each viewed separately without heed being paid to the other.

The usual calculation is involved in constructing this table. Column (b) is divided by column (a) to ascertain the output per man-hour of combined direct and indirect man-hour inputs. At the 100-unit level of production this joint output is only eight-thousandths of product per aggregate man-hour; this is because the fixed equipment is obviously being seriously underutilized. But at the 800-unit level of production output nears four-hundredths of a product per aggregate man-hour, showing that real progress has been made in using the fixed equipment adequately and in using the right number of men.

Now, Table 16–3 plainly shows that the advantage of using fixed plant and equipment more intensively overshadows diminishing returns to the variable input factor until a volume of production of 800

Table 16–3. Average Diminishing Returns Expressed with Reference to Both Fixed and Variable Inputs of Factors of Production

Man-Hours of Direct-plus-Indirect-Labor Input (a)	Total Units of Output (b)	Output per Man-Hour of All Labor Input (c)
10,000	0	....
12,000	100	.00833
13,500	200	.01481
14,500	300	.02071
15,000	400	.02666
16,000	500	.03125
17,500	600	.03429
19,500	700	.03591
22,000	800	.03636
25,000	900	.03601
30,000	1,000	.03333

product units has been reached. Thereafter the rate at which diminishing returns accrue to the variable factor of direct labor overcomes the advantage of more intensive utilization of the given plant and equipment.

At the 800-unit level of production the entrepreneur has reached his optimum yield in combining the productive factors. As a general proposition there is for each individual producer a determinate production level which for him is optimal, that is, represents his most favorable level of production from a physical-output point of view. Given the consumer demand, the rates of wages and so on, and his technological knowledge, this will also be his most profitable level of production. This may be appreciated by expressing the above insights about yields of production in the language of the money costs of production.

A Roster of Contractual Money Costs

When compared with income from sales, the money costs of production determine whether or not a profit is realized. The maximum profit position for an individual firm is at the point where there is the widest spread between aggregate income from sales and the total cost of production. But note that the maximum profit position is not necessarily indicated by the *margin* of profit which an entrepreneur realizes on the sale of each unit of product. A low per-unit profit margin can be offset by a large volume of sales. An entrepreneur is interested in aggregate sales income, not necessarily in how much he can earn on each unit of product. If he charges too high a margin of profit, he might not be able to sell much of the product!

The minimum average cost of producing any one unit of product does not fix the maximum profit position either. Although cost is increasing least when the *per unit* cost of producing a good is at the minimum, this indicates nothing about how the *total revenue* is increasing. *Both aggregate sales income and total cost* must be taken into account to arrive at the maximum profit position for the firm.

Total money cost of production is the arithmetical sum of all the particular outlays which an entrepreneur makes, or contracts to make, for purchasing and hiring productive services directly and in the form of fixed plant and equipment. As more and more is produced, total money cost must naturally rise as more productive services must be purchased or hired.

Table 16–4. Total Cost of Production of a Firm
(at $1.00 per man-hour)

Quantity Produced (a)	Total Cost (b)	Fixed Cost (c)	Direct Cost (d)
0	$10,000	$10,000	$ ....
100	12,000	10,000	2,000
200	13,500	10,000	3,500
300	14,500	10,000	4,500
400	15,000	10,000	5,000
500	16,000	10,000	6,000
600	17,500	10,000	7,500
700	19,500	10,000	9,500
800	22,000	10,000	12,000
900	25,000	10,000	15,000
1,000	30,000	10,000	20,000

Total cost under given conditions. Table 16–4 presents a total cost schedule. It is constructed on the basis of data on inputs of direct man-hours, given in Table 16–1; on data of inputs of indirect man-hours, given in Table 16–2; and on the data of combined direct and indirect man-hour inputs, shown in Table 16–3. For simplicity's sake, a uniform cost of $1.00 has been assumed for every direct man-hour as well as indirect man-hour used in production. Observe that total cost starts at the level of the cost of the fixed investment, which is a cost even when not a single unit of a commodity is produced. Thereafter, total cost necessarily rises continuously. (Attention is directed to column [b]; columns [c] and [d] have been included only for reference.)

The total cost schedule of Table 16–4 is pictorialized in Figure 16–1.

Figure 16–1. Total Cost for an Individual Firm

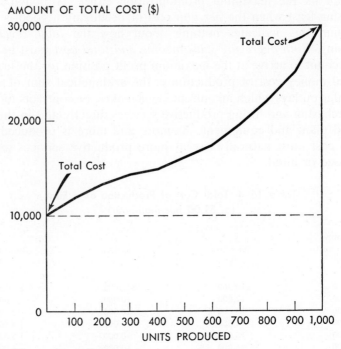

AMOUNT OF TOTAL COST ($)

SOURCE: Column (*b*) of Table 16–4.

Aggregate sales income under given conditions. The reader is asked to bear carefully in mind that the figures here presented furnish a basically *static* picture of the firm's situation, of what happens consequent upon a change in its rate of plant and equipment utilization. The data in no respect reflect any dynamic growth of the firm. This does not prevent us, however, from making various assumptions about the *magnitudes of the given factors.* Here we shall assume that there are two different price levels at which the product might sell: a price of $32.50 a unit and $27.50 a unit. Table 16–5 (columns [b_1] and [b_2]) shows what sales income would be at several levels of output for each of these different prices. It is assumed that the particular firm is one which operates in competition with numerous other plants making the same basic product. Hence the price of the product remains as given no matter how much output the competitive firm produces; it is too small a firm among many others to be able to influence the price of the product by its output variations.

Figure 16–2 visually presents the hypothetically given data of Table 16–5.

Table 16–5. Aggregate Sales Income of a Firm at Two Prices
of Its Product

Quantity Sold (a)	Income from Sales When Product Sells, per Unit, at	
	$27.50 (b₁)	$32.50 (b₂)
200	$ 5,500	$ 6,500
400	11,000	13,000
600	16,500	19,500
800	22,000	26,000
1,000	27,500	32,500

Figure 16–2. Aggregate Sales Income for an Individual Firm

AMOUNT OF TOTAL REVENUE ($)

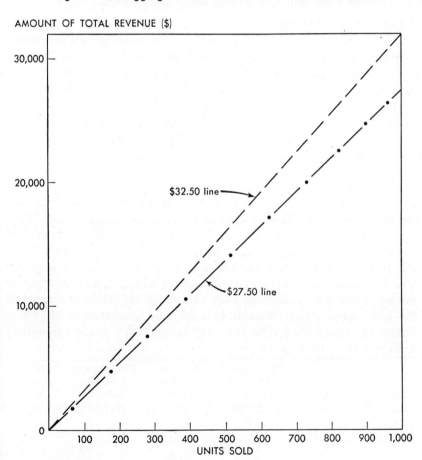

SOURCE: Table 16–5.

Observe that there is linear increase of aggregate sales income at each price per unit. This is because we have assumed the firm to be competitive, too small to influence the price of the product whether or not it produces much or little. With the price remaining constant, sales income is bound to increase in direct proportion to the increased volume of sales; that is, sales income is bound to grow in a linear fashion. The elasticity of the demand *for the firm's product* (not for that of the industry) is infinite. This is to say that it can sell as much as it can produce or wishes to produce at either one of the two prices, that is, at whichever one of them happens to be current in the market, or at any other price. Infinite demand for the product of the firm causes its sales income to rise in a linear fashion, that is, in direct proportion to the increased volume of sales. To say this is merely an alternative way of stating that the firm is operating under competition.

PROFIT MAXIMIZATION

The easiest way in which to appreciate how a single firm maximizes its profits while operating under competition is to compare its total costs and aggregate sales revenue visually. This is done in Figure 16–3, by simply superimposing the total cost curve (*TC*) of Figure 16–1 on the two hypothetical sales income curves of Figure 16–2.

The firm maximizes its profit when producing 800 units of output if the price current for the product is $27.50 a unit. The firm's aggregate sales revenue then just covers its total cost (which includes a 6 per cent profit on the investment). Mark well that at any other level of output, total cost would exceed aggregate sales income, thus involving the firm in a financial loss. If the price current of the product is $32.50 a unit, the firm must produce 900 units in order to maximize profit, for at that volume of output the largest of all spreads between total cost and aggregate sales income is found. By interpolating, from Figure 16–3, the aggregate sales value of 900 units of product when it is priced $32.50 a unit, we ascertain the amount of $29,250. Let us compare this aggregate sales value, and a few other relevant values of sales, with the total cost—which remains in each case unaltered as shown in Tables 16–1 and 16–4. The following calculation is made (subsidiary to Tables 16–1 through 16–5):

Units of Output:	Their total cost:	Their aggregate sales value @ $27.50:	Leaving surplus profit of:	Their aggregate sales value @ $32.50:	Leaving surplus profit of:
700	$19,500	$19,250	loss	$22,750	$3,250
800	22,000	22,000	normal profit	26,000	4,000
900	25,000	24,750	loss	29,250	4,250
1,000	30,000	27,500	loss	32,500	2,500

Figure 16–3. Profit Maximization for a Competitive Single Firm

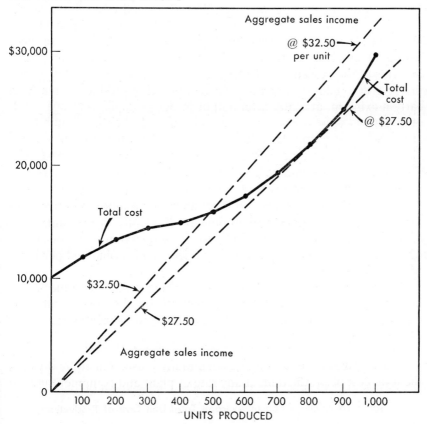

Clearly, when the sales price of the product is $32.50 per unit, production will be at the rate of 900 units of output per period of time. Observe that at this rate the entrepreneur is not operating at his optimal rate of production. This informs us that although an entrepreneur knows that a workable cost structure is essential for maximizing profit, sales income is considered, as well as cost, in determining the rate of output expected to be the most profitable.[2]

[2] In good times there is a tendency to become "receipts-conscious," in bad times, to become cost-conscious. Thus in a leading business journal, this ad appeared in 1958: "When business slows down, you get tough, tighten your belt, and cut back steel inventory because you free capital that way and save on costs of space, handling, taxes, obsolescence and wastage. . . . But when business speeds up again, do you soften and let these economies—plus your protection from risk—go out the window? . . . get the booklet *What's Your Real Cost of Possession for Steel?*" (*U.S. News & World Report,* October 3, 1958, p. 4.)

Other Ways of Viewing Cost of Production

The reader may have noticed that total cost, as portrayed in Figure 16–3, rises at three different rates. The *TC* (total cost) curve slopes gently upward toward the 400-unit rate of plant utilization level, and more steeply toward the 800-unit level. The *TC* curve then rises very steeply. This expresses the operation of the law of diminishing returns in terms of the movement of costs. Earlier, in Table 16–1, it was seen that average yields of direct man-hours applied in production reach an early maximum, at a 500-level output in our example. Average yields of direct and indirect man-hours combined reach their maximum later, at the 800-unit output level in our example. Now when these average yields successively taper off, there must be an increase of cost. The same wage rates continue to be paid to labor, the same salaries to management; and the prices of units of raw materials do not rise as the individual firm's production is expanded by a more intensive utilization of the given plant and equipment. Evidently, if the same rates of remuneration must be paid to factors of production, the money cost of production must increase as less and less yield is obtained per input of the factors of production.

To trace the growing effect of diminishing returns as reflected in increasing costs, it is useful to concentrate on the cost of any one typical unit of production when the rate of output is increasing.

AVERAGE COST (ALTERNATIVELY: AVERAGE TOTAL UNIT COST)

The average cost of a unit of a commodity is ascertained by dividing the total cost of production, at any rate of plant and equipment utiliza-

Table 16–6. Derivation of Average Total Unit Cost of Production

Quantity Produced (a)	Over-all Total Cost (b)	Total Fixed Cost (c)	Total Direct Cost (d)	Average Total Unit Cost [col. (b)÷(a)] (e)
0	$10,000	$10,000	0	....
100	12,000	10,000	$2,000	$120.00
200	13,500	10,000	3,500	67.50
300	14,500	10,000	4,500	48.30
400	15,000	10,000	5,000	37.50
500	16,000	10,000	6,000	32.00
600	17,500	10,000	7,500	29.20
700	19,500	10,000	9,500	27.90
800	22,000	10,000	12,000	27.50
900	25,000	10,000	15,000	27.80
1,000	30,000	10,000	20,000	30.00

tion, by the number of output units produced. Let this be done for the whole range of production, from the earliest unit to the thousandth unit in our example of the production costs of an individual firm. We then obtain the information in column (e) of Table 16–6; the other columns are inserted for reference purposes.

In Figure 16–4 the movement of average total unit cost (*atuc*)— alternatively called simply average cost (*ac*)—is shown in comparison with the movement of total cost (*TC*) for the individual firm. The data in Figure 16–4 are plotted on semilogarithmic graph paper, which is the only device by which two such greatly varying magnitudes as

Figure 16–4. Average Total Unit Cost of Production for the Individual Firm

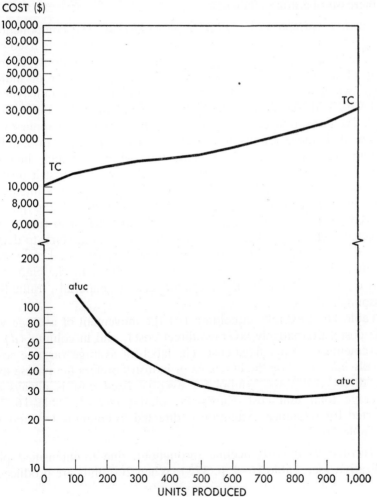

the total cost of all produced or produceable units and the average cost of a single unit can be directly compared.

Observe that average total unit cost (*atuc*) is at its minimum at that level of production where the plant and equipment are being used to produce 800 units of the firm's product. This is, indeed, what we should have expected. It could not be gleaned, however, by simply examining the total cost graph or schedule. When total cost is considered, the center of attention is on its relation to aggregate sales income. If this is a profitable relation, it is easy to overlook the possibility of increasing profit through widening the cost-income spread by reducing costs. But average cost directly invites re-examination of engineering procedures, restudies of personnel relations, and other types of research to increase operating efficiency.

Average variable cost and average fixed cost. The components of average total unit cost are average variable cost and average fixed cost. They correspond, in an inverse relation, to average output per man-hour of direct labor and average output per man-hour of indirect labor, which were given in Tables 16–1 and 16–2. Certain types of cost vary with the degree to which a given plant and equipment are used. As utilization becomes intensive, more material supplies must be handled, more repairs made, more provision made for handling human relations, and so on. This type of cost, which increases with the rate of operations, is called *variable cost.* At first it declines because improvements are made when a plant is used more intensively after having originally been understaffed. But before the plant is utilized in an optimal fashion the variable costs begin to rise, as was reflected in Table 16–1 as output per direct man-hour starts to decline after the 500-unit level of production. However, this is taken in stride because for a time there is more to be gained by using the plant more fully than is to be lost through mounting costs of materials, traffic-flow, personnel, and so forth.

Table 16–7 exhibits in column (*c*) the movement of average variable cost (alternatively, average direct cost), and in column (*d*) the movement of average fixed cost. The label for average variable cost is usually *adc* (because the language of industry prefers the phrase average direct cost); the symbol for average fixed cost is always *afc*. Average total unit cost, shown in column (*b*) of Table 16–7, is inserted for reference. Attention is directed to columns (*c*) and (*d*) of Table 16–7.

Average fixed costs decline throughout, due to intensified plant utilization (see Table 16–4, p. 373). When 200 units are produced at

COSTS OF PRODUCTION AND SUPPLY SCHEDULES

Table 16–7. Types of Average Cost

Quantity Produced (a)	Average Total Unit Cost (b)	Average Direct Cost (c)	Average Fixed Cost (d)
0	....	....	....
100	$120.00	$20.00	$100.00
200	67.50	17.50	50.00
300	48.30	15.00	33.30
400	37.50	12.50	25.00
500	32.00	12.00	20.00
600	29.20	12.50	16.70
700	27.90	13.60	14.30
800	27.50	15.00	12.50
900	27.80	16.70	11.10
1,000	30.00	20.00	10.00

a total fixed cost of $10,000, the fixed cost burden on each unit of production is $50, but when 1,000 units of the product are manufactured, the average fixed cost is only $10. This characteristic behavior of fixed cost is referred to as "spreading the overhead." It constitutes an advantage of increased production, but it is an advantage which wanes. In column (d) of Table 16–7 it is seen that producing 200 units instead of only 100 reduces average fixed cost by $50; but producing 1,000 units instead of only 900 reduces average fixed cost per unit by only $1.10.

THE CONCEPT OF MARGINAL COST

When operating under diminishing returns, the entrepreneur can do many things to learn how to live with this economic principle. He can turn the principle to his advantage by understanding that it is really a reflection of his own limitations and those of his plant and equipment. Thus he will interpret manifestations of diminishing returns as warning signs to inform him that he must either curtail his operations or change his methods of organizing these operations.

Entrepreneurs do not usually determine this limit in terms of theoretical concepts. Instead they make cost studies, ask supervisors to report on potential "bottlenecks of production," receive reports on rising internal costs by their cost-accounting department, and use numerous other practical means. Economists, however, think in terms of a general concept of "incremental" or "marginal" cost. This is simply the total additional cost, or the extra cost of expanding operations —regardless of the specific practical factors causing bottlenecks which require progressively more costly applications of effort to get out added production.

The burden of incremental, or marginal, cost naturally varies with changing amounts of output. To increase production at an early stage requires no great extra effort. But as the limit of the given plant and equipment is approached, the additional cost of extra output tends to rise steeply. By observing the effect of diminishing returns at various margins of production, corresponding to changes from one level to another, it is possible to derive an entire schedule of marginal cost corresponding to different levels of output. Simply take the total cost of producing an increased output and subtract from this the total cost of the previously produced smaller output. Thus if 600 units of product cost $17,500 and the 500 units produced before that cost $16,000, the aggregate incremental cost is $1,500. Dividing this $1,500 by 100 —the number of extra units of output—yields $15 as the marginal cost of each extra unit. (Strictly speaking, each additional unit after 500 has a different marginal cost, the 502d unit a higher one than the 501st, etc.) Using the figures employed in previous illustrations in this chapter, Table 16–8 shows how the marginal cost of an entire run of production develops.

Table 16–8. Hypothetical Schedule of Marginal Costs at Different Levels of Output of a Firm

Quantity Produced (a)	Total Cost (b)	Incremental Cost (c)	Marginal Cost [col. (c) ÷ 100] (d)
0	$10,000		
		$2,000	$20.00
100	12,000		
		1,500	15.00
200	13,500		
		1,000	10.00
300	14,500		
		500	5.00
400	15,000		
		1,000	10.00
500	16,000		
		1,500	15.00
600	17,500		
		2,000	20.00
700	19,500		
		2,500	25.00
800	22,000		
		3,000	30.00
900	25,000		
		5,000	50.00
1,000	30,000		

The meaning of marginal cost. Marginal cost is the epitome of the entrepreneur's cost calculations. Indeed, it is not really a cost, at least in the sense of an expense which is met by paying money. Instead, *marginal cost is a way of thinking about all other costs.* It shows the entrepreneur how well or badly he is faring in regard to rates of cost of operation and/or how effectively he can manage his costs. Thus it could be seen (if one had access to some actual cost data) that marginal costs will be lower in a plant in which resources are cleverly organized and labor relations are mutually satisfactory than in a poorly run firm with ineffective industrial relations. Or a plant may be distantly located with inferior access to the markets for materials, labor, and capital. This plant will have higher marginal costs than one which is favorably located.

From these considerations of marginal cost, as a concept, it emerges that an efficiently organized, well-situated plant can deliver more output at any price current than a less well-organized plant can. In a way, that is only common sense; but the concept of marginal cost highlights and states it more informatively. Poor organization, inferior location, and the like will be reflected in steeply rising costs. The entrepreneur is confined to furnishing a limited output at any given level of price for the product. When marginal costs rise gently, as they do for an efficient firm, the entrepreneur can be in the market to supply a relatively large volume of goods and will be able to augment his supplies considerably when the market price for the product rises.

MARGINAL COST AS SUPPLY PRICE

Marginal cost determines the amount or the supplies of a commodity which individual firms will bring to market. This inquiry into costs began with the question: How does an entrepreneur decide whether to accept or to reject an offer for additional units of the type of product he manufactures? The question can now be answered by saying that he will decide on the basis of whether the price offered by the consumer will cover the entrepreneur's marginal cost of production, that is, whether it will be worthwhile to incur the extra toil and trouble and expense of furnishing the additional supply. When the price equals the marginal cost of production, an entrepreneur will be indifferent to any further offers, and he will reject them as soon as marginal cost exceeds the price consumers are willing or able to pay. Alternatively stated, the entrepreneur has a whole schedule of marginal costs at which he will deliver certain corresponding outputs of his product. This is his supply schedule. Marginal cost informs customers at what amounts of output the entrepreneur is marginal, i.e., indifferent to doing more business in response to different price offers.

For the entrepreneur this is a vital matter, which partly determines what his rate of capital accumulation will be. If he can freely supply the market, his net income will be large even though his margin of profit on every unit of his product may be low. But for society the state of marginal costs in industry is also a vital consideration. Human welfare can be expanded only when resources are efficiently utilized. Just as charity begins at home, efficient utilization of resources begins in the many places of work throughout the nation. This study of costs has been aimed at acquainting the reader with the entrepreneurial cost criteria of bringing supplies to market. The general rule is this: *Supply is determined by marginal cost.*

For Discussion

1. In the President's *Economic Report of 1958* it is said, among other things: "In 1957, our gross national product rose 5 per cent, but four-fifths of this increase was accounted for by rising prices. There are critical problems here for business and labor, as well as for Government." Can you discuss some of these problems in real-cost terms? Do you think the President did so? Prepare a tentative outline of your real-cost discussion, then check page 5 of the President's *Report* to see how closely yours and the official one are related.

2. Which of the following assumptions are necessary for the working of the law of diminishing returns? (*a*) All resources used must be increased proportionately. (*b*) All capital goods which have been installed must be used fully before diminishing returns can set in for an individual firm. (*c*) The quality of land must be held constant. (*d*) The quantity of land must be held constant. (*e*) The units of the variable factor or factors of production, which are successively added to the fixed factor or factors, must be (1) of homogeneous quality, (2) of equal size. (*f*) There must be a given state of the industrial arts. (*g*) All the factors of production in a given situation must be subject to diminishing yields.

3. When an entrepreneur installs multiple units of a given type of industrial equipment, what is the chief effect so far as diminishing returns are concerned? Does the installation of multiple units increase the firm's optimum point of production? Does it increase the range of output over which optimum efficiency may be secured? The latter is the effect as accurately stated. *Why* is this more accurate than simply saying that installing multiple units of productive equipment increases the firm's optimum point of production?

4. The implication which the law of diminishing returns has for social policy directed toward the most economical use of our resources is this: Resources should be applied to all their possible uses in such a way as to minimize their diminishing yields in alternative uses. Discuss.

5. *Cost schedules.* Complete the following cost table of an imaginary firm with the indicated cost structure. Marginal cost (col. [*h*]) is the change in total cost (col. [*d*]) resulting from a unit change in output.

Output (a)	Total Fixed Cost (b)	Total Variable Cost (c)	Total Cost (d)	Average Fixed Cost (e)	Average Variable Cost (f)	Average Total Cost (g)	Marginal Cost (h)
1	$12	$ 8					
2	12	15					
3	12	21					
4	12	26					
5	12	30					
6	12	33					
7	12	36					
8	12	40					
9	12	45					
10	12	52					
11	12	61					
12	12	72					
13	12	85					
14	12	100					

6. *Cost curves.* On the graph below plot the average fixed cost, average variable cost, average total cost, and marginal cost curves from the data computed in the table of Question 5. Begin with the 2-unit output; the graph is not ruled to permit starting with the 1-unit output. Notice that the marginal cost in this exercise is identical for two different amounts of total output. This requires

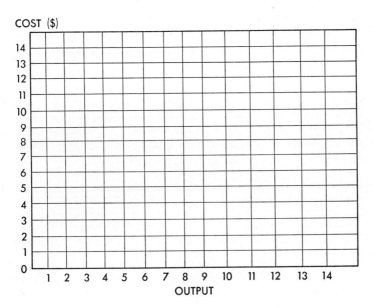

us to plot the marginal cost curve *between* our output units; otherwise the marginal cost curve will not pass through the average total unit cost at its lowest point. So plot the marginal cost of the third unit at an output of 2.5, the *mc* of the fourth unit at an output of 3.5, etc.

7. *Break-even charts.* Label the curves on the accompanying graph. At what output would the first break-even point occur? At an output of how many units would profits be at a maximum?

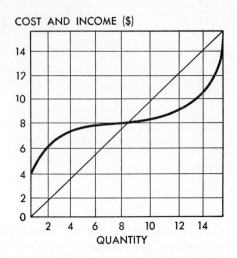

COST AND INCOME ($)

QUANTITY

17

Elementary

Theorems

of Price Determination

$\mathbf{M}$arginal cost is the determinant of supply. Marginal utility and disposable income determine consumer spending. These are complex forces of human behavior. Equipped with a general knowledge of the demand behavior of consumers and of how costs influence supply, one may *meaningfully* say that "demand and supply determine prices"!

This chapter explains their relationship—that is, the interaction of demand and supply in an abstract setting. All of the theorems developed here assume the existence of pure competition, a condition which is entirely hypothetical. Thus the approach resembles that of physicists who sometimes employ the concept of a frictionless machine as an aid to thinking about the complex problems raised by actual motors. For the economist, too, the real world of brute fact is far too complex to understand without first constructing a simplified pure model.

Price Determination Under Conditions of Pure Competition

THE CHARACTERISTICS OF A PURELY COMPETITIVE MARKET

There are many sellers and many buyers. The output of each *seller* is so small that whether he sells it or withholds it, his output will not appreciably influence the price which will be set upon the commodity. Likewise, the purchase of each *buyer* is so small that whether or not that amount is spent will not affect the market price of the commodity. Each seller knows this and does not expect to raise the price by withholding his output. If a seller does withhold, it is because he thinks a higher price is in the offing owing to *general* supply conditions and not because of his dropping out of the market. Likewise a buyer will purchase when he is satisfied with the price and refrain when he is dissatisfied, but not because he thinks the latter will make any difference in bringing down the price. Of course, *all* buyers and sellers together fix the price, those who are actively in the market as well as those who drop out. But it is the *general* conditions of demand and supply which determine the price current at any one time in a purely competitive market.

THE PURELY COMPETITIVE PRICING PROCESS VISUALIZED

A sequence of price-determining events is always confined to a "market day." In actual life this may be a period of short or long duration. It will depend on the type of commodity involved, on customary business practices, on facilities for communication, and the like. It has already been seen that a market is not necessarily a specific place; likewise, a market day is not one certain time period but varies case by case.

To bring a typical pricing process to view, one simply plots basic (actual or hypothetical) demand and supply schedules on graph paper. Each point plotted on the graph represents the relation between a certain level of price and quantity demanded on the one hand and the quantity offered to be supplied at that level of price on the other. We know that quantities offered (the supply) depend upon marginal cost.

Figure 17–1 plots an aggregate industry-wide supply schedule of all firms. The supply curve slopes upward because as output increases, productivity drops. As productivity declines, costs rise. Thus, to elicit more production, a higher and higher price is necessary.

Next, the market demand schedule for the commodity is recorded and plotted, as in Figure 17–2. The demand curve slopes downward, reflecting the downward pull of diminishing marginal utility and diminishing freely spendable income (especially in the case of low-income recipients).

In actual practice, market trading involves price bids and price offers closely gravitating around some previously established price; for example, $3.90 to $4.10 a unit for a commodity which in a previous market period had sold for $4.00. For theoretical purposes we

Figure 17–1. Supply Curve for a Commodity Drawn from
Its Industry Supply Schedule

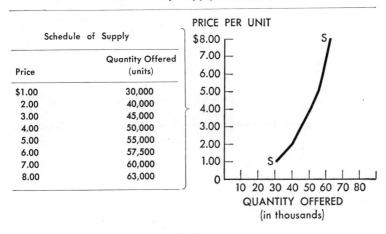

Schedule of Supply	
Price	Quantity Offered (units)
$1.00	30,000
2.00	40,000
3.00	45,000
4.00	50,000
5.00	55,000
6.00	57,500
7.00	60,000
8.00	63,000

Figure 17–2. Demand Curve for a Commodity Drawn from
Its Market Demand Schedule

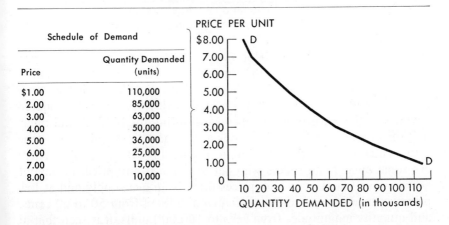

Schedule of Demand	
Price	Quantity Demanded (units)
$1.00	110,000
2.00	85,000
3.00	63,000
4.00	50,000
5.00	36,000
6.00	25,000
7.00	15,000
8.00	10,000

present the entire range of possible price bids and price offers; in other words, we show the entire lengths of the demand and supply curves on a graph.

The market pricing process, under pure competition, can now be visualized. Simply superimpose on a graphed market demand curve an industry schedule of supply. Then note where they intersect. This locates the price current which will be established in the market and the quantity of the commodity traded at that price. Under given conditions this price will last, all other things being equal.

Figure 17–3A shows that in a competitive market there can be only *one* point of price, $4.00, and this point must lie coextended on the demand and the supply curves. Suppose that consumers offer the lower price of $3.50 for a quantity for which the producers ask the price of $6.00. The consumers will desire the amount of 57,500, but only 47,500 will be forthcoming. However, at the price of $4.00, 50,000 will be wanted and supplied.

Figure 17–3A. Supply and Demand Determining Price

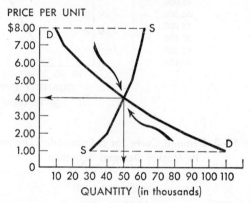

PRICE PER UNIT

QUANTITY (in thousands)

A close observation of theoretical market-price determination can be made by assuming, for the purpose of illustration, that quantity offered and quantity bid for change at identical rates in response to price trends in the market, on a market day. The quantity offered declines as the price trend is downward during the bidding and offering; the quantity asked for increases at the same time and at the same rate as quantity offered is declining. Figure 17–3B shows this. There are some buyers and sellers who get together at any price, no matter how high or low. But at high prices there is an oversupply and at low prices an overdemand. Using price magnitudes of from 50 to 60 cents, and quantity magnitudes from zero to 160,000 units, it is seen that at 55 cents the rectangles of supply and demand precisely coincide, with 120,000 units of product being exchanged.[1]

The reasoning of sellers and buyers who bring about the 55-cent balancing price, with a turnover of 120,000 units of product, is as follows: There are some sellers who stand ready to dispose of their product at 55 cents. They cannot afford to permit the price to rise higher than this—not even one cent higher. For at 56 cents the quan-

[1] This illustration is based on Fred M. Taylor's classic example, in *Principles of Economics* (New York: The Ronald Press Co., 1922), pp. 283–87.

Figure 17-3B. Prices Equating Supply and Demand

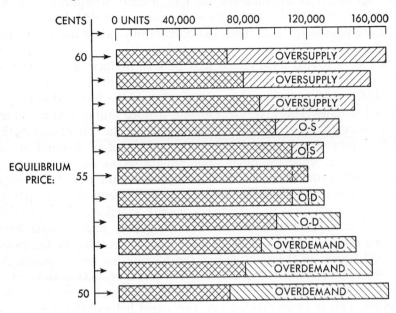

tity demanded is 10,000 units smaller but the quantity which will be brought to market is 10,000 units larger. This constitutes an oversupply of 20,000 units. Should the 56-cent price become established, some sellers will be unable to dispose of their wares. This would include sellers who are willing to trade their supply of the commodity at 55 cents. To ensure that they will not be left holding all or a part of their supplies, these sellers who can afford to trade at 55 cents will bid the price down to that amount. This diminishes the supply by 10,000 units as sellers unwilling to part with their commodity at less than 56 cents leave the market without selling their products. At the same time, the quantity demanded increases by 10,000 units. Thus the sellers who stand ready to sell at 55 cents are successful in disposing of their supplies.

The reasoning of the buyers is similar, though differently oriented. There are some buyers who are willing to pay 55 cents per unit of the product. They cannot afford to let the price fall lower than that, not even one cent less. For at 54 cents there would be a quantity of 130,-000 units asked for but only 110,000 units would be available from the sellers. If the 54-cent price were established, the supply available at that price might be absorbed by the buyers willing to pay only up to 54 cents, leaving the buyers who are willing to pay up to 55 cents without the goods they want. These buyers will consequently bid the price up to 55 cents; then the cheaper bidders withdraw, reducing quantity wanted by 10,000 units at the same time that 10,000 extra units are offered for sale. Thus the 55-cent buyers are assured of the supplies they desire.

In Figure 17–3B these effects may be seen by focusing on the 56-, 55-, and 54-cent bars in the graph. At 56 cents the excessive supply of 20,000 units is indicated by the portion of the bar having only a parallel shading. This excess rectangle is divided into two equal shares by a broken vertical line. The small square at the left measures the 10,000 units of oversupply due to the falling off of demand at the 56-cent price, while the other small square shows the 10,000 over-supply units brought to market by producers willing to sell at a price down as low as 56 cents but for no less. At 55 cents these particular sellers have withdrawn, but buyers willing to take another 10,000 units have appeared on the scene. Now supply and demand have become equated; the marginal 10,000 units are recorded by the cross-hatched square at the right end of the 55-cent bar in the graph. At 54 cents, however, there is an excessive demand of 20,000 units, indicated on the graph by the portion of the bar with only a parallel shading. This is again divided into two equal halves. The one on the left shows the falling off of supply at this relatively low price; the small square on the right shows the increase in quantity demanded.

From this explanation and illustration there emerges the law of supply and demand.[2]

THE LAW OF SUPPLY AND DEMAND

Given a typical demand and supply schedule, price must tend to rise so long as demand is in excess of supply and to fall so long as supply is in excess of demand; it must therefore move up or down till it reaches a figure which equates supply and demand; and at this point it can rest, since here the price-moving forces become quiescent.

Corollary 1. *The equilibrium price, once reached, will continue as the price current, market-day after market-day, so long as the conditions of the supply and the demand of the product remain unchanged.*

This is because the price which equates supply and demand clears the market. Unless the excluded sellers can reduce their production costs, they will not further trouble to enter this market, because the equilibrium level is unprofitable so far as they are concerned. Likewise, unless in the excluded buyers' budgets the marginal utility of the product changes, or their incomes increase, they will not further

[2] *Ibid.*, p. 286.

trouble to enter the market, because the clearance price, or equilibrium price, is too high for them.

Corollary 2. *The excluded sellers and buyers continue to exert a price leverage which maintains the equilibrium price, even though they are no longer actually offering to sell or bid for units of the product.*

It is known that extra sellers will make their appearance if the price rises, and extra buyers will come into the market if the price falls. This potential competition of outside sellers and buyers acts to support the price current at its equilibrium level.

Corollary 3. *Shifts of the demand schedule, up or down, theoretically move equilibrium price in the same direction (but not proportionately); shifts of supply schedules cause price movements in an opposite direction.*

This is because a change in any of the given conditions, say an increase of demand, opens the door to the re-entry of sellers who have previously been excluded from the market. Thus in Figure 17–3B the horizontal bar representing the 56-cent price level showed an oversupply. A portion of this was due to an excessive number of product units brought to market; another portion of the oversupply was due to quantity demanded falling short as the price mounted to 56 cents. When consumers want more of the product and are willing to make an extra sacrifice to obtain it, the demand obviously ceases to fall short and the extra supply is salable. In our example, 110,000 units are wanted at 56 cents a unit, but 130,000 units were originally offered by the sellers. If the consumers now wish to enjoy 130,000 units and offer to pay 56 cents a unit, the price current becomes readjusted at the level of 56 cents a unit.

Validity of the law of supply and demand. The market process of pricing commodities, as described, is evidently a rationing process which acts to exclude certain sellers and buyers, thus reserving for those buyers and sellers who can come to terms of exchange agreeable amounts of goods and the resources needed to produce them. There are of course other methods of rationing goods, services, and resources. But insofar as people are legally free to reach exchange agreements, markets exist and the described pricing process is found.

MARKET PRICE DETERMINATION VERBALIZED

The price of 55 cents is the only price which will last. Why is this so? At the price of 55 cents, and at no other price, there are just as many buyers who are willing and able to purchase the total amount of goods, 120,000 units, as there are goods offered by a certain number of sellers, namely the quantity of 120,000 units.

At any other price there is an excess of goods for sale over the quantity demanded, or more goods are wanted than are for sale. When either of these situations occur, tentative price quotations with which trading started on a given market day are revised. Some persons become dissatisfied with the direction in which price seems to be moving. They drop out of the market. The rest adjust their bids and offers in line with the observed trend; they see that they cannot get as good a bargain as they had hoped for but find the price trend reasonable. Consumer offers and producer bids come closer to each other. Finally, the unique price is established which *clears the market* of the goods still for sale.

The Social Meaning of the Pricing Process

Thus far nothing more has been said than that prices are determined by the interaction of consumers and producers, each seeking to maximize personal gain. But how is the public interest served?

To be socially significant, prices must accomplish more than a mere balance of the quantities of desired commodities with the quantities offered to be supplied. That in itself tells us nothing about how well the economy is likely to fare. What we want to know is whether this is also a balance of the aggregate of marginal utilities which society attaches to the goods exchanged, and the marginal *real* costs of producing them. If so, our resources will be ideally allocated, for this is merely a technical way of stating that:

1. Consumers (other than the poverty-stricken) have carried their free spending to the point at which, under the given circumstances, they are getting their money's worth.
2. Producers are efficiently managing our valuable resources and earning enough, at the current prices, to maintain these resources intact instead of exhausting them.

These considerations of marginal utility and marginal cost are not the only welfare criteria. We also want to know whether the market pricing process is contributing to the maintenance of full employment or helping to bring it about. What is the effect of the higgling and bargaining in the market on the national income distribution? Is any particular price high enough so that producers of the commodity can be paid adequately—paid enough to maintain a moderate and decent standard of living? Alternatively, does the price which we pay for a unit of a good include a heavy surcharge of excess profit, more than enough to induce the producers to bring the supply to market? If so, who reaps the profit—the absentee owners of the concern? or the management? or the union? or all of them combined, at the expense of the consumer?

These are questions which come to mind, and they are questions which it is proper to pose. For American society is a mutual aid association formed to enhance the general welfare and common defense. The pricing process must serve these aims as one of many social processes which determine the quality of national life.

To ascertain how a model competitive pricing process would perform with reference to efficiency, income distribution, and employment, it is necessary to observe its theoretical impacts on the various work places where supplies are manufactured and where incomes are distributed. Now, the economic motivation of the individual entrepreneur is to maximize profit so as to achieve optimum capital accumulation. Hence for the market pricing process to operate in the public interest it must:

1. Permit only efficient entrepreneurs to earn profit.
2. Assure that only extraordinarily efficient firms gain surplus profit. Surplus profit is any return of more than 6 or 7 per cent on the owners' investment.
3. Induce entrepreneurs to furnish maximum employment.

Profit Maximization for the Individual Firm

SHORT-RUN AND LONG-RUN DECISION-MAKING

There are two points of view from which profit maximization is to be seen, corresponding to two kinds of business decisions which must be made. First there is the already noted *short-run* point of view. This is adopted by an entrepreneur when he contemplates accepting orders, or rejecting additional ones, in consideration only of the costs of operating his existing plant and equipment. In other words, short-run price analysis envisions the entrepreneur as responding to changes of consumer demand solely by varying the rate of utilization of the productive facilities which he has on hand.

It follows from the definition of the short run that the *long run* must be a period of time over which the entrepreneur can enlarge the existing scale of his productive capacity by acquiring new plant and equipment. In practice, the two types of decision-making become imperceptibly blended. Upon feeling the pressure of additional demand, an entrepreneur will weigh whether to accommodate it by intensifying the use of his given facilities, working double shifts, and so on; or whether to add a new wing to the factory, install more machinery, and the like. For theoretical purposes, however, it is useful to make a sharp distinction between business decisions which affect the rate of utilization of a given capacity of plant and equipment, and business decisions to multiply or diminish the scale of plant and equipment.

PROFIT MAXIMIZATION OF THE INDIVIDUAL FIRM IN THE SHORT RUN

In Chapter 16 it was noted that profit maximization consists in observing where the widest spread lies between aggregate sales income and aggregate total cost, then producing up to that point. However, this general concept does not afford us the precise view which can be obtained by analyzing the matter in terms of the *unit* costs of production and of the sales revenue *per unit* of product. We begin with marginal cost.

Previously, the marginal cost schedule was computed by subtracting the total cost of production of a smaller output from the total cost of an enlarged one; this gives the additional cost of producing the larger output. The same result can be obtained in unit-cost terms. When more is produced under conditions of diminishing returns, each unit of product will be somewhat more costly. These procedures are illustrated diagrammatically in Figure 17–4.

Figure 17–4. Computing Marginal Cost

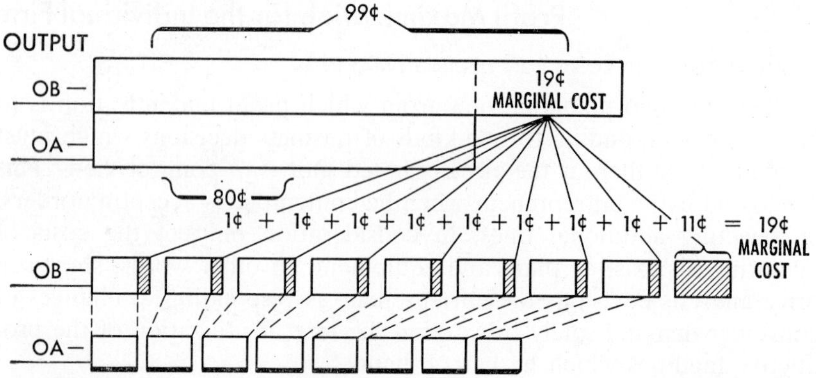

Suppose that it costs 10 cents on the average to produce an output A of eight units and 11 cents on the average to produce an output B of nine units. The marginal cost can be computed as in Chapter 16 by subtracting the smaller total cost of output A from the greater total cost of the enlarged output B.

$$9 \text{ units @ } 11\text{¢} = 99\text{¢ (Output } B)$$
$$8 \text{ units @ } 10\text{¢} = \underline{80\text{¢}} \text{ (Output } A, \text{ subtrahend)}$$
$$\text{Marginal cost:} \quad 19\text{¢}$$

Alternatively, the marginal cost can be computed as follows. When nine units are produced instead of eight units, it costs an extra penny for each of the previously produced eight units, and 11 cents for the ninth unit which was not heretofore produced. Eight extra pennies on the units of the previous output *plus* 11 cents on the newly added unit of output yields 19 cents as the marginal cost of the ninth unit. Had it not been produced, the other eight units could have been produced more cheaply. So the ninth unit must bear the entire added cost burden (its own cost plus the additional cost of the other units). This is the measure of the toil and trouble of increasing production.

UNIT SALES REVENUE

Under pure competition the entrepreneur cannot control the price of his product. He must accept the current market price as a given datum. At this price he can sell as much as he pleases. But if he attempts to charge one iota more than the price current, he will presumably have no customers at all; there are many other sellers who will serve the consumers on the established market price basis. This characteristic attribute of a purely competitive market price situation is shown graphically by simply drawing a horizontal line across the graph at whatever level the going market price happens to be. The line is called *average revenue curve* because it shows the revenue which the entrepreneur will receive *per unit* of his product. Under pure com-

Figure 17-5. Average Revenue Curve Equals Marginal Revenue Curve

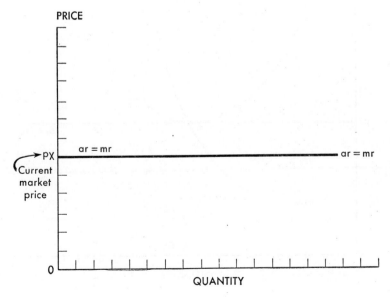

petition the average revenue curve is also the marginal revenue curve. This is explained by the fact that every additional unit sold brings the same revenue as the preceding one. That is to say, the last unit sold is worth no more than all the units on the average. Figure 17–5 exhibits an average revenue curve which is also a marginal revenue curve; this is always the case under pure competition.

A "close-up" view of short-run profit maximization can now be taken. This is done simply by showing the unit cost curves and the unit revenue curve in juxtaposition (see Figure 17–6).

The exhibited price and cost relationship has a significant social implication. The established price, px, covers the firm's costs of production—average and marginal, but nothing more. However, the aver-

Figure 17–6. Price and Cost Relationship of an Individual Firm
Under Pure Competition

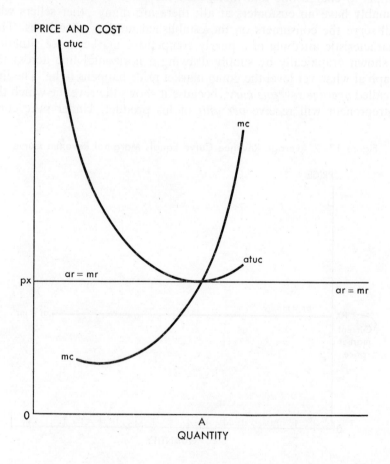

age cost includes 6 per cent of profit. This informs us that the firm in question is operated by an entrepreneur of average efficiency. Entrepreneurs who are run of the mill so far as productive efficiency is concerned must earn this much profit; otherwise they would spare themselves the toil and trouble and risk of conducting their own business. At least 3 per cent can be earned simply by placing one's money capital in a savings deposit, and more can be earned by investing in stocks or bonds. If a person of ordinary efficiency could not earn at least twice as much as he can by simply lending his money, he would be ill-advised to conduct his own business. (Many people, of course, do so for other than economic reasons, such as the wish to be independent.)

A pricing criterion. When an entrepreneur operates at a rate at which he realizes his lowest average total unit cost, he is doing the best he can under his circumstances to use society's resources efficiently by keeping his real costs to the minimum. However, it has been seen that the entrepreneur fixes his rate of operations with reference to marginal cost, not in terms of average total unit cost. So long as the customers of a firm are willing to pay for the extra expense of producing more output, the entrepreneur is willing, within reasonable limits, to proceed. In doing so he may surpass the rate of plant and equipment utilization which corresponds to his least average cost.

To prove that this is possible let us suppose that there is a change in one of the given conditions, namely, in the preference of the consumers for one commodity and/or in consumer incomes. Let it be assumed that the consumers develop a stronger preference for a product and/or that rising national income permits some persons to purchase the product who had previously been unable to do so. Because of this increase of demand the price rises from, say, px to py. Now it will pay the firm to expand its production from OA to OB units. That will carry the firm beyond its least average cost of operation. But although this entails relatively high-cost production, extra revenue is to be gained by multiplying sales turnover when demand is increasing. This is graphically demonstrated in Figures 17–7 through 17–9.

First is shown, in Figure 17–7, the extra revenue which accrues to the firm by expanding output in response to an increase in demand. Of course, in reality this entails a rising cost of production. But we ignore this momentarily, to see what would happen if the per unit cost of production did *not* rise. The reason for making this artificial procedure, followed in constructing Figure 17–7, is to dramatize the action of marginal cost in the next graph, Figure 17–8. By first ignoring the rise of cost, we observe in the hatched rectangle in Figure

Figure 17–7. Effect of Increased Demand on Price and Sales Income
(Constant-Cost Production)

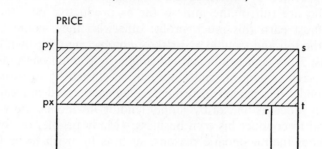

17–7 the added revenue gained by expanding output in response to
increased demand after it has raised the price of the product.

Figure 17–7 shows the effect of rising price on sales income when
production is expanded. When output OA is sold, total sales revenue
is OA multiplied by the price px, which was current before demand
increased. Total sales revenue at price px and output OA is represented, moving clockwise in Figure 17–7, by the rectangle:

When increased demand raises price to py and output to OB, the new
and larger sales revenue is computed by multiplying OB by py. The
graphical result in Figure 17–7 is the larger rectangle:

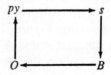

The additional revenue is represented on the graph by:

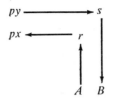

However, an increased sales revenue could have been obtained by the firm's simply augmenting to *OB* its output and selling the output at the lower price *px* (the price of output *OA*); this extra revenue would have been:

Hence the truly additional revenue obtained by producing more output in response to increased demand, at a higher price, is (as shown in Figure 17–7):

Figure 17–7 reckons sales income, artificially, without reference to production cost. Figure 17–8 takes rising cost into account. Marginal cost is the criterion of rising cost to be selected. It registers the full impact of the extra cost of producing the enlarged output *OB*. The output *OB* is comprised of old output *OA* plus additional *AB* units of output. Marginal cost records the additional toil and trouble of producing the extra *AB* units of output. That is all with which Figure 17–8 is concerned. This extra cost is measured by the striped area

which lies under the marginal cost curve between the price indicators of *px* and *py* (Figure 17–8).

Figure 17-8. Increased Demand, Price, and Cost

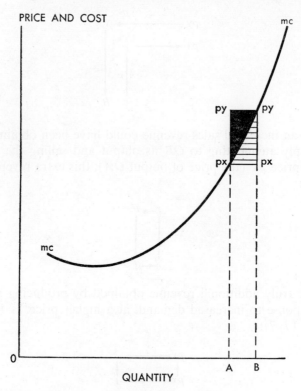

The solid black area (in Figure 17-8)

is the amount of net sales income the firm would have foregone
had it persisted in producing output OA only, after demand increased
and price rose. The firm might have persisted in output OA because
it is the output which can be produced at least average cost. Mark
well that the firm would still have earned a substantial extra revenue
by producing OA but at the new, higher price of py. This revenue is
computed by multiplying output OA by the excess of the new price py
over the original price of px. In Figure 17-9 this yields the rectangle:

$$py \longrightarrow q$$
$$\uparrow \qquad \downarrow$$
$$px \longleftarrow r$$

Figure 17–9. Short-Run Production Increase of the Firm

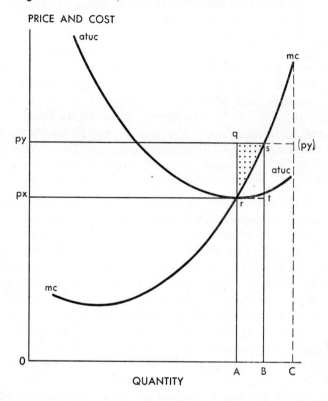

PRICE AND COST

QUANTITY

However at this rate of production the firm would not have *maximized* its profit. To do so it must produce output *OB*, realizing the extra profit shown in Figure 17–9 as the area:

$$\left(\begin{array}{c} q \longrightarrow s \\ \raisebox{0.2em}{$\uparrow$} \!\!\nearrow \\ r \end{array} \;=\; \begin{array}{c} py \longrightarrow py \\ \raisebox{0.2em}{$\uparrow$} \!\!\nearrow \\ px \end{array} \; \text{in Figure 17–8} \right)$$

Implication of short-run profit maximization. From society's point of view it is not desirable that the firm should produce the output *OB*. To be sure, the firm's profit is increased if it does so, and the consumers of the product are accommodated in their desire for more of the product. But output *OB* is produced at a relatively high real cost. This is shown in Figure 17–9 both by average total unit cost at the *OB* output level, and by marginal cost even more dramatically. Average total unit cost is above the firm's minimum, and marginal cost has risen markedly. Some people in the economy are better off, but valuable resources are inefficiently employed. If there were no other use for them, this might be tolerable. But if the extra manpower and raw materials input required to produce the extra amount of output AB is diverted from more productive uses, the economy is harmed. The damage might appear to be trivial but it could mount to significant proportions if practiced in many work places.

In a boom hasty efforts to expand production can involve a high toll of general welfare. What of it, the reader may ask; the producers are doing the will of the sovereign consumers. Granted, but waste should not go further than it absolutely must. Normally we strive to control and distribute social consumption to prevent overutilization of resources in one place and underutilization in others, or at least to keep this inefficiency to a minimum.

Curbing short-run waste. In Figure 17–9 observe that the output is not expanded in response to increased demand as far as it might be. Conceivably, production could be carried to the outer absolute limit of plant and equipment, which, in our example, lies at output OC. In other words, in addition to the extra quantity of AB, produced with relative inefficiency, another quantity of BC units could be produced, with even less efficiency. At OC of output, the price py still exceeds substantially the average cost *atuc* for OC units of the product. This is the case even though marginal cost, at OC, is excessive.

By limiting his output to the point where the price py equals the marginal cost *mc*, the entrepreneur is rationing his consumers although he indulges them—and himself, profit-wise—by producing with relative inefficiency the output OB rather than the least-cost output of OA. The medium of curbing unhealthy industry booms is the charging of a high price for forced production wrested from given plant and equipment. If the rate of output is to be beyond the optimum rate, the consumers are theoretically (and in practice should be) asked to bear the *full* extra cost burden of operation above the point of least average cost.

ECONOMICAL EXPANSION OF PRODUCTION

Nothing said so far permits any inference that consumers should not be accommodated in their desire for the additional enjoyment to be secured by consuming more of a given product. However, the economical way to accomplish this is by placing added productive capacity into operation—if possible. This can happen only in the long run, the period during which the entrepreneur has an opportunity to contract for new construction and have it finished, to order additional equipment and have it installed, and to train his personnel in working under the new conditions.

The entrepreneur will not engage in plant and equipment expansion unless he is assured that the increased demand of consumers is more than a passing whim. He will want to be reasonably certain that increased demand for his product will last over a period long enough to afford him some latitude in carrying out an expansion of capacity, so that he is not forced to acquire and install new plant and equipment under hectic circumstances. Also, the entrepreneur must have a reasonable expectation that the increased demand will last for a period of years long enough to permit him to write off the depreciation and eventual obsolescence of the new plant and equipment according to a normal schedule of amortization. Obviously, the time period involved must vary case by case for different entrepreneurs. However, Bain has estimated that the long run can be said to involve intervals of approximately three to ten years.[3]

When a long-run expectancy of demand remaining at an increased level is not given or cannot be reasonably entertained, it is certainly in society's interest that consumers be rather strictly rationed in their momentary desires for additional production of a given commodity or service. But even if there be every reason to believe that there is a permanent change in consumers' preferences for a product, the short-run procedure theoretically is (and practically should be) to hold the price rein tight on the consumer until additional productive capacity has been added after a long-run period of construction, installation, and personnel training.

A DEFINITION

The long run is that chronological period of indeterminate length during which entrepreneurs can freely and advantageously vary the scale of their plant and equipment, as well as the amounts of the other factors of production. What can be done in this respect, and how soon, depend in the first place on the availability of natural, human, and man-made resources. By availability is meant not mere physical access to resources but access on favorable real cost terms, so that efficiency rather than waste is encouraged, and therefore a rise of living standards. In the ensuing discussion of long-run adjustments made by entrepreneurs, different circumstances which typically surround individual firm and industry expansion are considered.

Long-run Pricing Under Rigidly Restricted Conditions

Additional supplies of basic factors of production, such as high-grade cropland or rich ore or oil deposits or suitable factory locations,

---

[3] Joe S. Bain, *Pricing, Distribution, and Employment* (New York: Henry Holt and Company, 1953), p. 110.

are frequently difficult if not impossible to find even over long periods of time. In those cases we have conditions of tight resources. As has been seen in Chapters 5 through 8, conditions of tight resources are by no means rare. Production can be augmented by straining the rich resources or resorting to inferior grades of land, low-grade ore deposits, or the like.´ But real costs must rise. Here is the pricing aspect of the previously described circumstances of forced high-cost production.

THE ABC'S OF STRAINED PRODUCTION

There is really no difference in short-run and long-run price trends under conditions of tight resources. To highlight the nature of pricing under such "anticonservationist" situations, let the tight factor of production be considered as being *absolutely* fixed. This simplifies the exposition without rendering the analysis fallacious.

If a basic production factor is absolutely fixed, the short-run marginal cost curve—the fundamental short-run supply curve—also constitutes the long-run marginal cost curve. It is, therefore, the industry's supply curve under any time period. That is to say, marginal cost as given in the short run determines output response to increasing consumer demand at any moment, whether in the short run or long run. In fact, whatever is the short-run price will remain as the long-run price.

Suppose there is an increase of demand. The price will then rise, according to the marginal cost schedule, the industry's long-run supply schedule under tight scarcity conditions. All the firms in the industry would have been operating at their respective optimum-yield, least-cost points, and the original price would have covered this cost, including a normal 6 to 7 per cent profit. The new, higher price would then afford the firms more than normal profit, for a larger output. Since the resource base cannot be expanded, there is no reason for the producers to alter this price and profit situation.

The sequence of events is pictorialized in Figure 17–10. The cost curves shown are those of a firm we shall consider to be a typical and representative enterprise in its particular industry (this can be any industry, provided that, for the purpose of this analysis, it uses a tightly fixed resource, or several rigidly given resources). The original level of price is pictured by the lower horizontal line at px. It touches the firm's average cost curve at the lowest point. At the new, higher price level of py, extra profit income is realized. This is shown by the shaded area in Figure 17–10.

Conditions of tight resources and income distribution. Entrepreneurs typified by the example firm could not retain the extra income for

Figure 17–10. Long-Run Price and Output Under Conditions of
Tight Resources

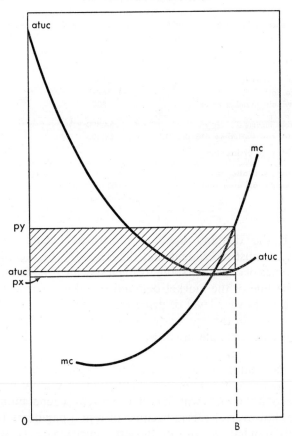

long. As soon as their leases or other types of property contracts expired, they would have to pay increased rents to the owners of the absolutely fixed resource. If an entrepreneur owned his stock of the fixed factor—for example, land—he would retain the extra gain of, say, $1,600. But he would treat that as rent which he pays to himself (imputes), on the grounds that he could lease the land and receive that same $1,600 as rent.

Whether an entrepreneur actually pays rent to a property owner or imputes it to himself, the amount by which marginal cost exceeds average total unit cost is henceforth considered a cost of production rather than an operating profit. When added to the previous costs, the actually paid or imputed rent has the effect of raising the average total unit cost. This is clarified in Table 17–1.

Table 17–1. Emergence of Rent from Ownership of an
Absolutely Fixed Resource

Sequence of Events Before and After an Increase in Demand for the Product
Using the Resource

	Before	After
Price of product (per unit)	$6.00	$8.00
Average cost	$6.00	$6.20
Quantity sold (number of units)	800	900
Gross income	$4,800	$7,200
Total cost (including 6% profit)	$4,800	$5,580
Rent (paid or imputed)	0	$1,620
Extra profit after rent	0	0
Average cost after rent	$6.00 (no rent paid or imputed)	$8.00

Although the demand increase illustrated occurs between two
points only, it must be evident that theoretically the increased desires
and/or incomes of consumers, regarding a specific product, are reflected
all along the line of the market demand schedule. Consequently, rent
must increase at every level of price for the product, and with regard
to every quantity of the product which is sold. If that is necessarily so,
the average cost schedule must, by reason of rent paid, rise all along
the line. By contrast, the marginal cost schedule will not change. The
reason is that real costs of production are not altered by the entrepreneur's paying rent (or imputing it to the absolutely fixed productive resource when he owns it). The entrepreneur's money cost of
production, however, is raised because of rental payments (or imputa-
tions). This is what the rise of the *atuc* curve records, whereas the
marginal cost is left unaffected. The *atuc* curve slides upward on the
marginal cost (*mc*) curve, so to speak. This may be observed in
Figure 17–11.

Sleight of hand must have been used in the construction of this
graph! For it seems to indicate that as more production is squeezed
from the absolutely limited factor, the output continues to be produced at least cost. But we know that the entrepreneurs are operating
beyond the points of least cost. The answer to the reader's natural
query is this: Assuming as we did that the previous location of least
average cost represented the industry operating in the *best possible*
manner, we actually portrayed a minimum *real cost* point. The new,
higher level of average cost therefore represents only the best manner
of production *available* under the circumstances of demand having

Figure 17–11. Emergence of Rent from Ownership of an
Absolutely Fixed Factor

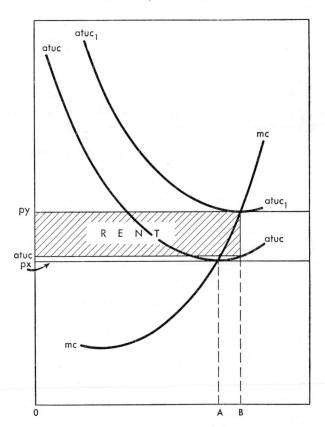

increased. Average costs have been marked up to reflect it. If that
were not done, a false impression of abundance might be given to
consumers. Hence they might wonder why they should be so tightly
rationed by a high price, one which apparently favors the producers
with surplus profits.

In noting these surplus profits, producers outside this field might be
misled into believing that there is room for expansion. In this belief
they might even persuade investors to "grubstake" them for the purpose of entering the field. This would be feasible only if in the industry
using the fixed factor a discovery had been made on how to use the
fixed resource more economically, so that there would in effect be
more of it to go around, leaving room for expansion. Also, a transportation improvement might bring new resources into reach.

But Figure 17–11 clearly shows that nothing has happened to reduce real costs of operation. All that did occur is that under the pressure of increased demand some extra production was squeezed from the given factor. This was more costly, so that the levels both of price and of cost must move higher. Marking a higher point on the industry's marginal cost supply curve could have no effect on the form or location of the curve.

The higher price and cost levels only warn consumers and producers that they are making more strenuous demands on the fixed resource and must therefore be more tightly rationed, lest they use the resource to the point of ruination.

Conditions of Flexible Resources

In the long run the existence of many freely reproducible resources —bricks for building, cement, machinery, electrical energy, and so forth—makes it possible to augment many types of production without duress. To the extent that there are flexible supplies of resources which can be used, real costs need not rise in long-run expansion, or if they do, they need rise but little.

THE ABC'S OF LIGHTENED PRODUCTION

Under conditions of flexible resources, costs of production have a much gentler movement in the long run than they do in the short run. In the short run (which typically lasts from six months to three years), the entrepreneur can accommodate extra demand only by varying the rate of utilization of his given factors of production. Consequently, he encounters diminishing returns in an accentuated form. In the long run, the entrepreneur can vary both the *rate* of utilization of plant and equipment and the *scale* of plant and equipment. Moreover, new entrepreneurs can enter a field of industry when there is pure competition. In other words, under conditions of flexible resources additional resources can be put into the service of the consumers if their demand warrants it.

It is important to bear in mind that in long-run price analysis we are still adhering to the characteristic assumptions of given conditions —principally, given methods of production, given supplies of the factors of production, and given tastes and incomes of consumers. However, in order to trace the course of long-run price adjustments, we shall take consumer tastes and incomes as given at two different levels—an original level of demand and then an increased demand.

An increase of demand, all other things being equal, brings into play an extension of the best-known method of production in an industry. This may be done by the firms already established in an industry by building another factory wing of a known serviceable type, by installing additional batteries of machines of types already in use, and so forth. Alternatively, or in a supplementary fashion, new firms may enter the industry using its known and tried methods of production. Under pure competition this is entirely possible. One of the prime postulates of pure competition is that there shall be free entry to an industry. Now the economic meaning of free entry is that newcomers to an industry shall be able to use the established method of production. This is not an unrealistic assumption. In Chapter 16 it was seen that standard cost ratios for achieving efficiency rapidly become common knowledge once they have been tried and tested.[4]

In this discussion it is posited that the increased demand, expected to be permanent, will be accommodated by a moderate expansion of firms already existing in the industry as well as by the entry of new firms into the line of production. It is also postulated that the increase of demand is not of a drastic nature, but is rather a gradual rise such as occurs in a growing community. Thus the entrepreneurs in the expanding industry will be able to hire needed additional labor without raising wages, and will be able as well to procure additional amounts of raw materials, machinery, and the like, without having to pay higher prices for these or any other factors of production.

Under these circumstances the real cost of producing a unit of the product will not rise in the industry as a whole. To be sure, the new firms will be somewhat better equipped with the most modern facilities and may thus have something of an advantage over the existing firms in the industry. However, there are in every industry a few very old concerns which are declining; they have seen their day and are on the way out of the industry. Nevertheless, they will try to secure some advantage from an increasing demand. This they will do, not by installing additional equipment, but by using their present equipment more intensively—that is, hiring more labor to operate old machinery that they might have retired from use had not the demand for the product increased. Of course, their real cost of producing a unit of the product is raised. Thus there are in the oldest part of the industry rising real costs, while in the newest part of the industry the firms which are just entering it have relatively low real costs. The bulk of the producers in the industry continue to operate with unchanged real costs.

REPRESENTATIVE FIRM FOR AN INDUSTRY

With a few firms declining, many soundly established, and some just beginning, it is possible to summarize a competitive industry's cost

---

[4] See above, pp. 365–66.

situation by conceiving of a *representative firm*.[5] This is a well-established concern operating with average efficiency. It has under pure competition a small share of the total market for the commodity. But the representative firm's share of the market is in a satisfactory relation to its output capacity. That is to say, the representative firm can usually operate at 85 per cent of its capacity or better. Also the firm is able to expand moderately when demand for the industry's product increases, having both the knowledge and the capital necessary for doing so, or being able to attract the capital. In short, the representative firm can extend the industry's production, by the use of the best known methods, without having to use more labor per unit of a larger output or more raw materials per unit of its product. The representative firm can gradually expand its output without a rise in real cost.

The new firms also can have access to needed labor and raw materials without extra expense. They may experience some early struggles in becoming established in the industry, ironing out initial difficulties (like a ship's company on a "shakedown cruise"). But the new firms can, and do, look forward to becoming representative businesses. They aim at participating in the ranks with ordinary ability, and with free access to the customary methods of production and sales outlets, at any time and over the long pull, as the industry grows. On the other hand, some old firms which are declining attempt to stay as close as possible to the standards set by the representative business, even though they are on the way out. They cannot rejuvenate their operations, and their total volume of business diminishes, but the declining amount of activity is not carried on carelessly.

It emerges that the structure of real costs of the representative firm describes the cost situation of the industry. Likewise, the decisions which the managers of the representative firm make on long-run plant expansion govern the response of the entire industry to an increase of demand which is expected to be permanent. In the following remarks and graphical illustrations, there is traced in terms of the behavior of the representative firm the path of business response to a supposedly lasting increase of demand for the industry's product.

Sequence of long-run price determination. The first response to increased demand is a short-run expansion of output by the existing firms in an industry. Under pure competition the new price and output can be ascertained by comparing the increased-demand schedule with the representative firm's marginal cost schedule, which is the firm's supply schedule. If the representative firm stands for 100 firms, as will

---

[5] Alfred Marshall, *Principles of Economics,* 8th ed. (London: Macmillan & Co., Ltd., 1930), pp. 317, 342, 377, 459–60, 805, 809n.

be assumed, one can readily calculate the industry supply schedule, that is, the aggregate of marginal costs of firms in the industry. In this case one simply multiplies by a hundred the marginal cost of the representative firm at each possible level of output. The resulting supply schedule can then be directly compared with the demand schedule at any level of demand. In Table 17–2 the bases of such comparison are furnished for demand at two different levels of intensity.

The new, higher price which now equates supply and demand, *in the short run,* is $8.00 per unit of the product, with a turnover of 900 units. This is the equivalent of marginal cost for the 900-unit production level.

Table 17–2. Change in a Demand Schedule with a Given
Industry Supply Schedule

List Price of the Product per Unit (a)	Quantity Demanded		Industry Supply Schedule
	Before Demand Increases (b)	After Demand Increases (c)	
$13.00	300	500	Insufficient capacity
12.00	350	550	" "
11.00	400	625	1,000
10.00	460	700	970
9.00	530	800	940
8.00	600	900	900
7.00	700	1,000	850
6.00	800	1,100	800
5.00	900	1,225	730
4.00	1,000	1,400	640

In this illustration we assume an original price of $6.00 as an equilibrium price which equated supply and demand and cleared the market. After the demand increases, the representative firm in the industry will at first produce beyond the point of minimum average cost (*atuc*). Beyond the point of least cost, marginal cost must necessarily be higher than average cost (*atuc*). In the short run this is true because *beyond the optimum rate of production the effect of diminishing returns to the variable factors of production outweighs the benefits of making more intensive use of the given and fixed plant and equipment.* In the long run the law of diminishing returns does not apply to the representative firm, because there is no fixed plant and equipment; both can be varied in scale. But now we are centering attention on what first happened when demand increased.

The representative firm expands its production from 8 to 9 units, which means that the industry now realizes excess profits. Table 17–3 provides the relevant data in columns (*b*) and (*c*). The demand and supply schedules for the product are shown for reference (over a range of output which is pertinent in this illustration).

The average cost (*atuc*) for the equilibrium output of 900 units is $6.20, while the marginal cost is $8.00. The equilibrium price must equal marginal cost, and does, at $8.00. With sales revenue per unit at $8.00 and average cost at $6.20, there is an excess profit of $1.80 per unit of the product. This yields for the representative firm an aggregate of $16.20 excess profit, or for the 100 firms for which the representative firm stands, an aggregate profit of $1,620.00, compared with, and in addition to, a total cost of $5,580 for producing 900 units of the product at an average cost (*atuc*) of $6.20.

Table 17–3. Short-Run Excess Profit of the Representative Firm

Quantity of the Product in Units for the Industry —Representative Firm × 100 (a)	Applicable Equilibrium Price (b)	Average Cost— atuc (c)	Supply Schedule— mc (d)	Demand Schedule (e)
600	....	6.50	4.70	11.50
700	....	6.15	5.70	10.00
800	....	6.00	6.00	9.00
900	$8.00	$6.20	$8.00	$ 8.00
1,000	....	6.70	11.00	7.00

Expansion of existing firms. Let us assume that the representative firm finds its enlarged output of 9 units satisfactory but in the long run does not desire to squeeze it from existing plant and equipment. Consequently, the firm adds to its plant and equipment until it has a production capacity at which it can turn out 9 units for the same average cost (*atuc*) of $6.00, the cost at which it previously could produce only 8 units. This is possible according to the postulate that the industry bidding for more management, labor, equipment, and materials is too small to raise any of the rewards to these factors of production.

On the basis of this long-run expansion which renders the representative firm in the industry more efficient, the industry is prepared to sell its product at a price cheaper than the high price of $8.00. This high price was exacted, after all, in order to accommodate immediately an increased demand by working extra shifts or longer hours. By competitively reducing the high price of $8.00, each firm in the industry may seek to attract new customers or please old ones and thus retain them. How far the price may drop because of this intra-industry rivalry among the established firms would be difficult to know a priori. However, the price-cutting effect of pure competition is not exhausted by the actions of already established firms.

Entry of new firms. When excess profits are earned in an industry, the entry to which is free, additional firms will be attracted. For, if investment funds are available in the economy, they will be entrusted to entrepreneurs wishing to enter this lucrative field.

Now as the new firms enter the industry, the supply of the commodity naturally increases. Let us suppose that eleven new firms enter, each modeled after the representative firm of the industry and therefore producing 9 units at an average long-run cost of $6.00. The existing firms have already added units of output (by expanding from 8 to 9 units of output per firm). Eleven new firms, each producing 9 units, add roughly another 100 units. Consulting the demand schedule in column (*e*) of Table 17–3, it is seen that for 1,000 units of the product the consumers are able and willing to pay at a rate of only $7.00 a unit.

A price of $7.00 a unit still affords excess profits. The representative firm—which now stands for 111 concerns—can produce 9 units at an average cost (*atuc*) of $6.00. Thus $1.00 of excess profit is earned on every unit of the product which is sold.

As long as any excess profit is earned in the industry, more new firms continue to enter it under pure competition. Like the firms which entered before them, they are able to use the best known methods of production. Thus they closely simulate the representative firm, by turning out 9 units each at a minimum average cost (*atuc*) of $6.00 a unit. Of course, the new firms, which swell the ranks, make available an increased aggregate output of the product of the industry.

Under the circumstances of pure competition we can ascertain exactly how far the industry's aggregate output will be augmented and what the final level of the equilibrium price will be. Let us suppose that eleven more firms enter the industry, in addition to a previous number of eleven new entrants. The output schedule is now:

   100 established firms produce 900 product units
   11 additional firms produce roughly 100 units
   11 of the most recent newcomers produce about another 100 units, for total output of 1,100 units

What is the equilibrium price at which 1,100 units can be sold? Table 17–4 informs us that the price which will clear the market of 1,100 units is $6.00 a unit. This is enough to cover the minimum average cost (*atuc*) of all the producers, old and new. Although this least cost includes a normal 6 per cent of profit, it permits of no *excess* profit. Consequently, the entry of new firms now ceases. There is no longer an incentive to attract them.

Observe that the price has returned to its original level of $6.00 in the above example. Output, however, has increased from an equilibrium amount of 800 units before the demand increased, to an equilibrium amount of 1,100 units after the completion of entrepreneurial long-run adjustments. Carefully bear in mind that this is

Table 17–4. Long-Run Equilibrium Price, 122 Firms in the Industry, Each Producing 9 Units of the Product

Quantity of the Product in Units for the Industry —Representative Firm × 122 (a)	Applicable Equilibrium Price (b)	Average Cost of the Representative Firm— atuc (c)	Increased Industry Supply Schedule— mc (d)	Demand Schedule (e)
800	....	6.20	2.00	9.00
900	....	$6.00	3.00	8.00
1,000	....	6.10	4.50	7.00
1,100	$6.00	6.50	$6.00	$6.00
1,200	....	7.30	8.00	5.00
1,300	....	9.00	11.00	4.60

possible only under conditions of flexible resources, when enough of them are available at given prices which are not raised by an industry's expansion. If real costs of extracting and developing economic resources increase, long-run prices of products using the resources must rise also. But even then, the cause of the rise of prices would lie in the poor management of our national resources; high prices could not be blamed on the management of the representative firms in the different industries which use our economic resources—except insofar as they personally extract and develop the resources they use.

This significant conclusion about the action of pure competition returns the discussion to the problems of national resources management which was introduced in Part II of this book. There it was seen that national resources management is the proper object of social policies of conservation, education, and research. Of course, the entrepreneurs who use valuable resources can exploit them wastefully. But it has now been shown that under pure competition this would force them to leave an industry, for their real costs would rise. Consequently, they could not make ends meet at a price which covers the minimum average costs of production of the representative firm in an industry. The representative firm itself might be wasteful in the use of social resources. But this is inconceivable under enlightened policies, private and public, of conserving known resources and discovering new ones.

The findings of this analysis of long-run price determination under conditions of flexible resources may now be stated in the form of a theorem.

Axiom: *When under the regime of pure competition demand increases, price must in the long run return to the level from which in the short run it departed, but output will have been augmented.*

This is a useful theorem to have in mind when coping with actual economic problems of a growing community or nation. For the purpose of theory, however, it is possible to draw from this axiom an implication which permits us to state the matter of long-run price, under conditions of flexible resources, in the form of a general principle of the relation of cost and equilibrium price.

The Cost-Price Principle: *The equilibrium price of a commodity not only clears the market but also tends to encourage the production of a maximum aggregate output of the commodity at the representative firm's least cost of production.*

Earlier it was seen that at some tentatively quoted prices the buyers in the market are unwilling to absorb the entirety of the supply offered by sellers at these prices, while at other prices the buyers wish more of the product than the sellers are willing to part with at those prices. Now this can be restated so as to emphasize that at certain relatively low prices the buyers of the product do not offer to meet the full costs of production of the commodity, while at relatively high prices more than enough to cover the production cost (including the normal 6 per cent profit) would be earned by the producers. However, at the relatively high prices the quantity demanded is not sufficient to keep the producers fully occupied. At least some producers feel that they might be forced to operate at dangerously low volumes of output; unable or unwilling to take this chance, they bid the price down, in the direction of average cost of production (*atuc*). On the other hand, some buyers fear that because of a shortage of supplies available at low prices, they might be unable to obtain any, or a sufficient amount, of the product which they want to consume. This risk cannot be assumed, so there are buyers who bid the price up to its equilibrium level—at which level the price covers the representative firm's full average cost of production (*atuc*).

This analytical sequence to explain long-run price determination obviously resembles the explanation of equilibrium price made previously. But the present sequence relates supply and demand in terms of the representative firm's average total unit cost of production, rather than relating supply and demand simply in terms of quantities of goods brought to market after they have already been produced, which must be sold for whatever price is found acceptable.

Figure 17–12 presents a graphic illustration of the general principle that price must equal full cost if, over the long pull, an adequate supply of a product is to be forthcoming. On the left-hand side of the graph is portrayed the output adjustment of an industry's representative firm to demand of two different levels of intensity. At the lower level of demand, the representative firm stands for 100 firms, together producing an aggregate output of OA units of the product. This is shown on the right-hand side of the graph as a point on the original supply curve labeled S–S. The right-hand side of the graph expresses the industry's cost-price adjustments; output is labeled with the sign of sigma (for example, ΣOA), to distinguish it from the individual output of the industry's representative firm.

Explanation of Figure 17–12. The demand increase may be observed on the right-hand side of the graph. The demand curve shifts to the right and is now labeled D_1–D_1. This shift of the demand curve to the right is due to the fact that when consumers are willing to pay a price py instead of the price px per unit for ΣOA units of the product, the point that records the new price-quantity demand relationship must necessarily lie higher on the graph. This is true of all points on the new demand schedule. The intersection of the new demand curve, D_1–D_1, with the given supply schedule S–S, indicates the industry's short-run price and output adjustment. Tracing the short-run price back to the left side of the graph, we see that the representative firm is meeting its marginal cost at the new price py and is producing OB instead of OA units of the product.

The long-run price adjustment under conditions of flexible resources is best observed beginning at the left-hand side of the graph. Here the representative firm's average cost (*atuc*) and marginal cost curves are seen shifting to the right as the firm decides to increase its capacity to enable it to produce OB units at a minimum average cost (*atuc*) of px rather than OA units. That this is possible is explained by the fact that neither wages nor raw materials nor equipment costs rise because of one industry's expansion.

When the existing firms in an industry expand their production and new firms enter the industry, there is an increasing supply of the

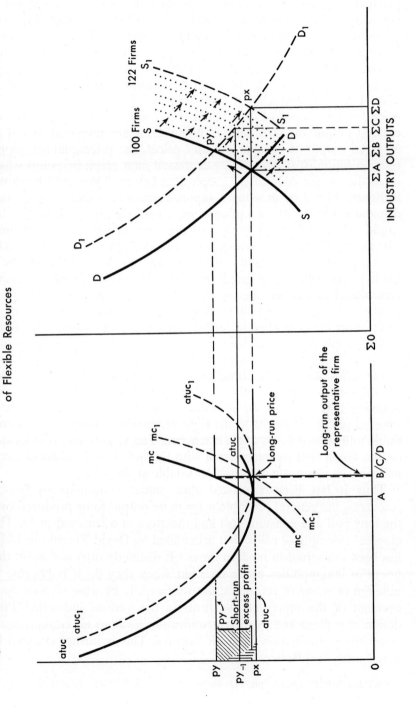

Figure 17–12. Price Determination for the Representative Firm and the Industry, Pure Competition Under Conditions of Flexible Resources

product. Real costs per unit of the product do not rise, so the marginal cost curve of the representative firm (which the newly entering firms emulate) does not change in form, but more marginal cost curves are to be aggregated to arrive at the supply curve for the industry. Thus when eleven new firms have entered and the existing firms have expanded their output capacity, $\Sigma B - \Sigma C$ additional units of the product are available. The mutual rivalry of firms, old and new, causes a decline of price for the output of ΣOC units (as compared to a short-run increased output of ΣOB units). When firms are prepared to sell an enlarged output at cheaper per-unit prices, the price-quantity supply relationship must necessarily be expressed on a graph by points which lie farther to the right of the graph than before. This could be shown in Figure 17–12 by drawing a supply curve which intersects the new demand curve $D_1 - D_1$ at a price of py_{-1} for $\Sigma O'C$ units. However, that would still afford excess profits, so the entry of new firms continues. The entry of new firms continues until at an aggregate output of ΣOD units a price of px per unit of the product is realized. Tracing this to the left-hand side of the graph, note that px (which includes a 6 per cent profit) just covers the representative firm's full cost of expanded production. Hence there is no longer an incentive for new firms to enter or for existing firms to further expand their productive facilities.

The supply curves which emerge as the industry is adjusting its output in the long run are transitory. This is shown in Figure 17–12 by a whole series of dotted but unlabeled supply curves, all of them having the form of the representative firm's marginal cost curve, but together denoting that more of the product is available to the consumers at lowered prices. The drift to the right of transitory supply curves continues until a final $S_1 - S_1$ curve is reached. The $S_1 - S_1$ curve is so located on the graph that its intersection with the new $D_1 - D_1$ demand curve indicates an aggregate output ΣOD salable at the price px.

Thus it has been visualized that, under conditions of flexible resources, the general principle is for more output to be produced over the long pull at a constant cost and therefore at a constant price. This classical principle of price, first articulated by David Ricardo in 1817, has been reasserted in modern times.[6] It distinctly does *not* mean that prices of commodities never rise; but when they do it is because of inflation or waste of resources, not intrinsically because of poor management of the representative firms in the various industries. Poor design of a plant and inefficient utilization leads to an entrepreneur's competitive elimination from an industry. This is further clarified by a new analytical device.

[6] See Joe S. Bain, *op. cit.,* pp. 142–46.

ENTREPRENEURIAL PLANNING CURVES

When existing plants in an industry expand their output capacity, or new firms enter the industry, the entrepreneurs who are to manage the plants envision a whole roster of different-sized plants which they might operate. Each enlarged plant or new plant that could be put into operation is estimated by the entrepreneur as involving a different structure of total costs, average costs, and marginal costs. Some potential plant sizes are really too small; others are expected to become increasingly difficult to manage. Somewhere along the line of possible plant sizes is the best possible plant which a particular management could handle. Bear in mind that these estimates exist only at the moment when a decision must be made about extending the present plant or building a new one. Estimates of this kind may change from time to time, for instance when the growth of a community brings with it new transportation, power, and communication facilities which enable an entrepreneur to operate on a larger scale than he had previously thought to be feasible.

With this understood, we can portray entrepreneurial planning for expansion, *at any one time,* by a whole series of *atuc* curves applicable to a given management at the time, as shown in Figure 17–13.

Figure 17–13 is called a "planning curve" because it shows what the entrepreneur has in mind when he contemplates expansion. Economists refer to this sort of graph as an "envelope" curve because it literally envelops a whole set of short-run *atuc* curves, each pertaining to a different size of plant which, once built, can be used at different rates. To illustrate the meaning of the envelope curve let us suppose that an entrepreneur is about to enter an industry. His aim will be that of emulating the representative firm. He can do this and still undertake some individual variations.

Upon his entry into the field, the entrepreneur might build a plant somewhat smaller in size than that which on first consideration would seem to be the most adequate. This might be done in the hope that the relatively smaller size would serve him well during his struggle to win acceptance as a going concern, and with the intention of expanding his facilities once the firm is fully established. Thus he might select the plant whose average cost (*atuc*) structure in Figure 17–13 is $atuc_1$. Observe that if this size of plant is chosen, the entrepreneur cannot, for the time being, operate at minimum average cost; this is shown on the graph by the fact that the $atuc_1$ curve is tangent to the envelope curve at a higher-than-minimum average cost; yet the point of tangency indicates the probable rate of operations. This particular entrepreneur might expect to reach the minimum cost point later, after he

Figure 17–13. "Envelope" or "Planning" Curve of Feasible Plant Sizes for an Entrepreneur

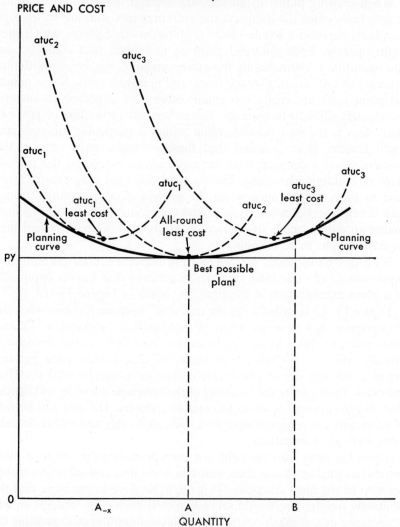

has become settled in the industry. Still later, he could expand his original plant to reach what for him is the best possible size of plant— indicated in Figure 17–13 by the *atuc₂* curve.

Another entrepreneur newly entering the industry might build a relatively large plant to begin with. If we let the envelope curve in Figure 17–13 stand for the planning curve of this other entrepreneur, he may be conceived as selecting the plant whose average cost structure is $atuc_3$. Inspection of the graph will show that when operating with this plant, the entrepreneur would experience a higher-than-minimum average cost; this is indicated by the point of tangency of the $atuc_3$ curve to the envelope curve, lying to the right of and higher than the minimum point of the $atuc_3$ curve. Thus the entrepreneur would from the outset operate under some pressure. However, he may consider it worthwhile to win acceptance—through aggressive selling and other means.

Bear in mind that envelope curves pertain solely to individual entrepreneurs. That is to say, all three plant sizes indicated for an entrepreneur in Figure 17–13 may be small compared with the representative firm, or they may be larger. We know that any particular entrepreneur strives to emulate the well-established representative firm, while indulging in some individual variations. In addition we know that whatever plant size is chosen by an entrepreneur, it cannot be radically different from the size of the representative firm in an industry. Thus supermarkets can and do vary in size, but no entrepreneur would attempt to build one so small as the average corner grocery of the early 1900's; nor would an entrepreneur attempt to build a supermarket the size of a metropolitan railroad station. To go to either extreme would be to invite competitive elimination.

Now the representative firm in any established industry also changes in size from time to time. In American economic history there has been a gradual growth in the size of the representative firms in the various industries: the typical foundry is larger than one considered a huge installation a hundred years ago; enamelware factories are larger; even highly specialized tool and die shops have grown from cubbyholes to fair-sized modernistic structures. On each historical occasion when the size of the representative firm changed, the entrepreneurs in the industry have envisioned an envelope curve, deciding among other things whether to enlarge the given plant or build a new and larger one.

A ready means of appreciating the device of the envelope curve is to be aware of the fact that it analyzes the average and marginal cost aspects of different *total* costs involved in building plants of different sizes. Thus the $atuc_1$ curve in Figure 17–13 is derived from a smaller total cost than are the $atuc_2$ and $atuc_3$ curves.

Although there are different-sized plants in every industry, most industries are characterized, at any time, by a prevailing type of plant and are recognizable by this size of plant. It would be surprising to find a foundry the size of a steel mill, or an oil refinery the size of a gasoline station. Bear in mind, however, that the representative firm varies in size at different periods of history.

If it were not for the fact that the structure of any particular industry tends to converge on a typical plant size, it would be difficult to discern the existence of a general cost-price principle. That is to say, if the size of firms in an industry varied at random and showed no tendency toward a standard optimum size, a random scatter of cost-price relationships, firm by firm, would forbid making any finding about an efficient pricing principle applicable to the majority of firms.

Summary

To recapitulate the major propositions of the price theory of pure competition:

1. In the short run, prices ration consumers in their use of given and temporarily fixed resources. For the time being the rate of production of many commodities cannot be adjusted rapidly to significant changes of demand. Hence people's free spending has to be throttled, by relatively high prices, until necessary changes in the production lines can be made.

2. In the long run, prices theoretically tend to conserve basic resources, whose supply is absolutely fixed, at least in the sense that such *ersatz* as very low-grade ores could be used only at prohibitive costs. By marking the cost high, and therefore the price of scarce strategic resources, the price system can act to prevent their use to the extent of ruinous exhaustion or depletion. (So far, however, the performance of our price system in this regard has been by no means impressive.)

3. When basic resources can be readily multiplied, long-run prices tend to move toward the lowest possible cost of production. The *one* market price which will last (all other things being equal) lies at that point at which the supply curve intersects the demand curve. But we have seen that this point is in the identical position of the low point of the representative firm's average cost (*atuc*) curve—*after the long run*. Thus the long-run price formula under pure competition is $p = atuc \ (= mc)$ for every firm in the industry. This also means that under theoretically conceived pure competition, production is carried on at least cost in the industry as a whole; we may express this by a long-run industry price formula: $P = ATUC \ (= MC)$ with a corresponding aggregate industry output which is the one that can be most efficiently produced of all the possible outputs, given the supply and demand conditions.

4. Ideally, under pure competition and with flexible conditions of resources, with full employment, and using given methods of production, more of any commodity can be produced in the long run at constant cost and, therefore, at a steady price.

5. Insofar as entrepreneurial planning curves are shaped in consideration of standard operating ratios, industry by industry, the rule of $P = ATUC \; (= MC)$ is universally applicable, for the operating ratios are implementations of the competitive cost equals price principle.

Organization of production by market prices is not unique to the American form of economic organization; thus price theory has a broad field of application. Anthropologists have found evidence that forms of competitive price determination existed in very early times and currently exist under fairly primitive production conditions. For instance, in certain parts of Guatemala[7] Indians use an early technology which has not changed since long before Columbus. The products of this early technology are exchanged in conformance with the theory of market price. On the other hand, a socialistic state, in which the government owns and operates most of the plants and equipment, would find price theory applicable insofar as there was free consumer spending.

Also bear in mind that the least-cost principle of price determination leaves open the question of whether all the industries in an economy, when operating together, have a sufficiently large aggregate output capacity to furnish full employment to the nation's labor force. It would be cold comfort if all our industries were operating at their respective least costs if there were so limited an aggregate of national output that an appreciable number of the labor force remained unemployed.

In Conclusion

The elementary principles of price determination must always be recognized as being purely theoretical. They define abstract *standards of performance* which, under appropriate circumstances, can be used to appraise the effects of the decisions which entrepreneurs actually make. The principles of price are tools of thought; they do not pretend to describe reality. They can no more be prescribed as direct solutions to practical problems than can theories of vision in making eyeglasses for an individual, or general theories of cognition to tell a particular student how to meet a specific study problem under concrete conditions.

In brief, the elementary theorems of price, like other scientific thought, are standard frameworks of reference; as such they are useful. However, tools of analysis must not be allowed to *dominate* our practical thinking. Practical economic judgments must be based on

[7] Sol Tax, *Penny Capitalism—a Guatemalan Indian Economy,* Smithsonian Institution, Institute of Social Anthropology, Publication No. 16 (Washington, D.C.: Government Printing Office, 1953).

many aspects of complex reality from which the theorems of price abstract. In the remaining chapters of this book many factors will be examined which influence resources allocation but have so far been ignored in abstractly conceiving the pricing process as a means of resources allocation. Throughout it will be demonstrated how the theory of price is properly used as a general reference framework without interfering with broader efforts of economic understanding.

For Discussion

1. What are the assumptions upon which economic model building, as discussed in this chapter, is based?

2. Why do economists bother with models rather than concerning themselves with a description of the actual world?

3. What are the distinguishing characteristics of competition (pure)?

4. The theory of pure competition is purely formal; its equilibrium-price concept is an idealized construction of the mind, and the setting of the theory is not the ever-changing structure of human affairs but rather a model economy in a more or less stationary condition. Obviously, therefore, the theory must not be judged in terms of its adequacy in describing the American economy as it actually operates. Rather, its validity must be appraised by the use to which it is put as a guide to action with respect to the practical economic problems that arise daily. To what kinds of problems is the theory of pure competition oriented? What kind of practical action is it supposed to guide?

5. Does competition qualify for acceptance as a desirable economic arrangement for economic efficiency? Why?

6. Which of the following graphs is for the competitive industry and which is for the individual firm in the competitive industry? Label the parts.

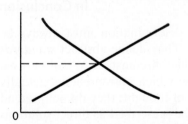 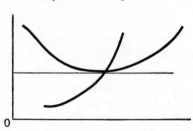

7. What is the distinguishing characteristic of short-run competitive pricing as contrasted with long-run competitive pricing?

8. Explain:
    a. "In the fixed-supply case, demand is determinant of price."
    b. "The setting of price above the equilibrium level results in a problem of surplus disposal."

9. How does this chapter support the remarks made about the rationing function of price which were made in Chapter 1?

10. Is there any evidence that countries with socialistic economies, e.g., Poland or Yugoslavia, make use of the price mechanism? If so, to what extent is the price mechanism used?

18   Monopoly

Exclusive of commercial farming and professional services, which together total 6 million businesses, there are more than 4 million business firms in the United States, serving 175 million consumers. Three million out of the more than 4 million nonfarm and nonprofessional businesses report to the Social Security Administration, providing data on the employment which they furnish to 40 million wage- and salary-earners (out of a total labor force of 70 million persons employed by either themselves or someone else). The data received by the Social Security Administration are categorized to show the different sizes of business concerns. Table 18–1, which is based on these data, reveals the typical proportions of American small, medium-sized, and large businesses in terms of (1) the number of going concerns and (2) their relative importance, as measured by the amounts of employment each category furnishes. These twin aspects of the structure of the business population must be considered together.

In column (c) of Table 18–1 it is to be seen that there is an evident concentration of industry—slightly more than 1 per cent of American business firms hire as many employees as do the 96 per cent of firms comprising the small-business sector. Particularly striking is the fact that our 200 largest concerns, out of a total of more than 4 million firms, hire one out of every five employees. This does not mean that these large firms have absorbed many small ones. Some lines of industry must be conducted on a large scale or not at all. Nevertheless, the data in Table 18–1 reveal a significant degree of business concentration. Table 18–2 illustrates this in more detail by exhibiting industries

Table 18–1. Typical Percentage Distribution of Nonfarm and Nonprofessional
Business Firms of Different Sizes

Size Category (a)	Percentage of Firms in Each Category (b)	Percentage of 40 Million Employed Persons Hired by the Firms in Each Category (c)
Small firms	96.0	34.0
Less than 4 employees	58.0	7.0
4 to 50 employees	38.0	27.0
Medium-sized firms (50 to 1,000 employees)	2.8	28.0
Large firms	1.2	37.0
1,000 to 10,000 employees	1.13	19.0
The 200 largest concerns, each hiring more than 10,000 employees	0.07	18.0

NOTE: This percentage distribution is typical of the 1950's.
SOURCE: U.S. Department of Commerce, Bureau of the Census, *Statistical Abstract of the United States, 1958* (Washington, D.C.: Government Printing Office), Table 609, p. 490.

in which 20 firms or less do most or all of the business. Observe, in column (b) of Table 18–2, the large volume of business done by the industrial giants; for example there is no industry which approaches the amount of $12 billion of shipments made by the petroleum refining industry.

Table 18–2 lists some of the industries with a large amount of production concentrated in the hands of a few concerns. There are also industries with a moderate degree of concentration; these include the producers of such commodities as leather footwear, television sets, radios and phonographs, canned fruits and vegetables, drugs and medicines, beer and ale, worsted and woolens—and numerous other industries including meat packing—in which 1,000 or fewer firms typically do $1 billion or more of business. Industries with a low degree of concentration include those baking bread and related products, manufacturing nonupholstered furniture, performing millwork, dressing poultry, printing commercially, stamping metal, making garments, and so forth. In the industries of low-degree concentration, from 3,000 to 10,000 firms typically would be required to do $1 billion worth of business.

Table 18–2. Percentage of Total Volume of Business Done by the
Twenty Largest Firms in Selected Industries, 1954

Industry (a)	Value of Shipments ($ billion) (b)	Percentage of Shipments Accounted for by the Twenty Largest Companies (c)
Petroleum refining	12	84
Motor vehicles and parts		
(8 companies = 80%)	6	87
Steel works and rolling mills	4	85
Aircraft		
(8 companies = 75%)	3.3	96
Blast furnaces	2.8	96
Organic chemicals		
(8 companies = 73%)	2.2	87
Inorganic chemicals	1.9	74
Tires and inner tubes		
(8 companies = 90%)	1.8	99
Cigarettes		
(8 companies = 99%)	1.6	100
Motors and generators	1.4	75
Tin cans and tinware		
(8 companies = 88%)	1.4	96
Copper rolling and drawing	1.3	90
Wire drawing	1.3	74

SOURCE: U.S. Department of Commerce, Bureau of the Census, *Statistical Abstract of the United States, 1958* (Washington, D.C.: Government Printing Office), p. 786.

THE QUESTION OF MONOPOLY

Industrial concentration is not synonymous with monopoly. However, there is a question of long standing as to whether competition among just a few large concerns, or relatively few, must not inevitably lead to monopoly; it matters not whether the drift in this direction is intentional or unintentional. Starting with Adam Smith, the founder of modern economics, many persons have contended that when businesses grow large and get ahead of their competitors, they will be tempted to relax their internal cost controls and marketing research. May not a large business embrace bureaucratic routines and, in the colorful words of a business editorial writer, "think with rubber stamps and get along on sheer momentum"?

Society's interest is in economic growth by the development of new ideas and their practical industrial application. Traditionally, Americans have believed that the best means to this end is the private-enterprise, private-profit system *under competition*. Will the profit motivation operate in the public interest when the number of com-

petitors becomes limited, perhaps necessarily, for technological reasons? This is a question not only for the present but also for the future.
Conventionally, Americans are probusiness-minded and habitually
against monopoly.

Monopoly Defined

A fitting definition of monopoly, given by Professor Frank H.
Knight, states to the effect that a monopoly enterprise can always be
recognized by its profits being "too high, too long." The virtue of this
plain definition is that it does not confuse monopoly profits and large
windfall profits. A rich harvest of unexpectedly high profits can sometimes be reaped by entrepreneurs because the economic scene is one
of relative uncertainty. Or high profits may be the special rewards
to entrepreneurs of exceptional ability. Again, there are pioneering
profits, the returns of aggressive innovation. Windfall, bonus, or pioneering profits are not properly to be considered as monopoly profits.

Profits that are "too high, too long" can only be realized by the
unreasonable exercise of economic power. Monopoly power arises
from the control of the whole or a substantial portion of the supply
of a commodity. Possession of this power places the monopolist in
the position of forcing the consumer to buy certain quantities of a
product at a dictated price or to go without that commodity altogether. Few persons may be able to follow the course of abstinence,
particularly in regard to articles of needed daily consumption.

To illustrate, let us suppose that instead of being able to shop
around freely for good bargains in butter or oleomargarine, the housewife finds that wherever she shops she must pay an unreasonably high
price for butter and is unable to obtain oleo at all. Having no alternative, she will pay the exorbitant price (although she will grumble).
Subsequently she will have less to spend on other things and
may even have to do with a reduced amount of butter—while yet
spending the same total amount as she had formerly budgeted for a
greater quantity. In general, a dollar may buy ten units of production
under competition but only nine units under monopoly. Thus, when
a buyer is pressed by monopoly, he is not free to spend his dollar so
broadly as he would under competition. There is a price guidance
of consumption and production under monopoly, as there is under
competition, but it is not of the same free nature.

The Demand Curve for a Monopolist

By definition, the monopolist is in full possession of the particular
field of production. The demand curve for the industry is therefore the

demand curve for his output. Suppose that he varies his price; what will happen?

We know by experience that the typical demand curve for an industry is negatively inclined; that is, a greater quantity can be sold only if the buyers are given the inducement of a lower price. Therefore if the monopolist lowers his price, he can, of course, sell the quantity which buyers will stand ready to take at that lower price. This, we have seen, is also true of the single firm in a competitive industry; the single firm which would lower the price to less than the price current in the market could probably sell all it could produce.

But with respect to raising the price, the experience of the single firm in the competitive industry and that of the monopolist would be radically different. We have seen that the former would not be able to sell anything at a price higher than the market price. The monopolist, being in entire possession of the industry, would be able to sell the entire output which buyers stand ready to take at the higher price. Thus, suppose that at $5.00 the buyers are willing to take 100,000 units of the particular commodity and at $6.00 they stand ready to take 85,000 units. The monopolist, when raising the price to $6.00, could still sell the 85,000 units, whereas when the ruling price was $5.00, the attempt of the single firm in the competitive industry to raise the price to anything at all above $5.00 would mean that the firm could not sell anything.

A monopoly may exist where a few or even many sellers (the cooperative association in certain circumstances) associate to get the same results as the monopolist; or where one firm "leads" in setting a price and the other firms in the industry "follow the leader." The price of the commodity or service monopolized would evidently bear no direct relation to the cost of production. Under actual competition nobody controls the traffic in a particular commodity even though everybody may have earmarked for himself a small portion of the total revenue flow from the sale of the total production of that kind of article. Under monopoly the whole flow of the economic traffic in that commodity or service *is* controlled, and it is therefore possible to "charge what the traffic will bear."

THE DETERMINANT OF MONOPOLY POWER

The elasticity of demand is the foundation from which any power of monopoly grows. A high elasticity of demand means that consumers either choose to substitute other commodities for a given article when its price rises, or they are forced to do so because at a high price this article does not fit into their budgets. A monopolist is by definition the sole supplier of a commodity. But if he is producing a commodity for which the demand is highly elastic, he is in strong competition with producers of alternative products even though he has no competitors in his own line of industry.

The less elastic the demand, the stronger the hold which the monopolist has on his customers. Economists of past generations illustrated this by making reference to commodities for which the demand is inelastic because people simply cannot go without them— transportation services, natural gas and electricity, petroleum, and, in earlier days, items such as spices and tea which the British East India Company once monopolized. When great natural treasures such as copper and oil deposits are monopolized, it is still customary to speak of *natural monopoly,* since the concentration—for example, of rich mineral treasures in a few places—is a fact of nature. Transportation and communication facilities also are regarded in the category of natural monopoly, since it does not pay to install several railways in an area with limited population, or several bus lines in a city, or to have competing telephone companies.

In addition, there are *legal* and *capitalistic monopolies.* Legal monopolies are conferred by the government, for example, in the form of patents or copyrights. The grant of legal monopolies was once based on favoritism, but in later history the purpose has been to encourage invention and creative writing. Capitalistic monopolies arise when a person, or a group of persons, has control of extraordinarily large volumes of money or has a superior credit standing. This permits the monopolist, whether an individual or an associated group, actually to produce things on a large scale and more cheaply than small-scale producers, or to buy supplies more cheaply. By this means he may be able to keep competition at bay, though he must sell at relatively low prices to keep latent competition in a state of dormancy.

Legal and capitalistic monopoly sometimes occur in a combined form. It has been observed that some government regulatory commissions tend to issue licenses only to a limited number of firms. The firms with the largest amount of capital are likely in that case to obtain the limited number of franchises. This is especially the case where there is not much room for competition because of technological conditions which require a business to be operated on a large scale or not at all. In such cases there is really a combination of natural, legal, and capitalistic monopoly.

The possession of exclusive control of a supply of a commodity, whether for legal, natural, or financial reasons, obviously confers monopoly power. It enables the monopolist to exact a toll from the consumers either in the form of absolutely high prices for his product or in the form of a price which is high for the type of service rendered. In the days of the horse-drawn streetcars in New York City, straps were attached to the sides of the cars so that many people standing on a narrow ledge could hang on outside, while a lesser number of persons could be seated inside. This was so profitable that there originated the saying, "Dividends depend upon straphangers." The fare was low, but the quality of service rendered was even lower. The railroads which served farmers in outlying districts charged exorbitant rates, knowing that the farmer must ship his crop. Because high monopolistic railway rates were charged without consideration of the cost of the service, a descriptive phrase was coined: "Charging what the traffic will bear."

In the past the exclusive control of a vital supply furnished the most obvious examples of monopoly power. But monopoly occurs in a much more pervasive form, applying to a greater or lesser degree to many articles of staple consumption.

MODERN MONOPOLY POWER

We live in a society of massive and varied production, so that substitution of articles in the consumer's budget is quite feasible. How, then, is monopoly possible?

The ideal foundation for monopoly in articles of mass consumption is control of the demand for an article which is either naturally or artificially differentiated from other articles which can serve the same general purpose. This means that the consumers must believe that there is something unique about the given commodity, either because of some intrinsic characteristic or because of its distinguishing label. To acquire its distinctive reputation the article must be widely used and therefore be produced in large quantities—for example, a select line of luggage or greeting cards, cash registers, basic aluminum products, and for industrial consumption a certain type of mechanical governor or airplane generator. Also, the monopolized commodity cannot be grossly overpriced, else it cannot be used widely. But a moderate monopoly profit reaped on many units of a product will go a long way in enriching the monopolist. More can be gained by earning a modicum of monopoly profit on a large sales turnover than by selling a few units at an enormous profit.

Unitary elasticity, the basis of monopoly. Economists explain the anatomy of modern monopoly by pointing out that the strongest monopoly power can be acquired by producing a commodity up to the point where the elasticity of the demand for the commodity is equal to unity, or at the first level of output beyond unitary elasticity. When this is accomplished, the monopolist can rely on a large total consumer expenditure for his product, *an aggregate outlay which will not change although he raises his price.*

To illustrate, when demand elasticity is unitary, a 10 per cent rise of price, roughly from $1.00 to $1.10 a unit, means that only 900,000 units of the product will be purchased when previously a million units had been bought by the consumers. Now if the monopolist always has the benefit of the same total amount of consumer spending, no purchasing power of his customers will be diverted to suppliers of alternative products. The monopolist need have no fear that his customers will desert him when he raises the price of his product. They will pay more per unit and acquire a lesser number of units, but they will not develop habits of consuming other commodities in the place of the monopolist's product. What does it benefit the monopolist if he always receives the same total income from sales? The smaller amount of production costs him less, a saving which augments his net profit.

Table 18–3 traces the path of monopoly price-fixing. In column (*e*) of Table 18–3, the elasticity of demand for a product is crudely cast. The product may be naturally unique or it may have acquired a distinctive reputation by dint of strenuous advertising. The monopolist begins with a relatively low price, at which the demand is inelastic. This means that the low price has no special appeal; it does not induce people to acquire many more units of the product. Realizing this, the monopolist raises the price. Will he push the price upward indefinitely? Certainly not. A point is reached (that is, a price and volume of production) beyond which the demand becomes elastic. If the monopolist continues to raise the price, many customers will desert him. This point is shown, in Table 18–3, where the elasticity of demand changes from 0.9 to 1.7.

In Table 18–3, it is shown that the elasticity of demand for the monopolist's product is less than unitary for any two-point range on the demand schedule (column [b]) until that range is reached where at the one end 12,000 units are demanded when the price is $1.90, and at the other end 11,000 units are demanded at a price of $2.00. In this situation the monopolist would raise the price to $2.00, because he could not be quite certain in advance at which exact point on the demand schedule there is a unitary elasticity of demand.

Once the monopolist reaches the point where the elasticity of demand is equal to unity, or the first point beyond that, there is no return to a lower level of price. Nor is there any incentive to raise the price higher. Having become elastic, the demand will become increasingly elastic as column (*e*) of Table 18–3 shows. This means that any further attempt to push the price upward would be met with progres-

Table 18–3. Elasticity of Demand and Monopoly Power to Raise Prices

Price of the Product (a)	Number of Units Demanded (b)	Percentage Change in Quantity Demanded (c)	Percentage Change in Price (d)	Elasticity of Demand [Col. (c) ÷ Col. (d)] (e)
$1.40	15,000			
		— 6.80	+13.0	0.5
1.60	14,000			
		— 7.30	+ 9.2	0.8
1.75	13,000			
		— 8.90	+ 8.0	0.9
1.90	12,000			
		— 8.65	+ 5.1	1.7
2.00	11,000			
		— 9.50	+ 5.0	1.9
2.10	10,000			
		—10.50	+ 4.8	2.2
2.20	9,000			
		—11.75	+ 4.6	2.6
2.30	8,000			

sively stronger sales resistance—meaning that the monopolist would lose customers to suppliers of alternative products.

Measures of Monopoly Gain

If one had a pure monopoly and were inclined to make the most of it, here is how it would be done. (1) The monopolist would estimate the extent of the market for the particular product. This may be done more or less informally; perhaps a regular demand schedule would be ascertained and a demand curve drawn, though probably not. (2) The monopolist would now take into consideration the effect that increasing his sales volume would have on the per-unit price of the product at differing volumes of output. This is indicated by the demand schedule.

THE CONCEPT OF MARGINAL REVENUE

The monopolist next counts the *marginal revenue* of increasing sales volumes. This means nothing more than that he estimates how much each additional unit of sales adds to the total income from sales. To learn what marginal revenue is, we take the sales revenue at any given volume of sales and *deduct* from it the previous total revenue at the preceding lower level of sales. Notice that in Table 18–4 marginal revenue is typically a "declining function" of sales volume.

Table 18–4. Income from Sales

Units of Article Sold, in Thousands (a)	Average Price (or Revenue) at Which Sold (b)	Sales Revenue, in Thousands (c)	Marginal Revenue, in Thousands (d)
5	$2.60	$13.0	......
6	2.50	15.0	$2.0
7	2.40	16.8	1.8
8	2.30	18.4	1.6
9	2.20	19.8	1.4
10	2.10	21.0	1.2
11	2.00	22.0	1.0
12	1.90	22.8	0.8
13	1.75	22.8	...
14	1.60	22.4	— 0.4
15	1.40	21.0	— 1.4
16	1.20	19.2	— 1.8

In itself this is precious little information; it merely discloses how the monopolist in selling a greater quantity of goods is, so to speak, turning the terms of trade against himself. Thus, when he sells 9,000 units instead of 8,000, he does not realize $20,700—as he would if he could sell 9,000 units at the same price of $2.30 a unit which he received when he sold only 8,000 units.

The entrepreneur now has to sell at $2.20 a unit, according to the industry demand schedule, which is also his demand schedule because he operates the only firm in the industry. Nine thousand units at $2.20 yield a sales income of $19,800, which is $900 less than if he had been able to sell as many units at the previous price of $2.30. On the other hand, the total income from sales increases. It was actually $18,400 when the entrepreneur sold 8,000 units at $2.30, now it is $19,800. Thus a marginal revenue of $1,400 has been added.

The marginal revenue schedule. The distinguishing characteristic of marginal revenue is that the extra income derived from selling another unit of a product must always be less than the average price of all the products sold (including, of course, the product last sold). This is because the last product sold is charged with the full impact of the declining price of all the products previously sold. If eight units of a product had been sold at 11 cents a unit and nine units must be sold at only 10 cents a unit, what is the marginal revenue in this case? It is 2 cents, a figure arrived at by the following calculation:

a. Eight units originally sold at 11 cents = 88 cents
b. Nine units now selling at 10 cents   = 90 cents

    Marginal revenue equals (b)
    minus (a)   = 2 cents

Another way of viewing the matter is to charge the ninth unit of product sold with the "loss" accruing to the earlier units now that they have to be sold at a lower price. Thus:

a. The ninth unit sold brings in 10 cents; but
b. The eight earlier units bring in a penny less than they formerly did, or a total of 8 cents;
c. Subtracting 8 cents from the 10 cents realized on the ninth unit leaves 2 cents as the marginal revenue of the production and sale of nine units of the product.

The market price of the product is referred to as average revenue, to distinguish it from the marginal revenue. Average revenue is quite evidently more than marginal revenue in the above example. This relationship can be observed at any level of production and sales.

It follows that when a marginal revenue schedule is shown on a graph, it will lie below and to the left of the average revenue schedule. The points on the graph of a marginal revenue and average revenue schedule relate different quantities of output to the money values of the marginal revenue and the average revenue. When nine units are sold, one reference of the average revenue schedule is to these nine units and the other reference is to the price of 10 cents. Thus the point on the graph which is located by these two references is 9 (units), 10 (cents). The marginal revenue curve refers, however, to 9 units of the product and only 2 cents as the marginal revenue from the sale of this much production. The point on the graph which locates the marginal revenue curve is, therefore, 9,2, which lies lower than the point located by 9,10. When a series of points are plotted for the average revenue curve and the marginal revenue curve, the marginal revenue curve gives the impression of lying to the left of the average revenue curve, as Figure 18–1 shows.

Figure 18–1. Monopoly Average Revenue and Marginal Revenue

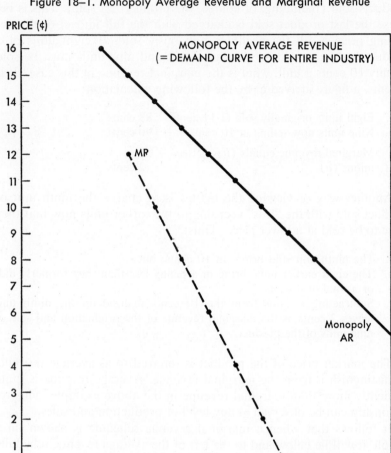

PRICE (¢)

MONOPOLY AVERAGE REVENUE
(=DEMAND CURVE FOR ENTIRE INDUSTRY)

MP

Monopoly
AR

MR (=0)

UNITS OF PRODUCT

Marginal cost. The sole entrepreneur in the field now knows how his sales revenue increases "at the margin." He observes that in a relative manner of speaking he is "turning the price against himself" by increasing his volume of sales. (If he were one of many sellers, this effect would be infinitesimal and he would therefore not be guided in his decisions by marginal revenue considerations at all.)

At this stage the entrepreneur will wish to know how declining marginal revenue affects his *net* profit income. That is to say, so far he is informed only as to what happens to his net *sales* income, which is only one element of his net profit income. To get from sales to profits he has to consult his cost schedule to see how rising costs might impinge on his profits. The most relevant measure of cost encroachment is marginal cost, shown in column (*d*) of Table 18–5.

Marginal cost compared with marginal revenue. In Table 18–5 we see the monopolist turning the terms of trade against himself; the more he produces the greater the cost "at the margin." Previously it was seen, in Table 18–4, that the more the monopolist sells, the greater is the price concession he must make to induce the consumer to accept

Table 18–5. Cost of Production

Units of Article Sold, in Thousands (a)	Average Total Unit Cost (b)	Total Cost, in Thousands (c)	Marginal Cost, in Thousands (d)
5	$2.50	$12.50	......
6	2.25	13.50	$1.00
7	2.05	14.40	0.90
8	1.90	15.23	0.83
9	1.79	16.00	0.77
10	1.70	16.95	0.95
11	1.63	17.90	1.00
12	1.62	19.30	1.40
13	1.61	20.80	1.50
14	1.60	22.40	1.60
15	1.75	26.00	3.60
16	2.00	32.00	6.00

more of the product. Of course, the rising marginal cost of production, as well as the declining marginal sales revenue, diminishes only the *rate* of profit. The monopolist considers this only one factor, for what he is maximizing is net profit income, which is determined by the rate of profit times the amount of turnover. Thus it becomes necessary to determine the point up to which the advantage of increasing turnover outweighs the disadvantage of a declining rate of profit, and beyond which point this advantage is lost, so that there is thenceforth a net disadvantage of further extending production.

As long as marginal cost registers lower than marginal revenue, there is a net advantage in augmenting production, even though marginal revenue is declining and marginal cost is rising. Thus, using the figures in Table 18–5, it will be seen that at 8,000 units of production the total cost is $15,230, whereas at 9,000 units it is $16,000. The marginal cost of producing 9,000 units is therefore $770 (column [*d*], Table 18–5). The entrepreneur could avoid the expenditure of $770 by producing only 8,000 units. But by doing so he would forego a marginal revenue of $1,400. (See Table 18–4, column [d].) Per contra, if the monopolist were to produce 13,000 units of the product, he would incur a marginal cost of $1,500 but would add nothing to his sales revenue. He would still realize a monopoly profit. At the 13,000-unit level of production and sales, the average cost is $1.61, but the average revenue, the price which can be realized per unit of product, is $1.75. However, at the lower production level of 12,000 units, the average cost is $1.62 and $1.90 is the average revenue.

If at some rates of plant utilization it pays the monopolist to increase output and at other points the reverse is true, there must clearly be a point where the output is optimal from the viewpoint of the monopolist who is maximizing his monopoly profit. This is the point at which marginal cost and marginal revenue are equal. Here is where the effect of diminishing returns to the monopolist's given plant and equipment is offset by the extra sales revenue to be realized by proceeding to this level of output. The entrepreneur operates under diminishing returns; also, the sales-appeal of his product is declining. But where the marginal cost and marginal revenue are equal, these two effects will be absorbed by the entrepreneur in an optimal fashion. Table 18–6 makes this plainly apparent by comparing marginal cost and marginal revenue.

A caution. Where $mc = mr$, the monopolist does not lose any net financial advantage because of diminishing returns and diminishing sales-appeal of increasing outputs of his product. But from this one must not infer that he will charge, for the product, a price which equals marginal cost or marginal revenue at the level at which they are equal.

Table 18–6. Equality of Marginal Cost and Marginal Revenue

Units of the Product, in Thousands (a)	Marginal Cost, in Thousands (b)	Marginal Revenue, in Thousands (c)	
5	......	......	
6	$1.0	$2.0	Range in which
7	0.9	1.8	diminishing
8	0.83	1.6	returns are
9	0.77	1.4	overshadowed
10	0.95	1.2	
11	1.0	1.0	
12	1.4	0.8	Range in which
13	1.5	...	the monopolist
14	1.6	—0.4	has no net
15	3.6	—1.4	financial advantage
16	6.0	—2.0	

This is by no means true. He observes the level of output at which *mc* = *mr* merely to determine how much he should produce. Then he determines how much to charge for this amount of output—that is, what the traffic will bear. This is done by referring to the demand schedule (the average revenue schedule). Thus, according to Table 18–6, *mc* = *mr* at $1,000 for an output of 11,000 units. Checking column (*b*) of Table 18–4 discloses that for an output of 11,000 units, $2.00 can be charged per unit. In Table 18–5, column (*b*) shows that the average cost (*atuc*) is $1.63 a unit. That this relation of cost and price yields the maximum amount of monopoly profit income is shown in Table 18–7, where total income from sales is directly compared with total cost, the difference constituting total monopoly profit income.

Table 18–7. Total Monopoly Profit

Units of the Product, in Thousands (a)	Total Sales Revenue (b)	Total Cost (c)	Net Monopoly Profit Income (d)
5	$13,000	$12,500	$ 500
6	15,000	13,500	1,500
7	16,800	14,400	2,400
8	18,400	15,230	3,170
9	19,800	16,000	3,800
10	21,000	16,950	4,050
11	22,000	17,900	4,100
12	22,800	19,300	3,500
13	22,800	20,800	1,950
14	22,400	22,400	....
15	21,000	26,000	— 5,000 (loss)
16	19,200	32,000	— 12,800 (loss)

The Social Meaning of Monopoly Price

Marginal costs, and the competitive supply schedules based on them, are the "barometer readings" of the pressures of fundamental relative scarcities under given social-economic arrangements. Thus marginal costs, which determine prices through supply schedules, convey the scarcity facts of economic life to the consumers. The consumers are rationed to the extent that the conditions of natural and institutional relative scarcity require. Table 18–8 shows what appears when attention is concentrated on the cost-price relationship of a monopoly firm at its output and price equilibrium.

When monopoly price stands above marginal cost, consumers are rationed more severely than is necessary. That is, monopoly price not

Table 18–8. Monopoly Equilibrium

Equilibrium Monopoly Output (number of units)	Equilibrium Price (per unit)	Marginal Cost of Equilibrium Output (per unit)	Average Total Unit Cost of Equilibrium Output
11,000	$2.00	$1.00	$1.63

only informs consumers of the fundamental relative scarcities situation but in addition restrains consumption because of increased relative scarcity artificially imposed upon the consumers by the monopolist.

It follows that the basic measure of scarcity which is inevitable under given conditions of desire, income, and technology is not revealed by monopoly prices; the impression is given that there is more relative scarcity than there actually needs to be. Monopoly prices are false messages and are therefore antisocial.

GRAPHIC VIEW OF MONOPOLY EQUILIBRIUM

It is perhaps natural for any person—not just a monopolist—to be skeptical about this way of getting at "what the traffic will bear." Hence the $mc = mr$ monopoly price-determination formula must be proved; this can be done visually. In Figure 18–2 the cost-price relationship of a monopoly concern is shown, using the data of the preceding Tables 18–4 to 18–8. The graph records: (1) the demand for the monopolist's product, that is, the average revenue schedule; (2) the marginal revenue schedule; (3) the average total unit cost for the firm; and (4) the marginal cost. The shaded rectangular area indicates the amount of monopoly profit, computed by multiplying the amount of the monopoly output by the excess of monopoly price over the average cost of the monopoly output.

Figure 18–2 shows that monopoly price will not be adjusted either to marginal cost or to average total unit cost, as it would be under competition. The monopoly price is established at a level higher than either mc or $atuc$. Unlike the competitive entrepreneur, the monopolist is seen not to use marginal costs as bases of a supply schedule. In fact, the monopolist has no supply schedule, properly speaking. He is interested in what the traffic will bear, not directly in costs of production. Thus he determines the quantity he will supply, using marginal cost only as a point of reference. The crucial consideration is how strong a hold the monopolist has over his customers, either because of their psychological attachments to his product or because they simply cannot go without it.

Figure 18–2. Monopoly Output and Price Equilibrium

PRICE AND COST

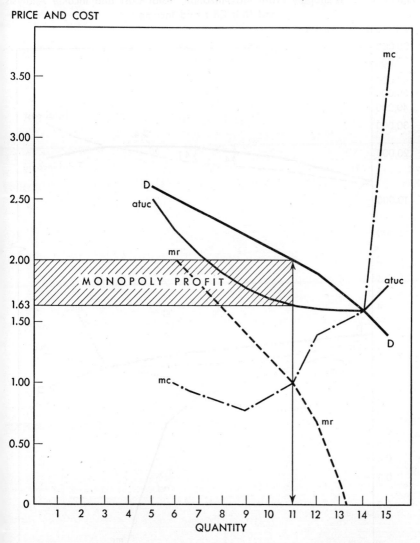

The observation that demand is at the root of monopoly, not supply, can also be emphasized by showing how the monopolist ascertains the widest possible spread between total sales revenue and total cost. This is shown in Figure 18–3, drawn on semilogarithmic graph paper so that the total income and total cost analysis can be compared with the per-unit income and cost analysis of Figure 18–2.

Figure 18–3 proves the general rule of pure monopoly pricing: (1) to find where $mc = mr$, (2) to ascertain to what level of produc-

Figure 18-3. Monopoly Profit Maximization, Total Cost and Income Analysis, and Unit Cost and Income

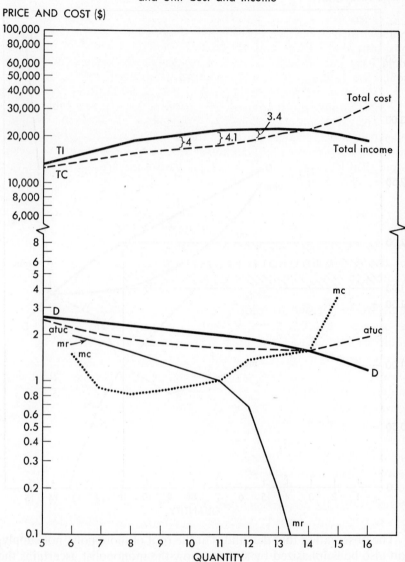

tion this applies, (3) to determine from the demand schedule what the consumers are willing to pay for that amount of production. Or one can simply compare the monopolist's total sales income at different levels of output, and the total cost at each level, and then find where the widest spread lies.

Observe that in the example the following extremely greedy prac-tices were followed by the hypothetical monopolist:

1. There was a severe restriction of production: one-fourth less was produced than would have been under competition, that is, only 11,000 units, instead of 14,000 units, the level of output at which a price of $1.60 would have just covered the cost of production, including a 6 per cent profit. (See Tables 18–4, p. 436, and 18–5, p. 439.)

2. The monopoly price of the product was $2.00 instead of $1.60, the price which would afford ordinary but not excess profit. (See Table 18–5.)

3. The excess profit, reckoned as a percentage of sales (which always understates profit), was 19 per cent. Added to the normal 6 per cent profit, this yielded the monopolist four times as much profit for producing less output than he might have, had he been content to earn the ordinary rate of profit. (See Table 18–7, p. 441, cols. [d] and [b].)

Such extreme use of monopoly power would be the logical outcome of what one might do if one had exclusive control of an industry. In practice it would involve behavior which generally has received public condemnation. It would mean hiring land, labor, and capital on a grand scale while denying other producers the opportunity to earn a living in this field of enterprise. Patents would be hoarded instead of being freely licensed to selected developers. Political pressure would be used to keep out foreign competitors, and community pressure would be exerted to keep down would-be domestic competitors.

Obviously the foregoing analysis of monopoly behavior is as "purely" theoretical as the explanation of pure competition. Both analyses have the virtue of exposing the anatomy of a particular economic process in its most logical form.

History is not made of logical extremes. In the matter of monopoly, when business concerns grow large they provide the managers with the opportunity to adopt a long-run, evolutionary outlook. Thus it becomes well-nigh self-contradictory for the managers of concerns which are "here to stay" to hazard the long future by short-sighted practices bound to undermine "public relations." Is it possible to assume that businessmen have not learned the lessons of history? In 1376, almost six hundred years ago, John Pecche, a London merchant with a patent for the exclusive right to sell sweet wines at retail, was charged by Parliament with abusing his privilege "to the great damage and oppression of the people." He was sentenced "to be imprisoned, to make fine and ransom to the king, and also to give satisfaction to the parties complaining of extortionate prices." He spent only a short time in prison and was forgiven most of his fines, but he did lose his monopoly. Not even Queen Elizabeth I could succeed in granting her groom a monopoly of manufacturing and importing playing cards; the Court of the King's Bench voided the patent and in doing so stated, interestingly:

All trades, as well mechanical as others, which prevent idleness (the bane of the commonwealth) and exercise men and youth in labour for the maintenance of themselves and their families, and for the increase of their substance, to serve the Queen when occasion shall require, are profitable for the commonwealth and therefore the grant to the plaintiff to have the sole making of them is against the common law and the benefit and liberty of the subject.[1]

Statutory law has long since taken the place of the common law's abhorrence of monopoly. In the United States the Sherman Antitrust Act of 1890 actually "went far beyond the common law when it authorized injured persons to sue, and the Attorney General to indict violators of the Act, making it possible to enforce competition actively."

The concept of pure monopoly is actually a very abstract one. But it is a useful one because it does describe the anatomy of monopoly. Actual monopolistic practices are far less rigid than the described skeletal structure might suggest, not least because the problem of monopoly has been thoroughly dissected, and the findings made common knowledge.

Federal Antimonopoly Legislation, 1890-1958

When in 1890 the first session of the fifty-first United States Congress passed its Public Law No. 190, and the twenty-third President of the United States approved it, not every member of Congress eagerly voted for what has since been popularly called the Sherman Antitrust Act. To be sure, some members of Congress were bent on curbing the strident monopolies of that time—such as the sugar, whiskey, oil, and even the cattle feeders' trusts. The "trust" was a device by which stockholders of operating enterprises handed over their stocks with voting rights to a board of trustees, receiving "trust certificates" in return. By this means numerous formerly competitive enterprises could be brought under central management. The owners, having sold their voting rights or given them up under threat, were impotent to protest the conduct of the enterprise.

[1] This quotation and the one preceding and the one following it are from William L. Letwin's "The English Common Law Concerning Monopolies," in Pamphlet No. 1 of *Law and Economics Studies,* issued by the Law School of the University of Chicago, and originally printed in *The University of Chicago Law Review,* Vol. 21, No. 3, Spring, 1954.

According to Senator Orville H. Platt, the political party then in power wanted to win support for planned high tariff legislation to curb foreign competition in the interests of certain manufacturing groups. This required soliciting the votes of farmers and general consumers in addition to those which could be counted on among the manufacturing interests. The tactic decided upon was to appeal to the many individual voters who were vociferously disgruntled with the activities of the trusts. These people would get an antitrust law, in return for which they would be expected to accept high tariff legislation desired by certain economic interest groups. Actually, the antimonopolists got an "act to protect trade and commerce against unlawful restraints and monopolies" right before the election; and the others got their high tariff—the so-called McKinley Bill—after the election. The tariff backfired, though, when the cost of living rose for the man on the street. As a result President Harrison soon lost his control of Congress and two years later was not re-elected. But the Sherman Antitrust Act has been in effect since that time, and so, for that matter, have tariffs that range from high to very high.

From this thumbnail sketch of the immediate historical background of our basic antitrust law it must be evident that it was not a very incisively worded legislative enactment. This was, indeed, the case— in fact, to such an extent that Supreme Court Justice Oliver Wendell Holmes once characterized the law as being vague to the point of being irresponsible. But that is looking at it only as a law. The Sherman Act appears rather more significant when we recognize it as an expression of deep-rooted antimonopolism.

Antimonopolism was, of course, not a new direction of American thought in the 1890's; the attitude is as old as the Republic and had much to do with our early difficulties with England, the mother country. Moreover, since the 1870's a series of laws had been enacted for the regulation of common carriers in interstate commerce. So the Sherman Act really only put our traditional antimonopoly outlook in writing. To prove that, one may take note of the fact that even to this day many competent foreign observers of the American scene voice the belief that Senator John Sherman's slim statute has helped to maintain in the United States economy a much stronger preference for competition than can be found in Great Britain, that traditional motherland of antimonopolism.

Our ingrained social psychology of antitrustism was first explicitly expressed in the following document of only about 1,200 words—a record of brevity hardly excelled in the annals of statecraft. It is herewith reproduced in full.

THE SHERMAN ANTITRUST ACT[2]

Be it enacted by the Senate and House of Representatives of the United States of America in Congress assembled,

Sec. 1. Every contract, combination in the form of trust or otherwise, or conspiracy, in restraint of trade or commerce among the several States, or with foreign nations, is hereby declared to be illegal. Every person who shall make any such contract or engage in any such combination or conspiracy, shall be deemed guilty of a misdemeanor, and, on conviction thereof, shall be punished by fine not exceeding five thousand dollars, or by imprisonment not exceeding one year, or by both said punishments, in the discretion of the court.

Sec. 2. Every person who shall monopolize, or attempt to monopolize, or combine or conspire with any other person or persons, to monopolize any part of the trade or commerce among the several States, or with foreign nations, shall be deemed guilty of a misdemeanor, and, on conviction thereof, shall be punished by fine not exceeding five thousand dollars, or by imprisonment not exceeding one year, or by both said punishments, in the discretion of the court.

Sec. 3. Every contract, combination in form of trust or otherwise, or conspiracy, in restraint of trade or commerce in any Territory of the United States or of the District of Columbia, or in restraint of trade or commerce between any such Territory and another, or between any such Territory or Territories and any State or States or the District of Columbia, or with foreign nations, or between the District of Columbia and any State or States or foreign nations, is hereby declared illegal. Every person who shall make any such contract or engage in any such combination or conspiracy, shall be deemed guilty of a misdemeanor, and, on conviction thereof, shall be punished by fine not exceeding five thousand dollars, or by imprisonment not exceeding one year, or by both said punishments, in the discretion of the court.

Sec. 4. The several circuit courts of the United States are hereby invested with jurisdiction to prevent and restrain violations of this act; and it shall be the duty of the several district attorneys of the United States, in their respective districts, under the direction of the Attorney General, to institute proceedings in equity to prevent and restrain such violations. Such proceedings may be by way of petition setting forth the case and praying that such violation shall be enjoined or otherwise prohibited. When the parties complained of shall have been duly notified of such petition the court shall proceed, as soon as may be, to the hearing and determination of the case; and pending such petition and before final decree, the court may at any time make such temporary restraining order or prohibition as shall be deemed just in the premises.

Sec. 5. Whenever it shall appear to the court before which any proceeding under section four of this act may be pending, that the ends of justice require that other parties should be brought before the court, the court may cause them to be summoned, whether they reside in the district in which the court is held or not; and subpoenas to that end may be served in any district by the marshal thereof.

Sec. 6. Any property owned under any contract or by any combination, or pursuant to any conspiracy (and being the subject thereof) mentioned in section one of this act, and being in the course of transportation from one State to another, or to a foreign country, shall be forfeited to the United States, and may

2 Public Law No. 190 of the 1st Session, 51st Congress; approved July 2, 1890; in *U.S. Statutes at Large*, vol. 26, pp. 209–10.

be seized and condemned by like proceedings as those provided by law for the forfeiture, seizure, and condemnation of property imported into the United States contrary to law.

Sec. 7. Any person who shall be injured in his business or property by any other person or corporation by reason of anything forbidden or declared to be unlawful by this act, may sue therefor in any circuit court of the United States in the district in which the defendant resides or is found, without respect to the amount in controversy, and shall recover threefold the damages by him sustained, and the costs of suit, including a reasonable attorney's fee.

Sec. 8. That the word "person," or "persons," wherever used in this act shall be deemed to include corporations and associations existing under or authorized by the laws of either the United States, the laws of any of the Territories, the laws of any State, or the laws of any foreign country.

This, then, is the grandfather document of a long line of antitrust legislation that sprang from a moral heritage implanted in the history of Western civilization. No less than sixty additional laws and public resolutions have followed since 1890. Not all of them were truly expressive of the original intent of the Sherman Act, to be sure.) Mark well the triple damage penalty provided for in Section 7.

AN ACT CREATING A FEDERAL TRADE COMMISSION[3]

This Act, after defining the composition, pay, and duties of the Federal Trade Commission, significantly declares in Section 5 "that unfair methods of competition in commerce are hereby declared as unlawful." Then, on a note of wisdom, and in the realization that trade practices must inevitably change with passing times, Congress simply leaves it to the Commission to determine what is and what is not unfair competition on a case-by-case basis.

Since this is not, however, a simple matter, the Act sets forth, in detail, the ways in which the Commission must *proceed,* so that the private rights of entrepreneurs may be safeguarded whenever they do not come into conflict with the announced public policy of preserving competition. At the same time the Commission is given powers and authority commensurate with its responsibility to protect the public interest in competition.

Chief among these powers is that entitling the Commission to issue "cease and desist" orders after public hearings have been duly held to determine whether and where an offensive unfair trade practice exists. "The findings of the commission as to the facts, if supported by evidence, shall be conclusive." But any party which feels itself aggrieved by an order of the Commission may appeal to the circuit court of appeals of the United States. "The jurisdiction of the circuit court of

[3] Public Law No. 203 of the 2d Session, 63d Congress; approved September 26, 1914; in *U.S. Statutes at Large,* vol. 38, pp. 712–24.

appeals of the United States to enforce, set aside, or modify orders of the commission shall be exclusive." Failure of a party upon whom an order has been issued to abide with the order of the Commission entitles the latter to ask for an enforcing order in any federal district court of the United States. To disregard such an enforcing order constitutes contempt of court, punishable in the usual manner. Naturally the same is true in the case of any final order issued by the circuit court of appeals, when an appeal has been made. To speed matters in this latter respect: "Such proceedings in the circuit court of appeals shall be given precedence over other cases pending therein, and shall be in every way expedited."

In practice, the Federal Trade Commission relies on its expert ability to sort the good from the bad in the matter of business practices. Rather than relying on court support, the Commission counts on the good will of the overwhelming majority of entrepreneurs; this good will the Commission has so far succeeded in winning by basing its arguments solidly on established fact. Numerous "cease and desist" orders have been issued, particularly after the enactment of the so-called Wheeler-Lea Act, in 1938,[4] which placed the advertising of pure food and drugs under the supervision of the Federal Trade Commission.

The issuance of "cease and desist" orders notwithstanding, it is noteworthy that the Commission has sought to engage in preventive conciliation, so-to-speak, rather than merely to take remedial actions after damage has already been done. To the end of prevention, rather than cure, the Commission sponsors fair trade practice conferences at which industry representatives are freely invited and fully consulted. These conferences lay an objective foundation for defining in advance fair trade practices *on the basis of popular consent* so that entrepreneurs might know where they stand.

ROBINSON-PATMAN ACT OF JUNE 19, 1936

This law is generally referred to as the Price Discrimination Act.[5] Section 2(*a*) states:

That it shall be unlawful for any person engaged in commerce, in the course of such commerce, either directly or indirectly, to discriminate in price between different purchasers of commodities where . . . the effect of such discrimination may be substantially to lessen competition or tend to create a monopoly in any line of commerce, or to injure, destroy, or prevent competition with any person who either grants or knowingly receives the benefit of such discrimination, or

---

[4] Public Law No. 447 of the 3d Session, 75th Congress; approved March 21, 1938 in *U.S. Statutes at Large,* vol. 52, pp. 111–17.

[5] Public Law No. 692 of the 2d Session, 74th Congress; approved June 19, 1936 in *U.S. Statutes at Large,* vol. 49, pp. 1526–28.

with customers of either of them: *Provided*, that nothing herein contained shall prevent differentials which make only due allowance for differences in the cost of manufacture, sale, or delivery resulting from the differing methods or quantities in which such commodities are to such purchasers sold or delivered.

The Robinson-Patman Act reflected findings of the Federal Trade Commission that large buyers of products from manufacturers, especially chain stores, were enjoying unfair buying advantages over small buyers, for example, independent retail stores. For an illustration of this, the abuse of "cumulative quantity discounts" may be cited.

The ordinary discount to a buyer is determined by the quantity bought at any one time. For example, when buying less than 100 units of a product, the buyer must pay $1.00 a unit, whereas when 100 or more units are bought the price is 98 cents a unit. But the cumulative quantity discount is granted on the amount of products bought over a period of time, regardless of the specific number of units bought at any one time. Thus it would be possible to buy only 50 units at a given time and yet receive a high discount if over a period of time 500 units, say, of the product were purchased.

Now the reason for granting quantity discounts is that by being able to fill large orders at a given time, the manufacturer is able to reduce his packing and shipping costs. He can thereby diminish his operating costs by planning his production more accurately than when he must rely on a fluctuating volume of many small orders. The *cumulative* quantity discount, however, is granted on the basis of delivering goods in small lots, so that packing and shipping costs are not greatly reduced, while production is spread out over a period of time instead of necessarily being augmented significantly at any one time. The large buyer thus receives his deliveries in small lots just as does the small buyer. But the larger buyer's total purchases outweigh the total purchases of the small buyer. By threatening to withdraw his patronage, the large buyer can therefore face the manufacturer with a crisis, whereas the loss of the business of one small buyer might not be felt. Thus without necessarily buying more than many small buyers combined, the large purchaser can extract concessions which no one small buyer can gain. The outcome is that the large purchaser not only obtains money savings, but he also acquires a competitive advantage over the small buyers to the extent that he passes his savings on to the consumers. Forceful elimination of competition does not benefit consumers in the long run. When competition is reduced because a powerful merchant gains unmerited cost advantages which reduce the earnings of the manufacturer, the consumers are jeopardizing their sources of supply even though for the moment they may be able to buy goods more cheaply from the large merchant who does not hesitate to exercise his economic power coercively when dealing with manufacturers.[6]

Under the Robinson-Patman Act, the Federal Trade Commission has the authority to fix the maximum quantity upon which discounts can be increased, but after which the rate of discount must remain stable. This has the effect not only of ruling out the cumulative quantity discount but also of confining, within reasonable limits, the superior buying advantage of the large purchaser at any one time. In exercising its authority to limit quantity discounts, the FTC is not required to show that a cumulative quantity discount is discriminatory; instead, the burden of proof that it is not rests upon the businessman who grants cumulative quantity discounts. If, say, a manufacturer cannot prove that his cost savings justify the amount of discount granted by him, the FTC issues a cease and desist order against the seller as well as the buyer.

This power of the Federal Trade Commission has not, so far, eliminated the practice of granting cumulative quantity discounts. One reason is that the FTC must proceed on a case-by-case basis and is therefore constrained by the sheer amount of work to be done from reaching many sources of trouble. As late as 1958 there was considerable popular sentiment in favor of imposing a heavy money penalty on merchants and manufacturers found using discriminatory discount practices. This furnishes evidence that the practices had by no means ceased.

In general, the Robinson-Patman Act is too hedged about with exemptions, and too vaguely worded, for ready enforcement. For example, in Section 3 it is stated that ". . . to sell, or contract to sell, goods at unreasonably low prices for the purpose of destroying competition or elimination of a competitor, exposes the offender to a fine of not more than $5,000 or imprisonment for not more than one year, or both." The extremity of this penalty, in the light of the vagueness of the phrase "unreasonably low prices," means that courts and juries must contemplate enforcement of Section 3 with the greatest hesitation.

THE MILLER-TYDINGS RESALE PRICE MAINTENANCE LAW[7]

This law, which was passed in 1937, legalizes "contracts or agreements prescribing minimum prices for the resale of a commodity which bears, or the label or container of which bears, the trade-

[6] See Charles F. Phillips and Delbert J. Duncan, *Marketing—Principles and Methods* (Homewood, Ill.: Richard D. Irwin, Inc., 1954), pp. 662–65.
[7] Public Law No. 314 of the 1st Session, 75th Congress; approved August 17, 1937; in *U.S. Statutes at Large*, vol. 50, pp. 694–94.

mark, brand, or name of the producer or distributor of such commodity and which is in free and open competition with commodities of the same general class produced or distributed by others." The Federal Trade Commission is directed not to consider the making of such contracts or agreements as an unfair method of competition *provided* such contracts or agreements are not made between entrepreneurs who are in competition with each other. In other words, an entrepreneur is allowed to "protect" the price of his product—from its origin to its final delivery to the end consumer; but an entrepreneur cannot get together with a competitor to fix a common price for the product, or force the competitor to do so by causing the competitor to produce the product under a common brand, trademark, or label. Economists by no means agree that this legislation is a sound one, for it gives the manufacturer the right to patrol the pricing of his product far beyond the factory gate and may therefore damage the interest of the consumer, by denying him possible advantages of competition among wholesalers and retailers.

THE McGUIRE ACT OF 1952

This was another act of Congress which many persons, including numerous merchants and manufacturers, considered inimical to the consumer's interest. The Act exempted from the federal antitrust laws the practice of a manufacturer's signing a resale price agreement with a single dealer, then binding all other dealers handling the manufacturer's product to charge the same price. On penalty of losing their franchise to handle the manufacturer's product, the other dealers could be required to charge the manufacturer's fixed price, whether they had signed a resale price agreement with the manufacturer or not. Specifically, the McGuire Act amended the original Federal Trade Commission Act, with this stated purpose:

... to protect the rights of States under the United States Constitution to regulate their internal affairs and more particularly to enact statutes and laws, and to adopt policies, which authorize contracts and agreements prescribing minimum or stipulated prices for the resale of commodities and to extend the minimum or stipulated prices prescribed by such contracts and agreements to persons who are not parties thereto.[8]

Holding a person legally responsible under a contract that has been made between two other people seems like a far departure from any known canons of free enterprise. Economists are well agreed that this is strange economics, if indeed it is economics at all. Many members of the business community share this view, so that the McGuire Act

[8] Public Law No. 542 of the 2d Session, 82d Congress; approved July 14, 1952; in *U.S. Statutes at Large*, vol. 66, pp. 631–32.

was a dead letter even at the moment of its passage. In 1952 many trade-marked products had for a number of years been sold below manufacturers' list prices. Although one leading manufacturer of household appliances spent $5 million prosecuting 3,000 of his dealers for selling below his fixed list price, most manufacturers found it inadvisable to penalize their dealers for such a violation by revoking their licenses or suing them in court. In several states the courts refused to enforce these strange contracts, on the ancient precedent of Anglo-Saxon law that some practices which are not unlawful ought nevertheless to be denied the sanction of legal enforcement. The ubiquitous discount house played a strong role in ignoring the so-called Fair Trade contracts. Starting as dealers in off brands and odd-lot shipments of standard brands, they soon burgeoned into sizable enterprises whose patronage manufacturers often came to appreciate more than that of department stores. Economists pointed out that the so-called discount house was nothing other than a new firm entering the retailing industry. Early in 1958 the firm which had most adamantly tried to enforce manufacturer's resale price maintenance abandoned its policy on the ground that it was inoperable.

The fate of the McGuire Act reveals why competition persists in the American economy. The general knowledge that the Sherman Antitrust Law exists undoubtedly plays an important role, as does the Federal Trade Commission. The FTC's activities should be regarded in somewhat the same perspective as the role which municipal fire departments play. The reason there is relatively little fire damage is not that firemen are available for putting out fires before they burn very far, but that people generally keep their houses in a condition which prevents fire. Similarly, the Federal Trade Commission is capable of reducing some of the worst abuses of our competitive system. But it cannot really enforce competition. Competition works because the overwhelming majority of producers and consumers want it to work. Without popular preference for competition, the Commission would be as a feather to the wind.

The same holds true of the Antitrust Division of the Federal Department of Justice, which administers the Sherman Act in terms of its various amendments, particularly in terms of the so-called Clayton Act.

The Clayton Act[9]—The Policing of Monopoly

The family names of Roosevelt and Taft in a real sense symbolize the nation's economic history during the first half of the twentieth

[9] Public Law No. 212 of the 2d Session, 63d Congress; approved October 15, 1914; in *U.S. Statutes at Large,* vol. 38, pp. 730–40.

century. What is particularly interesting is that the Roosevelts and
Tafts, for all their feuding in the political arena, always stood as one
in their opposition to trusts. Theodore Roosevelt went after the trusts,
speaking softly but carrying a big stick. Then, when William Howard
Taft succeeded as President, he initiated more antitrust suits than any
President before or since. The writings of both Theodore Roosevelt
and William Howard Taft reveal that both contemplated a Federal
Trade Commission of broad scope, a much more pervasive body than
exists at mid-twentieth century. This shows that our redoubtable fore-
bears placed more faith in the method of education and joint consultation than in the method of prosecution. And in this they had the
intellectual support even of Judge Elbert H. Gary, that masterly
architect of the modern large consolidated concern. Tired of being
called to Washington, D.C., to be investigated by Congressional committees, he exclaimed, on at least one occasion, that he would rather
have a Federal Trade Commission keep its eyes on the affairs of large
business than to have big business repeatedly carry its records to the
nation's capital for investigation. Judge Gary was persistently being
wooed by Samuel Gompers of the American Federation of Labor with
a siren song that if big business and big labor could get together in a
working scheme of industrial democracy, government interference
with either group could be kept at a minimum. But Samuel Gompers,
too, seems to have favored the idea of a competent Federal Trade
Commission, for he says in his *Autobiography* that in addition to
corporations and labor unions, a consumers' interest should also be
organized—which is, of course, what the Federal Trade Commission
endeavors to be.

Thus it may be seen that there was at one time widespread support
for a fundamentally educational and consultative approach to antitrust policy, using the device of an administrative commission. But
there remained also a strong sentiment in favor of just plain policing
the domain of trade and industry. This requires stopping monopolistic
abuses by prosecutions based on definitions that are made by the
legislature in suitable statutes. The policing approach was favored by
persons who were not as yet convinced that an ounce of working
harmony between business, labor, and government may be worth a
ton of printed legislation.

The Clayton Act "got into business" barely three weeks after the
Federal Trade Commission Act had been passed (October 15, 1914,
as compared to September 26, 1914, when the act establishing the
FTC was passed).

Compared with the organic Sherman Act of 1890, the Clayton Antitrust Act is exacting legislation which lists certain specific monopolis-

tic abuses that were occurring in the 1900's. Section 2 of the Act rules against price discrimination (although in no such specific terms as does the Robinson-Patman Act of 1936). Section 3 of the Clayton Act forbids tie-in contracts under which the distributor of a given product is restrained from handling a like product made by a competitor of the manufacturer, whether or not the dealer gets a special price concession, a discount, or a rebate for entering into such a "tie-hands" agreement.

Holding companies. Section 7 of the Clayton Act tries to get at holding companies. A holding company is a device by which a financial group owning 51 per cent of the voting stock of some basic operating concern sets up a new company, which will have for its assets the financial group's ownership of 51 per cent of the operating concern's stock. The new company is the holding company. It issues its own shares. It then sells some of these newly issued shares—not more than 49 per cent of them. The financial group that began the manipulations thus retains control of the holding company and, therefore, of the underlying basic operating concern. Having sold about half of its shares in the holding company, and receiving cash for them, the financial group has now really only a 26 per cent ownership in the operating concern. The free cash realized by the owners of the holding company, when selling a part of their holding-company shares, is now available for similar financial ventures. Thus financial groups could, and did, acquire additional ownership without investing much money. Inasmuch as the stockholders of the underlying operating concerns, and of the minority stock of the holding companies, were often quite separated from each other, it sometimes required very little *concentrated* ownership to run the affairs of important basic operating companies, with layers of functionless holding companies heaped on top of them. Sometimes 5 per cent ownership might do, since no other group of stockholders would ever get together to form a 5 per cent countervailing power bloc.

Section 7 of the Clayton Act decrees that:

No corporation shall acquire, directly or indirectly, the whole or any part of the stock or other share capital of another corporation engaged also in commerce where the effect of such acquisition may be to substantially lessen competition between the corporation whose stock is so acquired and the corporation making the acquisition ...

Then again:

No corporation shall acquire, directly or indirectly, the whole or any part of the stock or other share capital of *two or more* corporations engaged in commerce where the effect of such acquisition or the use of such stock by the voting or granting of proxies or otherwise may be substantially to lessen competition. ...

Then, in Section 8 of the Act, Congress tried to prevent interlocking directorates. This is a self-explanatory term. Congress first provided that:

... no person shall at the same time be a director or other officer or employee of more than one bank ...

then went on to require that:

... no person at the same time shall be a director in any two or more corporations, any one of which has capital, surplus, and undivided profits aggregating more than $1,000,000 ... if such corporations are or shall have been theretofore, by virtue of their business and location of operation, competitors, so that the elimination of competition by agreement between them would constitute a violation of any of the provisions of any of the antitrust laws.

The other sections of the Act—there are twenty-six of them—deal principally with coverage, procedures, penalties for violation of the Act, rights of the parties to court review, and the duties of the enforcing agency—in this case the office of the United States Attorney General. The triple damage provision to parties injured by monopoly was retained, as under the Sherman Act, along with the $5,000 penalty to be paid to the government.[10] Also retained was the provision for issuing injunctions against any party held to be threatening irreparable damage to some other party when the behavior of the first party is deemed to be in violation of the antitrust laws.

IMPACT OF THE CLAYTON ACT

One of the provisions of the Clayton Act had a curious outcome. Section 20 of this Act seemed specifically to exempt labor unions from coverage under the Sherman Antitrust Act:

... no restraining order or injunction shall be granted by any court of the United States ... in any case between an employer and employees, or between employers and employees, or between persons employed and persons seeking employment, involving, or growing out of, a dispute concerning terms and conditions of employment, unless necessary to prevent irreparable injury to property, or to a property right. ...

Then again:

And no such restraining order or injunction shall prohibit any person or persons, whether singly or in concert, from [doing practically all of the things that labor unionists could think of doing in the normal, lawful, and peaceful pursuit of their legitimate activities]; or from doing any act or thing which might lawfully be done in the absence of such [labor] dispute by any party thereto; nor shall any of the acts specified in this paragraph be considered or held to be violations of any law of the United States.

[10] This was raised to $50,000 on July 7, 1955.

Whoever got this Section 20 into the law (no doubt Samuel Gompers) surely thought he had covered the field; indeed, organized labor celebrated this section of the Clayton Act as "Labor's Magna Charta." But as it developed, this section proved to be completely ineffective after World War I when the Clayton Act was first put to the test. During the 1920's injunctions were freely issued by federal courts against labor unions, though triple damages were rarely imposed or collected. (The injunction performed the *main* task of preventing concerted labor action that was unwanted by employers.) It is not too much to say that Section 20 was virtually emasculated by lower courts and the Supreme Court.

William Howard Taft, then Chief Justice of the Supreme Court, did try to instill a "rule of reason" into the application of the Sherman Act to organized labor, such as that which had already been developed for the business community. Under the rule of reason, as developed by the courts in interpreting the Sherman Act, bigness does not amount to badness *provided that* any damage caused by a big concern moving about on the economic scene was not intentionally inflicted to repress competition but was merely incidental to a concern's growth. Consequently, under Justice Taft's tenure, it was held that if a labor strike interfered with the shipment of goods in interstate commerce, it could not be enjoined outright for that reason alone. One would first have to find whether the interference with the free flow of commerce was merely an inescapable incident of the work stoppage, or whether the labor union had planned to diminish commerce for the purpose of driving up prices, and then getting paid higher wages. Needless to say, this still left the labor unionists aghast, as the Clayton Act seemed so definitely to have removed them from coverage under the Sherman Act that if they *were* to be regulated, it would have to be done by separate legislative enactment.

Monopolistic mergers. Whereas the Clayton Act was being applied to labor in the 1920's, it would appear to have had but little effect on the business community. When applied there, the "rule of reason" seems to have been flexible enough to permit holding companies, for example, to grow luxuriantly. At the same time the device of the *merger* was widely employed. Merging amounts simply to combining the actual physical assets of formerly separate concerns.

If one measures the degree of monopoly in the United States economy as a whole by the simple device of comparing variations in the excess of sales revenues over basic prime costs of manufacturing, the degree of monopoly would seem to have increased by about 20 per

cent from 1923 to 1929.[11] The merger movement of the 1920's was
encouraged by what has become known as a loophole in the Clayton
Act, which a vigilant Eighty-first Congress then tried to close by the
O'Mahoney-Kefauver-Celler Act of 1951. This Act was specifically
designed to "amend the Clayton Antitrust Act to close loopholes and
prohibit corporations purchasing assets of competing corporations."
The loophole in the Clayton Act was that one could circumvent its
requirements by simply buying a competitor's *physical assets,* his plant
and equipment, instead of merely buying all or a controlling part of
his stocks or share capital. Section 7 of the O'Mahoney, Kefauver-
Celler Act of 1951 states that:

> No corporation shall acquire, directly or indirectly, the whole or any part of
> the stock or other share capital and no corporation subject to the jurisdiction of
> the Federal Trade Commission shall acquire the whole or any part of the assets
> of one or more corporations engaged in commerce, where in any line of com-
> merce in any section of the country, the effect of such acquisition, of such stocks
> or assets, or of the use of such stock by the voting or granting of proxies or
> otherwise, may be substantially to lessen competition, or to tend to create a
> monopoly.[12]

The O'Mahoney-Kefauver-Celler Act does not forbid mergers made
in the normal course of technological development (Section 7):

> Nor shall anything contained in this section prevent a corporation engaged
> in commerce from causing the formation of subsidiary corporations for the
> actual carrying on of their immediate lawful business, or the natural and
> legitimate branches or extensions thereof, or from owning and holding all or
> a part of the stock of such subsidiary corporations, when the effect of such
> formation is not to substantially lessen competition.

It is the responsibility of the Federal Trade Commission to judge
what the case might be, either upon complaint of any person who
may feel himself injured, or on the Commission's own motion. A bill
reported to Congress on May 28, 1957, foreshadows a requirement
that proposed mergers be justified to the FTC in advance.

[11] This method of comparing sales revenue with basic prime costs of wages and
raw materials can only be used for an economy as a whole, for then the supplementary costs of overhead replacement and expansion reduce to the costs of the labor
and materials used for making capital goods. One must, of course, assume that the
composition of the total industrial output for the nation will not have changed
drastically between the base year of the calculation and any other year. Studies of
the structure of the U.S. economy show that it does not radically change from decade
to decade, so that one can use a "chain-index" method of comparing the degree of
monopoly during rather long periods during which no major industrial revolution
occurs. See Michael Kalecki, *Theory of Economic Dynamics* (New York: Rinehart
& Co., Inc., 1954), pp. 13–23.
[12] Public Law No. 906 of the 2d Session, 81st Congress; approved December 29,
1950; in *U.S. Statutes at Large,* vol. 64, pp. 1125–28.

Antitrust Legislation at Mid-twentieth Century

These excerpts from the leading antitrust laws show that the framers of the Sherman Act and of the Clayton Act and its subsequent amendments tried to put a halt to certain specific tactics of combination that had evolved since 1890. These were malpractices which were universally held to be fraught with danger to the survival of competition—not in every case, but in some perhaps very important ones. Obviously, then, the tactic of amending and further amending the Sherman Act is one of trying to interdict new malfeasances of monopoly. The trouble with that sort of policing approach is threefold.

1. It is a static approach, which seems to assume that certain abuses develop and then remain constant, so that they can simply be swept out. This overlooks the fact that such entrepreneurs as may be willing to spend a lot of time getting around competition, instead of getting into it, will also spend time trying to outwit the Antitrust Division of the Department of Justice. To the extent that they might be successful, the Division will always be merely catching up.

2. There is a difficulty in deciding "who is trying to get around what." For example, it has recently been observed that a number of separate corporations have acquired *joint* subsidiaries. That is to say, the different parent corporations jointly own and operate certain facilities of which they can make common use, even though the parent corporations are in competition with each other. Is this an abuse? Is it an attempt to get around the antitrust laws? Or is it a practice intended to avoid wasteful duplication of facilities which would have to be separately established in the absence of jointly controlled subsidiaries? If there is blame to attach, who is to be blamed—the sellers of the facilities or the buyers?

3. Since only a minority of producers spend their time trying to get around the antitrust laws, the trouble with trying to police monopoly (except in outrageous isolated and short-lived instances) is that it is apt to end by also policing actual competition; then "the rain falls on the just and the unjust alike."

The situation is likely to occur because of the *dynamic* nature of modern forms of competition. That is to say, actual competition emerges in ever changing forms; hence, it is quite impossible to select a favorite form of competition and expect it to persist. In other words, the real problem of monopoly is *not one of form*. It is a problem of knowing how to prevent, on an evolving, up-to-date basis, any sort of private *or* public economic control which might interfere with the efficient utilization of our natural resources and human skills.

For Discussion

1. Which of these definitions of monopoly do you prefer, and why?

   a. "... a monopoly ... is nothing else than a business not limited by competition." (Richard T. Ely, *Outlines of Economics*, 1st ed., 1893.)

   b. "The monopolist is coerced by conditions in fixing his prices, not according to his own caprice, but in conformity with certain broad principles over which he has no control." (F. M. Taylor, *Principles of Economics*, 1922.)

   c. "A single-firm monopoly is most easily defined as the case in which one firm has an output for which there are no close substitutes." (Joe S. Bain, *Pricing, Distribution, and Employment*, 1953.)

2. Modern monopoly theory emphasizes control of demand for a commodity rather than control of its supply. Are these two approaches mutually exclusive? What is the advantage of the newer approach? Do the above quotations reveal the trend in this direction?

3. "The tendency of monopoly price to rise above the competitive normal price varies inversely with the elasticity of the demand for the monopolized commodity." Explain.

4. Explain the following chart, and label it fully. What length on the horizontal axis shows the quantity produced at monopoly equilibrium? If quantity *OA* were produced, where would the price be marked on the vertical axis of the graph? What length, anywhere on the graph, shows the net monopoly income? Why are the two tangents which are drawn to the two curves parallel?

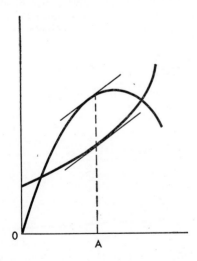

5. Complete the following table and plot the results on a graph. Label all the curves. Determine the monopoly equilibrium price and the output. How does this unit-cost and unit-price analysis add to what can be learned by simply comparing total cost and total price in order to ascertain monopoly price and output?

P (AR)	Q	TR	MR
$13	1		
12	2		
11	3		
10	4		
9	5		
8	6		
7	7		
6	8		
5	9		
4	10		

6. The monopolist seeks the largest return; so does a competitive firm. What, then, is the difference between monopoly and competition?

7. Government regulation has in given instances fostered monopoly, yet government regulation aims to control monopoly. How can this be?

8. What is the result of attempts to regulate monopolies by law? Why?

9. The Robinson-Patman Act of 1936 seeks to prevent large buyers of commodities from obtaining them at unfairly low rates, and thus being able to sell at lower prices. But does not this practice furnish the consumer better bargains? By what reasoning could action instituted against large buyers by the Federal Trade Commission be justified as monopoly control?

10. Establish some criteria of monopoly control by the government which you consider would be realistic and therefore acceptable to the business community so that only a minimum of enforcement action would be required.

19

Limited
Competition

In regarding the relation of pure price theory to practice, the reader may feel moved to remark, as Shakespeare's Hamlet did: "There is more in heaven and earth than is dreamt of in your philosophies!" That is not the point. The relevant fact is that knowledge of the logically extreme cases of pure competition and monopoly can be applied as an aid to understanding the bewildering terrain of actual price situations.

To establish an intellectual continuity between pure competition and pure monopoly we shall make the economist's customary use of the concept "degree of monopoly." This means classifying actual price situations according to the extent to which they depart from the model situation of pure competition. Of course, one might also approach the analysis of economic life situations in terms of the "degree of competition."

We shall follow the customary usage and speak of degrees of monopoly in given actual price situations which are typical. First the situations will be described, and then the concept of "degree of monopoly" will be articulated.

Monopolistic Competition

Low degrees of monopoly are encountered in cases in which entrepreneurs have won a clientele not easily swayed by competitors because of psychological resistance. The word "client" has among its connotations "dependent," "frequenter," "supporter." In economics the word "clientele" is applied to steady customers of a concern who patronize it even though superior shopping alternatives are available. In other words, the entrepreneur can count on a body of loyal customers who are willing to pay relatively high prices for goods which are substantially similar in quality, serviceability, and so forth to goods being sold elsewhere at lower prices. Of course, when two products serving the same general purpose are quite unlike in quality and so forth, they must be considered as being two different commodities. Here we shall speak only of cases in which there is no significant difference between goods which are nevertheless sold at different prices.

The origin of a clientele in the psychological "loyalty" sense may be in consumer indifference or ignorance regarding alternative buying opportunities, or it may be a matter of consumer pride in buying at reputable establishments or acquiring goods marked with an exotic label. However, we often encounter, in addition to these forms of consumer behavior, purposeful entrepreneur conduct designed to attract a clientele—for example, by the practice of "creative selling." Illustrations of this abound in any issue of various consumer's research publications available to the general public. For example, we find in one such publication (in an issue and at a page picked purely at random), the following revealing statements:

For esthetic reasons, some consumers who are buying both an automatic washer and a clothes dryer will want two matching units, rather than units which differ in dimensions and appearance. If the esthetic considerations are not worth $70 to $100 to you, it would be more economical to purchase one of the color-checked washers and the relatively low-priced Best Buy electric clothes dryer, the XYZ Company's ET-8. However, if you are willing to pay the price premium, you can select any of the seven color-checked washers (recommended below) and its matching electric dryer, or gas dryer if it has one, and obtain an effective laundry pair.

What this statement clearly allows one to infer is that some producers will be able to get an extra high price for an article, a clothes dryer, which has a certain attraction in that it matches another article, but which is not designed to do the job any better than a lower-priced dryer for the housewife who is really interested only in getting her work done. In other words, we have here a case in which some producers have apparently succeeded in differentiating their product from those of other firms without remodeling the product to such an extent as to make it a *truly* different one.

Making an extra profit without furnishing the consumer an equivalent amount of extra *economic* satisfaction is possible only if there is a way of limiting entry to the field. Nowadays that would be difficult to accomplish by sheer force or by prevarication. In the words of a conservative member of the advertising profession: "Today out-and-out fraud in advertising no longer exists . . . The abuses of today are more difficult to handle than fraud, because they are within the law as now written." What is meant is that a manufacturer who has a technologically superior product to offer the public may find himself checked by psychologically potent advertising of relatively inefficient competitors.

THE ECONOMIC ANALYSIS OF MONOPOLISTIC COMPETITION

An induced or self-inspired clientele confers only a low degree of monopoly on the entrepreneur. There are a number of reasons: (1) Even though each seller may have a clientele, there still remains a large number of sellers, as, for example, in the case of shops selling ladies' garments. (2) It remains possible for new firms to enter the industry—for instance, the hotel and restaurant trade. (3) The products offered in the market have a "differentiated" sales-appeal, but close substitutes exist. (4) Although each seller is able to vary his prices, he cannot stray far from the "price current" for the basic type of product. As an illustration consider the men's clothing business. Despite the fact that different prices are charged for well-nigh identical suits, there are really three standard price levels of suits: the low-priced $35.00 variety, the $60.00 suit for the aspiring middle-income recipients, and the $90.00 garment for college students and members of the upper-income classes. The middle-priced suit may vary from $55.00 to $70.00 depending upon where one buys it—at the University Shop or in a downtown department store. The $90.00 garment may rise in price according to the degree of custom tailoring bestowed upon it.

Price trends are still determined by the interaction of many sellers serving many buyers. The monopoly element of "charging what the traffic will bear" does not exert the major price-determining influence. This is why economists speak of monopolistic *competition*—in cases where clienteles have been won but can only be retained by psychological manipulations.

The economic analysis of this prevalent price situation leads to a singular conclusion, namely, that monopolistic competition may be no more profitable than pure competition. This is paradoxical, for the motive in monopolistic competition is to earn surplus profit. The means to achieve this end is to divorce oneself from the general merchandising or manufacturing market, to rule instead one's own little submarket. These tiny submarkets are, however, closely related—so closely that in the case of a gas station, for example, a single penny of extra price markup might drive the customers to other stations. Nor is there any way to keep somebody else from putting up a station; entry into the field is almost entirely free to anyone who wants to risk his time and money.

Under these circumstances, if any producer of ordinary efficiency is earning more than normal profit, this will almost immediately attract competition. The new competition may not drive the original operator out, but it may very well diminish the demand for his particular services. The original dealer's personal relationship with his steady clientele may last, but marginal buyers who do not know about him and do not greatly care what brand of the article they buy will give some of their trade to the newly established entrepreneur. To generalize: when there is no profound basis for product or service differentiation, the over-all result may be that all the dealers (or any kind of producer in similar circumstances) may sell enough to cover their average total unit costs of production, but no one dealer (or producer) may be able to use his plant to its optimum capacity. In other words, $p = atuc$, but not at that optimum yield (or least cost) point where $atuc = mc$. (See Figure 19–1.)

To the economist this sort of possible situation would reveal a waste of social resources. The rule of efficiency is that $P = ATUC \ (= MC)$. Whenever that is not the case, either too much or too little use is being made of the given productive capacity. In this case there is underutilization of fixed plant and equipment, a familiar spectacle on the United States economic scene. The attempt to realize excess profits results only in excess productive capacity.

Monopolistic competition interferes with the optimal functioning of the nation's capital markets because the cost of risk-bearing is artificially increased. Formerly there was only the risk of selling a standard product; now there is the added risk of sales fluctuations for *each label* of that basic product. A variety of small risks is expensive to handle.

Under monopolistic competition the supply of a commodity is splintered without being improved. Note that in the absence of monopolistic competition a great variety of different garments, suits, and other articles would be available. But they would be truly differentiated, not nominally so. Competition would take place in terms of quality, durability, aesthetic appeal, and so forth. Advertising would be con-

Figure 19–1. Price Determination and Resource Utilization Under
Crowded Service Competition

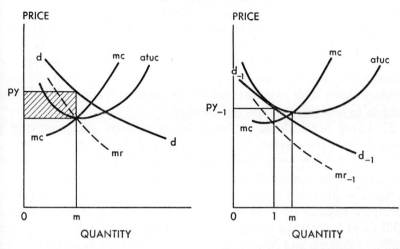

(A). SHORT-RUN EXCESS PROFIT OF
MONOPOLISTIC COMPETITION
(SHADED AREA)

(B). LONG-RUN EXCESS CAPACITY, MEAS-
URED BY POTENTIAL OUTPUT *l m*, WITH-
OUT SURPLUS PROFIT AFTER ENTRY OF
NEW FIRMS

fined to conveying information about genuine differences in goods and
services. It is annoying to hear promotional selling, pompous public
relations, and inane TV commercials extolled as competition. "That's
a great deal to make one word mean," said Alice in Wonderland in a
thoughtful tone. "When I make a word do a lot of work like that,"
said Humpty Dumpty, "I always pay it extra." "Oh!" said Alice. She
was much too puzzled to make any other remark.

Oligopoly: Monopoly or Competition?

This unfamiliar term is compounded of the Greek word *oligos*
meaning "few" and *poleo* meaning "seller." An oligopolist is therefore
one of a few sellers in an industry.

Competent observers will not deny the *fact* that oligopoly exists in
certain leading United States industries. The most prominent instances
are those of automobile and tractor manufacturing, typewriter manufacture, cigarette production, petroleum refining, and basic steel production.

Unlike monopolistic competitors, established oligopolists are shel-
tered by objective economic barriers which hold competition at bay,

and they do not have to rely on the psychological techniques of advertising and selling (though these are certainly not spurned). As a matter of fact, oligopoly is a natural condition in the mass production industries. That is to say, there is not room for many sellers as a consequence of modern technology. In a general way, the following factors operate.

1. The high cost of constructing and efficiently managing an optimally sized plant mounts up to a half *billion* dollars in the auto industry. Such high capital requirements naturally act as formidable barriers to new entrants into the industry.

2. Large firms already existing in an industry and supplying a great share of the market enjoy strong prestige among the consumers, making it difficult for a competitor to become accepted even when he can raise the required large amount of capital. A spectacular illustration was provided by the P. Lorillard Company when, in 1926, it attempted to enter the field of cigarette production with a new brand, "Old Gold." After an initial lavish advertising outlay of better than a million dollars, and further heavy outlays after the launching of the venture, "Old Gold" reached a position of fifth-best seller in the industry. (The success of filter cigarettes, in 1956, was not due to their being new brands, but rather to the lung cancer alarm, although this was, of course, not mentioned in the advertising.)

3. A firm which had an early start in a mass production industry requiring much capital is in a favored position of staying ahead of its competitors. In serving the needs of modern technology, the firm can keep abreast of the latest technological developments. And having massive funds of capital, the firm finds no difficulty in attracting additional capital.

Because the firms in our oligopolistic industries manifestly serve the needs of modern technology, it has been argued that we should abandon the term *oligopoly* in describing them, because it is reminiscent of the term *monopoly,* with its antisocial implications. It has been suggested that we use, instead, a neutral term such as "competition among the few" (William Fellner).

Economic theory must not be emasculated by considerations of semantic nicety. We require a well-rounded theory of oligopoly, one which neither stigmatizes the producers in a field that will not naturally tolerate the existence of many sellers, nor merely echoes uncritical paeons in praise of our industrial giants' mass production.

Curiously, a theory of oligopoly was developed with great refinement over a hundred years ago, in 1838, by the French mathematician

Augustine Cournot.[1] True, he accomplished this by a method of deductive logic—he could hardly have done so by observation at that early date! The findings of modern experience, however, do not invalidate Cournot's early reasoning; they strongly tend to confirm it.

THE ECONOMIC ANALYSIS OF OLIGOPOLY

Cournot gave an early explanation of how profits are theoretically maximized under a variety of mixed situations which exist in real life between the polar opposites of pure monopoly and pure competition. In certain of these intermediate zones the nature of an industry causes the profit-maximizing entrepreneurs to approximate more closely the behavior of the monopolist rather than the conduct of the competitive firm. This is the case when the entrepreneurs in an industry, instead of considering price as given and only output as subject to their control, endeavor to control the price of the product as well as the amount of output. An entrepreneur may attempt to do so in an effort to eliminate his competitors, in the course of a price war. If victorious, the surviving entrepreneur would thereafter occupy the position of a single-firm monopoly. Far more likely, the limited number of entrepreneurs in an oligopolistic industry reach agreements, openly or tacitly, to fix the price of the product for their greatest *mutual* benefit. Under these circumstances the price which is fixed tends to approximate the level of monopoly price.

Cournot meticulously shows how and why entrepreneurs come to open or tacit understandings to limit competition for their mutual benefit, and why this leads to price-setting more in conformance to monopoly theory than to competitive price theory. The chief virtue of Cournot's analysis is that it demonstrated that pure price competition does not guarantee that the price of a product will be established at exactly the point where it covers, for the producer of ordinary efficiency, the full average total unit cost of production, so that no excess profits are earned. Cournot demonstrates that price competition may carry price below this level, inflicting financial losses on all the producers in an industry. This is one reason why entrepreneurs tend to reach agreements to limit price competition—open agreements sometimes, but tacit agreements in most instances. The fear of destructive price wars leads to open or tacit price fixing, which may overshoot the mark and move price in monopolistic directions.

To understand these tendencies in real economic situations, particularly that of oligopoly, it is necessary to trace the course of a

---

[1] *Mathematical Principles of the Theory of Wealth* (New York: The Macmillan Co., 1897).

theoretical price war; to show that this danger can be averted only by producers coming to open or tacit agreements; and to demonstrate (1) that such agreements are theoretically monopolistic in their effect on prices and outputs, and (2) that once established at monopolistic levels, prices tend to remain at these relatively high levels.

PRICE WAR THEOREM

Each firm disregards the production trends of the other firms in its industry and seeks to maximize its profits independently. Suppose that there are only two business rivals and that one of these firms seeks to attract some of the other firm's customers by increasing its own output and lowering its prices. The other firm is now forced to also increase its volume of production and to lower its price in retaliation against the rival concern. This forces the rival to increase his output and to reduce the price in reprisal. The "price war," as we call it, continues—not only up to the point where excess profit is eliminated, and ordinary profit thereafter, but beyond this into the area of financial losses to all concerned. Cournot has shown that competition not only may eliminate profit but, as "cut-throat competition," can continue the point of entailing operating losses.

To illustrate let us assume that two producers constitute an industry, that they have identical cost schedules, and that the market demand schedule for the product appears as in Table 19–1. In columns (a) and (b) the demand schedule is shown, and in column (c) the total revenue schedule (computed by multiplying columns [a] and [b]). Column (d) shows the aggregate cost schedule of the two producers, and in column (e) the vertical bar graphs express the amount of excess profit to the industry at different levels of output. Since the industry's output is by assumption equally divided between two producers, who have identical costs, each naturally receives half of the industry's total profit; this is shown in column (e) by the two vertical bars being of equal size.

First move. Producer 2 becomes restive with any output and profit which merely equals that of his rival, Producer 1. Producer 2 estimates that by lowering the price of the product and offering to sell more of it, he can get ahead of his rival. Suppose that both producers have been producing 2,000 units *each,* gaining a profit income of $2,250 *each* (column [e], Table 19–1). The combined industry output was 4,000 units which, according to the demand schedule for the product, could be sold at $4.00 a unit.

Producer 2 now lowers the price to $3.75 and produces another 1,000 units, half of which is sold to former customers of Producer 1; thus Producer 1, who formerly sold 2,000 units, can now sell only

Table 19–1. Demand for the Product, and Costs and Profits for Its Two Producers

Price of the Product per Unit (a)	Quantity Demanded (for the combined output of the two producers) (b)	Total Revenue (c)	Total Cost (d)	Excess Profit (+ or —) Producer 1	Excess Profit (+ or —) Producer 2
$5.50	2,000	$11,000	$ 8,000	+$1,500	+$1,500
4.65	3,000	14,000	9,600	+ 2,200	+ 2,200
4.00	4,000	16,000	11,500	+ 2,250	+ 2,250
3.75	4,500				
3.50	5,000	17,500	14,200	+ 1,650	+ 1,650
2.85	6,000	17,000	17,000	0	0
2.00	7,000	14,000	24,500	— 5,250	— 5,250

1,500. But Producer 2 now sells 3,000 units. The industry output is 4,500 units which can be sold at $3.75 a unit, according to the demand schedule shown in columns (a) and (b) of Table 19–1. Bear in mind that Producer 1 must accept this price of $3.75. What is now the profit record of each of the two rivals? To ascertain this, it is necessary to break down the cost situation which confronts them under the supposed circumstances. This may be done by dividing column (d) of Table 19–1 by 2, thus revealing the separate costs incurred by Producer 1, who now has an output of only 1,500 units, and by Producer 2, who now sells 3,000 units. The relevant costs are underlined in Table 19–2.

Table 19–2. Total Cost for Each Producer

Output of Each Producer (a)	Total Cost of Production	
	For Producer 1	For Producer 2
	(b)	
1,000	$4,000	$4,000
1,500	4,800	4,800
2,000	5,750	5,750
2,500	7,100	7,100
3,000	8,500	8,500
3,500	12,500	12,500

Now a tally of the profit gains of the aggressive Producer 2 and of the affected Producer 1 can be made.

Producer 2 sells 3,000 units at $3.75 a unit = $11,250
His cost of production   =   8,500

Net profit income   = $ 2,750
as compared with $2,250 previously (an
increase of approximately 20 per cent).

Producer 1 sells 1,500 units at $3.75 a unit = $ 5,625
His cost of production   =   4,800

Net profit income   = $ 825
as compared with $2,250 previously
(approximately a two-thirds profit decrease).

In Figure 19–2, the original situation is pictorialized by the bars at the left-hand side of the graph, the new situation by the bars at the right-hand side.

Figure 19–2. Profit Impact of Price Rivalry, First Move

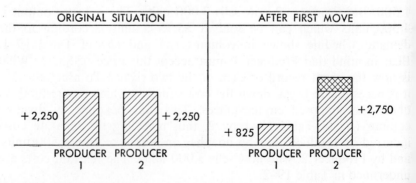

Second move. With his profits reduced by 63 per cent, Producer 1 cannot afford to stand by. He is forced to take retaliatory action against the aggressive Producer 2, and does so by doubling his production and offering to sell his new output of 3,000 units at $2.85 a unit. Producer 2 must accept this price for his products because the industry's output is now 6,000 units; columns (*a*) and (*b*) of Table 19–1 show that 6,000 units of this product can be sold for no more than $2.85.

The result is that neither producer now gains excess profit.

```
Producer 2 sells 3,000 units at $2.85 a unit  =  $8,500
    His cost of production                     =   8,500
                                                  ───────
    Net profit income                         =      0

Producer 1 sells 3,000 units at $2.85 a unit  =  $8,500
    His cost of production                     =   8,500
                                                  ───────
    Net profit income                         =      0
```

Third move. According to Cournot, and practical observation, the rivalry of two or more producers[2] does not stop here, unless an agreement is reached between them. If they cannot agree, either producer may, in desperation, throw another 500 units on the market, offering to sell his entire output of 3,500 units at the low price of $2.00—in the hope that when his rival is forced to sell at that low price, he will be driven into bankruptcy. Because both producers in our example entertain this hope, both are most likely to end by experiencing actual financial losses. This is pictorialized in Table 19–1 by the two bars at the bottom of column (*e*).

Price war won. Let us assume that the aggressive Producer 2 succeeds in forcing his rival into bankruptcy and thereupon acquires the plant and equipment of Producer 1. He will now control the industry as a single-firm monopoly. What amount of output will he choose to produce, and at what price?

Chapter 18 explains that the sole survivor of the price war will ascertain the point at which marginal revenue and marginal cost are equal, or nearly so, and then produce the output indicated at this point, charging what the traffic will bear. In Table 19–3 the demand schedule for the product and the marginal revenue and marginal cost schedules are shown, as well as the total revenue schedule for the product.

The monopoly equilibrium price for the victor in the price war is $4.00 a unit, with an output of 4,000 units. This is twice as much as

---

[2] Griffith C. Evans has shown that Cournot's price-war analysis applies to a large number of rivals as well as to a small number. See *Mathematical Introduction to Economics* (New York: McGraw-Hill Book Co., Inc., 1930), p. 28.

Table 19–3. Demand, Marginal Revenue, and Marginal Cost Schedules
for the Single-Firm Monopoly

Price of the Product (a)	Quantity Demanded (b)	Marginal Revenue* (c)	Marginal Cost† (d)
$5.50	2,000	....	....
4.65	3,000	$3.00	$1.60
4.00	4,000	2.00	1.90
3.50	5,000	1.50	2.70
2.85	6,000	0 (approx.)	2.80
2.00	7,000	— 3.00	7.50

*Marginal revenue is derived by dividing the increments to the total revenue schedule shown in Table 19–1, column (c), by 1,000.
†Marginal cost is derived by dividing the increments to the total cost schedule shown in Table 19–1, column (d), by 1,000.

the aggressive Producer 2 of our example produced originally, when both he and the now-defunct Producer 1 did business side by side, each producing 2,000 units. And the price which is re-established by the sole producer after it had dropped to $2.00 is again $4.00, as it had been originally. Of course the victorious producer now enjoys all the income of the industry, $4,500 per period of time rather than $2,250. The consumer will have received no lasting benefit from the price war.

COURNOT COOPERATION

The imminent threat of ruinous price war suffices to bring about formal or tacit agreements to refrain from competitive price-cutting.

Money price rigidity is characteristic of industries where only a small number of firms operate. Cournot's basic analysis shows why this is necessarily the case. Formal agreements to limit price competition are not necessary. When there is only a small number of business rivals in an industry, it is possible for each to observe when his aggressive competitive behavior is becoming offensive to the rest and stop right there.

Outright agreement. Reverting to the example of two producers in an industry, it is conceivable that they might meet and formally adopt a price agreement. In this case *they would agree to maximize the income for the industry on a monopoly basis.* Cournot shows by the use of mathematical analysis that when this is the case, the output and price of the product will be identical to the output and price selected if the industry were operated by a single monopolist. The cooperators would agree to produce 2,000 units each so that the combined industry output would be 4,000 units, to be sold at the price of $4.00 each. If perchance the two producers had operated at that level of output and price prior to engaging in a price war, they would thereafter return to their original positions. The test of force would have demonstrated, to each, its futility. However, formal and overt price agreements among entrepreneurs are rare.

Another type of Cournot cooperation. Another result is obtained when business rivals do not formally agree to limit competition but refrain from competitively reducing prices for fear of precipitating a price war. On this assumption: *Each producer tries to determine the amount of his production, for any given period of time, so as to maximize his total profit without encroaching on the other producer's production and marketing.*

Success in this effort for any producer depends, of course, upon the amount of information he can obtain about the plans of his competitors. We shall posit that every producer has an equal opportunity to obtain this information about the other producer so that no differential advantage exists in this respect. On this assumption, there is a process of accommodation under which each competitor varies his output and price quotations until it is observed that all producers are satisfied that they are not upsetting the plans of the other producers. Mathematically expressed, there is a continuous function by which the outputs and prices of the different producers are related at different levels. The function has an absolute limit in that the different producers do not experiment to the point of producing an unwieldy aggregate output for the industry. And the function has a maximum value; that is, there is some level of price and a level of output for the industry at which each producer in the industry gains more of a "profit of cooperation" than at any other levels.

Reverting to our example of two producers in an industry who have identical costs of production, it was seen that they would produce 4,000 units, per unit of time, at $4.00 a unit *if they overtly agreed to cooperate.* It is now postulated that they will not do this, but will only "feel each other out."

Tacit agreement of entrepreneurs causes an equilibrium situation, for the industry, in which the output is larger and the price is lower than it would be under either single-firm monopoly, or under outright agreement. In terms of the present example, the most likely outcome of indirect cooperation is that the industry will produce 5,000 units and sell them at the price of $3.50—the price which consumers are prepared to pay for this quantity of output. This means that each of our two producers would produce and sell 2,500 units. At this rate of output and price, each producer would earn, per period of time, $1,650 on the sale of 2,500 units. The situation is pictorialized in Table 19–1, column (e), by the fourth set of bars, reading from the top of the table.

A profit of $1,650 is less than the $2,250 that each producer could gain were the two producers formally to reach a price agreement. However, when each must guess about the plans of the other, a gain of $1,650 is the only maximum which promises to remain a *stable* value. In this case, the aggressive Producer 2 is able to expand his production and sales up to 2,500 units without offending the rival producer, for at a combined output of 5,000 units, both entrepreneurs are still able to earn excess profits. If Producer 2, in our example, were to produce another 500 units, turning out 3,000 units in all, we have posited that he will do so at the expense of Producer 1—who now can sell only 1,500 units. Even though Producer I could sell these 1,500 units at $3.75, the price quoted by Producer 2, the excess profit of Producer 1 would be severely diminished (Figure 19–2). Thereby his retaliation would be invited.

On the other hand, at the 2,000-unit level of production, Producer 2, the aggressive one, would always feel restive; therefore Producer 1 could not be sure that a price war might not break out at any moment. Accommodating Producer 2 by allowing a 500-unit expansion of production and sales for each would benefit Producer 1, although his excess money profit would be reduced. However, it would be an economical price to pay for business peace. Observe that under this mutual accommodation of producers, the consumers would derive an advantage by being furnished 5,000 units of the product at $3.50 a unit, rather than 4,000 units at $4.00.

It must also be observed that this outcome is not the same as would be the case if the two producers were to act as they would if they were engaged in pure competition. This is demonstrated in Table 19–4 where the schedule of average total unit cost of production is shown along with the schedule of marginal cost and marginal revenue. Because the two producers in the industry are assumed to have identical costs, the schedules in Table 19–4 apply to each of them equally. What would be the price and the industry's output if the two producers acted as if they were engaged in pure competition? In Chapter 17 it was explained that under pure competition the formula which determines price and output is: price equals the least average cost of production and at the same time equals marginal cost.

Table 19–4. Competitive Price and Output

Price of the Product (a)	Quantity Demanded (b)	Average Cost— atuc (c)	Marginal Cost— mc* (d)	Marginal Revenue— mr† (e)
$5.50	2,000	$4.00	....	....
4.65	3,000	3.20	$1.60	$3.00
4.00	4,000	2.90	1.90	2.00
3.50	5,000	2.84	2.70	1.50
2.85	6,000	2.83	2.80	0 (approx.)
2.00	7,000	3.50	7.50	— 3.0

*Increments of total cost, column (d) of Table 19–1, divided by 1,000 units.
†Increments of total revenue, column (c) of Table 19–1, divided by 1,000 units.

At the level of output of $6,000 units, the price which consumers are prepared to pay covers the least average cost of production and therefore the marginal cost as well. The price is $2.85 a unit. But under *informal* Cournot cooperation, only 5,000 units are produced, and sold at $3.50.

Summary. Under pure monopoly 4,000 units of the product would be produced, and sold at $4.00. Under collusive oligopoly, that is, formal Cournot cooperation, the same would be the case. Under ordinary oligopoly, that is, informal Cournot cooperation, 5,000 units would be produced, and sold at $3.50. Under pure competition, 6,000 units would be produced, and sold at $2.85 a unit. This illustrates how Cournot's early analysis lays the foundation for tracing the price phenomenon from the one pole of pure monopoly to the opposite pole of pure competition.

EXPANSIVE OLIGOPOLY AND PRICE LEADERSHIP

The industries in which oligopoly is the rule are those in which net *internal* economies can be achieved by managerial competition within the firms, each manager of a production department seeking to maximize his contribution to the firm's over-all rate of return on total investment. Because of their ample staffing and strong command of capital, oligopolistic concerns are able to plan, experiment, and develop innovations on a much broader scale than a farmer can, for example. A large concern, whose supply is a major part of the total supply of an industry, is also aware of, and ready to take advantage of, net *external* economies. For instance, it will locate branch plants in areas where cheap power becomes available because of the completion of a public multipurpose development project.

From these considerations it follows that an alert oligopolist will not rest content with dividing the market for the commodity with his rival. He will "run a race" of output expansion with his competitors rather than concentrate on "fairly shared" output restriction. Policies of output restriction predominate only when the total market for a product is declining, as was the case in certain industries in Great Britain during the interwar, depressed period of 1919–39. Agreements to set restrictive quotas on the production and sales volumes of individual steel producers, for example, were quite common at that time. Even chemical and oil companies in the United States were bound by such agreements so far as their overseas operations were concerned. On the other hand, certain American oligopolists have been known to curtail, or at least to limit, the operations of foreign concerns in the United States, not by signing agreements but by exerting direct pressure or threatened law suits for patent infringements and by other coercive means.

Even in times of depression it is a wise policy for the entrepreneur in an oligopolistic industry to improve his methods of production so that he may be among the first to take advantage of available external economies. In that way he can at least widen the spread between his total money cost and his sales revenue, although operating at a low rate of capacity utilization, say 35 to 50 per cent, instead of 80 or 90 per cent of a given capacity of plant and equipment. During past depressions technological change never ceased; indeed, it was hastened by efforts of entrepreneurs to reduce real costs in order to endure low prices. The oligopolistic entrepreneurs are usually in a favored position to adopt improved methods, because of their ample command over capital, even during depressions. As a matter of fact, depressions tend to accelerate industrial concentration.

During good times there are many steps which an oligopolistic entrepreneur can take in order to get ahead and stay ahead of competition by expansion, rather than by static output restriction. For example, he can exchange ideas on how to reduce costs. In practice this takes the form of quality control engineers' visiting plants of competitors to see how certain types of equipment or processes which they all use are being managed in the different plants, and with what results. Intimate production "secrets" are not likely to be shared, but there are many types of procedures which all know are being used by entrepreneurs generally and which can be evaluated in common.

Another method which an aggressive oligopolist can use without encroaching on the profits of his competitors is "institutional advertising." This means boosting the basic product of the industry as a whole, not simply the particular concern's trade-marked variety of the product. In this case the aggressive oligopolist wins the approval of his competitors, especially the smaller ones who cannot afford to carry on expensive advertising campaigns.

There is much to be gained by acquainting competitors with the use of improved technology, and this is also a way to keep an industry in good standing with consumers. If producers who have a first-rate knowledge of how to produce the industry's basic commodity hoard their insights, they stand in danger of having the rest of the producers in the industry turn out inferior versions of the product, thereby bringing even the first-rate producers into disrepute.

We have proceeded far beyond the simple practice of producers carving static shares of a *given* market. However, Cournot's approach remains fundamental. More output is produced under expansive oligopoly, but at higher prices than would be charged under competition.

THE PRICE CONVENTION

In any situation of industrial expansion it would be infeasible, if not impossible, to cooperate by observing another's output with the aim of readjusting one's own output. The other entrepreneurs' outputs could be observed at any moment, but there is no practical or moral way of knowing what the expansion *plans* of other entrepreneurs might be.

Direct price manipulation is the way out of this "predicament" of oligopolists in an expanding industry when they have the mutual desire to maximize the industry's growth and their joint profits.

The logical policy for the few producers in the industry is to hold prices stable and, when they must be raised or lowered, to take such action as a body, not competitively. Say that one oligopolist finds an improved method of production, the intimate details of which he does not care to share. Thus he will be realizing more output per unit of factor input. We shall assume that this reduction of real cost was accomplished by installing an amount of improved capital equipment, without scrapping all the old equipment, or even a major part of it.

Under pure competition the savings would be passed on to the consumers in the form of reduced prices. If an established entrepreneur maintained his prices, he would earn increased income. But in the long run this would serve to attract outsiders who, buying the new type of equipment, would move into the high-income industry. The competition would cause prices to decline to the point at which entrepreneurs would cover the costs of producing with the improved

capital equipment. The old-fashioned equipment would now be obsolete, its continued use unprofitable at the new, lower prices. The firms
saddled with the old equipment could do no better than to minimize
their losses by producing whatever volume of output can be produced
at a marginal cost which equals the price of the product, even though
marginal cost is lower than average total unit cost. This seemingly
harsh finding only expresses the law of economics: Society must be
served by the best equipment, at the least cost of using that equipment
—not at the cost of using obsolete equipment. Only thus can price
reflect the determining influence of marginal cost on the supply side
of the market and thereby reveal the *true* state of relative scarcity to
the consumers.

Under oligopoly there is no automatic force operating to cause an
entrepreneur to pass on to the consumers, by lower prices, the full
savings made by a firm when it reduces its real costs of production.
This statement must be qualified to allow for the circumstance of an
oligopolist placing a novel product into mass production after the new
article has gone through the pioneering stage of development. An
example is cellophane, which, after having first been used as a wrapping for expensive jewelry, is now being inexpensively utilized for
wrapping meats and vegetables. Here we are only examining the more
common cases of well-established products being made by the use of
improved capital equipment.

Competition, to repeat, would force the producers using old equipment to take their losses. No one producer being sufficiently large to
exert control over the price, the influence of real cost reductions
would make itself felt through the medium of producers using the
improved equipment and lowering their prices to attract new customers at the lower prices. But under oligopoly each of the few sellers
controls enough of the supply of the product to be able to influence
the average price charged for the product. By lowering the price one
seller would force the others to follow suit; if he raises the price, they
will be glad to do the same. And if all act in unison, the consumers
are faced with a situation reminiscent of monopoly: either they must
buy units of the product at the price commonly charged by the producers, or they will buy none of the product at all. When oligopolists
cooperate the consumer has no real opportunity to shop around.

Presumably no ordinary businessman relishes taking a loss on old
equipment by reason of its obsolescence, but only the oligopolist is
in a position of not having to do so. For upon making real-cost reductions he can, instead of reducing price, simply allocate the savings to
an obsolescence account on his books, which he now augments. He

s thereby treating his extra income as a cost coverage instead of entering it on the books as increased operating profit.

Of course our hypothetical oligopolist will seek to realize his relative low-cost production advantage over an increased volume of sales. This he will attempt not by reducing his prices but by various means of nonprice competition such as intensified selling effort to include more personal services to consumers; adding more design, accessories, and other special "qualities" to the basic product; engaging in public relations through radio and TV advertising as well as printed "institutional" advertising to benefit the entire industry; augmenting his welfare benefits and personal health services and so on to the employees—in short, by practically any means other than making actual price reductions. Thus his original degree of monopoly will be preserved, as well as the opportunities of the competitors to earn excess profits. At the same time the progressive oligopolist will be inviting the competitors to share all but the most intimate advantages of his improved manner of production.

By all these methods and others which comprise the arts of persuasion—including instalment credit financing!—the oligopolist broadens the market for the particular product. Thus he is able to spread his cost advantage over an augmented sales turnover without breaching the unwritten agreement not to cut prices competitively. Consequently he may be crowned as the price leader to whom the rest of the producers will look for guidance—instead of to their marginal-cost supply schedules, as they would do under competition.

Whatever may be said pro or con in this matter of oligopoly, this fact remains: Prices will be arbitrarily set at higher levels than under competition. And prices will not emerge freely in response either to the independent spending pattern of people uninfluenced by sales pressure and "instalment debtistry" or to the spontaneous distribution of the benefits of achieved technological cost reductions, but only at the producers' private discretion. Under oligopoly, price stands higher than marginal cost no matter how efficiently the output may be produced. The oligopolist may hide this fact from himself by treating obsolescence and selling expense as costs. These may be considered as private costs, but the economist must ask if they are socially necessary. Is it necessary that the existing entrepreneurs and such newcomers as they may choose to admit to the industry protect themselves from taking losses on obsolete equipment? Or is it necessary that they spend lavish sums on "keeping the product before the public" by artificial means of psychological appeal rather than the natural means of offering an improved product at a lower price? Do not the high and inflexible prices of oligopoly convey a false message of scarcity—to a lesser degree than but in a manner kindred to monopoly pricing?

In Conclusion

With monopolistic competition existing in the merchandising sector of the American economy, and oligopoly in important key lines of manufacturing, Americans are becoming accustomed to uniform prices, and price movements. But although price competition is on the decline, living standards for many people continue to advance.

The foregoing analysis would warrant an inference of progressive stagnation in living standards only if its basic theoretical assumptions were facts of actual economic life. One of these is the assumption of given incomes. But with increasing productivity have come increased incomes (especially in years since World War II) to the industrial classes of American society. And technological advances have taken the form not only of improving the means of producing existing commodities, but also of new-product development. Thus the negative price impact of a "degree of monopoly" has been offset to varying extents by positive developments in the fields of income distribution and production pioneering.

To summarize the findings of this chapter:

1. Monopolistic competition is a form of competition rather than of monopoly. Yet to the extent that monopolistic competition successfully strives toward monopoly, it detracts from social efficiency without enriching the private producers.

2. Oligopoly *in its price impacts* is akin to monopoly, and in this regard detracts from social efficiency. But oligopoly is also that form of United States business organization under which much managerial product-development takes place. The reader is therefore asked to delay his judgment until this aspect of the question has been presented

For Discussion

1. What is the difference in demand as seen by purely competitive firms and by firms engaged in monopolistic competition? How do the altered circumstances of monopolistic competition work to the advantage of the monopolistic firms' Is it a lasting advantage?

2. "The causes of the preference shown by any group of buyers for the product of a particular firm are of the most diverse nature, and may range from long custom, personal acquaintance, confidence in the quality of the product, the possibility of obtaining credit, or the reputation of a trade-mark, to special features of modelling or design in the product which, without constituting it a distinct commodity, have for their principal purpose the distinguishing of a

commodity from the products of other firms." For the purpose of defining monopolistic competition, what is the most significant phrase in this sentence? What do all the stated reasons for consumer preference have in common?

3. Does monopolistic competition reduce the freedom of consumer choice?

4. Three leading experts in testing consumer response to advertising find that most advertising campaigns are only faintly successful, and many fail utterly. One of these experts finds that as many as one-third of the people who, when interviewed, remembered many of the details of a television performance, had no idea what product or brand was being advertised. Why, then, is there so much monopolistic competition?

5. The automobile industry is commonly considered oligopolistic; yet price wars do not occur. Does this mean that the industry is not really oligopolistic? What is the situation in the petroleum industry? Do the gasoline price wars constitute events of the nature described theoretically in this chapter? If so, why? If not, what are the differences?

6. Businessmen who operate in industries with only a small number of firms characteristically frown on the term *oligopoly* when applied to them. Can you think of some reasons for this response? How would you argue the case that they are oligopolists?

7. If oligopoly does not block technological progress, why is concern felt about this phenomenon?

8. Price leadership is one means of preventing destructive competition. Is price leadership, therefore, a socially beneficial practice?

20

Product

Competition

Thus far in Part IV we have studied the price mechanism to see how it functions to help conserve human as well as natural resources, and how it relates and balances people's selected wants and activities. There is another aspect of the topic of price, namely, how specific prices are involved in the creation and spread of new wants and activities, their genesis and proliferation. This subject has not been carried nearly so far as price analysis of the conservation and selection type. Perhaps the main reason is that observations of the actual genetic and proliferative processes in industry have been hard to come by. Consequently economics, with its bit-by-bit marginal analysis approach, was for many years forced to discuss the subject of economic *change* in a peripheral fashion, explaining the residues of history but not having much to say about its making. This is not to imply that the "first things first" conservation and selection approach of economics should be discarded or even treated lightly. But when opportunities present themselves to watch genetic and proliferative economic processes in operation, the acquired information should be classified and assimilated into the body of accepted economic doctrines.

Concept of Product Life Cycles

Modern economies have as one prime characteristic the evolution of new products. At first new products take their place in serving wants along with old products, then replacing them, and finally becoming old—to be replaced by other products which by then have grown to maturity. Joseph A. Schumpeter named this a "process of creative destruction." To illustrate, about half of the products manufactured by chemical companies in 1950 were unknown, or had barely been in their infancy in 1925, only a generation before. For a contrasting example, one of decline, we cite the production of steel rails. It reached its peak at the end of World War I; since then there has been no net expansion in the demand for rails, but rather for the replacement and betterment of existing trackage. On the other hand, highway travel and truck transport are in a mature phase of growth, whereas air travel and transport are at a vigorous early stage of growth.

The emergence and subsequent decline of particular commodities suggests the concept of "product life cycles." In Figure 20–1, a historical graph, we illustrate this in the framework of a parent category of production—namely, steel fabrication.

Explanation of Figure 20–1. In the broad parent category of finished rolled iron and steel production continual growth is observed. When scrutinizing the constituent parts of total production, we note that rail production has completed most of a life cycle.

Rolled sheet and plate production is still in an early phase of mature development. Since the 1880's there has been an all-embracing mechanization of production—first in automobile production, and most recently, a new high level of military production in the United States.

The fabrication of structural shape is, relatively speaking, new; on a large volume basis it dates only to 1901, when girder construction became common, first for skyscrapers and then for ordinary structures. The continuing upward trend of structural shapes is amply explained by urbanization. Structural shape production will not—at least need not—reach a stage of aging for years to come. At mid-twentieth century there remains an urgent need not only to build more housing for our rising population, but also for great quantities of structural shapes to be used in the replacement and betterment of existing slum structures in presently blighted areas.

PRODUCT COMPETITION

Science, practically applied to industry, is the mainspring of product life cycles. Modern man has so combined his motivations to work and to investigate the laws of nature that new goods are unrelentingly challenging old goods, then superseding them. Thus, to the concept of competition a new dimension of economic growth has been added.

This is to say that, as individuals, we habitually think of competition as taking place among entrepreneurs in a given industry and

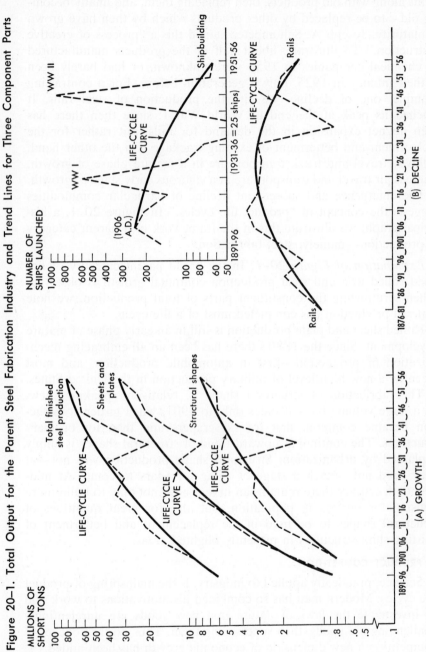

Figure 20-1. Total Output for the Parent Steel Fabrication Industry and Trend Lines for Three Component Parts

NOTE: Each year listed above is the last in a five-year span. Solid curves are the product life cycles; dotted lines connect points

between entrepreneurs in different industries. It is also useful to think of new products competing with older products. Before we exploit the full economic implications of product life cycles, a thumbnail sketch is given of major types of product competition in modern times. Product life cycles have been exhaustively studied for an entire economy, the British economy, from 1700 to 1950.[1] Three product development stages have been identified:

1. The stage of industrial expansion, characterized by a rising *rate* of growth in output
2. The stage of industrial development, when the *rate* of growth in output declines although total output continues to increase
3. The state of industrial regression, when a decline of output occurs

Stage 1. The first stage of a product's industrial expansion is characterized by a rising *rate* of the growth of output. A good example of this was the British cotton goods industry during the years 1699 to 1800. Raw cotton had been brought into England from Syria since 1580; it was used to make a sturdy corduroy-like product called fustian, with a linen warp and a cotton weft. Thereafter the East India Company imported finished cotton goods into England, and a demand for all-cotton goods arose. Thus the stage was set for the development of a *native* British all-cotton cloth industry. Up to 1760 the industry, located in Lancashire, was small. Large production units did not really come into being until after 1760, when spinning machines were invented. Because of that innovation, the early rate of growth of the industry was high. An increase of output of from 1,000 pounds of yarn to 2,000 pounds is not difficult to achieve; yet it is a 100 per cent increase. All this time long-staple sea island cotton was used as raw material, being imported from Syria, the West Indies, and Asia. The cotton warp began to replace the linen in 1780, and the production of all-cotton cloth was under way in earnest. The rate of growth at this time was 8 per cent—approximately three times the normal rate which long-established industries feature.

Stage 2. In the second stage of a product's life history the total output continues to increase, but it does so at a *decreasing rate*. The new industry is now making its way ahead. Originally it may only have filled an inadequately met demand for the products of an older industry. Later, as the new industry grows, it may actually be creating its own new demand, both because the new product may have distinguishing characteristics which make it desired in its own rights,

---

[1] Walther G. Hoffman, *British Industry, 1700–1950* (Oxford: Basil Blackwell & Mott, Ltd., 1955); see especially pp. 176–226.

instead of being accepted only as a substitute or a complement to older products; and because through its low-cost technical efficiency the new product may reach markets that the older rivals could not penetrate. All-cotton cloth production of the early 1800's placed washable garments within the reach of masses of consumers at relatively low prices, just as nylon later made "silk stockings" generally available. In its second stage of industrial development, many a new product is no longer merely a way of adding to the production of an old thing. Instead, a new product at its second developmental stage usually is rapidly coming into its own. Today few women would speak of nylon as being a substitute for silk, let alone referring to rayon as "artificial silk."

The necessary condition for a product to enter the second stage of production is that there shall be an ample supply of the basic raw material. Thus it was the cultivation of short-staple cotton in the southern United States that ushered in the second stage of industrial development for the cotton goods industry, not only in Britain but in New England as well.[2]

The second stage is also originally characterized by a noticeable fall in the real cost of the product; in the case of cotton products this was made possible by the external economy of being able to devote broad acres of land to cotton and by the internal economy of the cotton gin, the handy mechanical device for cleaning cotton which was invented in 1793 by Eli Whitney, that great forefather of modern mass production. Because of the drop of real cost as external and internal economies develop with increasing experience, the expansion in volume of a new product in the second phase of its life cycle is normally accompanied by a reduction of the price. In the nineteenth century this actually meant lowered *money* prices; thus, prices per pound of cotton fell from 25 cents at the beginning of the century to 7 cents at the end of the century. This second stage of competitive product development, when total output is increasing—even if at a decreasing rate—may last a long time. In 1956 cotton was still in its second stage of development. In the later phases, however, real costs no longer decline; the law of diminishing yields in fairly stringent form takes over; the

[2] Small quantities of short-staple cotton were raised before 1775, but even in 1784 the supply was so small that an amusing incident took place: the Liverpool customs officers seized eight bags of U.S. short-staple cotton on the grounds that this much could not have been raised in the United States. See Chester W. Wright, *Economic History of the United States* (New York: McGraw-Hill Book Co., Inc., 1949), p. 220. The limiting factor on upland cotton was the difficulty of extracting the seeds of the boll. Before Eli Whitney's cotton gin only one pound could be cleaned with one day's labor; the invention immediately made it possible to clean fifty pounds in the same time.

product now becomes a fully mature one.[3] Technological improvements may still reduce real costs, and probably will, but it now becomes a question of whether it is worthwhile to spend much money and resources in improving the product rather than using at least some of that time and money to develop other new products which ought by now to be making their appearance as close rivals to the presently matured one. In other words, even with progressively lowered real costs for the product there arrive what may be called "rising alternative (or opportunity) costs" for the further development of that product— vis-à-vis the possible development of some improved rival for that product.

Stage 3. The third stage in the life cycle of a product, when output declines *absolutely* (not just its rate of growth), will obviously be reached when the rate of growth has declined to zero. This automatically marks off the end of the second phase and the beginning of a third stage, that of decline. Shipbuilding, both in the United States and Great Britain, furnishes a good example of an industry which reached its peak in both countries about 1900 and has shown declining outputs ever since. (For American shipbuilding, see Figure 20–1B.)

ORGANIZATIONAL IMPACT OF PRODUCT DEVELOPMENT

Growth competition between new and old products favors the large firm. Of 111 steel works and rolling mills which in 1947 fabricated the products whose life cycles were sketched in Figure 20–1, the four largest companies handled 45 per cent of the total industry output; the first eight firms produced 65 per cent of the output; and the twenty largest firms 80 per cent of the output. Large concerns in modern key industries not only have ample financial means to sponsor basic and applied research, but they usually conduct a variety of integrated productions. This makes it possible to explore a wide range of possible commercial applications in research findings. The United States Steel Corporation, for example, has in its employ 1,000 research workers.

[3] Statistics on United States cotton acreage and output after 1936 would seem to indicate a fall of real costs, since output per acre has increased. This has not been reflected in lower prices owing to two facts: (1) the increased productivity of cotton cultivation is largely due to mechanization, so that instead of measuring output per acre we ought to measure it as output per combined acre-machine input; (2) since 1936 the cotton farmer has enjoyed a better position on the personal income ladder— but only because of the fact that prices have been tampered with to bring about that result. Parts of the supplies were withheld in given years. This was not the original intent of the framers of farm programs that have been in effect since 1936. But for the miscarriage of an original plan to *diversify* and improve farm production technologically, not to curtail supplies, cotton supply curves, shifting downward to the right, would have brought lower prices, without diminishing the cultivator's income below what it is now.

At the end of 1957 there were 1,000 specific projects under way, including further refinement of a method of rolling wide and thin-gauge stainless and alloy steel sheets; such sheets for aircraft and missiles mean fewer joints, less weight, and greater operating efficiency for airflight devices. Another new product, in 1958, was the aluminum-coated barbed wire and farm fence which is virtually free from progressive corrosion. Another example of a concern exploring a wide range of commercial applications of its basic technology is that of a major American firm which handled fuels and energy and acquired a research and development firm which produces propellants and solid fuels for use in missiles and rockets.

The large firm is also in a favored position to take advantage of external economies. These are general developments which benefit the economy of an entire region. For example, upstate New York is receiving a threefold benefit from (1) the development of the St. Lawrence Seaway; (2) a 430-mile north-south superhighway known as the New York State Thruway; (3) the Niagara River power project of the Power Authority of the State of New York. By 1957 the development of the New York State Thruway had already added a half billion dollars' worth of new industrial plants and business facilities to the region's economy. The power company operating in the region was adding 20,000 new customers each year, the equivalent of a sizable city. By 1967, this company has estimated, its peak load production of kilowatt-hours of electricity will be 5 million, as compared with 3 million in 1957 and 2 million in 1947. While all types and varieties of industry and business benefit from regional development, it is not surprising that the establishment of two new aluminum reduction plants, an automobile plant, and new chemical plants in this particular region will be undertaken by existing large firms.

Integrated firms. When entrepreneurs operate in terms of product life cycles, the tendency is to integrate many productive processes, that is, to place them under general *policy* direction of a single board of directors (not necessarily under central technical direction of the firm's chief production manager). There are several types of integration. One, called *horizontal integration,* features combining a number of similar operations. This is the case when several producers of automobiles or refrigerators merge. *Vertical integration* exists when a large firm combines different steps in the production of a product, for example, when steel companies acquire ore mines and fleets of Great Lakes ore boats. There is also *lateral integration,* which is the handling of different kinds of products under one head. Lateral integration may be the result when a large corporation has surplus funds which it chooses to invest in acquiring other plant and equipment rather than investing the funds in securities of other corporations. However, lateral integration may also occur because a large company is conducting research and desires to apply the findings in another line of production than it has conventionally pursued.

Of these forms of integration, lateral integration is the most controversial, because it seems to shrink the sphere of opportunity for small business—which happened, for example, when the erstwhile highly competitive steel barrel drum industry was absorbed by the major basic steel-producing companies.

Managerial competition. An integrated concern is not a simple aggregation of formerly separately owned and separately managed plants. The integrated firm is, rather, an economic complex of which each part must be brought into balance with the other operations so that the parent concern can gain a satisfactory rate of return on its over-all investment.

In the integrated firm many former market transactions are supplanted by internal exchange transactions among the constituent units of the total enterprise. In one integrated concern, for example, 15 per cent of all business done is carried on inside the firm, at prices which are negotiated between different department managers. Internal exchange transactions of the integrated firm are not conducted for profit, but department managers are usually permitted to acquire needed supplies from the outside, in the market, if they can do so more advantageously than by trading supplies internally.

An important problem of the integrated firm is that which arises because certain costs of production which were formerly reflected in prices quoted in the market now become internalized cost factors. These internalized costs the integrated firm must carefully control at the hazard of losing rather than gaining by integration. The more integrated a firm becomes, the greater is the risk of disruptive internal imbalances in the flow of materials, the deployment of personnel, the routing of capital funds, and so forth. An integrated firm bears some analogy to a jet-plane motor with its delicately balanced turbine blades, each shaped individually. When a foreign object strikes one of these blades, it not only damages that blade but sets up a cumulative process of destruction, in which each damaged blade destroys another until the whole interlaced mechanism is ripped asunder. The integrated firm is not in quite so delicate a position, but it cannot afford to relax its efforts to detect bottlenecks of production and to eliminate products which do not pay their way. For this reason the integrated firm requires for its management a special type of skill, one which emphasizes workmanlike competition in fostering constructive product development and innovation.

Concept of technology administration. Integrated concerns do not, properly speaking, produce congeries of separate product lines. It is more accurate to conceive of integrated firms as managing substantial flows of basic technologies—metallurgy, electronics, types of chemistry, and so forth. The specific products of these technologies are only embodiments of these technologies, and the effort is continuously made to give the basic technologies increasingly refined expression. In other words, the managers of integrated concerns have as their primary task that of routing technical processes along related existing and emerging product lines. In a sense there is no final end product. The end product is a verb rather than a noun. *Cellophane* connotes the activity of using organic chemistry in a certain way. *Stainless steel* means using metallurgy a certain way, rather than denoting a thing that is given and self-contained in distinction to other things.

With an increasing integration of industrial production in and around the main lines of modern technology, managerially administered product development in core concerns must provide much of the price leverage once furnished by the competition of many sellers. Thoughtful persons are bringing their thinking about competition up to date. They are not necessarily disturbed by the fact that many enterprises are large and command substantial shares of the markets for their respective products. The more relevant question is whether a particular concern, or group of concerns, which has a broad hold on a given basic technology—in aerodynamics, electrical equipment, chemistry, metallurgy, and so forth—is progressively and economically finding improved (not merely trivial) industrial and/or household applications. Another relevant question is whether managerially administered product competition is conducive to price flexibility, the traditionally cherished attribute of pure competition. In a deeper sense, does product competition tend to carry prices into equality with the least cost of production, so that we might have efficient resources utilization?

Pricing Under Product Competition

SHORT-RUN PRICE

The short-run function of price is to ration consumers to the use of temporarily fixed plant and equipment. This principle is not changed by planned product development, but the *mode* in which the principle of short-run price operates does differ. To understand why this is so, and how, it is necessary to recall how product development would occur, spontaneously, under pure competition.

Earlier it was seen that when demand increases under pure competition, there is a rise of price to equal the marginal cost of an enlarged output which is produced at less than optimum efficiency. An excess profit arises, and serves to attract new firms to the industry. Over the long pull, the price of the product returns to the level of minimum average cost (*atuc*), but more output is produced.

Now the first phase of a product's life cycle can be conceived as a series of short runs, for it is characteristic that demand successively increases while a product is gaining acceptance. Assuming a given method of production of the commodity, there would be a zig-zag movement of its price from the level of its minimum average cost (*atuc*) level, up to a high level of marginal cost, and down again to the minimum *atuc*. This would continue until the product matures and the demand for the product no longer increases but remains stable. In the course of the successive short-run price adjustments, the industry's output capacity would be expanded to meet the demand at its final stable level. Parts A and B of Figure 20–2 illustrate this sequence of events. It is assumed that the product has been developed to the point where it can always be produced over the long run at a $3.00 minimum average total unit cost, for increasing amounts of output. Part A of Figure 20–2 shows that as the demand increases from D_1-D_1 to D_2-D_2 (shown in Part B), the representative firm first increases its output on a short-run basis, from 40 to 45 units of the product. The charge per unit is now $3.60, the amount which meets the marginal cost of producing 45 units in the representative firm. Since $3.60 exceeds the average cost (*atuc*) of 45 units, new firms are attracted to the industry. Production for the industry, having increased from 4,000 units (for 100 firms) to 4,500 units, in the short run, now increases to 5,000 units in the long run for 122 firms. This is sold at $3.00 a unit, as is indicated by the new demand schedule D_2-D_2. Thus no lasting excess profit is earned. The same is true when the demand increases once more, from D_2-D_2 to D_3-D_3.

LONG-RUN PRICE

There is no theoretical reason why after the first phase of a product's life cycle its price should not equal the least average total unit cost permanently, including a 6 or 7 per cent profit. In the first phase, which has just been illustrated, the movement of price from minimum *atuc* of $3.00 to the marginal cost of $3.60, then back to $3.00, creates earnings higher than 6 or 7 per cent. But in the declining years of a product, earnings will be less than 6 per cent, and may turn negative; that is, losses may be incurred. This indicates that the efficiency rule of $P = ATUC (= MC)$—or price equals average cost

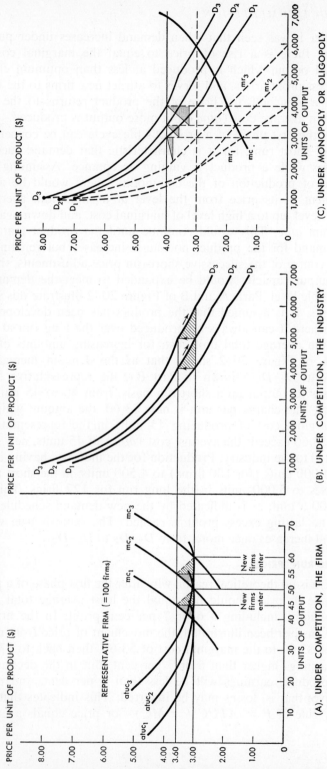

Figure 20–2. Price Movement and Output Increase in First and Second Phase of a Product Life Cycle

(A). UNDER COMPETITION, THE FIRM

(B). UNDER COMPETITION, THE INDUSTRY

(C). UNDER MONOPOLY OR OLIGOPOLY

which in turn equals marginal cost—is not expected to be applicable at every moment. Instead it is an *average* figure running from the time a product is ushered in until the time when it wanders into the limbo of forgotten products. As reflected in profit gained, this means that a normal profit of from 6 to 7 per cent on the capital invested (not on sales volume) will be earned in producing the commodity for, say, 30 years, as shown in Table 20–1.

Table 20–1. Rate of Return on Investment During Several Growth Phases of a Product

Growth Phase of the Product (a)	Average Rate of Return for the Phase (b)	Weighted Average Profit Rate (c)
First 4 years	15%	+ 60%
Second 4 years	10	+ 40
Mature 12 years	6	+ 72
Final declining 10 years	3	+ 30
Total, 30 years divided into		202%=6.7%

DEGREE OF MONOPOLY

In practice it is likely that a higher gain than 6 or 7 per cent will be realized on a component of an integrated firm's product mix over that component product's life cycle.

Stage 1. Part C of Figure 20–2 demonstrates that in the first phase of the product's life cycle, a firm which has a degree of monopoly— as most integrated firms do—can charge from the outset a price higher than would be realized if the product were developed under competition. Part C of Figure 20–2 is directly comparable with Parts A and B. The difference is that whereas under competition the price is always cost-determined, that is never the case under monopoly or oligopoly. Here cost is only a reference point, along with marginal revenue, to determine what the traffic will bear. Thus in Part C of Figure 20–2, the intersections of mc and mr_1, mc and mr_2, and mc and mr_3 show that upon each increase of demand—from D_1–D_1 to D_2–D_2, then from D_2–D_2 to D_3–D_3—the price remains undisturbed at \$4.00 a unit.

The adjustment of the monopolist product developer, or of formally cooperating oligopolists, is to make more units of the product available as demand increases, but always at the same price. And this is the relatively high price of \$4.00 a unit, which at a 3,000-unit level of output includes an excess profit for each unit of 20 cents above a \$3.80 average cost (*atuc*) of 3,000 units; when production is at a rate of 3,400 units, an excess profit is realized of 40 cents per unit and when 4,000 units are produced the excess profit is 75 cents or each unit. See Table 22–2. (This assumes that the monopolist or the oligopolists have from the outset had the same long-run capacity and cost structures as does the representative firm under competition after its expansion in response to the increase of demand up to D_3-D_3.)

Stage 2. Having begun a product's development with a gain of monopoly profit, the product's developer would continue realizing excess profit during the mature stage of the product's life cycle. During this second phase, when the demand no longer greatly increases, a large integrated firm could improve the method of producing the commodity, thus lowering its real costs of production. The integrated firm could thereupon lower the price of the product and still maintain its degree of monopoly, even enhance it.

Let us suppose that the average cost of production (*atuc*) has been reduced so that old and new costs compare as shown in Table 20–2.

Table 20–2. Cost Reduction for the Firm

Number of Units Produced (a)	Old Average Cost—atuc (b)	Old Marginal Cost—mc (c)	New Average Cost—atuc-1 (d)	New Marginal Cost—mc-1 (e)
2,000	$4.70	......	$4.15	......
3,000	3.80	$1.5	3.10	$1.0
4,000	3.25	2.0	2.70	1.5
5,000	3.05	2.5	2.55	2.0
6,000	3.00	3.0	2.40	2.5
7,000	3.20	4.5	2.57	3.5

If the new marginal cost schedule shown in column (*e*) of this table were to be plotted on Part C of Figure 20–2, it would be seen to intersect the mr_1 and the mr_2 and the mr_3 curves there shown in a manner to indicate that the maximum monopoly or cooperative oligopoly income can now be achieved by lowering the price of the product and expanding sales, at any level of demand, whether D_1-D_1 or D_2-D_2 or D_3-D_3. Table 20–3 shows precisely by how much price would be lowered and sales expanded, in comparison with the profit maximizing policy applied under the conditions of the old cost structure.

Referring to Table 20–2, it will be seen that under the old cost structure the *atuc* for 4,000 units was $3.25, which, with a $4.00 sales price, resulted in an excess monopoly or cooperative oligopoly profit of 75 cents a unit. Under the new cost structure the *atuc* for 4,350

Table 20–3. Change of Price and Output Because of Cost Reduction, Under Monopolistic Profit Maximization

Demand (a)	Price Indicated for Profit Maximization		Output Indicated for Profit Maximization	
	Under Old Costs (b)	Under New Costs (c)	Under Old Costs (d)	Under New Costs (e)
Lowest Demand (D_1–D_1)	$4.00	$3.80	3,000	3,300
Medium Demand (D_2–D_2)	4.00	3.80	3,400	3,700
Highest Demand (D_3–D_3)	4.00	3.80	4,000	4,300

units is $2.62; with a sales price of $3.80, the excess profit is $1.18 for each unit. (At 4,350 units: $mc_{-1} = \$1.7 = mr_3$.)

Stage 3. Product development, when carried on by a large firm having a degree of monopoly, permits relatively high returns to be realized on investment even in the state of a product's decline. This is because a firm operating on monopoly principles, or cooperative oligopoly principles, can abandon a product before financial losses are incurred in its production.

Such is not possible under competition, where the product is sold at the minimum average cost (*atuc*) during the mature phase of the product's life cycle. When demand falls off, as the product enters its declining phase, its price under competition falls below average total unit cost. How far below? The price declines to the level of marginal cost. Now at any amount of output less than that which can be produced at minimum average total unit cost, marginal cost is less than the full average cost of production. Consequently, although price equals marginal cost, it is not sufficiently high to permit entrepreneurs to remain in business after the long run. Nevertheless, decreasing quantities of output of the product will be produced so long as marginal cost is higher than *average direct cost* (*adc*), that is, so long as the price covers the out-of-pocket costs of wages and materials.

Only when not enough income is earned to pay daily wages and cost of materials is the production of a commodity fully abandoned under competition. Figure 20–3 is a simplified illustration of this. Where marginal cost equals average direct cost, both being less than average total unit cost, the cessation point has been reached for a product under competition.

Figure 20-3. Product Decline Under Competition

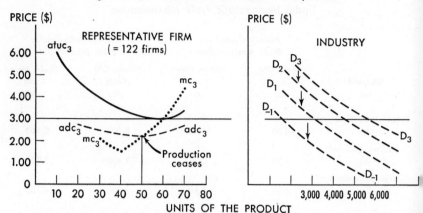

UNITS OF THE PRODUCT

Let us revert to Figure 20–2 to examine the behavior of a monopolist or of cooperating oligopolists who realize that a component commodity in the product-mix is entering its stage of decline. The demand curves in Figure 20–2 would then be viewed as shifting downward to the left, beginning with the top demand curve D_3–D_3, and ending not necessarily with D_1–D_1 but perhaps with a demand curve even below that. Now the monopolist or the formally cooperating oligopolists supposedly are selling 4,000 units of the product at $4.00 a unit; this is the output indicated in Part C of Figure 20–2 by the intersection of mc and mr_3 when the demand is D_3–D_3. How will the monopolist or the cooperating oligopolists respond when the demand now decreases as the product starts to decline?

A hasty and incorrect answer to this question is that the entrepreneurs will curtail output and try to continue to charge $4.00 a unit for the product. This would merely be reading the intersection points of mc and the three mr's backward, as compared to the manner they were examined when Part C of Figure 20–2 was used to describe the first stage of product development under monopoly or oligopoly. In real life, however, there is more to the pricing process than geometry. A monopolist, or the oligopolists, must face the fact that the product is declining and cannot possibly command a high price in the future. The informed monopolistic producer of the commodity, or the oligopolistic producers, will eventually lower the price to $3.10 and thereby still sell 3,000 units (after having sold only 4,000 units at $4.00). The reason is that so long as the producers receive a penny more than $3.10 a unit for an output of no less than 3,000 units, there is a positive monopoly profit greater than zero. In other words, there remain some excess profit, although it gradually dwindles from its original high amount of 75 cents a unit. Whatever excess profit can be salvaged, however, can be applied to assist the development of new products.

Observe that 6,000 units sold at the minimum average cost (*atuc*) of $3.00 a unit is the normal condition under competition, after the initial adjustments during stage 1 of the product's life cycle, as shown in Parts A and B of Figure 20–2. Yet for the monopolist or the oligopolists $3.10 is the cessation point for the production of the commodity. What in theory is the terminal point of a liquidation for the monopolist or oligopolists would be for the competitive entrepreneur only the point of departure for the liquidation of the product.[4]

Mark well that the declining profits on the product in its later years are explained by the emergence of other products in the economy, perhaps within the integrated firm itself. If a firm engages in product development, it will not halt the practice in favor of its own products; indeed, it cannot do so without abandoning the practice of product development. The effect is to provide product development with some of the automatic force of competition, similar to that of the entry of new firms into new industries under conditions of pure competition. This similarity appears paradoxical, since the integrated firm is typically an oligopoly. One would therefore, theoretically, expect the firm to behave restrictively in the matter of price and output, rather than to approximate, expansively, pure competition. Of course there is no paradox involved. An expansive oligopoly engaging in product development can retain a degree of monopoly and yet deliver more goods at lower prices than can competitive entrepreneurs who cannot afford costly product developments.

Summary

When a product is in an early stage of growth, an innovating firm can gain considerable pioneering profit, even under competition. When the product matures, the rate of return will normally be 6 or 7 per cent on the proprietors' investment. But if a firm has a degree of monopoly, a higher profit can be earned during the mature phase of a product. The firm will enter into this mature stage of one of its products while, from the outset, receiving for the product a high price compared with what it would be under conditions of competition. Then, during the mature stage of a product's life cycle, an oligopolistic

---

[4] In real life a monopolist, or a group of oligopolists, might well continue the production of a declining commodity although the return on investment might be less than 6 or 7 per cent, perhaps being willing to accept 4 or 3 per cent. This would be done for the sake of good customer relations while the customers were becoming accustomed to purchasing a new product which can be produced with greater gain. Monopolists or oligopolists hardly ever continue to produce at zero profit or at a loss.

or monopolistic firm can lower the price of the product to reflect savings made in the cost of producing it. This can be done while the firm can yet hold its degree of monopoly constant.

Thus it may be seen that under product development, monopoly or oligopoly does not entirely abolish that flexibility of price and of output which is characteristic of pure competition. In the first stage of the life cycle of a product, output increases. Although the product tends to be sold at a rigid price, increased demand is nevertheless accommodated. Price is flexible in the mature stage of a product's life cycle, to reflect reduced real costs of operation. As more output is realized for each unit of labor and materials input, the consumers gain although the firm retains its degree of monopoly. In other words, during the mature phase of a product, price tends to move in conformity with costs as it would under pure competition. Of course the *level* of price is higher than cost, but the *movement* of price is, significantly, of the nature of price movements under competition. A marked difference appears when a product enters its final stage of decline. When an integrated firm has a degree of monopoly, as it usually does, the production of any particular component of the total product-mix will be abandoned as the excess profit dwindles to zero, whereas under pure competition the process of liquidation would set in only when financial profit had been replaced by loss.

Industrial integration tends to go hand in hand with oligopolistic pricing practices. However, in the mature phase of a product's life cycle, the fundamental efficiency rule of price still applies, namely, that price and cost should be related in their movements. The *equality* of price and cost is, however, eliminated. To the extent that integrated firms which have a degree of monopoly aggressively engage in product development, the problem which faces the consumer is whether he is better served by integrated firms which gain excess profits but offer improved and cheaper products, or by many competitive firms too small to afford product development. Price bargains offered by small firms selling at a loss might still represent higher prices than must be paid under the oligopoly of integrated firms. There is no easy answer to this question. Much must depend upon whether the product innovations of integrated firms possessing a degree of monopoly are truly serviceable products or merely articles which cater to trivial wants.

Growth and Price

In complex matters it is a good idea to refer to reality. In the following pages the attempt is made to present certain practical insights into managerial growth and pricing policies. The method of presentation is (1) to describe certain aims and tactics of managing the Du Pont Corporation;[5] (2) to view these procedures in the light of established economic efficiency criteria.

Articulate aims for growth. The corporation's growth objectives can be described by a three-dimensional analogue:

First, there is the dimension of breadth, which means that the company will seek to accomplish *product diversification* by (1) developing new products, as well as by (2) establishing more diversified uses of existing products. An illustration of the former approach is the discovery of nylon; an illustration of the latter is furnished by the expanded use of cellophane.

The second dimension of growth is depth. By that is meant the attempt to penetrate any given field of production to any extent to which that field appears as an attractive investment outlet.

With respect to these two growth dimensions it should be noted that what we are talking about here is carefully regulated growth, growth by proportion, not haphazard growth. Product diversification is not considered to be an end in itself; for taken as such, it would dilute energy and ability. Depth, if taken by itself, would engender a "war of all managers against all managers," each seeking to route a major flow of internal finance in his particular direction.

The third growth requirement is the level of profit. This is the height dimension. It is an apposite expression. For though profit is indeed the vanguard of growth, it is by no means the entire substance of growth. So we shall see—perhaps to the astonishment of some readers who in their thinking make growth depend entirely upon profit.

Actual growth. The present average long-term growth of the Du Pont Company is at a rate of 9 per cent annually in terms of physical production, and at a rate of about 10 per cent in terms of the financial return on investment. The 9 per cent increase factor, where growth is considered in terms of physical output, is comprised of a 4 per cent increase in employed labor force and a 5 per cent productivity im-

[5] E. I. Du Pont de Nemours & Co., of Wilmington, Delaware; established in 1802. In 1957 this corporation did a $2 billion business in products of chemistry. Its principal customer is the textile industry, but Du Pont also serves the rubber and plastics industries; the petroleum products and refining industry; the mining industry and agriculture; industries producing such products as foods, drugs, automobiles, chemicals, household furnishings and appliances, sporting goods, military powders, and iron and steel; and to a minor extent, the printing and tobacco industries.

Sources of these and subsequent observations are, unless otherwise noted: (1) analysis of the company's annual reports, the latest as of March, 1958; (2) reprints of speeches delivered by company officials; (3) current periodical literature; (4) lectures of, and interviews with, company officials on the occasion of the educators' and company officials' conference of 1954.

provement factor. The productivity increase rate is thrice the average national long-term productivity increase rate of 1.75 per cent annually. In real-cost terms this means that the company uses economic resources with extraordinary effectiveness to produce output.

Some Insights into Enterprise Growth

Helping to guide the company's actual development are some vital empirical generalizations of a unique nature. These guidelines are unique because, for the run of enterprises, growth is largely a matter of being benevolently slapped by Adam Smith's "invisible hand" of competition, rather than acting articulately in a recognition of basic growth conditions.

PRODUCT LIFE CYCLES

Highly important among these empirical generalizations is the observed life cycle of individual products or particular product lines. Every entrepreneur realizes that the attractiveness to the public of specific product or product *lines* (we are not talking of product *genera*) grows and subsides. This does not mean that products literally become extinct, but it does mean diminished profitability. George Richardson Porter long ago, in 1833, put the case forcefully when arguing for diversification in tropical agriculture:

Some of the more important articles of commerce . . . from their earliest settlement, have always been cultivated in the greater number of English colonies within the tropics. One of them—coffee—is still an object of great interest in many of those colonies; . . . while others have, from a variety of causes, ceased to offer their former interest to the planter.[6]

Regarding the "waning product" and speaking of the planter:

. . . what course would he then necessarily adopt? Would he persist in the expensive and forced cultivation of that for which an adequate demand no longer existed? Would he not rather betake him to some less costly tillage, and seeking to acquire the best means of producing other articles for which a market was still open to him, endeavour to guard as much as possible against those accidents and changes to which all human pursuits are in some degree exposed?[7]

Figure 20–4 illustrates the rise and decline in profitability of a specific commodity (in this case, a chemical product).

In Figure 20–4, *taking it as applying to one product* (or a narrowly specialized product line), we have a perfect illustration of the

---

[6] George Richardson Porter, *The Tropical Agriculturalist: A Practical Treatise on the Cultivation and Management of Various Productions Suited to Tropical Climates* (London: Smith, Elder and Co., 1833), p. ix.

[7] *Ibid*, p. viii.

hazard of nondiversification. Notice that the volume of sales keeps on increasing, *but so does investment.* If this process were continued at an increased investment trend rate, it would mean ruinous "forced cultivation."

Figure 20–4. Profit Cycle of One Selected Chemical Venture

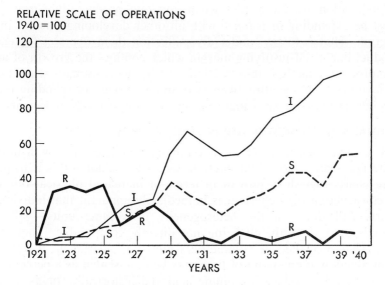

RELATIVE SCALE OF OPERATIONS
1940 = 100

CODE: *I*=Investment, including working capital
S=Sales
R=Percentage return on investment—net after all costs, expenses, and income taxes

SOURCE: Chaplin Tyler, *Chemical Engineering Economics* (New York: McGraw-Hill Book Co., Inc., 1948), p. 280.

One might perhaps argue that the increasing sales shown on Figure 20–4 signify that the entrepreneur is attempting to serve the public by extending the market even though his rate of return on investment, after reaching a peak in the early years of production, is now consistently poised at a lower but apparently quite stable rate of return. Such an argument might hold true of a product which, after having been somewhat of an innovation, has become a staple article of consumption for which there exists no ready alternative. But if there were profitable alternatives, then the entrepreneur would not really be serving the public as well as he might, simply by persisting in developing his original line. The very existence of alternatives would indicate public preference in other directions.

In other words, growth, considered in terms of increases in physical output along any given line of production, does not tell us much. It satisfies only one growth dimension, that of depth penetration. However, when we can assume that entrepreneurs are alert and imaginative in *diversifying,* as well as in suitably *penetrating* given fields, *then* the growth of any line of physical output describes more than the particular fate of any one particular venture. For under well-managed diversification we know that when any one product line grows, it must be expanding *in balance* with all other developing lines of production. That is to say, under diversification there operates for each product line a self-justifying margin which confines the growth of any one product, exactly within the limits set by the consumers when they compare the relative attractiveness of different ways of spending their incomes in the context of their particular cultural needs and wants.

TOTAL GROWTH PICTORIALIZED IN PHYSICAL TERMS

It is obviously desirable to have tangible evidence of growth in the material means of want-satisfaction. One way of doing this is to prepare charts that show growth in terms of increased physical output. In constructing such charts it is immediately apparent that individual charts will differ in the heterogeneity of volume units—gallons, pounds, and so forth, all being not directly comparable. Therefore a translation of the raw volume data must be undertaken. A volume of production at any point of time may be represented as a percentage of the highest production volume achieved historically, or as a percentage of any other base volume that may be chosen. However the choice of base-volume of production is made, the translation, in each case, permits assembling the separate growth indexes on one master chart. This is shown in Figure 20–5.

Figure 20–5 illustrates the location of any one point of physical growth of output, by the method of adding ordinates of the component product life-cycle curves. At any chosen moment, X, a perpendicular line is drawn to the horizontal bottom axis of the graph, the perpendicular line intersecting all the product curves shown on the graph. The separate magnitudes of the ordinates of the product curves are then ascertained and added, as shown on the right-hand side of Figure 20–5. This locates the point of growth at the moment X. Similar points can be ascertained for every moment of any chosen period, that is, a whole series of points.

When all growth points are ascertained for various products at different times and are connected by a line, that line describes the movement of the total physical output of the firm investigated, for the period of time chosen. If there were never any production setbacks owing to

Figure 20–5. Growth in Terms of Physical Output

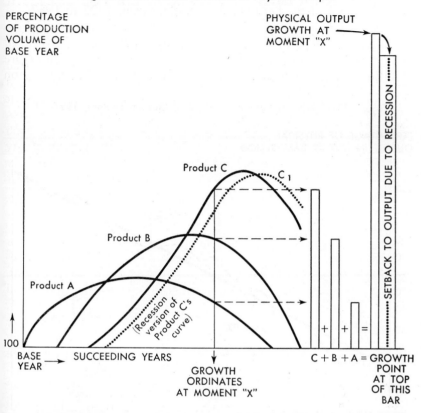

PERCENTAGE
OF PRODUCTION
VOLUME OF
BASE YEAR

PHYSICAL OUTPUT
GROWTH AT →
MOMENT "X"

SETBACK TO OUTPUT DUE TO RECESSION

Product C

C_1

Product B

Product A

(Recession version of Product C's curve)

100

BASE YEAR → SUCCEEDING YEARS

GROWTH ORDINATES AT MOMENT "X"

+ + =

C + B + A = GROWTH POINT AT TOP OF THIS BAR

recessions, the line connecting all the points on the graph of physical output growth would be a smooth curve rising upward to the right. Inasmuch as there are recessions in total economic activity, however, the output growth of a given firm is interrupted. All the product life-cycle curves reflect this by shifting downward and to the right; in Figure 20–5 this is illustrated by only one curve, the dotted C_1 line for product C, but it would be true of the other two curves. Even when illustrated only with reference to one product, the evident outcome is that the growth point of physical output is lowered for the moment X if it is a moment of time during a recession. This is shown on Figure 20–5 by the bar at far right. To its left is the total growth bar for all products if there is no recession at moment X. In a recession the growth point must lie lower than had been expected.

In reality, the occurrence of recessions means that when we connect the growth points of physical output with a line, this will be a serrated line moving upward in zig-zag fashion, rather than rising as a smoothly rounded curve. This is line *A* of Figure 20–6, which shows the rise of physical output of the Du Pont Corporation, from 1927 to 1957.

When a trend line is fitted to the serrated line showing rise of physical output, the slope of the trend line measures the rate of growth of physical output, from year to year, over the period surveyed. In Figure 20–6 line *B* is the computed trend line. Since the data are plotted on

Figure 20–6. Rate of Growth of Physical Output, DuPont, 1927–57

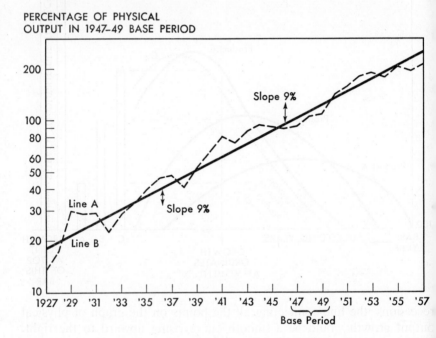

PERCENTAGE OF PHYSICAL
OUTPUT IN 1947–49 BASE PERIOD

semilogarithmic paper, the trend line appears as a straight line. It has a slope of 9, which means that from 1927 to 1957 the rate of growth of Du Pont's physical output has been 9 per cent annually.

Product "S" curves. Using the foregoing technique we engage only in historical narration; it could happen that the factors that accounted for the graphically depicted growth will already have changed in their mode of operation by the time their previous effects have been graphed. But it is most unlikely that *basic* changes should overtake all the factors that influence enterprise growth. Hence it is possible to derive distinct benefit from information about past growth, *provided* that one is prepared to proceed from the level of historical narration to the level of empirical generalization. This requires that one make assertions about what factors in the previous growth of an enterprise will continue to operate in much the same manner as before.

In attempting to project a growth chart into a reasonably predictable future, we do not have to resort to mere guessing. Chaplin Tyler informs us that:

Experience shows that the period of high return in any branch of the [chemical] industry is relatively short—sometimes as short as 5 years and certainly no more than 10 to 15 years. Moreover, profits do not as a rule commence with production, even though years of research, development, and semiworks operation may have preceded factory-scale production.

He cites that:

. . a careful examination was made of eight products which were developed through scientific research. At the time of the study, these eight products had been operating commercially a total of 115 product-years, or an average of 14 years.[8]

The findings of this study are shown in Table 20–4.

Table 20–4. Operating Profit History of Eight Products

Product	Years Required to Attain Normal Operations*	Years of Normal Operation
A	5	11
B	1	4
C	4	11
D	4	16
E	2	21
F	6	6
G	2	14
H	1	7
Average	3	11

* "Normal operations" means sustained production at substantially the projected cost and quantity.
SOURCE: Chaplin Tyler, *Chemical Engineering Economics* (New York: McGraw-Hill Book Co., Inc., 1948), p. 283.

Information such as this, and a wealth of other information available to any enterprise able and willing to study basic growth conditions, permits us to construct empirical S-curves depicting the rise and predicting the decline of given products. Naturally, "the accidents and changes to which all human pursuits are in some degree exposed"

[8] *Chemical Engineering Economics* (New York: McGraw-Hill Book Co., Inc., 1948), p. 281.

bring some real surprises. Some products "explode" into profitabilit\
and physical productivity; others persist most actively for a time afte\
they were supposed to have "settled down."

Mechanisms of Growth

Research. This is the chief growth mechanism for a large, integrated
concern. It is also one main reason for the existence of large firms
The expense of carrying on applied research is great, but even more
so is the expense of conducting pure research. In no known technol
ogy is there room for many firms to employ, as Du Pont did in 1957
2,200 scientists, of which 400 were engaged in fundamental research
done without regard to specific commercial objectives. The case of the
production of polyethylene illustrates the manner in which a concern
which performs a central research function almost naturally grows. To
produce polyethylene as a raw material for the fabrication of various
types of housewares requires heavy investment and continuous re
search to improve the product and process. The fabrication is undertaken by independent molders, many of them operating a relatively
small firm. The finished polyethylene houseware is sold by thousands
of retailers. The fabricators frequently turn to Du Pont for assistance
in solving fabrication problems, and the retailers are advised by Du
Pont with regard to selected marketing problems. Thus an interdependence has come to exist between the large firm providing the basic
resource on the basis of research, and the smaller firms performing the
fabricating and marketing functions.

Handling obsolescence. Research means not only finding new
methods of production but also standing guard against obsolescence.
Du Pont does this by earmarking depreciation reserves for growth
purposes. That is to say, the main purpose for creating depreciation
reserves is not to make up for wear and tear, but to prevent obsolescence by continually modernizing permanent assets. Of course
there are outlays for repairs and renovations of damaged parts, but
these expenses are charged to current operations. As a result, the
funds specifically designated for depreciation and obsolescence are
almost in their entirety available to modernize and improve plant and
equipment. The outcome is that Du Pont's oldest plants are as good
as new.

"We prefer to do our own obsolescing"—this is the way one executive describes the policy of not waiting until competitors overtake the
firm with superior plant and equipment. The policy is reflected in a
unique accounting procedure. Most business concerns carry their

permanent assets on their books at a net value, that is, at the original cost minus the amount of accumulated depreciation. Du Pont shows its plant and equipment at the *undiminished* value of its original cost— the accounting manner of stating that the permanent assets are always as good as new.

This method of accounting for growth funds can be criticized as technically understating profits, inasmuch as money plowed back into a business is conventionally considered to be a part of profits. But the money is not taken from the stockholders, even when it is not called profit, for what is good for a business is ultimately good for its owners. Technical understatement of profits is practiced by some other large concerns which report profit as a percentage of sales rather than as returns on the proprietors' investment. Sales income usually is higher than proprietary investment, so that if profit is taken as a percentage of sales, it appears as a relatively small percentage. By whatever method accomplished, any technical understatement of profit is a mechanism of entrepreneurial growth. The possibility of understating profit is accessible, of course, only to entrepreneurs who earn more than the normal, competitive 6 or 7 per cent rate of return on investment; at or below this rate, any understatement of profit would drive capital away from the enterprise.

Biological growth. To what extent can growth be financed from internal funds, and to which extent shall it be stimulated by outside funds? The Du Pont company, if it wished, could have ample outside funds almost for the asking—for instance, from the great insurance companies, participating with some of their wealth of institutionalized saving. Thus far, however, the company has not gone into bonded indebtedness, although it has had some recourse to outside funds through the medium of stock issues. The emphasis has been on pre-ferred stock that by its very nature involves the investor, personally, without committing him to active management participation (except in times of crises). This financial procedure, when taken in connection with the fact that Du Pont manages a substantial portion of the whole technology of organic chemistry, has resulted in the company's growth being to a remarkable extent "biological," that is to say, self-generative.

Seen solely by analogy of the technology of organic chemistry, Du Pont's growth is biological in the following sense. The basic tech-nology is similar to the fertility power of an original bed of soil. Upon being cleverly called into action, this fertility will ripen the "seed" of say, 25 cents' worth of cash invested at the outset of a venture in a dollar's worth of ultimate investment—at the same time r⎯ more of the "seed of cash" required for launching further⎯

Pricing for Growth

In this demonstration we can start with the knowledge that Du Pont's general managers are free to price their products as they see fit; they are accountable to the executive committee not for their *methods* of pricing, but only for the *results* of pricing in contributing to the corporation's earning a profit. This remote control does *not* constitute a noncompetitive constraint on the managers, as might be inferred. For in holding the managers responsible for results in contributing to the company's *over-all* rate of return on investment, the executive committee only preserves in a conscious and articulate manner a common purpose of assuring a satisfactory income. In a crowded auction market this common purpose emerges inarticulately. This is because there is in every market a generally understood minimum rate of return on investment which is acceptable to the run of producers.

Using cost estimates and market surveys, each of Du Pont's twelve general managers may discover that it is possible to earn 10 per cent on investment

While operating at:	And charging, per unit:
50%	$1.25
60	1.20
70	1.15
80	1.10
90	1.05
100	1.00

But here is where classification and practical decision-making part ways. Arithmetically it may make no difference at all whether one operates at 50 per cent capacity, charging $1.25, or at the 100 per cent capacity, charging a $1.00 price. Arithmetically one earns 10 per cent on the investment in either case. But in the world of realities, of customer relations and personnel relations, it makes all the following differences:

1. The combination of 100 per cent capacity and a low price enlarges a firm's particular clientele and therefore means reaching the limit of what that firm can feasibly claim as its share of the *total* market for that product. For example, in the market for tetraethyl lead many commercial users of the product prefer to have more than one supplier. Thus there is always a chance for each entrepreneur making tetraethyl lead of realigning his respective share of that market even though he can never expect to capture the entire market.

2. A high-capacity output means eliminating customer resentment at not being able to get things, even when prices may not be *the* major consideration, as is sometimes the case.

3. On the other hand, having a clear view of its capacity-price relationship prevents a firm from *lowering* price beyond its potential capacity. That is to say, an entrepreneur may lower his prices to arouse a great deal of interest in his wares and then find that he cannot serve all of the people whose attention he has attracted. He has then the unhappy choice of serving his old-established customers first and not serving some newly attracted ones at all, of serving both categories partially, or of neglecting the old customers in whole or in part. Economists treat this matter rather loftily as "a short-run adjustment problem"; new firms will come into the field until everybody is well served. It might happen that new firms not only move in to take up the production slack of the short run, but in moving in they even take over some of the customers of the established firms.

4. Operating at high capacity keeps one's personnel fully employed and therefore in a state of high morale. It is the sort of thing a wise football coach does in giving all the potential players on the varsity a chance to get into the game for at least a few minutes before the end of the half or the end of the game.

5. Operating at high capacity keeps one alert against trying to penetrate any new line of endeavor unless the firm's technology is really superior to the production methods of the entrepreneurs already in the field. By contrast, the entrepreneur who runs at low capacity and charges high prices in his own field is easily tempted to "spill over" into some vaguely related high-price field with his unused capacity, adapting it for that purpose. But he may discover, too late, that with his adapted equipment he is an inferior operator in the other field. A familiar example is that of the early ill-fated ball-point pen ventures; not until the established fountain pen companies entered the field was success assured.

These are only some of many available illustrations to show that an entrepreneur cannot really be indifferent as to how he earns his rate of return on investment. But what about the high rate of return that might conceivably be realized when operating at 100 per cent capacity *at high prices*? In the illustration a price of $1.25 at 100 per cent capacity utilization would yield no less than a 35 per cent rate of return on investment. Two questions come to mind: Under what circumstances would this be possible? and how long could it last?

It could probably happen in a pronounced "sellers' market," for example, after a war. Or, a company might offer a product that caught the people's fancy to the extent that cost would be "no consideration" (within limits, of course). Other eventualities of this sort come readily to mind. In those cases an entrepreneur might be inclined to say to himself, "If you can get it, why not take it?"

Even so, how long can a frenzied demand situation persist for any particular product? The upper limit could ultimately be a "buyers' strike"; the lower limit an influx of enterprise that would sooner or later glut that particular field of enterprise. From the standpoint of growth a producer can well afford to let an outside spontaneous (fly-by-night) auction market absorb the temporary windfall gains of speculative fever and secure to himself instead the good will of steady customers that will stay with him. He can do this by serving them at moderate prices that are nicely correlated to an ample utilization of capacity which will permit him to fill his orders without fail. After World War II the Du Pont company sold nylon at $6.75 a pound at a time when some speculative resellers were being paid as much as $26.00 a pound by certain processors.

ECONOMIC DRAGNET DEVICE

So long as a general manager continually achieves a satisfactory rate of return on investment, the company's executive committee cares not which of the various price alternatives he selects to achieve his earnings. The executive committee sees the enterprise as a whole, and from that viewpoint it is interested not in this or that product, but in the profitable product-mix. New products are always flowing in, while old ones are being abandoned by the operation of a "dragnet" device for weeding out unproductive investments. This device is a simple one of having available for the executive committee and the general managers a comparison of actual results with written estimates of the results the manager expected to achieve at the time he presented the committee with data justifying a budgetary request to support a projected undertaking and won the committee's approval. At that time the manager stated what he wanted, why he wanted it, and what he expected to accomplish. That was then. Now, the venture having been launched, the discussion goes: "What I claimed, what I did, and what I would have done if outside variables had not intervened" (for example the imposition of government price controls in a war crisis).

Suppose then, that a 20 per cent rate of return on investment was expected, but only 12 per cent is realized. So long as the rate of return continues at or above 10 per cent, the executive committee is not likely to persist in wanting to know whether this venture should be continued—particularly if the factor depressing earnings is an outside variable, such as price control or a cost-increasing factor beyond the manager's control. In the latter case there is in operation an *external* diseconomy of production, operating on all similar enterprises. The company can therefore "escalate" (pass on) this cost-increment to the consumer without fear of competitive recoil. In the case of price control or profits taxation the company, along with all its rivals, must simply "take its licking and would certainly not whip its manager."

But suppose a certain type of production continually shows a lower rate of return than expected. Then its general manager must keep on explaining. Perhaps it is a matter of *internal* diseconomies that had not been foreseen. In that case it is not a matter of finding *who* is to blame, but *what* is to blame; in other words, what are the internal cost-raising factors, and what is to be done about them?

One thing that will *not* be done is to raise prices to consumers to cover losses resulting from *internal* diseconomies. Instead, there will be analytical appraisals that may "read like doctoral dissertations." That member of the executive committee who is the special advisor to the industrial department involved—each department has such an advisory committee member—will be in charge of that appraisal and will be in a scientific (not a biased) sense the advocate of the general manager when the latter appears before the committee. This procedure of review and loss-searching has great disciplinary value in the constructive, not the authoritarian, sense of the word. For the search may reveal loss factors that could not reasonably be foreseen—as when a technically excellent detergent simply failed to "take" with the public simply because it didn't bubble. What a waste of talent it would have been to foam at the manager, instead of developing a bubbling detergent! Again, a business may be potentially profitable, yet fail to recommend itself, as for instance, the zinc products business which the Grasselli Chemicals Department sold to four different companies, transferring the employees to titanium development. Finally, a product may become "old"; that was the case of lithophane, to get rid of which the Du Pont company actually paid money.

In all these cases the low-end dragnet has come into operation to enrich the company's product-mix by siphoning off dregs and making room for new products at a high rate of investment return. The reader may note that this "dragnet device" of continual review and persistent probing for loss positions functions much the same as does the competitive elimination of relatively inefficient product lines through the timely withdrawal or bankruptcy of small producers. Only the "dragnet device" features prevention rather than cure and would therefore seem to be less costly and rather more educational than bankruptcy due to outside pressures that can sometimes be only vaguely understood.

Indeed we have now come to the kernel of this analysis of D Pont's built-in mechanisms for economic growth. By definition healthy kernel contains a life-giving essence. In this case it is th essence of competition manifested in the form of product competition

In Conclusio

The foregoing illustrates the probable behavior of prices whe price-determination is seen as a process operating in the context o enterprise growth, rather than as a mechanism to conserve give social resources in a context of fixed consumer wants and incomes The two ways of viewing price-determination are not incompatible The given data of mechanistic price analysis can be varied, one at time, to show in which directions price and output tend to move when for example, demand increases. In the early part of this chapter w have applied conventional price analysis to gain an elementary under standing of the prices of a product at different phases of its life cycle However, the necessarily delimited nature of this approach forbid that the findings be applied lock, stock, and barrel to the comple: realities of life.

Life is growth, and therefore there are deviations, major and minor from logical predictions based on slight changes in basically give conditions of wants, resources, and methods of production. When group of entrepreneurs specializes in maximizing the profit opportu nities inherent in *changes of* wants and methods of production, th economic results for the firm and the community as well are worth of notice. These complex results of real operations under conditions o change, and with the aim of economic change, have been illustrate with reference to an actual industrial operation. The practices in volved, and their results, are not to be classified so easily as ar theoretical propositions. But they do throw light on price as a *proces* of resources allocation under changing economic conditions, rathe than on price as a mechanism of resources allocation under give conditions. There is much yet to be learned about price as a proces rather than as a mechanism.

For Discussio

1. Which of the two types of competition, price and product competition do economists conventionally prefer?

2. "The ultimate consumer and the whole of American industry benefit fror having business units of all sizes." Do you agree? If so, on what bases do yo agree, i.e., in terms of what assumed consumer protection would you agre with the above statement?

3. Where pure competition interferes with the most efficient size of plan

for performing one or more industrial functions, the attempt to enforce pure competition would be self-destructive. Illustrate.

4. Product competition has the effect of keeping prices in some relation to costs, though by no means necessarily equal to them. Also, outputs are larger under product competition than they would be otherwise, even when there is not much price competition. Ascertain some leading instances of how product competition operated in these ways in the last 25 years (for example, the introduction of the air-coach).

5. If you were a member of a Congressional committee investigating the practice of large corporations in administering prices, what sort of critical questions to be asked of witnesses at the hearings would a reading of this chapter sugges'? List at least six questions.

6. What is the difference between the concept of a "product life cycle," as discussed in the early part of the chapter and illustrated in Figure 20–1, and the concept of "product S-curves," as illustrated in Figures 20–4 and 20–5?

7. With more than a thousand specific product lines produced for use in fifteen main lines of American industrial production, the Du Pont company has a broad base of diversification against which to appraise the possibilities of commercializing the various compounds synthesized in its laboratories. To illustrate, certain findings on synthetic resins led to the development of "Duco" lacquer because Du Pont had experience in the paint business. Likewise, its established rayon business made the company conscious of the commercial possibilities of silk-like fibers; this in turn encouraged research and development of other fibers such as Dacron and Orlon.

Can you think of other cases in America where this advantage of diversification exists? In your opinion, is it an automatic by-product of "lateral integration"? In industries in which the structure of organization does not favor concentrated research, how might the advantage of diversification be realized by a mass of small producers? For example, in agriculture?

8. "High prices delay growth." In which sense is this statement true, given that high prices also provide revenue needed for carrying on research functions?

Recommended Further Reading for Part IV

Demand

MARSHALL, ALFRED. *Principles of Economics.* 8th ed.; London: Macmillan & Co., Ltd., 1930. (A 1936 reprint is available.) See Bk. III: "On Wants and Their Satisfaction."

MEADE, J. E. *Trade and Welfare.* New York: Oxford University Press, 1955. Vol. II, Part 1. Excellent introduction to welfare economics.

MENGER, KARL. *The Principles of Economics.* (Trans. Frank H. Knight) Glencoe, Ill.: Free Press, 1950.

SMART, WILLIAM. *An Introduction to the Theory of Value—On the Lines of Menger, Wieser, and Boehm-Bawerk.* London: Macmillan & Co., Ltd., 1914. The reader who wishes to delve into some more detail of the "utility" economics school of thought may do so by consulting any card-catalogue for works by Stanley S. Jevons, Karl Menger, Friedrich von Wieser, and Eugen von Boehm-Bawerk.

SCHULTZ, HENRY. *Statistical Laws of Demand and Supply, With Special Application to Sugar.* Chicago: The University of Chicago Press, 1928. A pioneer work.

TAYLOR, FRED M. *Principles of Economics.* New York: The Ronald Press Co., 1921. A teaching text not as yet improved on for purposes of demand analysis. See chaps. xx, xxiv, and xlviii, especially.

U.S. DEPARTMENT OF AGRICULTURE. *Marketing.* The Yearbook of Agriculture, 1954. Washington, D.C.: Government Printing Office, 1955. Gives many practical aspects of demand.

Costs and Supply

BROWN, HARRY GUNNISON. *Basic Principles of Economics and Their Significance for Public Policy.* Columbia, Mo.: Lucas Bros., 1942.

CANNAN, EDWIN. *A History of the Theories of Production and Distribution in English Political Economy, from 1776–1848.* London: P. S. King & Son, Ltd., 1924. For rich background material read the sections on "Diminishing Returns" and "Tendency to Diminishing Returns," chap. v, pp. 147–82.

CASSELS, JOHN M. "On the Law of Variable Proportions," in *Readings in the Theory of Income Distribution.* Sponsored by a committee of the American Economic Association. Philadelphia: The Blakiston Co., 1946, chap. v.

CLARK, JOHN MAURICE. "Diminishing Returns," in *Encyclopedia of Social Sciences.* New York: The Macmillan Co., 1931, vol. V, p. 144.

LEFTWICH, RICHARD H. *The Price System and Resource Allocation.* New York: Rinehart & Co., Inc., 1955. Chap. viii, "Costs of Production."

PATTON, FRANCIS LESTER. *Diminishing Returns in Agriculture.* New York: Columbia University Press, 1926.

PETERSON, GEORGE MARTIN. *Diminishing Returns and Planned Economy.* New York: The Ronald Press Co., 1937.

RICARDO, DAVID. "An Essay on the Influence of a Low Price of Corn on the Profits of Stock, 1815." In Piero Sraffa and M. H. Dobb (eds.). *The Works and Correspondence of David Ricardo.* London: Cambridge University Press, 1951, vol. IV, pp. 1–47.

SRAFFA, PIERO. "The Laws of Return under Competitive Conditions," *Economic Journal* (organ of the Royal Economic Society), vol. 36, pp. 535–50. Very basic reading.

STIGLER, GEORGE J. *The Theory of Price.* New York: The Macmillan Co., 1952. Chaps. vi, vii, viii.

VINER, JACOB. "Cost," in *Encyclopedia of Social Sciences.* New York: The Macmillan Co., 1931, vol. IV, p. 466.

Price Under Pure Competition

ALLEN, CLARK L. *Prices, Income, and Public Policy: the ABC's of Economics.* New York: McGraw-Hill Book Co., Inc., 1954.

AMERICAN ECONOMIC ASSOCIATION. *Readings in Price Theory.* Homewood, Ill.: Richard D. Irwin Co., Inc., 1952. See especially Part 2, pp. 180–263.

BAIN, JOE S. *Pricing, Distribution, and Employment.* New York: Henry Holt & Co., Inc., 1953.

BECKWITH, BURNHAM P. *Marginal-Cost Price-Output Control; a Critical History and Restatement of the Theory.* New York: Columbia University Press, 1955.

EITEMAN, WILFORD J. *Price Determination; Business Practice versus Economic Theory.* Ann Arbor: School of Business Administration, University of Michigan, 1949

HENDERSON, HUBERT D. *Supply and Demand.* New York: Harcourt, Brace & Co. Inc., 1932. One of the Cambridge University Handbooks.

KNIGHT, FRANK H. *The Economic Organization.* New York: Augustus M. Kelley Inc., 1951. Pages 67–96 on "Demand and Supply and Price."

MARSHALL, ALFRED. *Principles of Economics.* 8th ed.; London: Macmillan & Co., Ltd., 1930. Recently reissued. See Bk. V, "General Relations of Demand, Supply, and Value."

PETTENGILL, ROBERT B. *Price Economics.* New York: The Ronald Press Co., 1948.

STIGLER, GEORGE J. *The Theory of Price.* New York: The Macmillan Co., 1952.

WILSON, THOMAS, et al. *Oxford Studies in the Price Mechanism.* London: Clarendon Press, 1951.

WRIGHT, DAVID McCORD. *A Key to Modern Economics.* New York: The Macmillan Co., 1954.

Monopoly

ADAMS, WALTER, and GRAY, HORACE M. *Monopoly in America: the Government as Promoter.* New York: The Macmillan Co., 1955.

BRADY, ROBERT A. *Business as a System of Power.* New York: Columbia University Press, 1943.

FETTER, FRANK A. *Masquerade of Monopoly.* New York: Harcourt, Brace & Co., Inc., 1931.

KEYES, LUCILLE S. *Federal Control of Entry into Air Transportation.* Cambridge, Mass.: Harvard University Press, 1951.

MACHLUP, FRITZ. *The Political Economy of Monopoly; Business, Labor, and Government Policies.* Baltimore: The Johns Hopkins Press, 1952.

NUTTER, G. WARREN. *The Extent of Enterprise Monopoly in the United States, 1899–1939.* Chicago: University of Chicago Press, 1951.

REYNOLDS, LLOYD G. *The Control of Competition in Canada.* Cambridge, Mass.: Harvard University Press, 1940.

ROBINSON, E. A. G. *Monopoly.* Student Economic Handbooks, XI. London: Cambridge University Press, 1941.

STOCKING, GEORGE W. *Basing Point Pricing and Regional Development: a Case Study of the Iron and Steel Industry.* Chapel Hill: University of North Carolina Press, 1954.

STOCKING, GEORGE W., and WATKINS, MYRON W. *Monopoly and Free Enterprise.* New York: Twentieth Century Fund, 1951. With the report and recommendations of the Committee on Cartels and Monopoly.

WESTON, FRED J. *The Role of Mergers in the Growth of Large Firms.* Berkeley: University of California Press, 1953.

ZIMMERMAN, L. J. *The Propensity To Monopolize.* Amsterdam: North Holland Publishing Company, 1953.

Antitrust Legislation

BERNSTEIN, MARVER H. *Regulating Business by Independent Commission.* Princeton, N.J.: Princeton University Press, 1955. Findings of this book are based on study of the experience of the Civil Aeronautics Board, the Federal Communications Commission, the Interstate Commerce Commission, and the Securities and Exchange Commission.

DIRLAM, JOEL B., and KAHN, ALFRED E. *Fair Competition: The Law and Economics of Antitrust Policy.* Ithaca, N.Y.: Cornell University Press, 1954.

FEDERAL TRADE COMMISSION. *Report on Corporate Mergers and Acquisitions.* Washington, D.C.: Government Printing Office, 1955. Has special reference to the Clayton Act, Sec. 7.

GLOVER, J. D. *The Attack on Big Business.* Boston: Harvard University Graduate School of Business Administration, 1954.

KAYSEN, CARL. *United States v. United Shoe Machinery Corporation: An Economic Analysis of an Anti-Trust Case.* Harvard Economic Studies, vol. XCIX. Cambridge, Mass.: Harvard University Press, 1956.

MOULTON, HAROLD G. *Economic Systems; Free Enterprise . . . Regulation Compatible with Free Enterprise.* Washington, D.C.: The Brookings Institution, 1948.

PAPANDREOU, ANDREAS G., and WHEELER, JOHN T. *Competition and Its Regulation.* Englewood Cliffs, N.J.: Prentice-Hall, Inc., 1954.

Report of the Attorney General's National Committee to Study the Antitrust Laws. Washington, D.C.: Government Printing Office, 1955.

ROBERTSON, DENNIS H. *The Control of Industry.* London: Cambridge University Press, 1949.

THORELLI, HANS B. *The Federal Antitrust Policy: Origination of an American Tradition.* Baltimore: Johns Hopkins Press, 1955.

Limited Competition

BAIN, J. S. "Economics of Scale, Concentration, and the Condition of Entry in Twenty Manufacturing Industries," *The American Economic Review,* March, 1954, pp. 15–39.

BREMS, HANS. *Product Equilibrium Under Monopolistic Competition.* Cambridge, Mass.: Harvard University Press, 1951.

BUCHANAN, NORMAN S. *The Economics of Corporate Enterprise.* New York: Henry Holt & Co., Inc., 1940.

CHAMBERLIN, EDWARD. *The Theory of Monopolistic Competition.* Cambridge, Mass.: Harvard University Press, 1936. The American classical work in this field.

CLARK, JOHN MAURICE. "Toward a Concept of Workable Competition," *The American Economic Review,* June, 1940.

FELLNER, WILLIAM J. *Competition Among the Few; Oligopoly and Similar Market Structures.* New York: Alfred A. Knopf, Inc., 1949.

KAPLAN, A. D. H. *Big Enterprise in the Competitive System.* Washington, D.C.: The Brookings Institution, 1954.

LILIENTHAL, DAVID E. *Big Business: A New Era.* New York: Harper & Bros., 1953. A spirited defense of bigness in business; on a popular level—not designed as a scholarly economic analysis.

MCLEAN, JOHN G., and HAIGH, ROBERT W. *The Growth of Integrated Oil Companies.* Cambridge, Mass.: Harvard University Press, 1954.

NATIONAL BUREAU OF ECONOMIC RESEARCH. *Business Concentration and Price Policy.* Princeton, N.J.: Princeton University Press, 1955.

ROBINSON, JOAN. *The Economics of Imperfect Competition.* London: Macmillan & Co., Ltd., 1933. The English classic.

VATTER, HAROLD G. *Small Enterprise and Oligopoly: A Study of the Butter, Flour Automobile and Glass Container Industries.* Oregon State Monographs, Studies in Economics, No. 4. Corvallis: Oregon State College, 1955.

V

DISTRIBUTION OF
THE NATIONAL INCOME

21

Income and

Wealth Distribution

Preliminary Summary

Consumer income and what it can purchase depend upon the efficiency with which we use our national resources. However, the volume and the distribution of consumer purchasing power play a leading role in guiding the further use of productive resources. The incomes received by consumers determine what goods and services are produced and in what proportions, and which workers are employed and how fully. Consumer income also affects tax revenues of federal, state, and local governments—revenues to be spent for maintaining and expanding schools and roads and public health and other community facilities.

Because the flow of national and personal income largely guides the performance of the economy, it is imperative that we know the channels through which this flow passes and the processes by which it is distributed. The possession of this knowledge enables businessmen to estimate the demand for their products and permits lawmakers to levy taxes without damaging production or diminishing personal incentives. Students of living standards can trace poverty to its origins by observing where and how income flows cease, or are diminished, for certain persons and groups in given local areas or regions. Generally speaking, any effort to come to grips with basic economic problems requires thorough understanding of the distribution of wealth and income among the various groups of the nation's consumers. In other words, the economy's survival and growth depends upon the distribution of purchasing power as much as on sustained and efficient production.

Purchasing power is acquired by exerting one's labor for pay or by receiving payment for the use of owned or controlled productive property. One criterion of an adequate income and wealth distribution is whether enough purchasing power is generated so that a sufficiently high aggregate effective demand can sustain full employment and encourage efficient production. This is the quantitative view of the matter.

There is another criterion, one which is qualitative. Does the economy's system of rewards furnish individuals with opportunities and incentives for self-realization through creative workmanship in the common good? A modern technological society is, as a matter of fact, a vast cooperative undertaking. This reality is well understood by the participants in the economic process, regardless of the particular tasks they perform whether by choice or force of circumstances. People grow restless if they observe that as much, or more, money can be made by self-aggrandizement (which damages production by unproductive speculation, featherbedding, waste of resources, and so on) as can be earned by creative participation in the economic process. A system of income and wealth distribution must reward creative workmanship and punish mere self-seeking. For the one serves the life-interest of the community, while the other is its enemy.

It may be seen that the subject of income and wealth distribution raises two major questions:

1. Is purchasing power so broadly dispersed under given systems of distribution that the power to consume equals the power to produce? In this connection it is important to note whether poverty is being eliminated now that the productive power to do so exists.

2. How equitable is our income and wealth distribution? This is a controversial question. Every individual must face and resolve it in terms of his personal and social value judgments. Part V of this text furnishes a background of objective information which permits approaching the distribution question in the light of the facts.

Chapter 21 describes the quantitative aspects of American income and wealth distribution—what the American standard of living is, and how widely it is enjoyed and accessible. In Chapters 22 to 27, the specific processes of income and wealth distribution are explained, chief among them, the determination of property incomes through the price mechanism and the determination of wages and salaries through individual and collective bargaining.

Standard, Plane, and Mode of Living

A standard of living is the minimum list of goods and services to which individuals or groups have become accustomed and toward which they aspire. A plane of living is the list of goods and services actually consumed, whether or not it falls below or exceeds the desired standard of living. *Mode of living* refers to distinguishing types of individual or group consumption habits, knowledge of which helps to explain given social problems. In regard to health, for example, the dominance of degenerative heart disease as a cause of death in the industrialized high-income sections of the world is in significant part explained by the types of food consumed in these areas.

In practice, the term living standard is used loosely to describe that which is commonly considered a minimal accoutrement of goods and services, required not only to meet basic needs but also in order to keep up appearances. It is not difficult to establish in objective terms a "minimum standard of comfort and decency." This is done in the broadest sense by listing major conditions of life to which citizens of a nation, or in an area of the world, have become accustomed, then comparing the conditions either with conditions elsewhere at present or with domestic living conditions in the past. In Table 21–1 the first type of comparison is made.

Table 21–1 reveals the American-European standard of living by showing that American-European people expect to eat well without having to use the largest part of their income for the purpose; that they expect to live long without being struck down by epidemics; that they not only know how to read and write but favor higher education; that they are amply attuned to receive the daily news of the world; and that they expect to have privacy in their homes. These are not unreasonable expectations in our industrialized civilization, as Table 21–1 shows. Table 21–1, however, does not emphasize some of the hazards of living in a technologically advanced society. There is, for example, the risk of accidental death; in this regard the United States leads the world, especially in transport fatalities. Another example of the hazards of technology is the toxic effect which insecticides used in agriculture may have when traces are left on food that reaches the table; there may also be toxic effects of certain food additives and other chemical products ingested into the body. Air pollution in industrialized and heavily settled urban regions is dramatized by the "smogs" of London, Los Angeles, and the Ruhr Valley in Germany. Then there is the whole problem of the genetic effects of artificial irradiation.

Table 21-1. Some Components of the Current American Standard of Living, in the Perspective of World Conditions

Element of the Standard of Living	U.S. and Canada	Europe	Latin America	Asia	Africa
FOOD					
Expenditure on food as percentage of total personal expenditure	32	32	45	50	....
Calories, daily and per capita (minimum required, 2,500)	3,100	3,100	2,200	1,900	2,000
Percentage of calories derived from starchy foods	40	50	65	80	80
Annual meat consumption, pounds per capita	165	110	65	10	....
Annual milk consumption, quarts per capita	250	200	75	50	....
HEALTH AND EDUCATION					
Years of life expectancy at birth (both sexes)	71	67-72	45	35 in India, Burma, Philippines	....
Deaths from infective and parasitic diseases per 100,000 population	20	25	150 Yellow fever is endemic	Smallpox, cholera, yellow fever, are endemic	Endemic yellow fever, diseases by worms in blood vessels; "river blindness."
Inhabitants per physician	750	900	5,000	50,000	50,000
Percentage of population 15 years and over which is literate	98	98	50-75	15-20	5-10
Enrollment in institutions of higher learning per 100,000 population	2,000	500	150	50-100	10
Radios per 1,000 population	800	300	100	10	3 to 30
HOUSING					
Percentage of population living more than 1.5 persons to a room	5	5	65	85	85

SOURCES: Most figures are based on: (1) *Report on the World Social Situation* (New York: United Nations, 1957); (2) "Trends in Economic Growth," a study prepared by the Legislative Reference Service for the Joint Committee on the Economic Report, 83d Congress, 2d Session (Washington, D.C.: Government Printing Office, 1955), pp. 220–21, for data on housing.

THE AMERICAN LIVING STANDARD IN TIME PERSPECTIVE

Figure 21–1 exhibits a comparison of middle-class living standards in 1957 with the standards of a century earlier, in 1857. The comparison is made in terms of the distribution of a hypothetical dollar's worth of the consumer's expenditure for various goods and services. To compare the actual amount of dollars expended at the two dates would be meaningless because of the great change in the purchasing power of the dollar during the century.

Figure 21–1. Distribution of the Consumer Dollar, 1957 Compared with 1857

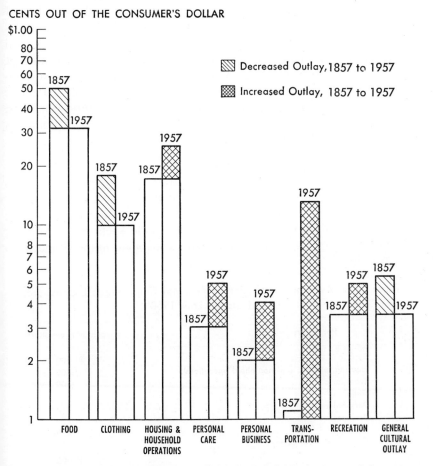

CENTS OUT OF THE CONSUMER'S DOLLAR

SOURCE: Recent information based on official data of the Department of Commerce. For the earlier period, based on Ernst Engel, "Die Lebenskosten," *Bulletin of the International Institute of Statistics* (Rome), ed. 1, vol. IX (1895), first part.

The comparison made in Figure 21–1 reveals, strikingly, that Western civilization has become a roaming culture with its automobile, and means of sea and air travel; this is the meaning of the large modern transportation item of expenditure, which was minimal in 1857. Noteworthy, too, is the increased amount of money spent for recreation, personal care, and personal business; the latter consists of legal, insurance, home finance, and banking expenses; and the increase of this item of outlay therefore proves that more Americans now possess insurance and homes and savings accounts than was true a century ago. An increased number of cents out of each consumer dollar is spent for housing and household operations, showing that the home is still the center of American social organization. Many of the improvements in the 1957 living standard, as compared with that of 1857, are due to the two facts. (1) Food expenditure now absorbs only 32 cents out of the consumer dollar (or approximately one-third of the consumer's budget), whereas it used to absorb 50 cents (or one-half the consumer's budget). (2) Outlay for clothing has diminished, from 18 cents out of every consumer dollar to only 10 cents. A regrettable decline is that of outlay for general cultural purposes, which now absorbs only 3.5 cents out of every consumer dollar as compared with 5.5 cents in the past.

AVERAGE CONSUMPTION EXPENDITURE

In mid-1958 total consumer expenditure for all income classes was $288 billion after payment of taxes. As there were 57 million households of families and of individuals with no dependents (including persons living alone), each American household spent $5,000 on the average. This amount was arithmetically distributed in the proportions shown in Table 21–2.

Table 21–2. Average Distribution of Personal Consumption Expenditure, United States, Late 1950's

Item of Expenditure	Amount of Expenditure
Food and tobacco	$1,600
Housing, utilities, and household operations	1,300
Transportation	600
Clothing	500
Personal care	325
Personal business	250
Recreation	250
General cultural outlay	175
	$5,000

SOURCE: Department of Commerce, Bureau of the Census, *Statistical Abstract of the United States, 1958,* Table 388, p. 308.

DIFFERENCES IN CONSUMER INCOMES AFFECT EXPENDITURES

Not all consumers are able to express their wants with the same effectiveness in the markets of the nation. High-income families or individuals are able to bring more purchasing power to bear than families or individuals at low-income levels. Table 21–3 shows how this distinction directs production along somewhat different lines than would be the case if every family had the same income.

Table 21–3. Food, Clothing, and Shelter as Proportionate Shares of Total Family Expenditure, by Income Classes in Three Representative American Cities

| Income Class | Percentage of Family Income After Personal Taxes Spent for: | | |
	Food (not including tobacco)	Clothing	Housing (including upkeep)
Category I (15% of families)			
Under $1,000	34	7	29
$1,000 – 1,999	35	9	27
Category II (75% of families)			
$2,000 – 3,999	34	12	21
$4,000 – 5,999	31	13	19
$6,000 – 7,499	29	16	16
Category III (10% of families)			
$7,500 – 9,999	26	18	14
$10,000 and above	25	17	18

NOTE: The three cities are Denver, Detroit, and Houston (Tex.).
SOURCE: Department of Labor, Bureau of Labor Statistics, *Family Income, Expenditure, and Savings in 10 Cities*, Bulletin No. 1065 (Washington, D.C.: Government Printing Office, 1952).

More detailed information reveals that there are significant differences within the broad categories shown in Table 21–3. As buying power increases, a shift takes place from starchy foods—bread, potatoes, corn pone—to meat, milk, and fresh vegetables. Housing expenditures at higher income levels purchase more privacy, room for gardening, separate rooms for members of families, and so forth. In the matter of cars the higher-income person need not tinker with his car to keep it running, nor need he repair his shoes instead of buying a new pair or mend his trousers after they have become worn. The general difference is brought to light in Table 21–4, which exhibits the contrast in how a dollar of income would be used if it were spent by low-income, middle-income, and high-income recipients respectively.

Table 21–4. Size of Income and Proportionate Consumer Expenditures

Expenditure Item	Allocation of a Dollar of 1957 Consumer Income		
	By a Family with a 1957 Income of $1,000 to $2,000	By a Family with a 1957 Income of $5,000 to $6,000	By a Family with a 1957 Income of $10,000 and over
Food and tobacco	38.4¢	32.0¢	25.5¢
Housing, utilities, household operations	26.4	18.5	22.5
Furnishings and equipment	4.9	7.2	8.4
Clothing and clothing services	9.3	12.3	14.1
Medical and personal care	7.8	7.0	6.0
Recreation, reading, education	3.7	6.3	7.8
Transportation	7.9	15.4	12.8
Miscellaneous	1.6	1.4	2.9
	$1.00	$1.00	$1.00

SOURCE: Department of Commerce, Bureau of the Census, *Statistical Abstract of the United States, 1958,* Table 396, p. 315. The constituent items of this table are a little differently arranged than the items in Figure 21–1 and Table 21–2.

LEVEL OF DISPOSABLE PERSONAL INCOME AND CONSUMER EXPENDITURE

Major differences in consumer proportionate outlays can be expected to result from variations in the aggregate disposable income of consumers. This is plainly seen during a major depression. In 1929 the aggregate personal disposable income was $83 billion; by 1933 it had fallen to $46 billion. On the basis of estimates prepared by the National Resources Committee, it is possible to gauge the probable effects of increasing the low volume of 1933 consumer spending of $46 billion (there were no net savings) to $82 billion of personal consumption expenditure out of $93 billion personal disposable income (which means that $11 billion would have been saved). Table 21–5 estimates the proportions of depression spending as contrasted to moderate prosperity spending.

Table 21–5 shows the average directions of consumer expenditure as affected by recession. We must, however, be mindful of the information conveyed by Table 21–4, which shows that food and shelter become increasing proportions of incomes as incomes diminish. In a depression this impact is accentuated, so that it is not unusual for low-income families to spend, for food alone, two-thirds or even more of their meager incomes. Necessarily, housing is neglected, as is, frequently, clothing expenditure. In postwar recessionary periods this trend has not been so apparent until the onset of the 1957 recession

Table 21–5. Level of Aggregate Disposable Income and Proportionate
Consumer Expenditures, on the Average

	Expenditure of $46 Billion out of a Disposable Income of $46 Billion (no savings)		Expenditure of $82 Billion out of a Disposable Income of $93 Billion (net savings of $11 billion)	
Item of Expenditure	Amount ($ billion)	Percentage	Amount ($ billion)	Percentage
Food and tobacco	17	37	26	32
Housing, utilities, and household operations	14	30	25	30
Furnishings and equipment	1	2	2	3
Clothing and clothing services	5	11	9	11
Medical and personal care	2	5	5	6
Recreation, reading, and education	2	5	5	6
Transportation	4	9	9	11
Miscellaneous	1	1	1	1
	46	100	82	100

SOURCE: Based on Table III of: *The Structure of the American Economy,* prepared by Gardiner C. Means for the National Resources Committee (Washington, D.C.: Government Printing Office, 1939), p. 14.

in business activity. Between September, 1957, and March, 1958, personal disposable income dropped $3.7 billion and retail sales dropped 7 per cent. The cutback of retail sales was centered largely in durable goods, with a sharp drop in automobile sales and a slackening of consumer demand for large-ticket items in furniture and appliance lines. The availability of government unemployment insurance benefits, as well as of privately negotiated supplement unemployment benefits, tempers the impact of recession on consumer spending in modern times but does not alter the fundamental nature of the findings presented in Tables 21–4 and 21–5.

GREATER NATIONAL INCOME MORE EVENLY DISTRIBUTED

In recent times there have been significant changes in the income structure in America. This is plainly evidenced when columns (*b*), (*c*), (*d*), and (*e*) of Table 21–6 are compared—especially column (*b*) for 1929 and column (*e*) for 1957. This comparison reveals that, in terms of dollars of stable purchasing power, only 41 per cent of American households were receiving $3,000 a year or over in 1929,

Table 21–6. Distribution of American Households by Total Money Income—
1929, 1935/36, 1944, 1957
(in dollars of 1954 purchasing power)

Money Income (a)	Per Cent in Income Category			
	1929 (b)	1935/36 (c)	1944 (d)	1957 (e)
Less than $1,500	21	29	23	21
$1,500 – $3,000	38	40	22	16
$3,000 – $4,500	19 ⎫	18	21	18.5 ⎫
$4,500 – $6,000	9 ⎬ 41%	7	16	17.5 ⎬ 63%
$6,000 and above	13 ⎭	6	18	27 ⎭

SOURCE: Department of Commerce, Bureau of the Census. Adapted from various issues in Series P–60 of *Current Population Reports, Consumer Incomes.* The 1957 figures are estimated from issue No. 29, June, 1958, and *Federal Reserve Bulletin,* September, 1958, supplementary Table 1, p. 105.

whereas 63 per cent of American households were receiving $3,000 or over in 1957.

The primary meaning of America's new structure of personal incomes is the considerably extended market for goods and services. The recession year of 1954 serves as an example.

If personal income had been distributed in the same proportions in 1929 as in 1954, $166 billion of consumption (in 1954 dollars) would have been undertaken. Actual consumer spending was $128 billion in 1929. Alternatively, if personal income distribution in 1954 had been in the same proportion as in 1929, only $180 billion would have been spent by consumers in 1954 instead of the $238 billion actually spent. With only $180 billion of goods and services being sold, the demand for labor would have declined more sharply than it did. Sixteen million persons would have been wholly or partially unemployed in 1954, instead of an actual 5 million.

From 1929 to 1947 some redistribution of income occurred. American trade unions have now grown strong: (1) because of their own and successful organizational efforts; (2) because of winning recognition from manufacturers in key lines of American industry; and (3) as a result of federal and state legislation favoring collective bargaining between labor and management. (This is discussed in Chapters 24 and 25.) At the same time, American management proved itself willing and able to adapt to the new order of things in the labor market. It might be said that from 1936 onward, people went to work at union wages, which employers were prepared to match and sometimes exceed, even though their workers were not

epresented by a labor union affiliated with the American Federation
f Labor (AFL) or the Congress of Industrial Organizations (CIO),
ow merged into the American trade union center (AFL-CIO).

Also contributory to the rise in the economic status of low income
roups and lower-middle income groups has been the social security
ystem, with its retirement, disability, and unemployment benefits.
This has caused the "transfer payments" element of aggregate per-
onal income to rise from 2 per cent of personal income, in 1929, to
7 per cent in August, 1958. In 1929 transfer payments were mainly
comprised of military pension and civil service retirement benefits; in
1958, although these benefits had grown in volume, they were far
overshadowed by transfer payments taking the form of old-age and
urvivors' insurance benefits, payments made under public assistance
programs, expenditures for public health services, unemployment and
workmen's compensation payments, and other types of payments
cushioning the shocks of income losses to the individual and the
nation alike.

RECENT DEVELOPMENTS IN INCOME DISTRIBUTION

Since World War II great impacts have been made on living standards by successive increases in output and employment, rather than
by income redistribution. A way to summarize recent changes in
relative income distribution is to compare relative increases in nine
out of ten equal-size groups of American spending units. That is,
we divide the 56 million spending units of 1957 into ten equal sections, each containing 5.6 million spending units. Turning from this
numerical array for a moment, let us find out how many spending
units fall into income categories of, say, under $1,000 a year, $1,000–
$2,000 a year, and so forth. In 1957, approximately 4.5 million
spending units had an income of $1,000 or less and 7.3 million spend-
ing units were in the category of from $1,000–$2,000, for a total of
11.8 million spending units receiving $2,000 or less. This makes it
evident that the income of the lowest tenth (5.6 million) of the 56
million spending units was more than $1,000 and less than $2,000 a
year. If we have income data in sufficiently detailed form, we can
determine exactly the highest income of that lowest tenth. The federal
government has these detailed data, and the income information for
all but the highest tenth of the spending units is given here in Table
21–7.

The reason for the lack of data on the highest tenth is that such data
are not based on the income of every spending unit but on limited
samples, and it is difficult to arrive at a representative sample in the
high-income group. The inclusion of only a few spending units having

Table 21–7. Absolute and Percentage Change of Income Distribution,
1935/36 to 1947, and 1947 to 1957, Shown by Income Tenths
(in current dollars)

Rank	Highest Income Within Tenth			Percentage Change	
	1935/36	1947	1957	1935/36 to 1947	1947 to 1957
Highest tenth	*	*	*	*	*
Second	$2,800	$5,700	$9,050	+ 104	+ 59
Third	2,050	4,200	7,190	+ 105	+ 71
Fourth	1,675	3,500	6,010	+ 109	+ 71
Fifth	1,373	3,000	5,140	+ 119	+ 71
Sixth	1,160	2,550	4,350	+ 120	+ 71
Seventh	970	2,100	3,600	+ 116	+ 71
Eighth	800	1,700	2,760	+ 113	+ 62
Ninth	610	1,200	1,890	+ 97	+ 58
Lowest tenth	410	750	1,140	+ 83	+ 52

* Data not available.

SOURCE: For 1935/36 data, *Consumer Incomes in the United States—Their Distribution in 1935–36* (Washington, D.C.: National Resources Committee, 1938), Tabl 6B, p. 96. For 1947 data, *Federal Reserve Bulletin*, June, 1955, supplementary Tabl 5, p. 616. For 1957 data, *Federal Reserve Bulletin*, September, 1958, supplementar Table 4, p. 1053.

extremely high incomes might distort the picture considerably. Govern ment statisticians find that, in guarding against this, "the share o income received by high-income recipients is probably understated." So it is just as well to omit the highest tenth of American incom recipients from our considerations.

Data on the highest incomes received in all but the highest tentl of American spending units can be used to shed light on recen changes in relative income distribution. If all incomes had increase proportionately in the recent past, the percentage changes in the highes incomes received by each of the nine income-tenths considered woul have been equal, from year to year or for any other time interva chosen. Table 21–7 shows that this has not been the case. The dat show, instead, that from 1935/36 to 1947, the middle-income spend ing unit tenths gained additional income at a greater rate than did th second- and third-highest income tenths and the two lowest incom tenths. If this period is more closely analyzed, it will be found tha most of the strikingly greater relative gains of the middle-incom tenths of spending units occurred between 1935/36 and 1941. Durin World War II the lower-income spending units experienced th greatest gains in income positions; this ceased in 1944 (as reliabl

[1] *Federal Reserve Bulletin*, September, 1958, Technical Appendix, p. 1046.

lata, not here shown, prove).[2] As noted, since World War II gains
have been made in living standards by successive increases in national
output and employment, rather than by income redistribution.

Pockets of Poverty

The foregoing survey must not blind us to the fact that poverty
persists, even though it occurs in isolated pockets throughout the na-
ion. The fact remains—to challenge us—that there is a lower seventh
of American families and unattached individuals receiving incomes
which are inadequate for sustaining a minimum living standard of
comfort and decency.

In 1956, a year of prosperity, there were 43.5 million families and
9.5 million unattached individuals. How many of these families and un-
elated individuals experienced absolute need? Bench marks to denote
poverty for different types of families and individuals are required to
answer this question. It is possible to estimate such bench marks by
he use of selected budgets prepared by private and government agencies. These budgets define the minimum income necessary for a "modest but adequate plane of living." Poverty bench marks to indicate
incomes below which there is absolute need are shown in Table 21–8.

Table 21–8. Definitions of Need for Spending Units of Different Sizes, 1956

Size and Type of Unit	Minimum Income Required To Prevent Poverty
Single person	
farm	$ 500.00
nonfarm	1,000.00
Families	
farm	1,000.00
nonfarm rural	1,500.00
urban	2,000.00

SOURCES: Estimated on the basis of: (1) Studies of the Heller Committee, University
of California, at Berkeley; (2) WPA Budget, 1935; (3) City Worker's Family Budget,
U.S. Bureau of Labor Statistics, 1946 and revised. See also, Hearings before the
Subcommittee on Low-Income Families of the Joint Committee on the Economic
Report, Congress of the United States, 84th Congress, 1st Session (Washington, D.C.:
Government Printing Office, 1955); "Selected Materials Assembled by the Staff of
the Subcommittee on Low-Income Families," Joint Committee on the Economic
Report, 84th Congress, 1st Session (Washington, D.C.: Government Printing Office,
1955).

[2] See Selma Goldsmith, George Jazi, Hyman Kaitz, and Maurice Liebenberg, "Size
Distribution of Income Since the Mid-Thirties," *Review of Economic Statistics* (Har-
ard University), vol. 36, No. 1 (February 1954), pp. 1–32.

Applying these bench marks of poverty to the official data on the 1956 income distribution, we arrive at Table 21–9, which discloses the poverty situation.

Table 21–9. Mid-twentieth Century Poverty

Size and Type of Unit	Receiving less than:	Number, millions
Single person		
farm	$ 500.00	.2
nonfarm	1,000.00	3.6
		3.8 million
Families		
farm	1,000.00	1.1
nonfarm rural	1,500.00	1.2
urban	2,000.00	2.9
		5.2 million
At 4 persons a family, total impoverished individuals		24.6 million

SOURCE: Department of Commerce, Bureau of the Census, *Current Population Reports, Consumer Income,* Series P–60, No. 27 (April 1958), Table 1, p. 2.

When Franklin D. Roosevelt was President in the 1930's, he stated, on the basis of documented fact, that "one-third of the nation is ill-fed, ill-housed, and poorly clothed." A recent figure is 14.6 per cent, one-seventh of the nation (1956 population = 168 million).

MAJOR CAUSES OF POVERTY

Regional maladjustments, racial discrimination, educational deficiencies, lack of skill, as well as poor health and broken homes, create pockets of poverty throughout the nation. A paradox of modern economic society is the continuation, during periods of full employment, of geographic pockets in which chronic unemployment and underemployment are excessively high.

Temporary layoff and sporadic employment as poverty factors. Steel and automobile production centers are not characterized by chronic unemployment, but temporary layoffs of hundreds of thousands of workers are not uncommon. Workers at any skill level experience this as a definite income-deteriorating factor; this is why the demand for a "guaranteed annual wage" has been so insistent in those areas.

Intermittent employment is the rule for many workers in the age-range beyond 45; practically every major labor market has a complement of such workers who count on employment only when their locality's economic activity is unusually high.

Long-run depressed areas. Coal mining and the textile industry have een subjected to long-term cutbacks and have been characterized by hronic unemployment, especially in New England textile production nd in Pennsylvania anthracite coal production. In the northern Great _akes area there has been chronic unemployment owing to the deple- ion of the Mesabi iron ore range. The lumber regions of upstate Visconsin and Michigan have similarly declined.

In agriculture 1.25 million farm families have money incomes of ess than $1,000. Approximately two-thirds of these families are ocated in the South, as Table 21–10 shows.

Table 21–10. Rural Farm Families in the United States and Their Total Money Incomes in 1954, by Region and by Color in the South

Region	Total (millions)	Under $1,000	$1,000 to $2,000	$2,000 and over
Northeast	.457	.049	.091	.317
North Central	2.064	.396	.432	1.236
South	2.329	.933	.628	.768
white	1.851	.622	.530	.699
nonwhite	.478	.311	.098	.069
West	.376	.054	.064	.258
Total	5.226	1.432	1.215	2.579

SOURCE: "Characteristics of the Low-Income Population and Related Federal Pro- grams," selected materials assembled by the Staff of the Subcommittee on Low-In- come Families, Joint Committee on the Economic Report, 84th Congress, 1st Session (Washington, D.C.: Government Printing Office, 1955), Table 7, p. 12.

Race and poverty. Racial economic handicap is difficult to measure, nor does it apply merely to Negroes. However, if the percentages of southern white and southern nonwhite farmers in the three income categories in Table 21–10 are computed, it is seen that 65 per cent of the southern nonwhite farmer families earn under $1,000, as com- pared with 34 per cent of the white farm families. The nonwhite southern farm families comprise only one-tenth of the nation's farm families but account for one-fifth of all farm families in the lowest income group.

Education. There is a striking relation between education and the poverty level. One in every twelve college graduates earns $2,000 or less; for high school graduates the proportion is one in every eight; but almost one in every two people earning less than $2,000 has only a grade school education. During the Korean war the Armed Forces rejected 14 per cent of persons between eighteen and twenty-six years of age for reasons of intellectual and educational deficiency; not included in this percentage are mentally diseased persons. This high rate of rejection occurred despite the fact that the educational standard for rejection was less than a third-grade education.

Lack of skill. The recession year of 1954 illustrates how low skill or absence of skill correlates with unemployment. Of the unemployed persons who claimed and received government unemployment insurance benefits, two-thirds were unskilled workers. The total acknowledged unemployment was 5 per cent of the civilian labor force. But unemployment among unskilled workers was 10 per cent.

Broken homes. This is a prime cause of poverty. One out of every seven low-income families in American cities has only one adult taking care of one or more children, but only one out of every twenty middle-income families is in this unfortunate position. Usually the income of a family broken by death, divorce, or desertion is half or less of the income of the ordinary family. This is most often due to the fact that the sole head of the family must spend time with the children and cannot afford to accept a full-time paying position. Or if this can be done, the job must be near the home, often in a low-paying menial occupation.

Illness. Some 2 million persons have long-term physical disabilities about half of these persons cannot work at all. The rest are frequently employed at low wages because of the disability and are under the constant hazard of losing their jobs as a result of their condition.

It is apropos to summarize our total poverty situation in the words of former President Truman, who informed Congress in his January 1953, economic report that:

The problem of low income families is no longer caused by general unemployment, or generally substandard wages, or very low prices for farm products The problem centers in families with special disabilities: racial minority families, broken families, families with sickness, families where there is lack of sufficient training and education for the principal wage earner, and farm families on substandard farms. . . .

It is feasible within a decade [by 1963] to raise all the families whose incomes are now below $4,000 annually to that level plus providing all the new families with this much income, in a full employment economy. We should set this as a target for a basic American standard of living for all within a decade. In fact this would require less than half the total gain in personal incomes that we can achieve, leaving more than half for raising still further the incomes of families already above this basic standard.[3]

[3] *The Economic Report of the President,* transmitted to Congress, January, 1953 together with a report to the President, "The Annual Economic Review," by the Council of Economic Advisers (Washington, D.C.: Government Printing Office 1953), p. 25. Also see subsequent *Economic Reports of the President,* for example that of January 24, 1956, where in part similar statements will be found.

The Wealth of Families and Individuals

Although income is the prime determinant of aggregate effective emand, a strong secondary influence is exerted by the store of peo-le's possessions; specifically, by the ownership equity they have in hese possessions. Personal wealth includes tangible items as well as ntangible ones. Just as there are producers' durables so are there onsumers' durables—a home, a deepfreeze, a car, a partially auto-ated kitchen, and so on. Intangible consumer assets are comprised f cash on hand or deposits in the bank, private and public securities wned, shares in savings and loan associations, and other financial ssets. Cash and readily marketable securities, as well as savings eposits, are termed "liquid assets."

Table 21–11. Growth of Consumers' Assets, United States, 1957
(in $ billions)

New Tangible Consumer Assets and Related Transactions		
New housing	$15.2	
New consumers' durables	35.0	
Construction and equipment by nonprofit bodies	2.4	
Increase of mortgage debt	8.3	
Increase of instalment debt	2.6	
Total of tangible assets and related transactions		$63.5
New Intangible Consumer Assets		
Liquid assets		
Currency and deposits	$ 6.0	
Shares held in savings and loan associations	4.8	
U.S. savings bonds	—1.9	
Normally marketable securities		
Securities of private corporations	4.4	
Government securities	3.7	
Not readily marketable assets		
Private insurance and pension reserves	7.9	
Government insurance	2.3	
Total of intangible assets		$27.2
Grand Total		$90.7

ource: Based on *Statistical Abstract of the United States, 1958,* Table 390, p. 309, ut using a different concept of saving.

Quite apart from the influence of currently earned income, there ; a distinct impact of consumers' wealth on total national spending. his was dramatically brought forth after World War II, when a epression would have transpired had consumers confined their spend-g within the limits of their current incomes while holding on to their artime savings.

In 1946 manufacturing employment declined by 6 per cent and payrolls by 8 per cent after both had already diminished in 1945 subsequent to the German surrender. Unemployment reached a figure of 2.5 million; at the same time 3.5 million women returned to their roles as homemakers. Despite this, 2.5 million more jobs were filled in 1946 than in 1945 as returning veterans were absorbed into industry. That is the number of people who might well have gone without work had Americans used only their current incomes for spending. However, they not only spent their current incomes but drew on their wartime savings as well. Furthermore, they went into debt, through the medium of massive instalment buying, in an effort to procure the many durables which had been denied them because of wartime rationing. Table 21–11 shows that personal wealth is not static.

Tangible Consumers' Assets

HOME OWNERSHIP

Of newly married families whose head is from eighteen to twenty-four years of age, 10 per cent own their homes; the figure is 40 per cent when the family head is twenty-five to thirty-four years old. Two out of every three middle-aged spending units own a home, as do three out of every four persons between the ages of fifty-five and sixty-five. In view of the increasing life-span it is good to note that two out of every three married couples above the age of sixty-five are home-owners able to spend their last years in familiar surroundings.

It would be hasty to conclude that the housing problem has been solved. Annual surveys of consumer attitudes toward present housing

Table 21–12. Housing Status of Nonfarm Families, 1958

Home Ownership	Percentage
By Income Groups	
Low income (under $2,000)	40
Lower middle income ($2,000–$5,000)	45
Upper middle income ($5,000–$10,000)	68
High income ($10,000 and over)	76
By Occupation	
Unskilled and services	38
Semiskilled labor	46
Skilled labor	63
Managerial persons	72
Self-employed	79

SOURCE: *Federal Reserve Bulletin*, July, 1958, supplementary Table 12, p. 773.

arrangements suggest that one-third of all home-owners either are positively dissatisfied or are not fully satisfied with their present arrangements. Fully one-half of the people who rent homes feel that way.

HOUSEHOLD EQUIPMENT

The household investment habits revealed in Table 21–11 and Table 21–12 suggest that the American home is well equipped. Two n every 3 urban dwelling units have central heating. Only 1 per cent of houses are not heated at all. In most cities practically every house has a kitchen sink, although in a few cities up to 40 per cent of the houses do not. If there are homes without radios, it is by choice, and television antennas obtrude wherever one looks. Refrigerators are durable household staples, and in some cities up to 98 per cent of the houses are equipped with them; the average for all cities is 80 per cent.

AUTOMOBILES

The auto is a most important symbol of social status (besides being useful in getting around). It is therefore interesting to observe how car possession is distributed among spending units in relation to their incomes (see Table 21–13).

American automobile buyers show the rest of the world a new form of economic behavior in that cars are bought chiefly in terms of "trade-in value." The reason is a practical one: the trade-in value constitutes the down payment on a new car. Careful shopping is done to ascertain which of many dealers will offer the most advantageous price for one's used car. Approximately two-thirds of all cars, new

Table 21–13. Automobile Ownership Within Income Groups, 1958

Groups by Income Before Taxes	Percentage Owning Cars		Percentage Owning a Car 10 or More Years Old (1957)
	1 Auto	2 or More	
Less than $1,000	31	1	24
$1,000–1,999	36	2	26
$2,000–2,999	54	6	13
$3,000–3,999	61	7	12
$4,000–4,999	69	9	12
$5,000–7,499	75	14	8
$7,500–9,999	69	25	5
$10,000 and over	59	34	....

SOURCE: *Federal Reserve Bulletin*, July, 1958, supplementary Tables 8 and 9, pp. 771–72; June, 1957, supplementary Tables 11 and 12, pp. 642–43.

and used, are bought on credit. And in the big automobile sales year of 1955 fully 85 per cent of new cars, as well as half of the used cars which were purchased, were bought on a trade-in basis.

Credit buying on a trade-in basis is not limited to car purchases. One-half of the furniture, TV, refrigerator, and washing machine business is done on credit terms, though trade-in values so dwindle in those cases that they resemble a modest discount offered with the added courtesy of the merchant hauling the old equipment away. The Singer Sewing Machine Company has conducted much of its business on a credit basis since 1857. Curiously, it was only in the late 1920's that instalment buying of consumer goods became respectable. Since that time it may be said it has become indispensable.

Intangible Consumer Assets

These are liquid assets: cash balances usually held in a checking account at the bank, postal savings, bank savings accounts and time deposits, United States Government savings bonds, shares in savings and loan associations, and shares in credit unions. Cash balances are perfectly liquid; they represent generalized purchasing power. The other items are illiquid to the extent that they have to be turned into cash before constituting purchasing power, but the degree of illiquidity is low for these items.

With normal peacetime production it is in no way disturbing for people to hold liquid assets as financial line-backing in case an emergency should develop or an opportunity presents itself to make a good buy or do a good deed. In fact, it is wise home economics to do so. And from the point of view of society liquid assets that are held when production is in full swing do not represent hoarding of the kind that draws purchasing power out of circulation. The reason is that under conditions of full employment cash balances held at the bank are invested by the bank in productive short-term loans to businessmen who need temporary financial accommodation in marketing things that have already been produced.

Government bonds, when issued for economic development purposes, are backed by public wealth in the form of parks, museums, highways, and other projects the fruits of which families and individuals can enjoy as part of their plane of living. Shares in building and loan associations are certificates of participation in quasi-cooperative home development projects, while shares in credit unions reveal that people are lending funds to their immediate work associates. The credit union is a truly cooperative venture under which money is lent ₙnder the very closely controlled condition of everybody's work ncome being known to all the others.

It is because one can normally expect real physical wealth, wrought ɔy production, to back up liquid assets that it is both safe and wise ₒ hold some liquid assets. For even though they are only intangible ϲlaims to wealth, the point is that tangible wealth is there to be real-zed if a need or want arises.

At least three-quarters of American spending units have some ιquid assets.[4] About half of the holdings are worth $750 or less; 90 ɔer cent are worth less than $5,000. The size of holdings for each ːamily or for each unrelated individual, or whether any liquid assets ∪re owned at all, varies with the income earned. Table 21–14 illus-ːrates this.

Table 21–14. Liquid Asset Holdings and Their Composition,
by Income Groups, 1958

Groups by Income Before Taxes	Percentage with Savings Accounts and Savings Bonds Worth $500 or More	Percentage with No Liquid Assets
Less than $1,000	8	62
$1,000–1,999	13	50
$2,000–2,999	16	37
$3,000–3,999	17	32
$4,000–4,999	18	25
$5,000–7,499	23	13
$7,500–9,999	32	2
$10,000 and over	40	1

SOURCE: *Federal Reserve Bulletin,* September, 1958, supplementary Table 7, p. 1054; see pp. 1049–50 for explanation of difficulties of estimating values of checking accounts, which are therefore not included in this table.

Ownership of corporate securities. Savings deposits and government savings bonds are truly liquid assets because they can readily be cashed without appreciable loss. By contrast, corporate stocks may fluctuate widely in value, their lows being reached precisely when family incomes may be diminished by loss of earnings during a depres-sion. A sound economic approach for individuals to follow is, there-

[4] Government statisticians experience difficulty in appraising the aggregate amount of liquid assets owned by all American spending units or by various groups of spending units. The difficulty stems in large part from inadequate reporting; it is most pronounced in the case of corporate stocks. Stock ownership is quite concentrated, so that the chance exclusion of a few large holders from a sample can significantly understate the estimated total of stock ownership. See *Federal Reserve Bulletin,* September 1958, Technical Appendix, especially pp. 1050–51.

fore, to first acquire tangible home ownership, then put away something in the form of insurance, savings deposits and savings bonds, and only then get into stock ownership. This is also sound business economics, for it spares the investment house the costs of handling accounts of people who cannot really afford to be in the market. And it is good national economics because mere stock speculation by masses of persons who do not have sufficient funds is a factor that accentuates unhealthy booms that are sooner or later followed by busts.

As a matter of fact, one out of nine spending units (11 per cent) owns corporate stock. However, practically no spending unit earning less than $5,000 a year is among this 11 per cent of all spending units.

LIFE INSURANCE

Four out of five American spending units carry life insurance, that is, 80 per cent. In more than half of the cases, premium payments range from $100 to $500 annually. These are national statistics. In a more intimate view, Table 21–15 shows different amounts of life insurance contracted for by 977 families of four persons, the adults being typically aged thirty-five, earning typically $5,400 a year (in 1954) as compared with a national median family income of $4,100.

Table 21–15. Life Insurance Provisions of 977 Families Surveyed in 1954, Including Group Insurance and GI Policies

QUESTION: Do either you (or your wife, husband) have any life insurance? If "yes," about how much in all, including group and GI policies?

	Total	Male	Female
Number of Respondents	977 (100%)	492 (100%)	485 (100%)
YES, have life insurance	83%	89%	77%
Less than $5,000	15	15	15
$5,000–$10,000	27	29	25
$10,000–$15,000	19	21	16
$15,000–$20,000	10	11	10
$20,000–$25,000	7	8	6
$25,000 or more	5	5	5
NO, do not have life insurance	4	4	4
Don't know	10	3	18
No answer	3	4	1

SOURCE: "The First 100,000 National Homes Families," A Survey by Elmo Roper and Associates, for the National Homes Corporation, builder of prefabricated homes (1955).

In addition to privately contracted insurance and GI insurance, most Americans also make payments on federal social insurance. In connection with social insurance, employers also make a contribution, as they do on private group insurance policies frequently taken out for the employees. Many an American therefore receives more insurance protection than he pays for personally. Insurance premiums paid by employers may be taken out of profits, but they may also be passed on to consumers as added costs of production, or paid by the employer in lieu of wage increases.

Protection of dependents is the major reason for carrying life insurance so far as spending units earning $3,000 or more are concerned; for spending units earning less than $3,000 provision for burial or pre-mortem medical expense warrants carrying life insurance. The higher-income spending units tend to purchase policies which in addition to protection for dependents carry savings features to provide later retirement pensions or provision for the children's college education; many such policies have "cash-surrender values," which means that the fund of savings can be drawn on should the need arise. Most of the persons with medium or lower incomes tend to carry ordinary term life insurance without cash surrender values; this means that the insurance must be renewed at future dates, at higher premium rates corresponding to the advancing age of the policy holder. These policies are cheaper and are in some circles considered to provide the most economical form of purchasing life insurance protection.

The purchaser of life insurance acts upon the recognition that there is safety in numbers. The risk of income loss by premature death of the family's breadwinner is large if it must be individually assumed, but it is relatively small if many persons in different age categories jointly assume it. By analogy, a home-owner would have to store a great quantity of water to guard against fire, but the incidence of fire is small for any community. Pooling funds for financing centralized fire protection demands only a small contribution from each member of a community. It is sometimes said that in buying life insurance one gambles against other policy-holders. For if they outlive us, they must continue to pay premiums without receiving benefits. But the benefit is daily provided in the sense of security achieved upon purchase of insurance. And the risk involved is a natural one; it is not one which is created as is the case with gambling.

The ownership of life insurance policies and the amount of premium payment vary directly with the income of spending units, as Table 21–16 shows.

Table 21–16. Life Insurance Premiums Within Income Groups, 1956
(Percentage distribution of spending units within income groups)

Income Before Taxes	All Spending Units	Does Not Own Policy	Owns Policy	Average Annual Amount of Premium Payment (Mode)
Under $1,000	100%	57%	43%	$ 50
$1,000–2,000	100	47	53	75
$2,000–3,000	100	33	67	100
$3,000–4,000	100	19	81	150
$4,000–5,000	100	9	91	200
$5,000–7,500	100	7	93	250
$7,500–10,000	100	3	97	350
$10,000 and over	100	4	96	750

SOURCE: *Federal Reserve Bulletin*, August, 1957, supplementary Table 12, p. 898; column 5 is an inspection mode based upon a detailed breakdown in the original source.

For Discussion

1. If the income trends which characterized the period 1935/36 had continued to the present and were to be resumed in the future, would poverty be eliminated? Would people lose their incentives to get ahead?

2. Among the causes *not* listed as producing poverty is the personal factor of laziness. Would you include it as a major factor?

3. Do you think consumer capitalism is a fortunate expression to describe our present economic system?

4. What is the impact of a depression on the *directions* of consumer expenditures? What is the impact of prosperity?

5. What light do actual statistics shed on the assumption that there can be general overproduction because basic wants for housing, food, and clothing are limited?

6. Could we get along without the present high level of military spending?

7. "The poor are always with us." Does this ancient sentiment gain support from the data which show that in 1929, in 1935/36, and in 1957 some 20 per cent of income recipients were earning $1,500 or less?

8. "The rich and the poor are really equal, because when they spend their dollars they are expressing their preferences in terms of the same dollar yardstick." Comment.

9. Why are savings accounts and savings and loan association shares considered as part of liquid consumer assets, in view of the fact that banks and savings and loan associations can legally demand advance notice for a period of time prior to withdrawal of the money?

10. Late in 1957, construction on new residential housing dropped from an annual rate of 1.3 million to 970,000 units. Is this normal and desirable in view of the fact that prices of consumer goods were rising and that a good deal of concern was being expressed about continuing "inflation"?

11. How can a family's home economics be conducted rationally without iving up the new concept of savings; i.e., the practice of paying on the instalnent plan and considering this a part of savings?

12. Ownership of stocks is fairly closely restricted; perhaps not more than ne in ten spending units own any corporate securities. What would be the best vay of spreading stock ownership: more aggressive salesmanship? permitting tocks to be bought on the instalment plan? improving the income-positions of ower-income recipients? or any combination thereof? What other means come ɔ mind? Why do college graduates have a higher percentage of stock ownerhip than people generally?

22 General Theory

of Distribution

The gross national product (GNP) is the source of all income. GNP, the value at market prices of the annual national production, cannot in its entirety be distributed in the form of money incomes to persons. A part of the gross national product must first be set aside by entrepreneurs to provide for depreciation; some of it is withheld from consumers by the medium of indirect business taxes; and entrepreneurs retain a part of dividends gained for business expansion.

The remainder, after these financial provisions have been made, is the grand total of consumer incomes before taxes. This large sum of money is comprised of: (1) wages and salaries that private entrepreneurs and public agencies pay; (2) incomes paid to owners of property used in production; (3) transfer payments received by qualifying persons, principally veterans, aged persons, dependent children, and registered unemployed persons. Americans also make social security contributions; these are deducted from the paycheck of wage-earners by their employers, or paid by self-employed persons directly to the Social Security Administration. Table 22–1 illustrates total consumer income before taxes.

Comments on Table 22–1. The amounts shown were not actually distributed in the single months of August, 1957, and August 1958. These amounts show what *would have been paid out* during the

546

entire year 1957 or 1958 had incomes been earned and distributed throughout the year at the same rate as during the month of August. Seasonal factors which uniquely affect the distribution of income during the month of August have been allowed for; that is, they have been statistically "eliminated."

Table 22–1. The American Distribution Ledger, August, 1957,
and August, 1958

(In $ billions of stable 1958 purchasing power)

AUGUST, 1957			AUGUST, 1958		
Type of Income	Amount	Per Cent	Type of Income	Amount	Per Cent
Proprietors' and rental income	$ 57.0	14.9	Proprietors' and rental income	$ 56.4	15.0
Personal interest income and dividends	32.6	8.5	Personal interest income and dividends	31.9	8.5
Labor income	256.0	67.0	Labor income	247.5	65.6
Social security contributions	14.4	3.8	Social security contributions	14.5	3.8
Transfer payments	22.0	5.8	Transfer payments	26.7	7.1
Income before personal taxes	$382.0	100.0	Income before personal taxes	$377.0	100.0

SOURCE: *Federal Reserve Bulletin,* September, 1958, pp. 1122–23.

The sum totals of consumer income before taxes are not identical with the amounts which government statisticians report as *personal income* (see Chapter 2). In the government's computation of personal income, social security contributions of employees (nearly $7 billion) are deducted, and the contributions of employers to social insurance (somewhat more than $7 billion) are not recorded at all. This procedure is warranted in the government's national income accounting, which is primarily oriented toward problems of full employment. In this context income distribution is naturally viewed in terms of the contribution it makes to the stream of spendable income available for buying the results of current production. However, one can also view income distribution from the standpoint of how equitable it may be, and how sound it is *qualitatively* speaking. In both these aspects the social security contributions of employees and self-employed persons, as well as the contributions made by employers, must be taken into account. The social security system makes a real difference in the way we share national income today as compared to the way it was shared before 1937. At present, practically every employed and self-employed person can look forward to retiring on an annuity which in earlier times would have cost him, on a rough calculation, $40,000 and upwards to purchase.

Supply and Demand Theory of Income Distribution

Economic theory contemplates that the sum of available consumer incomes is disbursed by private entrepreneurs and public agencies in paying for productive services or contracting to pay for them. These income payments will be made out of sales revenue and, in the case of government, out of tax revenue, augmented at times by government deficit borrowing. Thus in a general view of the process of income distribution, entrepreneurs and public officials may be seen as standing at the center of the nation's monetary circulation. They receive inflows of purchasing power and disburse this power in the form of money incomes to the factors of production—land, labor, capital—and to the recipients of transfer payments. The ensuing explanation of income distribution is confined to income payments made for productive services; these income payments of course constitute more than 90 per cent of consumer incomes.

ECONOMIC EQUIVALENCE OF PRODUCTIVE SERVICES

There are literally millions of different types of productive resources, although these many varieties can be classified under only three broad distribution categories, namely, land, labor, and capital. A book-keeper is a type of human resource, a machinist is another type, and so forth through the many pages of the Labor Department's *Dictionary of Occupations*. Similarly a bookkeeping machine is a type of man-made resource, a steamshovel is another type, and so forth. Then again, there is cropland suitable for the cultivation of avocados, land suitable for wheat growing, for pasture, and so on.

Incomes paid to owners of these different resources differ first of all in accordance with the supply and demand for the various specialized types. In older schools of economic thought the refined differences between specialized types of land, labor, and capital services were ignored. Distribution was analyzed from separate viewpoints of three different types of compensable sacrifices, made, respectively, by owners of land, by labor, and by owners of capital resources. Working people and managers in performing their services incur a real cost measured by fatigue and by the sacrifice of leisure. For this toil and trouble labor must be rewarded by at least a minimum subsistence wage— if labor supplies are to be continuously forthcoming. The cost incurred by owners of capital, which must be compensated, was held to be the inconvenience of abstaining from consumption in order to possess loanable capital. To allow one's land to be used productively was considered as only entailing an "opportunity cost"—the "cost" of foregoing alternative avenues to gain when renting one's land to a particular kind of user.

Except in the case of capital, this classical approach is by no means wrong. Detailed explanations of income distribution continue to be made under the three headings of Rent, Interest, and Wages. However, a *general* theory of income distribution has been developed which places on the same footing the ability of land and labor and capital services to gain income. All income gained is in modern *general* theory measured by opportunity cost incurred by each owner of any type of resource. This is, as has been said, the "cost" of foregoing income that might be earned by permitting use to be made *in alternative ways* of one's specialized personal efforts and/or one's specialized property resources.

To clarify this generalized viewpoint let each owner of any unit of a valuable resource, of any type, be seen as exchanging units of the resource for units of purchasing power. Now the amount of purchasing power which a wage-earner or a property-owner demands will depend upon the reward which he considers just worthwhile. A wage-earner or salary-earner may have to be given a financial incentive for working at all rather than remaining at leisure; a property-owner may need an incentive for permitting his land to be used rather than letting it lie idle. As regards any particular type of labor, a wage-earner must be assured that in a given occupation he can earn at least as much as on other jobs available to him; likewise an owner of land on which avocados can be grown must receive as rental at least as much as he could gain by permitting the land to be used for orange cultivation.

Productive Services Supply Schedules

Given the basic supplies of resources, that is, of factors of production, greater or lesser amounts *of the services* of these resources can theoretically be obtained, *depending upon the reward which is offered.* At a relatively high rate of interest, for example, more money capital may become available for loan. This effect is within the limit of money which has been saved, by persons and institutions; loan funds are also circumscribed by the banking system's limit of credit creation. However, the point is, that at a high rate of interest some persons or institutions will make their savings more extensively available for investment, and banks will feel encouraged to lend freely. The question of whether or not a high rate of interest also encourages people to *save* more money is not involved in this analysis, for the total supply of savings will be assumed to be fixed and given. The only problem is to explain how freely or reluctantly this given supply of savings is made available for loan, depending on different terms at which it might be lent.

Similarly, when wages are high it is presumed that some people, not all, will wish to work longer hours; at the same time a number of persons may enter the labor market who had previously preferred to remain at leisure. Per contra, a diminution of wages would be expected to diminish the supply of work services offered by the members of a given number of population eligible to work. The size of this eligible population, however, is not analyzed; it is simply taken as given. (The classical economists of the eighteenth and early nineteenth centuries represented population as a function of wages, holding that population would increase when wages passed the subsistence minimum and decrease when wages fell below minimum subsistence requirements; this approach has long been abandoned by economists.)

Again, when rentals are high, it is presumed that additional land or subsoil resources will be offered for use, instead of being kept idle. In this case, too, the basic supply of land and subsoil resources is in modern analysis taken as given. (The classical economists also took the basic supply of land as given, arguing that there is an "original fertility of the soil" not created by man nor capable of being renewed when once it is exhausted by poor land utilization or mining practices.)

To summarize, for the purposes of modern distribution analysis there is a *given* limit to the amount of capital, a given total amount of land (to include subsoil resources), and a given population. The owners of these given and basic amounts of resources are motivated to gain profit. They decide on the extent to which they will make the services of their resources available for use. The amounts of productive services offered will vary at different levels of wages, interest, and rentals that might be earned.

By this reasoning one necessarily arrives at service-supply schedules of the factors of production. They will be similar in appearance to supply schedules of finished commodities. The higher the reward offered by entrepreneurs for the use of a unit of a resource, the more of it will theoretically be offered, and vice versa. Table 22–2 exhibits a hypothetical service-supply schedule for a factor of production.

When plotted on a graph, a factor of production supply schedule resembles a commodity supply schedule, rising upward to the right of the graph's point of origin, as is seen in Figure 22–1.

Table 22–2. Service-Supply Schedule of Resource z

Hypothetical List Price per Unit (cents)	Quantity Available at That Price (units)
2	4
3	8
4	11
5	14
6	16
7	18
8	20
9	22
10	23

Comments on Figure 22–1. The locus (location) of a service-supply curve of a resource, and the curve's elasticity have two determinants. First, both the locus of the curve and its elasticity depend on the subjective preferences of the owners of resources, on whether they wish to use their labor, in one or another fashion or wish to have their property used in one way or another. Second, the supply offers of

Figure 22–1. Service-Supply Schedule of Resource z

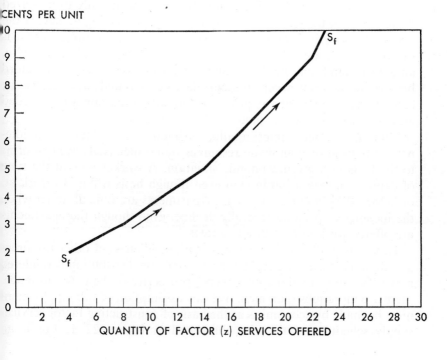

CENTS PER UNIT

QUANTITY OF FACTOR (z) SERVICES OFFERED

owners of resources depend upon their need for income. To illustrate both factors, when operating in conjunction, one may consider the case in which disagreeable work will normally discourage a service-supply of labor. This would be true of the onerous task of handling rotted vegetable cargo in the holds of ships. But if there are many persons who must either perform this work or go without means of subsistence, the work may be performed at very low wages. (This is so, of course, only if there is not a strong stevedore's union which can demand and receive relatively high basic wages plus penalty rates for unloading rotted cargo. The difference may be observed by comparing the conditions of longshoremen in certain North African ports, for example, and in North American ports.) In general, the location and shape of a service-supply schedule for a resource depends on the opportunities open to the owners of the resource for recovering the cost of exerting personal effort, or the pure opportunity cost of letting their property be used in one way rather than in others.

ASSUMPTION OF FULL EMPLOYMENT

A factor service-supply schedule is presumed to reflect comparative evaluations of alternative means of gaining income. This implies among other things that if any unit of a resource remains idle, it is by the free choice of its owner. For if only a poor opportunity exists for gaining income, that is still an opportunity; it needs only to be seized if the owner of the resource is at all interested in making money. If the reward to be gained does not appear worthwhile, the presumption is that a worker, for example, remains *voluntarily* unemployed. Likewise, an acre of land may be deliberately withheld from use by a landlord because he will not accept the current rate of rental, not because he cannot find a tenant at any price. Or money capital might be hoarded although interest is being paid for the use of money.

Now this stringent interpretation of human unemployment or idleness of natural or man-made resources by no means always conforms to the facts of a given economic situation. A worker may at the time of depression seek a job in vain even though he is willing to work at, or below, the going rate of wages. Apartments are difficult to let when the incomes of persons generally decline, even though the apartments are offered for rent at "attractive rates."

By defining all human unemployment or idleness of other resources as voluntary, the theoretical analysis of income distribution is rendered applicable only to times of general prosperity—when, for instance, there are more jobs than men. Yet this assumption of full employment must be made by economists as the basis of constructing factor service-supply schedules of the type illustrated in Figure 22–1. For if an increasing amount of the services of factors of production can be attracted at the same rate of reward or even a declining remuneration, the theoretical conditions under which productive services are supplied do not obtain.

An aid to understanding the theoretical full employment assumption is to conceive of resource-owners as themselves determining the amount of employment of their resources, even though they let for hire, or lend or rent their resources. This again warns us not to overlook the abstract nature of the general theory of income distribution which is being explained. The theory, as will be shown, is useful in understanding the manner in which incomes are based on productive efficiency considerations, to the extent that they are so based. But the general theory of income distribution does not warrant the assertion that a man can always find a job, or a store can always be rented. This is simply not the case when the national income has not reached a full-employment level.

Now the assumption of full employment, which is the foundation of the customary factor service-supply schedule, does not inform us what will be the actual amount of resources utilization under given circumstances. It tells us only that the owners of resources will permit greater or lesser amounts of them to be used, depending upon the rewards which can be gained. Nor does the mere assumption that there is full employment furnish a clue of how any current rate of reward is established. To determine what a going factor-market rate of reward shall be we must take into consideration, besides supply, the *demand* for resources.

Demand for the Factors of Production

Qualitative demand for resources. The demand for resources has two fundamental aspects. One of these is qualitative, in that the demand for productive services depends upon the *kinds* of goods and services which consumers desire. This is a qualitative consideration because desire expresses a relationship, one which exists between a person's aims in life and material objects or services of other persons. These goods and services are expected to contribute toward a realization of the person's aspirations. In the earlier discussion of demand for commodities, the qualitative aspect of demand was labeled "utility." Consumers do not directly ascribe utility to resources, as they do to commodities. But commodities can only be produced by a transformation of resources into utilitarian goods and services. (Let us recall that a commodity may be utilitarian without being necessarily useful—as is the case with many goods that are acquired only to keep up appearance.)

Economists express the relation of consumers' preferences for goods and services to the demand for the resources needed to produce them by saying that the demand for resources is a *derived* demand. The direct approach to owners of resources is usually made by the entrepreneurs. Only in rare instances will factors of production be directly used by the consumers. For example, most people prefer to have their house built by contractors instead of buying their own lumber, cement, roofing, and so on, and then hiring different types of construction workers to assemble the materials.

Quantitative demand for resources. Given the qualitative aspects of the derived demand for resources, the important consideration is how many units of them shall be used and in what combinations. Here the entrepreneur interposes his skill in combining resources to round out the demand for the resources. That is to say, it does not suffice for consumers to desire goods and services; there must also be a technology for producing them. The entrepreneurs manage the technology. If they understand how to manage it well, there will be a stronger demand for factors of production than in the opposite case.

Eighty per cent of the incomes which Americans gain are paid to factors of production by managers of private enterprises which are operated for profit. This means that most units of American resources will be placed into production only so long as their use promises to be profitable. By what criteria does a private entrepreneur judge whether it is profitable to use resources, and to what extent?

Principle of Marginal Revenue Productivity

In strict income distribution theory (as in strict commodity price theory) the aim of the entrepreneur is to maximize profits. This depends in the first place on his ability to sense the qualitative aspect of the demand for finished products and personal services, that is, to know what kinds of goods people desire, or can be persuaded to want.

Beyond this, however, is a physical constraint which operates on the entrepreneur. This is his technical ability to combine factors of production in least-cost combinations. If he is to survive in an industry, he must be able to produce at least with average efficiency, that is, must be able to produce at the least cost of production of the representative firm in the industry. This means that each factor of production, which is relevant to the entrepreneur, must be hired to that extent to which units of the particular resource not only aid in production but assist in reducing the average cost (*atuc*) of an individual firm to the minimum average total unit cost of the industry's representative firm. When it is recalled that literally thousands of specialized subspecies of land, labor, and capital are utilized in the production of complicated modern goods, this practical business of isolating the separate factor-varieties and imputing to each an economic significance would seem impossible to perform. In the overwhelming majority of cases, output is "an omelet."

Nevertheless, it is necessary to unscramble total cost of production in order to attribute, to each amount of cooperating factor used, a separate value. For if this cannot be achieved it would be mere chance that when hiring various amounts of different resources, the entrepreneur should arrive at that sum total of rewards paid to the factor which equals his optimum total cost of production, not some higher total cost of production.

DOSING METHOD OF IMPUTING FACTOR VALUE

Conceptually, by conducting experiments the entrepreneur can isolate the contribution made to total revenue and the addition made to total cost by each factor of production. He can take as fixed and given all factors of production other than one single factor, the use of which can be varied. Then the entrepreneur can add equal and homogeneous doses of the one variable factor, observing what the effect on total sales revenue is.

Under the law of diminishing returns, successive additions of homogeneous units of a variable factor to a fixed and given amount of the other factors entail a proportionately decreasing increment of physical output. The extra output realized by adding another unit of the variable factor is the marginal *physical* product of that factor.

Now under pure competition an individual firm can sell as much or as little of a product as it wishes without changing the price of the product. In other words, whatever the output of the individual firm may be, the price of the product remains constant. If the marginal physical product which results from adding successive doses of a variable factor is multiplied by the constant price of the product, we obtain the *value* of the marginal product. Alternatively stated, each additional unit of a product which is sold brings in additional sales revenue. Multiplying the marginal physical product of a variable factor of production by the additional sales revenue realized from the sale of the marginal physical product yields what in modern terminology is called the *marginal revenue product* (*mrp*).

When the price of a finished commodity is constant, as it would be under pure competition, the marginal revenue product of the variable factor added to the fixed factors must necessarily decline under di-minishing returns. This is the necessary consequence of a proportion-ately declining marginal physical product being multiplied by the constant price of the finished commodity.

When there is pure competition among entrepreneurs in the hiring of units of factors of production, an individual firm can employ few or many units of a factor without changing the price of the factor. Thus we have three basic facts: (1) the individual firm can sell as much or as little of its product as it wishes without changing the price of the commodity; (2) the individual firm can hire as few or as many units of the variable factor of production without changing its rate of remuneration; (3) the marginal revenue product of a variable factor declines under diminishing returns, as more and more units of the variable factor are added to a fixed complement of the other factors.

Under these circumstances how far will an entrepreneur proceed in adding successive doses of the variable factor? The obvious answer is that the entrepreneur will not employ additional units of a variable factor beyond the point at which an additional factor unit costs more than the equivalent of the extra sales revenue contributed by the last-added amount of the variable production factor. Alternatively stated, units of any type of resource will be employed by an entrepreneur up to that point at which its cost equals its marginal revenue product. This is a fundamental, theoretical rule in the hiring of units of all factors of production. Expressing this rule symbolically:

$$mrp \text{ (its marginal revenue product)} = pf \text{ (price of the factor)}$$

Economists conceive of entrepreneurs as determining *for each factor of production* the point at which $mrp = pf$. The entrepreneur hypothetically conducts a series of experiments in which all relevant and costly production factors are variably applied, each in its turn, while all the other factors are in their turn held fixed and constant.

Now suppose that enough units of each factor of production are employed so that in every instance the marginal revenue product of a factor equals its per unit money cost to the entrepreneur. In that event the total amount of money paid to all the factors of production cannot exceed the total revenue received from sales. For if *no single factor* gains a reward greater than the additional sales revenue which it contributes, at the margin of its utilization, *all the factors* together cannot absorb as an aggregate reward more than the total sales revenue which is created by the cooperation of all the factors.

Illustration. For simplicity's sake assume that a farmer can have all the land he wants free of charge and that to work this land he uses his own labor, hires some amounts of labor, and rents mechanical arm equipment (such as a combine or other types of equipment which he does not care to purchase). Since the land is free, it presents no problem for economic analysis. The labor is costly, as is the rented equipment. By labor we shall understand, in this example, not only labor which the farmer hires but the personal effort that he exerts as well.

It is postulated that the money cost of renting a unit of mechanical farm equipment is $1.00 an hour for every hour that the equipment is used. The wage rate for skilled farm labor is taken at $1.90 an hour, which is also what the farmer implicitly considers his time to be worth. Finally, we shall posit that the price for which the farmer's product can be sold is 50 cents a unit.

Suppose now that when using a given amount of free land, the farmer applies to it nine units of rented mechanical equipment and fourteen units of his own and other people's labor. The hourly output of his product, k, we arbitrarily assume to be seventy-four units. The farmer does not consider this to be sufficient, so let us say that he decides to apply another unit of rented equipment. The result is that the output increases to seventy-six units of his product k. To express these facts somewhat differently:

| | Factor Combination | | |
Units of Output	Units of Factor A (rented equipment)	Units of Factor B (labor)	New Output
74	9	14	
	10	14	76

The increase of from seventy-four to seventy-six units of his commodity farm output appears to the farmer hardly worth the extra toil and trouble. However, he notices that in his new combination of the factors of production he lacks sufficient labor to realize optimum gain from the use of ten units of mechanical equipment. He needs another hired hand, or he must apply himself more intensively. We shall suppose that he hires another experienced farm worker. Now his production increases from seventy-six bales of product k to eighty bales an hour. Otherwise expressed:

| | Factor Combination | | |
Units of Output	Units of Factor A	Units of Factor B	New Output
76	10	14	
	10	15	80

With this performance the farmer rests content.

When adding the tenth unit of mechanical equipment, the farmer augmented his output by two bales of product k. This is the marginal *physical* product of the tenth unit of equipment (factor A), leaving undisturbed the amount used of labor (factor B). Multiplying this by 50¢, the unit market price of product k, we obtain as the marginal *revenue* product of mechanical equipment when ten units are used $1.00 for an hour of use of the equipment.

When the farmer next added an extra unit of labor, the fifteenth unit, output increased by another four bales an hour. This is the marginal physical product of labor (*mp*) *when fifteen units are used* Multiplying this *mp* of four bales by 50¢, the farm product's market price, gives $2.00 an hour as the marginal revenue product of labor Evidently, a unit of labor is twice as efficient as a unit of mechanical equipment at this particular eighty-unit output rate of operation. Bear in mind that this is a matter of economic *imputation*. It is not a matter of technological causation. Without other units of factor A, and without units of factor B, the application of any units of factor A equipment would be useless; the application of, say, only one unit of labor to the farmer's free land would be relatively fruitless. Technologically production is joint, but economically the *results* of production may be separately *imputed* to the two different and costly factors of production.

Having imputed $1.00 as the marginal revenue product of an hour's use of rented farm equipment and $2.00 as the marginal revenue productivity of labor, let these *mrp* data be compared with the prices of these factors. The hourly rental price of the equipment is $1.00. The hourly wage of the farmer's labor (or the implicit value of his own labor) is $1.90. With ten units of rented farm equipment used total outlay is $10.00 an hour. Fifteen units of labor are used; hence total outlay for this purpose is approximately $28.00. Total outlay is therefore $38.00 an hour. (It is assumed that the land which is used costs the farmer nothing.)

Now the amount of farm commodity k produced each hour is 80 bales. Each bale sells for 50 cents; hence total income from sales is $40.00. The farmer, by hiring ten units of mechanical equipment and employing fifteen units of labor, breaks even (or does slightly better) In real life, normal profit of 6 to 7 per cent would be included in his income from sales. Consequently, he would benefit from increasing his sales turnover as a result of augmenting his hourly output from seventy-four to eighty bales.

In this illustration it has been assumed that the farmer conducts his affairs so as to obtain for each dollar's worth of factor-input a dollar's worth of sales revenue. A unit of rented equipment costs him $1.00 an hour; the marginal revenue product of the unit of equipment is also $1.00. A unit of labor is rewarded at $1.90 an hour; its marginal revenue product at $2.00 is of approximately the same amount. The interesting implication of this state of affairs is that the farmer could not possibly benefit from changing the proportions of ten units of equipment used on his cost-free land along with fifteen units of labor. Were he to use an eleventh unit of equipment, its marginal revenue product would be less than its cost of $1.00; the marginal revenue product of labor would also decline with a relatively increased utilization of labor.

How to bring entrepreneurial affairs to such profitable fruition is in the final analysis a matter of acquiring practical experience, studying, doing research, attending conferences, and so on, to keep advanced in the field of knowledge. Yet we have seen that under pure competition an entrepreneur would be required in the long run to operate always at the point where his average cost (*atuc*) equals the minimum average total unit cost of his industry's representative firm. This can be accomplished only by making sure that every dollar spent for acquiring units of resources shall yield a dollar's worth of marginal revenue. In other words, the concept of marginal revenue productivity is but the other side of the coin of marginal-cost efficiency.

Difficulty with the dosing method. The dosing method of imputing factor productivity is easy to conceive for broad categories of resources, land, labor, capital, and management. But modern production, in industry or agriculture, involves the use of literally thousands of specialized varieties of these basic factors of production.

Now this is not a major obstacle to the conceptual use of the dosing method of factor-productivity imputation in the case of the utilization of human resources. Labor and management services fall into a relatively limited number of job classifications. Although there are thousands of particular job titles, most of them are different names for a comparatively limited number of basic functions performed by human beings—essentially the work of executives, of professionals, of routine administrators, of supervisors, foremen, skilled, semiskilled, and unskilled labor. In Chapter 23, which deals with the theoretical determination of wages, the dosing method of imputing economic significance to units of labor will be explained in greater detail.

The millions of types of *natural* and *man-made* resources which are utilized in production are not like human effort. Consequently, they cannot readily be placed into broad categories. Take the case of a machinist and his kit of tools. The machinist's particular job description may be one of many, but it is not difficult to classify him as a skilled laborer who fits into one of the top grades of, say, fifteen job grades in a factory. But when we look into his tool kit, it is seen to be filled with several dozen minor items of equipment of different sorts. When we observe the different machines he may operate during a day and their component parts which can be replaced by ordering from a catalog, a forbidding complexity of minor factors of production becomes manifest.

Simultaneous Productivity Imputation

Because it is inordinately difficult to imagine revenue productivity being imputed in turn to every means of production, say, in an automobile factory, we may employ a simple method of simultaneously imputing to several factors of production their respective marginal productivity values. Let us assume for theoretical purposes that in the entire economy only three commodities are produced, P_1, P_2, and P_3. Furthermore, these three commodities are assumed to be produced without the intervention of any intermediate man-made resources, by three primary factors of production alone—labor, management, and a given type of natural resource (x, y, and z.)

We know that at long-run equilibrium the three factors of production, x, y, and z, must gain the same reward regardless of whether they are used to produce commodity P_1, P_2, or P_3. This is due to the operation of the principle of opportunity cost, which tells us that units of the three production factors, x, y, and z, will be shifted by their owners until there is no more advantage in doing so, that is, until their reward in every use is equal as fully shown on pages 575–80.

We also know that at long-run price equilibrium production in the three industries which produce the commodities P_1, P_2, and P_3 takes place at minimum average cost (*atuc*). Combining this theoretical insight with the one immediately above, it is seen that, theoretically, all of the three products are produced at minimum average cost (*atuc*) by each representative firm precisely because only by operating efficiently can each industry effectively compete in attracting productive services that must be paid for at certain rates.

In the case of each product, P_1, P_2, and P_3, we now have two basic facts at our command. First, we not only know the price of the product, but it is also understood that this price measures the least average total unit cost of production. Second, we can in the case of each product ascertain, by observation, the proportions in which factors x, y, and z are actually combined. The respective combination, n the case of each of the three products, is known to be the most efficient combination. Thus:

1. In the production of commodity P_1 the optimum factor combination is four units of resource x combined with three units of resource y and eleven units of resource z. This combination yields one unit of product, which costs 86 cents and can be sold at that price.

2. In the production of commodity P_2, the optimum combination is four units of x with ten units of y with two units of z. The cost of each unit of commodity P_2, when produced with these resource proportions, is 60 cents, which is also the unit price that can be realized under conditions of long-run equilibrium.

3. The least-cost production of commodity P_3 is accomplished by combining, for each unit of P_3, ten units of x with three units of factor y and three units of z. The money cost for a unit of the finished commodity P_3 is 50 cents, which is also the price received for a unit of P_3 at long-run equilibrium.

We have now three simultaneous equations; they are:

$$4x + 3y + 11z = 86 \text{ cents} \qquad (1)$$
$$4x + 10y + 2z = 60 \text{ cents} \qquad (2)$$
$$10x + 3y + 3z = 50 \text{ cents} \qquad (3)$$

Bear in mind that factors of production x, y, and z are used equally well in the three different industries. And each is equally rewarded, wherever utilized. We have therefore only to solve the above simultaneous equations in order to be informed what is the value productivity of each of the three types of resources.

When equations (1), (2), and (3) are solved simultaneously for the unknown values of x, y, and z, the result that is.[1]

$x = 2$ cents, which is the marginal revenue product of x
$y = 4$ cents, the marginal revenue product of y
$z = 6$ cents, the marginal revenue product of z

Substituting these *mrp* values in equations (1), (2), and (3), we obtain the results shown in Table 22–3.

The economy-wide marginal revenue product of factor x is 2 cents. Knowing this, we can by simply reading column (a) determine that

---

[1] The solution is obtained by first subtracting equation (2) from equation (1). This gives the equation: $-7y + 9z = 26$ cents. Then equation (2) is multiplied by 5, and equation (3) by 2. This allows us to eliminate, by subtraction, the factor x. That leaves the simpler equation: $44y + 4z = 200$ cents. When the above two derived equations in y and z are similarly cleared of z, we arrive at a final equation: $-424y = -1,696$ cents, or, $424y = 1,696$ cents. Dividing, y is seen to equal 4 cents. This value is substituted in equations (1) and (2), which are then cleared of x by subtraction. This yields: $9z = 54$ cents, or, $z = 6$ cents. Substituting in equation (1), 4 cents for y and 6 cents for z shows that x must be worth 2 cents.

Table 22–3. Total Marginal Revenue Products of Three Factors

(a)		(b)		(c)		
4x (= 8¢)	+	3y (=12¢)	+	11z (=66¢) = 86¢		(1)
4x (= 8¢)	+	10y (=40¢)	+	2z (=12¢) = 60¢		(2)
10x (=20¢)	+	3y (=12¢)	+	3z (=18¢) = 50¢		(3)
Total: 18x		Total: 16y		Total: 16z		

eighteen units of x will be demanded by entrepreneurs whenever the price of a unit of factor x is 2 cents. This follows from the fundamental hiring rule that units of factor x will be demanded by entrepreneurs up to the point at which the marginal revenue product equals the price of the factor ($mrp = pf$).

The marginal revenue product of factor y has been ascertained at a value of 4 cents. A glance at column (b) of Table 22–3 informs us that sixteen units of factor y will be demanded throughout our hypothetical economy whenever the price per unit of factor y is 4 cents. Similarly, upon inspection of column (c) it may be seen that sixteen units of factor z will be wanted in the entire economy whenever the price of factor z is 6 cents a unit.

These findings are shown in a different arrangement in Table 22–4 where the total quantity demanded of each factor of production is added in rows P_1, P_2, and P_3 rather than, as in Table 22–3, by columns.

Table 22–4. Entrepreneurial Resources Demand at Given Factor Prices

Per Unit Price of Factor (a)	Demanded Quantity of the Resources			
	For Commodity P_1 (b)	For Commodity P_2 (c)	For Commodity P_3 (d)	Total (e)
Resource x at 2 cents	4	(+) 4	(+) 10	(=) 18
Resource y at 4 cents	3	(+) 10	(+) 3	(=) 16
Resource z at 6 cents	11	(+) 2	(+) 3	(=) 16

Having observed how great a quantity of factors x, y, and z is wanted at their respective unit prices of 2, 4, and 6 cents, a question naturally arises. What happens if the price of any one of the factors of production changes? If the price of units of factor z increases from

6 to 8 cents, what would be the response of the entrepreneurs in industries P_1, P_2, and P_3?

Principle of Substitution

When the price for any finished commodity is given, the entrepreneurs, as they combine factors of production to make units of the commodity, seek to substitute units of cheap resources for units of expensive resources. To illustrate, all the representative firms in our hypothetical economy use units of resource z. Consequently, a rise of the price of units of factor z would raise the prices of all of the commodities in our hypothetical economy, *all other things being equal.* This may be confirmed numerically by substituting 8 cents as the value of a unit of factor z for the previous value of 6 cents. When this is done in the three equations on page 561, we find that a unit of commodity P_1 now costs $1.08 instead of 86 cents; commodity P_2, which uses the least amount of z for a unit of product, now rises from 60 cents to 64 cents in cost for a unit of product; commodity P_3, which uses more z than P_2 but less than P_1, rises from 50 to 56 cents unit cost of output. (Per contra, if resource z were to decline from 6 cents a unit to 4 cents, then commodity P_1, which uses the most of z, would drop in cost for a unit of output by 25 per cent, that is, from 86 cents to 64 cents; commodity P_2 would drop from 60 to 56 cents in unit cost, or 6 per cent; commodity P_3 would drop by 12 per cent, from 50 cents to 44 cents.)

These computations depend, however, on an assumption that in the production of finished commodities the ingredient resources cannot to any extent be substituted for each other. In other words, to obtain the above arithmetical results the implicit assumption has been made that for the production of each commodity, P_1, P_2, and P_3, there is in each instance one and only one technologically feasible combination of production factors, or, alternatively stated, there is in each case a given and fixed *method of production.*

Now this is rarely the case. Usually it is possible to replace to some extent a resource which becomes expensive with one whose price does not change and which, therefore, becomes relative cheap. The engineers in a plant might prefer one particular way of combining the factors of production, but the entrepreneur views engineering formulas as means to the end of gaining at least normal profit. Consequently, entrepreneurs readily substitute for expensive resources those which are relatively inexpensive.

Let resource z be a given type of cropland. Should the rent of this land increase, the effort will be made by farmers to use more labor to cultivate more intensively land which is already in cultivation. The aim would be to abandon the use of some acres of land presently in use, thus reducing the rent burden. If this substitution of intensive for extensive cultivation is quite feasible, total yield of the agricultural product of land would not decrease. Neither would the total cost of cultivation increase, since relatively inexpensive labor is used to obtain higher yields from a reduced amount of crop acreage.

Per contra, suppose that land is relatively cheap in comparison to labor. In that case, extensive cultivation will be preferred to intensive cultivation. In the history of American agriculture, many illustrations of this type of substitution can be found.

The principle of substitution is not limited in its application to simple and direct factor substitution. The substitution may also be accomplished indirectly, by a relative curtailment or expansion, as the case may be, of finished commodities which require for their fabrication much of an expensive factor, or per contra, much of a relatively cheap factor. Thus with an increase in the unit cost of resource z, the production of our hypothetical commodity P_1 might be severely restricted, for P_1 is assumed to rely heavily upon the use of factor z. Commodity P_2 would be the least affected, since it requires but little use to be made of factor z.

We observe that there are two apparent effects of a change in the reward gained by the owners of one or several factors of production. Insofar as direct factor substitutions may readily be made, entrepreneurs continue to produce about the same amount of any given product but seek to use less of the resource whose cost to them has been raised, while making greater use of resources whose cost has relatively or absolutely diminished. The second type of effect of a factor of production changing in price is a change in the comparative amounts of finished commodities produced.

A generalization. When the money cost of units of a productive factor rises, fewer units of the factor will be demanded; when the money cost of units of a resource declines, more units of that resource will be demanded. If this is the case, it is quite evidently possible to schedule the demand for a factor of production by listing the number of units of a productive resource which will be demanded at different rewards for each unit that might be paid to the owners of the productive resource. This scheduling of factor demand can be illustrated by preliminarily probing the course of events when the reward of resource z changes from 6 cents to 8 cents, then to 4 cents for a unit of the resource.

Table 22–5. Entrepreneurial Demand for Factor of Production z
at Three Different Prices

Per Unit Price of Resource z (a)	Commodity for Which Resource z Is Used (b)	Entire Production Function for One Unit of Output (c)	Quantity of Resource z Demanded (units) (d)
Part I			
6¢	P₁	4x + 3y + 11z	11z
	P₂	4x + 10y + 2z	2z
	P₃	10x + 3y + 3z	3z
		Total:	16z

Part II

Upon a rise of the unit price of resource z to 8 cents, the production functions of commodities P₁, P₂, and P₃ are altered as shown in column (c).

8¢	P₁	6x + 4y + 9z	9z
	P₂	6x + 12y + 1z	1z
	P₃	11x + 3y + 2z	2z
		Total:	12z

Part III

The unit price of resource z declines to 4 cents, whereupon the production functions of commodities P₁, P₂, and P₃, are altered in the manner shown in column (c).

4¢	P₁	3x + 2y + 14z	14z
	P₂	3x + 8y + 3z	3z
	P₃	3x + 2y + 5z	5z
		Total:	22z

Summarizing the demand for resource z as shown in column (c) of Table 22–5 and arraying it in ascending order, a regular demand schedule appears:

Per Unit Price of Resource z	Quantity Demanded, in Units
4¢	22
6¢	16
8¢	12

Other observations can be made of how under the principle of substitution other factor combinations are made at prices of resource z, ranging from 2 cents to 10 cents a unit. When this is done, the following demand schedule for factor z units is disclosed, always on the

Table 22–6. Hypothetical Demand Schedule for Units of Resource z,
on an Economy-wide Basis

Per Unit Price of Resource z (cents)	Quantity Demanded (units)
10	9
9	10
8	12
7	14
6	16
5	18
4	22
3	26
2	30

assumption that the rewards for each unit to the other factors, x and y, remain constant.

When Table 22–6 is plotted on a graph (Figure 22–2), the demand curve for the services of factor z has a similar appearance to demand curves for finished commodities.

Figure 22–2. Service-Demand Schedule for Resource z

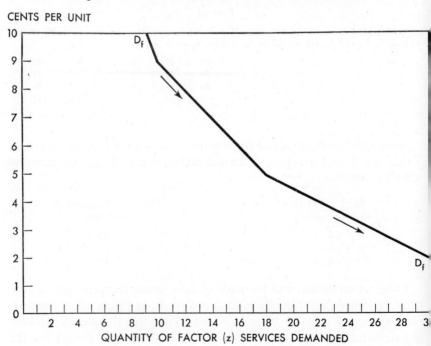

CENTS PER UNIT

QUANTITY OF FACTOR (z) SERVICES DEMANDED

Resource Supply and Demand Seen in Conjunction

Let us summarize the analysis which has been made thus far. First, every entrepreneur has a scheduled demand for different quantities of factors of production which he will use at corresponding list prices for each unit of the resource. The separate demand schedules of individual entrepreneurs can be aggregated, provided, of course, that the demand is for homogeneous units of given resources. It is important to notice that the aggregation of entrepreneurial factor-demand schedules is made on an economy-wide basis, not only on an industry-by-industry basis. That is, insofar as resources are freely transferable between industries, or transferable at all, the totality of entrepreneurs in the economy must be conceived as competitively bidding for units of resources. The principle of substitution is, within broad limits, universal in its application.

The economy-wide demand curve for any given resource, that is, any factor of production, slopes downward and to the right of the origin of a graph. This reflects diminishing utility to the consumers of finished commodities into the manufacture of which particular resources enter. Diminishing purchasing power of consumers for particular commodities also influences the location and elasticity of the entrepreneurial resources demand which in part derived from consumer demand for finished products. The character of resources demand is also influenced by diminishing returns *to the entrepreneur* when he uses more and more units of any given resource in combination with fixed amounts of other resources. In other words, an entrepreneur's demand for resources depends in part on his managerial ability. Also, in general, the demand for specific factors of production depends upon the principle of substitution, under which entrepreneurs seek to substitute units of cheaper resources for units of resources which are becoming increasingly expensive, and vice versa. The principle of substitution really encompasses the first two considerations of diminishing salability of finished commodities, and diminishing returns to managerial ability. Therefore, the resource demand curve, and its elasticity, may be summarily explained simply in terms of the principle of substitution.

Next, we may summarize the conditions under which supplies of given stocks of our basic human, natural, and man-made resources are made available in varying amounts of productive services. But the reasons why the basic labor force (in its constituent varieties) is *given*, in an amount of, say, 70 million persons, are not analyzed. Neither is an analysis made of the causes of the *given* supply of exploitable natural resources, of the *basic* supply of capital which is free to be invested in man-made resources. The factor-service supply schedules with which the above income distribution theory operates only represent how and why more or less use is made of given amounts of basic resources. This is an important reminder, one which furnishes the warning that the type of income distribution theory presently explained must not be carelessly applied to actual problems concerning income distribution under conditions of *growing* (or declining) amounts of the basic human, natural, and man-made resources.

Given the amount of basic resources, every owner of units of the resources schedules the quantities which he will offer to bring to market at a corresponding list of rewards. The separate service-supply schedules of individual resource owners can be aggregated. This can be done on an economy-wide basis, not simply on an industry-by-industry basis. That is possible because the owners of units of resources seek profitable employment for them anywhere in the economy. The owners of resources are not in principle partial to any particular use which might be made of units of their resources. The economy-wide supply curve of any given resource slopes upward to the right of the origin of a curve. This visualizes the increasing toil and trouble experienced by marginal suppliers of a productive service in furnishing additional units of productive services, as measured by opportunity cost. For example, as more and more work is supplied by labor and management, the alternative of withholding further services in order to enjoy leisure becomes increasingly attractive.

Comparison of factor supply and demand. Mindful of the complex psychological, sociological, physiological, and technological elements which underlie resource supply and demand schedules, we can, without fear of performing a merely mechanical action, determine factor rewards (1) by comparing a typical factor supply with a typical factor demand schedule (Table 22–7), and (2) by portraying the relationship on a graph of the typical factor-service supply and the typical factor-service demand schedule (Figure 22–3).

The equilibrium price of resource z is 6 cents a unit, with sixteen units of the resource exchanged. The exchange is made between owners of resource z units and entrepreneurs who in our example use resource z as one of the ingredients for producing outputs of commodities P_1, P_2, and P_3. The reward to owners of resource z cannot under the given conditions be less than 6 cents a unit. If the rate of reward were lower than 6 cents a unit, some entrepreneurs who are willing to pay for units of resource z at a higher rate of reward would fear that they cannot obtain a sufficient amount of the resource to meet their requirements. Consequently, they would bid up the rate of reward for each unit of the resource.

Table 22–7. Factor-Price Determination for Units of Resource z

List Price (cents per unit)	Supply Schedule— Quantity Available at Corresponding List Price (units)	Demand Schedule— Quantity Demanded at Corresponding List Price (units)
2	4	30
3	8	26
4	11	22
5	14	18
6	16	16
7	18	14
8	20	12
9	22	10
10	23	9

SOURCE: Tables 22–2 and 22–6.

Figure 22–3. Equilibrium Price of Resource z

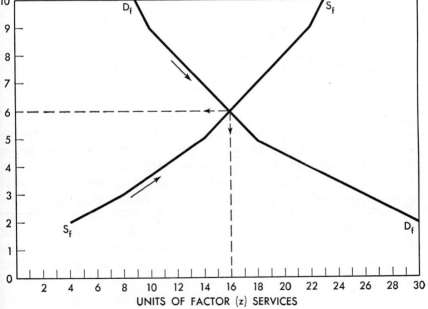

CENTS PER UNIT

UNITS OF FACTOR (z) SERVICES

On the other hand, the rate of reward for units of resource z cannot be higher than 6 cents. For if it were higher, some suppliers of the resource would fear unemployment of some units of their resource, the control of which units they are willing to relinquish at 6 cents a unit. Accordingly, these marginal suppliers will bid down the rate of reward until, at 6 cents a unit, they can supply the number of units they care to exchange for money.

Thus, in the markets for resources, just as in commodity markets, a single price becomes established at the point at which the quantity which suppliers stand ready to make available equals the quantity of the resources demanded by entrepreneurs. This price will last until any or several of the given conditions change. All units of factors of production which are not exchanged between resource-owners and entrepreneurs are presumably held out of use by voluntary choice by owners and entrepreneurs rather than by the force of circumstances. This follows from the fundamental assumption of full employment and of pure competition in the factor markets. Figure 22–3 pictorializes these findings.

FULL-EMPLOYMENT NATIONAL INCOME

In real life so perfect a consummation of equilibrium factor-service price and amount exchanged as is illustrated in Figure 22–3 is not attainable. To prevent this there is in actual affairs too much of imperfect competition in factor-service markets as well as commodity markets. No perfectly free flow of economic information exists to enable entrepreneurs and resource-owners to make with certainty their day-by-day investment and employment decisions. There is always some involuntary unemployment to render supply schedules of factor-services somewhat unpredictable, and, of course, there is time lost merely in making economic adjustments. Moreover, it is at any one moment easy to believe that affairs are proceeding as usual. But social change has a way of creeping in unnoticed, then suddenly becoming manifest with startling implications. Who would have predicted in the 1920's the powerful role which modern trade unions presently play in income distribution? One can count on one's hand the persons who in earlier years predicted the mid-century "population explosion."

Notwithstanding unexpected social change and the many imperfections of economic affairs, an economy-wide tendency exists for factor-services to be exchanged in equilibrium amounts and at equilibrium prices. Like the fundamental 4/4 rhythm of a popular tune, this tendency underlies the most imaginative flights of entrepreneurial imagination. As in music the "breaks" created by an individual firm or industry always return to the fundamental theme of economics, that of efficient resources allocation. It could not be otherwise, for what we call our economic system is really a way of approximately relating all economic processes, including income distribution, to the society's basic need of preserving (within reasonable limits of deviation) the American economy's inherited state of material abundance. In other words, we are not simply confronted by a list of haphazardly made income distribution when we inspect, for example, the President's *Economic Report* which estimated that in 1957 public employees and those of private business gained $254 billion of income, farmers gained $12 billion, and so forth. There is a relationship between incomes paid and economic efficiency. This is not to say that all the goods and services produced in the American economy, or the amounts thereof, rate high by the broader criteria of *cultural* efficiency. Economic efficiency only means that whatever goods are made, however culturally rated, are made efficiently. And they are made by people whose incomes appreciably depend upon their personal or their property's marginal revenue productivity.

Now the amounts of income shares shown in national income accounts are, of course, aggregate amounts. That is to say, the tendency which factor-service pricing has to implement efficient resources allocation is expressed through millions of separate transactions. The largest electronic computer could be overloaded if it were taped with all of the nation's service-supply and factor-service demand schedules, then asked to solve for the numerical values of all equilibrium factor-service amounts and prices. Yet what might lie beyond the numerical comprehension of an electronic brain is readily grasped symbolically by the average individual human brain. We have only to imagine that *each* factor of production tends to be priced, and used in equilibrium amounts, by matching the supply and demand for its services in the manner explained for a single factor of production.

RESOURCES RATIONING THROUGH FACTOR PRICES

Let us return to the simple example of an economy which uses only three resources, x, y, and z, utilizing units of these production factors to produce only three commodities. Next we concentrate on the use made by all the entrepreneurs in the economy of only one resource, namely, factor z. We then stipulate that the representative firms in the three industries use resource z with differing degrees of efficiency. Let us say that in making use of resource z the entrepreneurs producing commodity P_1 are extraordinarily efficient; the producers of P_2 are comparatively the least efficient; and the producers of commodity P_3 are in the utilization of units of resource z moderately efficient.

If we are to be realistic it must be granted that not all industries can use the same amounts of any factor of production. In our example it could well be that the entrepreneurs producing commodity P_1 use resource z as a basic ingredient, whereas in the production of P_2 and P_3 the use of resource z is not so important. Accordingly, the entrepreneurs producing P_2 and P_3 could not possibly absorb so many units of resource z as the producers of P_1 can and must utilize. The proper use of leather is of utmost importance in the shoe industry but not so crucial in the automobile industry (where leather is used for several purposes other than seat-covering).

Nevertheless, it is usually reasonable to surmise that if the producers of commodities P_2 and P_3, in our example, understood how to use factor z more abundantly and efficiently, they could substitute some units of resource z for certain units of factors x and y.

The demand schedule for the services of a factor reflects the marginal efficiency with which it is used. In our example, the strongest demand for resource z would emanate from the representative firm which makes commodity P_1; the least demand would be that of the representative firm producing P_2; and the representative firm in industry P_3 would have only a slightly stronger demand for units of factor z. Assuming that we have these three demand schedules on hand, we proceed to plot them on a graph. This yields, in Figure 22–4, three separate demand curves for the services of resource z. Knowing that the equilibrium price of a unit of factor z is 6 cents (Figure 22–3), we also draw across Figure 22–4 a straight horizontal line at the 6-cent level of the price of factor z. This horizontal "price-line" is seen to intersect the three demand curves. At each point of intersection, drop a perpendicular line to the x-axis of the graph. Then by simple inspection it is seen that the 6-cent price for one unit of factor z rations the producers who make commodities P_2 and P_3 more tightly than the producers of commodity P_1.

The pricing of factors of production has now been seen as a means of rationing the representative firms in different *industries* in their use of valuable national resources. But factor price rationing operates not only to ration resources among different industries. Factor-service pricing also rations resources among the individual firms in any *one* industry. That is because each producer in an industry can use only as many units of resources as he can manage while yet keeping his average cost (*atuc*) to the minimum standard established by the representative firm. If any one entrepreneur in any industry becomes abnormally inefficient, the result is a financial loss. Over the long pull this means that the abnormally inefficient firm is absorbed by a more efficient firm, or group of highly efficient firms. In general, control over

Figure 22–4. How Factor Price Rations

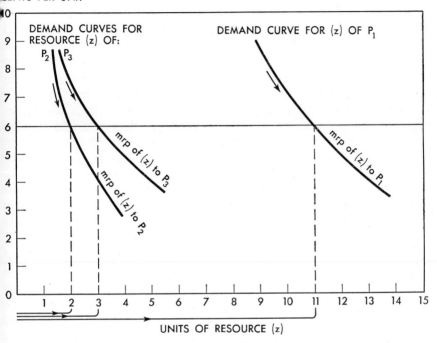

UNITS OF RESOURCE (z)

resources passes in the long run from inefficient firms to efficient concerns, and from inefficient industries to relatively more efficient ones.

Unifying Effect of Factor Pricing

A brief recapitulation is in order before we proceed with this discussion, to demonstrate how competitive factor pricing tends to unite the economy in an efficient over-all scheme of utilizing resources. For this to happen it is not enough that each entrepreneur produces to the best of his ability. He might still be producing an excessively large amount of output at an average cost (*atuc*) far above the minimum possible. This could be profitable for the entrepreneur, but for society it would signify a waste of resources.

In Chapter 17 it was seen that under pure competition each entrepreneur in the long run produces no more or less than he can manage at his minimum average total unit cost, that is, where *atuc* = *mc*. Moreover, this minimum *atuc* (=*mc*) should be equal to, or less than, the standard of least cost for the industry, a standard set by the industry's representative firm. If these conditions are fulfilled, an efficient entrepreneur in an industry will produce a large output, and a relatively less efficient firm must rest content with producing a small output of the particular commodity. From this we can infer the criterion of how to judge whether an entrepreneur combines in a socially significant manner the resources under his control in optimal proportions. "Optimal" clearly refers to the entrepreneur in the act of hiring just the right amounts of different resources to enable him to produce output at the standard least cost for his industry.

Under pure competition in the markets for commodities, any entrepreneur cannot possibly produce more output than he could manage at his industry's least cost of operation. For under pure competition the price of a commodity is in the long run equal to the representative firm's minimum average total unit cost, the cost to which each firm in the industry must conform (see Chapter 17). A greater or lesser amount of production would doom the entrepreneur to elimination, for then his money costs would in their totality exceed the total revenue from sales.

This is a reassuring proposition, even though it describes an ideal situation. However, the demonstration of optimal resources allocation under pure commodity-market competition is also a *limited* proposition. This proposition only reassures us that all the firms *in an industry* shall conform to their representative firm's least-cost standard. It could happen that the representative firm in any given industry could itself be wasteful in its use of resources. This could happen if every separate industry in the economy used resources which it alone can use and which cannot be used by any other industry. Then each industry would be its own judge of efficiency. No uniform test by which to determine whether or not any given industry *as a whole* is doing its best to conserve resources could be applied to all industries.

Fortunately, this is not the condition of real-life circumstances. The fact is that most basic types of human, natural, and man-made resources and many of their subvarieties can be used in a large number of different industries. Consequently, the entrepreneurs in any one industry are in a large measure actively in competition with entrepreneurs in other industries. All entrepreneurs must seek to attract units of many universally applicable resources. For theoretical purposes it is not too much to say that *each* entrepreneur in the total economy competes for factors of production with *all* the other entrepreneurs in the economy. This statement may be clarified by understanding *from the viewpoint of the owners of resources* the nature and scope of the entrepreneurial competition for units of resources.

PRINCIPLE OF OPPORTUNITY COST

In distribution analysis the costs which owners of resources seek to recover are not objective costs such as the fatigue incurred in working in a coal mine or the loss of the scenic beauty of land converted to use in open-strip iron mining. Such considerations may lie at the foundation of the rewards which owners of resources demand, but economic analysis of the modern vintage does not trace resource supply schedules to their psychological or physiological roots. Instead, all resource owners are conceived as persons who seek to maximize commercial returns on their personal effort or for the use of their property. All owners of resources are regarded as seeking the most favorable employment or investment opportunities which are available.

If all standard units of resources are freely interchangeable, all owners of any given type of resource must receive the same money value for a unit of the resource, regardless of the use to which the resource may be put. For if in any given single use the reward is higher than in equally feasible alternative uses, it will pay owners of units of that resource to shift a marginal (transferable) number of resource units to the field of utilization in which the rate of reward is abnormally high. This marginal transfer process would theoretically continue until the reward in the abnormally high-paying field of utilization is reduced to the point at which it is equal to the reward in all the alternative uses of the resource. Those rewards of course rise somewhat as units of resources are withdrawn from the other fields of utilization in order to be applied in the abnormally profitable field. Thus by the process of transferring marginal units of resources an equalization of rewards to owners of homogeneous units of resources ultimately results. The units of any given resource have theoretically the same money value in whatsoever manner they are utilized.

Figure 22–5 illustrates the equalization of rewards to four types of factors of production—*A, B, C, D*—used in the production of five commodities—I, II, III, IV, V. The relative amounts of each resource used in the production of each commodity is in this illustration of no consequence. The matter of notice is that all entrepreneurs in the five different industries must pay, for each unit of each resource, the going rate of reward for the particular type of resource. This is highlighted in Figure 22–5 by the fact that straight lines emanating from each commodity sector converge on each of the four triangular symbols representing a different resource and its unit price.

Figure 22–5 envisions an ideal theoretical eventuation. In the real world odd patterns of income distribution can be found —for example, the so-called "white collar differential." Scientific studies have proved

Figure 22–5. Equalization of Rewards to Units of Resources

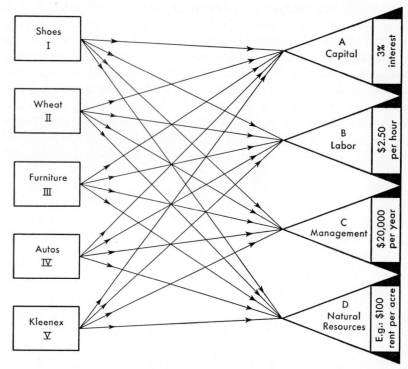

that there is no substantial difference in the quantity or quality of work performed by a typist and a semiskilled manual worker; yet the typist in many instances receives less pay. Then again there are adjacent geographical regions in which the cost of living is equal, or almost equal; yet rates of remuneration for identical work done in both regions differ appreciably. The rent for land of equal capability is apt to vary in contiguous counties although the same product is cultivated on the land. Urban rentals frequently differ in a manner inexplicable on the assumption that persons having property to let really act on the principle of opportunity cost, that is, seek to obtain from committing their property to one type of use at least as much return as they could from alternative uses of their property. There are puzzling differences in the levels of the rate of interest on money capital, that most fluid and mobile type of resource.

Nevertheless, there exists a persistent *tendency* for homogeneous units of resources of standard classifications to gain the same reward in any use whatsoever which may be made of marginal units of these resources. The tendency is sufficiently pronounced to warrant econo-

1ists in ascribing to it the operation of a fundamental principle of *pportunity cost. However, the operation of this principle cannot in 1odern times be ascribed simply to individual action of owners of esources. The measure of opportunity cost is in many instances de-2rmined by the consensus of the members of an organized group. *rade unions, for example, shape their demands on employers at union 1eetings and/or wage committee meetings. On these occasions the nterest of a majority of union members rises paramount to the par-icular wishes of every single member. Thereafter, the individual 1ember deals with his employer not directly but through the union epresentatives of his choosing. Collective definition of opportunity ost for the group is not practiced exclusively by trade unions. Farmers 1ave associated to secure federal legislation under which they may >ecome qualified for income aid through a system of farm parity >ricing (to be examined in Chapter 23). In administering their end of arm legislation, farmers vote to control acreages planted to certain :rops. When the farmers decide on acreage allocations, they are defin-ng opportunity cost in an organized manner. Many other forms of :ollectively determining opportunity cost exist.

Whether enforced by individuals or by collective action, the prin-:iple of opportunity cost tends to effectuate the equalization of the ewards gained respectively by each species of the general land, labor, and capital factors of production. The more highly organized is the letermination of opportunity cost by a specific class of owners of esources, the more likely is this particular factor price to be equalized >n a national scale. Some economists profess to foresee in the collec-ive determination of opportunity cost by a group the ruin of our economic system. There is nothing to fear so long as the collective letermination of opportunity cost by a group of owners of resources s made by applying the proven principles of representative democracy.

OPPORTUNITY COST AND THE ECONOMY

The opportunity cost principle which guides the owners of resources 1as a simple meaning for the entrepreneurs in any given industry. They must match the terms and conditions of hiring resources which are >eing met by the entrepreneurs in the rest of the economy. What if the group of entrepreneurs which comprises a given industry cannot meet these terms and conditions? Then the entire industry will in the long run be eliminated. This is the necessary consequence of the industry's inability to further command resources.

Earlier, in the examination of how commodity prices would be established under pure competition, it was seen that a declining or bankrupt individual firm is one whose minimum average cost (*atuc* is in the long run higher than the market price of the product. Such firm would be absorbed by its competitors. Now an inefficient *industr* is necessarily one in which the minimum average total unit cost of th *representative firm* is higher than the market price of the industry' commodity, not just the minimum *atuc* of any particular firm.

The theory of commodity pricing cannot explain how such an in dustry as a whole could be denied the further use of valuable resource The theory of income distribution furnishes this missing explanation When they were prosperous, the entrepreneurs drew to a substantia extent on the national economy's common pool of resources. Whe the market-price of their commodity no longer covers their representa tive firm's minimum *atuc,* the losing industry must suffer its resource to be returned to the common pool for use by the other industries This return is effectuated under conditions of full employment b persons who previously permitted their personal and/or propert resources to be utilized in the industry which is now losing out. Thes persons can no longer expect to be compensated in the losing industr for their cost of foregoing alternative opportunities to employ or inves their resources.

It may now be appreciated how and why the concept of opportunit cost completes the explanation of how an economy is theoreticall linked in an efficient over-all scheme for the utilization of resource under conditions of full employment. The principle of opportunit cost performs this final explanatory function by establishing the con nection between the separate processes of commodity pricing and factor-service pricing. The linkage is the flow, back and forth to th common pool of national resources, of particular units of these re sources.

Visual demonstration. The foregoing remarks can be graphically illustrated in two steps. First, we pictorialize, as was done in Chapte 17, how the pricing of finished commodities under pure competition requires the representative firm in an industry to operate with optima efficiency, that is, at its least average total unit cost, which equals th long-run equilibrium price for the commodity. This is shown i Figure 22–6 for two of our three hypothetical commodities, namely P_3 and P_2. The equilibrium price of P_2 is taken as being lower than th long-run equilibrium price of P_3, but the actual magnitude of th difference does not matter in this symbolic illustration. In each case a rise of demand is postulated which first raises the price to a new short-run high. Thereafter by the influx of new firms the price return to its previous long-run level, but more output is permanently pro

Figure 22–6. Commodity Price Equilibrium

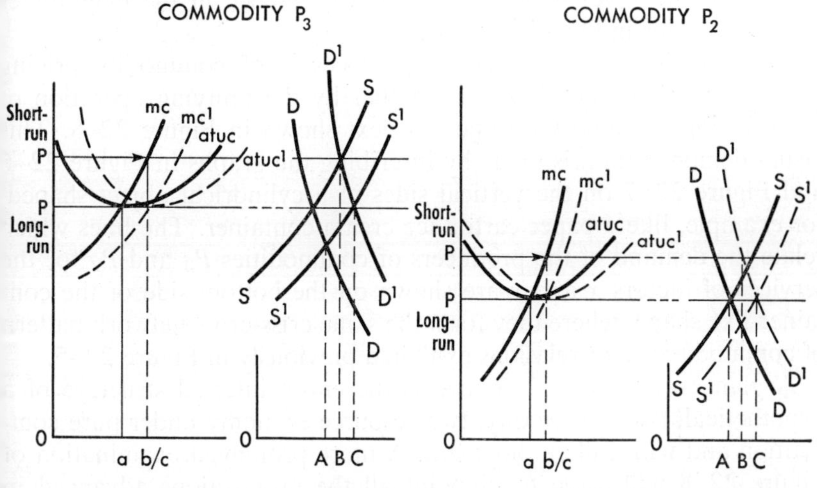

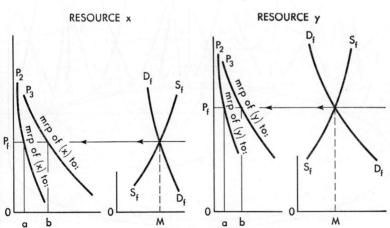

luced. Always over the long pull the representative firm operates in a condition of its minimum *atuc* equaling the price of the commodity.

Next there is shown, in Figure 22–7, how the pricing of the factors of production assigns respectively to two representative firms, one producing P_2 and the other P_3, those amounts of two factors of production, x and y, which the representative firms can efficiently manage. These are the amounts of the two resources which the respective representative firms can employ while yet producing their

Figure 22–7. Factor Price Equilibrium

commodities P_2 and P_3 at the respective minimum average total uni
costs. The price of a unit of resource x is taken as being lower thar
the unit price of resource y; the actual difference in the magnitude:
does not matter in this illustration.

The way in which the separate processes of commodity pricing
and factor pricing are brought together by the unifying operation o
the principle of opportunity cost is next shown in Figure 22–8. This
visual demonstration is made by inscribing the graphs in Figure 22–6
and Figure 22–7 on the vertical sides of a cylindrical object shaped,
for example, like a paper-carton ice-cream container. The lines which
relate the demand of the producers of commodities P_3 and P_2 for the
services of factors x and y are shown on the bottom side of the con-
tainer-like shape, where they form the same criss-cross network pattern
of commodity-factor relations exhibited previously in Figure 22–5.

A glance at Figure 22–8 reveals the entire internal structure of a
hypothetical, two-commodity, two-resource economy under pure competition and with full employment. A more prolonged examination of
Figure 22–8 will serve to pinpoint all the propositions advanced in
this chapter, as well as their conceptual relations. Finally, purely in
the imagination one may multiply the equilibrium prices and equilib-

Figure 22–8. General Equilibrium

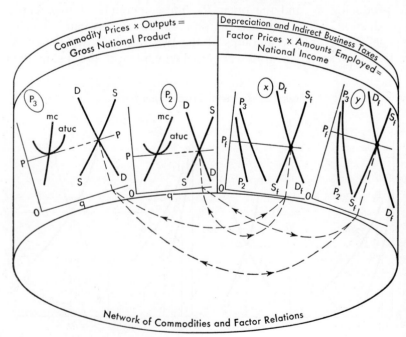

rium amounts produced not only of commodities P_3 and P_2 but of millions of commodities. Adding these imaginary results will yield an equilibrium gross national product (GNP), the market value of aggregate national output at equilibrium prices. Of course this would not represent any actual GNP in a real world of imperfect competition and involuntary unemployment, which is why the author insists on the use of the imagination. Likewise, imagine multiplying equilibrium factor prices by equilibrium amounts of factor-services utilized, not for resources x and y alone but for all resources used in an economy—hundreds of thousands of them. The result of conceptually adding the imaginary data is a hypothetical equilibrium national income at factor prices. Thus it has been shown how under assumed conditions of full employment and pure commodity and factor competition, the national income is exhaustively distributed on a marginal efficiency basis.

Further Considerations

So far, only the *mechanics* of income distribution are explained. But these mechanical principles do not operate in a social vacuum. They apply in the broad context of human relations, which are expressed through social institutions—the customs, the laws, and the political as well as the ethical practices by which men live and hope to prosper. To end the analysis of income distribution after having examined only the abstract principles of income distribution would be to represent as sufficient, for understanding the warmth and glow of a living being, the X-ray picture of his skeletal structure.

The social institutions which primarily influence contemporary income distribution in the United States are (1) legally sanctioned private ownership of land and other natural resources, (2) legally sanctioned private ownership of money capital and of capital goods, (3) collective bargaining between organized labor and management —a practice encouraged by the law as a constructive alternative to disruptive labor strife. These primary social institutions set the stage for the operation of the described marginal efficiency principles of income distribution. In the succeeding Chapters 23 through 27 the following processes are explained, not only by the application of the foregoing analytical principles but never without reference to them: (1) the determination of rent on land which can be privately owned, (2) the determination of interest on privately owned money capital, and (3) the determination of wages and salaries under conditions both of individual and collective bargaining. Raised, and discussed, will be the leading ethical and political problems, as well as certain sociological problems which historically have arisen in connection with the purely economic determination of the national income shares which are received in the forms of rent, interest, profit, wages and salaries, and transfer payments.

For Discussion

1. The concept of *consumer income* is properly applied in studying income distribution, but *personal income* as computed by government statisticians is a concept better suited to the analysis of employment problems. Why? What concept in national income accounting is best adapted to the study of production problems?

2. The president of a large local trade union rents IBM equipment which his paid assistants use for keeping dues-paying records. On what basis did this labor leader win the consent of his members for the use of union funds in this manner? Elaborate your answer.

3. During World War II in the building of airstrips in northern India, human labor was used for clearing and filling instead of the usual construction equipment. The pay received by this labor would be considered a pittance by an American. Yet supply officers were aware that it would have been cheaper to use expensive American equipment operated by Americans receiving at least soldiers' pay. Does this experience negate the principle of substitution?

4. Occasionally one sees the following sign in a restaurant window: "Dishwasher Wanted." How is this possible inasmuch as automatic dishwashing machinery can be bought?

5. Illustrate the principle of *opportunity cost* by imagining how you will respond as a second-semester senior to different job interviews you will have at your university's placement office.

6. On page 571 it is stated that "economic efficiency only means that whatever goods are made, however culturally rated, are made efficiently." This statement does not render trivial the study of economic efficiency by the use of marginal methods. Why not?

23 Property Incomes

Interest is income which is received, or calculated, for the use of money. If a person has money which he lends to another person he *receives* interest in return. When the banking system creates money by the process of multiple credit expansion, the individual bankers also *receive* interest. But if a person uses his own money in his business, he *calculates* interest. "Imputing" interest (that is, calculating interest) is necessary in order to determine whether the business is earning profit. If the income of a business from sales only exceeds the total cost of production by the equivalent amount which could have been earned by lending the firm's money capital at interest, a profit will not have been earned.

It is important to distinguish interest from risk premiums which are usually charged by lenders of money. These are in addition to interest; they are insurance-type payments which the borrowers must make. Likewise, any cost of making a loan—a service charge, a charge for reinsuring the loan, and so forth—must be held apart from the concept of interest. Loan costs are frequently averaged over the period of the loan and included with the total amount of interest plus payment of principal which a borrower must make, say, on the first of every month. This inclusion does not transform loan-service charges into interest. Interest must also be carefully distinguished from profit. Properly understood, profit is a reward for individual or team performance. Unlike interest, it is not a standard cost paid to, or calculated by, people using money. That is to say, profit varies from case to case; its origin is, so to speak, biographical. But interest originates impersonally; it is a standard rate or percentage of money capital, a rate determined in the money market. Interest is a *price*, whereas profit is a residual amount after costs have been incurred and incomes received from the sale of goods at current market prices. In other words, interest is a price, but profit is a result of prices.

In brief, interest must be understood as a pure payment for owner- ship of money capital or, in the case of the banking system *acting as a whole*, for action in creating money capital.

Why Is Interest Paid?

To the modern American this may appear to be a strange question; yet for many centuries the payment of interest was frowned upon by the highest ecclesiastical authorities. Traffic in usury might not con- demn a soul to Hell but it depreciated his social standing. What this reveals is that interest is not a natural arrangement but an institutional one—that is, a social custom which has only recently achieved general sanction. Today the payment of interest is a condition of having access to bank credit or to money, either other people's or one's own by calculation. Persons who borrow must pay the market rate of interest. Persons who can use their own money in a business venture do not consider this to be worthwhile unless they can earn something in excess of the rate of interest.

The fundamental reason for the institution of interest, as a condi- tion of obtaining supplies of money, is that money is an asset which can be privately owned or controlled. Money can be withheld from use, or placed in use, at the owner's discretion. Credit can be extended or denied at the banking system's discretion. There is no law which requires a person or banker to place liquid money into circulation. If he desires, he can abstain from doing so when at any time he be- lieves it more advisable to hold his wealth in money form, waiting for an investment bargain which he thinks may become available in the future. Most people would prefer to withhold their money, it is generally believed, at any rate of long-term interest below 2 per cent per annum.

WHY ENTREPRENEURS PAY INTEREST

The basic reason entrepreneurs are willing to pay interest is that money capital gives an entrepreneur access to the society's technology, specifically, to plant and equipment and research services, and so on. To clarify this, an extremely simplified situation may be imagined. Let us join Robinson Crusoe and his man Friday somewhere in the neighborhood of Pitcairn Island. Robinson was of course forced to "go native," but that did not deprive him of all the knowledge he had acquired when he was a member of civilization. Thus he carried with him the important knowledge that it pays to take time off from merely grubbing for food to construct productive equipment and thus, for example, to multiply his catch of fish. By doing so for eighteen days, he was able to raise his catch of fish from two to four a day. But by taking off twenty days, he found that he could raise this again, to six fish a day. When Friday appeared Crusoe was able to pay him two fish a day for services and continue to consume four fish himself. He now had the advantage of Friday's paid services to relieve him of some routine chores, without diminishing his accustomed consumption. The time gained by Robinson was again spent in improving his methods of production. In effect, Robinson found it worthwhile to pay Friday in order to achieve further access to technology which he remembered or newly invented and innovated. If Robinson Crusoe had acquired from Friday an outrigger canoe which only Friday was able to construct, Robinson in his turn would have gained access to a new technology. Applying this new technology to augment his catch of fish, Robinson would have been enabled to pay, for the cost of the canoe, a share of his newly gained surplus. The payment would have been interest.

From this seemingly primitive example the modern investment process may be derived by entering only a few complications. The first is that entrepreneurs do not take time off from manufacturing consumers' goods to build new plant and equipment. Some entrepreneurs are always producing consumers' goods, and others are producing capital equipment. Thus we have a *continuous* flow of production of capital goods, not just occasional production. Of course capital goods do not exist for themselves; though they do not immediately contribute end-consumption goods, they do so as they wear out in providing goods for the use of consumers. Earlier it was seen that plant and equipment are really temporary stores of indirect man-hours. As by reason of wear and tear and obsolescence the capital goods depreciate in value, the services of labor which were applied to their production must be renewed to produce equipment for replacement and modernization. Thus in a real sense work performed in constructing and maintaining man-made resources, as well as improving them, is always, and ultimately, performed in the service of the consumers. Let us consider the manufacturing of electric dishwashers.

This effort indirectly assists in the performance of a service which in earlier times a kitchenmaid rendered directly, although a great deal less effectively. Many girls who in yesteryear might have worked as kitchenmaids, today can be found working in the production line where household appliances are assembled. Because this labor, al though indirectly applied to home service, is highly effective, more people today enjoy the services of labor in their homes than was the case in earlier times, when menial servants were employed. Today if one wishes to hire personal home services one must pay, according to the principle of opportunity cost, at least the minimum rate of wages or salary which is earned by the employees of industry or business. The modern rule for consumers to be served more amply but less directly by the use of intermediate capital goods. Entrepreneurs are limited in their use of these by the rate of interest, in the following manner.

VALUATION OF INDIRECT SERVICES

The fact to be emphasized in this connection is that plant and equipment are durable. Now this is but another way of saying that plant and equipment embody resources whose services will be gradually released. But how shall we evaluate, at any time during the active life of the plant and equipment, those services which still remain to be released? An entrepreneur needs to be informed of the worth of his existing productive facilities. Even more to the point, what shall the entrepreneur pay for *new* plant or equipment? In their case, *all* the indirect productive services will be performed in the future. What is their present worth?

We need only to reverse our time-perspective in order to solve this problem. So far, attention has been drawn to the productivity which is built into the plant and equipment. This will be released over a period of years, until all of it has been enjoyed by the consumers. Now, let us assume that we have already reached this future date and are looking backward to observe what amount of income has been realized by the entrepreneur annually, while the plant or equipment lasted. Supposing that by the use of a machine an entrepreneur gained a *net* income (above cost of repair and operation) of $200 annually. Thus, over a period of twenty years, the machine will have contributed an aggregate net income of $4,000.

Was this the purchase price paid by the entrepreneur when he acquired the machine originally? Certainly not. Had he paid $4,000 in order to gain $4,000 after twenty years, he would have invested money without gaining interest. He would have been better advised to place his money in a savings bank or buy $4,000 worth of stocks, bonds, or real estate. In that event a dollar invested at the present moment at, say, 5 per cent interest, would, if it were left untouched for twenty years, have earned interest of $1.65. Consequently, a total amount of $2.65 would be due after twenty years, the original dollar plus the compound interest.[1] Now, if $2.65 can be possessed in the future by investing $1.00 at the present, surely $4,000 will not be paid by an entrepreneur for a machine which merely returns the $4,000 in twenty years, and no more. What, then, is the amount up to which, but not above, the entrepreneur is willing to pay for the machine? From Chapter 22 we know that it is an amount which is measured by the marginal revenue product of the machine, its *mrp*, in relation to the price of the machine, *pf*. The representative firm in an industry will, under conditions leading to equilibrium, buy the machine only if its marginal revenue product is equal to, and no less than, the price of the machine; that is: *mrp = pf*. However, this insight does not advance the understanding beyond the broad scope of Chapter 22. Here we are concerned in making a specific application, to a particular type of specialized factor of production (a machine), of the general finding about the demand-price for productive resources, of any type whatsoever.

Now the mere fact that an entrepreneur expects to earn at least as much from the use of a machine as he could by lending its purchase money at interest tells us that the rate of interest enters crucially into the determination of the demand-price for a capital good—in this case a machine. Interest is a price. Hence, like all prices, the rate of interest must perform the characteristic function of rationing entrepreneurs in their use of valuable resources. In the case of durable capital goods, however, price in the form of interest performs this function in a complicated manner. The rate of interest does not in this instance come to bear directly and openly on the entrepreneur, but yields its influence only by the role it plays in determining capital value, through a process called *capitalization*. The procedure of capi-

[1] The calculation of how money grows at compound interest proceeds according to the simple formula: $(1 + r)^t$, where r symbolizes the rate of interest and t stands for the period of time over which the money accumulates. What is the amount of $1.00 at 5 per cent compound interest for twenty years? The formula is: 1.05^{20}. In round figures this amounts to $2.65. Observe how the accumulation proceeds, year by year.

Future Year	Amount	Future Year	Amount	Future Year	Amount
0	$1.0000	7	$1.4070	14	$1.9800
1	1.0500	8	1.4770	15	2.0790
2	1.1025	9	1.5510	16	2.1830
3	1.1576	10	1.6290	17	2.2920
4	1.2155	11	1.7100	18	2.4070
5	1.2763	12	1.7960	19	2.5270
6	1.3400	13	1.8860	20	2.6530

talization—finding the capital value of a durable producers' good—is a simple mathematical process; but in examining it, it is easy to become lost in mathematical details, thereby losing sight of what really matters to the economist, namely, how interest, through capital value, rations entrepreneurs in their use of productive equipment. To prevent becoming sidetracked, we shall first review the rationing function of interest through capital value, then show how capital value is established, by capitalization, under the influence of the rate of interest— seen as one of many types of prices.

Rationing Function of Interest

This may be illustrated by the case of an entrepreneur who is deciding whether or not a machine which he contemplates purchasing will pay for itself. The demand for the product of his industry is given and is expected to last. What if the entrepreneur decides that by buying and using the machine he cannot gain as much income as he would by lending at interest the equivalent of the cost of the machine? The entrepreneur would in effect be deciding that he cannot manage with ordinary efficiency a single unit or another unit of the technology which this particular type of machine embodies.

Seen from the entrepreneur's viewpoint this is a simple profit-or-loss decision. But let us view the same decision from the outside, from the standpoint of the national economy. Then rationing of a man-made resource is observed. The entrepreneur's negative decision was prompted by the price of the machine being too high. Now this could be because the entrepreneur believes that in the future the demand for his industry's product will decline or cease. However, we have stipulated that he expects the demand to remain at its present level. On this assumption the entrepreneur's decision whether or not to buy the machine is merely a matter of whether or not he understands how to use it for his profit. If he feels that he cannot do so efficiently, and foregoes the purchase of the machine, the effect is the same as if he had been informed that he cannot have the machine because he is not qualified to use it.

This train of thought may be clarified by imagining, for a moment, that a specially appointed group of persons directly rations the use of the factors of production among the many firms in the national economy. This group would undoubtedly approach its task by trying to imagine how much production would be gained by allowing certain firms to acquire new plant and equipment while at the same time denying to other firms access to man-made resources. The productivity which the representative firm in every industry could add by using given man-made resources would be the opportunity cost which any given firm in each industry must meet to be able to qualify for using the particular type of man-made resource.

American entrepreneurs are not normally granted or denied access to man-made resources by a body of rationing administrators. The individual entrepreneurs ration themselves, so to speak, under our predominant market-exchange type of economic organization. This does not imply, however, the absence of a social standard to guide in a uniform manner our *indirect* rationing of man-made resources. Entrepreneurs who wish to utilize units of man-made resources must comply, although not strictly, with a common criterion of efficiency in order to gain access to technologies which are embodied in new plant and equipment. The social yardstick is the long-term market rate of interest.

CAPITALIZATION

We return to the entrepreneur who contemplates the purchase of a machine which will last twenty years and over that period contribute a net income, above cost incidental to its operation, of $200, year by year. Thereafter it will not even have a scrap value. The rate of market interest is 5 per cent per annum.

Observe what the entrepreneur is doing. He is in effect deciding whether to acquire the right to gain an expected net additional income of $200 per year, based on the physical and marginal revenue productivity of the machine over a period of twenty years. However, the condition of buying a right to an expected $200 over a period of twenty years is that the entrepreneur pay for this right at the present. The successive $200 incomes are, so to speak, built into the machine because it is constructed for twenty years of service. In other words, to realize the particular $200 income that is expected to be realized twenty years hence, he must pay for it at the present moment; the expected income of the nineteenth year must be purchased now as well as that of the eighteenth year, the seventeenth year, and so on. This is the same as: (1) investing a certain amount at the moment in order to realize $200 a year hence; paying another amount, now, in order to realize $200 in two years, and so on.

Now we may appreciate how the rate of interest enters. We know that the entrepreneur will not pay more to acquire the right to one year's expected income than he could gain by simply lending his money at interest. At a going rate of interest of 5 per cent, an amount of $190.48 will grow to $200 at the end of a year. This is the limit of what the entrepreneur would pay were he able to buy a machine which promises a net income of $200 and lasts only one year. But in our example the machine is stipulated to last twenty years, after which it will not even have a scrap value. What will the entrepreneur pay now for the right to receive an expected income of $200 two years hence, another $200 three years hence, and finally, twenty years hence?

To determine these respective amounts, it is necessary to ascertain, in each case, the amount of money which would grow to $200 if invested, at the present, at 5 per cent, with the understanding that the interest which accrues will be left untouched for twenty years. When interest earned is continually reinvested—as is the case if it is not withdrawn—it gains interest itself; there is "interest on interest." This is described by saying that the original amount of money invested accumulates at *compound* interest.

When an entrepreneur invests in *durable* plant or equipment, he necessarily invests money at compound interest; for he obviously cannot withdraw interest gained by the use of the machine, as he could had he lent his money instead of investing it in the machine.

The accumulative effect of compound interest begins necessarily with the second year of an investment, for during the first year no interest has as yet been gained on which further interest may be paid. (This assumes that interest is compounded on an annual basis; it may of course, by arrangement be compounded on a semiannual or quarterly basis.) For example, let $181.40 be invested for a period of two years. After the first year, $9.07 is earned on the principal amount at the 5 per cent rate of interest. At the end of the second year, $9.07 is again earned on the principal amount of $181.40. In addition, 5 per cent interest is also earned on the interest of $9.07 gained during the first year and reinvested during the second year. The "interest on interest" amounts to 46 cents. Thus we have, at the end of the second year:

$181.40 = the amount originally invested
9.07 = interest earned during the first year
9.07 = interest earned for the second year
.46 = interest on the interest of the first year
$200.00 = total due at end of second year

On this principle of compound interest, the right to acquire an expected income of $200, *after* twenty years, earned interest being left untouched over that period, costs at the present only $75.38. Figure 23–1 shows, in rounded figures, the different amounts of money which must be invested in order to receive $200 one year hence, two years hence, three years hence, and so forth.

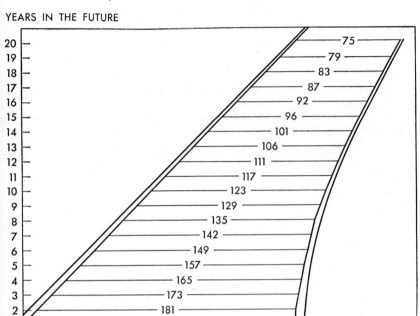

Figure 23–1. Present Values of $200 to Be Received at the End of a Specified Number of Years in the Future

YEARS IN THE FUTURE

20	75
19	79
18	83
17	87
16	92
15	96
14	101
13	106
12	111
11	117
10	123
9	129
8	135
7	142
6	149
5	157
4	165
3	173
2	181
1	$191

PRESENT VALUE

PRESENT VALUE

The amounts which for different years will yield $200 when growing at compound interest are called the "present values" of the future expected earnings. One can ascertain each separately by the use of a simple formula.[2] When in our example the twenty separate present values shown in Figure 23–1 are added, the sum total of (roundly) $2,500 is obtained. This is the present value of a machine which wears out over a period of twenty years, but which is expected to contribute an aggregate net sales revenue of $4,000 during this period—$200 year after year until the machine's service life has been exhausted.

The sum of $2,500 is, therefore, the amount of money *up to which* the entrepreneur will pay for the machine. If $2,500 is the long-run

[2] To generalize the situation, one may refer to the firmly expected net income as *a*, while the rate of interest is symbolized by the expression *r*. Present value, that is, capital value, is labeled *V*. Then:

$$V = \frac{a}{(1 + r)} + \frac{a}{(1 + r)^2} + \frac{a}{(1 + r)^3} \cdots \frac{a}{(1 + r)^n}$$

equilibrium cost of the machine, the entrepreneur would be unable to make the purchase at a lower price. If, on the other hand, the machine were priced at more than $2,500, it would not pay the entrepreneur in our example to acquire it. For then he would be earning less than 5 per cent on his investment. Another entrepreneur might be able to buy the machine at a higher price than $2,500, but to do this he would have to be more efficient than the entrepreneur in our example. Thus it has been illustrated that the rate of interest rations entrepreneurs in their use of man-made resources, each according to his efficiency.

ECONOMIC IMPLICATIONS

By purchasing plant and equipment, an entrepreneur gains access to the specific technologies embodied in particular man-made resources. The services of these technologies are managed by the entrepreneur and the labor force which assists him. Productivity stemming from technology is the reason entrepreneurs can afford interest to themselves and/or to their creditors. By investment of money capital in new plant and equipment, productivity is added *year after year* so long as the particular man-made resources last. The money itself does no work. But it enables the entrepreneur who invests it to extend his own and the economy's application of technology and thus to generate additional productivity.

The traditional explanation was that lenders of money could demand interest because they were required to wait for the returns on their money, which presumably they could have spent immediately. The fallacy of this reasoning is that waiting is not a sacrifice. It is done purposefully for the sake of sharing the benefits of technology in the form of interest received.

How Current Rates of Interest Are Determined

Particular levels of current interest rates are determined at different times in a simple manner. The level of the pure market rate of interest, considered as a performance par for entrepreneurs generally at any time, is established by the entrepreneurs themselves. That is to say, the rate of interest, which may be called the price of capital used during a given time interval, is set by demand and supply, as is any other price. But in the process the supply of capital plays a passive role, whereas the demand for capital is the active determinant of the level of the rate of interest. Now, the demand for capital evidently emanates from the entrepreneurs. If they are skilled and aggressive in trying out new ideas, their demand for capital will be high. Consequently the

level of the rate of interest will be higher, *all other things being equal,*
than it would be in the case of entrepreneurs who are sluggish as a
group, the same supply of capital being given in either instance. This
is illustrated in Figure 23–2.

The chart shows a given supply of capital by the vertical *S* line.
The demand price entrepreneurs are willing to pay as interest is
measured along the vertical axis of the graph; the quantity of capital
demanded, along the horizontal axis. The *D–D* curve is one of a
sluggish body of entrepreneurs, the D^1-D^1 curve that of an aggressive
group. The actual interest rate is evidently determined by the demand
factor.

Figure 23–2. Capital Demand Determining Interest

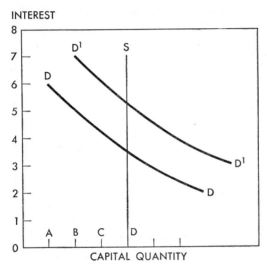

In the graph of Figure 23–2 the supply of capital is shown as given,
that is to say, the same amount will be available regardless of whether
the rate of interest paid is high or low. Some economists prefer to
think that at high rates of interest people will save more, but this
incentive is not likely to be strong.

Moreover, it is equally likely that while some people may save
more at a higher rate of interest, others will save less. To set aside a
given amount of money requires less saving when one is more liberally
rewarded for the act of saving. Compromising the issue, we might
assume that with higher rates of interest there may be a little more
saving, expressed on the graph by slightly tilting the *S* supply curve
of capital to the right. As Figure 23–3 shows, this would make little
difference in our principal assertion that it is the demand for capital

which determines the level of the rate of interest, the supply being passive over any limited time interval.

The supply of capital is in reality markedly different from the supply of finished commodities or the supply of labor and land. These are entirely independent of the demand, but the supply of capital is very much dependent upon the demand for capital. The simple reason for this is that in the United States economy the demand for capital is as much for the purpose of improving our technology as for merely maintaining any given state of the industrial arts. Improved methods

Figure 23–3. Capital Demand Still Determining Interest

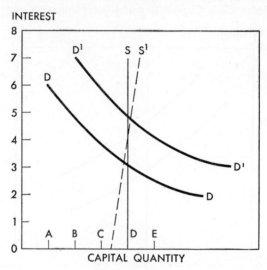

of production, however, make it possible for people's real incomes to increase. This permits them to make increased savings, so that the supply of capital available to entrepreneurs is also increased. Alternatively stated, improved technology augments the national income; and out of an increased national income more can and will be saved. The demand for capital to introduce new technologies which increase productivity increases the national income which, in turn, increases the supply of capital. The evident interdependence of demand and supply, true of capital alone among the factors of production, is pictured in Figure 23–4, in which an increased demand for capital is depicted as causing a shift of the supply curve to the right. Of course technological improvement takes time; hence this type of graph differs from others by involving an implicit time dimension as part of the "secret of progress."

The *D–D* curve in Figure 23–4 pertains to the *S* curve and does not (as in the previous graphs) depict sluggish entrepreneurs. The *D¹–D¹* curve informs us that the same entrepreneurs as those depicted by the *D–D* curve have become conscious of technological improvements which may be made and are therefore more anxious to obtain capital. At first the rate of interest increases, as shown by the point p^1. Thereafter the technological improvements, having been made and having increased the national income, have also increased the supply of capital, so that a new supply curve, S^1, now pertains to the

Figure 23–4. Technology and National Income Really Determine Interest

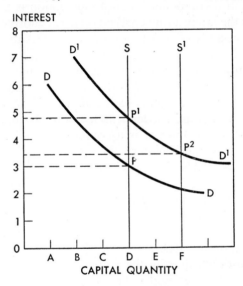

D¹–D¹ curve, the resultant rate of interest finally being lower, at p^2, though, in this illustration, not as low as the original rate *p*.

The theory of interest rate determination just portrayed may be articulated to emphasize certain interesting implications. Above all, the foregoing explanation of how the interest rate is determined makes clear that its level depends largely on the total state of economic activity rather than on any one particular factor such as personal or business saving. Old-school economists believed that investment depends upon saving which, in its turn, was represented as being dependent upon the rate of interest. Savings were thought to increase in response to a high price being paid for the use of savings. But today we know that when people have the *means* to save, they need no special inducement to do so. Prosperity (that is, a full-employment national income) affords the means to saving. That being the case, high interest rates are not required to maintain the economy in full motion.

In fact, when the economy is operating at high levels of national income, output, and employment, high interest rates constitute a redistribution of real and money income which tends to diminish the stream of spending and investing. Thus an entrepreneur who is confronted with high rates of interest cannot undertake projects other than those which have a high marginal efficiency of capital, although they may have a low social priority. For example, at a high rate of interest it is difficult to undertake low-cost housing to reach the lower-income market. If a compound interest calculation is made, it is seen that a change in the interest rate charged on home mortgage loans, from 4 to 5.5 per cent, adds several thousands of dollars to the cost of the home, placing it out of reach of many potential buyers. Needed public works projects are also retarded; for example, state and local governments in the recent past deferred even normally lucrative toll highway projects, and uncertainty has been growing about the development of the much-promised federal highway program.

Actually, the rate of interest is a complex "bundle" of short-term money market rates and long-term investment market rates on gilt-edged securities. All rates of interest are related, so that what is called the "interest rate" is really a moving average of rates of interest on debt-certificates having different maturities. Thus the federal government, acting in cooperation with the Federal Reserve System, has some influence on the rate of interest, even though it has but little control over long-term rates.

The degree with which even the limited power of government over interest rates can be exercised is largely a political consideration. It may well be that the government is unable to stem the tide of rising interest rates at a time of prosperity. The only hope for socially necessary projects at such a time, and under given political conditions, is the mere accretion to the supply of capital which naturally results from prosperity and could be a means for holding interest down. Unless this natural result is boosted by government policies to influence interest rates in a downward direction, there is a danger of high prices and relatively high interest rates associated with increasing unemployment and residual hard cores of poverty.

The argument for low interest rates is particularly strong in times of recession. At such times the public, acting through democratic government, contributes much to the reactivation of economic activity through public works construction. Hence there could be no justification for rising interest rates to scoop the financial cream of recovery.

The stated facts being increasingly well understood, and by an increasing number of persons, there is every reason to expect a long future in which interest rates will be purposefully kept low to permit the nation to become better equipped with high-priority public and private durable goods such as schools, hospitals, highways, and housing. The only question is whether the economy will reach this goal in the sunlight of prosperity or approach it by first traversing the valley of depression.

Figure 23–5 exhibits a comparison of productivity and the short-term rate of interest in the United States for three major historical

Figure 23–5. Productivity and the Federal Reserve Rediscount Rate

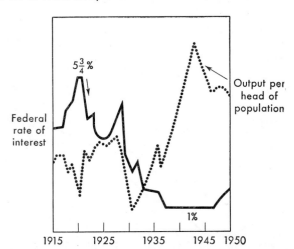

SOURCE: *Economic Report of the President*, January, 1958.

"short" periods—1915 to the Great Depression, the 1930's, and World War II and postwar times. Observe that, in the period of prosperity, short-term interest rates declined as productivity rose. During the depressed 1930's, productivity necessarily declined, as did the rate of interest. A low rate of interest, however, was not sufficient to induce recovery. For, to the entrepreneurs, the marginal efficiency of capital was even lower than the rate of interest. This of course reflected a lack of business confidence which occurred for many reasons, but among these was undoubtedly the steeply falling rate of productivity, as shown in Figure 23–5 for the period.

The short-term interest rate, that is, the Federal Reserve System's rediscount rate, is a price of money funds which is politically administered. This institutional fact explains why for many years after

1935 the rediscount rate remained fixed at the horizontal 1 per cent level shown on the graph in Figure 23–5.

The next historical graph, Figure 23–6, shows the relation, in recent years, between productivity and the long-term interest yield of grade *Aaa* corporation bonds; the price of these bonds is established in the free and competitive private capital market. In the years following World War II the long-term rate of interest rose, although there was a continual increase of productivity. This exemplifies the post-World War II situation in which there is a great deal of consumer spending to which the entrepreneurs are anxious to cater, being thereby dis-

Figure 23–6. Productivity and the Long-term Rate of Interest

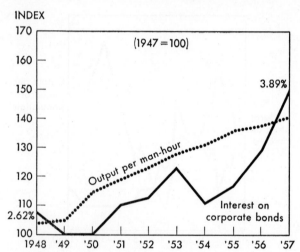

SOURCE: *Economic Report of the President,* January, 1958.

tracted from remedying a relative shortage of capital goods. (In this case this shortage of capital goods dedicated to civilian production was the heritage of depression and of hot and cold war.) Notice that in the years immediately preceding the recession which began late in 1957 the rate of increase of productivity declined, yet the rate of interest increased sharply.

Rental Incomes

A rental income is money received or calculated for the use of real property. The concept also embraces royalties paid to holders of patents, copyrights, and exclusive rights to the use of certain natural resources. Persons who own their own homes are considered to be renting their homes from themselves.

It is interesting to note that rent, as a share of the national income, has been steadily declining. It stood at 6 per cent in 1929 as against 3½ per cent a generation later.

THE DIFFERENCE BETWEEN ECONOMIC RENT AND CONTRACTUAL RENT

The actual amounts which people pay or calculate as rent are contractually specified sums of money for the use of real property over periods of stipulated durations. Now, these contractual amounts of money may include payment not only for the use of property but also for the expenses which a landlord incurs to maintain property in repair, for paying interest on his mortgage, etc. The landlord also receives interest on his investment in structures and equipment. Thus it may be seen that much of what is called "rent" represents other categories of income—interest and wages (where the landlord performs personal services for the tenants).

Economists classify as "rent" only the scarcity value of property. This may be a scarcity of certain types of fertile land, of favorably located urban sites, or of patented processes, and so on. Now, the degree of real and corporeal property changes from time to time in conformance with general economic developments. For example, a rapid settlement of a section of a city may make a given site location scarce where once the land had been of little value. Figure 23–7 illustrates this.

Suppose that an owner of pasture land had rented it to a tenant on a twenty-year lease basis. Urbanization causes the pasture land to be

Figure 23–7. Land Values Before and After Urbanization

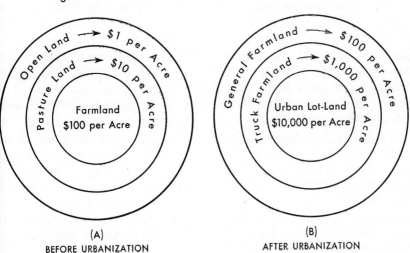

(A)   (B)
BEFORE URBANIZATION   AFTER URBANIZATION

used for truck farming, thus greatly increasing its scarcity value. But the landlord cannot claim a share or all of this increased value until the lease has expired. At that time, he can inform the tenant that he must either pay an increased rent or vacate the land. For there will be other persons, i.e., truck farmers, willing to pay a premium for the use of pasture land which can be converted to truck farming. Even if the original occupant had taken up truck farming, he would have to meet the competition of other truck farmers willing to pay a premium to occupy land located so near the new and presumably still growing city.

What Is Economic Rent?

Like interest, rent is an institutional arrangement, not a fact of nature. A wanted crop which grows on the land gives it its value, but the fact that part of this value is received by the owner of the land is a matter of economic organization. In other words, the land itself requires only the farmer to cultivate it but "is indifferent" to whether or not a landlord owns it. Evidently, then, rent is an income-distributional category, not a natural factor in production. In this respect it differs from wages; these must be paid as a condition of society's having a supply of labor.

However, as an *institutional* condition of supplies of land (and other rent-yielding assets) becoming available for use, rent plays a crucial role. Thus, unless a landlord is satisfied with rentals offered, he might withhold his land altogether; this would create not a natural scarcity but a proprietary one—which for all practical purposes would be indistinguishable from the former kind.

Rent may also be understood in terms of the alternative opportunities of a landlord for using his property. He will decide whether he wants it to be used for barley cultivation, orange growing, or perhaps for subdivision into urban building lots—depending upon which use promises to yield the highest relative rental income. If a farmer wishes to use the land for barley cultivation, he must be prepared to pay at least as much rent to the landlord as could be obtained from an orange grower. When a city "moves into the orange groves," as recently has been happening in California, it means that at no future expected price for oranges could the growers see a profit in paying rents to match the income which the landlords could obtain by making the land available for residential building lots. (This would be true in the case of the orange grower who owns his land and calculates rent instead of actually paying it; he would sell the land to a real estate development concern and take up orange cultivation elsewhere; at California real estate prices he would probably retire.)

DIFFERENTIAL ECONOMIC RENT

Earlier chapters on resources showed that physically identical goods, for example bushels of wheat, are produced at different real costs depending on the fertility, general capability, and situation of the particular land on which particular bushels of wheat are grown. Or oil of the same kind may have to be lifted from different depths, so that increasing the total supply involves increasing real cost as drilling and lifting has to be progressively deeper. Here we shall employ the concept of land capability to illustrate the nature of differential economic rent.

The reader is referred to Chapter 5 on natural resources for our previous classification of land capability grades, from grade I, the highest, to grade VIII, the lowest. For use in growing crops we can go no lower than grade IV land which requires that cultivation be carefully safeguarded by conservation practices, these may be quite expensive. Class I land requires only ordinary good farming methods if used moderately; but it also has to be safeguarded if worked intensively. Therefore, it may be no more expensive to produce wheat on grade IV land if it is done carefully and sparingly, than on grade I land if this land is worked to the point of exhaustion. Generally speaking, though, a bushel of wheat raised on the best land costs less to produce than a bushel of wheat on expensive "marginal land."

The price of wheat is determined by demand and supply, with the marginal cost schedule defining the terms on which wheat will be supplied. If the demand is sufficiently strong to require using lands of lower capabilities, say grade II land as well as grade I land, it will be the marginal cost on grade II land which must be covered if sufficient supplies are to be forthcoming. Because cultivation on grade I land is, however, less expensive (assuming it to be moderately used, not exhaustively), a surplus revenue will accrue to the cultivators on grade I land who are receiving a price based on the more expensive cultivation of grade II land. Each bushel of wheat, being identical with the others, will command the relatively high price based on the cultivation costs for grade II land, since it would be impossible to differentiate the various sources of identical goods coming into markets. If, then, with increasing demand, land of the lower capabilities III and IV has to be put into cultivation, it is obvious that: (1) rent will be created on grades II and III of land successively, while (2) the rent on land grade I will keep increasing.

There is nothing objectionable about this, the conventional manner of explaining the origin and rise of rent in the context of price analysis, where the problem is that of rationing consumers through price so as to prevent the waste of valuable resources. (See Table 17–1 and accompanying discussion on pages 407 to 410.) However, this production emphasis is apt to be misleading in the present context of income distribution.

From this point of view, rent as a share of national income has the peculiarity of being a *deduction* from value added in production, rather than constituting itself a value added in production. To appreciate this, one need only recall that, in its origin, rent is measured by the spread between marginal cost (*mc*) and average total unit cost (*atuc*)—before *atuc* has been revised upward by an entrepreneur to reflect the increased money cost due to the necessity of paying rent. (See Figure 17–11, page 409.)

David Ricardo, one of the original formulators of the theory of rent, gave as neat an illustration as any of the characteristic of rent being a deduction from value added in production, rather than itself constituting value added. Ricardo assumes the economic situation of a country which is in an early stage of settlement during which rich land can be had for the asking (as under our homestead laws). For purposes of illustration he postulates that an annual output of 300 quarters of wheat (2,400 bushels) can be obtained on this rich land by an investment which in monetary value equals an amount that could be realized by selling 200 quarters of wheat (1,600 bushels) at whatever is the price current of wheat. With an investment equal to 200 quarters of wheat and an output of 300 quarters, there is a surplus of 100 quarters of wheat which accrues to the cultivator of the rich land; that is a profit of 50 per cent on the investment. (Actually, this is not all profit; some of it constitutes the wages of the farmer and his normal profit. But for the sake of simplicity we shall, with Ricardo, overlook this complication which in the present context does not really matter.)

As Ricardo's hypothetical country becomes settled (he was actually thinking of America), less fertile and/or less favorably located land must be taken into cultivation. To obtain an output of 300 quarters of wheat now requires an annual investment of an amount equal to the sales value of 210 quarters of wheat, at the price current, whether or not this price is rising. Of course the original settlers on the best land still need invest only the equivalent of 200 quarters of wheat in a year to obtain an output of 300 quarters. Their profit continues for a time to be 50 per cent, but the cultivators of the second-grade land, newly brought into cultivation, are realizing only 43 per cent (90 quarters of surplus product on an investment of 210 quarters).

Under this circumstance, it would be a matter of indifference to the cultivators of grade II land whether they cultivated it and realized

43 per cent profit, or cultivated grade I land and paid for this privilege a rent to the landlord who owns grade I land, provided of course this rent did not exceed 14 quarters of wheat. An investment of 200 quarters with a net return of 86 bushels yields the same profit of 43 per cent as does an investment of 210 quarters with a net product of 90 bushels. Presumably, therefore, some cultivators of grade II land will offer the landlords owning grade I land a premium to induce them to remove the present tenants from that land. At first the offer will be 5 or 6 bushels, let us say. This offer, however, places the landlords owning grade I land into a bargaining position vis-à-vis their present tenants, who are informed that they must at least match the offers made by other cultivators or, upon expiration of their lease, vacate the land. Thus a competition is set up between the present occupants and would-be occupants of grade I land. In theory, and under pure competition in the market for land leases, the landlords would succeed in reaping a full harvest of rent of 14 bushels, the amount which reduces the profit on grade I land to the level of that which on a cost-of-production basis can be realized on grade II land.

From this point on, with more and more land being settled, Ricardo's illuminating example proceeds as shown in Table 23–1.

This demonstration that rent is a *result of* value added in production, and not in itself value added, is meaningful in more than academic terms. For it shows that with rent being the result of scarcity —a reward which in comparison to labor and management income is "unearned"—owners of scarce resources may effect public policies to prolong a scarcity which might be overcome by importing the same kind of resources from abroad when they can there be extracted under more favorable, efficient conditions. But this is not the only example which might be given of how, in internal economic affairs as well as in international affairs, scarcity has sometimes been artificially accentuated in order to augment the rents of scarcity. This discussion reveals, in general, that one is always well advised to probe any practical economic issue to discover whether or not it has, besides a production aspect, a special meaning in the context of income distribution —that of a "special" or "vested" interest being opposed to the interest of every other economic group in the community.

The differential rent phenomenon may also be illustrated with regard to urban land sites. When the pueblo of Los Angeles was first established, land in what is now the downtown financial district could probably be had for the asking. Yet tremendous land values are now attached to sites in this downtown area, based on high rentals which can be charged and are paid by businesses in that location. Financial firms can afford to pay the high rentals because it is efficient to do

Table 23–1. Progress of Rent and Profit

Estimated Capital (quarters of wheat)	Profit (per cent)	Net Produce After Paying Cost of Production on Each Capital (quarters of wheat)	Profit (P) and Rent (R) of Portions of Land (in quarters of wheat)											
			1st Portion		2d Portion		3d Portion		4th Portion		5th Portion		6th Portion	
			P	R	P	R	P	R	P	R	P	R	P	R
200	50	100	100	none.										
210	43	90	86	14	90	none.								
220	36	80	72	28	76	14	80	none.						
230	30	70	60	40	63	27	66	14	70	none.				
240	25	60	50	50	52½	37½	55	25	57½	12½	60	none.		
250	20	50	40	60	42	48	44	36	46	24	48	12	50	none.

SOURCE: *An Essay on the Influence of a Low Price of Corn on the Profits of Stock* (London, 1815) in Piero Sraffa and M. H. Dobb (ed.), *The Works and Correspondence of David Ricardo* (London: Cambridge University Press, 1951), vol. IV, adapted from the table on p. 17.

business in this central location close to the stock exchange and other branches of the Southern California capital market. Likewise, merchants on any Main Street of the nation pay high rentals based on the advantage of being centrally located where townspeople, tourists, and farmers from the neighboring countryside congregate to do their shopping. Notice that it is the prices which consumers are willing to pay that determine what rents shall be—the fact that one pays high rental does not permit charging higher prices.

In other words, there are some central locations at which, given a certain level of prices, one can sell more and therefore realize more profit-income than in less favorable locations. The best sites for doing business therefore become "grade I land" as compared with outlying business locations. If a downtown firm does not wish to pay the high rentals of the downtown location, it can move, only to see its profit-income diminished. Therefore it will normally be willing to pay the higher downtown rental. Or when buying downtown real estate, the firm will pay more for it than for land sites away from the central shopping district. (The rise of decentralized supermarket shopping areas does not alter the fundamental principle of rent; instead of speaking about "downtown locations" we should think in terms of "express-way locations.")

PECULIARITY OF ECONOMIC RENT

Truly economic rent is not a cost of production in the ordinary sense of the word. The lands on which mankind produces its starchy foods were given by nature and had only to be settled—the wheat lands of the American prairies and Russian steppes, the millet lands of Africa, and the rice bowl lands of Indo-China. Again, human beings did not bury millions of years ago untold billions of tiny shelled (foraminifera) organisms, which, being crushed, produced subterranean oil deposits that sometimes give fabulous value to land above them—even when it is submerged offshore ocean-bottom land!

By contrast, labor of particular kinds and capital equipment of various types can be freely supplied in greater or lesser quantities. Human and man-made resources are not given by nature in fixed amounts. There is nothing fixed or given, for instance, about a battery of machine tools. More units or batteries can be made, or the existing supply diminished, depending only on the demand for the finished goods which the machine tools help to produce. And labor as well as management skills of particular types can be increased by suitable training and wage incentives. One must meet only the required cost of production.

Since most of the fertility of soil is given by nature and is not man-made, the site value of urban land is not created by individuals. That is to say, as the United States population grew, cities like Chicago were founded at important crossroads of the nation, at port outlets, or where iron ore or other natural resources were concentrated or could be shipped economically so that manufacturing could be under-taken. The resulting relative scarcity of urban and industrial sites was therefore of social origin; the basis of this type of land value was *general* economic activity, not the individual efforts of those land speculators who arrived early, bought the land cheaply, and then sold or rented it dearly. Croplands, oil lands, and urban sites bear the hallmark of economic value because of the pressure of demand, not because much, if any, effort was exerted as a cost of production.

COMPUTATION OF LAND VALUE

A fact of nature simplifies the determination of land values. With only ordinary care an acre of land can furnish a "perpetual" flow of physical product. Let us assume that this product of an acre of land can be sold at prices which will yield $100 net income forever. The purchaser of the land would therefore acquire a right to a perpetuity, income that can be realized as long as is desired. What would this acre of land be worth, at its present value, taking the rate of interest to be 5 per cent?

All of the payments which a person would make for a yearly income of $100, from here to eternity, would by the law of compound interest aggregate to $2,000. This figure is determined by applying a simple formula for ascertaining the present value of a perpetual asset. This formula reads:

$$\text{Present value} = \frac{\text{annual expected income}}{(1 + \text{ rate of interest})^n} = \$2,000$$

The result can be checked by expanding the simplified formula:[3]

$$V \text{ (present value)} = \frac{a}{(1 + r)} + \frac{a}{(1 + r)^2} + \frac{a}{(1 + r)^3} \cdots \frac{a}{(1 + r)^n}$$

shown in footnote 2 on page 591. When there is an infinite geometrical progression of smaller and smaller amounts of present values, as would

---

[3] This formula is an infinite geometrical progression with a first term $a/(1 + r)$, and ratio $1/(1 + r)$. The limit of such a series is:

$$\frac{a/(1 + r)}{1-[1/(1 + r)]}$$

This expression, when cleared, reduces to a/r; the formula for the present value of a perpetual asset is, therefore: $V = a/r$.

be true of a perpetually income-yielding asset, the capitalization formula reduces to:

$$\text{Present value} = \frac{\text{annual expected income}}{\text{rate of interest}}$$

In the present example, the perpetually expected annual income from the acre of land is $100; the rate of interest is 5 per cent. Therefore, the present value of the acre of land is $100/.05, which equals $2,000. Observe that this is exactly twenty times the amount of expected yearly income. By the same method of calculation, the price of this acre of land would be $3,333 if the rate of interest were 3 per cent instead of 5 per cent; this may be readily verified by the reader.

From this explanation emerges a simple rule of capitalizing land whose productivity, with ordinary care, is given to man forever. Simply multiply the expected annual income by the reciprocal value of the rate of interest at which the land is to be capitalized at the present moment.

WHAT IS THE ECONOMIC FUNCTION OF RENT?

One of the functions of wages, we know, is to act as an incentive to workers to engage in given types of production; likewise salaries induce managerial efforts in particular directions. In this sense rent has no economic function, for paying rent to an owner of land does not cause the land to become fertile or a city to be settled at that location. But stimulating production in an absolute sense is not really the function of price; hunger and the love of comforts would achieve that. The paramount function of price is not to create resources but to direct them to their relatively most productive uses. In this sense, the allocative sense, rent has a genuine economic function, as the following demonstration indicates.

Let us suppose that on a certain acreage of land a farmer produces a crop worth $7,500 above depreciation and maintenance cost of the equipment and conservation expense of the land. The equipment is worth $10,000 at original cost value. This means that at a market rate of 5 per cent interest he must earn $500 a year to cover interest (for otherwise he would have benefited by lending his $10,000 rather than buying equipment). The farmer hires one laborer to whom he pays $2,000 in wages. His own labor he figures as being worth $3,000 a year, which he could earn by working for someone else instead of managing his own farm. He must earn $1,000 as normal profit, for the toil and trouble of operating as an individual entrepreneur, risking his own money and managing it besides.

The sum of these costs is $6,500; if he failed to earn this sum, he would sell his equipment, discharge the laborer, and himself seek work elsewhere. Actually though, the farmer in our example has gross earnings of $7,500—a thousand dollars more than is required to cover his cost of production including normal profit. This is the surplus revenue which the land contributes, which we label rent, whether or not it is retained by the farmer or paid by him to a landlord who owns the land which the farmer is cultivating.

So long as the farmer can realize surplus revenue above $6,500 of cost and pay it to the landlord in rent, the landlord will see to it that the land is used only for cultivating the particular rent-yielding crop. Alternatively, if the price of the product grown on this land were only to yield $6,500 for the output, instead of $7,500, it would be a matter of indifference to the farmer or the landlord to have this land used for the cultivation of the particular crop, for it would yield no rent. But so long as land yields rent, say, when it is used to produce barley, it will be used for that purpose until some more productive use is found to yield a higher rental. Thus rent rations the use of land.

Illustration may also be given with regard to urban land sites. It is to society's interest to have the most effective entrepreneurs situated at the centers of commerce or on the best industrial sites near power and water sources and central transportation facilities. By requiring a graduated payment of rent, rising high for the best sites, only the most qualified entrepreneurs can afford to be located at the best sites. Thus rent may be seen as constituting a part of our fundamental price mechanism which rations resources to those producers best able to serve the public. Only those whose $mrp = pf$ may use the best resources.

The rationing function of rent being appreciated, the question has nevertheless been raised why rent should be paid to individual owners of land. Over a century ago the English economist John Stuart Mill asserted that because land brings constantly increasing income to the owners in a "prosperous country . . . apart from any exertion or expenditure on his part," rent should be "subjected to special taxation in virtue of that increase . . ."[4] Others, notably Henry George[5] and Harry Gunnison Brown,[6] went further and argued that not only increased rental but all rental should be taxed. Thus taxation would rest on natural wealth rather than on burdening the wage earner and the

---

[4] *Dissertations and Discussions* (London: Longmans, Green, Inc., 1869–75), vol. V, pp. 256–57.

[5] *Progress and Poverty* (New York: Robert Schalkenback Foundation, 1955). First published in 1879.

[6] *Economic Science and the Common Welfare* (2d ed.; Columbia, Mo.: Lucas Brothers, 1925), chap. vi.

businessman. Henry George thought the tax on economic rent would cover all government expenditure and would therefore suffice as a *single tax*. Official data show that if all rents were to be fully taxed, the total tax bill of federal, state, and local governments could possibly be reduced by $10 billion. The remaining advocates of rent taxation claim that it would make home ownership more accessible to persons of limited financial means, as well as reduce farm tenancy. Land values would decline in consequence of a tax on rent. Land values and rent once lay at the heart of the farm problem; but, as we shall see, this is no longer the farmer's view.

The Farmer's Income Problem

Of the American farmer it has been said that in good times he is a businessman and in bad times he is a laborer. During prosperity he is profit-conscious; at other times he hopes to be able to earn a minimum wage.

THE FARMER AS A BUSINESSMAN

Although American agriculture is highly commercialized, farming is still a way of life as well as a business. Whereas in industry it is relatively easy to change from job to job, a major decision is involved for the farmer when he is asked to abandon his farm, which is also his homestead. He may be cultivating crops on land which, from a conservationist's point of view is submarginal and which yields the farmer a meager income. There are farmers who cultivate tracts of good land but which are of too limited a size to permit the use of modern farm equipment and efficient methods of production. According to the 1954 census of agriculture, one out of every three American farms contains forty-nine acres or less.

Except in the case of high-priced specialty crops, the cultivation of only a small acreage places the farmer in a difficult market position. It is a position of immobility. The farmer is not bound to the soil, but because of his limited means he experiences difficulty in exploring alternative economic opportunities. The supply of the small farmer's produce is therefore quite inelastic. When farm prices are high, he produces to the limit, but it is a modest limit. When farm prices are low, he is forced to produce to the limit in order to exist.

The scope of farm enterprises can be ascertained in terms of their dollar volumes of sales. Table 23–2 shows that two-thirds of the nation's farmers, in the census year of 1950, had a sales volume of $5,000 or less. Together these 67 per cent of farmers realized 25 per cent of the total value of farm products sold.

Table 23–2. Percentages of Commercial Farms in Different Size Categories, 1950

Category, by Value of Farm Product Sold	Percentage of Commercial Farms in That Category	Percentage of Resident Farm Operators per Category	Percentage of Value of All Farm Products Sold per Category
$250 to $1,999	19.4	19.5	2.3
$2,000 to $2,499	24.3	24.4	7.4
$2,500 to $4,999	23.8	24.0	14.8
$5,000 to $9,999	19.5	19.6	23.1
$10,000 to $24,999	10.3	10.2	25.5
$25,000 or more	2.8	2.5	26.9

SOURCE: Department of Commerce, Bureau of the Census, *U.S. Census of Agriculture: 1950*, Vol. II.

From Table 23–2 an inference may readily be drawn that many farm families and individuals must supplement their farm incomes by accepting employment in nonfarm occupations. As a matter of fact, only 25 per cent of our rural-farm families could exist on their farm incomes in 1955. This is shown in Table 23–3.

Table 23–3 reveals, surprisingly, that 37 per cent of farm families had no *money income* at all from farm enterprise.

There are, of course, medium-sized and large farm enterprises in the United States which are managed with scientific precision and in which a great deal of money has been invested. The air traveler over eastern Colorado can see neat geometrically patterned contour farms, large wheat farms in Nebraska, huge, centrally managed fields of

Table 23–3. Rural-Farm Families by Source of Money Income, 1955

Money Income Situation		Percentage of Families
Having Farm Self-Employment Income, Total		63
With no other kinds of earnings	25	
With off-farm incomes	38	
Having No Farm Self-Employment Income, Although Living on Farms, Total		37
With wages and salaries earned elsewhere	17	
With other income combinations	20	
		100
Total number of rural-farm families = 5.3 million		

SOURCE: U.S. Department of Commerce, Bureau of the Census, *Current Population Reports—Consumer Income*, Series P-60, No. 24 (1957), p. 3.

cotton in Texas, and, for field crops, the "factories in the field" of California. One-half of the value of all farm products sold was produced by only 13 per cent of all farm operators, in 1950. In that year, a handful of 2.5 per cent of all farm operators, who individually had a sales volume of $25,000 and above, produced somewhat more than did another 67 per cent of our farmers, that is, the small farmers.

These data reveal that the farmer's income problem is not primarily a problem of price. It is pre-eminently one of inadequate size of many of our farms, their poor location on submarginal land, and the lack of capital equipment and funds with which to buy equipment.

The farms which are of sufficient size to be efficiently operated yield their owners good financial returns. The land is treated with sound conservation practices, and productive farm equipment is used. It is these farms of ample size which have contributed most to a productivity breakthrough which practically doubled agricultural output in the single decade between 1947 and 1957. The well-located American farm of adequate size is not burdened by heavy mortgage indebtedness. Never before in American history has the economically and geographically well-situated farmer been as independent as he is at present. Thus the farm problem reduces to the plight of the small farmer who, in the parlance of business, works with inferior physical assets and does not have enough capital really to be in business.

Farm history. American farmers, large and small, for many years until World War II experienced difficulty in earning adequate incomes. Although the farmer is reputedly a rugged individualist, farmers cooperated politically, as early as 1867, in the effort to secure by the power of their massed vote beneficial federal farm legislation. In that year the Patrons of Husbandry (National Grange) was founded to secure regulation of burdensome railroad rates as well as storage rates charged at warehouses and grain elevators. A veritable rash of farm organizations occurred in the 1880's, outstanding among them being the National Farmers' Northwest Alliance and the National Farmers' Cooperative Union of America, a southern organization. These organizations joined with an early national-scale labor organization, the Knights of Labor, to form the Populist Party. To be sure, the farmer wing of this historic party was concerned mainly with securing cheap money—by federal legislation for the free coinage of silver at a ratio of 16 to 1 to the value of an ounce of gold. The labor wing of the Populist Party was rather more interested in having the federal government place social controls on the strident big business of that era. Together, farmers and laborers forged a program of demands, pressing for institutions which we now have and take for granted. Among these is the graduated income tax, the direct election of senators, postal savings banks, and, of course, cheap money.

The Populist Party was lost in the sweep of the silver oratory of William Jennings Bryan; it fused, in 1896, with the presently existing Democratic Party. Thereafter the farmers steered their political course independently of organized labor, although farmer-labor parties persisted in Scandinavian-German areas, for example, Minnesota and North Dakota, well into the 1920's. For the most part, however, the farmers exerted organized political pressure up to the mid-1930's with the primary aim of securing agricultural credit on reasonable terms. Many agricultural credit acts were passed by Congress (for example, the Agricultural Credits Act of 1923); Joint Stock Land Banks were established under the auspices of the federal government to facilitate farmers' borrowing at cheap long-term mortgage rates. In 1927 they strongly agitated for a bill, the McNary-Haugen Bill, which attempted to deal with what had by then become the still existing "farm surplus problem."

Under the McNary-Haugen Bill, prices of agricultural products were to be raised in the home market by selling farm surpluses in foreign markets for whatever price they might bring. Farmer exporters of specified crops who lost money on the transactions were to be reimbursed. This was to be accomplished by levying a fee on all those American farmers who were expected to benefit by the augmented home prices of agricultural produce. The fee was called an "equalization fee." The proposed practice of selling abroad regardless of the domestic (and foreign) cost of production is known to economists as "dumping." The McNary-Haugen Bill was twice vetoed by President Coolidge, so it never became effective.

President Hoover in 1929 approached the so-called "farm surplus problem" in a different manner. Under his regime a Federal Farm Board was established, with a revolving credit fund of $500 million for loans to marketing "cooperatives." These were in reality quasi-voluntary organizations which bought produce from the farmers and, by storing it, held this produce off the market. By thus reducing domestic supplies of specified crops, principally wheat and cotton, domestic prices were to be raised. But the knowledge that the stored supplies could be offered in the markets at any time tended to *depress* prices.

PARITY PRICE

Among the principal measures promulgated by the Roosevelt Administration were several "Agricultural Adjustment Acts," the first being enacted in 1933. This Act laid the foundation of the present type of farm policy.

The general intention of past and present parity price legislation is to restore the relation which existed, from August, 1909, to July 1914, between the purchasing power of farmers and the purchasing power of city dwellers. It was argued that after that period the farmer had been forced to pay monopolistic prices for the products of industry, while selling his produce to urbanites at competitive world market prices. The presumably equitable relationship of city and country purchasing power of 1909–1914 was therefore to be restored under the rubric of "parity."

The principal instrumentation of "farm parity" is the purchase of "surpluses" of specified types of crops by the federal government. Actually, the farmers were supposed to receive loans on surplus portions of their crops, pledging the produce as security. Since the crop loan was not repaid by the farmer, the transaction amounted to the farmer selling his crop to the government, which then held it in storage. During and after World War II some agricultural surpluses were sent as gifts to our Allies.

When the supply of specified types of farm produce was reduced in the domestic market, prices naturally rose. In return for this aid, given by government at the expense of the consumer, farmers were expected to reduce their acreages of those crops that were declared to be overproduced. The crops principally involved were cotton, wheat, corn, and tobacco. These are crops whose intensive cultivation exhausts the soil. For this reason, the policy of the Roosevelt Administration, in urging acreage reductions of soil-exhausting crops, had a more constructive aim than that of simply raising farm prices. As a matter of fact, the intention of Henry Wallace, the head of the Department of Agriculture at the time, was to encourage farmers to diversify their production.

The original AAA legislation of 1933 (Agricultural Adjustment Act) was declared unconstitutional by the Supreme Court in 1936 because it placed a tax on middlemen who first handle a crop after it has left the farm. The Supreme Court declared that the processing tax was an instance of the power to tax being the power to destroy.

The original legislation of 1933 was immediately replaced by the Soil Conservation and Domestic Allotment Act of 1936. This made available to farmers cultivating specified crops—not only soil-exhausting crops—federal subsidies on the condition that farmers reduce the planting of specified crops, and plant instead soil-building legumes, grasses, trees. Farmers could also qualify for benefits by adopting recommended practices of soil conservation. Then, in 1938, another

Agricultural Adjustment Act was passed by Congress, which omitted the unconstitutional processing tax. Under this legislation, farmers who reduced their planting of specified "surplus" crops, and observed recommended soil conservation practices, qualified for receiving parity price aid. That is to say, if, after the acreage reductions undertaken by subscribing farmers, a farm surplus was still declared to exist, the farmer could make crop loans against the security of a part of the crop which he delivered to the government for storage. Since these loans did not have to be repaid, this amounted to the farmer selling "surplus" portions of the crop to the government. The government's store of farm produce was labeled an "ever-normal granary," that is, a revolving reserve of farm produce. Crops which the government thus acquired began to be held in the familiar corrugated iron bins which now greet the eye of the motorist in the midwest.

Under the 1938 AAA, specific allotments of acreage to individual farmers were made by the farmers themselves upon the recommendation of government agricultural agents. The farmers met, and continue to meet, at an annual meeting of their respective conservation districts. At these meetings, the majority decides whether or not the allotment plan should be continued.[7] If the majority vote is in the affirmative, the individual farmer consults with the government's agricultural agent in order to determine his specific allotment of acreage for the crops covered by the general plan. Any individual farmer can withdraw from the plan, but by doing so he becomes ineligible to receive benefits under the plan. Of course he still gains from the rise of the price of subsidized crops. But this places him in the position of being a "free rider." That is a dubious distinction which few farmers desire.

The combination of parity benefits, based on the reduction of specified types of farm produce supplies, with soil conservation benefits still forms the essence of American farm policy. What has been the impact of this type of policy on the farmer's income position?

The answer is implicit in the explanation, given at the beginning of this section, of the nature of the farm problem. Parity pricing has not greatly aided the small farmer. Because his enterprise is of inadequate size, the amount of subsidy he receives under the parity program is not substantial. For example, the median income of farmers was $2,340 per farm family in 1955, and this included earnings made away from the farm. A few hundred dollars of parity payment added to this still left a farmer far short of the $4,500 required to sustain a family of four at a moderately decent and comfortable standard of living. The increment of the farm price caused by artificially render-

---

[7] In November, 1958, farmers voted in a national referendum to end the 25-year-old production controls on corn, the nation's largest-value crop.

ing scarce the supply of the crop adds a bit to the income of farmers, whether they subscribe to the parity program or not. This still leaves the small farmer short of an adequate family income.

The large farmer, on the other hand, could probably do well under unrestricted market competition. His farm is mechanized, of proper size, and the land is properly treated and is therefore bursting with productivity.

IN CONCLUSION

Our national agricultural policies, although oriented toward conservation, have accorded aid to farmers in the form of price support. This is to regard the farmer solely in his role of businessman. But in the case of the small farmer it disregards his family income needs. Moreover, it ignores the needs of our most precious natural resource, the land. The hope of the agricultural policy-makers seems to be that when once the farmer earns a little more, he will invest money in improving the land and acquiring capital equipment. This is often a great deal to expect. For instance, farmers on severely eroded lands are almost without exception "ill-fed, ill-clad, and ill-housed." The pittance of parity support which they may receive is most likely to be spent rather than invested.

We must separate the income aspect and the production and price aspects of the farm problem by the following:

1. Providing a legislated *income* parity formula which will afford a moderate comfort and decency standard of living to a person tilling soil which is worth using.
2. Assisting people to get off hopelessly submarginal land—by suitable incentives, not by forcing them off.
3. Giving *conservation aid* to farmers in the forms of actual equipment, materials, rare seeds, and specialized research services, rather than in the form of cash.

This is what Dr. H. H. Bennett learned in a lifetime of experience as a farmer, scholar, and government expert: "Government aid in the interest of permanent soil conservation is really effective only when scientifically applied on the basis of the needs and capabilities of the land itself."

Profits

From the viewpoint of economics, profit is any residual amount left in a business after it has met all money costs that were contracted to be paid for services of labor, management, land, and capital. Ordinary salaries paid to management personnel do not form a part of profit; the salaries must be paid before profit is counted. There are some owners of unincorporated businesses—small merchants, farmers, and so on—who mistakenly believe that they have gained more profit than is actually the case. This is because they fail to impute to their own services a salary commensurable with what they might earn by working for another entrepreneur.

FUNCTIONAL TYPES: NORMAL PROFIT

Normal profit is as a matter of fact a misnomer. The 6 or 7 per cent which is earned by the representative firm, at long-run equilibrium, is really interest on the firm's own investment. Let us say that the pure long-term rate of interest is 3 to $3\frac{1}{2}$ per cent. In real life a premium to allow for special risks peculiar to any given business is customarily added to the pure rate of interest. Only a concern of great consequence can expect to borrow money at the pure rate of long-term interest; that is, only the largest firms can float their *Aaa* bonds at 3 or $3\frac{1}{2}$ per cent. The rest must pay a risk-premium to lenders, the amount of which is calculable on the basis of the special risks attached to any given line of production, or peculiar to particular types of firms—for example, those which have not as yet become fully established as going concerns, those possessing only limited assets, and so forth.

Now let us look at this matter of risk, not from the viewpoint of a lender of money, but from the standpoint of a person who invests his own money in his business. He too requires to be paid a premium in addition to earning the pure rate of interest on his money. This is not a risk-premium, for the businessman trusts himself; else he would not put money into the business. But there is toil and trouble involved in using personally owned funds in one's business, rather than lending it at interest. To compensate himself for assuming the toil and trouble of financing the business with his own money, an entrepreneur customarily adds to the cost of pure interest on his investment an amount equal to the pure rate of long-term interest.

This is a custom of long standing; it is reflected in the Code of Justinian (the sixth-century Byzantine emperor).[8] Adam Smith in 1776 stated that: "Double interest is in Great Britain reckoned, what the merchants call a good, moderate, reasonable profit; terms which I apprehend mean no more than a common and usual profit."[9] In modern

---

[8] Gibbon informs us that by the amended Code "persons of illustrious rank were confined to the moderate profit of four per cent; ... ; eight was allowed for the convenience of manufacturers and merchants; ..." This resembles the difference, at present, between the rate on gilt-edged bonds and what is called "normal profit." See *Decline and Fall of the Roman Empire* (New York: Random House, Inc., Modern Library, 1932), II, p. 370.

[9] *The Wealth of Nations*, Bk. I, chap. ix.

times, the long-term rate of interest gravitates towards a level of 3 to 3.5 per cent. Six to 7 per cent is generally considered to be normal profit. It can now be appreciated that this gain of 6 to 7 per cent on investment is really the pure rate of long-term interest, augmented by a conventional premium for the trouble of using money owned, by individuals or groups, to conduct their own business.

NONCOMPETITIVE PROFIT

Chapter 19 shows that monopolistic competition does not enable a firm to gain excess profits. A concern which "differentiates" its product by the use of a trademark may realize surplus profit. This is accomplished by artificially creating one's own submarket, in which the firm will possess a degree of monopoly power. However, the other firms can, by advertising their brand name, also create their own markets and raise their prices. When many or all of the firms in an industry do this, the quantity demanded of the output of the entire industry necessarily diminishes according to the basic commodity's market demand schedule. This forces each member firm of the sundered industry to produce at an average total unit cost which is less than the minimum. Thereby the extra profit which was gained originally by raising the price monopolistically is ultimately eliminated.

Profits of monopoly. A pure monopoly is a theoretical construct. In real life single-firm monopoly can only exist: (1) when a natural resource is found in a unique location; or (2) when heavy investment is required to produce a commodity on a large scale or not at all. In that case, the output of the single firm may suffice to serve the entire market for the commodity. For instance, in the case of power and light utilities excessive profit could be realized, all other things being equal. In the American economy natural monopolies are regulated by public authority. They are customarily allowed, by public control commissions, to earn a "fair rate of return," not more. The "fair rate of return" is defined as one which permits the single firm to earn a sufficient amount of profit so as to be able, competitively, to attract capital. This theoretically implies that the single concern would, at long-run equilibrium, earn the normal profit of from 6 to 7 per cent. In practice, a higher return may be allowed; how much the actual return may be must be determined on a case-by-case basis.

Monopoly profits may be earned by reason of a grant of patent made by the government. This confers upon a private business concern the privilege of making exclusive use of a superior method of production to produce a commodity which is unique. The firm possessing the patent may legally charge a monopoly price for its unique product. The grant of legal patent monopoly is purposely made to encourage the development of new products, by assuring the developer "pioneering profits." In the United States, the term of a patent is seventeen years, which means, in practice, that the firm enjoys about eleven years of legally protected monopoly profit. It is estimated that three years, on the average, are required for a new product to win acceptance in the market. A wise firm will lower its price during the last three years of a patent. For at the termination of the patent other firms will enter the field and sell the same product at a much lower price.

In wartime, profits of monopoly could be enjoyed by the sellers of civilian goods, most of which are in short supply because productive resources must be diverted to the war effort. War automatically creates "sellers' markets." However, modern governments impose price controls and rationing of commodities; in addition, they levy taxes on excess profits. If this were not done, people during this time of absolute scarcity would be rationed "by their pocketbooks" rather than in terms of their basic needs. The result would be a diminution of the entire morale of the war effort.

Profits of monopoly are in times of peace occasionally reaped because competitive adjustments of prices and outputs take time. Short-run profits which are gained because goods can be sold at a marginal cost which is greater than minimum average total unit cost are, in a manner of speaking, monopoly profits. But by the same token, where competition is technologically feasible, monopoly profits tend to be of short duration.

PROFITS OF OLIGOPOLY

Competition depends upon the freedom of new firms to enter an expanding industry. In that case existing firms may expand output and keep price constant in the long run, thereby simulating competition. However, there are numerous modern technologies which in order to be efficiently applied must be operated on a large scale. The cost of entry which would have to be met by a new firm may be forbidding. The stage is then set for oligopoly—competition among only a few large firms which already exist in an industry.

Under these conditions patterns of tacit or open collaboration in price and output determination make their appearance. "Cournot-competition," as described in Chapter 19, becomes the rule of the game. It is a game in which a limited number of firms rival each other in securing customers but refrain from overt price competition for fear of unleashing a price war. Restraint of trade does not occur because the high-cost technology, which limits the number of firms, also prompts them to make the greatest use of the technology. To make the most of the required heavy investment goods are produced in abundance. However, the administered prices of the goods are relatively high in comparison with their theoretical competitive level. The interesting question arises of whether under pure competition there would be sufficient incentive or financial ability among many producers to cooperate in jointly developing an expensive technology—a technology which, by its very nature, requires the concentration of an industry's output in a few, heavily financed centers.

There is one certain outcome of oligopoly when it is viewed in the context of income distribution. The share of profits will *at any moment* be higher in an economy which is structured to include oligopolies than it would be under pure competition. However, the findings of static analysis must be modified when we adopt a realistic perspective. The profits of corporate oligopoly are taxed by the federal government. Substantial amounts of corporate profits which remain after taxes are plowed back into the business. Surplus profit becomes a means of corporate self-financing when this is done. Finally, organized labor successfully claims its share and thereby reduces, in effect, the degree of oligopoly.

To the extent that surplus profits which are plowed back are used to improve the technology managed by the oligopolist, material abundance is increased. To the extent that surplus profits are used to sustain expensive advertising and selling cost, nothing of material worth is added.

INCALCULABLE UNCERTAINTY

The preceding remarks summarize explanations of profit which were separately made in the different chapters of Part IV. In the structural view of the origin of profit, no residual amount of sales income would be left to a firm, over the long pull, under pure competition or under imperfect competition. (Bear in mind that so-called normal profit is really interest surcharged with an "inconvenience premium.") Thus it would appear that profit, defined as income above the economic total of money costs, can only be realized under conditions of monopoly or oligopoly.

This is a theoretically constructed finding, too strictly conceived to be applicable as a direct interpretation to the facts of economic life. The element of error in the making of economic judgments enters into the day-by-day traffic of business; so does the "personal equation." That is to say, the mind of an entrepreneur is not the simple analogue of a universal digital computer which, upon being taped with all pertinent information, flawlessly casts out irrelevant data and unswervingly comes to a perfect maximum-profit solution.

Then, too, an entrepreneur is rarely able to obtain all the information which in the short run and long run will have a bearing on the outcome of a business decision made at any moment. The entrepreneur must take chances. In doing so, he may make costly errors— or he may later find himself faring better than he anticipated. Of course the entrepreneur attempts to take only risks which are calculable, so that they can be insured either by buying protection from specialized insurance agencies, or by setting aside a financial reserve for the contingency of loss or unexpected increases of necessary expenditures. But after all cost and risk has been estimated, there remains the need for taking the *calculated* risk, that is, the *incalculable* risk of overevaluating or underestimating future profit. The art of entrepreneurship is distinguished not by a submission to risk, but by an understanding of when a calculated risk should be taken.

Observe that the act of venturing, in the face of incalculable uncertainty, is not to be construed as gambling. The risk of overevaluating or underestimating the profitability of innovation is inherent in the economic situation, unlike the gambling risk, which is artificially created. Of course this remark does not apply to promotional projects which are designed to take advantage of consumer gullibility. The author's framework of reference is that of entrepreneurs who wish to innovate an improved use of the community's technology and who find that in order to do so they must take calculated risks.

The Modern Entrepreneur

The "personal element" naturally enters into economic decision-making, but it can be dramatized out of proportion. As was pointed out in Chapter 20, product innovation in the key lines of basic industries is the specialized function of large firms which occupy a nuclear position at the source of the industry's technology. The managers of these firms act as a coordinated group to administer the development of the basic technology; they are not concerned with products in a static sense, but with seeking commercial outlets for the products of an evolving technology. Theirs is the task of turning to account the use of technological improvement, whatever may be the source of the improvement—the findings of their own research departments, practical experience, published articles, and so forth. The common aim of the managers is to maximize the over-all rate of return of their firm by accelerating the rate of innovation and thus, by "getting ahead and staying ahead," to reap continuously the profits of pioneering.

In this common endeavor there is, of course, much room for rivalry among the individual managers which provides the fine edge of individual self-expression to the joint action. However, it must be understood that this individual rivalry does not determine the calculated risks which the firm will take in making innovations. That is decided by *pooling* individual judgments. Every manager of a department of the firm states his case before the firm's executive committee, but he does not attempt to *manipulate* the situation for his exclusive benefit, or that of his department. The firm as a whole takes chances, not any individual within it. Managerial competition is of a marginal form, the morale of cooperation is the essence of the firm's survival and growth.

This modern manner of conducting enterprises requires us to adapt the traditional conception of profits gained, or lost, due to incalculable uncertainty. By *inviting* calculated risks on an extended scope, firms which act as nuclear centers of their industry's evolving technology are advancing into virgin territories of technology. There the returns are rich. In general, when a number of competent persons organize not merely to exploit a technology, but to foster its evolution, incalculable uncertainty ceases to be a contingent liability. It becomes, instead, a contingent asset.

Mark well that this is not an attribute solely of capitalism. The public entrepreneurs who administer publicly owned and operated technologies in economies which are striving towards socialism must possess the same ability for taking calculated risk on a group basis; otherwise they would vegetate in a state of socialist stagnation. However, as between the countries of socialism and capitalism, the prime motivation differs significantly. The search for profit continues to be the chief inducement for American entrepreneurs to supply goods and services. It is therefore at the best, utopian, and at the worst, insincere, to launch an attack on the profit-system. One must understand the general role and the particular origin of profit. However, it is also utopian, or insincere, to argue that the members of our democratic citizenry should not look to their elected representatives in government to take steps for securing full employment on a nonprofit basis if and when capital accumulation through the gain of profit does not suffice to make jobs available for all persons who are willing and able to work.

For Discussion

1. "For Robinson Crusoe to augment his catch of fish by adopting Friday's outrigger-canoe technology, only the canoe and the man were necessary. The arrangement under which Friday was paid a share of the surplus catch, in the

form of interest for the loan of the canoe, was a social arrangement based on an institutional practice familiar to Robinson. Yet, it has been argued that the payment of interest is a *natural* necessity." Controvert this assertion *pro* and *con*.

2. Productive services are utilized in constructing new plant and equipment. Productive services are gradually released after the plant and equipment go into operation. These are not the same productive services that were used to construct the plant and equipment. They are the services of the *technology* which was embodied in the plant and equipment. But the technology is the product of human effort and imagination. Does this suggest that, in the ultimate analysis, all economic value is of human origin?

3. If an entrepreneur has money funds which he personally owns and can invest in his business, why should he trouble to impute interest to his personally owned money capital? Can he not escape the rationing effect of the rate of interest? If not, why not?

4. A series of old, but substantial stone mill buildings, located near a large town in Massachusetts, had in the spring of 1933 a burden of $5,300 in unpaid taxes upon it. The buildings had tight roofs, solid floors, and unbroken windows. There was also machinery for generating water power. The selectmen of the town offered to take over title to the mill and then to resell the whole for only $2,000—on one condition. The purchaser who would obtain this seeming bargain would have to operate the mill for some manufacturing purpose so that employment would be given to the inhabitants of the mill village, many of them unemployed. But there were no buyers. Apply the principle of capitalization to explain why there were no purchasers, making reference both to expected future income and the rate of interest; this you can assume to have been 3 per cent per annum.

5. (a) Find the present value of $3,000 due in 3 years, at 5 per cent interest compounded annually. (This can be computed by the use of data given in this chapter.)

(b) A manufacturer wishes to acquire a small piece of equipment which will wear out in five (5) years, having then no scrap value. The equipment is expected to contribute $100 of net income (above cost of maintenance and operation), year after year for the five years of its duration. How much can the manufacturer afford to pay for it? (The data and formula for this computation are also available in the text of this chapter.)

6. "The determination of the rate of interest differs from the establishment of other types of rewards, because in the determination of the interest rate, it is the *demand* for capital which specifies what the level of interest shall be, the *supply* of capital being passive." Can it, therefore, still be said that supply and demand determine the rate of interest?

7. In Figure 23–5 it may be seen that after 1935 the Federal Reserve System's rediscount rate remained, politically set, at a low level. If the rate had not been fixed politically, but had been determined in a free money market, would it still have been established by the money market at a low level? In 1947 the rediscount rate was 1 per cent; in 1957 it stood at 3.12 per cent. What accounted for this pronounced rise?

8. A person is offered a piece of property for $11,600 cash, or for $8,000 cash and payments of $2,000 at the end of one year and two years. If he can afford to pay cash, but can invest money at 5 per cent, compounded annually, should he pay cash?

9. What is there about the capitalization of land which tends to encourage real estate speculation?

10. This chapter has explained that the supply of an ordinary type of farm product is characteristically inelastic. Is the demand for farm produce of staple consumption also inelastic? If not, why not? If it is inelastic, what are some of the principal reasons?

11. "One agricultural expert has described the farm problem as one which is characterized by the price mechanism operating so as to eliminate marginal farmers from the field of agricultural production. But it can also be argued that low prices tend to tie many farmers to the soil." Explain.

24   Labor Incomes

The Nature of Labor Problems

Must work be considered a necessary evil? Or can it be an interesting human activity performed during the best hours of one's waking day? Some kinds of work will always remain dull and uninspiring as well as a portion of everybody's lot. But much of the work assigned to human beings can be made creative, designed to appeal to one's imagination. Imagination is mankind's greatest talent, a unique one. Therefore to enrich people's work experiences by allowing for creative expression in industry is to make "human use of human beings."

Is it idealistic to hope that every person willing and able to work shall enjoy the six "L's" of civilized existence: a bit of luxury consumption; leisure time; literacy; longevity; laws to protect us; and a bit of higher learning? If this hope is idealistic we have been practical dreamers for a long time. Since the grimy days of the early industrial revolution we have seen (1) wages increasing to permit the ordinary person a share of our cultural benefits; (2) hours being shortened to the universal forty-hour week; (3) almost all of the people learning the three R's; (4) laws being enacted to protect our wage-earners, as well as working rules being more democratically made and administered at places of work; (5) safe and healthy working conditions being established to prolong the worker's span of life, with pensions at retirement; (6) opportunities being furnished for advanced learning. (Getting an education for himself or his youngsters is no longer the workingman's dream; it is something he *does*.)

This progress being fully acknowledged, we must not forget that our previous survey of the structure of wants, and their satisfaction, revealed that 14.6 per cent of Americans still live under poor conditions. As for the rest, many remain plagued to one extent or another by impersonalization, urbanization, cultural vulgarization, hero-identification, class-stratification, and occasional highway or wartime decimation. Our manifold labor problems arise from people being resentful of mass standardizations meant for morons; most people wish for work experiences which have individual meaning. After all, Americans are brought up to think of themselves as dignified individuals; small wonder that they will demand to be treated as such whenever possible.

The Nature of Work and Wages

WHAT IS WORK?

Let us adopt the definitions of the United States Labor Department's Wage and Hour Division, as upheld by our courts of law. Human work is time and energy which a person freely places at the disposal of a managing entrepreneur. This is done irrevocably for a period of specified duration, a day, a month, a year, and sometimes for a longer period. The reward for placing one's services under the control and supervision of a managing entrepreneur is a wage or a salary. A wage or salary must be paid by an employer to his employees, even though no work may have been performed, *provided that* the wage-earners stood prepared to perform the work after having been hired. The reason for this requirement is that by contracting to work for an employer wage-earners must give up opportunities to work elsewhere. Having foregone alternative job opportunities, it would hardly do to be told, at the chosen place of work, that there is, after all, no work to do. To discourage this, many union-management agreements now provide that wage-earners who report for work, not having been instructed otherwise, be paid four hours of "call-in time" for reporting but having no work assigned to them.

WAGES AND SALARIES COMPARED

Wages are customarily paid on a straight-time hourly basis, by the week. Overtime payments are computed in terms of the regular hourly rate, usually at 50 per cent of that rate and sometimes at 100 per cent and even 200 per cent of the straight-time hourly rate. Thus, if the regular rate is $2.00 an hour, work after 40 consecutive hours may be compensated at $3.00 for each overtime hour worked; on Sundays or holidays every hour of work may be paid at $4.00, that is, at "double time," if this has been stipulated. Sometimes after excessively long hours have already been worked, say 56 or 60 hours, a "golden-hour" premium may be awarded which doubles the "double-time pay" itself. The intent of such a provision is obviously to discourage employers from requiring their employees to work for excessively long periods. To a lesser extent this is also the intent of overtime pay provisions at the ordinary time-and-a-half or double-time rates. In the latter case, the aim is usually to discourage work on days, or at hours, when work interferes with the pursuit of leisure-time social activities. Wages may also be paid on a piece-rate basis—so much for so much work turned out. In whatever manner paid, the basic wage unit is the hourly rate of pay or equivalent thereof. The latter can easily be computed by taking the total amount earned under piece-rates, or by the week, and dividing this amount by the number of hours worked.

The fact that a weekly or monthly wage may be called a "salary" does not necessarily make it such. The difference between wage and salary does not lie in the name. Properly speaking, salaries are paid to employees who have responsibility for making company policies; or who can hire and fire; or who use independent, creative judgment, as in doing research; or who work with some substantial degree of independent discretion in any manner whatsoever.

This differentiation of salaried workers from wage-earners, who work largely under direction and are paid by the hour, is a sound distinction. In the case of the person exercising independent discretion the amount of time spent is not necessarily the true index of the work performed. Thus an executive may stay at the office after regular hours and is expected to do so if he has not reached crucial decisions; a professional worker may take some problem home; a research worker may puzzle over his work on a Sunday. Most modern companies and government agencies distinguish on this basis between "wage-roll" and "salaried" employees. Salaried work is principally executive, supervisory, and professionally specialized work.

For practical purposes we may say that in 1958 most of the people who were working in industry and earning $7,000 or less per year were wage-earners (counting only straight-time hourly earnings, not overtime pay). Most persons earning over $7,000 (when not self-employed) were salary-earners. Salary-earners typically think in terms of how much they earn per year. Even so, it is sometimes interesting to compare yearly earnings with wages paid on an hourly basis. Thus a salary of $7,500 a year corresponds to $3.60 an hour; $10,000 corresponds to an hourly wage rate of $4.80; and an awesome $50,000 a year comes to about $24.00 an hour, assuming that a forty-hour week is worked. But that is just the point: men or women earning $50,000 a year are not expected to work by the clock.

WHAT WAGES INCLUDE

Thus far we have considered wages from the viewpoint of money paid by the employer. But it must be realized that included in the concept of wages are many things other than the amount of money received. The contributions which an employer makes to a pension fund, established for the benefit of qualified employees, are part of wages. Contributions of employers to medical health plans are also part of wages. Also to be considered as part of wages are such merit increases which may be earned by *any* employee under stipulated conditions, such as regular attendance at work, punctuality, absence of "blue slips" (warnings) in his record, and other normal evidences of competent performance. By contrast, merit increases which are awarded for unusually high quality performance, clearly beyond the line of duty, do not readily fit under the rubric of wages. This is because extraordinary performance on a job is not to be expected time after time if the job has been properly defined. In general, any type of remuneration which any employee can regularly expect to receive is a part of wages, whereas the type of reward which at any time can be withheld at the discretion of an employer is usually called a bonus.

The reason for defining a wage as an expected payment is simple and economically sound. For, what is the basis on which a wage-earner chooses to work for a given employer rather than for all the others for whom he might work? It is obviously a broad basis of selection, including not only the hourly wage rate, but also pension benefits, promotional opportunities, and so forth. Not only does the wage-earner, when shopping for a job, react to the hourly rate offered, but in addition he considers all of the benefits which are offered competitively by different employers—medical benefits, insurance and retirement benefits, perhaps a stock-option purchase plan, and so on.

Not all beneficial working conditions can be expressed in dollars and cents. Nevertheless, many benefits can be counted. In June, 1958, the average straight-time hourly wage rate for the nation was $2.12. An additional minimum of 40 cents represented the worth of various direct benefits such as retirement and health plans.

If, then, wage-earners ultimately make their choices of particular employers under the influence of fringe benefit considerations along with the money rate of wages that are offered, we must consider the fringe benefits as part of wages. Failing to do so, we would be quite unable to explain how the United States labor force is distributed among different employers and why.

LABOR MARKETS

The term "labor market" describes any place, method, or medium for employers and wage-earners to get together and, if possible, to agree on terms and conditions of employment. To speak of a labor market is in one sense misleading, because human labor is not a commodity to be bought or sold. In the so-called labor market managers representing owners of capital meet wage-earners seeking work. Terms of productive cooperation in industry, trade, agriculture, and government service are worked out.

A specific labor market may be located in the personnel office of a corporation, in the administrator's office of some government agency, at the headquarters or field office of a state employment office, or even at some street corner where itinerant workers wait for an employer to pick them up with his station wagon for a day's work.

As is the case of capital markets, no *visible* bargaining may occur in labor markets. Some persons seeking work will accept it on the terms offered; some will perhaps wait to see whether the terms will improve; some will only check in long enough to find out what the terms are and, being dissatisfied, go elsewhere. Yet, if we take only a city-wide view, we may observe movement of labor in, out, and between jobs at practically every moment. (Sometimes there are more people willing to work than will be hired on almost any terms.)

Elementary Principles of Wage Determination

THE GENERAL WAGES-FUND

Having defined wages to include money rewards plus welfare benefits, it would seem that the general level of wages in the United States economy at any one time must be the weighted average of what all the separate employers, the businessmen and government agencies, pay together.

Now, it is an interesting fact that for at least a century the nation's aggregate wages-bill has amounted to a constant 65 per cent of the total national income (not the gross national product). In other words, no matter what the national income may be, labor obtains roughly two-thirds of its financial value, year after year.

However startling such a constancy in percentage may be, it poses no special economic problem. The curious statistical fact is really but another way of talking about the sum total of all separate wage payments made throughout the nation during a year. It is in connection with these *separate* wage payments that practical labor problems arise and must be settled, if work is to go on uninterruptedly. Consequently, the following explanation of wage determination is made in terms of wages paid for *particular* kinds of work-services by *particular* employers, private and public.

PERFECT COMPETITION IN THE LABOR MARKET

Perfect competition in any labor market would mean that all the employers act *entirely* independently of each other in bidding for labor. So would all job-seekers. The latter would therefore competitively bid wages down in order to get jobs, while the employers would competitively bid wages up in order to attract labor.

Actually, perfectly competitive labor markets do not exist. Competitive wage-cutting to obtain work is looked down upon by workers as "scabbing"; competitive wage-raising is frowned upon by employers as "labor pirating." Unless absolutely desperate, wage-earners dislike "spoiling the market" for each other, as do businessmen and government personnel administrators. Why, then, trouble to depict what might happen in a perfect labor market?

Analyzing Wages

The theory of wages which follows is based on the assumption of perfect competition because that is a simple way of thinking about how prices and wages are related. It has been seen that prices *do* tend to ration goods and personal services to the consumers who possess the most effective purchasing power, even though there is not much obvious price competition. (A great deal of service competition, however, does take place.) Similarly, wages tend to ration the use of labor to those entrepreneurs who have the greatest ability to pay wages, including welfare benefits. It has already been shown how, theoretically, prices and capital values function as instruments of the economy's basically indirect rationing system. The pure theory of wages attempts to show wages as another set of prices geared into commodity prices in cog-wheel fashion.

WAGES IN THE SHORT RUN, AT FULL EMPLOYMENT

Supply in theory. To avoid confusing human beings with commodities we shall speak of "the supply of *work-services*" rather than "the supply of labor." Work-services fall into literally tens of thousands of job classifications. The supply of work-services in each classification depends upon:

1. The number of persons available for doing the particular sort of work, whether they are presently performing it or not.
2. How much work each of the actually or potentially available persons wishes to perform at different rates of wages, including fringe benefits.

First, as to the number of available persons. The circumstances which determine this over-all number are tremendously numerous and complex. So great is the difficulty of tracing the various causes that modern wage theory simply takes the number of workers as *given*.[1] In past times economists postulated a functional relationship between wages and population; when wages went up, population supposedly increased, and vice versa. This "hog-breeding" theory has been rejected for a long time.

Accepting some number-supply of labor as given, we next ascertain how much work is likely to be performed, at different rates of wages. This will depend upon decisions made by individual wage-earners in the following hypothetical manner.

At any one time or place a worker has presumably made up his mind as to the amount of work-service he will make available at different hourly rates (plus benefits) or at different quoted piecework rates. Then, when a particular rate is quoted in the actual labor market, he merely responds, one way or the other. For example, if $2.00 an hour is quoted for his kind of labor at some place where he would wish to work, he may decide to take the job, perhaps quitting some other job to do so.

The wage-earner's response at the moment is predetermined by a consideration of various alternatives. In deciding whether he wishes to work at all, or for longer than a certain number of hours, the wage-earner weighs: (1) the attractiveness of leisure against the anticipated pleasure of having more money to spend or save; (2) the extra physical strain of additional work effort; (3) the psychological stress of changing jobs; and so forth. Acting rationally, the individual worker will attempt to bring all the relevant factors in his choice situation into balance. He will avoid making any change that would leave him worse off.

This rational behavior assumption is expressed by economists in the following theoretical terms:

1. *Utility of wage-income.* This refers to any kind of enjoyment a wage-earner expects to derive from spending money earned by work activity.
2. *Disutility of work.* By this we must understand every reason which might lead a wage-earner to withhold his work-services rather than to accept wages and hours which he considers substandard.

---

[1] This remark should be understood as applying only to the supply of work-services as a general proposition. In particular instances a study of the work-services supply in a given area at a given time may be of great practical value. But it is a good idea to consult a sociologist when making such studies.

3. *Marginal disutility of work.* The burden of the last hour's or last-added day's work, having in mind the alternative of the leisure that is foregone.

From these definitions emerges this theoretical proposition: *A wage-earner will accept work up to that point at which the utility of the wage is equal to the marginal disutility of that amount of employment.*

When viewed practically, this theoretical finding has the following meaning. Suppose a wage-earner is trying to sustain a plane of living which costs $90.00 a week, but the standard of living he strives for is priced higher than that. On the other hand, we shall assume this worker to believe that 40 hours of work a week is about right. If the rate of wages were $2.25 an hour and his scheduled work-week 40 hours, he might rest content. He would be interested in raising his plane of living, but only if he could receive more per hour, or an overtime premium for working longer hours. If his employer managed inefficiently and asked him to work for only $1.75 an hour, this particular wage-earner would undoubtedly look for another employer. His present employer might be able to replace him, provided he could find some needy person willing to work at the lower wage. In theory he would be able to find needy persons who would not lose much utility in consuming goods they would not have at all if they refused to work at the relatively low wage rate, and who would not mind working perhaps 50 hours to earn something like $90.00 a week.

On the other hand, suppose that this particular employer manages his business more efficiently and is willing to pay $2.75 for work of the particular job classification. He might attract more persons offering work-services than he needs.

Theoretically, the higher a wage rate the employer offers, the greater the amount of work people offer to do for him. On the other hand, it is quite likely that he will experience difficulty in staffing his plant as he lowers his wages.

The theoretical demand for work services. In trying to keep their real cost of production to a minimum, employers ask themselves what amount of human work services they can efficiently handle. If another man, or crew of men, is hired, will there be added production? If so, will the sales receipts from this extra production cover the additional wages to be paid? Sometimes this problem is not involved. When probing his real costs, a businessman may discover that it is only necessary to shift some workers so that they might be used more efficiently. At other times, however, the indicated action may be that of hiring additional employees, or of discharging some. When either is the case, the employer's demand for labor is naturally affected.

The following examples indicate how employer demand would be shaped if there were pure competition. The reader is asked to bear the theoretical nature of the ensuing discussion carefully in mind.

Let us assume that in a certain town there are five machine shops. We take the size of the shops and their respective equipments as given. We also assume that they employ the same classification of machinists. Two of the shops are very similar in every way, and the following is observed:

Number of Machinists	Units Produced per Week
15	7,500
20	9,500
25	11,000
30	12,250
35	13,250

In the other three machine shops the operations are not as efficient. Fifteen men can turn out 6,000 units; twenty men 7,500; twenty-five machinists can handle 8,750 units; thirty men 9,750; and thirty-five men can produce 10,500 units. For simplicity's sake we assume that in all five shops identical refrigerator parts are produced which will be sold at identical prices.

Notice that the law of diminishing yields is in operation. The more machinists that are hired, the less the production of each machinist. In the two efficient shops, for example, production declines from 500 units a man when fifteen men are employed, to 378.5 units a man when thirty-five machinists are employed.

If the price at which each item of production is sold is uniformly 50 cents a unit, the managers of the two more efficient shops, beginning with fifteen machinists *at a given wage rate* of $125 a week, would observe the following when hiring more machinists.

Number of Men Hired	Sales Revenue	Wage Bill	Difference	Additional Business Income for Each Man of the Last Five Men Hired
15	$3,750	$1,875	$1,875	....
20	4,750	2,500	2,250	+ $75
25	5,500	3,125	2,375	+ 25
30	6,125	3,750	2,375	0
35	6,625	4,375	2,250	− 25

The example shows that hiring another five men after twenty-five men have already been employed brings no extra net business income —the additional men just earn their wages. This can also be illustrated by noticing the added total sales revenue as machinists are added, then dividing this by the number of men added in order to determine the extra, or *marginal revenue product* of each man:

Number of Men Hired	Total Sales Revenue	Marginal Revenue	Marginal Revenue Product for Each Man of the Last Five Men Hired
15	$3,750	....	....
20	4,750	$1,000	$200
25	5,500	750	150
30	6,125	625	125
35	6,625	500	100

This method of demonstration shows even more clearly than the preceding one that it will not pay the employer to hire more than thirty men, for if he did, the wages-bill of each of the last five men added would be $125, but the extra income produced by each of these five men would only be $100, producing a loss of $25 each, or a total loss of $125.

From such demonstrations economists deduce the following hiring rule for employers: *The quantity of labor demanded is determined at that point where the marginal revenue product of the last man (or last batch of men) added equals the wage-bill.* Or, in abbreviated form: $mrp = pf$ (where pf stands for "price of factor").

If wages were $150 a week, each efficient shop would hire twenty-five machinists only; correspondingly, if wages were only $100 a week, thirty-five machinists per shop would be hired, all other things being equal. On the other hand, if prices declined to 40 cents for each unit of product, the marginal revenue product of the machinists would decline also; therefore only thirty men would be hired in each efficient shop even when wages were only $100 a week.

When similarly computing the data for the three less efficient shops, we stipulate that at wages of $125 a week with the product selling at 50 cents a unit, each can hire only twenty-five men in comparison to thirty hired by the other two shops. Upon a rise of wages to $150 a week they could use only twenty men each, and so on. In general, therefore: The amount of employment offered to wage-earners increases with lower wages or higher prices, and vice versa, the more efficient entrepreneurs always being able to offer more employment than relatively inefficient entrepreneurs.

This theoretical finding permits us to draw a labor demand curve which has the same slope-direction as any ordinary commodity demand curve—downward and to the right.

Readers of this book will not misunderstand the meaning of the principle of diminishing labor productivity when used as a factor in a theoretical explanation of wage determination under absolutely given conditions. After what has been said, it must be evident that diminishing labor productivity does not necessarily mean that as more and more workers are hired, the quality of work-services deteriorates until "the bottom of the manpower barrel is scraped." That might be one factor, or it might not. In any case, however, other factors are involved in causing diminishing labor productivity. One such factor is factory layout, which may become cramped with the successive addition of machinists. In this regard the ability of management to plan and to administer production and personnel relations is of utmost importance.

Insofar as diminishing yields affect production, we speak of diminishing *physical* productivity; as the demand-price drops for every commodity, we speak of diminishing *revenue* productivity. Usually we simply use the term "diminishing marginal labor productivity" or just "marginal productivity."

WAGES THEORETICALLY DETERMINED

We have a supply of work-services which characteristically means that more work is forthcoming in response to rising wages, and vice versa. As regards demand, employers stand prepared to hire more wage-earners at low wages than at high wages. What must happen in the labor markets for particular kinds of labor is, therefore, easy to grasp.

Numerous persons who would seek work, or would work longer hours if the terms were "right," will stay where they are when they see that employers are obtaining work-services on lower terms. To return to our numerical example: Let us suppose that in this town there are 135 machinists working at $125 a week, and 5 more might come to work if the wages were $150. On the other hand, 5 machinists who are now working can and will quit if wages should decline. If wages do decline, say to $100 a week, 130 machinists will be left; we shall assume that they have no choice but to go on working. But at $100 a week it would pay the employers, altogether, to hire no less than 160 machinists. In a theoretically perfect labor market the employers, who would be disadvantaged by only 130 machinists wishing to work at that low wage, bid the wages back to $125 a week. This is assuming, of course, that prices have not dropped. Table 24–1 summarizes the discussion.

On the other hand, wages would not rise to $150 under given conditions. If they did, employers as a group would not want to employ more than 110 machinists. Yet, according to our calculations, 140 men would offer their services. By competition among the workers, wages would be bid down to $125 again. Eventually 135 machinists would be at work, as before. The 5 extra men, who are prepared to work only if the weekly rate is $150, would drop out of the market.

Table 24–1. Static Analysis of Specific Wage Rate Determination

Number of Men	Sales Revenue @ 50 Cents Market Price Per Unit of Product		mrp for Each Man of the Last Five Men Hired		Wage Rate Per 40-hr. Week	Total of Men Wanted by All the Five Firms	Available Supply of Machinists at Given Wage Rate
	2 Efficient Firms	3 Inefficient Firms	2 Efficient Firms	3 Inefficient Firms			
15	$3,750	$3,050	....	....	....	......	......
20	4,750	3,800	$200	$150	$150	110	140
25	5,500	4,425	150	125	125*	135**	135**
30	6,125	4,925	125	100	100	160	130
35	6,625	5,300	100	75	75	185	100
40	7,000	5,550	75	....	....	......	......

*Theoretical equilibrium wage rate.
**Theoretical microeconomic amount of employment under assumed conditions, including economy-wide full employment.

The situation can be described by saying that under given conditions in a perfect labor market there is a theoretical equilibrium rate which clears the market. Whichever way wages move, some employers, or alternatively some wage-earners, drop out of the market when its terms turn against them. Those who remain in the labor market conclude employment contracts. The market is cleared by these two processes. Notice that this description is identical to that of a commodity market under perfect competition.

What Is the Practical Usefulness of This Kind of Theory?

This theory of wage-determination in perfectly competitive labor markets has one great virtue. It allows one to think about wages not just in terms of what people want to pay wage-earners or in terms of what wage-earners wish to receive. Rather, one is talking about wages in the context of the law of diminishing yields, our basic principle of regulating efficiency. Thus:

1. Marginal productivity reflects diminishing *physical* yields to production which entrepreneurs experience by hiring more men to "push" production.
2. Marginal productivity also reflects diminishing *utility* yields as experienced by consumers. It does this by registering the influence of a falling demand price on the value of labor's marginal product.
3. Labor's own marginal disutility of work reflects diminishing physical and utility yields, which develop with the prolongation of work activities.

Economists point out that this theory is useful in that it delineates not only how employers and wage-earners are accommodated in their private desires, but also how society is served. It is to society's interest:

1. Not to allow entrepreneurs to be crowded, or to crowd themselves, beyond their optimum yield rate of production (by letting them have work-services too cheaply).
2. Not to force products on consumers (which might happen if too many persons were employed in producing products that are not really desired by consumers who would, however, be told or persuaded through expensive advertising to use the extra products).
3. Not to exploit workers by requiring them to work against their wills (as would happen if they were forced to work at less than the values of their marginal products).

In Conclusion

With this brief survey we must realize that effective thinking about wage determination—meaning wages in a broad sense inclusive of benefits—can only *begin* with perfect theorizing. Just as the theory of perfect price competition furnishes only the skeletal outlines of real life situations, so does this theory of perfect wage determination necessarily overlook the economic growth factors in the United States economy. Yet change, growth, and the expectations of people for better things to come are the most powerful wage determinants in the real world. Moreover, ethical human relations, rather than commodity-type transactions under given circumstances, shape the course of day-by-day living in industry.

The theory of wage determination in a perfect labor market, like all other perfect theories, is "out of this world." But by no means is it therefore useless. For it sharpens our wits in thinking about economic necessities, along with dreaming about how much pie we would like to extract from the sky. Economists who have learned to use this theory wisely, employ it, however, only as a point of departure. They go on to broader considerations, such as will be made in the following chapters.

For Discussion

1. How does the definition of work, which is given in this chapter, illustrate the principle of opportunity cost?

2. Classify the labor market areas which exist in your region of the nation. Would you say that there are, in strict theory, as many labor market areas as there are different occupations which can be substantively differentiated (not merely nominally)? But if this is so, how can the Department of Labor maintain that in the United States there are 149 primary labor markets? (Check the publication *Labor Market* in the Documents Division of your University Library.)

3. Is anything stated in the explanation of the supply and demand theory of wage determination at odds with the explanation of general factor-service supply and demand theory given in Chapter 23?

4. Which of the following are, or are not, a part of wages: (a) a turkey given to each employee at Christmas time; (b) an automatic increase to the standard rate paid for a job classification, after a probationary on-the-job period of sixteen weeks for any new employee; (c) an incentive bonus paid an employee on the basis of the employer's personal appraisal of an individual employee's extraordinary performance; (d) an incentive bonus paid under a group-bonus plan; (e) the contribution made by the employer to the Social Security Administration for each of his employees; (f) dividends on stocks individually owned by employees under a "profit-sharing" plan which: (i) offers the individual employee an opportunity to acquire stock on favored terms; (ii) allows employees to authorize the employer to deduct a given amount from their wages and place it in an individual savings fund to be spent for acquiring more of the firm's stock; and (iii) provides for the employer matching the amount placed in individual savings funds by employees, thus doubling the rate at which the employees can acquire their firm's stock.

25 Modern Methods of Wage Determination

A Realistic Analysis of the Demand for Labor

When we raise our sights, from considering labor power as a commodity which is bought and sold in a "labor market" to the whole personality of a man or woman who works, the definition of the demand for labor changes quite considerably. Modern employers think in terms of the contributions a well-trained, steady, reliable, and satisfied employee can make in circumstances under which he is free to make suggestions about the work process, as well as feel free to voice his occasional grievances, confident of having them speedily and justly settled. A trained, motivated employee who confidently participates in solving the company's production problems, is a low-cost employee even though his hourly wage rate may be high. An uneducated, sullen, and distrustful employee is a high-cost employee from this point of view, no matter how low his wage may be. The truth of this matter can easily be grasped by reminding oneself that more is required to operate a modern enterprise successfully than a set of engineering blueprints. There must also be "behavioral engineering"—a term used to emphasize the need for understanding and for mutual trust among the participants in production, from janitor to works manager.

SPECIFIC ELEMENTS OF THE DEMAND FOR LABOR

Skill. Let us begin by acknowledging that in our times the demand for labor is for staffs of workers to supervise the operations of machines in a managerially scheduled flow of productive operations. That is to say, the "principle of substitution," which represents men as competing to do the work of machines, applies only in unusual circumstances. At the heart of the industrial process in the United States men are seen to complement machinery, not to do its work. Moreover, man-machine combinations are related by plan to each other in a total flow of work processes. For instance, in an automobile plant auto bodies arrive with perfect timing from one assembly line to be attached to chassis that have been assembled along another line. To appreciate how obsolete is the concept of men competing for work with machines, consider the case of transferomatic machines which pass work between more than 400 built-in operations which no human operator touches. There is one man who starts the line and one who supervises it; for more than these there could be no demand. Labor is combined with the automated line in a fixed proportion. In addition, the whole plant operates on a fundamental layout design made in terms of standardized parts, gauges, and dimensions, so that there is little room for substituting labor.

A new type of skill is required to man these operations. The human operator must have an understanding of his particular task, but in addition he must possess a quality of attentiveness and he must feel a social motivation to work with other operators under special conditions of noise, lighting, and speed of work. He is not required to be a craftsman who gives the product a personal touch; neither is he a robot. His skill consists in being alert to prevent a "bottleneck" from developing at his work-station and in being able to understand why orders are given so that he adopts them rather than merely follows them.

The important implication is that the fundamental design of a modern plant, shop, and office defines the scope of the demand for labor in advance. Layout architects, engineers, and technicians plan a complete flow of operations for a factory well in advance of the ground having been broken on which the plant will be built. The reader will appreciate that the demand for labor in these typical instances will feature a strong emphasis on a worker's mental and social ability to fit into a *sequence* of operations, in addition to performing a given task or handling a given tool.

Demand for labor in terms of demand for the end-product. Common sense as well as the theory of wages affirm that there is a connection between the volume, sensitivity, and seasonality in the demand for a product and the demand for the labor needed to make the product, however remote the connection may be.

Petroleum refining may serve as an example. During World War II new production records were set, and were greatly exceeded in postwar years. Yet, though the output of refinery products increased by 60 per cent between 1945 and 1955, the number of persons employed increased at most by 20 per cent. Automatic panel-board flow controls to regulate new equipment have replaced human operators but have stabilized the jobs which remain. Modern production scheduling and stability-oriented marketing techniques are reducing temporary layoff rates in industries formerly characterized by seasonally fluctuating labor demands, as, for instance, in garment manufacturing and automobile production. Conducive to employment stabilization is the employer's necessity of paying a tax on his payroll for the support of the state unemployment compensation system. A refund of a part of this tax is made to employers who have good records of maintaining stable employment.

Demand for labor in terms of modern personnel programs. The new dimension of "teamwork skill" in many industries requires that careful selections among job-applicants be made and that job-entrants be subsequently trained in the work process of the particular plant. Required attentiveness and ability to work with others, without becoming personally disturbed or disturbing to fellow workers, are not natural traits. The quality of industrial self-discipline must be cultivated. Under modern personnel relations this is accomplished by studying the workers' needs rather than by imposing direction by force or fiat.

Modern personnel relations programs originated in 1895 with Frederick W. Taylor's theories of scientific management. He claimed that workers believed it to be in their interest to limit the amount of work done in a day.[1] Therefore Taylor proposed to stimulate the individual worker to produce without restriction. This was to be done by scientifically establishing production standards which, when exceeded, would entitle the worker to premium pay.

Now, these standards were not to be established in an abstract manner, but on the basis of observing optimum worker performance under favorable working conditions. It was this emphasis on devising incentives and arranging for favorable working conditions which gave rise to the modern art of personnel relations.

What Taylor actually observed was waste and inefficiency in labor utilization. In part, this was caused by not acquainting the individual worker with the needs of the industrial situation. Because Taylor mis-

[1] Frederick W. Taylor, *Scientific Management* (latest ed.; New York: Harper & Bros., 1947).

takenly attributed labor waste entirely to the working person, rather than to the total work organization throughout an enterprise, his efforts contributed to the rise of the modern personnel manager in the curious role of "shop disciplinarian."

Notice, however, that the person designated as shop disciplinarian was to enforce working rules based on scientific observation rather than on an arbitrary assertion of management authority. In fact, the disciplinarian's function was that of an industrial peacemaker. To assist him, time and motion studies of worker performance were to be made on new or changed jobs. On the basis of these studies the disciplinarian would then readjust a worker's wages in conformance with the scientific findings. If a worker complained about his rate of pay, the findings would be explained to him; or if no study had been made of the job, it would be promptly undertaken. If retraining were required, this would be given the worker. Taylor also urged scientific planning for accident prevention and for reducing industrial fatigue.

This emphasis on paying workers by the measured physical results of their efforts and on training them to achieve these results revolutionized earlier conceptions of the demand for labor. No longer were workers to be hired simply on the basis of the cheapness of the wage they would accept. The prime element in labor demand now became the worker's adaptability to training and his steadiness and reliability on the job. The actual money wage that would be paid became an afterthought rather than the determining consideration in the hiring of labor. An employer would not mind paying high money wages if the worker, by efficiently handling materials and equipment, helped the entrepreneur to reduce real costs of production.

This productivity emphasis came increasingly to the fore in later years, when it was recognized that a worker's needs are psychological to an extent greater than the simple physiological need for knowing how to use one's mental and muscular capacity efficiently in order to earn more money. Thus one of the first textbooks on personnel administration defined the aim and implementation of the new approach as focusing on the human element. It was asserted that this had become the crux of the production problem. To cope with the problem, a new division of the labor of management was recommended, namely, the institution in each place of work of a specialized administrative agency to be known as the personnel department. From this institutionalization a new science of management techniques for improving human relations in the plant was to arise.[2]

[2] Ordway Tead and Henry C. Metcalf, *Personnel Administration* (1st ed.; New York: McGraw-Hill Book Co., Inc., 1920).

One of the first important evidences of the new science was the series of seven personnel studies made at the Hawthorne, Illinois, plant of the Western Electric Company. These studies, published in 1927, were conducted by members of the faculty of the Harvard Business School.[3] The original purpose was to determine the effects upon output of changes in illumination, rest periods, and other working conditions. The specialized research (even though not conducted by the Company's personnel staff) revealed the importance to workers not only of individual incentives but also of group goals of achievement. Thus another dimension was added to the conception of demand for labor, a social psychological dimension. Henceforth it was appreciated that desirable *social* work situations contribute to optimum production. This called for leadership in providing satisfaction of group needs.

During the 1920's many employers endeavored to serve the group needs of workers by the practice of "collective dealing" with their employees, having regard to such commonly felt needs as (1) benefit and insurance provisions; (2) employee education about the needs of the business and the economic situation; (3) recreational facilities; (4) cooperative buying arrangements; (5) thrift plans and employee stock ownership; (6) company housing; and other types of welfare arrangements. The handling of grievances was also standardized and facilitated, instead of being left for each individual foreman to attend to in his peculiar fashion. While these provisions had a moral basis of regard for the welfare of workers, frequently they were made in order to pacify workers and attach their loyalty to the firm rather than to an "outside" labor organization.

Then, in the late 1930's the orientation of personnel administration underwent a significant change, when labor militancy as well as a rise of public opinion favorable to independent trade unionism brought union-management collective bargaining to the fore. As American Federation of Labor (AFL) and CIO unions demanded and won recognition, top management executives soon shifted the responsibility of conducting wage negotiations to their personnel departments.

From this change in the structure of employment policy-making by management emerged the modern practice of personnel relations, which encompasses participation in collective bargaining as well as day-to-day personnel administration. The aim is to establish systematic programs for improving job methods and job relations. Many concerns have found that strong trade unions, when capably led, may serve as

[3] See Elton Mayo, *Human Problems of an Industrial Civilization* (New York: The Macmillan Co., 1933); Fritz J. Roethlisberger, *Management and Morale* (Cambridge, Mass.: Harvard University Press, 1941); Arthur B. Goetze, "Tomorrow's Management" (New York: Western Electric Co., 1958).

a valuable aid to management by effectively representing the workers in the plant in joint efforts to carry out constructive personnel programs.

Does this mean that we have industrial co-determination in the American economy? No, the practice is one of joint consultation, with management having the final say. But the influence of worker opinion, expressed through trade union channels, does make itself pervasively felt in the formulation of management policies. That is true even in some significant instances where workers are banded together in local plant employees' associations instead of being affiliated with national unions. The employers are under a constant pressure to meet or exceed the terms of labor agreements concluded in other enterprises where union and management have selected collective bargaining rather than collective dealing as the means of achieving working harmony.

Actually, collective bargaining between trade unions and managements sets the pace of modern wage determination because twenty million workers are organized in unions constituted on a region-wide or national coverage basis—as against less than 1 million workers organized in local plant employee associations. Of course millions of workers are not represented either by trade unions or employee associations and for that reason do not set the pace in wage determination. Before explaining how collective bargaining works, it is well to examine how the pace-setting regional or national trade unions are structured and motivated.

TRADE UNIONS

To understand unions one must ask why people join them. Some persons do so without taking thought; some because they must, even though they might not choose to. Most people, however, join unions because they expect to derive job protection and earnings advantages. Wherever impersonalization has become a characteristic of the employer-employee relationship (as in the mass production industries), or where a strong craft tradition persists (as in the building or typographical trades), some twenty million men and women have chosen to deal with their employers conjointly through representatives, rather than to bargain for wages, hours, and work-benefits individually.

A common experience of impersonalization, or a common craft tradition, causes people at a place of work to make a common interpretation of labor problems; thus the stage is set for organization. At first a committee of employees may be formed to speak for many workers in the plant; soon an advantage may be seen in affiliating with an established labor organization. In doing so, the local unionists will enjoy the benefits of having representatives who are not on the employer's payroll and can speak without fear of losing their jobs or promotional opportunities. Then again, large unions have their own research staffs and political lobbyists; most importantly, they can mass the strength of a large organization of workers in an industry in supporting strike action at any particular place of work or throughout a community and sometimes even the nation.

It is important to realize that in the United States economy, and in Canada, choice of union representation by a worker does not typically alter his economic aspirations but is only a means of implementing them more effectively. The American worker is job-conscious rather than class-conscious; that is to say, he expects his union to serve him in improving the terms and conditions on which he supplies his labor to an employer, not as a political agency to take over the management of industry. Consequently American unions have job-conservation and job-sharing as their main objectives. Unions strive to attain these goals chiefly by a strategy of bringing economic pressure to bear on employers. What does this involve?

Trade unions use strike action as a last resort; yet the threat of strike is always a "silent partner" to any bargaining sessions between labor and management. Indeed, most unionists would hardly expect to be taken seriously by the employers if they lacked the ability to strike. In practically 95 per cent of labor-management negotiations, however, the economic pressure of potential strike action is subtly transmuted. A well-established, responsible union will, through its officials, make every effort to impress the employer with the *positive* benefits of uninterrupted cooperation, rather than attempt to frighten him. Thus the union, in return for obtaining beneficial terms of employment for its members, will offer cooperation in reducing labor turnover, in improving morale, in maintaining shop discipline, and in encouraging workers to participate in increasing productivity. This does not mean that union officials take the place of management supervisors; it means only that they are business-minded.

To illuminate the primarily businesslike, job-conscious outlook of the typical American unionist, the following modern definition of "supply of labor" is given. It lists (1) what a wage-earner expects of an employer; and (2) how he expects his union to serve him when he supplies his labor to an employer.

A supply of any particular kind of labor is an offer by any given person to commit his or her time to the control of an entrepreneur for a period of specified duration, in return for money and benefits to be earned during that period.

Under our laws against involuntary servitude, an employment contract cannot be held to be binding; the wage-earner can leave at any time, without giving a reason, and he can be discharged at any time for good cause. Not even the individual worker himself can bind himself in·o servitude under our laws, let alone a union indenturing him. (See the 13th Constitutional Amendment.)

The rate of pay which a worker normally expects is one which will be in balance with pay rates for similar kinds of work in the plant, and with rates for the same or similar work in the area. It is expected to be in line with the cost of living.

The rate of pay is expected to be based on the value of the work done for the employer, not on how urgently one happens to need money at the moment or based on any consideration other than the content of the job, objectively classified in such a way that the worker can understand the system of classification and verify the results by comparing them with what is paid elsewhere in the shop and in the labor market area.

American workers also expect to be able to move along promotional lines and not to be led into blind alleys where no further advancement is possible. They desire, in this connection, that adequate training facilities be available to enable them to advance if they are willing to make the effort.

Seniority is a prime consideration in the thinking of wage-earners. They realize that as they age their opportunities for changing jobs decrease, at the same time that their worth to a firm increases because of their background of experience in working for that firm. Hence they consider it fair that their length of service with a given concern be rewarded by increasing their job security in proportion to past service rendered.

From our earlier discussion of the personnel management programs of employers, it must be evident that these aims of employees are not incompatible with the long-run interest of employers in having a steady, well-trained, and reliable labor force at their command. And it is easy to see that unions, in serving these needs of their members, can play a constructive role in effectuating the personnel policies of the employers. True, some firms remain unorganized, recognized labor unions never having gained a foothold. Many of the top managers of these firms feel that unionization among employees occurs only when management neglects the employees; hence these managers have instituted personnel programs so comprehensive as to provide benefits which exceed those granted by competing employers who deal with autonomous trade unions. (Is this *de facto* recognition?)

THE STRUCTURE OF UNIONS

Classifying trade unions by size and economic power, we encounter the following categories, progressing from weak to strong unions.

1. *Single-firm unions.* In most instances these are unions whose membership is confined to the employees at a given place of work, unaffiliated with any parent union of larger scope. They exist primarily where the management is striving to keep the employees satisfied in

order that neither a basis nor the excuse will be provided for the entrance of AFL-CIO trade unions. Total membership of single-firm unions is not known but probably does not exceed 500,000 to a million.

2. *Federal charter unions and local industrial unions.* These are local unions which are directly affiliated with the top American Federation of Labor–Congress of Industrial Organizations (AFL-CIO) trade union center at Washington, D.C. They were so organized when no local or regional, craft, or industry-wide parent body was considered acceptable by a group of local workers who nevertheless wished to be affiliated with the AFL-CIO. Total membership in this type of structure is minimal; it is about 150,000.

3. *Independent trade unions.* These are large federations, such as two Railway Brotherhoods and the United Mine Workers of America, which are not affiliated with the AFL-CIO. Included in this group are some industrial unions expelled from the CIO in 1949 or from the AFL-CIO in 1957. Total membership is over 3 million.

4. *Nationally affiliated AFL-CIO unions.* This category includes a great variety of craft unions and industrial unions. Craft unions are based on the type of work done, such as the Glass Bottle Blowers Association of the United States and Canada, the United Brotherhood of Carpenters and Joiners of America, the Pattern Makers' League of North America, and so on. Membership in industrial unions, by contrast, is not according to the type of work done within an enterprise, but comprehends all wage-earners working "in and around" a place of work. Examples are The United Automobile, Aircraft & Agricultural Implement Workers of America (UAW), the United Packinghouse Workers of America, and the United Steelworkers of America. The AFL-CIO has 1 million Canadian members.

Membership of AFL-CIO unions in the U.S. in 1958 was in the neighborhood of 15.5 million. Some 44 million persons were employed as non-farm wage-earners. Adding the membership in the four categories of unions, it will be seen that approximately 20 million people, or 45 per cent of wage-earners, belong to unions, most of them to unions affiliated with the American Federation of Labor–Congress of Industrial Organizations (AFL-CIO) trade union center. This total figure is, however, somewhat misleading. As a matter of fact, the degree of organization is very high in United States manufacturing, up to 80 per cent in the steel industry and the automobile industry, for example. The unions in these industries have over one million members each. By contrast, probably not more than 10 per cent of retail trade employees are organized.

Collective Bargaining

In the United States economy, as in that of Canada, Great Britain, Australia, and the Scandinavian countries, law and order in industry is established in the final analysis by management officials, but not without many concessions being made to the representative viewpoints of the employees. Collective bargaining is the process by which agreements are made between labor and management. It includes various *negotiations,* the drafting of the terms of agreement, and numerous responsibilities of the company and union in the administration of the agreement during the life of the agreement (which is one year at the minimum).

NEGOTIATIONS

Conferences at which the agreement on terms of remuneration and working conditions are explored may be held at a national, regional, city-wide, or local plant level. If negotiations are on a national, industry-wide scale, it is usual for the employers to be represented by personnel officials of some of the leading concerns in the industry, advised by an informal committee of top management executives. The union will be represented by its national president and staff assistants, with a national wage policy committee comprised of delegates from various districts standing by to give advice. Since in the United States there are no national collective bargaining negotiations involving many industries, neither the national federations of employers (such as the U.S. Chamber of Commerce) nor the AFL-CIO national trade union center enter into negotiations (as is the case in Sweden).

Regional collective bargaining, sometimes referred to as multi-employer bargaining, takes place in such instances as longshore operations on the West Coast, between the Teamsters Union in an area and associations of their employers, or in the building trades between, say, the Carpenters Union and the contractors in a region such as the Denver metropolitan area.

The reason for large-scale collective bargaining is historical. It is characteristically encountered in large industries in which a limited number of concerns furnish a product or a line of related products for a regional or national market. Or it may take place where separate entrepreneurs form employers' associations to act in concert when confronted by the demands of some powerful union or unions. Industry-wide bargaining on a national scale does not entirely supersede direct bargaining between a specific employer and the wage-earners at his place of work. An industry-wide agreement on a national basis is too broad to cover all the detailed arrangements which have to be made at a given place of work, and thus has to be adapted to the needs of the local situation.

Generally speaking, the personnel officials of a firm will also be the bargaining representatives of the firm, although top executives may sit in and will sign the final agreement. On the union side of the bargaining table there will usually be found a national union representative, staff experts to present data, and some elected, nonpaid union officials. Sometimes in local bargaining a rank-and-file shop bargaining committee takes its place at the table.

An agreement to govern terms and conditions of employment (including benefits) is reached after negotiations have resolved differences between the union's demands and management's counterdemands —or in rare instances after a strike has put both parties to "the test of force." A typical, mid-twentieth century union-management agreement usually contains clauses which provide for the following:

1. Recognition of the union as the sole bargaining agent for the workers in the plant, whether or not they belong to the union.
2. Union security provisions according to which the employer undertakes to assist the union in maintaining its membership by discharging a worker who does not pay his dues or fails to join the union after a period of 30 to 90 days of continuous employment.
3. The checkoff. Upon authorization by an individual worker, the employer deducts union dues in the same manner as income tax and worker social security contributions.
4. The grievance procedure. This sets up a system under which a worker can protest what he considers to be unjust treatment and bring his case before a jury made up of employer and union representatives.
5. Arbitration and means of selecting an arbitrator. This provides for an impartial outsider to come in when union and management representatives become deadlocked in trying to settle a grievance. Very rarely is an arbitrator used to specify terms and conditions of a new contract (labor agreement).
6. Specific limitations on arbitrary discipline and discharge, binding the company to show good cause and absence of personal discrimination.
7. Seniority provisions affording long-service employees special consideration when layoffs and transfers are concerned, or in the matter of first chances at promotional opportunities.
8. Agreements on the mechanics of job evaluation, which has a direct bearing on the wages paid for particular kinds of work. In general these provide for the management to have the final say, but for union officials to be represented and consulted. The effort is often made to make these mechanics understandable to the worker; even

so, 25 per cent of major labor disputes in the recent past have been over "time and motion studies" which are used in evaluating particular jobs.

9. Wage-rates to be paid. These are usually listed separately in a supplement to the agreement, but *wage increases* are usually cited in the body of the agreement.
10. Vacation plans and the enumeration of paid holidays.
11. Methods of calculating overtime pay and sharing overtime work among the workers.
12. Provisions for sick leave and securing any type of leave and absence, paid or unpaid.
13. Statement of company responsibility in the matters of safety and sanitation.
14. Retirement pension plans.
15. Supplemental unemployment benefit plans (paid in addition to state unemployment compensation). These are sometimes referred to as "guaranteed annual wage plans," as for instance in the automobile industry.
16. Welfare, insurance, and medical care plans.
17. Military leave plans and re-employment rights under them; special contributory life insurance plans and thrift plans or provisions under which the company will contribute to an employee's expenses in acquiring a higher education.
18. Profit-sharing plans usually taking the form of the employee receiving a profit-bonus or being allowed to purchase company stock at reduced rates or with the company making part of the payment. In the United States as a whole, 13 per cent of office workers enjoy this type of benefit, and 7 per cent of plant workers. The practice is mentioned here because it will undoubtedly become much more prevalent. At present it is more frequently encountered in areas where large multiplant concerns have branches, as for instance in Chicago, where 21 per cent of office workers and 13 percent of plant workers are party to profit sharing. It is interesting to notice that in the majority of cases the wage-earners covered by these plans prefer not to receive their dividends in cash, but have them added to the amount of money which the employer sets aside to finance retirement pay, thereby increasing their future pension. Thus profit-sharing plans are primarily savings plans.

This list of agreement provisions is by no means exhaustive. Years ago agreements were brief and terse—and sometimes jotted down on a piece of wrapping paper! In the 1940's perhaps the most revealing provision was the "attitudes clause" found in contracts between locals of the CIO Steelworkers' Union and various steel companies; it stated:

The Company and the Union encourage the highest possible degree of friendly, cooperative relationships between their respective representatives at all levels and with and between all employees. The officers of the Company and the Union realize that this goal depends primarily on attitudes between people in their respective organizations and at all levels of responsibility.... They believe that these attitudes can be encouraged best when it is made clear that Company and Union officials, whose duties involve negotiation of this labor Agreement, are not anti-union or anti-company, but are sincerely concerned with the best interests and well-being of the business and all employees.

In the 1950's the concern of the parties to collective bargaining was more directly with technological than with psychological problems of cooperation, as is revealed by the following excerpts from an agreement reached in 1955 between the Owens–Corning Corporation and the Glass Bottle Blowers Association at the Newark, Ohio, plant where fibrous glass products were being produced:

All of the parties to this contract are fully aware of the many problems involved and the necessity for the greatest cooperation in recognizing each other's needs as solutions are attempted. It is recognized that the manufacture of fibrous glass products is a new business and it is a mutual aim of the parties to assist in the building of this business into a kind which will be able to carry on its sales and manufacturing operations at a profit and in such a constantly improving manner as to create the greatest possible number of steady jobs for all the parties.

DAY-BY-DAY LIVING UNDER THE AGREEMENT

The work of the personnel and the union officials has just begun after a labor agreement has been reached. Differences over the interpretation of the agreement arise and find expression as well as resolution through the grievance machinery. It is the grievance procedure which provides for the day-by-day operation of the terms of the collectively bargained instrument. Unsolved grievances are referred upward through various levels of joint consultation, involving at successive stages more responsible officials of the contesting organizations, until the difference is finally settled or is ultimately referred to an impartial arbitrator whose decision is final and binding.

The majority of grievances are brought by workers, not by the company. Steps in the appeal of grievances to progressively higher levels of management are these:

1. The "shadow step"—a level of informal discussion between the foreman, the aggrieved worker, and his union steward. No records are kept, but the discussion is expected to be conducted in a friendly, courteous atmosphere. Often it is found that when the issue is really extracted from other side issues, by merely discussing the matter, the grievance can be readily settled in terms of established practices and therefore requires no further handling.

2. If this is not the case, a *written* presentation of the grievance is made by the worker, the issue now being clearly defined. At this

stage the general foreman and the personnel director or his representative may take part. Often at this stage the aggrieved worker will be found really to be a spokesman for others having a similar grievance, so that processing at this stage is a matter of minor policy-making rather than a personal adjustment to cover the case of one worker. Records are kept, since the grievance may reveal a "weak spot" in the labor agreement which ought to be reconsidered at the next negotiation period. (For example one plant had in a few years 129 seniority grievances, proving that something was wrong with the seniority clause of the agreement, as was subsequently seen and remedied.)

3. If the grievance cannot be settled at step 2, a grievance committee usually convenes to consider it. Members of the committee are designated by management and elected by the union. The personnel director of the company and a paid union official are almost certain to attend such meetings. Previous testimony is not rehashed, foremen and aggrieved workers now appearing as witnesses rather than as contestants. Stenographic transcripts may be made. At this level of grievance handling policy matters perhaps covering an entire department of a plant are sure to be involved.

4. If a major policy decision has to be made by either the union or management, or both, representatives of the national union and top executives may either attend at stage 3 or set up a stage 4 meeting. This might happen when the company is charged with misinterpreting the layoff provisions of an agreement which in this respect is standard for many locals of the union throughout the nation. The national officers of the union will be concerned with preventing peculiar practices in one enterprise from setting an eccentric pattern; the company's top officials will not wish to come under criticism by following practices which are clearly out of line with general community practices.

5. If a grievance becomes deadlocked at all the preceding stages, an impartial third party (or board of arbitrators), agreed on by the parties, is given the final responsibility for resolving the grievance. However, all agreements stipulate (and it is generally understood) that the arbitrator must interpret the agreement and not add anything to it! In other words, an arbitrator is expected to be a peacemaker, but not a peacemonger.

Unions and managements do not cooperate simply on annual occasions when negotiations take place, or when there is conflict within the place of work. There is a great deal of "preventive conciliation" in which labor and management cooperate as in production committees grappling with problems of technological change; safety committees trying to prevent industrial injuries and diseases; joint participation in apprenticeship training programs; joint social and recreational activities; joint appearances before legislative bodies; or joint participation in civic affairs, blood donor programs, Red Cross and Community Chest Drives, and so forth. Top management officials have been invited to union banquets and labor leaders have addressed the American Management Association. In several cities cerebral palsy clinics have been constructed by managements donating materials, equipment, and direction, while labor donated productive services of members who volunteered and continued to serve with management officials on the boards of trustees for such institutions.

It is through these broader contacts, as well as in direct economic consultations, that American managers and workers alike experience a sense of mutuality.

The Impact of Collective Bargaining

THE PURELY ECONOMIC IMPACT

Most economists are agreed that collective bargaining assures workers that they will receive the value of their marginal product as a minimum wage. Lacking organization, some workers, particularly unskilled ones, might receive less. Thus Alfred Marshall wrote long ago:[4]

It is more difficult for them [unskilled workers] than for skilled artisans to form themselves into strong and lasting combinations; and so to put themselves on something like terms of equality in bargaining with their employers. For it must be remembered that a man who employs a thousand others is in himself an absolutely rigid combination to the extent of one thousand units among buyers in the labour market.

Since the formation of the Congress of Industrial Organizations (CIO, now merged with the AFL), the unskilled and semiskilled worker in manufacturing industries has overcome the handicap pointed out by Marshall, but the situation still holds true of migratory farm workers, of small cities where there may be only one or two major employers, and of depressed economic areas of the nation. Chapter 21 pointed out that substandard bargaining power among unskilled workers and those in certain racial minority groups, as well as among workers stranded in declining labor market areas, accounts for some of the millions of Americans who still live in "pockets of poverty."

Trade unions protect the wages of the rest of the wage-earning population, assuring them that they will at least be equal to the value

4 *Principles of Economics* (8th ed.; London: Macmillan & Co., Ltd., 1936), p. 568. First published in 1890.

of the marginal product of their labor. However, where organization is strong, it will be the value of the marginal product of a whole group of workers in any one given job classification which is protected, not necessarily that of every individual worker. That is to say, the superior worker may, in a manner of speaking, "carry along" a somewhat inferior worker by working at the same union rate. To the employer this will make no difference, for on the average he will be paying no more than if he paid the inferior worker less and the superior worker more. To the superior worker the sacrifice is more nominal than real, for he rests secure in the knowledge that his wage is protected against desperate underbidding by inferior workers. And, of course, the superior worker can, and frequently does, move up the promotional ladder, especially when adequate training facilities exist.

If the group value of the marginal product of workers in different job classifications sets the minimum wage rate when workers are organized instead of splintered, what sets the upper limit? Here again modern economic theory has not much to add to what Alfred Marshall wrote years ago:

If the employers in any trade act together and so do the employed, the solution of the problem of wages becomes indeterminate; and there is nothing but bargaining to decide the exact shares in which the excess of its incomings over its outgoings for the time shall be divided between employers and employed. Leaving out of account industries which are being superseded, no lowering of wages will be permanently in the interest of employers, which drives many skilled workers to other markets, or even to other industries . . . ; wages must be high enough in an average year to attract young people to the trade. This sets the lower limits to wages, and upper limits are set by corresponding necessities [to attract] the supply of capital and business power. But what point between these limits should be taken at any time can be decided only by bargaining. . . .[5]

In brief, the upper limit to wage demands which the trade unions can expect to have fulfilled are set by the anticipated profit incomes of capitalists and managers in the sense that if wages encroach on what is considered a reasonable profit income, further investment will not be undertaken. However, this should not be understood to mean that capitalists, acting through managers, arbitrarily estimate what they should earn and are therefore not prepared to consider wage demands of unions. Actually, the situation is entirely the reverse. Management experts estimate what net profits can be earned *after* wage demands are reasonably accommodated and often seek for ways of meeting increased wages-bills by improving efficiency in their plant. In their turn, responsible trade unions modify their demands when

[5] *Op. cit.*, pp. 627–28.

convincing evidence is presented that this is the reasonable course of action.

In this connection it is well to bear in mind that there is a marked distinction between money wages and real wages—what money wages will buy. Sometimes it is possible for trade unions to obtain large increases in money wages, only to witness the cost of living rise so as to absorb a substantial portion of the money wage increase. However, one must be careful not to jump to hasty conclusions. In the post-World War II "inflationary" economy of the United States, the consumer price index rose 18 per cent between 1947/49 and 1957, but spendable wage income (after taxes) rose by 55 per cent, three times as much as the cost of living. Thus real wages increased (as did profits), largely because the lion's share of postwar productivity gains went to labor and management instead of being passed on to consumers in the form of lower prices or being awarded to owners of land and other types of property in the form of increased rents and interest payments. Indeed, the shares of rent and interest in the national income decreased considerably.

Trade union bargaining for wages has a special effect in lowering the degree of monopoly throughout the economy by lowering excess profit income. When monopolistic profits are high, the unions are placed in a strong position to demand higher wages, since these will encroach not on normal profits but on excess profits. Public opinion therefore tends to favor trade union action, especially when prices are raised in excess of what is required to meet increased wage costs. Thus a policy of lower profit ratios may be adopted, which of course means that the degree of monopoly has been lowered.

Thus far only beneficial results of trade unionism have been mentioned. There is a minority of economists who believe that collective bargaining decreases wages on the average. This point of view has been expressed by Fritz Machlup as follows:

> It is the chief purpose of a trade union to obtain monopolistic advantages for its members. [These advantages] can be maintained . . . in the long run only at the expense of less fortunate laborers and consumers. In the short run, labor may exploit chiefly the owners of the immobile capital sunk in certain enterprises. In the long run, however, the beneficiaries of monopolistic wage policies exploit their fellow laborers. This exploitation takes several forms: (1) fewer laborers will find employment in the industries which pay the monopolistic wage rates; (2) in the other industries, which absorb some of the laborers who cannot get the more attractive jobs, wage rates will be lower than they would be otherwise; (3) some of the displaced laborers will remain unemployed and their subsistence will have to come out of assessments made on the others; and (4) as consumers, all will have to pay higher prices for the products made with the dearer labor.

An elimination of monopolistic wage determination would open up the better jobs—which would then of course be somewhat less attractive than they are now—and would relieve the congestion in the low-wage industries and occupations. As a result, *wages in general would be higher* if the low wage rates were permitted to rise in consequence of mass migrations of workers into the higher-wage jobs.[6]

This minority view among economists is impossible to verify statistically, for in reality the general level of wages is always rising, except during depressions. At such times it is unlikely that cutting wages would increase employment. However, in particular instances one can sometimes observe what Machlup asserts:

1. There are cases of certain types of skilled craftsmen in largely nonmechanized industries making it difficult for new workers to join the union or obtain needed apprenticeship training. In one metropolitan area the average age of a particular kind of craftsman was observed to be steadily increasing, which is not normally the case when young persons are allowed to enter the craft.

2. "Vested interest situations." In one such instance breadwagon driver-salesmen were charging commissions when simply delivering bakery products to chain-store outlets without having to exert any selling effort. Because of the high cost, the chain stores were constructing their own bakeries. Had ordinary truck drivers, working at hourly rates (instead of rate plus commission) been used, a better allocation of resources would have been achieved than was the case when the chain stores built bakeries while the regular bakeries had sufficient capacity to produce all the needed bread. Likewise, the demand for truck drivers would have increased, although the demand for driver-salesmen would have decreased (since they were not really needed for chain-store delivery service).

3. Monopolistic wage determination occurs when, sometimes, craftsmen and their employers act together to raise costs to consumers by restricting production. Cases have been known of union electricians and electrical contractors, for instance, causing city ordinances to be adopted which require persons having a home built to use more expensive cable than would be required on consumer-oriented safety standards; or union craftsmen have been known to refuse to install equipment not manufactured by certain favored entrepreneurs.

The question is, can such malpractices be observed *generally* throughout industry, rather than here and there in particular instances?

[6] "Monopolistic Wage Determination," in George P. Schultz and John R. Coleman (eds.), *Labor Problems: Cases and Readings* (New York: McGraw-Hill Book Co., Inc., 1953), chap. xliv.

In answering this question we must note that with some important exceptions—teamstering and the building trades—trade unionism is mostly concentrated in the mechanized and mass production industries. But in these industries *expansive* membership policies characterize the unions, just as expansive rather than restrictive oligopoly is the rule among entrepreneurs. Moreover, the wage demands of unions in our modern industries provide one of many stimuli for managements to adopt improved methods of production, while, on the other hand, the unions *must* support technological progress enabling the employer to pay higher wages.

In the mass production industries the unions usually represent all the workers in and around the place of work. They have therefore no interest in keeping some people out of work or in restricting productivity for the benefit of only some workers in the entire bargaining unit. An automobile workers' union, a rubber workers' union, or a steelworkers' union would quickly collapse if special privileges were negotiated for the workers in the higher labor grades at the expense of the workers in lower job classifications. Thus in an exhaustive study of seven industries in which industry-wide collective bargaining is the rule, Richard Lester and Edward Robie found no evidences of monopolistic or collusive labor practices with regard to wages or technological change. Instead: ". . . elimination of wage-cutting has tended to stress efficiency of management as the most important factor of competition."[7] The industries studied were glassware, pottery, stoves, hosiery, silk and rayon dyeing and finishing, flat glass, and pulp and paper. In all of them there are some skilled workers (for instance, glass cutters) who could conceivably organize narrowly to try to obtain high wages at the expense of the rest. There are other industries in which it would be unfeasible for high-rated workers to practice discrimination against the rest. Thus in the hotel and restaurant trades, bartenders may not always feel sympathy for the waiters but will work with and for them in the knowledge that waiters can substitute for bartenders in the event the latter should go on strike to secure gains only for themselves.

Briefly, then, in the most modern industries restrictive labor monopolism is virtually impossible. In many other trades it is unfeasible. In yet other trades the unions are too weak to attempt any monopolization of job opportunities, as, for instance, among white collar office workers. Moreover, unions are not unaware of the necessity of maintaining good public relations; in addition, it would be a gross exaggeration to imply that the bulk of labor's rank-and-file and union

[7] Richard A. Lester and E. A. Robie, *Wages Under National and Regional Collective Bargaining* (Princeton, N.J.: Princeton University Press, 1946), p. 95.

officialdom is bereft of moral sentiments. These are some of the reasons why a majority of economists accept the beneficial impact of collective bargaining as a general proposition, although freely granting the existence of abuses in particular instances.

United States government policy in this matter of labor and management relations follows the majority view among economists and therefore encourages collective bargaining at the same time that public policy strives to prevent abusive labor practices. How the American labor code emerged, and how it is presently implemented, will be the subject of Chapter 26.

Appendix:

Structure of the AFL-CIO

MEMBERSHIP

The American Federation of Labor and Congress of Industrial Organizations (AFL-CIO) is made up of 139 different national and international unions, which in turn have more than 50,000 local unions. The combined membership of all the unions affiliated with the AFL-CIO, as of 1958, was 16,500,000 workers, including Canadian members.

AFFILIATED ORGANIZATIONS

In addition to the national and international unions, the AFL-CIO has state and city central bodies and special trade and industrial departments. There are *state central bodies* in each of the 49 states, Puerto Rico, and Hawaii. The state bodies, composed of and supported by the different local unions in the particular state, function to advance the state-wide interests of labor and represent labor on state legislative matters. Similarly, in each of more than 1,000 communities, the local unions of different national and international unions have formed *city central bodies,* through which they deal with civic and community problems and other local matters of mutual concern.

POLICY DETERMINATION AND APPLICATION

The basic policies of the AFL-CIO are set by its *convention,* which is its highest governing body. The convention meets every two years, although a special convention may be called at any time to consider a particular prob-

Figure 25–1. Structural Organization of the American Federation of Labor and Congress of Industrial Organizations

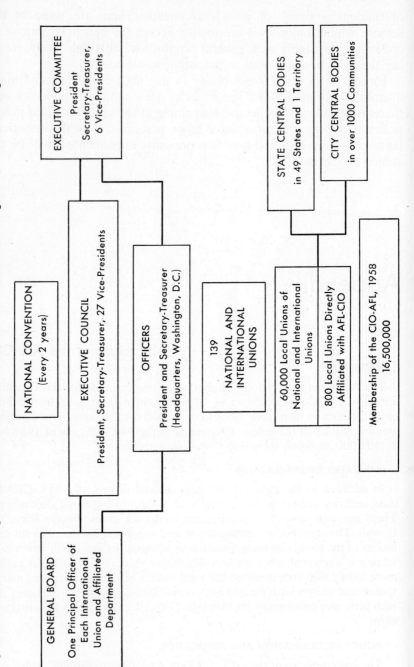

lem. Each national and international union is entitled to send delegates to the convention; the number of delegates is determined by the size of the union. Other affiliated organizations are entitled to be represented by one delegate each.

The governing body between conventions is the *Executive Council,* which is made up of the federation's President, Secretary-Treasurer, and 27 Vice-Presidents, all of whom are elected by majority vote of the convention. The Executive Council carries out policies laid down by vote of the convention and deals with whatever issues and needs may arise between conventions. It meets at least three times a year.

The *executive officers* of the AFL-CIO are its *President* and *Secretary-Treasurer.* They are responsible for supervising the affairs of the federation. The President appoints a number of *standing committees* on particular subjects and directs the committees and staff departments in providing services to labor through organizing, legislative, international, public relations, educational, economic research and other activities.

There are two other official bodies: (1) The *Executive Committee,* made up of the President, Secretary-Treasurer and six Vice-Presidents, meets every two months to advise the executive officers on policy matters. (2) A *General Board,* made up of the Executive Council members and a principal officer of each national and international union and each trade and industrial department, meets at least once a year to consider policy questions referred to it by the officers of the Executive Council.

For Discussion

1. It is incorrect to assess the labor cost of a firm by the wage rates paid to the employees. Why? What is the proper measure?

2. How does the concept of "personnel management" represent a progressive departure from Frederick W. Taylor's concept of "scientific management?"

3. A warehouse employee who belongs to a union is promoted to a job in the office of the same firm; office workers in this firm are not represented by a union. Does the promoted employee no longer experience any impact of the union to which he formerly belonged on his economic affairs as an office worker?

4. "Impersonalization of the work relationship sets the stage for labor organization." Explain.

5. "American unions are job-conscious, not class-conscious." Discuss.

6. At the present time what are some of the newest provisions to be found in union-management agreements? What additionally new features do you think might be incorporated in union-management agreements in 1965? 1970?

7. The president of one of America's large international unions takes advantage of every suitable opportunity to remind his officialdom that unions were formed as grievance committees in the service of the individual worker and that as such they must fundamentally remain. Is not this a negative approach? If it is not, why not?

8. The share of the national income which labor receives has been 65 per cent, give or take, as far back as trustworthy statistics reach—approximately

100 years. The collective bargaining power of trade unions has waxed strong since 1937, but labor's share remains approximately 65 per cent of the national income. Does this suggest that collective bargaining is "much ado about nothing"? Does it suggest that although organized labor has made great strides, it has done so at the expense of unorganized workers? If the latter were the case, would it pay the unorganized persons to "be wise, and organize"? These topics are controversial, so spare no effort to consider various sides of each question, i.e., management's viewpoint, that of organized labor, unorganized labor, and the viewpoints of persons or groups not directly involved in labor and management relations.

26   Public Policy

and Collective Bargaining

Evolution of Public Policy

Collective bargaining postdates the American Revolution, largely because British colonial policy discouraged industry in North America, so that few occasions for collective bargaining existed. Industrial disputes of a modern nature featuring organized labor unions first became prominent in the 1790's in the shoe-making, hat-making, and printing industries. In one such dispute involving the Philadelphia shoemakers (cordwainers) in 1806, some organized employees struck to secure from their employer an agreement that he would hire only members of their society. A mayor's court ruled that in seeking a closed shop agreement (as it is now called), the cordwainers were attempting to mass economic strength so as to be able to raise wages. Any combination to raise wages and to "injure" others in pursuit of this aim the mayor's court ruled to be a criminal conspiracy under English common law. However, workmen's combinations continued to function.

In 1842 the conspiracy doctrine was significantly altered by the ruling of the Massachusetts Supreme Court in the case of *Commonwealth* v. *Hunt*. The Boston shoemakers were trying to enforce a closed shop in their trade. The Massachusetts court ruled that the union's objective was lawful, since the mere acquisition of power constitutes no evil, but only a proved abuse of power does.

Actually this removal of the criminal conspiracy doctrine did not so much open the door to unionism as it enabled the courts to intercede in labor disputes to determine the legality of the means and ends of union action in given instances. If the findings were adverse to the union, it was still held to be a conspiracy, although a civil damage judgment would be rendered rather than a criminal conviction.

THE LABOR INJUNCTION

Civil damage suits against unions were found to be inadequate by employers opposed to unions or aggrieved by their actions. They did not wish to be compensated for damage done so much as they wanted to prevent it from being done. Hence there was resort to the injunction. This is a device of Anglo-Saxon common law which erects sanctions against specific kinds of damaging actions such as assault, trespass, fraud, libel, purported damage to another's property, and so forth. An injunction is a court order which seeks to prevent actual or threatened wrongful invasion of property which, if not prohibited, would result in irreparable damage to property for which there is no apparent practical restoration.

Now, if we include under the concept of "property" a businessman's right to do business without being troubled by labor strife, union activity is bound to be severely curtailed, since its aim, among other things, is to make it difficult for an entrepreneur to do business as usual if he will not award the union recognition or deal with the union's representatives when they present demands. Injunctions in labor disputes, freely issued by local courts at the behest of private employers, sometimes even forbade the mere mention of an existing labor dispute lest this cause some potential customers of a firm to buy elsewhere for fear of not having their orders filled should a strike develop at the particular plant. Unionists were quick to point out that while this practice of issuing injunctions protected the employer's business it threatened to destroy the union's business.

The power of the injunction to repress organized labor activity was strengthened when, after 1890, the Sherman Antitrust Act was applied to labor. Whether or not Congress intended unions to be covered by the Sherman Act is an interesting but moot question. The fact is that the courts held unions to be covered. This meant that injunctions could now be issued against unions for threatening to act as if they were conspiracies in restraint of trade. Obviously, almost any strike activity could be prevented under this doctrine, for work stoppages inevitably diminish the flow of commerce. Since the Sherman Act is a federal statute, however, its main effect was to curb large-scale *interstate* strike action designed to bring about industry-wide collective bargaining. But localized bargaining also stood under the shadow of the ban against interference with interstate shipments of goods should any union official incautiously suggest that this might be a way of bringing pressure to bear on a local employer.

As public policy in labor and management relations, the labor injunction was felt to be especially onerous by the unionists because it aimed so directly at depriving them of their power of last resort, the strike and the boycott. This is economic power, not political power. Samuel Gompers, the founder of the American Federation of Labor, had deliberately chosen the path of economic power, rather than that of political power, as the means to labor's ends of improving wages, hours, and working conditions. Gompers' philosophy was one of *voluntarism,* working directly with employers rather than relying on the government or the courts to enact and enforce laws beneficial to labor. Of course, when gains were achieved from employers, Gompers counseled political action of labor to secure laws to protect the gains of labor wrung from the employers in action "on the economic field."

The Sherman Antitrust Act, when applied to labor, was an enactment that labor interpreted as potentially depriving labor of gains already made or which could in the future be made by the direct use of economic power. Hence Gompers led the trade union movement in support of an amendment to the Sherman Antitrust Act, the Clayton Act passed by Congress in 1914. Sections 6 and 20 of the Clayton Act met many of organized labor's protests against labor injunctions as expressed in the AFL's "Bill of Grievances" in 1906. Section 6 stipulated, in part, that nothing in the antitrust laws shall be construed (1) to forbid the existence of labor organizations; (2) to forbid or restrain individual members from lawfully [*sic*] carrying out the legitimate objectives of labor organizations; (3) to hold labor organizations to be illegal combinations or conspiracies in restraint of trade under any antitrust laws. The preamble to the Clayton Act, incidentally, stated that the labor of a human being is not a commodity. With Section 6, and with Section 20 purporting to limit federal courts in their issuance of injunctions, organized labor in 1914 believed it had won "Labor's Magna Charta."

Labor's hopes were further raised during World War I, when Gompers and other labor officials were consulted freely by the government to help in various ways to minimize labor unrest in the interest of the effective prosecution of the war effort. Most promising in rewarding labor for its loyal participation were the "principles" of industrial relations agreed upon by employers as well as by union representatives and administered through the medium of the National

War Labor Board. These "principles" asserted the right of workers to organize into trade unions in order to bargain with employers through freely chosen representatives without employer interference; discharge of a worker by reason of union membership was prohibited; and closed shop agreements between unions and managements were protected if they had been made before the war.

With the end of World War I, however, labor's advance was suddenly halted; and some of its wartime gains were lost when the United States Supreme Court, in some key decisions in the 1920's, interpreted the Clayton Act as *not* having removed unions from liability under the Sherman Antitrust Act. This the Court accomplished by the simple device of calling attention to the use of the word "lawful" in the wording of the Clayton Act. Thus where the Clayton Act stated that courts cannot restrain an individual member of a union from lawfully carrying out the legitimate objectives of the union, the Court held that it had in the past defined what is lawful for union members to do and what is legitimate for the unions to have as objectives. Thus Congress was considered as having in 1914 merely affirmed, and put into statutory form, all the existing court practices, including the issuance of injunctions. Besides this, the Supreme Court upheld as legitimate the "yellow dog contract," by which signing workers promised not to join an AFL or other outside union and often also promised to join a company union organized by the employer so as to deter the employees from joining a bona fide trade union. Small wonder that trade union membership declined steadily during the 1920's, after having reached a high level during World War I.

DEPRESSION AND THE RISE OF LIBERAL LABOR LEGISLATION

The 1929 depression stubbornly refused to cure itself; hence, by 1931, leading management groups advanced plans for recovery, if only to head off government planning. The best known "plan" at the time was that of Gerard Swope of the General Electric Company. Its fundamental intent was to modify the antitrust laws so as to permit greater cooperation among competitive enterprises through trade associations. Agreements would be made by firms in an industry to govern minimum prices, to regulate output, to standardize wages in the industry, and to define "fair" competitive practices. The agreements would be submitted to the federal government for approval. Mention was made of labor organization in the Swope Plan, but the reference was to employer-dominated company unions rather than to AFL or other bona fide unions. The Swope Plan did not, however, give full expression to the entire range of management opinion in the matter of labor relations. For instance, in the coal and garment industries depression had unleashed disruptive cutthroat price and wage competition which the employers seemed unable to control.

Consequently, in those industries entrepreneurs reluctantly accepted the union as a mechanism of stabilization; by imposing the same wage standards on all employers, price cutting based on wage cutting could be prevented. Thus, for example, *Coal Age* (an industry magazine) stated in September, 1931:

> In an industry compelled to carry the idle-capacity load of bituminous coal . . . stabilization [of wages, hours, and working conditions] without the interposition of some outside agency representing the workers presents insuperable obstacles. . . .

And *Coal Age* added that the outside labor organization must be accepted "by a sufficiently large percentage of the operators to give the wages and working conditions so established a controlling influence. . . ." In other words, industry-wide bargaining to bring about uniform wage standards was recognized to be an essential ingredient of industry stabilization along all fronts.

Now, if wage stabilization was a means to the end of price stabilization for the employer, wage stabilization was an end in itself for the wage-earner. Naturally he was keenly aware of the fact that industry-wide bargaining would have to be sanctioned by law in order to effect wage stabilization throughout an industry. Hence strong pressures were brought on Congress to pass anti-injunction legislation, since the injunction stood as a barrier against industry-wide bargaining across state lines. It is a notable fact that federal and state anti-injunction laws were enacted early in 1932 prior to the advent of the New Deal legislation. The federal law which drastically restricted the use of injunctions in labor disputes has come to be known as the Norris–LaGuardia Act.

Section 4 of the Act bans the granting of injunctions by federal courts unless unions use violence or engage in fraud during a labor dispute. Section 13 of the Norris–LaGuardia Act defines a "labor dispute" broadly, to include as participants not only people directly employed by an entrepreneur but also workers and union officials who have a direct economic interest in the outcome of a dispute in which they are not personally involved. This fully legalized industry-wide bargaining on a regional or national scale, since steelworkers, for example, could now apply economic pressure as a group on all their employers as a group. In subsequent decisions of the United States Supreme Court the Norris–LaGuardia Act was also interpreted as making the Sherman Antitrust Act inapplicable to union activity, barring only the case of unions and managements collusively acting together to raise prices to consumers.

THE NEW DEAL AND SECTION 7(a) OF THE
NATIONAL INDUSTRIAL RECOVERY ACT (NIRA)

When Franklin D. Roosevelt's administration took office in 1933 no specific recovery legislation had been prepared. However, three proposals enjoyed organized support and action could be taken on them. Senator Black (of Alabama) introduced a 30-hour work week bill to prohibit the shipment in interstate commerce of goods produced in establishments in which any person was employed more than five days in one week or more than six hours in one day. The bill, designed to spread work and prevent cutthroat competition for overtime work, was known to have the support of the American Federation of Labor. Second, to prevent distress selling at abnormal prices of "overproduced goods," there was the Swope Plan for relaxing the antitrust laws so as to permit trade association "planning" industry by industry; this proposal (no bill having been introduced) enjoyed the support of many persons and groups in the business community. Third, a large program of public works to stimulate re-employment was advocated by a group of Senators centering around Wagner (of New York), LaFollette (of Wisconsin), and Costigan (of Colorado).

The Black 30-hour work week bill passed the Senate but was rejected by the Roosevelt administration as being too rigid. An alternative proposal was made to regulate minimum wages and provide for time-and-one-half payment for overtime hours worked, to discourage using some workers for long periods while leaving others completely unemployed. Many conferences were held by administration leaders and members of Congress with influential business and labor leaders; out of these meetings emerged the National Industrial Recovery Act. This Act relaxed the antitrust laws on trade associations by providing for codes of fair competition to be developed by industry groups, establishing minimum prices and other trade protections against "chiselling." These codes were subject to government approval and to immediate cancellation upon abuse, for they were meant to prevent depression-distress selling, not normal competition. Adherence to the codes permitted an entrepreneur to display a poster with the imprint of the "Blue Eagle," to inform his customers that he was cooperating with the national recovery effort. In addition, each employer who subscribed to an industry code was expected to abide by the "President's Re-employment Agreement," under which he promised to maintain stipulated minimum wage and maximum hours conditions. In addition, the NIRA featured Section 7(a) which read in part as follows:

(1) . . . employees shall have the right to organize to bargain collectively through representatives of their own choosing, and shall be free from the interference, restraint, or coercion of employers . . . in the designation of such representatives. . . .

(2) . . . no employee and no one seeking employment shall be required as a condition of employment to join any company union or to refrain from joining, organizing, or assisting a labor organization of his own choosing. . . .

Considered at face value, this provision of the NIRA added little to the legal status already gained by organized labor and left employers ample opportunity to avoid bargaining with unions. It has been described as "a compromise among powerful employers, a weak trade union movement, and a government interested in a recovery program capable of promoting revival without overturning the long line of American institutional development or behavior."[1] Yet Section 7(a) was soon to provide the basis of America's first specific labor code.

The National Labor Relations Act (Wagner Act) of 1935

The immediate background. To implement the administration of Section 7(a), public labor boards were created by the New Deal administration. Many excellent persons did yeoman's work as members of the NIRA labor boards, attempting to bring about the peaceful settlement of labor disputes so that the national recovery effort might not be interrupted. The field was an unexplored one, although labor boards were not novelties on the American scene, since previous ones had operated in the price-regulated railroad industry or under wartime conditions. But to try implementing a depression-recovery effort was not only unprecedented but well-nigh forbidding.

There was nothing specific about the recovery effort. There was only the general idea that by industrial self-government under public supervision, industry would again become profitable and therefore able, among other things, to pay high wages. Naturally the industrialists argued that before paying high wages they ought to be sure of the *realization* of profits. So they were averse to working with labor boards who might recommend high wages in *anticipation* of high profits. On the other hand, the labor organizations feared that the

---

[1] See Grant N. Farr, *A Study of the Origins of Section 7(a) of the National Industrial Recovery Act.* (Ph.D. Dissertation, University of California, 1955).

NIRA labor boards would recommend that wages should be kept static until profits had sufficiently recovered. As a consequence the NIRA labor boards found very little acceptance. They had been designed to offer a friendly forum and to give expert advice to disputing labor and management groups who, taken together, knew all the facts bearing on the dispute. It was hoped that in a friendly atmosphere the parties to a labor dispute would jointly investigate all the facts bearing on the recovery of their particular enterprise to see what agreement could be reached by reasonable compromising in the light of known facts. Thus government-sponsored conciliation of conflicting but reasonable labor and management officials was hoped to take the place of industrial warfare.

The hope was premature. It was premature because the development of trade union psychology and of management behavior favorable to the holding of refined economic conferences requires both parties, labor and management, to approach power equality. In 1935 the majority of wage-earners were just organizing enough bargaining strength to confront their employers. The latter were as yet entirely skeptical of their employees' ability to organize any real strength of bargaining power. Hence the existence of the NIRA labor boards was more or less beside the point so far as the settlement of disputes over wages, hours, and working conditions was concerned. The employers could use their superiority of economic power to do fairly much as they wished, if they wished. And what the unions needed was aid in winning the employers' recognition, not offers of assistance in matters of refined bargaining that might perhaps ensue, but only *after* recognition had been won.

Observing the manifold failures and frustrations of the NIRA labor boards in their attempts to settle bargaining disputes, the Roosevelt administration split the functions of handling matters of union recognition and of trying to settle disputes over wages, hours, and working conditions. In the autumn of 1933 President Roosevelt created the National Labor Board, a centralized organization with headquarters in Washington, D.C., and branches in nineteen cities. The Board, headed by Senator Robert F. Wagner, dealt primarily with union recognition questions. Because its recommendations were rejected by employers, President Roosevelt issued executive orders giving the Board, among other things, the right to conduct elections among workers to determine their choice of a bargaining representative, if any.

This executive Labor Board was superseded by one having a statutory foundation when Congress in June, 1934, adopted Joint Public Resolution No. 44. Under the terms of this resolution President Roosevelt was empowered to appoint a new labor board, to be known as the National Labor Relations Board. Though given the mandate to deal with any and all violations of Section 7(a) of the NIRA, this new board was clearly intended to limit itself to recognition problems, that is, to effectuate the will of a majority of working people whenever a question of worker representation arose. As for bargaining disputes over wages, hours, and working conditions, the government beat a strategic retreat; it really abandoned the scenes of industrial conflict.

Then, in May, 1935, many sections of the National Industrial Recovery Act were declared unconstitutional by the United States Supreme Court.[2] The reasoning was that Congress had improperly delegated authority to the President to engage in price fixing, even though he had called upon the industrialists themselves to draw up the price codes under public supervision and with consequent public surveillance. However, Section 7(a) of NIRA was not declared unconstitutional, undoubtedly because it had no direct relation to price fixing. Thus the National Labor Relations Board setup could be continued.

Passage of the Wagner Act. Even before the NIRA was declared unconstitutional in most of its provisions, hearings had been held in both the Senate and the House of Representatives on bills introduced for the purpose of making the National Labor Relations Board a permanent institution. As such it was not to handle all labor disputes, but was to act primarily to protect the right of workers to self-organization. When releasing the news of the passage of the Act, President Roosevelt remarked that this would be a long step toward industrial peace. As a matter of fact, the Wagner Act of 1935 in its preamble goes a little further than merely asserting the right of workers to self-organization—a declaration already made in the Norris–LaGuardia Act of 1932. Section 1 of the Wagner Act states among other things that "it is hereby declared to be the policy of the United States [to remove sources of industrial strife and unrest] by encouraging the practice and procedure of collective bargaining."

In this effort to encourage collective bargaining the role cut out for the government was one of educator and guide, not of policeman. The Board was to encourage people to develop by their own resources the talent and skill for free collective bargaining. The government insisted on only one thing, namely, good faith in collective bargaining. The Board had at all times the power to take whatever *affirmative* action might be required to effectuate the basic policy of the government in the matter of encouraging free collective bargaining. But such affirma-

---

[2] *Schechter Poultry Corporation* v. *United States*, 295 U.S. 495 (1935).

tive action constituted only remedial intervention when necessary, never prosecution or punishment.

Under the 1935 Wagner Act the new National Labor Relations Board was not established as an arbitration board in any sense. Its only task was to carry out the intentions of Congress when passing the Act. These were (1) that workers should be free to bargain through representatives of their own choosing, and (2) that subsequent to such free choice there should be no employer interference in the internal affairs of the union, or no discharges of workers merely by reason of their belonging to a union and carrying on normal union activities. The reason for this latter provision was that a system of free elections can be brought to nought if subsequent employer interference with the unions undermines them. The intention of Congress in passing the Wagner Act was to make free election of worker representatives mean something. Now, intentions of Congress can only be carried out; they cannot be mediated or arbitrated, for they are the will of the people. Accordingly the new NLRB had the job, not of compromising, but of carrying out the *general will* by (1) supervising representation elections, and (2) being on the lookout for the unfair use of any employer's economic power destined to undermine the union and therefore abrogate collective bargaining if left uncurbed.

The latter task, as experience soon proved, meant disallowing by cease-and-desist orders (enforceable in the district courts) such unfair labor practices as industrial espionage financed by employers; threatening a worker with loss of his job by reason of normal union activity or, alternatively, promising benefits to workers agitating against the union. Bargaining in good faith was defined. It required an employer to make proposals and counterproposals during negotiations, instead of sitting aloof, with a reserved veto power over workers' demands. Among other things bargaining in good faith also meant putting agreed points into writing, and employers taking responsibility for the actions of supervisory employees in their relations with union members.

While not commonly known, the fact is that the National Labor Relations Board also had the power, and on proper occasions used the power, to compel unions to bargain in good faith. It could and did grant only tentative recognition to unions of whose integrity the Board was initially in doubt.

THE WAGNER ACT'S MAIN PROVISIONS

A ready way to remember the gist of the United States federal labor relations code is that the chief clauses bear the same number, no matter how the code is changed or amended. Thus the clause stating that the workers shall have the right freely to organize has carried the number (7) since NIRA days; the unfair labor practices clause is always number (8); and clause (9) gives the NLRB its powers to set up and conduct elections among employees to determine which union, if any, they wish to be represented by. The rest of the sections are either definitional or administrative procedure sections; they may contain some "sleepers," but in general one can sense the drift of federal labor relations codes by noticing changes in the three above-mentioned clauses. At present we shall examine the broad contours of the nation's first detailed labor code, the Wagner Act of 1935.

Section 7 of the Act is brief, to the point, and self-contained. It simply states: "Employees shall have the right to self-organization, to form, join, or assist labor organizations, to bargain collectively through representatives of their own choosing, and to engage in concerted activities, for the purpose of collective bargaining or other mutual aid or protection." This summarizes everything organized labor had gained in the eyes of the law up to 1935. Note well that it does not really add anything—a right is acknowledged which labor had always claimed and fought for, but no new rights are bestowed in Section 7.

Section 8 of the Act might perhaps be considered as adding rights to those already possessed by organized labor, but before drawing this conclusion the following provisions of Section 8 should be pondered.

1. "It shall be an unfair labor practice for an employer to interfere with, restrain, or coerce employees in the exercise of the rights guaranteed in Section 7." Observe that since Section 7 adds no new rights, neither can this part of Section 8. What then does this clause accomplish? It adds facilities for preventing employee coercion. How strong these facilities were we shall see immediately below.

2. An employer will be considered to be acting unfairly from the viewpoint of public labor policy if he dominates, interferes with, or in any overt manner tries to influence the formation or administration of *any* labor organization [not just AFL-CIO unions] or if he contributes financial or other support to any labor organization. This part of Section 8 was obviously designed to discourage company unionism or other attempts to "beat the union to it" by offering the employees the benefits of some company-organized and company-supervised welfare plan. The purpose of the Wagner Act was to promote industrial democracy. The only trouble with this part of Section 8 is that only crass employer domination is likely to come to the attention of the Board. If the employer uses a smooth, psychological approach to give his employees the general idea that he

would much prefer to deal with some kind of labor organization existing at his plant alone and only among his own employees, the NLRB would find it hard to prove, or accept purported proof, that the strictly local plant organization of labor was dominated or being supported by the employer.

3. It shall be an unfair labor practice for the employer "by discrimination in regard to hire or tenure of employment or any term or condition of employment to encourage or discourage membership in any labor organization." This is the principle that a wage-earner cannot be fired by reason of his performing normal union activities. The unions used to enforce this principle by striking against unfair discharges of members actively promoting the interests of the union. Now the unions could protest to the NLRB in such matters.

4. This part of Section 8 simply states that a wage-earner must not be fired or penalized for appealing to the NLRB or testifying before it in some other wage-earner's behalf. It supports the worker's freedom of speech.

5. It shall be an unfair labor practice for an employer to refuse to bargain collectively with the representatives of his employees. This does not mean that bargaining must go on forever, but only that an effort in good faith must be made to reach an agreement.

Commenting on Section 8 as a whole, it should be noted that insofar as it seems to add rights in subsections 2–5 to organized labor, it does so by considering abuses by employers as "unfair labor practices." In practice this means that the government will shake a warning finger. However, it may require up to six months to process a case before the NLRB. In unfair labor practices cases the employer can appeal—perhaps all the way to the United States Supreme Court. If the union proves its case against an employer, the latter may have to reinstate an unfairly discharged worker and perhaps cover the employee's financial loss. (That is, the employer may have to cover the employee's lost wages during the time the unfair labor practice was being committed, or the difference between lower wages the employee earned on some other job and the wages he would have earned at his regular occupation.) Or perhaps the employer may have only to post a notice in his shop that he had seen Uncle Sam's warning finger and thereupon promised to cease and desist from his unfair labor practice. Really to get in trouble and suffer any appreciable economic loss an employer would have to defy not the NLRB, but some court order which the Board had sought and obtained after having been defied by an employer. In other words, an employer would have to go far out of his way to suffer actual punishment under this unfair labor practices section of the Wagner Act.

Section 9 of the Wagner Act states that the spokesmen of a union selected by the majority of the employees in a unit appropriate for such purposes "shall be the exclusive representatives of all [*sic*] the employees in such unit for the purposes of collective bargaining in respect to rates of pay, wages, hours of employment, or other conditions of employment." This is the principle of majority rule. It is expressed in part (a) of Section 9. In part (b) of the same section the Board is given power to decide on what basis representation elections shall be held so that collective bargaining might be conducted in a practical manner—that is, with employee bargaining power being reasonably matched with employer bargaining power, however organized. Thus if the employers are organized on an industry-wide basis, an industry-wide bargaining unit may be certified, but denied where this is not the case. This is to assure the employees "the full benefit of their right to self-organization and to collective bargaining." But the "unit appropriate" for purposes of collective bargaining —whether the employer unit, craft unit, plant unit, or subdivision thereof—shall also be determined by the Board in order to "effectuate the policies of this Act." This is where the public interest in collective bargaining enters—together with many of the worst troubles the NLRB experienced.

EMPLOYER ATTITUDES TOWARD THE WAGNER ACT

It is a tragic fact that between 1935, when the Wagner Act was passed, and 1937, when it was upheld by the Supreme Court, numerous employers refused to act in accordance with the Act because of their belief that it would be held unconstitutional. Such violations of the requirement that a law must be heeded until legally declared invalid caused much bitter blood and led to some violent labor-management conflicts between 1935 and 1937. For, indeed, the workers took the Wagner Act seriously.

After the Act was upheld by the United States Supreme Court in 1937,[3] the American business community split in its reaction somewhat along lines of size. In some cases of medium-sized business concerns (or medium-sized branches of a few large concerns) opposition to union organization was actually violent: armed company guards were employed, ordinary civil decencies were ignored in dealing with labor organizers, rumors were spread that a plant on which a town might depend heavily for its prosperity would be closed down, and so forth. Almost invariably these hard-fisted methods were rationalized with an assertion that public law and order had broken down because

---

[3] *NLRB* v. *Jones and Laughlin Steel Corporation*, 301 U.S. 1 (1937).

the local public officials were playing politics, not wishing to lose the labor vote. In truth, this is really a back-handed way of acknowledging that public officials were trying to be impartial in labor disputes. Small businessmen in the particular communities affected by labor strife more often than not supported hard-fisted treatment of labor organizers whom they usually labeled "outside troublemakers"; in various instances so-called citizens' committees were formed independently by small merchants and manufacturers to drive out or keep out labor organizers. Not all merchants and manufacturers of small and medium size opposed the Wagner Act, and a few vehemently spoke out against community hysteria engendered spontaneously or deliberately to frustrate the Act.

The attitude of most of the large industrial concerns was in general more self-enlightened. Some large corporations with long-established schemes of company unionism or employee representation refrained from engaging in industrial warfare to keep unions out. Instead they relied on their employee organizations to stand up in competition with the AFL and CIO unions. In other important instances large corporations voluntarily granted the unions recognition, more often because some important public figure had prevailed upon a corporation executive to do so than because of any distinct preference for dealing with unions. For instance, the United States Steel Corporation's Myron C. Taylor undoubtedly opened the door to the Steelworkers' Union partly under some persuasion from his personal friend, Franklin D. Roosevelt, and from Sir Walter Runciman, head of the British Trade Commission, and partly also because of a personal respect he developed for John L. Lewis when the two were returning from Europe on the same ship in 1937. Walter P. Chrysler in the automobile industry was brought together with John L. Lewis under the auspices of Michigan's Governor Frank Murphy. In other instances, however, no reassurance of corporation executives by government executives was required to win the unions recognition; instead, straight pressure tactics worked, as in the case of the General Motors Corporation.

Now, whether the unions won recognition over bitter opposition or just because it would have been bad public relations to stand out glaringly against the Wagner Act, the fact remains that employers in granting the unions recognition were by no means converted to, or intended to become involved in, any farflung scheme of mutual trusteeship or industry-wide collective bargaining. The employers as a body continued to express a strong preference for localized collective bargaining on an employer plant-unit basis, over industry-wide, multi-employer bargaining. This preference when stated in the characteristically strong words of the National Association of Manufacturers (NAM) took the form of this recommendation:[4]

Our national policy must be revised, to permit free and successful bargaining between friendly labor unions and employers at a plant or company level. . . .

In practice the preference could be observed, for example, in the steel companies' refusing to enter into an outright scheme of industry-wide bargaining. Instead, the Steelworkers' Union worked out an agreement with the United States Steel Corporation, similar (almost identical) to agreements then being signed by the other companies and the local branches of the national Steelworkers' Union. Thus a follow-the-leader pattern took the place of industry-wide bargaining under which representatives of all the companies would have met with the representatives of all the union locals over one bargaining table. In some industries, however, industry-wide bargaining was established, notably, in the coal mining industry, in the West Coast paper and pulp industry, in West Coast longshore operations, and in the flat glass industry. In the garment industry multi-employer bargaining was strengthened. Notice that in those cases in which industry-wide bargaining was either established for the first time or strengthened after having been established earlier than the 1930's, the new or fortified bargaining practice helped to stabilize earnings of the industry by eliminating competitive wage-cutting leading to price-cutting. Thus in no instance were the unions or the Wagner Act accepted by the employers on a philosophical basis. It was found profitable to adopt a compliant attitude toward the existing national labor policy.

Had autonomous trade unionism of the AFL-CIO type really achieved a secure footing? The question was an important one to ask, and answer. Upon the answer depended the future course of the nation's public labor policy. In general, it was probably conceded, even by bitter opponents of unions, that "labor was here to stay." But unions would have to tread lightly; they would have to strive for respectability in every way. It was certainly known at the time that while the business community would in the future adopt and support New Deal innovations beneficial to business—for instance, currency management—anything reaching beyond localized, plant-wide (but not industry-wide) collective bargaining would not be desired except in a minority of instances where it prevented cut-throat competition among employers. The National Association of Manufacturers would continue to publish pamphlets attacking industry-wide bargaining and

---

[4] Quoted from Clark Kerr, *Employer Policies in Industrial Relations, 1945–47,* Reprint No. 11 (Berkeley: University of California Institute of Industrial Relations, 1949), p. 60.

the whole current administration of the Wagner Act—pamphlets perhaps in small part financed with funds contributed by organizations practicing some modified form of industry-wide bargaining but quite amenable to getting back, not indeed to localized bargaining, but to industry-wide wage determination without the participation of unions.

This is not to say that organized labor's new strength in membership and the Wagner Act were of no consequence in the life of the industrial worker. For one thing, labor's general status would henceforth not be subjected to repeated tests of naked force; employers generally realized that it was expected and required of them to cease and desist from using their powers of controlling concentrated economic wealth in coercive, open attempts at thwarting genuine, bipartisan collective bargaining. Henceforth labor's status in the United States community would be determined primarily on the legal and political level. To men and women of labor who had physically struggled and often had suffered bitterly in the hardboiled old days, their success in moving the labor-management relations problem onto the higher level of informal and formal parliamentary procedures was very significant. The reflective wage-earner of 1937 realized full well that further elevations of his status, in general and particular, would not be given for the asking. But the old contest over wages, hours, and working conditions would be carried out under more refined rules of the game—between professionally trained experts on both sides of the bargaining table instead of industrial warriors on different sides of a charged wire fence. The persons who remembered labor history felt that some types of gains which they had secured "with their fists," could in the future be won through parliamentary procedures and law.

Despite the advances made through the statutory labor code, the American trade union movement did not entrust its future solely to government administrative boards. It retained, and continues to retain, its primary emphasis on organization to make gains through economic pressure rather than political action. In fact, some long-time trade unionists feared that the Wagner Act would soften the will of the forthcoming generation of labor organizers more accustomed to soft chairs than picket lines.

For Discussion

1. Federal and state courts continue to have the right to issue injunctions in labor disputes, but they can do so only under controlled conditions. At present what are the restrictions placed by Congress upon the courts?

2. Debate, in the affirmative and the negative, this topic: Resolved, that the Sherman Antitrust Act shall once again be applied to labor unions.

3. Why was the Clayton Act in 1914 hailed as "Labor's Magna Charta"? By what logic did the Supreme Court of the United States emasculate the Clayton Act later, in the 1920's? Check your notes on political science and history to see whether the Supreme Court's interpretations of the Clayton Act, in the 1920's, gave expression to majority public sentiment toward organized labor.

4. Was Section 7(a) of the NIRA a "victory" for organized labor?

5. The Wagner Act, America's first labor code, is not to be interpreted as the long arm of government reaching out to police labor relations. It was intended, instead, to serve as an instrument of labor and management and the public's education. Education for what? In 1960 does it matter what the Wagner Act was intended to accomplish, or what it did accomplish or failed to accomplish?

27 The United

States Labor Code Revised

Stormy Weather for the National Labor Relations Board

No sooner had the National Labor Relations Board (NLRB) been established as a permanent institution in 1937 than it became enmeshed in labor's civil war— the AFL versus CIO split. This seriously diminished the Board's prestige and effectiveness as an agency of industrial peace. For the NLRB was set up to handle problems of union recognition by employers, not to adjudicate rival claims of different unions to represent rank-and-file wage-earners.

From its inception the NLRB refused to handle ordinary jurisdictional disputes between, say, millwrights and carpenters over the assignment of work that might be done by either craft. But the AFL versus CIO split went far beyond this dimension of industrial conflict. It was in many ways a business rivalry among powerful organizations and personalities, and it was in other ways a conflict of different philosophies of labor organization and collective bargaining. Whether it was one or the other, the imminent threat was that rank-and-file wage-earners would be jostled about in the battle of giants; that employers might benefit and for that matter also suffer by taking sides; and that, in general, the public interest in genuine free collective bargaining would not be served by letting the rival labor unions simply fight it out. Consequently, the Board intervened in order: (1) to make sure that the individual wage-earners would have the final say in who was to be their bargaining representative; (2) to ensure that a workable *unit* of representation might be chosen by wage-earners—a craft, a federation of crafts, an industrial unit including all workers in a plant, or even a regional representation unit—whatever might suit the requirements for effective collective bargaining.

For example, the Board might designate, as an appropriate bargaining setup, one covering all the workers in a plant in which neither the employer nor the employee had ever thought along craft lines of labor representation. To instruct workers in such plants to vote for bargaining representatives along, say, ten different craft lines was felt to be dangerously close to gerrymandering representation units in order to frustrate collective bargaining. For in the first place the craft unions might not get to first base in appealing to workers to join separate craft unions when these workers had not habitually thought along craft or occupational lines. If perhaps the employer nevertheless granted recognition to the craft unions, they might not be effective in collective bargaining because they lacked adequate support from the rank and file of the wage-earners. On the other hand, the NLRB might designate a craft union as an appropriate bargaining unit in cases where the CIO wished to represent all the workers in the plant but where the extent of its organizing efforts was not sufficient to have enlisted the support of all the workers in that plant. In such cases it was felt to be unjust and inappropriate to deny bargaining privileges to an already strongly organized craft union, forcing these craftsmen to wait for representation until the industrial union had a chance to organize most of the workers in that plant.

From the point of view of government labor policy, having to designate what form of organization might best serve the needs of individual wage-earners and the public interest was a sorry business indeed. One union was bound to lose out whenever an AFL and a CIO union contested for the representation of wage-earners in a plant. The proper form of union representation, whether craft or industrial, or even whether regional or local, was really something organized labor should have settled in its own ranks; or at least machinery for adjudicating rival claims should have been established within the parent AFL organization. But this the labor organizers had been unable to accomplish, and thus the government had been drawn into what at best can be described only as a "messy situation." It was a situation which had not been contemplated when the Wagner Act was passed.

Labor's internal strife over industrial versus craft unionism reflected the fact that there was not a majority of public opinion in favor of industry-wide collective bargaining. Industry-wide bargaining is the practice of a union representing all the wage-earners in a particular industry and negotiating the same over-all agreement (or identical separate agreements) with all the employers in that industry (with or without adjustments for regional differentials). Under industry-wide bargaining all of the employers are on a par so far as money-wage costs and the like are concerned. The union does not operate by getting all it can from one employer, then seeing how much it can get from the others in turn, all the while pitting one against the other in their competition for hiring labor. While "sacrificing" this whipsaw tactic, however, the industry-wide union gains the advantage of confronting the employers in that industry as a whole with the united bargaining power of the entire labor force of the industry.

THE AFL'S OPPOSITION TO INDUSTRY-WIDE BARGAINING

In the 1930's especially, employer sentiment could be said to be organized against industry-wide bargaining. Nor were, or are, all segments of the trade union movement reconciled to the practice of industry-wide bargaining. Traditional AFL organization tactics had been those of bargaining employer by employer, in the hope of ferreting out the "most favorable" employer, who would then be held up as a standard to the rest of the employers. This typical AFL approach may be referred to as localized bargaining to distinguish it from industry-wide bargaining. And to many employers it appeared to be a preferable alternative to industry-wide collective bargaining—if collective bargaining there must be, as seemed destined under the Wagner Act. Thus, in reality, there was no majority public opinion in favor of industry-wide bargaining.

Yet, here was a curious plight of public labor policy aimed at encouraging the practice of collective bargaining. In most of the industries (typically mass production industries) in which unionism had so far been successively held at bay, the employers of labor had for a long time stood together against the unions and therefore had followed essentially similar policies of paying wages and handling working conditions—lest a split in the ranks should invite the intrusion of labor organizers promising the workers standardized conditions and uniform wage increases. Then too, the employee representation plans of company unions organized for (but not by) the employees in most large industries had been based on company-wide or at least plant-wide worker representation, rather than on representation along craft lines.

It was this setup which the CIO wished to transform from something like industry-wide determination of wages and working conditions by the employers into bilateral industry-wide collective bargaining between the unions and managements of those industries. The simple device was to transform the company unions into locals of one autonomous industry-wide union. Since this was actually in many instances the only way in which effective collective bargaining could come into being, the CIO could naturally make a convincing case before the NLRB. The Board was merely taking the realities of the situation into consideration, giving the green light to that labor organization which had the will and ability to do the job that needed to be done in the public interest under the Wagner Act. However, in view of the fact that there was really no majority public opinion in favor of industry-wide bargaining (what with the AFL dissenting), the Wagner Act had got ahead of public opinion, rendering the NLRB's task of winning compliance a well-nigh impossible one.

Perhaps the most accurate manner of appraising the situation of the Wagner Act in the 1930's is to describe it as a dilemma—a situation which confronts one with two alternatives, but is equally conclusive against one whichever alternative is chosen. In other words, "you can't win." Had the NLRB designated only craft units as appropriate bargaining units, it would have brought on its head the bitter enmity of countless persons who would have considered this an abandonment of the effort to bring collective bargaining, *on an equality basis,* to the mass production industries where unilateral industry-wide wage determination was already the rule. But in approving industry-wide rather than localized bargaining units the NLRB stood strongly opposed by employers and vital segments of a disunited trade union movement.

As a real example, there was the case of the West Coast maritime industry. The companies employing stevedores and warehousemen, as well as the International Longshoremen's Association (AFL), claimed that the unit of bargaining representation should be restricted to those longshoremen and warehousemen working for a particular employer at each particular West Coast port. The International Longshoremen's and Warehousemen's Union (CIO) argued that all stevedores and warehousemen holding union cards should be represented on a coast-wide basis, through a central union negotiating committee elected from the several union locals at the different ports. Undoubtedly the AFL union would have won port-by-port elections. But the CIO demonstrated to the satisfaction of the NLRB that longshoremen freely wander from port to port so that port bargaining units would not be so strong as a union representing the dockworkers wherever they happened to be. Furthermore, it showed that the employers were organized on a coast basis, so that effective collective bargaining required a parallel coast-wide operating labor organization. Bitterness over this decision has not as yet been eliminated from the West Coast social atmosphere.

The Federal Labor Code Under Fire

PROPOSED AMENDMENTS

As might be expected, political attacks on the Wagner Act were primarily in the form of amendments proposed by employer interests to diminish the scope of the Wagner Act and to curb the powers of the NLRB. In attempting to get the powers of the Board curbed, the employer interests were joined by AFL interests wishing to halt the expansion of the CIO.

The numerous bills introduced in the Senate and the House (beginning in 1937) do not warrant citation. Most of the suggested revisions of the Wagner Act were actually incorporated in the nation's new revised labor code, the so-called Taft-Hartley Act of 1947. Suffice it to say that practically all the proposed amendments of the employer-interest type laid great weight on the NLRB's acting, in the future, in close conformance to formal court procedures rather than operating informally in the role of educator. Many of them also advocated government regulation of unions, as well as government intervention in the actual process of collective bargaining. As has been already explained, the Wagner Act only operated to set the stage for collective bargaining, and if it regulated unions at all, it did so only in regard to union-management relations and not with reference to the internal affairs of unions.

The AFL also suggested amendments. It wanted the NLRB to designate occupational craft units as worker representation units whenever "a craft exists, composed of one or more employees." The wage-earners in a plant would have been perfectly free to vote for a representative from whatever craft unit (if any) they fitted into. But they could not have voted on whether or not they wanted to be represented on a craft basis. Actually, though, the AFL had, even as early as 1937, organized many places of work on a plantwide basis. In all those cases the AFL would probably have waived the rule of designating craft lines as the basis of bargaining representation, for fear of upsetting worker morale. But that is not the vital consideration from a labor policy point of view. What about those industries, usually the mass production industries, in which the employers were in fact, if not by written treaties, associated to deal with labor on an industry-wide basis? Would the AFL, after allowing worker representation on a plantwide, industrial rather than craft basis, have gone on to form a wage policy committee of union delegates from an industry's various plants to deal with the employers as a group? Or would the AFL with its strong tradition of dealing with employers one at a time, have persisted in this practice? The latter would more likely have been the case. The tradition of dealing separately with employers was certainly a strong one. In one important instance an AFL union, after four wartime years of participating jointly with the CIO and the employers in a scheme of industry-wide bargaining, withdrew as soon as wartime regulations and pledges lapsed, in order to get back to dealing with its employers one by one, even though the wartime collaboration with the CIO was successful in the maintenance of good wages, hours, and working conditions. As a matter of fact, the AFL tradition is not only strong; it is also arithmetically sound. Getting the most from a leading employer and then whipsawing the rest of the employers up to the standards set by the leading one is apt to yield more overall financial benefit in the short run than negotiating with the employers taken altogether.

But what if employers refuse to be whipsawed and openly or tacitly combine to hold out against the union's attempted differential pressure? In that case it is the union which is apt to be whipped to the point of dissolution, so that collective bargaining ceases in that industry. Undoubtedly, that is what happened to the unions in most of the mass production industries, such as steel, rubber, and automobile, when, prior to the 1930's, they tried whipsawing employers instead of dealing the same with all employers—whether directly, or circuitously by signing the same kind of labor agreement with each employer.

At mid-twentieth century these questions had become somewhat academic, for now the AFL and CIO have merged; but it is interesting to note that the merger was least effective in just those places where the old AFL tradition against industry-wide bargaining had been strongest. To summarize, opposition to industry-wide bargaining was voiced from the very moment that the Wagner Act was declared constitutional in 1937. The employer line of attack verged on advocating the outright prohibition of the practice of industry-wide bargaining, while the AFL approach was to curb the powers of the NLRB to prevent it, in effect, from making key decisions favorable to the CIO. This would also have circumscribed the practice of industry-wide collective bargaining. It would have been strange, indeed, if upon the occasion of the amendment of the Wagner Act, in 1947, the effect of the concurrent, if differently motivated, employer and AFL attacks had not been registered in the formulation of the then revised labor code, popularly referred to as the Taft-Hartley Act (the formal title is Labor Management Relations Act of 1947).

The Revised National Labor Code: Taft-Hartley Act of 1947

THE PASSAGE OF THE ACT

After every war there is a loosening of the bonds of close social cooperation observed in the face of the common enemy. Once the enemy is defeated there is a veritable scramble for individualism—"let the rest of the world go by." Then, too, people were unsettled and resettled during the war; with its cessation the tight disciplines of military service, war production, and controls on civilians are abandoned while normal peacetime community life has not been fully resumed. When many people and situations are partially disorganized, a tightly organized interest group can go a long way. Such a group was the employer interest. As was seen, there had been pressure for restrictive labor legislation from this source since 1937.

The first proposed postwar legislation came as the legislative equivalent of a guided missile equipped with an atomic warhead. House Bill 3020, popularly known as the Hartley Bill, was introduced in the first session of the 80th Congress. It forbade unions from bargaining on an industry-wide basis. Since no similar prohibition was applied to corporate managements and/or employers' associations, it is evident that labor, being forbidden to match management's organized strength, would have been placed at a distinct bargaining disadvantage. The Bill purported to deal with labor abuses that had long made their victims cry for remedy and which Thurman Arnold, erstwhile United States Attorney-General, had once listed quite adequately as follows: (1) applying economic pressure to prevent the use of cheaper materials, improved equipment, and more efficient methods of production; (2) forcing employers to hire unnecessary labor; (3) using union power for extortion and graft; (4) colluding with employers to maintain high prices for certain commodities by refusing to furnish labor to competitors; (5) attempting to disrupt established collective bargaining between employers and unions, by competing unions.

The Hartley Bill, however, went beyond attempted control of occasionally occurring abuses of union behavior. Apparently the intention was also to control normal types of union functioning. The Bill would have reintroduced the use of injunctions issued directly to private employers by ordinary courts of law, sidestepping the NLRB. As a matter of fact, the National Labor Relations Board was to be abolished, its place to be taken by an Administrator and a labor court. The Administrator would act in the manner of a prosecuting attorney. The labor code was made markedly restrictive on unions by the introduction of "union unfair practices," so defined as to cover, in many instances, practices that had long been accepted as normal and necessary for the unions' functioning. Strikes were to be confined to local-scale matters of wages, hours, working requirements; terms of discharge, promotion, and so on; safety and health conditions; leaves and vacations; and details connected with the administration of these issues. Clearly, this was designed to render the union a sort of super-personnel department rather than a democratic force within industrial life. Trial of any charges either by or against employers was to be before a labor–management relations board, which was required by the terms of the proposed Act to behave very much in the manner of the ordinary courts with respect to the type of evidence that was acceptable, the conduct of hearings, and so forth.

Over and above this, however, the courts with their typical common law procedures—procedures not developed out of collective bargaining experience but derived from property law—were reintroduced as potent factors in labor relations. This was done not only in connection with damage suits for newly and loosely defined "unlawful concerted activities" (of labor unions only) but also in connection with alleged violations of collective agreements. In the latter context the unions were to be held responsible for the actions of their members whether or not these actions had been ratified either directly or by reason of the fact that the unions had taken no steps to prevent them. Not only did this represent an abnegation of the Norris–LaGuardia Act of 1932 in one important aspect, but the Bill in this regard restrictively amended the Clayton Act of 1914. Political action by unions was also to be prevented by making unlawful any union contributions *and expenditures* made in connection with any national political campaign. This was apparently predicated on the assumption that unions are mere job-brokerages, or at least should not be more than that.

The Hartley Bill was passed in its entirety by the House of Representatives on April 17, 1947. The vote was 308 to 107. Interestingly, such a large majority meant that Democrats must have crossed party lines to vote for the Republican Bill. By contrast, in the Senate Labor Committee, three Republicans joined with four Democrats to moderate a stringent omnibus bill to regulate organized labor which was proposed by the Labor Committee's chairman, Senator Robert A. Taft (Republican). It was a considerably milder Bill which the Senate Labor Committee reported to the Senate on April 17, 1947. But then the crossing of party lines which had been seen in the House of Representatives occurred on the floor of the Senate, as a majority of Democrats joined with a majority of Republicans to defeat the equable Committee-reported Bill by a vote of 73 to 19. In the stiff debate which ensued on the floor of the Senate, the majority of Senators evidenced a determination to support legislation for regulating organized labor in a stringent manner. The bill which emerged from the Senate was similar to the House-approved Hartley Bill in most of its essential features, with one major exception: it omitted Section 9(f)(1) of H.R. 3020 (passed by the House), which would have prohibited industry-wide bargaining in most instances. The industry-wide bargaining prohibition was, however, voted down in the Senate by the narrowest possible margin of *only one vote*. In one of the most exciting roll calls in the history of modern labor legislation, Congress showed that it was within a hair's breadth of carrying to its logical conclusion the emphasis which both employers and the AFL traditionally placed on localized collective bargaining in preference to industry-wide bargaining. Yet most experts in the field of labor relations agree that legislative prohibition of a naturally evolved practice such as industry-wide collective bargaining would not only spell government interference but might well disrupt normal economic development, increase disruptive labor strife, and set a precedent for government interference with forms of management organization that evolve in response to the needs of modern times, such as large integrated corporations.

The differences existing between the House (Hartley) Bill and the Senate (Taft) Bill were resolved in the Conference Committee of both branches of Congress, the House yielding on industry-wide bargaining, and the Taft-Hartley Bill was passed by both houses. President Truman vetoed the bill on the grounds that it would disrupt normal labor relations and thus hurt national unity, but the veto was overridden in the Congress and the Taft-Hartley Bill became law.

THE MAJOR PROVISIONS OF THE TAFT-HARTLEY ACT

The Taft-Hartley Act is an omnibus which contains, in one form or another, virtually every major limiting amendment suggested since 1937, with the exception of the prohibition on industry-wide bargaining. As in our analysis of the Wagner Act, we shall here examine the meaning of the Taft-Hartley Act in terms of the leading sections— 7, 8, 9, and the new fateful Section 14(b).

Section 7 remains brief, but adds to the statement that "employees have the right to bargain collectively . . . and engage in other concerted activities," the somewhat ironical qualification that "employees shall also have the right to refrain from any or all such activities." Here it would seem that public policy was blowing both hot and cold.

Section 8 was very significantly amended by adding to the old list of employer unfair labor practices, now called Section 8(*a*), a part (*b*) which lists and somewhat spells out "union unfair labor practices." These include: the coercion by labor people of workers to join their unions; a union's causing an employer to fire a man who has been expelled from the union on any grounds other than failure to pay dues; bringing pressure on one's employer to cease doing business with another employer until that second employer recognizes or bargains with a certain union (the so-called secondary boycott); forcing an employer to assign work to one craft rather than another; getting pay from an employer for work not performed; and in other ways, to be determined by the Board, using union power coercively against an employer or an individual employee.

In addition to parts (*a*) and (*b*) of Section 8, a part (*c*) was added which absolves the employer from any unfair labor practices charge if he, or his subordinates, express strong feelings against the union provided they do not threaten an employee with the loss of his job or possible future benefits by reason of his union activities. Finally, a part (*d*) was added to Section 8 on unfair union practices which requires the unions to go through a 60-day cooling-off period before going on strike, and accept compulsory mediation by the Federal Mediation and Conciliation Service for 30 days before going on strike.

Section 9 already had a part (*a*) and (*b*) under the Wagner Act. The Taft-Hartley Act carries these over. But part (*b*), having to do with bargaining unit designations, was now amended to exclude professional workers and foremen from union coverage in the same bargaining unit as manual or clerical workers. Plant guards were also not to be allowed to join the unions of the production or clerical workers. The Board shall not "decide that any craft unit is inappropriate . . . unless a majority of the employees in the proposed craft unit vote *against* separate representation." If any person or group proposes a craft unit to the Board, the Board must take a vote on whether the workers want it. In practice, the Board has insisted that a craft unit must be historically and reasonably well established, not just the product of an organizer's imagination. Section 9 was also amended by adding provisions for holding a *decertification* election when 30 per cent of the workers in a plant petition the Board to get a union out. Unions are required to file detailed statements about their internal affairs with the government; and unions are required to show that no official is a member of the Communist Party or "believes in, or teaches, the overthrow of the United States Government by force or by any illegal or unconstitutional method."

Congress prepared a self-contradiction by enacting Section 14(b), which paves the way for state "right-to-work" statutes—more accurately called anti-union shop statutes. (The union shop arises out of an agreement of management and the union that membership in the union shall be a condition of continued employment after a trial period of from 30 to 90 days; see page 648, item 2.) The Taft-Hartley Bill sanctions the union shop as national policy in Section 8(a)(3) but Section 14 (b) states:

> Nothing in this Act shall be construed as authorizing the execution or application of agreements requiring membership in a labor organization as a condition of employment in any State . . . in which [this] is prohibited by State . . . law.

The contradiction was compounded when Congress, in 1951, amended the Railway Labor Act to permit carriers and their unions to make union shop agreements, previously forbidden. In 1956 the U.S. Supreme Court interpreted this to mean that if an interstate carrier signs a union shop agreement it will govern his employees even in states that have right-to-work statutes[1] (19 states in 1959, none being heavily industrialized).

Conclusions

The changing character of production and the evolution of the labor code have contributed to the emergence of "big labor" in the United States. This phenomenon was an inexorable consequence of the evolution of the modern corporation. Nowhere is this relationship better emphasized than in a famous dissent in 1896 by Justice Oliver Wendell Holmes, who said:

> It is plain from the slightest consideration of practical affairs, or the most superficial reading of industrial history, that free competition means combination, and that organization of the world, now going on so fast, means an ever increasing might and scope of combination. It seems to me futile to set our faces against this tendency.
>
> .   .   .   .
>
> Combination on the one side is patent and powerful. Combination on the other is the necessary and desirable counterpart, if the battle is to be carried on in a fair and equal way. . .[2]

There can be no doubt that combination on the side of the working people has, incidentally, encroached on the absolute right of the

---

[1] *Railway Employees' Department v. Hanson,* 351 US 225 (1956).
[2] *Vegelahn v. Guntner,* 167 Mass. 92 (1896).

employer to run his shop as he might see fit. However, it can be argued that, far from threatening the institution of private property in the United States, the institution of trade unionism has helped to preserve it by demonstrating that working people can have a voice under private enterprise.

The reaction of labor leaders to the 1947 revised labor code has been one of wounded pride. But it would seem that they have failed to benefit from the example set by the business community of keeping abreast of legislative developments. Labor leaders instead have stood aside, crying for the repeal of the Taft-Hartley Act, after refusing to contribute positive suggestions to the formulation of a new law. But the simple fact is that unions cannot continue to grow larger and stronger without themselves undergoing a change in orientation by taking a more flexible attitude on broad questions of public policy. The following are some of the most important issues to which modern trade unionism must address itself.

First, as unions grow large they inherit the problem common to all large organizations—that of maintaining the individual member in contact and control. When unions were struggling for survival, it was assumed with considerable justice that every gain in trade union membership meant another victory for humanitarianism and democracy. But things do not continue that way forever. As with all large institutions, trade unionism will tend to become more bureaucratic because of natural concern of leadership for placing the survival of the union above some of the original aims of the union to serve the individual.

Second, as trade unions become large and conduct their affairs on an industry-wide basis, on a national scale—as so many unions now do—the unions must assume responsibility for economic stability and growth. When the struggle was only to catch up with a minimum standard rate of wages, every increase of membership meant more fighting strength to be expended in the battle for standards of health and decency in living. But under conditions of modern, large-scale collective bargaining the wages issue is related to problems of inflation, tax policy, employment stabilization policies, and productivity problems. In the old days, labor unions could raise wages for their members without setting a pattern throughout the nation. At present, labor-management negotiations do result in setting wage patterns, and these patterns have definite effects on the stability and growth of the economy as a whole.

In other words, organized labor finds itself somewhat in the same position as organized business. There was a time when businessmen were simply told to go ahead and sell all they could, at whatever the

traffic would bear—never mind the general economic picture. Increasingly, however, it became evident that some measure of coordination
was necessary, and so the Federal Reserve Banking System was
established, with the consent of the business community, to regulate
the supply of money. Later, during the Great Depression of 1929–40,
a more positive role was assigned the government: the Securities and
Exchange Commission was established, public works were undertaken,
and finally, in 1946, there was enacted the Maximum Employment
Act, which charges the government with responsibility to advise the
business community on economic trends so that investment might be
undertaken in a highly informed manner.

In a similar way, it was felt that all the unions had to do was to go
out and organize—never mind the general economic picture. But now
it is evident that the simple slogans ("Organize" for "more and more")
are no longer adequate. As Allen Flanders points out:

> The contents of a collective agreement can no longer be regarded as being only
> of concern to the signatories. *Laissez-faire* cannot be abandoned in other vital
> sectors of our economic life and retained on the wages front. Least of all can
> the trade unions, whose very nature has compelled them to seek an increasing
> measure of public regulation over the free-for-all scramble of each for himself
> which characterized economic activity in the last century, now claim that their
> own preserves should be exempted from the application of those principles
> which they have urged upon the nation.[3]

The implications of the Flanders statement are that political action
by labor pressure groups simply to protect labor's economic gains will
be insufficient. Yet organized labor in the United States has persisted
in a tradition of pressure group politics. This pressure group tradition
is reinforced by the recent labor code which, instead of giving sympathetic guidance to the use of powers, seeks to return to some by-gone
period of localism. This could be interpreted by labor only as an
attack on its fundamental position. Moreover, the revised labor code
has attempted to place obstacles in the way of political action by labor
(Section 304). Yet historical experience in other Western countries
has shown political action to be an effective means of assuring labor's
assumption of its broader responsibility. Political action necessitates a
definite stand on broad economic issues, as for example, the British
Labour Party's postwar wage-stop policy to prevent inflation or, on
the other hand, its program of national health insurance, low-cost
housing, and scholarship aid for higher education.

What is likely to be the result of the AFL-CIO merger, which
is to be completed at a regional and local level by 1959? At

[3] Article on Great Britain in Walter Galenson, *Comparative Labor Movements*
(Englewood Cliffs, N.J.: Prentice-Hall, Inc., 1952), pp. 99–100.

present it appears to be primarily a matter of administrative convenience to facilitate further organization and larger unit bargaining. But if historical experience is any guide, the very consolidation of organized labor's purely economic strength may lead to the recognition of the inadequacy of collective bargaining in regard to issues such as: employment security, taxation, cost-of-living stability; sickness and accidents not immediately service-connected; residential housing facilities; public works projects; resource conservation; National Security regulations; technological displacement; and so forth. In the older countries of our Western civilization, trade union movements were unfailingly converted into labor movements having recourse to democratic political action, in their attempts to cope with the problems posed by a mature industrialism or by a rather settled society, generally speaking.

Whatever may lie ahead in the United States of America, the reader will find much material for thought in the labor histories, especially of Great Britain, Sweden, Norway, Denmark, and in an even more comparable way, of Australia and New Zealand.

The preceding chapter revealed that organized labor has made substantial progress under voluntary collective bargaining. The present chapter shows that labor law, because of its late arrival, so far has contributed relatively little to the development of individual and community welfare standards. Nevertheless, it promises to be an avenue which organized labor seems bound to use increasingly, not only to swell its ranks but to benefit the society at large.

For Discussion

1. Are there at the present remaining evidences of "labor's civil war" which began in the mid-1930's? Who was, at the time, among its principal victims?

2. A perennial issue in America's institutionalized system of income distribution is the practice of industry-wide collective bargaining (as against multi-employer regional bargaining or local company-wide or single-firm bargaining). The issue has rankled deep within the ranks of labor; persons outside the ranks of organized labor have made repeated demands on Congress to abolish industry-wide bargaining by law; and some opponents of organized labor profess to see in the merger of the AFL and CIO an action designed to promote industry-wide bargaining. What, in the light of facts presented in this chapter, would appear to be the directions in which the American trade union movement will move in the calculable future? What is the structure of American entrepreneurial organization and its evolutionary trends? What light does this shed on the question of industry-wide bargaining, as well as on the broader question of the general direction of the American trade union movement?

3. Distinguish between: (a) affiliated union; (b) bona fide single-firm union; and (c) company union. Does the Taft-Hartley Act of 1947 put the employer-

dominated company union "back in business"? By what criteria would you judge whether or not there is employer domination?

4. What is meant by "whipsawing tactics of unions"? Can employers also adopt such tactics? By what means did Congress in enacting subsection (*b*) of Section 8 of the Labor Management Relations Act of 1947 attempt to come to grips with *union* whipsawing tactics?

5. In what general manner might Section 9 of the LMRA of 1947 be said to aim at strengthening internal union democracy? Can this be done by law? Or can the law reach no farther than to give protection to minorities which are subject to discrimination, not alone in union circles, but within any type of social-economic organization?

6. A list of important issues was stated in the concluding section of this chapter. To these issues the modern trade union movement must address itself. What major issues, if any, do you believe were not included that should have been included?

Recommended Further Reading for Part V

General Theory Distribution; Property Incomes

AMERICAN ECONOMIC ASSOCIATION. *Readings in the Theory of Income Distribution.* New York: McGraw-Hill Book Co., Inc., 1946.

BROWN, HARRY GUNNISON. *Economic Science and the Common Welfare.* Columbia, Mo.: Lucas Brothers, 1925.

BROWN, HARRY GUNNISON, et al. *Land-Value Taxation Around the World.* New York: Robert Schalkenback Foundation, 1955.

CASSEL, GUSTAV. *The Theory of Social Economy.* New York: Harcourt, Brace & Co., Inc., 1931. See Bk. II, chaps. vi, "Interest," and vii, "Rent."

FISHER, IRVING. *The Theory of Interest.* New York: Kelley and Millman, 1954. Reprint of the 1907 work.

GREBLER, LEO. *Experience in Urban Real Estate Investment.* New York: Columbia University Press, 1955.

KNIGHT, FRANK H. "Capital and Interest," *Readings in the Theory of Income Distribution.* New York: McGraw-Hill Book Co., Inc., 1946, pp. 384–417.

LERNER, ABBA P. *Essays in Economic Analysis.* London: Macmillan & Co., Ltd., 1953. Outstanding work on the Keynesian interest rate.

MITCHELL, RONALD L. *American Agriculture: Its Structure and Place in the Economy.* New York: John Wiley & Sons, Inc., 1955. Good contemporary introduction to land economics.

MORTON, WALTER A. *Housing Taxation.* Madison: University of Wisconsin Press, 1955.

NEVIN, EDWARD. *The Mechanism of Cheap Money.* Cardiff: University of Wales Press, 1955. A clear, modernly conservative criticism of the Keynesian interest rate.

SELTZER, LAWRENCE H. *Interest as a Source of Personal Income and Tax Revenue.* New York: National Bureau of Economic Research, 1955.
WRIGHT, DAVID McCORD. *A Key to Modern Economics.* New York: The Macmillan Co., 1954. See especially Pt. I, chap. xvii, "Stationary versus Dynamic Analysis in the Distribution of Wealth," continued in chap. xviii, Pt. II.

On Agriculture

BOULDING, KENNETH E. *Principles of Economic Policy.* Englewood Cliffs, N.J.: Prentice-Hall, Inc., 1958, chap. xiii.
SAMUELSON, PAUL, *et al.* (eds.). *Readings in Economics.* New York: McGraw-Hill Book Co., Inc., 1958, pp. 158–68.
UNITED STATES DEPARTMENT OF AGRICULTURE. *Yearbook of Agriculture, 1957.* Washington, D.C.: Government Printing Office, 1958.

On Profits

KNIGHT, FRANK H. *Risk, Uncertainty, and Profit.* London: London School of Economics and Political Science, 1933.
SAMUELSON, PAUL, *et al.* (eds.). *Readings in Economics.* New York: McGraw-Hill Book Co., Inc., 1958, pp. 300–307, 426–73.

Labor Incomes, Collective Bargaining, and Labor Regulation

BAKKE, E. WIGHT, *et al. Labor Mobility and Economic Opportunity.* New York: John Wiley & Sons, Inc., 1954.
BAKKE, E. WIGHT, and KERR, CLARK. *Unions, Management and the Public.* New York: Harcourt, Brace & Co., Inc., 1948. Selected readings.
CHAMBERLAIN, NEIL W. *Social Responsibility and Strikes.* New York: Harper & Bros., 1953.
CHINOY, ELY. *Automobile Workers and the American Dream.* Garden City, N.Y.: Doubleday & Co., Inc., 1955.
COMMONS, JOHN R. *The Economics of Collective Action.* New York: The Macmillan Co., 1951. Exacting reading but suitable for motivated beginning students; see especially Pt. I, chap. i, and Pt. IV, chap. xvi, "Capital-Labor Administration."
DERBER, MILTON. *Labor-Management Relations at the Plant Level Under Industry-Wide Bargaining.* Champaign: University of Illinois, Institute of Labor and Industrial Relations, 1955.
DUNLOP, JOHN T. *Collective Bargaining: Principles and Cases.* Homewood, Ill.: Richard D. Irwin, Inc., 1953.
GOLDEN, CLINTON S., and PARKER, VIRGINIA D. *Causes of Industrial Peace Under Collective Bargaining.* New York: Harper & Bros., 1955.
GREGORY, CHARLES O. *Labor and the Law.* New York: W. W. Norton & Co., Inc., 1952.
HABER, WILLIAM, *et al. Manpower in the United States: Problems and Policies.* New York: Harper & Bros., 1954.
HUTT, WILLIAM H. *The Theory of Collective Bargaining.* Glencoe, Ill.: Free Press, 1954. Marginal analysis is used in this essay to criticize trade unionism; best statement of minority economists' views on collective bargaining.
LESTER, RICHARD A. *Hiring Practices and Labor Competition.* Princeton, N.J.: Princeton University Press, 1954.
MELMAN, SEYMOUR. *Dynamic Factors in Industrial Productivity.* Oxford: Basil Blackwell & Mott, Ltd., 1956.

PETERS, EDWARD. *Strategy and Tactics in Labor Negotiations.* New London, Conn.: National Foremen's Institute, 1955.

PETERSON, FLORENCE. *American Trade Unions.* New York: Harper & Bros., 1952.

ROSEN, HJALMAR, and ROSEN, R. A. H. *The Union Member Speaks.* Englewood Cliffs, N.J.: Prentice-Hall, Inc., 1955.

ROSENFARB, JOSEPH. *The National Labor Policy and How It Works.* New York: Harper & Bros., 1940. The classical work on the Wagner Act.

ROTHSCHILD, KURT. *The Theory of Wages.* Oxford: Basil Blackwell & Mott, Ltd., 1954. A textbook presenting the pure theoretical marginal analysis view of labor incomes.

SCHULTZ, GEORGE P., and COLEMAN, JOHN R. *Labor Problems: Cases and Reading.* New York: McGraw-Hill Book Co., Inc., 1953.

SOULE, GEORGE. *Men, Wages and Employment in the Modern U.S. Economy.* New York: New American Library, 1954. A Mentor Book.

TAFT, PHILIP. *The Structure and Government of Labor Unions.* Cambridge, Mass.: Harvard University Press, 1954.

TAYLOR, GEORGE W., and PIERSON, FRANK C. *New Concepts in Wage Determination.* New York: McGraw-Hill Book Co., Inc., 1957. A collection of original essays.

ULMAN, LLOYD. *The Rise of the National Trade Union.* Cambridge, Mass.: Harvard University Press, 1955.

WILLIAMSON, S. T., and HARRIS, HERBERT. *Trends in Collective Bargaining.* New York: The Twentieth Century Fund, 1945.

General Index

Abstract thinking, economic understanding and, 77–78
Abundance, relative, defined, 4
Accountancy of Changing Price Levels, 51*fn.*
Accountants' Handbook, 72 *fn.*
Accounting
business, elements of, 65–75
national economic, 23–45
growing use of, in economic decision-making, 94–95
private enterprise
for capital accumulation, 62–65
nature and elements of, 65–75
Adams, Henry, 139
AFL, opposition to industry-wide bargaining, 680
AFL–CIO
affiliated organizations, 657
Executive Committee, 659
Executive Council, 659
executive officers, 659
General Board, 659
membership, 657
organization chart, 658
policy determination and application, 657, 659
structure of the, 657–59
Aggregate effective demand, 85–88
Aggregate supply schedule, 205
Agreement, labor, 648–52
Agricultural Adjustment Acts, 612–14
Agricultural Credits Act (1923), 612
Agriculture
extensive, 109
intensive, 109
American Federation of Labor; see AFL; AFL–CIO
Anti-monopoly legislation, 446–60
Assets
consumers'
intangible, 540–44
tangible, 538–40

current, 68
durable, 68
financial, 68
fixed, 60
liquid, 214, 216, 537, 540
"wasting," 60
Atomic energy
as economic resource, 150–51
as source of electricity, 147–51
problems, 148–49
Atomic Energy Act (1954), 149
Automation, 184, 188–92
benefits of, 191–92
Detroit, 189–90
electrothink, 190–91
feedback, 190
types of, 189
Automobiles, as consumer assets, 539–40

Bain, Joe S., 405 *fn.*
Balance sheet, 68–75
Banerjea, Pramathanath, 165 *fn.*
Banks
commercial, 295
reserves, 298–300
Barclay, Hartley W., 186 *fn.*
Behind the Scenes of Business (Foulke), 366 *fn.*
Benefits, employee, 627
Bennett, H. H., 615
Bonds, 10
Bonus, as method of payment, 627
Borrowing, 10–12, 13
government, 266–74
extraordinary, 267–68
ordinary, 266–67
intersector, 12
British Industry, 1700–1950 (Hoffman), 487 *fn.*
Broken homes, as cause of poverty, 534, 536
Brown, Harry Gunnison, 608

695

Capital
accumulation
business programing for, 83–85
defined, 49–62
picture of, on a national scale, 85–88
private, role of, 47–49
private accounting for, 62–65
private records of, 81–83
business, 50–61
decumulation, 64
fixed, 60
formation, 192–96
goods, 106
liquid, 61
marginal efficiency of, 237–45
aggregate schedule of, 241–43
concept of, 237–41
declining, implications of, 243–45
reserves, 61
working, 60
Capitalization, 589
Chemical Engineering Economics (Tyler), 502 *fn.*
Clayton Act, 454–59, 663, 664
impact of the, 457–59
Coal, as fuel for generating electricity, 143–45
Cohen, Morris R., 334
Coleman, John R., 655 *fn.*
Collective bargaining, 647–57
defined, 647
impact of, 652–57
industry-wide, opposition to, 680–82
public policy and, 661–77
regional, 647
Commercial and Financial Chronicle, 97
Competition
limited, 463–83
managerial, 491
monopolistic, 463–67
economic analysis, 465–67
perfect, in the labor market, 629
product, 484–515
pricing under, 492–99
pure, in the commodity markets, 387–88
Competitive market, characteristics, 387–88
Congress of Industrial Organizations; *see* AFL–CIO
Consumer income; *see also* Personal income
differences in, affect expenditures, 527
disposable, level of, and consumer expenditure, 528–29

Consumer spending, data on, 95–96
Consumers
assets
intangible, 540–44
tangible, 538–40
expenditures
affected by differences in consumer income, 527
average, 526
Consumption
aggregate, stimulating, 252–58
function, 209–17
community, 210
individual, 213–17
Cooperation, Cournot, 474–77
Corporate securities, ownership of, 541–42
Corporation income taxes, 281–83
Cost of living indexes, 28
Cost(s)
marginal, 438–39
as supply price, 383–84
compared with marginal revenue, 439–40
concept of, 381–84
meaning of, 383
money, 135–36, 362, 372
defined, 136
entrepreneurial, aggregating, 208
operating, 62
opportunity
economy and, 577–81
principle of, 575–77
production, 362–86
economical control of, 364
real, 133–35, 362–63
defined, 133, 362
tangible, 133
Cournot, Augustine, 469, 473, 474–77
Cournot cooperation, 474–77
Credit
commercial, creation of, 295–98
controls, 307–14
expansion, 295–302
Cultivation
extensive, 109
intensive, 109
Curtis, Myra, 290

Debt, national
extraordinary, 267–68
management in depression, 271
ordinary, 266–67
postwar, 269–70
Decline and Fall of the Roman Empire (Gibbon), 616 *fn*

Deflation, 229
  Federal Reserve action in controlling, 315–19
DeMan, Henrik, 163
Demand
  aggregate, 205–7, 209–25
    foundations of, 209–21
  commodity, individual choice and, 343–60
  effective, defined, 85
  elasticity of, 354–60
  for labor, 638–46
  for resources, 553–54
  government purchases, 219–20
  inelastic, 355–56
  individual schedules, 346–48
  investment, 217
  market schedules of, 348–53
    constructing, 351–53
Depreciation
  management of, 59–60
  reserves, 60, 71–72
Depression, debt management in, 271–74
Detroit automation, 189–90
Deutsche Volkswirtschaft im Neunzehnten Jahrhundert, Die (Sombart), 151 fn.
Dillard, Dudley, 233
Diminishing returns, principle of, 366–72
Discrimination, racial, as poverty factor, 534, 535
Dissertations and Discussions (Mill), 608 fn.
Distribution
  national income, 521–694
    recent developments in, 531–33
    supply and demand theory of, 548–49
  theory of, 546–82
Dorfman, 360 fn.
Dragnet device, economic, 512–14
Drainage, agricultural, 120–21
Duncan, Delbert J., 452 fn.

Economic History of the United States (Wright), 488 fn.
Economic information, major sources of, 95–98
Economic interdependence, 6
Economic Report of the President, 97–98, 251–52, 253, 286–87
Economic Science and the Common Welfare (Brown), 608 fn.
Economic stabilization
  monetary policy for, 289–330
  tax policy for, 283–87
Economic transactions, flows in, 7–8

Economic value, human effort and, 155–56
Economics
  as a social science, 4–5
  scope of, 5
Economics in the Public Service (Nourse), 249 fn.
Economy
  American, sketch of the, 6–14
  concept of, 3–4
  need for, 3
Education, poverty and, 534, 535–36
Education of Henry Adams, The, 139
Effective demand, defined, 85
Elasticity, of demand, 354–60
Electric power, 140–51
Electrical energy; see Energy, electrical
Electricity, 140–51
  consumption statistics, 141
  economics of, 142–43
  farms and, 141
  needs for, prospective, 141–42
  sources of, 143–51
Electrothink automation, 190–91
Employment
  determinants of, 203–26
  full; see Full employment
  levels of, 203, 206
  sporadic, as poverty factor, 534
  stabilizing, role of government in, 248–64
  theory
    applied to public works expenditure, 260–63
    problems in, 227–47
Employment Act (1946), 248–49
Employment and Equilibrium (Pigou), 90 fn.
Energy, 139–51
  atomic, 147–51
  as a source of electricity, 147–51
  electrical, 140–51
  fuels for, 143–47
  progress in production of, 140–41
Engel, Ernst, 214
Enterprise, growth of; see Growth, of enterprise
Entrepreneur, modern, 620–21
Equilibrium (balance) price, 337
Equilibrium employment level, 207
Erosion
  sheet, 111
  soil, 109, 111–13, 116, 119
  wind, 111–12
Essay on Population (Malthus), 161
Ethics (Nowell-Smith), 79 fn.
Evans, Griffith C., 473 fn.

Expenditure(s)
  consumer
    affected by differences in consumer
      income, 527
    average, 526
    level of disposable personal income
      and, 528-29
  federal, types of, 250-52
  local, 252
  public welfare, 252-53
  state, 252

Farmers
  as businessmen, 609-12
  income of, 609-15
Farming; see Agriculture
Farr, Grant F., 667 *fn.*
Federal Farm Board, 612
Federal Reserve Bulletin, 95
Federal Reserve System
  action in controlling inflation or defla-
    tion, 315-19
  background, 303-5
  index of "Consumer Attitudes and
    Buying Intentions," 95
  primary function, 305-7
  purpose, 302-5
  role of, in the money market, 312-14
  structure, 303-5
Federal Trade Commission Act, 449-50
Feedback automation, 190
Fertility, soil, 111-12
Final product, 35, 36
Financial transactions, 10-12
Financing
  deficit, 273
  public works, in peacetime, 272-73
  war, 268-69
Fiscal policies, 266
Fisher, Irving, 291
Fixed assets, 60
Fixed capital, 60
Flanders, Allen, 690
Flood control, 123
Ford, Henry, 186-87
Ford Production Methods (Barclay), 186
  fn.
Foulke, Roy A., 366 *fn.*
Fuels, for electrical energy, 143-47
Full employment
  conditions favoring, 221
  defined, 204
  problem of, 23
  traditional reasoning on, 88

Gas, natural, as fuel for generating electricity, 146-47

*General Theory of Employment, Inter-
  est, and Money* (Keynes), 216 *fn.,*
  241 *fn.,* 248 *fn.*
George, Henry, 608, 609
Gibbon, Edward, 616
GNP; *see* Gross national product
Gompers, Samuel, 455, 663
Goods
  capital, 106
  intermediate, 106
Government
  borrowing, 266-74
    extraordinary, 267-68
    ordinary, 266-67
  debt, 265-74
    extraordinary, 267-68
    management in depression, 271-74
    ordinary, 266-67
    postwar, 269-70
  fiscal policies, 266
  role of, in stabilizing employment,
    248-64
  war finance, 268-69
Government spending, 219-20, 250-52
Gross national product (GNP), 26
  measures, uses of, 39
  real, contrasted with nominal, 29-31
  relationship of national income to, 33-
    37
  source of all income, 546
Growth, of enterprise
  aims for, 501
  biological, 509
  insights into, 502-8
  mechanisms of, 508-9
  pricing for, 510-12
  pricing policies and, 500, 510-14
  total, pictorialized in physical terms,
    504-8

Hamilton, Alexander, 88
Harris, Seymour E., 274
Heller Committee of the University of
  California, 96
Hoffman, Walther G., 487 *fn.*
Home ownership, 538-39
Household equipment, as consumer asset,
  539
*Human Problems of an Industrial Civili-
  zation* (Mayo), 642 *fn.*
Human resources, 155-78; *see also* Labor
  defined, 106
Hydroelectricity, 147

Illness, as poverty factor, 536
Impact of Science on Society (Russell),
  161 *fn.*

Income
  business, 50–61
  farmer's, 609–15
  labor, 624–37
  national; see National income
  nonoperating, 62
    sources, 63
  operating, 62
  personal; see Personal income
  property, 583–623
  rental, 598–609
Income (or "input") prices, 18–19
Income statement, 66–68
Income taxes; see Taxes, income
Indexes
  cost of living, 28
  price, 29
  wholesale price, 28
Industrial Revolution, 107
Industry
  water and, 117, 121–23
  women in, 158
Inflation, 229–30
  Federal Reserve action in controlling, 315–19
  open market operations to curb, 310–11
Injunction, labor, 662–64
Innovation, 168
Instinct of Workmanship, The (Veblen), 167 fn.
Insurance
  life, 542–44
  unemployment, 256–57
Interest, 583–98
  calculating, 583
  defined, 583
  rate theory, Keynesian, 324–27
  rates, 88–91
    determination of, 592–98
    raising, 308–10
  rationing function of, 588–92
  reason for paying, 584–88
Intermediate goods, 106
Intermediate product, 35, 36
Invention, 168
Investment
  aggregate, stimulating, 258–60
  as a source of employment problems, 236–45
  autonomous, 196
  business, 216, 236
  demand, 216
  function, 217–19
  induced, 195

Irrigation, 115
  problems, 120
  water for, 117–19

Kalecki, Michael, 459 fn.
Kendrick, John W., 174 fn.
Kerr, Clark, 675 fn.
Keynes, John Maynard, 156, 216, 241, 248, 319, 322
Keynesian interest rate theory, implications of, 324–27
Knight, Frank H., 333, 430

Labor, 106, 155–78
  agreement, 648–52
  demand for, 638–46
    analysis of, 638–46
    in terms of demand for the end-product, 639–40
    in terms of modern personnel programs, 640
  division of, 6, 184–85
  force, characteristics of, 158–59
  incomes, 624–37
  injunction, 662–64
  legislation, liberal, rise of, 664–66
  market
    defined, 628
    perfect competition in the, 629
  problems, nature of, 624–25
  specialization, 6, 184–85
Labor code, U.S., revised, 678–91
Labor unions; see Trade unions
Land
  as a natural resource, 107–16
  capability, 108, 113
    classes of, 113–15
  categories of, 113
  clearing, 115
  drainage of, 115
  irrigation of, 115
  new, obtaining, 115–16
  planning associations, 116
  value, computation of, 606–7
Lending, 11–12, 13
Letwin, William L., 446 fn.
Liabilities, 70
Life insurance, 542–44
Linear Programming and Economic Analysis (Dorfman, Samuelson, Solow), 360 fn.
Liquid capital, 61
Liquidity preference
  combining with a fixed money supply, 322–24
  concept of, 319–22

Living
mode of, defined, 523
plane of, defined, 523
standard of
American, in time perspective, 525–26
defined, 523
Logical thinking, in economic matters, 78–80
Long run, defined, 405

Machinofacturing, 184
Machlup, Fritz, 654–55
Malthus, Thomas Robert, 20, 161–66
Malthusian law, 161–63
Management and Morale (Roethlisberger), 642 fn.
Man-made resources, 179–97
defined, 106
increase of, geometrical, 184–92
types of, 106
"Marginal efficiency of capital"; see under Capital
Marginal propensity to consume
concept of, 234–35
declining, implications of, 235–36
Marginal revenue
concept of, 436–41
marginal cost compared with, 439–40
product, 555
schedule, 436–37
Margins, concept of, 365–66
Market, competitive, characteristics of, 387–88
Marketing — Principles and Methods (Phillips and Duncan), 452 fn.
Markets, definition of, 15–16
Marshall, Alfred, 191, 412 fn., 652, 653
Martin, William McChesney, 291 fn.
Mass production, 185–88
Mathematical Introduction to Economics (Evans), 473 fn.
Mathematical Principles of the Theory of Wealth (Cournot), 469 fn.
Maximum Employment Act (1946), 690
Mayo, Elton, 642 fn.
McGuire Act (1952), 453–54
McKinney, Robert, 148 fn.
Metcalf, Henry C., 641 fn.
Mill, John Stuart, 608
Miller-Tydings resale price maintenance law, 452–53
Minerals
American position in respect to, 126, 127–30, 131
American potential position in respect to, 131–32

as source of power, 139
expanded production, cost impacts of, 136–38
imported, 131
international interdependence of, 126
money costs and, 135–36
real costs and, 133–35
situation in America, 138–39
wasteful exploitation of, 136–38
Mode of living, defined, 523
Modern Money (Curtis and Townshend), 290 fn.
Monetary control, 307–19
Monetary exchange equation, 291–95
Money
market, 310–11
role of Federal Reserve System in, 312–14
modern, human nature of, 290–95
monetary authority as the supplier of, 322
motives for holding, 319–20
supply of, altering the, 295–307
Monopolist, demand curve for a, 430–35
Monopoly, 427–62
anti-monopoly legislation, 446–60
defined, 430
degree of, 463
equilibrium, 442
gain, measures of, 435–41
power
determinant of, 431–33
modern, 433–35
price, social meaning of, 441–46
profits, 617–18
Monthly Labor Review, data on consumer behavior published in, 96
Mortgages, 10
Multiplier principle, 260–63

National Association of Manufacturers, 675
National debt; see Debt, national
National income, 31–32
concept of, 25
concepts in comparison with money-flow economic accounting, 37–38
distribution of, 521–694
recent developments in, 531–33
supply and demand theory of, 548–49
flow of, 230–33
full-employment, 570–71
measures, uses of, 39–41
national output as, 9–10
relationship of gross national product to, 33–37

National Industrial Recovery Act, 666–67

National Labor Relations Act (1935), 667–76
employer attitudes toward the, 673–76
passage of the, 669
proposed amendments, 682
provisions of the, 670–73

National Labor Relations Board, 669, 670, 678

National output, 6–7
as national income, 9–10

National product, gross; *see* Gross national product

National Recovery Administration (NRA), 84

National War Labor Board, 663–64

Natural gas, as fuel for generating electricity, 146–47

Natural resources
defined, 105
energy, 139–51
land, 107–16
minerals, 125–39
soil, 107–16
summary, 151–53
water, 116–23

Neo-Malthusianism, 163–66

Net worth, 73

Nonoperating income, 62
sources, 63

Nonoperating outlays, 62, 63

Norris-LaGuardia Act, 665

Nourse, Edwin G., 249 *fn.*

Nowell-Smith, P. H., 79

NRA; *see* National Recovery Administration

Nuclear fission, as a source of electricity, 147–51

OASI; *see* Old-age and Survivors' Insurance (OASI)

Obsolescence
estimates, 72
handling, 508–9
management of, 59–60
reserves, 60, 71–72
tax-allowable, 72

Oil, as fuel for generating electricity, 142–43

Old-age and Survivors' Insurance (OASI), 253–55

Oligopoly, 467–82
economic analysis of, 469–70
expansive, and price leadership, 477–79
profits, 618–19

O'Mahoney-Kefauver-Celler Act (1951), 459

Open-market operations, 310–11, 314–15

Operating costs, 62

Operating income, 62

Opportunity cost
economy and, 577–81
principle of, 575–77

Outlays, nonoperating, 62, 63

Output, national; *see* National output

Output prices, 18

Paley, William S., 133 *fn.*, 137 *fn.*

Par value, 73

Parity price, 612–15

Paton, W. A., 72 *fn.*

Personal income, 42; *see also* Consumer income
disposable, 43–45
measure of, 43

Personal taxes, 276

Personnel Administration (Tead and Metcalf), 641 *fn.*

Phillips, Charles F., 452 *fn.*

Pigou, A. C., 90

Plane of living, defined, 523

Planning curves, entrepreneurial, 421–24

Plant size, planning curves for, 421–24

Poll tax, 276

Pollution, water, 122–23

Population
as a resource, 156–59
problem of, 161–66

Porter, George Richardson, 502 *fn.*

Postwar debt, 269–70

Poverty, 533–36
causes of, 534–36

Power
electric, 140–51
minerals as source of, 139
sources of, 139
uses of, 139
utilization by types, 182–83
water, 139

Preferred stock, 73

Prentice, B. R., 144

Price analysis
explanation of, 333–41
policy recommendations and, 340
scope and method of, 334–37
welfare and, 341

Price controls, 16

Price current, 337

Price determination, 14–20
long-run, under restricted conditions, 405–24
managerial growth and, 500, 510–14

Price determination—*Continued*
  theorems of, elementary, 387–426
  under conditions of pure competition,
    387–94
  under product competition, 492–99
Price Discrimination Act; *see* Robinson-
    Patman Act (1936)
Price indexes, 29
Price war theorem, 470–74
Price(s)
  function of, 15
  income (input), 18–19
  leadership, expansive oligopoly and,
    477–79
  manipulation, direct, 479
  monopoly, social meaning of, 441–46
  output, 18
  parity, 612–15
  rationing, indirect, through, 17–18
Pricing, Distribution, and Employment
    (Bain), 405 *fn.*
Pricing factor, unifying effect of, 573–81
Pricing process, 14–20
  social meaning of the, 394–95
Principles of Economics (Marshall), 191
    fn., 412 *fn.,* 652 *fn.*
Principles of Economics (Taylor), 390 *fn.*
Product
  competition, 484–515
    pricing under, 492–99
  development, organizational impact of,
    489–92
  diversification, 501
  final, 35, 36
  intermediate, 35, 36
  life cycles, 502–4
    concept of, 484–92
Production
  costs, 362–86
    economical control of, 364
    defined, 362
    economical expansion of, 404–5
    factors of, demand for the, 553–54
    lightened, 410
    mass, 185–88
    strained, 406–10
    variable factors of, 364
Productive services
  economic equivalence of, 548–49
  supply schedules, 549–52
Productivity, 166–75
  changes in, 168–69
  defined, 167
  growth of, 168
  imputation, simultaneous, 560–63
  indexes, 170
    construction of, 174–76

marginal revenue, principle of, 554–60
  measuring, 169–74
  national, findings on, 176–77
Profit and loss statement; *see* Income
    statement
Profit maximization, 376–77
  for the individual firm, 395–405
Profit(s), 615–20
  defined, 620
  incalculable uncertainty, 619–20
  monopoly, 617–18
  noncompetitive, 617–18
  normal, 616–17
  oligopoly, 618–19
Progress and Poverty (George), 608 *fn.*
Promissory notes, 10
Property incomes, 583–623
Property taxes, 276, 277
Public assistance, 257–58
  economics of, 257–58
Public welfare expenditures, 252–53
Public works, 258–60
  expenditure, employment theory ap-
    plied to, 260–63
  financing, in peacetime, 272–73
Purchasing power, 522
  measuring the, 26–28
Purchasing Power of Money, The (Fisher),
    291 *fn.*
Pure ownership value, 73

Racial discrimination, as poverty factor,
    534, 535
Radioactive materials, problems pertain-
    ing to use of, 148–49
Rationing
  direct, by planned decisions, 16–17
  indirect, through prices, 17–18
Rent
  contractual, difference between eco-
    nomic rent and, 599–600
  economic
    defined, 600
    difference between contractual rent
      and, 599–600
    differential, 601–5
    peculiarity of, 605–6
    economic function of, 607–9
Rental incomes, 598–609
Report on Manufactures (Hamilton), 88
Research, 508
Reserves, 71
  bank, 298
  capital, 61
  depreciation, 60, 71–72
  obsolescence, 60, 71–72
  valuation, 72

Resource-allocation, 16
Resources
  classification of, 105–6
  defined, 105
  demand for, 553–54
    qualitative, 553–54
  description of, 105
  energy, 139–51
  flexible, 410
  human; *see* Human resources
  inventory of, 106–7
  labor, 155–78
  land, 107–16
  man-made; *see* Man-made resources
  mineral, 125–39
  natural; *see* Natural resources
  population, 156–59
  rationing through factor prices, 571–73
  structure of, 105–99
  substitution principle, 563
  supply and demand seen in conjunction, 567–73
  tight, 406
  use of
    abundant, 203–330
    efficient, 333–60
  water, 116–23
Ricardo, David, 340, 341
Robinson-Patman Act (1936), 450–52
Roethlisberger, Fritz J., 642 *fn.*
Russell, Bertrand, 161

Salaries, compared with wages, 625–27
Sales tax, 276
Samuelson, 360 *fn.*
Saving, 45, 91
  conception of, new, 93
  reason for, 181–82
Scarcity
  absolute, 3
  relative, 3, 4
  defined, 4
Schultz, George P., 655 *fn.*
Schumpeter, Joseph A., 485
Scientific Management (Taylor), 640 *fn.*
Securities, corporate, ownership of, 541–42
Sheet erosion, 111
Sherman Antitrust Act, 446–49, 454, 662, 663, 664, 665
  text of the, 448–49
Short run, defined, 395
Skill, lack of, as poverty factor, 534, 536
Smart, William, 344
Smith, Adam, 156, 184, 185, 258, 275, 502, 616

Smith, Warren L., 317 *fn.*
Social security system, 253–56, 547–58
  reserve fund problem, 255–56
Soil
  as a natural resource, 107–16
  fertility of the, 111-12
Solar radiation, 151, 155
Solow, 360 *fn.*
Sombart, Werner, 151
Specialization, labor, 6, 184–85
Spending
  business, data on, 96–97
  consumer, data on, 95–96
  government, 219–20, 250–52
Stabilization; *see* Economic stabilization
Standard of living, defined, 523
State taxes, 276–77
Steel, 125
Stock, 11
  preferred, 73
Study of Indian Economics (Banerjea), 165 *fn.*
Substitution, principle of, 563
Supply
  aggregate, 205, 209, 220–25
  foundations of, 207–9
Supply and demand, law of, 392–93
  validity of the, 393
Surplus, 74–75
Survey of Current Business, 97
Swope Plan, 664

Taft-Hartley Act, (1947), 682, 684–88
  passage, 684–86
  provisions, 686–88
Taxation, 274–87
  bases of, 274–75
  policy for economic stabilization, 283–87
  progressive-rate, 279–81
Taxes
  income, 277–83
    corporation, 281–83
    federal, on individuals, 278–81
  local, 277
  personal, 276
  poll, 276
  property, 276, 277
  proportional, 276, 277
  regressive, 276, 277
  sales, 276
  state, 276–77
  types of, 276–83
Taylor, Fred M., 390 *fn.*
Taylor, Frederick W., 640, 641
Tead, Ordway, 641 *fn.*

Technology, 92, 107
    administration, concept of, 492
    defined, 166
Theory of Economic Dynamics (Kalecki), 459 *fn.*
Thinking
    abstract, and economic understanding, 77–78
    logical, in economic matters, 78–80
    straight, 80
Townsend Movement, 257
Townshend, Hugh, 290
Trade unions, 643–46; *see also* AFL–CIO
    classification of, 645–46
    structure of, 645–46
Transfer payments, 42
Tropical Agriculturalist, The (Porter), 502 *fn.*
Truman, Harry S, 286
Tyler, Chaplin, 502 *fn.*

Unemployment
    defined, 204
    extent of, 159–60
    insurance, 256–57
Unions; *see* Trade unions
United States
    Commerce Department, 96–97
    Labor Department, 96
United States News and World Report, 97
Utility, 344–46
    marginal, 344–46
        diminishing, 345–46
        elasticity and, 358

Valuation reserves, 72
Value added, 34–36
Veblen, Thorstein, 167
Vermassung und Kulturverfall (DeMan), 163 *fn.*
Viner, Jacob, 249 *fn.*

Wages, 625–27

    analyzing, 629–35
    compared with salaries, 625–27
    concept of, 627
    determination of, 628–36
        modern methods of, 638–57
    in the short run, at full employment, 629–34
Wagner Act; *see* National Labor Relations Act
Wall Street Journal, 97
War finance, 268–69
"Wasting assets," 60
Water
    as a resource, 116–23
    industrial, 117
        problems, 121–23
    irrigation, 117–19
    management, 116, 123
    pollution, 122–23
    power, 139
    problems, 119–23
    users of, 116–17
Water Pollution Control Act (1948), 122
Wealth
    as service value, 180–82
    national, 179–81
    personal, 537
    records of, 179
Wealth of Nations (Smith), 156, 157 *fn.,* 184, 259 *fn.,* 616 *fn.*
Weighted average, 27
Wheeler-Lea Act (1938), 450
Wholesale price indexes, 28
Williams, Faith M., 216 *fn.*
Wind erosion, 111–12
Work, defined, 625
Working, Elmer J., 343
Working capital, 60
Works Progress Administration (WPA), 258
Wright, Chester W., 488 *fn.*

"Yellow dog contract," 664